WORLD IN CRISIS

WORLD IN CRISIS

A GLOBAL ANALYSIS OF MARX'S LAW OF PROFITABILITY

EDITED BY GUGLIELMO CARCHEDI
AND MICHAEL ROBERTS

Haymarket Books
Chicago, Illinois

Published in 2018 by
Haymarket Books
P.O. Box 180165
Chicago, IL 60618
773-583-7884
www.haymarketbooks.org
info@haymarketbooks.org

ISBN: 978-1-60846-181-3

Trade distribution:
In the US, Consortium Book Sales and Distribution, www.cbsd.com
In Canada, Publishers Group Canada, www.pgcbooks.ca
In the UK, Turnaround Publisher Services, www.turnaround-uk.com
All other countries, Ingram Publisher Services International, IPS_Intlsales@
ingramcontent.com

This book was published with the generous support of Lannan Foundation and
Wallace Action Fund.

Printed in Canada by union labor.

Library of Congress Cataloging-in-Publication data is available.

10 9 8 7 6 5 4 3 2 1

CONTENTS

PREFACE

World in Crisis has a specific aim: to provide empirical validity to the hypothesis that the cause of recurring and regular economic crises or slumps in output, investment, and employment in modern economies can be found in Marx's law of the tendential fall in the rate of profit. Marx believed, and we agree, that this is "the most important law in political economy."

The law is either ignored or disputed by mainstream economics, for an obvious reason: it suggests a fundamental flaw in the capitalist mode of production. Mainstream economics (whether neoclassical or Keynesian) starts from the assumption that capitalism is the best and, indeed, the only possible mode of production—that it can be improved but should be retained. The proposition that Marx's law provides the ultimate explanation of recurrent crises under capitalism is also denied by heterodox and many Marxist economists. They look to other explanations of crises. Much of the debate concerns what Marx actually wrote about crises in his works and what he meant. That debate continues. But far too often, alternative theories of underconsumption, rising inequality of income and wealth, surplus capital and overproduction disregard the law's empirical evidence.

This is where this book comes in. The book collates empirical work, mainly that of young Marxist scholars, from around the world (the Americas, Europe, and Asia) that supports the validity of Marx's law of profitability as a theory of crises and, in particular, of the recent Great Recession.

This empirical analysis has political consequences. The law reveals that crises arise from the very essence of capitalism—the fundamental contradiction inherent in technological progress, the motor of capitalism's development—namely, that technological progress, while increasing labor productivity, at the same time replaces labor with the means of production, thus decreasing the value of the greater output. If less value and surplus value is generated, less value and surplus value can be realized. This is the root cause of falling profitability and crises. It reveals itself as an ever-changing, complex articulation of the tendency and changing countertendencies, which give each crisis its own specific features. But the underlying cause is the same. Marx's law implies the unpalatable truth that capitalist crises cannot be permanently ended without ending the capitalist mode of production itself.

This book is academic in format: it is often dense in analysis, and it is flush with figures and numbers. This is a necessary drawback. Nevertheless, we believe that "the proof of the pudding is in the eating"; a theory, to be credible and useful, should rest on sound empirical evidence. And we believe that the evidence submitted in this volume is very robust indeed. As the old saying goes, *sapiens nihil affirmat quod non probat*: a wise man states as true nothing that he does not prove.

INTRODUCTION

World in Crisis is a collection of recent papers by Marxist economists from around the globe. Its purpose is simple. It is to compile evidence from recent developments in economies internationally to support the view that Marx's law of the tendency of the rate of profit to fall provides the best explanation of the cause of recurrent and regular crises (slumps) in global capitalism.

The authors of the papers we have included and commissioned start from that premise and, in our view, justify it through the evidence they generate from various economies. It is a controversial conclusion, denied not only by mainstream economics—which studiously ignores the Marxist narrative on crises—but also by heterodox strands in macroeconomics—which look to the theories of Keynes, Minsky, Kalecki, and others who deny the role of Marx's law in crises and instead rely on theories based on underconsumption, overproduction, financialization, excessive debt, or inequality of income and wealth. Indeed, even many economists who consider themselves Marxists consider that Marx's law of the tendential fall of the rate of profit has only a limited relevance to recurrent crises, and especially to the last major slump in capitalist production between 2008 and 2009, now called the Great Recession.

Several important Marxist economic works have established that Marx's theory of value and the concomitant law of the tendency of the rate of profit to fall are based on realistic assumptions and are logically consistent as a possible explanation for the movements in capitalist investment and economic output. This book aims to go a step further by presenting evidence that Marx's law "best fits the facts," as well.

Some Marxists reckon that trying to present quantifiable empirical evidence to support Marx's law is both impossible and unnecessary. For them, using the data provided by national and international statistical agencies will not provide any sort of close approximation to Marxist value categories or the Marxian rate of profit. And anyway, they say, the best proof is not statistical data but the very existence of recurrent and regular economic crises. We disagree.

1

The scientific method requires the analysis of data against categories to test any theory or law and, if necessary, to falsify it. Indeed, both Marx and his collaborator, Engels, tried to do just that by compiling data to support theory and using empirical analysis to develop theory further. In particular, when Marx developed his law of the tendency of the rate of profit to fall, he reckoned that a falling rate of profit was self-evident in the early nineteenth century, as the classical economists also assumed. But it was necessary to explain why the rate of profit fell, why it did not always fall, and what the implications of a tendency to fall meant for the capitalist mode of production and its ultimately transitional nature.

Without such analysis, science (and economics) cannot progress to a better understanding of social processes, nor, in the case of Marxism, know through what stage capitalism is passing and how the forces struggling for a new society, labor, should act accordingly to change the world.

We set several criteria in deciding which papers to include in this book. The first was that each had to make an empirical contribution to explaining and supporting Marx's law. Theoretical arguments were not enough.

Second, we required that the papers specifically deal with the Great Recession and its cause. While there are many excellent papers that we could have included that support Marx's law empirically, we wanted ones written after the end of the Great Recession. After all, there is nothing better than the benefit of hindsight!

Third, we wanted an international dimension to the contributions. Most papers on Marx's law and crises have based their evidence on the US economy alone. This is understandable because US capitalism remains the most important in the globe, and the US economy still offers the best "laboratory experiment" to test Marx's law and theory of crisis—just as Britain's economy did for Marx in the nineteenth century. The US statistics remain the most accessible and comprehensive globally. But the concentration on the United States alone does not serve as an adequate test for Marx's law—after all, the law and Marx's key value categories apply to the world economy, and not a national one as such. Also, we found plenty of papers that take up Marx's law using the evidence of national data in Asia, Latin America, and Europe, many of which we reckon have not been considered by the dominant Anglo-Saxon cartel in Marxist economic analysis. Thus this book brings together contributions from authors in the UK, Greece, Spain, Argentina, Mexico, Brazil, Australia, and Japan.

Finally, our contributors are mainly young scholars. We wanted this book to allow readers to discover the excellent work being done by young Marxist economists around the globe to show that it is not just aging (and possibly declining) Marxist economists (like the editors) who can fly the flag of Marxist economic analysis in the early twenty-first century. Indeed, we have deliberately excluded the continued fine work of many well-known scholars that could have been included over youth.

The book is divided into four parts. In part 1, the contributions concentrate on explaining the roots of the various crises in post-1945 US capitalism leading up to the Great Recession of 2008–2009.

In chapter 1 of this section ("The Long Roots of the Present Crisis"), the joint editors, Guglielmo Carchedi and Michael Roberts, start with the Marxist thesis that the ultimate cause of crises in capitalism is the fall in profitability. They present data from the postwar US economy to show that changes in the rate of profit on productive capital and in the whole economy support Marx's law of profitability as the ultimate driver of crises in the US economy, particularly the Great Recession.

Chapter 1 also considers the arguments of the Keynesians and Austerians (the supporters of "neoliberal" austerity measures). Both Keynesians and Austerians deny the determining role of profitability in crises. Carchedi and Roberts argue that this is the reason that their policy solutions for crises do not and will not work.

They counterpose to the Keynesian consumption, or spending "multiplier," as the model for the macro economy a novel concept: the Marxist multiplier, namely the notion that it is changes in the organic composition of capital in new investment that determine the final change in average profitability. And this change in profitability determines the efficacy of any new investment to boost growth. So Keynesian state-induced stimulus programs (redistributive, monetary, and fiscal) cannot overcome the underlying tendency for profitability to fall and thus cannot solve or "manage" recurrent crises. The authors critically examine the "success" of austerity policies applied in the weaker Eurozone states of the Baltics and Greece, as well as in the UK.

In chapter 2 ("The Old Is Dying but the New Cannot Be Born"), Carchedi focuses on the movement of the average rate of profit (ARP) in the productive sectors of the US economy. Carchedi shows that the US ARP falls from the end of World War II to 2015 due to productivity-increasing, but labor-shedding, technologies. Five objections to the law are considered and rebuffed. Carchedi tests Marx's law in value terms, rather than, as is usually done, in terms of prices. He finds that the law applies in both cases.

Carchedi shows that an upward profitability cycle generates from within itself a downward cycle. The latter, in turn, generates endogenously the next upward profitability cycle. Moreover, each cycle is a further station on the path of the long-term secular fall in profitability. Carchedi shows that crises emerge at the conjuncture of three elements: falling profitability, negative growth of new value generated, and employment. Conversely, recoveries are periods not only of growing profit rates but also of rising percentage growth in new value and employment.

In chapter 3 ("Investment, Profit, and Crises: Theories and Evidence") José A. Tapia reviews the major theories of business cycles. They are classified into two main groups, one emphasizing external (exogenous) factors and the other emphasizing internal (endogenous) influences. Tapia examines the role of investment in endogenous theories, presenting two contrasting views on the relation between investments and profitability. For Kalecki, Keynes, Matthews, and Minsky, changes in investment lead to changes in profitability. But for Marx and Mitchell, it is profitability that determines investments.

Statistical analysis supports the hypothesis that profits determine investment and, in this way, lead the economy toward boom or bust. Profits are much more volatile than wages and salaries. And, on average, profits peak and start falling several quarters before investments do. After the recession, investments reach their trough after the trough in profits. So the data support the thesis that the line of causation leads from profits to investments.

Part 2 goes beyond the United States to examine the international dimension. These chapters consider the measurement of a world rate of profit and its viability, before analyzing the movement in the rate of profit in Japan, Mexico, Brazil, Argentina, Spain, and Greece. Marx's model of capitalism assumes a world economy, or "capital in general"; however, in the real world, there are many capitals: not just one world capitalist economy, but many national capitalist states. Labor, trade, and capital restrictions, designed to preserve and protect national and regional markets from the flow of global capital, pose barriers to the establishment of a world economy and a world rate of profit. The essays included here ask: Can we realistically talk about a world rate of profit? And what would it tell us if we could?

Esteban Maito, with chapter 4 ("The Tendency of the Rate of Profit to Fall since the Nineteenth Century and a World Rate of Profit"), offers an ambitious project. Maito estimates the rate of profit for fourteen countries, employing data that in some cases stretches over more than a century, and that represents more than half of world production in the last seventy years and 62 percent of world gross domestic product (GDP) in 2010. Due to this geographic and economic comprehensiveness, these estimates can justifiably be considered a close approximation to the world rate of profit. Maito divides the core countries from the peripheral ones and finds that, on a secular basis, profitability falls in core countries. Profitability starts from higher levels in the peripheral countries but falls more rapidly, tending to converge with that in the core countries. A similar conclusion holds if China is included in the sample. China's profitability starts from a much higher level in the mid-

1970s but then follows the general downward trend. After a large increase from 2002 to 2008, it falls precipitously, nearing the world level in 2009.

In chapter 5 ("Japan's 'Lost' Two Decades"), Takuya Sato tackles two interrelated questions: the reasons for the prolonged stagnation of Japan's economy, and the causes of the recovery in Japan's profitability since the late 1990s in spite of poor economic conditions. Japanese capitalists halted and reversed the earlier fall in profitability by curbing productive investment. New investments came to a standstill, and there was no significant capital accumulation. The reproduction of capital took the form of simple, rather than expanded, production, and Japan entered two decades of economic stagnation.

Profitability then rose because Japanese entrepreneurs reacted to the slow growth of constant capital by increasing capacity utilization, the ratio of new value to constant capital, and the rate of surplus value. Employment and wages fell. Consequently, Japanese capital enjoys a much higher level of profitability than in the 1990s, and yet the economy is still depressed. State intervention has also played a role in rising profitability. In the era of neoliberalism, state intervention has increased, not lessened, but this has been to the advantage of big corporations and financial institutions, and to the disadvantage of labor. Due to the "trickle down" of new investments, non-financial corporations now have huge cash reserves so that their dependency on bank credit is considerably reduced.

Michael Roberts uses chapter 6 ("The UK Rate of Profit and British Economic History"), to analyze the movement in the rate of profit of capital in the UK since 1855 using a variety of data sources and methods. He finds that there was a secular decline over the last 150 years, interspersed with periods of upturn that sometimes lasted for decades. Roberts concludes that the movement of the UK rate of profit conformed with Marx's law of the tendency of the rate of profit to fall. He suggests that the biggest declines in the rate of profit coincided with the relative decline in the global supremacy of British industry. So Marx's law also provides an analytic tool for understanding the decline and fall of British industrial capitalism.

With chapter 7 ("The Long Depression in the Spanish Economy"), Juan Pablo Mateo estimates the Spanish rate of profit from 1970 to 2014. The trend is downward. Within this long-run period, he focuses on the 1995–2007 cycle, which also exhibits a declining profitability. In this period, investment, capital accumulation, employment, and wages rise; however, capital accumulation is largely explained by asset price inflation (which accounts for rising accumulation with falling profitability) and so has been distorted by the speculative boom in the housing sector and by a high debt level due to a net inflow of foreign capital. Government debt has fallen while households' and firms' debts have increased. Rising housing prices have meant greater profits for capital, but greater poverty for labor. From 2007 to 2012, the degree of mechanization accelerated and unemployment rose.

Thanasis Maniatis and Costas Passas, in chapter 8 ("Surplus Value, Profit, and Unproductive Labor in the Greek Economy"), follow the course of the Greek rate of profit through its different phases since the end of the 1950s. The first phase is the "Golden Age" of Greek capitalism. The fall in the rate of profit is explained by the interrelation of the rate of surplus value and the capital/output ratio (which the authors see as a proxy for the organic composition of capital). The former rises moderately, while the latter rises much more, meaning the rate of profit falls even in this phase of vigorous capital accumulation. A new phase starts in 1974: one of crisis and stagnation due to a fall in the rate of surplus value and profit share, and to a rise in the capital output ratio. Then in the mid-1980s, capital unleashes its attack on labor. This is the third, neoliberalist phase, a conscious measure to counter falling profitability. Profitability is restored, but not at the levels of the "Golden Age" due to the insufficient capital destruction and to the increase in unproductive labor relative to productive labor. Investments as a share of total output increase very modestly, and the lack of demand is partially countered by government deficit spending and financialization. The result is an unprecedented level of government, corporate and private debt. These are the roots of the present crisis in Greece.

In chapter 9 ("The Profit Rate in Brazil, 1953–2008"), Adalmir Marquetti, Maldonado Filho and Vladimir Lautert show that the Brazilian rate of profit exhibits a downwards linear trend from 1953 to 2008 due to the decline in capital productivity. This is explained by the rising cost of capital goods and by the declining real capital productivity. Within this long-term period, three phases can be distinguished. In the first phase, from 1953 to 1973, the rate of profit declines slowly. This is an era of import substitution industrialization. From 1973 to 1989 the rate of profit falls sharply. This marks the crisis of Brazil's import substitution/industrialization model. The rate of profit then rises moderately from 1989 to 2008 the neoliberal period, accompanied by a sharp decline in the wage share.

Chapter 10 ("The Chinese Economic Crisis"), is about China. Mylène Gaulard looks at the Chinese economy from the yardstick of Marx's law of profitability. She observes that a rising organic composition of capital has led to a secular fall in the rate of profit in China's industrial sector. This is leading to a growing contradiction between investment and productivity growth. The Chinese investment rate reached a world record in 2014, exceeding 45 percent of the GDP. However, Gaulard notes that this very strong accumulation, stimulated by the specific characteristics of the Chinese mode of production, could be extremely dangerous for future national investment.

Part 3 looks at the specific features of this current crisis. In particular, the papers here look at the massive expansion of private sector debt, and the subsequent transfer of that debt to the public sector after the bailout of banks globally following the global financial crash of 2008–2009. We also consider the rise of speculative capital in the decades prior to the crash.

In chapter 11 ("Debt Matters"), Roberts shows that the expansion of private sector credit was a major feature of the lead-up to the Great Recession, and that its overhang afterwards has contributed to the subsequent depression (or weak economic recovery). Roberts argues for an interpretation of Marx's view of credit (debt) as helping capitalist production take advantage of prospective profit opportunities, but also that this form of capital eventually becomes "fictitious" because its price loses connection with value and profitability in capitalist production. This disconnect leads to a bursting of the credit bubble, intensifying any economic slump. The problem of recovery under the capitalist mode of production is worsened when fictitious capital reaches such an unprecedented size because it takes a very long time to eliminate. Part of the task of the current depression is to deleverage debt in order to restore profitability so that companies will start a period of sustained investment in productive assets. Roberts provides empirical evidence for the advanced economies that private sector debt expanded at a rapid pace before the world financial crisis started in 2007. He also shows that the corporate sector is much more highly indebted than it has been at this point in previous business cycles, while deleveraging has been minimal so far.

Chapter 12 ("The Neoliberal Financialization of the US Economy"), presents an empirical analysis of the US economy by Sergio Cámara Izquierdo and Abelardo Mariña Flores. They estimate the profitability of "active capital" (productive) and "capital property" (financial) and show that the rate of return on the latter was consistently higher during the neoliberal period. The expansion of the financial forms of valorization appropriated and attracted a significant portion of the surplus value away from active-capital investment, which has tended to slow down productivity growth and, therefore, the dynamics of relative surplus value production mechanisms.

Similarly, with chapter 13 ("The Roots of the Global Crisis"), Murray Smith and Jonah Butovsky discuss the theoretical aspects of the measurement of the rate of profit, as well as its inherent difficulties. They measure profitability in the United States for both total and non-financial capital. On this basis, they conclude that the financial crisis of 2007–2009 has its roots in the persistent profitability difficulties of productive capital on a world scale. These problems date back to the profitability crisis of the 1970s, which, due to the determination of capital and capitalist states to avoid a major global depression, was never fully resolved. Three countertendencies are identified: a gradual but massive increase in the rate of exploitation; a shift of capital from the productive to the unproductive, especially the financial and speculative activities; and massive state interventions, especially in the monetary and fiscal spheres. The result has been unprecedented levels of state and private debt, and thus the private and sovereign financial crisis. Smith and Butovsky see these as expressions of a "historical-structural crisis" of the capitalist mode of production. Their conclusion—contrary to the view of many Marxist authors—is that the global slump that began in 2008 is an extreme manifestation of a longer-term crisis of capitalist profitability.

In chapter 14 ("Derivatives and Capitalist Markets"), Tony Norfield argues that the boom in derivatives trading in the decade or so before the global financial crisis was a product of the crisis of capital accumulation and of profitability in the productive sectors. Norfield traces the origin of derivatives to the instability of capitalist markets. Originally, derivatives were an instrument in hedging rather than in speculation, but over time, the division between hedging and speculation was blurred. Derivatives did not cause the crisis, but they extended the speculative boom and spread it far beyond the United States, thus making the crisis worse by connecting derivatives to commodity speculation, subprime mortgages and sovereign debt. Norfield concludes that stricter banking regulations will not correct the crisis-prone nature of this financial system.

Finally, Steve Nash, in chapter 15 ("High-Frequency Trading"), focuses on an extreme form of speculative capital, characterized by the tremendous speed of its executions: high-frequency trading (HFT). In HFT, stocks are bought and sold not according to firms' fundamentals, but based on the signals of the market. These signals can change rapidly and suddenly. HFT is thus inherently short term. Thanks to computers, high-frequency traders can buy and sell within a millisecond. HFT thus appears practically risk free: the transaction is so fast that there is no time for adverse changes in prices. However, computerized trading, as a new form of speculative competition, has played a role in financial crashes, promoting instability in a crisis-prone market while conveying no information about the economy.

Part 4 looks at how the global financial crisis and the Great Recession unfolded in Europe, and their impact on the great European project of a single-currency area.

In chapter 16 ("From the Crisis of Surplus Value to the Crisis in the Euro"), Carchedi argues that the euro crisis is a European expression of the global financial crisis. The precursor to the euro, the European currency unit (ECU), was borne as a strong currency, even if initially a virtual one. It had to be capable of challenging the US dollar's seigniorage. However, the recent crisis of the euro marked a pause in the struggle between the dollar and the euro. A strong dollar vis-à-vis the euro strengthens the dollar's seigniorage but hampers exports. Moreover, the disappearance of the euro would be preceded by the default of some states and financial corporations, which could be dangerous for the United States. So the United States wishes the euro to survive. Thus, two options are available: (1) to retain the euro as it is by rescuing states and financial corporations, and by letting labor pay for these policies; or (2) for the stronger countries (Germany *in primis*) to exit the euro and form a strong (Nordic) euro with the aim of expanding further, not south, but east—to Russia and China.

A key point is that the deficit in the trade balance of the weaker Eurozone countries is not caused by the inability to devalue their currencies, but by their inferior technological development. Lack of competitive devaluation only worsens it. Some member states' argument for exiting the euro is that it would be possible to resort to devaluation and its beneficial effects in terms of increased production, employment, and economic growth. However, greater exports do not necessarily stimulate production. And even if they did, greater production is not necessarily equal to sustained economic growth, because it almost certainly does not increase average profitability. This latter point is argued on the basis of the Marxist multiplier.

In chapter 17 ("The Euro Crisis Is a Crisis of Capitalism"), Roberts links the crisis in the Eurozone integrally with the general crisis flowing from the global financial crash and the subsequent Great Recession. Roberts finds a close statistical correlation between growth in individual Eurozone countries and the profitability of national capitals, while there is little correlation between cuts in government spending (austerity) and growth. Thus the Eurozone crisis owes more to the profitability crisis in capitalism than it does to the austerity policies of the Eurozone governments, as claimed by Keynesians.

The other factor was the buildup in private sector debt in the weaker Eurozone countries as they attempted to maintain profitability and growth. Roberts argues that the uneven development of capitalism, exhibited in varying productivity and investment growth, contributed to the fissures in the Eurozone when the crisis broke. Without full fiscal and economic union, such fissures cannot be bridged, and such union is impossible under the current structure and strategy of the European Union. Roberts argues that calculations on the different trajectories in the national rates of profit in Eurozone states are the best indicator of the centrifugal forces at play within the Eurozone. While the euro has survived this crisis so far, the existing structure of the euro will be under serious risk when a new slump arrives.

Finally, we must point out that the editors do not agree on all aspects of the contributions presented here. For example, we disagree on how to interpret the relation between profitability, capital productivity and capital efficiency, as well as on the inclusion of financial capital in the denominator when computing the rate of profit. Nevertheless, we have included contributions by authors who disagree with us on these points because we believe, in spite of these disagreements, that each of the authors in this volume makes an outstanding and empirically substantial contribution to the development of the law of the tendential fall of the rate of profit as the fundamental explanation of the Marxist theory of crises.

PART I

THE US ECONOMY

THE LONG ROOTS OF THE PRESENT CRISIS: KEYNESIANS, AUSTERIANS, AND MARX'S LAW

Guglielmo Carchedi and Michael Roberts

1. Profit Calls the Tune

Capitalism does not develop in a straight line upward. Its movement is subject to recurrent cycles of "booms and slumps" that destroy and waste much of the value previously created. For example, the 1880s and 1890s saw a massive destruction of US value and wealth, as did the Great Depression of the 1930s. Now we have suffered the first Great Recession and are in the Long Depression of the twenty-first century. We hold that the key to understanding the sequence of booms and busts is the movement of the profit rate.[1]

Individual capitalist businesses compete with each other to sustain and increase not only the mass of profits, but also their profits relative to the capital invested. To do so, they increasingly use new technology to boost the productivity of labor. On the one hand, this is capitalism's Achilles' heel: The accumulated cost of investing in new plants, equipment and so forth inexorably rises compared to the size and cost of the labor force. As only labor can create value,[2] the value and surplus value generated by the capitals investing in new methods of production then begins to fall. On the other hand, these capitals are more efficient and produce a greater output. By selling this output to other branches at the same price as the lower output of the technologically backwards capitalists, modernizing capitalists appropriate a share of the surplus value produced by the latter. Their rate of profit rises, but that of the technologically less efficient capitals—and of the economy as a whole—falls.[3] If other capitalists modernize as well, profitability falls even more. The less profitable capitals go bankrupt. Eventually the mass of profit falls as well, and a crisis ensues.

Capitalists try to avoid the crisis in various ways: by trying to exploit workers more; by looking for yet more efficient technologies; by speculating in unproductive areas of the economy (for instance, in the stock market, and in banking and finance, where they gamble for gain); and by increasing unproductive sales expenditures. National capitalist economies look for new sources of labor supply to exploit abroad and new foreign markets from which to appropriate (surplus) value. These are some of the counteracting factors to the main law of profitability, the "law as such." But these counteracting factors can only work for a while. Eventually, the law of falling profitability will operate.

Empirical evidence confirms this. We shall focus on the United States since World War II.[4] Figure 1.1 shows that the rate of profit has been falling since the mid-1950s and is well below where it was in 1947. There has been a secular decline; the rate of profit has not moved in a straight line. After the war, it was high but decreasing during the so-called "Golden Age," from 1948–65. This was also the fastest period of economic growth in American history. Profitability kept falling from 1965 to 1982, as well. The growth of gross domestic product (GDP) was much slower, and American capitalism (as did capitalism elsewhere) suffered severe slumps in 1974–75 and 1980–82.[5]

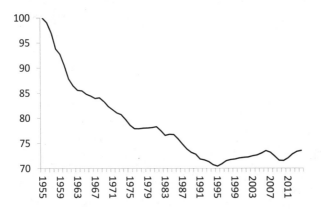

Figure 1.1 US average rate of profit, ten-year rolling annual average (%, indexed 1955 = 100), 1955–2011. Source: see appendix.

Then, as figure 1.2 shows, in the era of what is called "neoliberalism"—from 1982 to 1997—profitability rose. Capitalism managed to bring into play the counteracting factors to falling profitability: namely, greater exploitation of the American workforce (falling wage share), wider exploitation of the labor force elsewhere (globalization), and speculation in unproductive sectors (particularly, real estate and finance capital). Between 1982 and 1997, the rate of profit rose 19 percent, as the rate of surplus value rose nearly 24 percent and the organic composition of capital rose just 6 percent.[6]

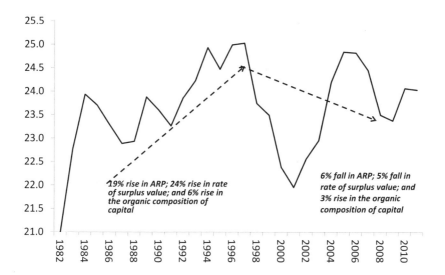

Figure 1.2. US average rate of profit (%), 1982–2011. Source: see appendix.

This "neoliberal period" had fewer severe slumps, although economic growth was still slower than in the Golden Age because profitability was still below that of the latter, particularly in the productive sectors of the US economy.[7] Much of the profit was diverted away from real investment and into the financial sector. Profitability peaked in 1997 and began to decline. Between 1997 and 2008, the rate of profit dropped 6 percent and the rate of surplus value fell 5 percent, while the organic composition of capital rose 3 percent.[8] This laid the basis for the Great Recession of 2008–2009. There was a mild contraction in the US economy in 2001, followed by a mild boom. Profitability started to fall again in late 2005 (fig. 1.2), and then we had the Great Recession of 2008–2009.[9]

The slump and the ensuing Long Depression were more severe than anything seen since the 1930s because of the huge buildup of debt and financial assets in the previous two decades (and particularly after 2002). This capital accumulation was what Marx called "fictitious" in that it did not create or represent real value; instead, there were credit-fueled bubbles, first in high-tech stocks (leading to the crash in 2000) and then in housing (leading to the crash in 2007). By 2007, the unproductive financial sector accounted for 40 percent of all US corporate profit. Finally, this credit bubble burst, bringing down the banking sector and the economy. The high level of private sector debt was compounded by the state having to bail out the banks.

Until this overhang of unproductive capital is cleared ("deleveraged"), profitability cannot be restored sufficiently to get investment and economic growth going again. Indeed, it is likely that another huge slump will be

necessary to "cleanse" the system of this "dead" (toxic) capital. The Long
Depression will continue until then. Despite the very high *mass of profit* that
has been generated since the economic recovery began in 2009,[10] the *rate of
profit* stopped rising in 2011. The average rate of profit remains below the
peak of 1997.

But the rate is clearly higher than it was in the late 1970s and early
1980s at its trough. That can be explained by one counteracting factor to
the secularly rising organic composition of capital, namely a rising rate of
surplus value since 1982,[11] as figure 1.3 shows. The story of US profitability
is also repeated for other major capitalist economies; various studies have
shown a similar trajectory for the rate of profit (Minqi Li 2008). The latest
analysis of the "world rate of profit" incorporating the G7 major economies
and the BRICs (Brazil, Russia, India, China) found that there was a fall in
the world rate of profit from the starting point of the data in 1963, and that
this never recovered to the 1963 level (Roberts 2012b).

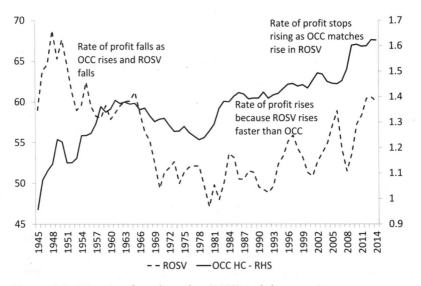

Figure 1.3. US ratio of surplus value (LHS) and the organic
composition of capital (RHS), 1945–2014. Source: see appendix.

The world rate of profit reached a low in 1975 and then rose to a peak
in the mid-1990s. Since then, the world rate of profit has been static or
slightly falling and has not returned to its peak of the 1990s. As shown in
figure 1.4, there is a divergence between the G7 rate of profit and the world
rate of profit after the early 1990s. This indicates that non-G7 economies
have played an increasing role in sustaining the rate of profit, while the G7
capitalist economies have been suffering a profitability crisis since the late
1980s, and certainly since the mid-1990s.

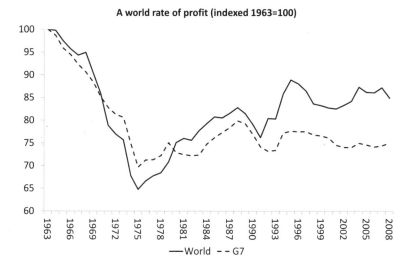

Figure 1.4. The world and G7 average rates of profit (%), indexed 1963 = 100), 1963–2008. Source: Roberts 2012b.

Globalization was the major force that enabled counteracting factors to dominate during the 1990s. Capitalism became truly global in the late twentieth century, a period in which it was similar to but far more encompassing than in the "globalization" period of the late nineteenth century. The huge increase in capitalist investment into so-called emerging capitalist economies brought into the capitalist mode of production for the first time a huge supply of peasant and non-capitalist labor, sometimes at a cost below the value of labor power in the dominant countries—what John Smith calls super-exploitation (Smith 2010).

However, the data suggest that countervailing factors are no longer sufficient to drive up the world rate of profit. To raise profitability, further destruction of capital will be necessary through another significant slump in global capitalism.[12] There is still a long way down to go for both US and global capitalism before they reach the bottom of their current downward phase.

2. The Keynesian Diagnosis

For many (but not all) Marxists, the key variable in understanding the motion of a modern capitalist economy is the rate of profit. The Marxist analysis recognizes that the underlying cause of the crisis begins with the failure of capitalist production to generate enough profit relative to capital invested. Then, capital must self-destruct in order to restore profitability and start the whole process again. This means that a sufficient mass of unprofitable, weaker capitals must go bankrupt; old technologies must be replaced by new,

more efficient ones; and sufficient employment must be generated at a higher
rate of exploitation. Until that point, capital will languish.

The Keynesians do not recognize profit, let alone the average rate of
profit (ARP), in the capitalist economy as the key variable. As do neoclassical
theorists, they start with the concept that capitalist production is for
consumption, not for profit. Consumption leads to investment in production.
Thus the key variables for Keynesians are consumption and investment.

The lack of demand can be caused by wage compression. But Keynesians
also rely on factors outside the economic process as an "explanation" for the
dynamics of the capitalist economy. If investors' and consumers' confidence
disappears, money is hoarded, demand falls, and investment stops. The state
is ascribed an important role in stimulating demand. Keynesian theory
concludes that higher profits depend on workers spending more, on the
economy exporting more and, failing that, on government dissaving or net
borrowing. So in a slump—when households are saving more and spending
less, especially less on foreign goods—the Keynes-Kalecki profit equation
argues that capitalism can be saved by more government spending, rather
than less (Kalecki 1942). However, as section 3 of this chapter will argue,
higher wages, and thus higher spending by workers, can only worsen the
crisis. Higher government spending in a downward phase leads eventually
to the financial crisis of the state.

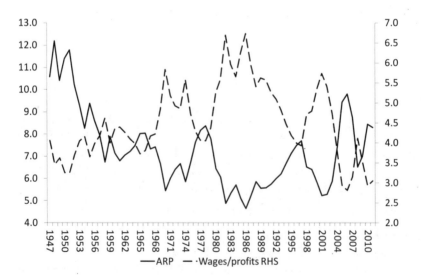

Figure 1.5. US average corporate rate of profit (LHS) and wages/
profit ratio (RHS), 1947–2011. Source: see appendix.

Indeed, there is no evidence that justifies the view that capitalism is beset
by a crisis caused by a lack of demand. Take, for example, the US economy.

The slumps of 1974–75 and 1980–82 were preceded not by a fall in wages relative to profits generating a "lack of demand." On the contrary, wages relative to profits rose, just as those major capitalist slumps were preceded by a decline in the average rate of profit for corporate business in 1973 and 1974, respectively (fig 1.5). However, after the 1980–82 slump, the average rate of profit rose, and wages fell relative to profits.[13] There was no serious slump for US capitalism after the early 1980s (the ones in 1990–91 and 2001 were mild compared with those of 1974–75 and 1980–82). So the data conform to the Marxist theory of crisis, and not to the Keynesian one.

All previous research on business cycles has concluded that the movement in investment is initially driven by movements in profit, not vice versa.[14] Our own analysis of the Great Recession confirms the conclusions of this earlier research. Profits fell for several quarters before the US economy went into a nosedive (fig. 1.6). US corporate profits peaked in early 2006—that's the absolute amount, not the rate of profit, which peaked earlier in 2005. From its peak in early 2006, the mass of profits fell until mid-2008, made a limited recovery in early 2009, and then fell to a new low in mid-2009. After that, the recovery in profits began and the previous peak in nominal dollars was surpassed in mid-2010.

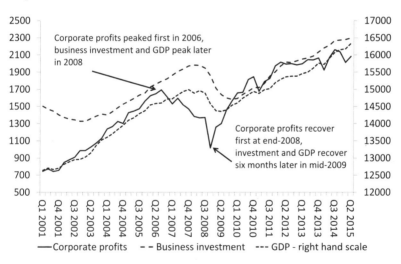

Figure 1.6. US corporate profits, real investment, and GDP Q1–2001 to Q2–2015 ($bn). Source: see appendix.

What was the reaction of investment to this movement in US profits? When US corporate profit growth started to slow in mid-2005 and then fell in absolute terms in 2006, corporate investment went on growing for a while as companies used up reserves or increased borrowing in the hope that profits would be restored. But when that did not materialize, investment growth slowed during 2007 and then fell absolutely in 2008, at one point falling at a near 20 percent year–over–year (yoy) rate. Profits started to recover at the end of 2008, but investment did not follow for a year. It was the same for GDP; GDP peaked well after profits did and also recovered after profits did. The movement of profits led the movement of investment, not vice versa. Profits were falling well before the credit crunch began. So the crisis was not due to a lack of "effective demand" but followed the Marxist law of profitability, even if the eventual trigger for the slump was in the financial sector.

3. The Keynesian Prescription

But can Keynesian policies restore an economy's profitability and end the slump? Civilian Keynesian policies can be defined as (a) state-induced, (b) capital-financed, and (c) redistribution or investment policies.[15] Let's consider redistribution first.

State-induced pro-labor redistribution

Suppose the state brings about a redistribution of value from capital to labor through pro-labor legislation, progressive taxation, or higher subsidies. Let us assume unsold consumption goods (the assumption behind Keynesian interventionism) and suppose that policies are introduced to raise net wages (direct, indirect, and deferred). More consumption goods are sold, and labor consumes more; this is why these policies are supposed to be pro-labor. Greater sales also mean fewer losses and thus the recovery of lost profits. The Keynesian argument is that these greater profits can (more than) offset increased wages, thus initiating the upturn. This is why these policies are supposed to be pro-capital as well. Both capital and labor would gain.

But does a policy aimed at increasing wages restore profitability? Let us divide the economy into the sector producing means of production (sector 1) and that producing means of consumption (sector 2).

Take first sector 1. Under the most favorable hypothesis for the Keynesian argument, the whole of the wage increase in both sectors is spent on unsold consumption goods (rather than being partly saved). On the one hand, sector 2 suffers a loss in profit due to higher wages; but on the other, it can sell the unsold means of consumption to its own laborers for an equal price. The numerator of the rate of profit is thus unchanged. But the denominator rises due to the higher investment in variable capital (labor). Labor's consumption increases, but sector 2's rate of profit falls.

Take next sector 2. Its numerator decreases (because of lower profits due to higher wages), and the denominator rises (because of higher investment in labor power). In this sector, too, labor's consumption increases, but the rate of profit falls.

Finally, higher wages in sector 1 (a loss for capital in sector 1) increase the sale of consumption goods by sector 2 to labor in sector 1 (a gain for capital in sector 2). Sector 2's gain is equal to the loss for capital in sector 1. There is no change in the two numerators.

Gains and losses in the numerators of the ARP offset each other, but the denominators in both sectors rise. So the ARP falls. Wages, and thus labor's consumption, can increase, but the ARP falls, confirming Marx's view.

Suppose now that wages keep rising up to the point where all consumption goods are sold. Supposedly, a further wage rise would spur the extra production of consumption goods, and this would stimulate the production of means of production. The economy would be revived. However, production will only increase if both demand for the extra output *and* profitability rise. But this is not the case: pro-labor redistribution raises demand, but lowers the ARP. At this new level of production, wages are higher, and profitability is lower. The Keynesian medicine fails because it assumes that the dynamics of the system depend on consumption, rather than on profitability. Even from the Keynesian perspective of profit, where the gains deriving from higher sales are supposed to offset the cost of increased wages, Keynesian policies fail because profits do not increase.

Up to this point, the implicit assumption has been that the profits are those of enterprises in the productive sectors. The conclusion has been that higher wages lower the firms' profits and profitability. But the brunt of higher wages can also fall on the profits of the firms in the unproductive sectors of the economy (commerce, finance, and speculation). In this case, labor gains from redistribution, but this policy threatens to accelerate, then burst, the financial bubble because profitability falls in these sectors. Profits in these sectors can be skimmed, but one should be aware of the consequences: your death, my life!

The brunt of a wage rise could also be borne not by the firm, but by the capitalists' own (unproductive) consumption. In this case, a pro-labor redistribution would increase labor's consumption but decrease that of the capitalists. Assuming that lower profit rates curb investments and that labor has a higher propensity to consume than capital, the investments induced by labor's higher consumption could increase by a greater amount than the decrease in investments caused by capital's reduced consumption. Both productive capital and labor would gain. This argument suggests a supposed community of interests between labor and productive capital against parasitic capital. However, it overlooks that, as a rule, the organic composition of new investments is higher, such that profitability falls. It also ignores that if, on balance, investments do increase, the more important question is whether, at the end of the chain of investments induced by the initial ones, the new average organic composition is higher or lower than the old one, and thus whether the ARP rises or falls as a result (see the Marxist multiplier below).

Most would argue in favor of a redistribution from capitalists' unproductive consumption to that of labor. This seems self-evident in terms of equity. But this is not the same as concluding that the policy would revive the capitalist economy. Higher wages reduce the capitalists' unproductive consumption and do not stimulate investments. The means of consumption that are not purchased by the capitalists are purchased by labor—a redistributive measure, which has been considered above.

Some capitalists—the more robust ones—might decide to increase production even at lower levels of profitability. However, on the one hand, if profitability keeps falling, investments will soon fall, too. And on the other, if profitability keeps falling, other (weaker) capitalists will go bankrupt and cease production altogether. It follows that capitalists will *reduce* their investments/output, in spite of the higher demand induced by pro-labor policies.[16]

State-induced investments and the Marxist multiplier

The strongest case for Keynesian policies is not the effect on the redistribution of national income, but the impact from state-induced investments. The first issue that is ignored by Keynesians (and some Marxists who advocate this policy) concerns who is supposed to finance these investments. There are two possibilities: either capital or labor.[17] Second, while the distinction is important from the point of view of who pays for these investments, the impact on profitability is relatively independent of which class initially pays for these policies.

Consider capital-financed investments. Let us distinguish between sector 1, the producer of public works, and sector 2, the rest of the economy. Let us say surplus value (S) is appropriated (e.g., taxed) by the state from sector 2 and channeled into sector 1 for the production of public works.[18] S is the loss for sector 2 and a deduction from its surplus value. Having appropriated S from sector 2, the state pays sector 1 a certain profit (p) and advances the rest ($S - p$) to sector 1 for the production of public works.

The state receives public works from sector 1 to the value of $S - p + p^\star$, where $p^\star$ is the surplus value generated in sector 1 (whether $p^\star$ is equal to p or not). Sector 1 realizes its profits because it has received p from the state, while $p^\star$ belongs to the state. Sector 2 loses S but sector 1 gains p. In sum, private capital loses $S - p$ to the state and the numerator of the ARP decreases by that much. So, initially, the ARP falls. In the case where labor finances the public works through taxation, the ARP rises because both capitalist sectors receive a share of the value of labor as surplus value.

But whether it is capital or labor that finances public works, the final outcome of these policies on the ARP will depend on what we call the Marxist multiplier.[19] To produce public works, sector 1 purchases labor power and means of production from other firms in both sectors. In their turn, these firms engage in further purchases of means of production and labor power. This multiplier effect cascades throughout the economy.

Under the most favorable hypothesis for the Keynesian argument, the state-induced investments are large enough to absorb the unsold goods and then stimulate new production. But given that the firms involved in the cascade effect have different organic compositions, three outcomes are possible for the ARP:

(1) In the first case, the initial investment by sector 1 (whether capital-financed or labor-financed) plus the further investments induced by it in both sectors are such that their average organic composition is equal to the average organic composition of the pre–public works economy. After these investments, the organic composition and the ARP do not change. *The policy fails to raise the ARP.*

(2) Alternatively, the chain of investments stops at a point at which the new investments' average organic composition is higher than that of the pre–public investments average organic composition. The new average organic composition has risen. This is the most likely outcome, given that new investments tend to incorporate new technologies with higher organic composition. *The ARP falls, and so the policy fails.*

(3) In the opposite case, where the new average organic composition falls because the new investments have a lower-than-average organic composition, the ARP can rise. But then the Keynesian policy has helped the less efficient capitals—those with lower organic composition (and thus lower efficiency)—to survive. In this case, *the crisis is only postponed* because eventually capital will rediscover its innate tendency, that of investing in more efficient, and thus high-organic-composition, techniques.

Most importantly, none of these three possible outcomes are policy options that can be determined a priori by the state. After the initial investment, the final result in terms of organic composition and ARP depends on the spontaneous activity of the system. The state can influence only the first step, by appropriating value either from labor or from capital, and by initially commissioning public investments to low- or to high-organic-composition capitals. *But more commissions will be given to the most efficient, and thus higher-organic-composition, capitals.* Figure 1.7 provides a summary of the above assessment of Keynesian policies.

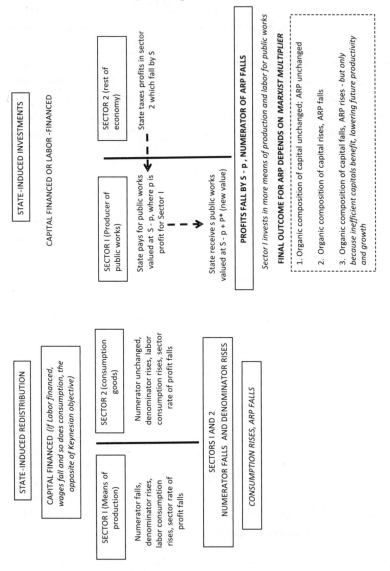

Figure 1.7. Keynesian policies and the Marxist multiplier. Source: authors.

Empirical evidence suggests that government spending (whether state-induced consumption or investment) has little impact on economic growth. Thus, the Keynesian multiplier is ineffective. In contrast, the Marxist multiplier, where changes in profitability lead to changes in real GDP growth, is much larger. (For further empirical evidence, see Carchedi, chapter 2, section 16 of this book).

The Keynesian multiplier would suggest that if governments tighten their fiscal balances that should lead to a corresponding contraction in real GDP growth. But if we look at the change in the real GDP between 2010 and 2015 against the degree of fiscal tightening, the result does show a negative correlation for the G6 plus distressed Eurozone economies between 2010 and 2015. But interestingly, there is positive correlation for the G6 alone. In other words, the tighter the fiscal impact, the better the GDP pick-up in the G6 economies—the opposite of the conclusions of the Keynesian multiplier (fig. 1.8).

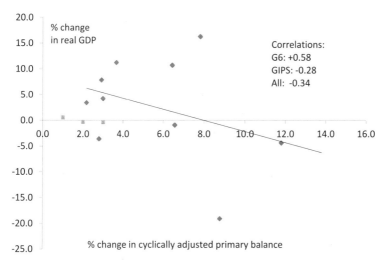

Figure 1.8. Changes in real GDP and cyclically adjusted primary balance 2010–15 (as % GDP). Source: see appendix.

If we compare changes in government spending to GDP against the average rate of real GDP growth since 2009 for the member economies of the Organisation for Economic Co-operation and Development (OECD), there is a very weak positive correlation, and none if Greece is removed.

Now let's consider the impact of changes in the profitability of business capital against economic growth (the Marxist multiplier). As shown in figure 1.9, there is a significant positive correlation between changes in profitability of capital and economic growth. The correlations are positive for G6 and the distressed Eurozone economies (GIPS), and at much higher levels than with the Keynesian multiplier. So we find that real GDP growth is strongly correlated with changes in the profitability of capital, while the correlation is only slightly negative with changes in government spending.

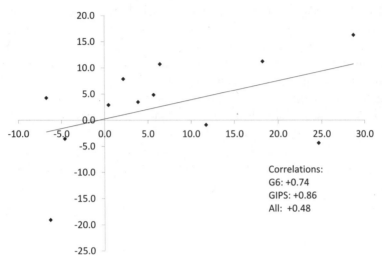

Figure 1.9. The Marxist multiplier: change in real GDP (vertical) and change in net return on capital (horizontal) (%), 2010–15. Source: see appendix.

If we compare the impact of the Keynesian multiplier (measured as the ratio of change in average real GDP growth to change in real government spending) for the top six economies against that of the Marxist multiplier (measured as the ratio of the change in average real GDP growth to the change in the net return on capital), the impact is much higher in the 1970s and from the 2000s to 2014, especially since the Great Recession, when you would expect the Keynesian multiplier to be strong. Only in the 1980s and 1990s is the Keynesian multiplier larger, and then only by a small margin (fig. 1.10).

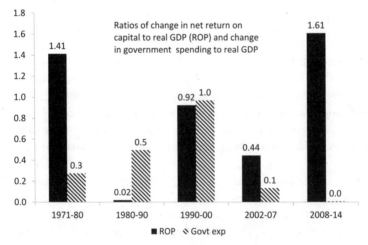

Figure 1.10. The Keynesian and Marxist multipliers in the United States, 1971–2014, change in ratios. Source: see appendix.

Would monetary policies help?

Rather than stimulate demand through state redistribution or state-induced investments, some Keynesians propose to do so by increasing the quantity of money.[20] Their assumption is that the ultimate cause of crises is a lack of "effective demand," such that a higher quantity of money in circulation could stimulate demand, investments, and growth.

Consider first the empirical evidence. Figures 1.1, 1.4, and 1.5 show unmistakably the secular falling trend in the ARP. If monetary policies have failed for more than sixty years to reverse the trend, why would they succeed now? Indeed, there is no reason to think they would. First, inasmuch as money is actually printed, no new (surplus) value is created. The economy cannot restart if, in spite of higher demand, the surplus value produced relative to the capital invested is unchanged. Printing money merely increases the *representation* of value. By printing money, the state redistributes value already produced, but no new (surplus) value is generated. We have seen that pro-labor redistribution cannot offer a way out of the slump; and we shall see in section 4 that pro-capital redistribution cannot do so either.

Second, by "printing money" what is really meant is expanding credit. The notion that credit is money is almost universally accepted and yet fundamentally wrong. By creating credit, one does not "create money out of nothing"—an absurd proposition. Out of nothing, one can create nothing. By creating credit, one creates debt, not money.

Central banks have increased the supply of money globally ("power money"), but the quantity of this money is tiny compared to the growth of credit or debt in the form of bank loans, debt securities, and their derivatives. Power money has risen from 4 percent of world GDP in the late 1980s to 11 percent now. But all forms of credit started at 150 percent of world GDP and are now over 350 percent of global GDP—some thirty times more than power money (fig. 1.11).

Eventually debts must be repaid. So credit expansion only postpones a crisis to the moment of debt repayment. The Keynesian argument is that debts can be repaid when, possibly due to Keynesian policies, the economy restarts and the appropriation of the surplus value needed for debt repayment no longer threatens the recovery. But this is wishful thinking. Pro-labor redistribution compresses profitability and thus worsens the crisis. State-induced investments can in principle raise profitability, but this is not a way out of the slump; rather, it is merely a postponement of the eruption of the crisis. By postponing the recovery, the policies are an *obstacle to*, rather than a *condition for*, the state's repayment of its debt.[21]

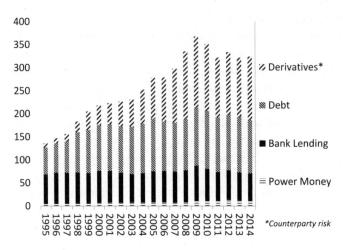

Figure 1.11. Global liquidity ($trn), 1995–2014. Source: see appendix.

The crisis must itself create the conditions for its own solution, namely the destruction of capital. Only when sufficient (backward) capitals have been destroyed (have gone bankrupt) can the more efficient productive units start producing again on an enlarged scale. It follows that if Keynesian policies postpone the impact of the crisis, they also postpone the recovery.

The idea that state-induced investment policies (possibly through state borrowing) could start a sustained recovery, provided that the scale is sufficiently large, is not only theoretically invalid (as we have outlined above) but also empirically unsubstantiated. The example commonly mentioned is the long period of prosperity that followed World War II, the so-called Golden Age of capitalism. Supposedly Keynesian-style policies, through government borrowing (budget deficits), made it possible to kick-start the long period of prosperity of 1946–70. But US gross federal debt as a percentage of GDP actually *decreased* during the Golden Age, from 121.7 percent in 1946 to 37.6 percent in 1970. The long spell of prosperity was due not to credit creation, but to the reconversion of military into civilian capital and to the liberation of pent-up purchasing power after the war.[22]

4. Austerians versus Keynesians

Nowadays, the dominant economic theory is the Austerian one. For it, the cause of crises is that wages are too high. In order to assess this thesis, we must start from a period of rising profitability; in fact, if we were to start from a period of falling profitability, we would *assume* a period of crisis, which is precisely what we want to explain.

The point is that higher wages cause a fall in profits only if the quantity of the new value generated (wages plus profits) is either stagnant or decreasing.

But this conjecture assumes that which has to be explained. On the other hand, in periods of rising profitability, if wages rise, profits do not necessarily fall; they may simply rise less. The theory is thus indeterminate: once the crisis has begun, higher wages worsen it, but that which worsens the crisis is not its cause. This is the root cause of neoliberalism's mistake.

What the Austerians propose are, in effect, various forms of pro-capital redistribution. They urge reductions in budget deficits and levels of public debt, most obviously by cutting wages. They oppose "quantitative easing" and instead propose to hike interest rates at the first opportunity. The purpose of these policies is clear: to restore profitability through a shift of value from labor to capital, while at the same time avoiding policy measures that interfere with the market.

If higher wages are not the cause of the crisis, wage compression cannot be its cure. Lower wages imply higher rates of exploitation. Under the assumption that constant capital is greater than surplus value, if the ARP falls by a certain percentage because of the rise in the organic composition of capital (OCC), the rate of exploitation must rise by a greater rate for the ARP to return to its previous level. It must increase even more for the ARP to rise above its previous level; that is to say, it becomes increasingly difficult for the rise in the rate of exploitation to counter the rise in the OCC. This is the nature of a countertendency: each time the OCC rises, the rate of exploitation must rise even more to bring the ARP back to (or above) its level before the rise in the OCC.

Critics of the law hold that the movement in the rate of exploitation is indeterminate. The rate of exploitation might, or might not, increase more than the OCC, such that it might, or might not, halt and reverse the fall in the ARP. But this is not the question. The question is whether an increase in the rate of profit due to a sufficiently high rate of exploitation is a step toward recovery.

A recovery presupposes the rise in the new value generated within the context of a rising ARP. A pro-capital distribution of value within the context of a falling ARP can revive the ARP, but this does not denote a recovery. This higher profitability hides the *decreasing* production of value and surplus value—that is, it hides the deterioration of the economy. This is why Austerian policies cannot succeed as anti-crisis policies.

A more detailed way to approach this is is by considering the two basic sectors of the economy. Sector 1 produces means of production, and sector 2 produces means of consumption. If one or both sectors innovate, usually the OCC rises and the ARP falls. All sectors realize tendentially the same, but lower, rate of profit. The capitalists might react to the lower ARP by lowering the level of wages, that is, by increasing the rate of exploitation across the board. This upsets the initial tendential equalization of the profit rates. *But this equalization presupposes full realization, which is impossible if stopping or reversing the fall in the ARP is to be achieved by raising the rate of exploitation.*

Suppose wages are reduced by the same percentage, Δ, both in sector 1 and in sector 2, represented by the equation $-\Delta v1 = -\Delta v2$. Then, sector 1 gains $\Delta s1$ (corresponding to the fall in wages, $-\Delta s1$). Sector 2 on the one hand gains $\Delta s2$ (corresponding to the fall in wages, $-\Delta v2$) but on the other loses $-(\Delta s1 + \Delta s2)$, the loss due to the unsold means of consumption to the workers both of sector 1 and of sector 2. On balance, sector 2 loses $-\Delta s1$, which is sector 1's gain. Means of consumption for a value of $\Delta s1$ are unsold. This is overproduction in sector 2.

The ARP is unchanged (what is lost by one sector is gained by the other), but the two rates of profit differ: that in sector 1 has risen by $\Delta s1$, while that in sector 2 has fallen by the same quantity. *The greater the fall in wages, the greater the fall of profitability in sector 2.* This spells crisis in sector 2. Sector 1's rate of profit rises. But this is not a sign of recovery in that sector. Sector 1's rate of profit rises not because more value and surplus value is produced in it, but because surplus value is appropriated from sector 2 within the context of a hidden fall in the ARP. Wage cuts can, at most, postpone the crisis.

Yet Keynesian economists perceive state-induced "austerity" (an ideologically laden word that should be carefully avoided) as the cause of the crisis. For example, Stiglitz (2002) criticizes austerity policies to the effect that wage cutbacks reduce income and thus profitability. If wage cuts were the cause of the crisis, the slump could be countered by raising wages. But if wage cuts merely postpone the crisis, then in the long run the policy is useless. *In sum, the tendency toward crisis will operate whether wages increase or decrease.*

Keynesians think that the economy can be revived by the Fed raising "expectations" (falsely), along with more government spending, enabled, if necessary, by more borrowing. The Austerians reckon that adding to debt will prolong the crisis. The Keynesians disagree.[23] Both sides continue to focus on the financial sector as the root cause of the slump, and not on the productive sectors that create (not enough) surplus value. Marxists reckon that you can tinker with more or less money creation, but that this will have little effect if the productive sectors of the economy are not recovering sufficiently to increase investment and employment.

Appendix: Sources and Methods

Figure 1.1. The ARP has been smoothed into a ten-year rolling average.

Figure 1.2. The US ARP measure is based on the whole economy. Profits = net national product (BEA, NIPA table 1.10) less employee compensation (BEA, NIPA table 6.2). Constant capital = historic cost net fixed private nonresidential assets (BEA, NIPA table 4.1). Variable capital = employee compensation (BEA, NIPA table 6.2).

Figure 1.3. The rate of surplus value = profit divided by variable capital. Organic composition of capital = constant capital divided by variable capital.

Figure 1.4. Data sources and methods can be found in Roberts (2012b).

Figure 1.5. Profits are from NIPA tables 6.17A, 6.17B, 6.17C, 6.17D: corporate profits before tax by industry. In the first three tables, utilities are excluded.

Fixed assets: The definition is "equipment, software, and structures, including owner-occupied housing" (http://www.bea.gov/national/pdf/Fixed_Assets_1925_97.pdf). The data considered in this chapter comprise agriculture, mining, construction, and manufacturing (but not utilities; see above). Fixed assets are obtained from BEA, table 3.3ES: Historical-Cost Net Stock of Private Fixed Assets by Industry ($ billion; year-end estimates).

Wages for goods-producing industries are obtained from NIPA tables 2.2A and 2.2B: wages and salaries disbursements by industry ($ billion). Employment in goods-producing industries is obtained from: US Department of Labor, Bureau of Labor Statistics, series ID CES0600000001.

The money ARP is computed by dividing profits of a certain year by constant and variable capital of the preceding year conform the temporal approach. It is computed for the productive sectors. The best approximation to this are the goods-producing industries. These are defined as agriculture, mining, utilities, construction, and manufacturing. However, utilities are disregarded (see above). Constant capital includes only fixed and not circulating capital because of difficulties of estimating the latter on the basis of the available statistics. The inclusion of circulating capital would only depress the ARP further. See note 4 in this chapter.

Figure 1.6. Data from FRED, Federal Reserve Bank of St Louis. GDP = real gross domestic product, BEA, NIPA ($ billion), chained 2005, GDPC96. Investment = real private nonresidential fixed investment ($ billion), chained 2006, PNFIC96. Corporate profits = corporate profits with IV and CC adjustments as annualized CPROFIT.

Figure 1.7. Developed from Carchedi (2012).

Figures 1.8, 1.9, and 1.10: Data from AMECO database: Net returns on capital stock (APNDK); gross domestic product at 2010 levels (OVGD); general government net lending (UBLG); cyclically adjusted primary balance (FMGOC%R).

Figure 1.11: BIS, IMF debt statistics compiled by the authors.

Notes

1   The authors support the view that the only meaningful rate of profit in Marxist terms is one based on measuring constant capital in historic costs. But there are differences among the supporters of this thesis. Kliman (2012) measures the rate of profit in historic costs and concludes that there was no significant rise in profitability during the so-called neoliberal period. Roberts (2011), using a different measure of profit but with constant capital based on historic costs, does find such a rise. Carchedi (in chapter 2 in this volume) also finds a rise after 1986 in the average rate of profit for productive sectors, but a fall if the increase in exploitation is factored out. Jones (2012, p. 7), "using a revised measure of historic

costs," also finds that there was a "recovery in the rate of profit following 1983 which was volatile, but significant."

2   This point is empirically substantiated in chapter 2 in this volume.

3   For a detailed analysis of the redistribution inherent in the process of price formation, see Carchedi (1991).

4   The empirical material in section 1 of this chapter concerns the whole of the US economy while section 2 focuses on the corporate sector and section 3 on the productive sector only (for the definition of the productive sector, see the appendix). The consideration of both the productive sectors the unproductive ones adds strength to our argument because, while the measures of the ARP and the shape of the cycle differ moderately according to whether the unproductive sectors are considered or not, the trends, the results, and the conclusions are the same.

5   All empirical research on the US rate of profit agrees with this statement. See Roberts (2009, 2011), Carchedi (2011a, 2011b, 2012; chapter 2 in this volume), and Kliman (2012), among others. See Roberts (2009, 2011) for references to other research. Basu and Manolakos (2010) applied econometric analysis to the US economy between 1948 and 2007 and found that there was a secular tendency for the rate of profit to fall with a measurable decline of about 0.3 percent a year "after controlling for counter-tendencies." Roberts finds an average decline of 0.4 percent a year through 2009 using the latest data.

6   The organic composition rose more in the productive sectors (see section 3).

7   See Carchedi (2011b) and chapter 2 in this volume for the causes of the rise and fall of the Golden Age.

8   Profitability peaked in 1997 (9.23 percent) and reached its lowest point in 2009 (4.45 percent). The organic composition rose from 1.75 percent in 1977 to 2.4 percent in 2008. The rate of exploitation fell from 25.38 percent in 1997 to 16.34 percent in 2009. But profitability in the productive sectors rose from 2002 to 2006. Thus, many analysts argue that the crisis cannot be due to falling profitability. This point is dealt with in Carchedi, chapter 2 in this volume.

9   Basu and Vasudevan (2011), like a number of other authors, argue that the "current crisis cannot be viewed as a crisis of profitability." Yet the authors also show that the cost of mechanization rose six times faster after 2000 than in the previous two decades. So the downward pressure on the rate of profit was resumed despite a rising rate of surplus value or exploitation. Therefore the authors conclude, "It was capitalism's dynamic drive to accumulate and innovate that led to the potential erosion of profitability."

10   Total US corporate profits reached a low at the end of 2008 of $971 billion at the depth of the slump, but then recovered to surpass the previous peak and reach $1,953 billion by the end of 2011, but profits have declined to $1,921 billion by mid-2012.

11   The rate of surplus value rose from 0.47 to 0.57, or 21 percent, up to 2005, while the organic composition of capital rose from 1.24 to 1.31, or just 6 percent. After 2005, the organic composition began to rise sharply, while the rate of surplus value tapered off. The rate of profit fell from 2006 onward, a good year or more before the credit crunch and two years before the recession.

12   Following Marx, by "destruction of capital" we mean, essentially, bankruptcies and unemployment.

13 The measure for the US rate of profit in figure 1.2 is based on the "whole economy" and not just the corporate sectors as in figure 1.5. Thus, the figures are based on different categories for the measurement of profit and fixed assets as a result. Figure 1.2 also starts in 1982, while figure 1.5 starts in 1947. While the turning points in profitability differ slightly, the same trends appear in both measures.

14 See Mitchell (1927), Tinbergen (1939), Haberler (1960), Feldstein and Summers (1997), Bakir and Campbell (2006), and Cámara (2010). More recently, Tapia (chapter 3 of this volume), using regression analysis, finds that over the duration of 251 quarters of US economic activity beginning in 1947, profits started declining long before investment did; he also find that that pre-tax profits can explain 44 percent of all movement in investment, while there is no evidence that investment can explain any movement in profits. Yet the Keynesians ignore this evidence and continue with the mantra that "it is investment that calls the tune," to use the phrase of Hyman Minsky.

15 We disregard military Keynesianism.

16 This, by the way, undermines conventional economics at its very foundations because it shows the fallacy of equilibrium: higher demand following higher wages does not cause an increase in supply if the profitability inherent in the greater investment and output falls. Lower profitability reduces purchasing power through lower employment and regulates the relation between effective demand and supply. The rate of profit determines effective demand and supply, and a change in the former changes also the latter.

17 Other classes receive their income from the two fundamental classes.

18 This is a simplification. The state appropriates surplus value, for instance, by taxing both sectors. The point is that sector 1 receives more surplus value to invest than it loses to the state.

19 See Carchedi (2012).

20 See Roberts (2012a).

21 There is no affinity between this conclusion and that of the Austrian school. For the Austrian school, the economy, if not tampered with, tends toward equilibrium (rather than toward crises, as in Marx), and government intervention is the cause of crises (rather than one of the many countertendencies).

22 See Carchedi (2011b). See also the IMF "World Economic Outlook," October 2012, chapter 3, on the reasons for the reduction in US federal debt after 1945. According to the IMF case study, high fiscal surpluses, strong GDP growth, and inflation accompanied the reduction in the debt ratio—not Keynesian cuts in interest rates or increased budget deficits (although the IMF tries to suggest the former as the cause).

23 In 2010, Krugman seemed to recognize that there could be "debt-driven slumps." He wrote a piece with Gauti Eggertsson (2010, p. 22) arguing that an "overhang of debt on the part of some agents who are forced into deleveraging is depressing demand." Yet more recently, Krugman appeared to deny the role of public sector debt in crises. Krugman says it does not matter in a "closed economy"—one where one man's debt is another's asset. For him, it would seem, it's only a problem if you owe it to foreigners.

References

Bakir, E. and A. Campbell (2006) "The Effect of Neoliberalism on the Fall of the Rate of Profit in Business Cycles," *Review of Radical Political Economics*, Vol 38, No 3.

Basu, D. and P. Manolakos (2010) "Is There a Tendency for the Rate of Profit to Fall? Econometric Evidence for the U.S. Economy, 1948–2007," Working Paper 2010–04, University of Massachusetts, Amherst.

Basu, D. and R. Vasudevan (2011) "Technology, Distribution and the Rate of Profit in the US Economy: Understanding the Current Crisis," University of Massachusetts, Amherst, http://gesd.free.fr/basuvasu.pdf.

Bourne, R. (2012) "Estonia: A Case Study: How and Why Estonia Embraced Austerity," pamphlet, Centre for Policy Studies.

Cámara I., S. (2010) "Short and Long Term Dynamics of the US Rate of Profit in the Context of the Current Crisis," paper presented at the Congrès Marx International VI, "Crises, Révoltes, Utopies."

Carchedi, G. (1991) *Frontiers of Political Economy*, Verso.

———. (2011a) *Behind the Crisis*, Brill.

———. (2011b) "Behind and beyond the crisis," *International Socialism*, No 132.

———. (2012) "Could Keynes end the slump? Introducing the Marxist multiplier," *International Socialism*, No 136.

Feldstein, M. and L. Summers (1977) "Is the Rate of Profit Falling?," *Brookings Papers on Economic Activity*, No 1.

Haberler, G. (1960) *Prosperity and Depression: A Theoretical Analysis of Cyclical Movements*, revised ed., League of Nations.

International Monetary Fund. (2012) "World Economic Outlook, October 2012," International Monetary Fund, World Economic and Financial Surveys.

Jones, P. (2012) "Depreciation, Devaluation and the Rate of Profit," paper to the WAPE/AHE/IIPPE conference, 2012, available at http://gesd.free.fr/jonesp12.pdf.

Kalecki, M. (1942) "A Theory of Profits," *Economic Journal*, Vol 52, Nos 206/207, pp. 258–67, available at https://esepuba.files.wordpress.com/2011/10/kalecki-1942.pdf.

Kliman, A. (2012) *The Failure of Capitalist Production: Underlying Causes of the Great Recession*, Pluto Press.

Krugman, P. (2011) "Debt Is (Mostly) Money We Owe to Ourselves," *New York Times*, February 6, https://krugman.blogs.nytimes.com/2015/02/06/debt-is-money-we-owe-to-ourselves/.

Krugman, P. and G. Eggertsson (2010) "Debt, Deleveraging and the Liquidity Trap," mimeo, Federal Reserve Bank of New York.

Minqi, L. (2008) *The Rise of China and the Demise of the Capitalist World Economy*, 4th ed., Harvard University Press.

Minqi, L., F. Xiao, and A. Zhu (2007) "Long Waves, Institutional Changes and Historical Trends," *Journal of World-Systems Research*, Vol 13, No 1.

Mitchell, W. C. (1913) *Business Cycles*, University of California Press.

———. (1927) *Business Cycles: The Problem and Its Setting*, NBER.

Norfield, T. (2012) "Finance, the Rate of Profit and Imperialism," paper to WAPE/AHE/IIPPE conference.

Roberts, M. (2009) "The Great Recession: Profit Cycles, Economic Crisis: A Marxist view," Lulu.com.

———. (2010), "The Causes of the Great Recession: Mainstream and Heterodox Interpretations and the Cherry Pickers," paper to the tenth conference of the Association of Heterodox Economists.

————. (2011), "Measuring the rate of profit, profit cycles and the next recession," paper to the eleventh AHE Conference.

————. (2012a) "Krugman and Depression Economics," *The Next Recession*, May 27, https://thenextrecession.wordpress.com/2012/05/27/krugman-and-depression-economics/.

————. (2012b) "A World Rate of Profit," paper to the WAPE/AHE/IIPPE conference.

Smith, J. (2010) "Imperialism and the Globalisation of Production," PhD thesis, University of Sheffield.

Stiglitz, J. (2002) "Is Keynesian Economics Dead?," *Project Syndicate,* May 7, https://www.project-syndicate.org/commentary/is-keynesian-economics-dead?barrier=accessreg.

Tapia, J. A. (2012) "Does Investment Call the Tune? Empirical Evidence and Endogenous Theories of the Business Cycle," reprinted in this volume as chapter 3, "Investment, Profit and Crises: Theories and Evidence."

Tinbergen, J. (1939) *Statistical Testing of Business-Cycle Theories*, Vol 2, *Business Cycles in the United States of America, 1919–1932*, League of Nations.

Tognonato, C. (2005) "Le fabbriche agli operai," *Il Manifesto* (journal), February 1.

CHAPTER 2

THE OLD IS DYING BUT THE NEW CANNOT BE BORN: ON THE EXHAUSTION OF WESTERN CAPITALISM

Guglielmo Carchedi

1. Some Basic Concepts

A fundamental tenet of Marx's theory of history and revolution is the contradiction between labor's productive forces and the capitalist production relation. In *A Contribution to the Critique of Political Economy*, he writes, "At a certain stage of development the material productive forces of society come into conflict with the existing relations of production. . . . From forms of development of the productive forces these relations turn into their fetters" (Marx 1970, p. 21). Traditionally, this passage has been read within the context of a theory of transition from capitalism to socialism or communism. But it applies just as well to the transition from one historical phase of capitalist development to the following one.

Let us begin with *labor's productive force*. This is labor's productivity, that is, the ratio of output to employment. The *relation of production* is the relation between capital and labor. Quantitatively, it is the relation between the capital invested and employment.

The contradiction between labor's productive force (productivity) and the (capitalist) relation of production is this. In a first stage, new investments in constant capital do not incorporate new technologies. Employment grows together with investments in constant capital, but after a while, due to technological competition, capital is invested in new technologies, which are labor-shedding. New technologies are productivity-increasing but labor-shedding. Thus, this greater labor productivity is the other side of the greater shedding of labor. Because only labor produces value and surplus value (a point to be shown shortly), as productivity *increases*, the labor shed by capital *increases*, the value and surplus value produced per unit of capital *decreases*, the organic composition of capital (OCC)— that is, the relation between constant capital (means of production) and variable capital (labor)—*increases*, and the profit rate *decreases*, ceteris paribus. The fall in the rate of profit is the synthetic manifestation of this contradiction: higher productivity but lower profitability. Within the context of a nation or a group of nations, what counts is the fall in the average rate of profit (ARP). The fall in the profit rate is the key variable to understanding not only economic crises, but also why and how the old—namely capitalism—is dying.

2. The Empirical Validation of the Labor Theory of Value

Let us consider the ARP of the United States, economically still the most important nation nowadays.[1] Statistical data show that while the OCC (i.e., the shedding of labor) grows tendentially, the ARP is in a state of irreversible fall. The fall is tendential, meaning it goes through upward and downward cycles. But the trend, the empirical measure of the tendency, is clearly downward.

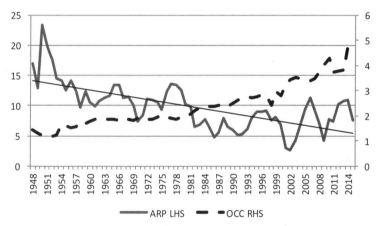

Figure 2.1. Average rate of profit (ARP) and organic composition of capital (OCC), 1948–2015.[2] Source: author's calculations.

The tendential replacement of labor by means of production causes the OCC to grow, from 1.4 in 1947 to 4.6 in 2015. At the same time, the ARP falls from 16.8 percent in 1948 to 7.6 percent in 2015, with a peak of 23.3 percent in 1950. If less labor (high OCC) means a lower ARP and thus a lower surplus value, more labor (lower OCC) means a higher ARP and thus a higher surplus value. It follows that only labor, and not the means of production, produces value and surplus value. Figure 2.1 is thus the empirical verification of the *labor theory of value's fundamental assumption*: that *labor and only labor is value and thus surplus value.*[3]

3. Monopolies and the ARP

It is usually assumed that the equalization of the rates of profits into an average
(ARP) requires capital mobility across sectors and (price) competition
within sectors. But in a monopolized economy, these conditions are lacking.
Supposedly, the tendency toward an equalization of the profit rate does
not apply to monopolies and thus to modern economies. Empirically, this
thesis is clearly wrong. Internationally, there has never been a greater capital
movement in and out of sectors (direct foreign investments), nor as much
interpenetration of capitals as there has been since the globalization following
the fall of the Soviet Union. Also, the financial sector contributes to the
formation of the ARP through the sale/purchase of shares with different
yields. Modern economies are oligopolistic rather than monopolistic.

But aside from this objection, assume for the sake of argument that
each sector of production is a monopoly (only one producer per sector)
and that there is no capital movement in and out of sectors. Then, there
would be no tendential equalization of the profit rates. However, it can
be argued that monopolies compete through technological innovations and
that they replace capital movement as the factor equalizing tendentially the
monopolies' rates of profit.

Under the assumptions above, each monopoly must sell its output not
only to the consumers but also to other monopolies (sectors). This does not
imply a lack of technological innovations.[4] On the contrary, if a monopoly
innovates (call it "M1") through labor-shedding and productivity-increasing
technologies, it produces a greater output but less value and surplus value.
Given a certain technical composition of capital, M1 must exchange the
same quantity of its products against the same quantities of the output of
other monopolies (call them "M2"). But M1's output has become bigger due
to productivity-increasing innovations. M1 cannot sell its entire product,
due to M2's lack of purchasing power. Therefore, M1 exchanges only a
share of its output, and thus a part of the value it has produced, for the same
quantity of output and value produced by M2. It gives the other monopolies
less value and surplus value and it receives from them the same value and
surplus value. The unsold commodities are a loss for M1. Thus on balance
its rate of profit remains the same. But in the next cycle, M1 invests less
constant and variable capital, in order to produce only the commodities it
can sell to M2. It produces less surplus value but appropriates surplus value
from M2. The unused capital is a reserve rather than a loss, as in the case
of unsold commodities. M1's rate of profit rises at the cost of the other
monopolies, which lose a part of their surplus value to M1.

M2's profitability falls, and they are forced to innovate to restore
profitability. Due to technological competition, the different profit rates
tend toward an average, even in the absence of capital mobility. This average

tends to fall because the innovators, by replacing the labor force with assets, generate less surplus value. The crisis is in the making. Marx's law operates in the same way as in non-monopolistic markets.

4. The ARP with Variable and Constant Rate of Exploitation: Why an Increase in Exploitation Cannot Hold Back Crises

Figure 2.1 shows that until the mid-1980s, while the OCC rises, the ARP falls, conforming to Marx's thesis. However, starting from the mid-1980s, while the OCC rises, the ARP rises, too, instead of falling. This has led some to question the general validity of the inverse relation between the ARP and the OCC. For Marx, a higher OCC leads to a fall in the ARP, and thus to crises. But figure 2.1 shows that since 1986, a higher OCC seems to lead to higher average profitability and thus to economic growth, while figure 2.7 shows that this period has been marred by several crises (1986, 1989–91, 2001–2002, 2007–2009). Not all crises would seem to be determined by falling profitability.

This critique neglects a fundamental point. The ARP can rise for two reasons. First, it can do so because surplus value rises due to employment rising more than assets. This is economic growth, where both profits and wages rise, and the OCC falls. This scenario presupposes an unchanged rate of exploitation (or a rate of exploitation lower than the increase in employment). Second, the ARP can rise because of a higher rate of exploitation with an unchanged or rising OCC. This is not economic growth; neither employment nor assets grow. In this case, a rise in the OCC is compatible with a rise in the ARP, but since there is no economic growth, crises can mature and emerge. They are only temporarily held back by a greater rate of exploitation.

Thus, to determine if higher profitability indicates economic growth (which would be incompatible with crises), we need a measure of profitability in which changes in the rates of exploitation are factored out. One such measure can be obtained by computing the rate of profit with a constant rate of exploitation (from now on, CE-ARP). If changes in the rate of exploitation are factored out, the ARP falls throughout, until 2015 (fig. 2.2).

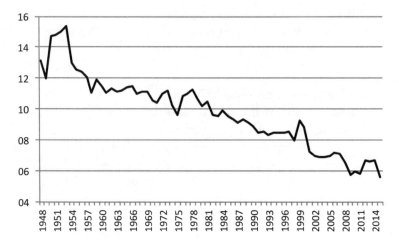

Figure 2.2. ARP with constant rate of exploitation (CE–ARP), 1948–2015. Source: author's calculations.

Figure 2.3 compares the two measures of the ARP: the ARP with variable rate of exploitation (VE-ARP, as in fig. 2.1) and the rate of profit with a constant rate of exploitation (CE-ARP, as in fig. 2.2).

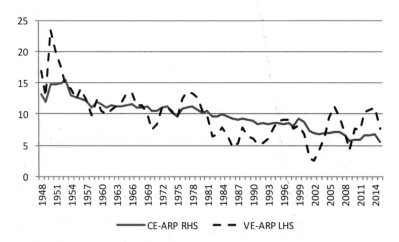

CE-ARP RHS   VE-ARP LHS

Figure 2.3. CE–ARP and VE–ARP, 1948–2015. Source: author's calculations.

Figure 2.3 shows two important points. First, starting from the mid-1980s, the VE-ARP rises while the CE-ARP falls. The generation of surplus value per unit of capital invested has fallen, but a greater proportion has been appropriated by capital through rising rates of exploitation. *The rise in profitability is due to higher rates of exploitation, rather than to employment rising more than assets (economic growth).* Second, the *VE-ARP fluctuates around the CE-*

ARP—that is, variations (increases) in the rate of exploitation cannot hold back the fall in the CE-ARP. Increases in the rate of exploitation are only a temporary countertendency. *Higher rates of exploitation cannot hold back the fall in the generation of profits relative to the capital invested and thus the emergence of crises.*

It has been objected that the CE-ARP does not measure "real" profitability, because in reality exploitation rates are variable. But this is true of all models of reality because they must abstract from certain aspects of reality (e.g., current versus deflated prices). The CE-ARP is one of the possible ways to isolate the temporary countertendential rise in the ARP within a tendential fall in profitability. The CE-ARP is no less real than the VE-ARP.

5. The Conversion of Money into Value and the Measurement of Value before Exchange

Statistical figures are monetary quantities, whereas Marx's categories are value—that is, abstract labor—quantities. Therefore, one needs to convert money into value to see whether the fall in money profitability is a manifestation of a closely correlated fall in value profitability. Supposedly, this conversion is impossible. But it can be made.

Suppose we want to calculate the *socially necessary* abstract labor contained in a commodity, say a computer. While the new value can be easily counted at the end of the production process (provided we dispose of a proper accounting system), the difficulty resides in computing the value of the means of production of that computer at the *beginning* of that process (the historical costs of those means of production).

Suppose the computer has been produced during period $t2 - t3$. Its input, a machine, has been produced during $t1 - t2$, the previous cycle. The point $t2$ is *both* the end of the production process of that machine as the *output* of $t1 - t2$ *and* the initial point of $t2 - t3$ as the process in which that *same* machine enters the production of the computer as its *input*.

We start our counting at $t1$ and count the hours of labor (or labor units) that have been needed to produce that machine from $t1$ to $t2$. This is the *new* labor (*NL*) gone into the production of that machine as the output of $t1 - t2$. This is also the value of that machine as the input of the production of the computer during $t2 - t3$. The quantity of money paid as wages (*W*) and profits (*P*) at $t2$ corresponds to this quantity of labor. Therefore, the following ratio can be computed at $t2$:

$$(1) \quad \alpha(t2) = NL(t1 - t2)/(W + P)t2$$

where $NL(t1 - t2)$ is the new labor (value) expended during $t1 - t2$ and $(W + P)t2$ are wages plus profits in money terms paid at $t2$. Then, $\alpha(t2)$ measures the units of new labor represented at $t2$ by one unit of money wages plus profits. For example, if at $t2$ new labor is 40 million hours and wages plus profits is 80 million euros, $\alpha(t2) = 0.5$. At $t2$, one euro (wages plus profits) represents 0.5 units of new labor.

Given that both money and abstract labor are inherently homogeneous, α can be applied also to the price of that machine at $t2$ as an output of $t1 - t2$, and thus as an input of the next period, $t2 - t3$. Thus, the valuation in labor hours of the money price (M) of that machine at $t2$, the start of $t2 - t3$, is

$$(2)\ \beta = M\alpha(t2)$$

For example, if at $t2$ the price of the machine is 150,000 euros, its labor content also at $t2$ is $150,000 \times 0.5 = 75,000$ hours. This is also the value transferred to the value of the computer during $t2 - t3$. Next we count the hours of new labor (NL) that have gone into the production of the computer during the $t2 - t3$ period. Suppose NL is 10,000 hours. This is added to the value of the input, which is determined at $t2$. Then, the value of the computer at $t3$ using that machine is

$$(3)\ V = \beta + NL$$

which in terms of the example above is $75,000 + 10,000 = 85,000$ labor hours. The price (P) and the value (V) of the output are

$$(4)\ P = c + v + s \text{ (in money terms) and}$$

$$(5)\ V = \beta + NL \text{ (in value, or labor hours, terms)}$$

Then,

$$(6)\ \gamma = V/P \text{ indicates the units of money representing one unit of value.}^{[6]}$$

We can now compute the ARP in terms of value (labor units or labor hours).

In the temporalist view, the value of the means of production is computed at the beginning of a period, and the new value and surplus value are calculated at the end of that period. These correspond to the total labor and the surplus labor at $t3$.

The new labor (NL) expended in $t2 - t3$ has to be split into necessary labor (nL) and surplus labor (sL). At $t3$ we compute wages as a percentage of $W + P$. We do the same with profits. If we multiply these percentages by the total of new labor units (NL), we obtain the value (i.e., in terms of labor) of labor power and of profits at $t3$. We now have assets in terms of labor at $t2$ as the initial point of $t2 - t3$, and wages and profits, also in terms of labor, at $t3$ as the end of $t2 - t3$. The temporalist ARP in terms of labor (value) follows.

Here are the two rates of profit:

$$(7)\ \text{Money rate of profit} = ARPm = p/(c + v)$$

$$(8)\ \text{Value rate of profit} = ARPv = sL/(\beta + nL)$$

A fundamental result emerges: *the two rates of profit track each other very closely*, as shown by the very high correlation coefficient (0.98) in figure 2.4.

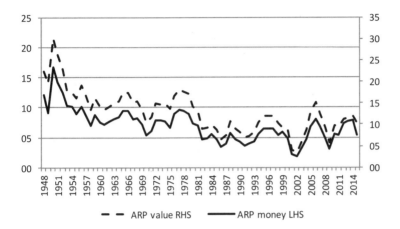

Figure 2.4. Money and value VE-ARP, United States, 1948–2015. Source: author's calculations.

Three conclusions follow. First, since money prices are closely correlated to value quantities, money prices can be safely used as labor quantities. Marx's money numerical examples can be read (as Marx did) both as money price and as value quantities. Second, it follows that the two rates of profit are only minimally quantitatively different; they are linked together in a single system. Third, the measurement of new labor (labor units or labor hours) also rebuts, besides the infinite regression critique, the "value form" interpretation—that is, the notion that value does not exist before exchange (and supposedly comes into existence only through, and at the moment of, exchange) or that, if it does exist, it cannot be quantified.[7] Value, if it can be measured before exchange, exists before exchange. Exchange only modifies a previously existing quantity.

6. The Exhaustion of the Present Historical Phase of Western Capitalism

As mentioned above, the CE-ARP is the fundamental indicator of the state of health of the economy. But there are other, *secondary* indicators. They are called secondary not because they are unimportant but because they are derived from the primary indicator, the CE-ARP. The first secondary indicator is employment as percentage of constant and variable capital invested, expressed as $v/(c + v)$.

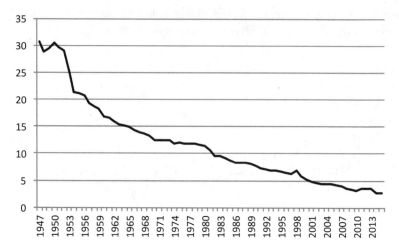

Figure 2.5. Labor units per million of invested dollars in constant and variable capital, 1947–2015. Source: author's calculations.

The relation between profitability (ARP) and $v/(c + v)$ is as follows. If the primary cause (OCC, or c/v) rises, constant capital rises and variable capital falls. The CE-ARP falls. Ceteris paribus, employment (v) falls. Then, $v/(c + v)$ falls, too, because the numerator falls, whereas percentagewise the denominator is unchanged ($c + v$ is always equal to 100 percent).

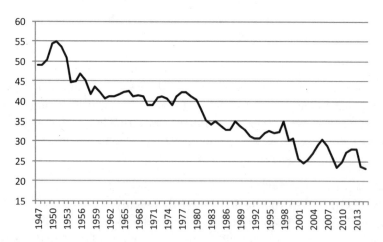

Figure 2.6. New value as percentage of total value, 1947–2015. Source: author's calculations.

The next secondary indicator is new value ($v + s$) as percentage of total value, $(v + s)/(c + v + s)$. Here, if the organic composition (OCC) rises, v falls and, given a certain rate of exploitation, $v + s$ falls. The numerator falls. The denominator falls less because c is now greater. The ratio falls.

The situation depicted in the previous charts is dramatic. Figure 2.2 shows the long, secular descent of average profitability. Figure 2.5 shows that each unit of capital invested in both assets and labor power generates less and less employment. Employment per unit of constant and variable capital invested falls from 30.7 in 1947 to 2.7 in 2015, a fall of -91.2 percent. In the Western economies, employment threatens to disappear from the productive sectors. New value relative to the total value falls, too, by -52.5 percent, as in figure 2.6. If the capital invested increases, then the average rate of profit, employment as percentage of constant and variable capital invested, and new value relative to total value all fall.

Two points follow. The present approach goes beyond the discussion between the advocates of the monocausality of crises (the ARP) and those for whom different crises have different causes. Besides the difference between the tendency (the rise in the OCC) and the countertendencies (e.g., the rise in the rate of exploitation), this approach introduces the difference between the tendency (the rise in the OCC as the primary cause of crises) and the secondary causes of crises (as in figures 2.5 and 2.6). The latter are *pro-tendential* causes of crises: aspects of falling profitability, rather than causes unrelated to falling profitability. They are *secondary* in the sense that they contribute to the emergence of crises while being themselves caused by the rise in the OCC (the primary cause). Crises explode when the countertendential forces cannot hold back anymore the tendential forces— *both primary* (the increase in the OCC) *and secondary, pro-tendential ones.*

Even more importantly, the above shows unequivocally *the progressive exhaustion of the present historical phase of Western capitalism.* No economic policy measure, whether neoliberal or (post-) Keynesian, has held or will hold back this process of decay. The writing is on the wall, and it is written in capital letters.

7. Crises and Recoveries

From the above, it follows that crises explode when the countertendential forces can no longer hold back the pro-tendential forces, both primary (the increase in the OCC) and secondary.

This is the *general context* within which crises have emerged since the end of World War II. But when *precisely* do they emerge? They emerge when *the rate of change of all these three causes—profitability, employment and new value—is negative.* Crises emerge at the points of intersection at which *all* these three indicators' rate of change is negative. These points of intersection are the

conjunctural manifestation of the persistent, long-term deterioration of the
US economy in the productive sectors, as shown by figures 2.1, 2.5, and 2.6.

On this basis, since 1945, the following twelve crises can be identified.
They match the periodization of the National Bureau of Economic Research
(NBER), with the exception of 1986, which the NBER does not consider
a crisis year.

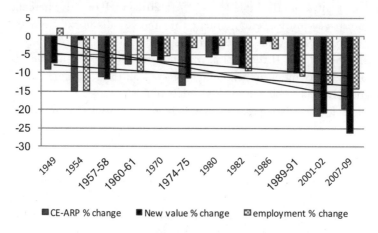

■CE-ARP % change   ■New value % change   ▨employment % change

Figure 2.7. Crises: percentage fall from pre-crisis to last
crisis years, 1949–2009.[8] Source: author's calculations

Conversely, recoveries are years in which the three fundamental factors'
rates of growth are positive. A less negative (but still negative) rate is an
improvement of the economy, but not a recovery. Notice that since the
end of World War II, crises have been increasingly severe (fig. 2.7), while
recoveries have been increasingly weak (fig. 2.8).

Table 2.1 shows the succession of crises and recoveries in the US from
the post–World War II phase of capitalist development. In the years that
are neither recovery nor crises, some indicators are positive but others are
negative. The economy is moving toward either one direction or the other.

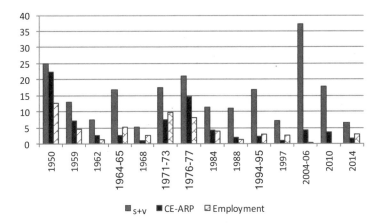

Figure 2.8. Recoveries: percentage rise from pre-recovery to last recovery years, 1950–2014. Source: author's calculations.

Crises	Recoveries
1949	1950
1954	
1957–8	1959
1960–1	1962
1964–5	1968
1970	1971–3
1974–5	1976–7
1980	
1982	1984
1986	1988
1989–91	1994–5
	1997
2001–2	2004–6
2007–9	2010
	2014

Table 2.1. Crises and recoveries, 1949–2014. Source: author's calculations.

8. Rising or Falling Profitability before Crises?

It is usually assumed that, aside from the secondary pro-tendential causes, if crises are (tendentially) determined by falling profitability, the latter should precede the former. However, that crises are *determined* by falling profitability in the productive sectors is not to say that falling profitability in those sectors must *precede* crises. The law of the tendential fall of the profit rate as the ultimate cause of crises (in the sense that it determines both the secondary pro-tendential tendencies and the countertendencies) does not say that the rate of profit must necessarily fall during the pre-crisis years. What the law says is that the ARP falls *in* the crisis year, meaning from the pre-crisis year to the crisis year (the same holds for the two other indicators). This is the case in all twelve crises (see fig. 2.7 above).

If the CE-ARP rises in the years before the crisis, the fall must have matured within this upward movement. More specifically, within the pre-crisis upward swing, either (1) *the rate of growth of wages falls while the rate of growth of assets rises;* or (2) *the rate of growth of wages rises less than that of assets.* What undermines profitability in the pre-crisis period is the different speeds at which assets and wages change prior to the crisis. Crises can be preceded either by falling profitability or by a *slowing down* of rising profitability. It is the latter that explains the sudden and unexpected change of direction in profitability. To see this, let us consider the time period from two years before the crisis to the pre-crisis year.

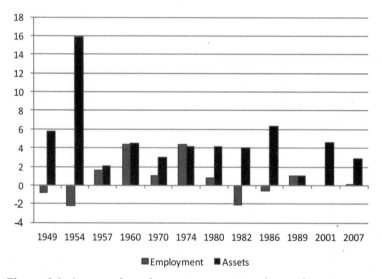

Figure 2.9. Assets and employment, percentage change from two years before the crisis to pre-crisis years, 1949–2007. Source: author's calculations.

In figure 2.9, there are four cases in which employment falls while assets grow. This is in line with the thesis submitted above. In six cases, the positive rate of change of employment is less than that of assets. This, too, is in line with the thesis submitted above. In one case, 1989, the test is indeterminate because both employment and assets grow by the same proportion of 1.1 percent. There are thus eleven cases to be tested. Of these eleven cases, the rate of growth of employment is greater (4.4 percent) than that of assets (4.1 percent) in only one case (1974). However, the difference is minimal. And this aside, the data are consistent with the hypothesis in ten out of eleven cases. On the whole, empirical evidence is very robust. *If from two years before the crisis to the pre-crisis year, the rate of growth of assets is greater than that of employment, then the crisis is maturing during the pre-crisis year in spite of the positive ARP.*

The percentage change of assets and employment in the pre-crises years fits into the general long-term picture of assets growing more than employment. In figure 2.10, up to 1979 (the year of maximum employment), employment rises by 43.3 percent while assets rise much more, by 291 percent. From 1980 to 2015, assets rise by 310.2 percent while employment falls by 18.6 percent.

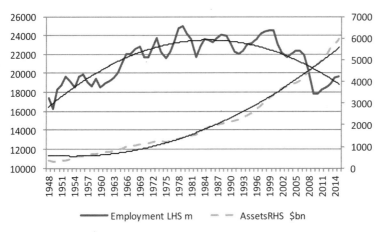

Figure **2.10**. Employment and assets, historical trends, 1948–2014. Source: author's calculations.

9. Rising OCC versus Falling Capital Productivity

The ARP falls because of the specific nature of technological innovations under capitalism, which constitute the main cause of its dynamism. On the one hand, innovations replace laborers with means of production. New labor falls relative to assets. Given the rate of exploitation, profits per unit of capital invested fall, too, and with them falls the rate of profit. However, given that constant capital grows, total profits grow as well. The former grows more than the latter. In the 1948–2015 period, the former grows by 1,557 percent, while the latter grows by 445 percent. On the other hand, innovations increase labor's productivity—that is, each laborer produces an ever-increasing quantity of output (use values) with the help of increasingly advanced means of production. *The fundamental contradiction is an increasing mass of commodities (use values) containing a decreasing quantity of value. There is an inherent overproduction of use values, which is not the cause of crises but the consequence of the fall in the average rate of profit.*

Some (also Marxist) authors challenge the thesis that *falling* profitability is caused by rising OCC. For them (and all those for whom value is use values) falling profitability is caused by *falling capital productivity*, defined as the ratio of output (use values) to assets (*O/A*). For example, "After 1970 [capital] productivity growth slowed markedly" (R. Gordon, 2012). The outcome is slow growth. Mokyr (2012), on the other hand, holds that new technologies will increase (capital) productivity again and that this will lift the economy out of its present predicament. There would be a positive relation between capital productivity and profitability. To show this, usually these authors decompose the ARP as follows:

(1) ARP = *profits/assets* = (*profits/output*) × (*output/assets*)

where the first term indicates the distribution of the output, and the second indicates capital productivity.

This formula lies outside the determination of the rate of profit as in Marx because labor (as the sole creator of value) is missing. This is a physicalist notion, rendered in terms of physical use values. It is inconsistent with the Marxist theory and as such useless to either support it or to reject it.

But let us assume for the sake of argument that the ARP is expressed in terms of value. How can we explain the high correlation coefficient (0.95) between profitability and capital productivity? As shown in figure 2.11, this would seem to indicate causation.

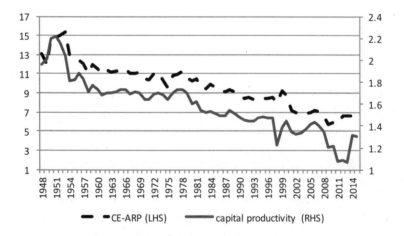

Figure 2.11. Ratio of output to assets (O/A) and average profitability with constant exploitation (CE-ARP), 1947–2015. Source: author's calculations.

In figure 2.11 both profitability (CE-ARP) and capital productivity (O/A) fall tendentially. Is there a relation of determination of one variable by the other? Does falling capital productivity determine a fall in the CE-ARP or vice versa? Actually, neither is the case, because movements in profitability (which are expressed in terms of value) are not causally related to movements in capital productivity (which are expressed in terms of use values). Less/more output as use values (as in formula 1 above) can be produced with one unit of new assets, but the effect on profitability depends on the OCC of the new assets.

So it must be the case that both indicators fall because of the action of a third variable, which determines both falling productivity and falling capital productivity. This is the rise in the OCC. This decreases the ARP because assets rise and labor falls. But a greater OCC also decreases capital productivity, provided capital productivity is seen as a value, and not as a use value, variable. In fact, if the OCC rises—that is, if assets rise—output must rise even more (a lower output would be irrational for capital). But due to the labor-shedding nature of new technologies, the value contained in this greater quantity of use values falls. Thus in value terms, the value of the output falls, too, and with it capital productivity. But this cannot be accounted for by formula 1, because of its physicalist nature.

The view that changes in capital productivity (measured in terms of use value) determine changes in profitability mirrors the perception of the technological leaders, those capitalists who increase output per unit of assets and thus *appropriate* part of the surplus value generated by the less efficient capitals. While for physicalism crises are determined by *falling capital productivity*, for Marx crises are determined by *rising labor productivity*, that is, by the shedding of labor inherent in greater labor productivity. The correlation between labor productivity and profitability is thus negative, not positive. In figure 2.12, tendentially, labor productivity rises and the CE-ARP falls.

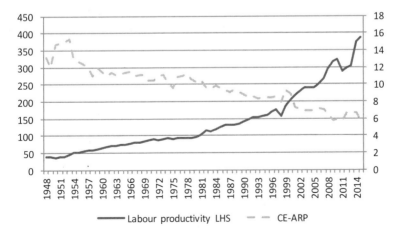

Figure 2.12. Labor productivity (output/employment) and the CE-ARP, 1947–2015. Source: author's calculations.

The same result holds if we consider percentage changes in labor productivity from the pre-crisis to the crisis year (fig. 2.13). The percentage change is positive in all cases (with the exception of 1949), conforming to Marx's hypothesis. For conventional economics, on the other hand, it remains a mystery why crises are preceded by a rise in labor productivity. What they cannot see is that the increased labor productivity is the other side of the shedding of labor, and thus of the decrease in the new value produced.

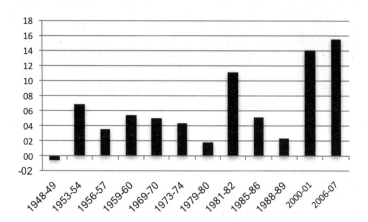

Figure 2.13. Labor productivity from pre-crisis to crisis years, (% pts difference), 1948–2007. Source: author's calculations.

10. The First Countertendency

The graphs above have shown that the ARP falls not in a straight line, but through shorter upward and downward cycles. The downward tendency is temporarily slowed and its direction possibly reversed due to the action of the countertendencies. But the countertendencies cannot prevent the falling tendency from asserting itself if the forces behind the countertendencies increasingly weaken. Three basic countertendencies are mentioned below.

First, due to greater labor productivity, technological innovations reduce the value of each unit of output, including the means of production. When these means of production enter a new production process as inputs, the denominator of the profit rate (the constant capital invested, or assets) falls, and the rate of profit rises on this account. Thus, the critics hold, if the OCC rises, the rate of profit does not necessarily fall. But empirical data show that over the long term the value of the assets as percentage of total value *rises* (fig. 2.14).

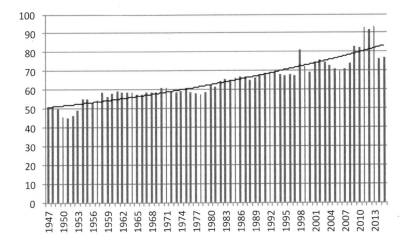

Figure 2.14. Value of assets as percent of total value, United States, 1947–2015. Source: author's calculations.

Figure 2.14 bears out what Marx had observed in the *Grundrisse*, namely that the price of a single machine can fall, but that the price of the system of machines that replace that machine grows both in absolute terms and relatively to the price of total output. But there is also another, more powerful, countertendency. This is that while the new assets, on the one hand, might incorporate less value, on the other, they shed labor so that constant capital also rises on this account. Figure 2.14 shows that both countertendencies have not overcome the tendency.

11. The Second Countertendency

The second countertendency is the increase in the rate of exploitation. Capitalists can increase their profitability by increasing this rate.

Consider first the VE-ARP. The correlation between rate of exploitation and the VE-ARP is strong and positive (0.67). If exploitation increases, profitability rises, and vice versa. From this positive correlation, neoliberalist authors conclude that the way out of crises lies in higher rates of exploitation, or in pro-capital redistribution, for example through budget cuts or wage compression. This implies that the rate of exploitation would *determine* the rate of profit. But this can be shown to be wrong. The point is that the rate of exploitation determines *variations* around the rate of profit as determined by variations in the OCC. The rate of profit follows its course (determined by the movements of the OCC) irrespective of the variations due to changes in the rates of exploitation. One way to see this is to hold the rate of exploitation constant. Then the rate of profit with constant rate of exploitation would display a tendential fall.

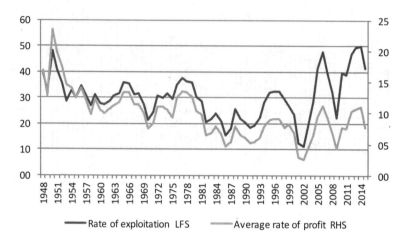

Figure 2.15. Rate of exploitation and VE-ARP, 1947–2015. Source: author's calculations.

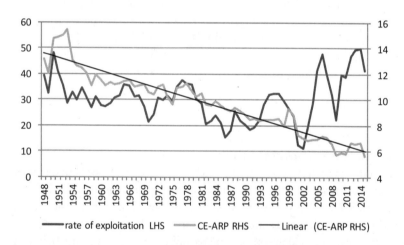

Figure 2.16. CE-ARP and constant rate of exploitation, 1947–2015. Source: author's calculations.

In figure 2.16 the correlation between the CE-ARP and the rate of exploitation is insignificant, 0.06. Variations in the rate of exploitation do not stop the tendential fall in profits relative to the capital invested, which in its turn is determined by the rise in the OCC. The rate of exploitation might increase, but the rate of profit falls if the OCC rises more. From 1949 to 2015, the OCC rises by 253.8 percent while the rate of exploitation rises by 24.2 percent. So this countertendency cannot stop the tendency, the increase in the OCC, nor the fall in the CE-ARP. The rate of exploitation might swing, but the OCC grows persistently.

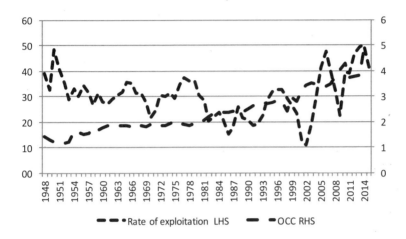

Figure 2.17. OCC and rate of exploitation, 1947–2015. Source: author's calculations.

Thus, while it is correct to hold, as in Marx, that higher rates of exploitation increase profitability, it is wrong to deduce that this higher profitability can help the economy to get out of the slump. This is a "doped" higher profitability; the economy exits the slump only if the CE-ARP recovers sufficiently. Figures 2.15, 2.16, and 2.17 belie the neoclassical orthodoxy.

Another neoclassical mistake concerns the positive relation between the rate of exploitation and employment. Neoliberal ideology holds that higher exploitation increases profits. Then, profits are accumulated, investments grow and employment grows, too. In short, in this view, higher exploitation increases employment; and vice versa: lower exploitation decreases employment through lower profitability and investments. There is thus a direct relation between exploitation and employment.

A fairly common critique of the thesis of the positive relation between employment and exploitation is that in an upward cycle of higher exploitation makes little sense, not only because the economy and profitability are already growing, but also because higher exploitation through lower wages curtails labor's purchasing power. In the downward cycle, these higher profits are not invested but saved, such that employment does not grow. And even if they were invested, the new productivity-increasing and labor-saving technologies would increase the absolute level of employment but would decrease employment relative to constant capital. Moreover, the question is whether the positive relation between employment and exploitation is empirically correct.

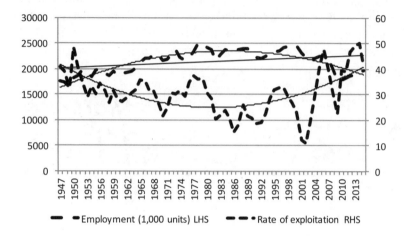

Figure 2.18. Employment and the rate of exploitation,
1947–2015. Source: author's calculations.

Figure 2.18 shows that in the long period, lower exploitation (up to the 1980s) does not lower employment but raises it. Vice versa, higher exploitation does not raise employment but lowers it. The relation is inverse. This chart belies the neoliberalist thesis and the hypothesis on which it is built.

The negative correlation also holds for the relatively shorter 2002–2015 period of austerity measures. While the rate of exploitation rises to unknown heights, from 11 percent in 2002 to 41 percent in 2015 (with a peak of almost 50 percent in 2014), employment falls instead of rising, from 22.189 million to 19.678 million. Given that labor "flexibility" and deregulation boil down to higher rates of exploitation, the above is also evidence that *flexibility and deregulation do not increase employment.*

The neoliberalist ideology rests on an optical illusion. For it, the line of causation goes from the rate of exploitation to employment. But actually, the line of causation goes the other way: *it is employment that determines the rate of exploitation.* This thesis is in perfect agreement with figure 2.18. Over the long period, if employment rises, labor's negotiating power rises and the rate of exploitation falls. If employment falls, labor loses negotiating power and rate of exploitation rises. This is shown in figure 2.18. Employment, in its turn, is determined by the cycle of capital accumulation (see section 13).

Recently this thesis has been corroborated by official institutions above suspicion. For example, the OECD (2016) states, "A new analysis of industry-level data shows that reforms lowering barriers to entry [read: lower wages] and the cost of dismissal induce non-negligible transitory employment losses" (p. 18). And the World Bank goes back on its previous position: "New data and more rigorous methodologies have spurred a wave of empirical studies over the past two decades on the effects of labor regulation [read: anti-labor legislation]. . . . Most estimates of the impacts on employment levels tend to be insignificant or modest" (World Bank 2013, p. 261).

It follows from the above that labor should not trade off higher exploitation for higher employment on condition that in a downward cycle the extra profits due to greater exploitation are invested. Labor's objective should be greater employment and thus the possibility to lower exploitation rates. It is greater employment that allows lower exploitation.

12. The Third Countertendency

Faced with falling profitability in the productive sphere, capital shifts from low profitability in the productive sectors to high profitability in the financial (i.e., unproductive) sectors. But profits in these sectors are fictitious; they exist only on the accounting books. They become real profits only when cashed in. When this happens, the profits available to the productive sectors shrink. The more capitals try to realize higher profit rates by moving to the unproductive sectors, the greater become the difficulties in the productive sectors. This countertendency—capital movement to the financial and speculative sectors and thus higher rates of profit in those sectors—cannot hold back the tendency, that is, the fall in the ARP in the productive sectors. Actually, profitability falls further in these sectors on this account. While in 1950 financial profits were 7.9 percent of real profits, in 2014 they were 24 percent, after reaching a maximum of 47 percent in 2009 (fig. 2.19).

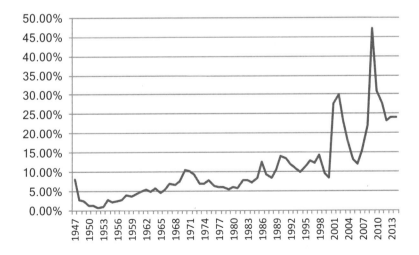

Figure 2.19. Financial profits as percentage of real profits, 1947–2015. Source: author's calculations.

The focus in this chapter is on the productive sphere of the economy (defined in the appendix). Some authors object that corporations in the productive sectors engage also in finance and speculation (which are not productive of value and surplus value). Since statistics do not separate the profits generated in the productive sectors from those realized in the unproductive ones, it would be impossible to know the profits in the productive sectors. Presumably the focus should be on the general ARP, that is, on profits in both the productive and unproductive sectors.

The point is that financial and speculative profits are not generated in those sectors, but rather are appropriated from the productive sectors. Therefore, the profits realized by productive capitals through their operations in finance and speculation must have been generated previously in the productive sectors, if not necessarily by the same capitals that have generated them, and not necessarily in the same time period. So the financial profits realized by the corporations operating in the productive sectors *should not be deducted* from the profits realized in these sectors.

Financial profits have been claiming an increasing share of real profits throughout the whole post–World War II phase. The growth of fictitious profits causes an explosive growth of global debt through the issuance of debt instruments (e.g., bonds) and of more debt instruments on the previous ones. The outcome is a mountain of interconnected debts (fig. 2.20). Real money (called "power money" in the graph) is the representation of value, labor congealed in commodities. As figure 2.20 shows, this is a very small percentage relative to the three forms of credit: bank credit, securitized debt and derivatives. But credit represents debt, not value. It is not money, even if it can have some of the functions of money.

As noted above, debt implies repayment. When this cannot happen, financial crises ensue. This huge growth of debt in its different forms is the substratum of the speculative bubble and financial crises, including the next one. So this countertendency, too, can overcome the tendency only temporarily. The growth in the rate of profit due to fictitious profits meets its own limit: recurring financial crises, and the crises they catalyze in the productive sectors.

But what are financial crises, what causes them and when do they emerge?

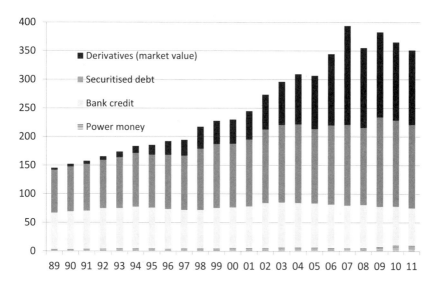

Figure 2.20. Money and debt as percent of global
GDP, 1989–2011. Source: Roberts 2009.

13. Financial Crises

The literature focuses on the size and number of financial bankruptcies, sets arbitrary criteria as to when these bankruptcies constitute a financial crisis, and concentrates on the specific features of each crisis. But the principal question is not identifying the different conjunctural causes of each financial crisis, but determining the common cause behind the specific characteristics of all these bankruptcies. By analogy with falling profitability in the productive sectors (for short, *real profits*) as the cause of crises in those sectors, this common cause is *falling profitability in the financial sectors*—the negative percentage growth of financial profits. Again, similarly to the productive sectors where not all falls in the ARP are crises years, not all years of falling percentage growth in financial profits are ones of financial crisis. Real profits must also grow negatively because of the increased difficulties to cash in the financial profits. Financial crises are due to the impossibility to repay debts, and they emerge when the percentage growth is falling both for financial and for real profits. On this basis, the following seven post–World War II financial crises are identified (fig. 2.21).

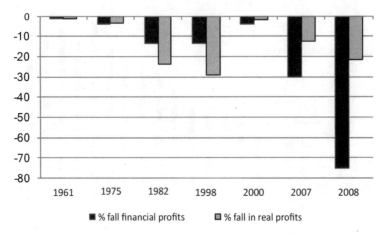

Figure 2.21. Financial crises, 1961–2008. Source: author's calculations.

The 2000 financial crisis marks a turning point because, contrary to the previous financial crises, the percentage fall in financial profits is greater than that in real profits both in this year and in 2007–2008. This is one element explaining the severity of these crises. Figure 2.21 shows that the first thirty years of post–World War II US capitalist development were free from financial crises, except for the relatively minor 1961 crisis. But in the forty-year period from 1975 to 2015, there have been six major financial crises. If the 2000 crisis is disregarded, these crises have been increasingly severe and culminate in the striking 75 percent fall in financial profits in 2008.

The root cause for the emergence of the financial crises afer 1975 should be sought in the productive sphere. After the war, with the liberation of the pent-up purchasing power of US labor and the transformation of the war economy into a civilian economy (see below, section 14), employment (in the productive sectors) grew from 17.417 million in 1948 to 24.970 million in 1979, an increase of 43.3 percent. But assets grew much more, by 291 percent (see fig. 2.10). The average rate of capacity utilization was at a high average of 83.3 percent, an indication that the increase in assets was not sufficient for the increased production of use values. There was expanded reproduction both of labor and means of production. In this first phase, there was no need to prop up the productive economy through the creation of fictitious capital and profits. However, beneath this surface the CE-ARP had already begun its long descent, from 13.1 percent in 1948 to 10.6 percent in 1979 (fig. 2.2). Employment as percentage of constant and variable capital invested fell from 28.7 percent in 1948 to 11.7 percent in 1979 (fig. 2.5). New value as percentage of total value fell from 48.8 percent in 1948 to 41.2 percent in 1979 (fig. 2.6). The Golden Age was being undermined from within.

In the second period, the CE-ARP continues its descent, from 10.6 percent in 1979 to 5 percent in 2015. Employment falls to 19.678 million in 2015, a fall of –21 percent while assets rise by 310 percent. Average capacity utilization falls to 79.2 percent. As assets grow and employment falls, new value as percentage of total value falls from 43.9 percent to 30.4 percent. Due to the worsening of all the relevant indicators, capital accelerates its migration to the financial (unproductive) sphere, which takes the upper hand over the real economy. Finance and its increasing reliance on debt becomes a way to escape decreasing profitability and production of (new) value. Financial crises follow.

A point of controversy is whether financial crises determine crises in the productive sectors, (for short economic crises), or vice versa. It is held that if financial crises *precede* the economic crises, the former *determine* the latter, and vice versa.

But this is not the point. The question is whether financial crises are *preceded* by a decline in the production of value and surplus value, which are not necessarily years of economic crises. These are years in which assets grow more than employment. Therefore, they are years of potential economic crises. But they are also years in which the financial sectors have increasing difficulties in appropriating surplus value from the productive sphere to sustain financial profits, due to the decreasing quantity of new value generated. Financial profits decline, and financial crises emerge. The reliance on debt increases. The financial bubble inflates and eventually bursts.

It follows that if financial crises emerge before economic crises, the former are the *catalyst* of the latter. Of course, financial and economic crises can emerge at the same time. The deterioration in the generation of new value is the factor determining both economic and financial crises, but it does not determine which appears first.

Five out of seven financial crises coincide with crises in the productive sectors (see fig. 2.9), where assets grow more than employment in pre-crisis years (fig. 2.22). The same holds for 1998, which is not a crisis in the productive sector. The 2000 financial crisis precedes the 2001 economic crisis. However, this does not imply that in this case the financial crisis determines the real one. In the two years preceding the 2000 crisis (from 1997 to 1999), assets in the productive sectors grow by 13 percent while employment falls by 1.6 percent. The 2000 financial crisis precedes the 2001 crisis in the productive sphere but is determined by the deterioration in the productive sector. The deterioration of the productive sector in pre-crisis years is thus the common cause of both financial and non-financial crises. If they have a common cause, it is immaterial whether one precedes the other or vice versa. The point is that the (deterioration of the) productive sector determines the (crises in the) financial sector.

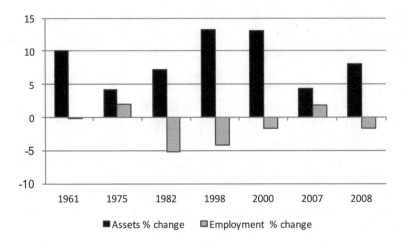

Figure 2.22. Assets percentage change and employment percentage change from two years before the financial crisis to the pre-financial crisis, 1961–2008. Source: author's calculations.

14. Capitalism Is on a Collision Course with Itself.

We are witnessing the following trends:

(1) There is a persistent tendential and irreversible fall in the (global) profit rate, even if with countertendential jolts.

(2) The share of the means of production to total value is growing: they are increasingly expensive instead of becoming cheaper (see fig. 2.14).

(3) There is a tendential fall in new value relative to total value since the end of World War II (see fig. 2.6).

(4) The increase of the rate of exploitation increases the variable exploitation rate of profit (VE-ARP), but this growth is neither cause nor effect of economic growth. It hides the fall in the constant exploitation average rate of profit (CE-ARP).

(5) The exponential growth of fictitious capital and fictitious profits inflate the speculative bubble and then cause it to burst, bringing about financial crises of increasing severity.

The conjunctural factors that could become the catalysts of the next profitability crisis include

(1) the first signs of commercial wars, which would reduce international trade, and thus first the realization, and then the production, of value and surplus value;

(2) the persistent growth of international debt and the inflation of the speculative bubble;

(3) local wars, especially in or over oil rich countries, which could easily spread to wars among the great powers. In this case, the producers of weapons (in the dominant imperialist countries) would increase their profits, but due to the Marxist multiplier (see below) the ARP in those countries would fall; in the war theaters, value and wealth would be destroyed; and

(4) the growth of right-wing, ultra-nationalist, racist, and fascist parties and movements—fanned also by austerity measures—which form a cultural background congenial to military adventures.

It could be held that even if capitalism cannot rejuvenate in the advanced capitalist world, it could get a new lease of life in the so-called emerging economies. The fallacy of this argument is that the same contradiction presently marring capitalism in the advanced economies is part and parcel of the economies of the emerging countries as well—namely, the contradiction between increasing labor productivity, on the one hand, and the shedding of labor inherent in the means of production imported from the technologically advanced countries of the West, on the other.

After a first period of enlarged reproduction, the tendency for the rate of profit to fall would emerge again, with its concomitant effects. The West thus transmits its technologically caused disease to the rest of the world. To mention only one example: the degree of dependence of the Chinese iron and steel industry on the technology of the advanced countries varies from 65 percent for the production of energy, to 85 percent for the casting and transformation of semi-processed goods, to 90 percent for the systems of control, analysis, safety measures and environmental protection.

15. The Impotence of Pro-labor Redistribution
Alternatively, it could be held that capitalism could go through a new phase of growth if Keynesian policies, namely, either pro-labor redistribution or massive investments in the civilian economy, were resorted to. Let us consider pro-labor redistribution first.

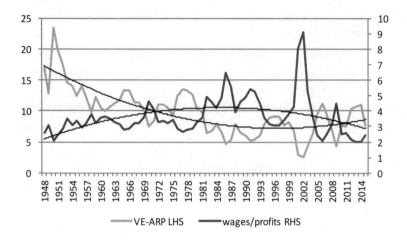

Figure 2.23. VE–ARP and ratio of wages to profits,
1947–2015. Source: author's calculations.

Higher wages relative to profits decrease profitability, according to Marx.
So any increase in labor's purchasing power is no antidote. Figure 2.23
confirms this. From 1948 to 1986, wages increase relative to profits, and
the ARP falls contrary to the Keynesian thesis. From 1986 to 2015, wages
relative to profits fall (with the exception of 2001–2002) and the ARP rises,
again contrary to the Keynesian thesis. Figure 2.24 tells the same story,
if the CE–ARP is considered. Profitability falls whether the wages/profits
ratio rises or falls. These two charts belie the Keynesian thesis.

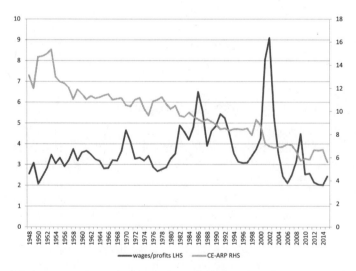

Figure 2.24. CE–ARP and ratio of wages to profits,
1947–2015. Source: author's calculations.

Marx had already noticed that crises are preceded by rising wages. This has not changed. Of the twelve post–World War II crises, eleven have been preceded by rising wages and only one by falling wages (the 1991 crisis).

		Wages		Wages		Wages		Wages
	1952	310.5	1955	357.9	1958	358.7	1968	581.1
	1953	341.2	1956	380.2	1959	391.0	1969	609
Crises	1954		1957		1960		1970	
	1972	632.0	1978	725.9	1980	716.6	1984	776.1
	1973	669.1	1979	725.9	1981	726.2	1985	806.8
Crises	1974		1980		1982		1986	
	1987	836.0	1989	869.8	1999	1067.5	2005	1108.1
	1988	872.3	1990	861.0	2000	1223.3	2006	1135.5
Crises	1989		1991		2001		2007	

Table 2.2. Falling rising wages precede crises (billions of deflated dollars; crisis years in bold), 1954–2007. Source: author's calculations.

Pro-labor redistribution has not worked and will not work. The theoretical argument is as follows. Suppose falling profitability and unsold commodities; these are features of crises periods. The government could print money or extend credit to households: "helicopter money," as it has fancifully been called. However, after an initial rise, the ARP would fall again, even with the full realization of previously unsold commodities, and even if this would spur new investments. The reason is that new investments would be labor shedding, such that the production of new value would find its limit in the Marxist multiplier (as discussed in the next section).

16. The Keynesian Multiplier versus the Marxist Multiplier

As for state-induced investments, the question is, who could finance them? The state can only appropriate the necessary value from either labor or capital. If it does not, it has to resort to debt. But in a crisis, debt is already very high; and, moreover, further debt would further inflate the speculative bubble. The Keynesian answer is that the state could *borrow* the necessary funds (value) *temporarily* in order to finance public (great) works of civilian investments.[12] These investments would spur other investments in the private sector, and these would spur still other investments, thus multiplying employment and profits. The economy would exit the slump. State revenues would increase, and the state debt could be paid back. This is in, short, the

Keynesian multiplier. However, both theory and empirical work show that it does not work. Let us see why.

First, under capitalism, higher profits are a condition for higher investments. But as argued above, in a period of economic crisis or stagnation, profits are not invested (or are insufficiently invested) in the productive sphere. Either they are saved, or they find their way into the higher profitability, but unproductive, sectors. The Keynesian multiplier fails right when it is most needed, in the slump. The Keynesians disregard the distinction between productive and unproductive (financial) investments: for them all investments can start the multiplier because all investments are productive. This is the first criticism.

The second and more fundamental criticism is that profitability moves not according to the Keynesian multiplier, but according to the Marxist multiplier.[13] Let us distinguish between the capitalists who receive the state orders (call them A) and other capitalists (call them B), who in their turn are commissioned by capitalists A. Let us focus on the means of production, which in what follows also encompass semi-finished products and raw materials. Capitalists B, who receive commissions for means of production from capitalists A, are as a rule those who can sell at cheaper prices—those whose workers are more productive because percentagewise more means of production than labor are employed. These are the capitals whose laborers produce more assets (a greater output of means of production), but less value and surplus value per unit of capital invested. The same holds if capitalists B commission capitalists C, and so forth. At each stage of the chain of investments, the more efficient capitals' employment might grow in absolute amounts but falls in relation to the means of production employed (as inputs), so that less surplus value is generated per unit of capital and the average rate of profit falls. Employment rises, but profitability falls.[14] This is empirically substantiated in figure 2.25: the correlation between government expenditures and the profit rate is strongly negative (−0.72).

Figure 2.25 shows that up to the early 1990s, rising government expenditure could not contain the fall in the ARP. Thus the Keynesian thesis fails. Starting from the early 1990s, the VE-ARP grows together with growing government expenditures. This would seem to support the Keynesian thesis. But the ARP grows because the rate of surplus value grows, and not because of growing government expenditures. In fact, as figure 2.18 above shows, the rate of exploitation rises from 11 percent in 2002 to 47 percent in 2006; it then falls to 22 percent in 2009 but shoots up to almost 50 percent (the highest rate since the end of World War II) in 2014. If the rate of surplus value is kept constant, the negative correlation holds for the whole secular period (fig. 2.26).

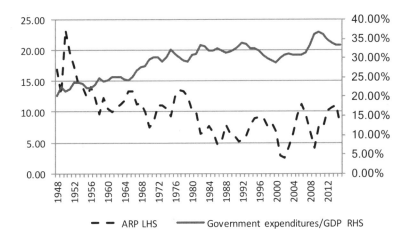

Figure 2.25. Government expenditures as percentage of GDP and ARP with variable exploitation, 1948–2015. Sources: (1) Government expenditure as percentage of GDP: fred.stlouisfed.org; (2) ARP: author's calculations.

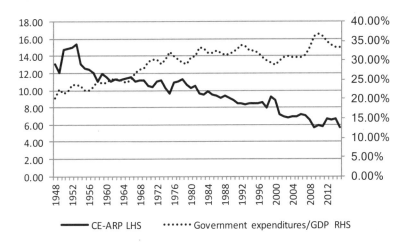

Figure 2.26. Government expenditures as percentage of GDP and ARP with constant rate of exploitation, 1948–2015. Source: government expenditure as percentage of GDP: fred.stlouisfed.org; (2) CE-ARP: author's calculations.

From the end of World War II to present, growing government expenditures have not reversed the tendential fall in average profitability. This result is replicated for each individual crisis: government expenditures rise from the year preceding the crisis to the last crisis years in all cases except 1954 (fig. 2.27). So rising government expenditures did not prevent the crises.

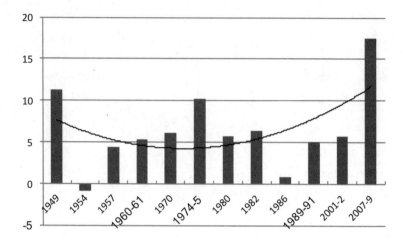

Figure 2.27. Government expenditure / GDP: percentage growth from pre-crisis year to last crisis year, 1949–2009. Source: government expenditure as percentage of GDP: fred.stlouisfed.org.

If government expenditures cannot avert crises, could they not be the factor for exiting the crisis? The test implies that both government expenditures and the ARP be measured from the pre-crisis years to the first post-crisis years. The Keynesian thesis holds only if both the ARP and government expenditures change in the same direction. It fails if government expenditures rise but profitability falls, or vice versa. Figure 2.28 shows that the correlation between government expenditures and the ARP is negative in ten out of twelve cases. Government expenditures do not reboot the economy.

It is fashionable nowadays to try to integrate Hyman Minsky and Marx. But two radically different theories cannot be integrated. For Minsky (1982), government spending (deficits) can offset private spending and increase profits. But the above has shown that this is erroneous: empirical data showing the nonexistence of the Keynesian multiplier are overwhelming.

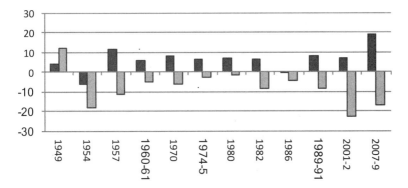

■ Government expenditure/GDP from pre-crisis years to first post-crisis years

☐ CE-ARP from pre-crisis years to first post-crisis years

Figure 2.28. Changes in government expenditures and CE-ARP, 1949–2009. Sources (1) Government expenditure as percentage of GDP: fred.stlouisfed.org; (2) CE-ARP: author's calculations.

17. The Destruction of Capital

If both Keynesian and neoliberal policies fail, the only way out of the crisis is that generated spontaneously by capital itself: its rejuvenation through a massive destruction of its less efficient units. The world economies exited the 1929–33 crisis with World War II, not through state-induced investments.

The story for the United States is different from that of the other warring parties. In the United States, destruction of capital meant principally the destruction and the regeneration of capital *as the production relation*—the relation between capital and labor. First, there was the transformation of the civilian economy—beset with high unemployment, low capacity utilization of the means of production, and a falling rate of profit—into the war economy—characterized by full employment both of labor power and assets, state-guaranteed realization of the output, and a high level of both profitability and savings. This was the destruction of capital in the civilian sphere and its reconstitution as a military economy. It acted as a powerful countertendency.

After the war, the economy was again reconverted into a civilian one. Capital was destroyed in the military sphere and reconstituted in the civilian one. Government expenditures as a percentage of GDP fell from about 52 percent in 1945 to 20 percent in 1948. The high level of labor savings imposed by the low production of civilian goods guaranteed the purchasing power needed for the new consumption goods, which in their turn required the production of new means of production. A whole range of war-related inventions was applied to the production of new civilian commodities.

While in the United States the productive apparatus remained unscathed, the other belligerent nations suffered a huge destruction of means of production and labor power. Capitalism was revitalized for a quarter of a century. But at what price? After a quarter of a century of vigorous growth (the so-called Golden Age, discussed above), the fall of the ARP, of employment (also as percentage of constant and variable capital invested) and of new value relative to total value accelerated.

The cost of this relatively short (golden) season of expanded reproduction was tens of millions of dead, atrocious suffering and terrible poverty. This is what labor, in addition to financing the war, had to pay to give new vitality to the system.

18. The Old, the New and the Decline of Western Capitalism

The above has argued that the descent of Western capitalism started right after World War II and is still continuing because it is inherent in the nature of the system. Are we approaching an inevitable breakdown, the end of capitalism?

This is not in the nature of the beast. Lacking a truly revolutionary change, capitalism will exit this long downward secular period. But first capital will have to be massively destroyed, in both the financial and the productive spheres.

Related to this question, there is Gramsci's 1930 reflection, which still applies nowadays: "[T]he old is dying [but] the new cannot be born" (Gramsci 1971, pp. 275–76). Gramsci meant the radically new: communism. If the radically new cannot be born, the old will survive, but in a new shape.

At present, it is difficult to foresee when and how a new historical phase will be ushered in, and the shape it will take. What is clear is that, as argued above, the present phase of capitalism in the West is increasingly exhausting its capacity to reproduce itself. It is dying. It might be replaced by a new phase of capitalism or by a superior society. But the latter will not be possible without the active and purposeful intervention of working-class subjectivity.

A condition for the emergence of this class consciousness within this society is that the struggle by labor for better living and working conditions is fought from the perspective of an irreconcilable antagonism between capital and labor, and not from the Keynesian perspective of class collaboration. Keynesian policies have not worked in the past and will not avoid the approaching end of this historical phase. This awareness is the condition for the rising of "the new," as Gramsci put it, of labor as "the full development of activity itself . . . [of the laborer's] rich individuality." (Marx 1973, p. 325).[15] Without this, capitalism will rejuvenate and will enter a new phase in which its domination over labor will be even greater and more terrible.

In this changed phase of capitalism, the new technologies being developed now will play a fundamental role. Marx noticed that "a crisis always forms the starting-point of large new investments. Therefore, from the point of view of society as a whole . . . a new material basis for the next turn-over cycle." (Marx 1967b, p. 186). New and massive investments will take the form of new technologies, which will not only be labor shedding and productivity increasing, but will also constitute new forms of domination of labor by capital. In Marx's words: "It would be possible to write quite a history of the inventions made since 1830, for the sole purpose of supplying capital with weapons against the revolts of the working class" (Marx 1967b, p. 436). Nothing could be more topical nowadays.

I have dealt with this question in past works (see Carchedi 2011; 2014, among others). Here I will mention only one recent example: wearable technologies. They make it possible both to increase the productivity of labor and at the same time to increase surveillance. For example, in warehouses,

> arm-mounted wearable computers in effect make the humans become an extension of the information systems that drive the supply-chain. The human is no longer given a list of products to find, and then be expected to use initiative and knowledge to find the products. Instead, the information system plans the best route for the human to take, and in effect pre-optimizes the human being's itinerary. Since the specific location of all products are known the system can be programmed to estimate the amount of time the human takes to obtains the products, and can build the item-by-item information into an asset-tracking process (the human is another machine asset in this type of business) that provides continuous and comprehensive performance information for managers. . . . If employees do not have to learn the layout of a warehouse, but are told where to go by instructions sent to computers that they "wear," then their training overheads are reduced, and the skill-set needed in reduced. . . . These technologies are strongly linked to the de-layering of staff, and in the de-skilling of staff. (Blackmore 2005)

Staff is reduced, and labor power is de-qualified and thus devalued. There is at the same time ubiquitous surveillance:

> The creation of a permanent awareness of being observed . . . ensures power to take effect automatically. . . . Everything an employee does can be recorded, filmed by CCTV or logged in databases: all conversations, the duration of conversations, timings and durations of meal and toilet breaks, personal searches when entering the premises. (Blackmore 2005)

To properly evaluate these technologies, consider the difference between old and new technologies in the past century. While old technologies (roughly, before World War II) forced human functions to adapt to the motion of machines (e.g., the conveyor belt), the new post–World War II, computer-based technologies replicate human functions in a machine-like fashion and thus replicate in a mechanized manner both bodily movements and the self-reflexivity of thought.

The class content of these technologies is that they mechanize human thought, human creativity, and human life itself so that they can be replicated (cloned) and better controlled. Consequently, these new technologies make possible the substitution of humans not only by machines (as in previous techniques), but by *human-like* machines. The ideological ramifications are all-pervasive. These new machines propagate a view of humans as highly skilled machines and elevate the machine-like mimicry of human functions to the ideal and most complete form of these functions. Since these machines can perform computational tasks that are impossible for humans, they propagate the notion that machines are the perfect form that can be reached by humans (and by human intellect). In the end, they secrete the notion that a perfect human is a machine-like human, a machine. If the perfect human is perceived as a machine, nature and thus life itself are seen also as machines and therefore subject to mechanical reproduction.

At present, large quantities of money capital are waiting to be profitably invested after the next large-scale destruction of capital. These capitals will be invested in the new technologies being developed since the end of the past century. For example, with biotechnology and genetic engineering (agribusiness, pharmaceutical chemicals, medical business, animal and human cloning, and so on) the mechanical reproduction of life achieves its greatest success. Nature is seen as programmed—and thus as programmable—matter. Already in 2000, the European Patent Office granted Amstrad, an Australian firm, the patent for the creation of "chimeric animals," that is, beings made up of human and animal cells. Other examples include nanotechnology (which aims to control matter on an atomic and molecular scale), bioinformatics (the application of information technology and computer science to the field of molecular biology), genomics (the determination of the entire DNA sequence of organisms), biopharmacology (the study of drugs produced using biotechnology), molecular computing (computational schemes that use individual atoms or molecules as a means of solving computational problems; in the long run, molecular computing is likely to replace traditional silicon computers), and biomimetics (the science of copying life, i.e., the transfer of ideas from biology to technology).

What is, then, the *class content* of all these new developments in science (and others to come)? I think it is the further fusion of nature and techniques, the melting of one into the other, in ways and forms such that the outcome will enormously increase the possibilities to control humans on behalf of capital and to shape their potentialities according to capital's rationality and interests. In this, they are no different from previous technologies, in the sense that only those techniques will be developed and applied that will be functional for capital's domination, even if the same techniques can be used by labor to resist capital's domination.[16]

These are some of the technological innovations that will become the hallmarks of the twenty-first century, just as the old technologies have been of the past century. After these new technologies have permeated society, society, as we know it, will have changed beyond imagination, just as the inventions and technologies introduced in the post–World War II period have caused a complete transformation of prewar capitalism.

Inasmuch as machines replace laborers, mental labor is bound to increase in importance. Much has been written on this topic, but almost never from the angle of Marx's labor theory of value. As I have argued elsewhere (Carchedi 2014), given certain conditions, mental labor can be productive of value and surplus value in the same way as objective labor—erroneously called material labor. Therefore, mental labor is subject to the same rules dominating objective labor. On the one hand, new forms of mental labor allow the introduction of new forms of exploitation together with greater rates of exploitation. On the other, new technologies replace mental laborers with means of production, just as in the case of objective labor, and thus affect negatively profitability. But perhaps the most important consequence of this analysis is that *mental laborers under capitalist production relations are part of today's proletariat*. The proletariat is not disappearing, but, contrary to a dominant thesis, is expanding, though with different features. In spite of its specific features, however, mental labor is not capitalism's elixir of life, but one of its potential gravediggers.[17]

Marx has shown masterfully that capitalism generates spontaneously unemployment, poverty, exploitation, wars and a host of other human predicaments. All this will not change. What will change is the form of these predicaments. Even if new and more fertile seeds are discovered, hunger will not disappear. New forms of wealth will arise, but they will be a tiny island in an ocean of new forms of poverty and destitution. Nanotechnology might eliminate some forms of pollution (as some supporters of green capitalism hold), but it will create new toxic waste. But even assuming a completely clean capitalism, the system would still be what it is: exploitative, destructive and insane in terms of human needs. The new technologies will be part of this system. Through them, capitalism will continue to shape the world in its own likeness and thus will shape—more than ever—human potentialities in forms consonant with capital's needs and rationality. Capitalism will not self-destruct. If labor does not destroy it, it will come out of this crisis stronger and more virulent than ever.

Perhaps the title of this chapter should have been "The Old Is Dying, but What Will the New Be?"

Appendix: Statistical Sources and Methods

Profits. Profits are from Bureau of Economic Analysis (BEA) tables 6.17A, 6.17B, 6.17C, 6.17D: "Corporate Profits before Tax by Industry" (billions of dollars). They include agriculture, mining, construction, manufacture and transport.

Profit rate. Following the temporalist approach, profits at time t2 (the end point of t1 − t2, the present period) are divided by the constant and variable capital at time t1, the starting point of the present period, which is also the end point of the previous period.

Fixed assets. The US Bureau of Economic Analysis defines fixed assets (constant capital) as "equipment, software, and structures, including owner-occupied housing." The data considered in this chapter covers agriculture, mining, construction manufacturing and utilities. Fixed assets are obtained from BEA, table 3.3 ESI: "Historical-Cost Net Stock of Private Fixed Assets by Industry" and the price deflator from table 5.3.4. Conforming to the temporalist approach, historical costs have been chosen instead of replacement costs.

Wages. Wages for goods-producing industries are obtained from Fred.stlouisfed.org (billions of dollars).

Employment in goods-producing industries. This is obtained from US Department of Labor, Bureau of Labor Statistics, series ID CES0600000001.

Financial profits. From BEA tables 6.17A, 6.17B, 6.17C, 6.17D: financial profits.

Government expenditures / GDP. From Fred.Stlouisfed.org.

Notes

1   The focus is on the productive sectors. Data are deflated. See the appendix.
2   This ARP is computed according to the temporalist method. See appendix.
3   Notice that the above presupposes only one capitalist per sector. If this assumption is dropped, the redistribution of surplus value inherent in the production price is such that the average rate of profit is realized by the capitalist with an average organic composition in their respective sectors, while the other capitalists realize different rates of profit according to their organic composition of capital in their sectors.
4   As held by the *Monthly Review* school.
5   This is the temporalist rate of profit. See appendix.
6   Notice that α refers only to new labor, while γ refers to both new and past labor.
7   Authors following this line of thought include, among others, Arthur (2004), Milios (2009), Murray (2000), and Heinrich (2004). For a critique see Carchedi (2011).
8   The only exception is employment in 1949. It rises by 2.1 percent from 1948. However, it falls by 4.5 percent from 1947.

9   Innovations are labor-shedding, rather then labor saving. "Labor saving" is an ideological term that should be avoided.

10   Output per laborer is determined both by productivity proper (the change due to more efficient means of production) and by the rate of exploitation (the greater output as a consequence of an increase in the rate of exploitation). In economic literature these two factors are not separated for ideological reasons. Here, productivity proper has been computed with a constant rate of exploitation for reasons similar to computation of the CE-ARP.

11   See Carchedi and Roberts, (unpublished) "Non-Equilibrium Prices, Overproduction and Profitability."

12   What follows holds also for military investments.

13   See Carchedi (2012a, 2012b) and Roberts, chapter 1 of this book.

14   If commissions are placed abroad, the beneficial effects on employment are lost.

15   Marx, K. (1973), *Grundrisse*, translated by Martin Nicolaus, Penguin Books.

16   See Carchedi (2011) for a full analysis of these topics.

17   Carchedi, "Old wine, new bottles and the Internet," *Work Organisation, Labour and Globalisation*, vol. 8, no. 1 (2014).

References

Albo, G., S. Gindin, and L. Panitch (2010) *In and Out of Crisis*, PM Press.

Basu, D. and P. Manolakos (2010) "Is There a Tendency for the Rate of Profit to Fall? Econometric Evidence for the U.S. Economy, 1948–2007," Working Paper 2010–04, University of Massachusetts, Amherst.

Basu, D. and R. Vasudevan (2013) "Technology, Distribution and the Rate of Profit in the US Economy: Understanding the Current Crisis," *Cambridge Journal of Economics*, Vol 37.

Bernstein, J., L. Mishel, and H. Shierholz (2006–2007) "The State of Working America," Economic Policy Institute, available at http://www.epi.org/.

Blackmore, M. (2005) *Surveillance in the Workplace: An Overview of Issues of Privacy, Monitoring, and Ethics,* briefing paper for GMB, September 2005, https://stopthecyborgs.org/2014/06/18/surveillance-in-the-workplace-an-overview-of-issues-of-privacy-monitoring-and-ethics/.

Brenner, R. and M. Probsting (2008) *The Credit Crunch: A Marxist Analysis*, The League for the Fifth International.

Izquierdo, S. C. (2007) "The Dynamics of the Profit Rate in Spain (1954–2001)," *Review of Radical Political Economics*, Vol 39, No 4.

———. (2010) "Short and Long Term Dynamics of the US Rate of Profit in the Context of the Current Crisis," paper presented at the Congrès Marx International VI, "Crises, Révoltes, Utopies."

Carchedi, G. (1971) *On the Economic Identification of Social Classes*, Routledge & Kegan Paul.

———. (2011a) *Behind the Crisis*, Brill.

———. (2011b) "Behind and Beyond the Crisis," *International Socialism*, No 32.

———. (2012a) "Could Keynes End the Slump? Introducing the Marxist Multiplier," *International Socialism*, No 136.

———. (2012b) "From the Crisis of Surplus Value to the Crisis of the Euro," *World Review of Political Economy*, Vol 3, No 3.

———. (2014a) "Krise und Fall der Profitrate – empirische Belege," *Das Argument*.

————. (2014b) "Old Wine, New Bottles and the Internet," *Work Organisation, Labour and Globalisation*, Vol 8, No 1.

Carchedi, G. and M. Roberts (2013) "The Long Roots of the Present Crisis: Keynesians, Austerians, and Marx's law," *World Review of Political Economy*, reprinted in this volume as chapter 1.

————. (2013) "A Critique of Heinrich's Crisis Theory, the Law of the Tendency of the Profit Rate to Fall, and Marx's Studies in the 1870s," *Monthly Review*, December 1.

————. (2013) "Marx's Law of Profitability: Answering Old and New Misconceptions," *Critique: Journal of Socialist Theory*, Vol 41, No 4.

————. (Unpublished) "The Rate of Profit and Circulating Capital," available at www.marx2010.weebly.com.

————. (Unpublished) "Non-Equilibrium Prices, Overproduction and Profitability"

Duménil, G. and D. Lévy (2004) *Capital Resurgent*, Harvard University Press.

————. (2011) *The Crisis of Neoliberalism*, Harvard University Press.

Foster, J. B. and R. W. McChesney (2012) *The Endless Crisis*, Monthly Review Press.

Freeman, A. (2009) "What Makes the US Profit Rate Fall?," Munich Personal RePEc Archive.

Gramsci, A. (1971), *Selections from the Prison Notebooks*, "Wave of Materialism" and "Crisis of Authority," International Publishers.

Gordon, R. J., (2012), "Is US Economic Growth Over? Faltering Innovation Confronts the Six Headwinds," NBER working paper series.

Grossman, H. (1992) *The Law of Accumulation and the Breakdown of the Capitalist System*, Pluto Press.

Harvey, D. (2010) *The Enigma of Capital and Crisis of Capitalism*, Oxford University Press.

Heinrich, M. (2013) "Crisis Theory, the Law of the Tendency of the Rate of Profit to Fall, and Marx's Studies in the 1870s," *Monthly Review*, Vol 64, No 11.

Husson, M. (2010) "The Debate on the Rate of Profit," *International Viewpoint*, Vol 426.

————. (2013) "A gauche de la crise : les discours heterodoxies," available at http://hussonet.free.fr.

Jones, P. (2012) "Depreciation, Devaluation and the Rate of Profit," paper to the WAPE/AHE/IIPPE conference.

Kaufman, H. (2009) *The Road to Financial Reformation*, John Wiley & Sons.

Kliman, A. (2007) *Reclaiming Marx's Capital*, Lexington Books.

Laderman, L. and S. Leduc (2014) "Slow Business Start-ups and the Job Recovery," *FRBSF Economic Letter*, July 7.

Maito, E. E. (Unpublished) "Income Distribution, Turnover Speed and Profit Rate in Chile, Japan, Netherlands and United States."

Maniatis, T. and K. Passas (2013) "Profitability, Capital Accumulation and Crisis in the Greek Economy 1958–2009: A Marxist Analysis," *Review of Political Economy*, Vol 25, No 4, reprinted in this volume as chapter 8.

Marquetti, A., E. M. Filho, and V. Lautert (2010) "The Profit Rate in Brazil, 1953–2003," Sagepub.com, reprinted in this volume as chapter 9.

Marx, K. (1967a) *Capital*, Vol 1, International Publishers.

————. (1967b) *Capital,* Vol 2, International Publishers.

————. (1967c) *Capital,* Vol 3, International Publishers.

————. (1968) *Theories of Surplus Value,* Part 2, Progress Publishers.

————. (1973) *Grundrisse*, Penguin Books.

Minsky, H. (1982) "Can 'It' Happen Again?," in *Essays on Instability and Finance*, M. E. Sharpe, pp. 64–65.

Mokyr, J. (2012) "Over innovatie," *Me Judice*, November 6.

Moseley, F. (2009) "The US economic crisis: causes and solutions," *International Socialist Review*, No 64.

Norfield, T. (2012) "Derivatives and capitalist markets: the speculative heart of capital," *Historical Materialism*, Vol 20, No 1.

Organisation for Economic Co-operation and Development (2016), *OECD Employment Outlook 2016*, OECD Publishing, http://dx.doi.org/10.1787/empl_outlook–2016-en.

Okishio, N. (1961) "Technical Changes and the Rate of Profit," *Kobe University Economic Review*, Vol 7.

Paitaridis, D. and L. Tsoulfidis (2012) "The Growth of Unproductive Activities, the Rate of Profit, and the Phase-Change of the U.S. Economy," *Review of Radical Political Economics*, Vol 44, No 2.

Reinhart, C. M. and K. S. Rogoff (2009) *This Time Is Different*, Princeton University Press.

Roberts, M. (2009), *The Great Recession*, Lulu.

———. (2012) "A World Rate of Profit," paper to the WAPE/AHE/IIPPE conference.

Shaikh, A. (1999) "Explaining the Global Economic Crisis," *Historical Materialism*, Vol 5, No 1.

———. (2011) "The First Great Depression of the 21st Century," *Socialist Register*, Vol 47.

Smith, M. E. G. and J. Butovsky (2012) "Profitability and the Roots of Global Crisis," *Historical Materialism*, Vol 20, No 4.

Tabuki, H. (2013) "Back in Power, Abe Aims to Spend Japan Back to Economic Vitality," *New York Times*, January 22.

Tapia, J. A. (2013) "From the Oil Crisis to the Great Recession: Five Crises of the World Economy," available at https://marxismocritico.com/2013/05/08/from-the-oil-crisis-to-the-great-recession-five-crises-of-the-world-economy/.

World Bank (2013) "Jobs," *World Development Report 2013*, World Bank Publications, p. 261.

CHAPTER 3

INVESTMENT, PROFIT AND CRISES: THEORIES AND EVIDENCE

José A. Tapia

> Analyzing business cycles means neither more nor less than analyzing the economic process of the capitalist era. . . . Cycles are not, like tonsils, separable things that might be treated by themselves, but are, like the beat of the heart, of the essence of the organism that displays them.

> —Joseph A. Schumpeter, *Business Cycles,* 1939

1. Introduction

American economists often talk about *the business cycle,* British authors generally favor *trade cycle,* and many in the profession dislike these terms and rather refer to *macroeconomic fluctuations.* Indeed, in the past two centuries, multiple terms have been used in the economic jargon to refer to this bipolar phenomenon: "boom-and-bust cycle," "expansion and contraction," "upturn and downturn," "mania and panic," "prosperity and depression." Terms such as "revulsion in trade," "commercial distress," "stagnation," "slump," "recession," or "crisis" were also used in the past to describe the phase of declining business activity of the "cycle."

Among authors who claim to be inspired to some extent by Marx's views, there are major disagreements about Marx's theory of crisis as well as on the nature and causes of the phenomenon.[1] The disagreements extend to how the Marxian concept of crisis is to be applied to twentieth-century periods of economic distress, and even to the terminology used to discuss these issues. Thus in the field of radical or heterodox economics, a common opinion is that the economic crises Marx discussed are entities different from the recessions identified by mainstream economics. While the National Bureau of Economic Research (NBER) identifies recessions of the US economy starting in 1895, 1899, 1902, 1907, 1910, 1913, 1918, 1920, 1923, 1926, 1929,

1937, 1945, 1948, 1953, 1957, 1960, 1969, 1973, 1980, 1981, 1990, 2001, and 2007, most heterodox economists and radical authors who write on economic issues refer to just four crises of American capitalism since the late nineteenth century. These four crises would be the Long Depression at the end of the nineteenth century, the Great Depression of the 1930s, another crisis in the 1970s–1980s, and the Great Recession that started in 2008. This is the view of Foley (2012), Duménil and Lévy (2011, p. 22), Panitch (2013), Shaikh (2016, p. 726), and many others. Dissenting voices that I know of are Perlo (1973), McNally (2010), and Cámara (2013). For historians like Arrighi (2003, pp. 527–39) or Wallerstein (2001, p. 23; 2011) economic crises may last many decades, even more than a century.

If, as often sustained by left-wing authors, crises can last many years, or even many decades, while business-cycle recessions as defined by mainstream economics never last more than several quarters or a few years, then theories used to explain business cycles and crises must be different theories. However, in discussions of these issues it is hard to find this distinction in authors like Marx, Keynes, Kalecki, or Minsky, who largely inspire the ideas on crises of present-day heterodox economists.

In the years since the eruption of the global financial crisis in 2008, there has been an increased interest in crisis theory, business-cycle theory, or macroeconomic dynamics—whatever we may call it. In these matters, a major issue is whether there exists a key variable (or variables) that exerts a major influence on the economy and serves as the major determinant of its dynamic condition of expansion or contraction. This chapter reviews some aspects of crisis theories, focusing on endogenous theories and, particularly, on the role of investment and profits. The general assumption is that crisis theory and business-cycle theory are the same thing because in economic matters, terms such as downturn, crisis, recession, or depression refer to different intensities of the same intrinsic phenomenon of capitalism. I disagree with the view of crises as phenomena that may last many years. My starting notion is that an economic crisis is a brief interruption of the accumulation of capital, a momentary solution for solving conflicts created by the internal dynamics of the system, a "violent eruption that reestablish[es] the balance that has been disturbed" (Marx 1981a, p. 357; 1968, p. 497). My view is that the essential qualities that for Marx characterize "economic crises" can be found in what modern economists call "recessions"; and what Marx called the "industrial crisis cycle" is precisely the same as "the business cycle," as generally defined by Wesley Mitchell and the NBER.

I accept, with some exceptions, the NBER chronology, which for me is basically a chronology of economic crises. Thus, focusing on the past half century, I see economic crises in the mid-1970s, early 1980s, early 1990s, around the turn of the century, and in 2008–2009. This is consistent with the NBER chronology for the economy of the United States, with the exception that the two recessions that according to the NBER occurred in the first semester of 1980 and between mid-1981 and late 1982 constitute for me a unique crisis. A recent publication of the International Monetary Fund dates four recessions of the world economy in 1975, 1982, 1991, and 2009 (Kose and Terrones 2015). I indeed believe that there were crises of the world economy in these years, and that the US recessions were part of them, but I also identify a crisis of the world economy around the turn of the century, corresponding to the NBER recession of 2001. For more details on all this see Tapia (2014).

This chapter starts with an outline of the development of theories of the business cycle and then focuses on some endogenous theories and the role of profits and investment in these theories. Next I present empirical evidence to assess to what extent the theories, particularly those of Marx, Mitchell, Keynes, and Kalecki, fit or do not fit with empirical data. I conclude with some general considerations.

2. General Aspects of Crisis Theories

The earliest conjectures on the business cycle were probably the underconsumption theories proposed at the turn of the eighteenth century by Lord Lauderdale, Thomas Robert Malthus, and Simonde de Sismondi. These authors attributed downturns in business activity to economic circumstances, that is, to endogenous factors (Mitchell 1927, ch. 1). "General gluts" occurred because purchasing power available in society was not sufficient to buy the output produced. Wages, being too low, would not be sufficient for labor "to buy its own product." These were therefore underconsumption theories in which insufficient purchasing power generates lack of consumption with unsold goods and depressed business.

David Ricardo, John Stuart Mill, and most economists of the nineteenth century—who agreed with Jean-Baptiste Say's idea that sufficient demand is always available to purchase the produced supply—rejected these theories. For Say the market represents an exchange of produced commodities, such that products exchange by products and, furthermore, as David Ricardo emphasized, nobody has any interest in hoarding money, which has no utility by itself. Therefore the production of commodities represents more purchasing power, and a general glut is impossible, though there may be an excess of a particular type of goods. This rationale, later baptized as Say's law, would be the supposed theoretical reason precluding the possibility of "general gluts," that is, crisis of overproduction.

For Gottfried Haberler, who in a major work reviewed the theories of the business cycle, underconsumption theories have a scientific standard significantly lower than other theories of the business cycle (Haberler 1960); and Joseph Schumpeter (1954, p. 740) suggested the same thing, asserting that underconsumption theory, "as Marx well knew, is beneath discussion since it involves neglect of the elementary fact that inadequacy . . . of the wage income to buy the whole product at cost-covering prices would not prevent hitchless production in response to the demand of non-wage earners either for 'luxury' goods or for investment." As we will see, Karl Marx had rejected Say's law, but his reasons for it were quite different from those of Malthus and Sismondi.

In the late decades of the nineteenth century, with the weapon of Say's law at hand, the nascent discipline of economics was quite aloof to the possibility of general gluts of markets and thus paid little attention to commercial crises and business-cycle issues. Indeed, apart from Marx and Jevons, economists were scarcely interested in this field (Morgan 1990, p. 15), and a major contribution such as *Des Crises commerciales et leur retour périodique en France, en Angleterre et aux États-Unis* came from a noneconomist, Clément Juglar, in 1862. For Juglar the crises were generated endogenously by the workings of the financial system propagating to commerce and industry. Economists paid little attention to it.

The years between 1870 and the start of the First World War saw major developments in economics. The "cycle" displaced "crises" in economists' language and minds, and crises theories were displaced by business-cycle theories (Besomi 2005; Schumpeter 1954, p. 1123). It was also the time when three exogenous theories that attribute business cycles to astronomical or biological influences were proposed. Thus in papers published by W. S. Jevons between 1875 and 1882 and in two books authored by H. L. Moore in 1914 and 1923, the fluctuations of the economy were attributed to weather, determined in turn by astronomical phenomena—sun spots in Jevons's view, the planet Venus in Moore's (Morgan 1990, pp. 18–33). In the schemes of Jevons and Moore, the causal chain runs from astronomical events to weather, which in turn impacts agriculture and thus the economy at large. However, the data on these causal links were considered very insufficient by the contemporaries as evidence to prove these theories; years later Wesley Mitchell showed that neither agricultural output nor crop husbandry prices, inventories, or shipments correlate with business cycles (Mitchell 1913, p. 239; 1951, p. 58).

A third exogenous theory of the business cycle was that of the geographer Ellsworth Huntington, who in 1920 proposed autonomous changes in the rate of death as the factor stimulating or depressing business. An upturn in mortality rates due to causes unrelated to the economy would cause sadness and thus a drop in spending, which would lead to a slowdown of the economy; conversely, a decrease in mortality would cause increasing spending and prosperity. The views of Jevons, Moore, and Huntington, today scarcely considered or even known, are typical examples of exogenous business-cycle theories in which the oscillations between prosperity and depression are attributed to phenomena external to the economy itself.

In the late 1920s, exogenous theories of the business cycle found an unexpected source of inspiration coming from the USSR in the work of the statistician Evgeny Slutzky, who showed that applying some mathematical operations to a series of random numbers could generate apparent cycles. Following Slutzky's idea, Ragnar Frisch (1933) was the first in proposing that the fluctuations of the level of activity in modern industrial economies may be due to the effects of erratic, uncorrelated shocks upon an otherwise interrelated system. Frisch proposed the separation of what he called the impulse problem (the discontinuous random shocks providing "oscillating energy" to the system) and the propagation mechanism (the inner workings of the system, balancing it back toward equilibrium). In the 1950s Irma Adelman and Frank L. Adelman showed that applying perturbations to the endogenous variables of the propagation mechanism as well as applying random shocks to "energize" the system enabled an econometric model of the US economy to show oscillations resembling the empirically observed business cycles. According to Irma Adelman (1960), she and her husband had not "proved that business cycles are stochastic in origin," though they had presented evidence creating "a strong presumption in favor of this hypothesis," which would be "especially significant in view of the absence (to date) of a completely satisfactory endogenous theory of business cycles."

To understand why Irma Adelman referred in 1960 to the absence "of a completely satisfactory endogenous theory of business cycles," it has to be mentioned that previous years had seen two major reactions of mainstream economics against endogenous theories of the business cycle. The first reaction was against Jan Tinbergen, the second against Wesley Mitchell.

Tinbergen went into research on economic issues from a background in mathematics and physics; he had not had formal instruction in economics. Thus in his research he was mostly an empiricist—he applied statistical methods to look for regularities in economic data that allowed him to infer economic laws. During the turbulent 1930s, he was charged by the League of Nations with investigating the cause of economic recessions. In his econometric studies on the business cycle, Tinbergen (1939) showed that investment is the key variable that oscillates upward in expansions and downward in depressions, a fact that was largely consistent with the view that John Maynard Keynes had recently exposed in his *General Theory of Employment, Interest and Money* (1936). The other key finding of Tinbergen was that profits have a major influence in endogenously determining investment, something that was at odds with Keynes's views.

In an episode that highlights the antiempirical proneness of economics, Tinbergen's pioneering investigation received heavy criticism from none other than Keynes and the nascent figure of the anti-Keynesian field, Milton Friedman (Friedman 1940, pp. 657–60; Keynes 1939, pp. 558–68). In brief, both Keynes and Friedman trashed Tinbergen's work.

The second attack against endogenous views of the business cycle took the shape of the "measurement without theory" debate. This debate started when Tjalling Koopmans reviewed the book *Measuring Business Cycles*, authored by Arthur Burns and Wesley Mitchell (Koopmans 1947, pp. 161–72).

Wesley Mitchell had published his views on the business cycle already in 1913, when he had conceptualized the cycle essentially as a fluctuation of the production of capital goods, that is, investment, which in turn followed the fluctuation of profits. His views had coexisted in mainstream economics with a variety of ill-defined ideas about the business cycle. Four decades later Mitchell was still convinced that business cycles are endogenously determined—as shown by the fact that in 1941 he republished, almost without changes and with the title *Business Cycles and Their Causes*, the theoretical part of his 1913 book. Furthermore, in 1944 he published an article in the *New York Times* in which he stated that no nation had yet found a solution to the problem of operating a system of free enterprise "without falling every few years into a spam of unemployment." (Mitchell 1944). For that problem, Mitchell said, "no nation has yet found a solution that does not involve the suppression of free enterprise itself." This kind of consideration was at odds with the claims of the Keynesian school, which, following the ideas of *The General Theory*, would soon be asserting that the business cycle could be put completely under control. Thus Paul Samuelson claimed in 1955 that by using proper fiscal and monetary policies, "our economy can have full employment and whatever rate of capital formation it wants" (cited by Bowles and Edwards 1985, p. 355).

In his review of *Measuring Business Cycles*, Tjalling Koopmans criticized Burns and Mitchell as just presenting "measurement without theory." From Keynesian quarters, Alvin Hansen (1949) echoed Koopmans, asserting that "the driving forces back of the cycle movement, Mitchell was never able to disclose," and similar views were exposed from the non-Keynesian field by Robert A. Gordon (1961). From the 1950s it was a common view in economics that Mitchell was just an empiricist who had described some interesting patterns, never going beyond the surface of economic phenomena. As a Marxist economist put it much later, Mitchell described the "ups and downs [of the economy] using little theory" (Devine 1986).

A more detailed explanation of the reaction of mainstream economics against Tinbergen and Mitchell goes beyond the scope of this chapter. It is sufficient to say here that it occurred in a context in which the economic

profession was increasingly adamant in denying precisely what Wesley
Mitchell asserted: that periods of prosperity and depression are endogenous
and unavoidable, and that profits are a key variable in the cycle—something
that was also supported by Tinbergen's econometric analyses. Keynesians
and anti-Keynesians disagreed on many issues, but they agreed that
business cycles could be eliminated—whether by the proper policies of
Keynes, or the laissez-faire "non-policies" of Friedman. In that context,
Tinbergen's and Mitchell's ideas were a hindrance to be removed, and they
were marginalized and forgotten. At the same time, the view that business
cycles are exogenously determined by random shocks became increasingly
influential in economics in the 1960s and 1970s. Disputes between Keynesian
and monetarist authors during the period of decline of Keynesian economics
can be seen as arguments about which parts of the propagation mechanism
proposed by Ragnar Frisch and the Adelmans were the most important
for the dynamics of the economy, but the idea that business cycles are
exogenously determined was almost never disputed. Business-cycle theories
based on monetarism and rational expectations were fully exogenous, and
New Keynesians increasingly adopted the view that recessions may be
caused by factors that are exogenous, though mediated by different kinds of
market failure, rather than by the animal spirits that Keynes had proposed.

After the decades that Paul Krugman called the dark age of
macroeconomics, the field was populated by an amazing variety of views,
and ignorance, on business cycles. An important school was that of the real-
business-cycle (RBC) theory, in which business cycles are conceptualized
as the consequence of a self-equilibrating economy responding to random
events. Supporters of the RBC theory often mention, in the tradition of
Schumpeter and Hayek, technological innovations or "shocks" as causes
of economic fluctuations. Other exogenous factors such as demographic
changes, political influences, or variations in relative prices have also been
proposed. This type of "shock" is often referred to without specifying its
nature, though James Hamilton (1988; 2011), for instance, has repeatedly
proposed oil prices as a key determinant of recessions.[2]

An important aspect of present views on the business cycle is that
they are often vaguely defined, which makes it difficult to differentiate
theoretical perspectives. Economists who support a theory of business
cycles determined by exogenous factors—Austrians, monetarists, and RBC
theorists—coexist with economists who view the fluctuations of the market
economy as perhaps determined by endogenous factors—Samuelsonians,
Keynesians, New Keynesians, post-Keynesians, institutionalists, and socialist
economists.[3] However, as will be promptly explained, many economists,
perhaps a majority, do not espouse any particular theory of the business

cycle. Educated in the kingdom of Say's law, in which crises do not exist, they are clueless about possible explanations of black swans.

It is known that the economic profession did very poorly in predicting the global crisis that was later baptized as the Great Recession and was totally unexpected for almost all macroeconomists. As Nicholas Mankiw (2010, B6) put it, in 2008 the Great Recession "caught most economists flat-footed." This led many noneconomists to inquire (as the Queen of England did) what was the usefulness of a profession that supposedly deals with economic issues but had been utterly unable to forecast a major economic disturbance such as the crisis that erupted in 2008.[4] Obviously, the presence or absence of "talent" to forecast economic distress is not connected with the presence or absence of psychic powers, but with the ability of economic theories to explain business cycles—and this is not very large, to put it mildly. This is demonstrated by the fact that in recent years distinguished economists have declared that the cause of recessions is not known and that recessions cannot be forecasted. For a famous econometrician, Edward Leamer (2010, pp. 31–46), economists' understanding "of causal effects in macroeconomics is virtually nil, and will remain so," and the Nobelist Eugene Fama declared that economists do not know what causes recessions (Cassidy 2010, p. 28). Nicholas Mankiw, who has had major roles as economic advisor of the US government, believes that it is basically impossible to predict recessions because economic fluctuations do not follow any predictable pattern (Mankiw 2009), such that future recessions will occur "at some unknown date for some unknown reason" (Mankiw 2010).

Though many economists would agree with these views, many others would disagree, as they sometimes vehemently argued about why crises occur, or more generally, about the causes of the business cycle. For many in the profession, the fluctuations of the economy—even when they are brutal—are to be seen in the framework of a built-in ability of the free enterprise system to balance itself, so that the swings of the economy between prosperous business conditions and ruinous downturns would be just the manifestation of the reaction of the economy to exogenous "shocks." What is the nature of these shocks? Many economists are happy leaving them undefined, but others, following the tradition of Friedman and Hayek, mention injudicious actions of governments or central bankers (Schwartz 2010; Butler 2010), or spikes in oil prices due to a variety of factors—wars, revolutions, or cartel activities (Hamilton 1988; 2009). Still others mention more abstruse causes, for instance idiosyncratic events impacting big firms and propagating through networks (Gabaix 2011; Acemoglu et al. 2012), or just miscellaneous circumstances that generate economic uncertainty (Bloom 2014). The alternative vision that economic crises have endogenous causes, so that business cycles are determined by the inner workings of the market system, is today hard to find in economics. This view is typical of two authors who largely theorized on economic crises, Marx and Mitchell, but because the ideas of these two authors are mostly ignored in modern economics, the view that business cycles are endogenous is today usually associated—in a quite improper way, as I will explain—with the left-wing components of the Keynesian school, represented for instance by Kalecki (1954), Robinson (1979), Minsky (2008), and the modern followers of post-Keynesian economics. However, the distinction between endogenous and exogenous theories of the business cycle is important because, as Thomas E. Hall put it very well, "they imply a very different behavior for an economy," so that authors supporting exogenous factors as causes of the business cycle tend "to view economies as being inherently stable but shocked by outside forces," while endogenous theorists "generally consider economies as being inherently unstable and subject to self-generating cycles" (Hall 1990, p. 10).

For quite a number of economists and economic commentators, wages are a key variable explaining recessions. Indeed, since wages constitute the largest portion of consumption, and consumption is the largest item in the national product, wages are often thought of as important determinants of the business cycle. Therefore the idea of too-low wages leading to insufficient consumption, which in turn would depress the economy, appears plausible and is common in explanations of economic crises. It is the traditional underconsumptionist view. But other authors who also claim an important role of wages in explaining the business cycle propose exactly the opposite mechanism, too-high wages, as the factor leading to recession. This was the view once maintained by Arthur Pigou (1927) that has been recently upheld by Lee Ohanian (2008), a qualified representative of the RBC school. In this theoretical framework, high wages—caused by an exogenous factor, namely the distorting influence of trade unions on the equilibrium of the labor market—cause unaffordable costs for business, which in turn will stifle production with the consequent economic decay. Thus, in this scheme a decrease in wages would increase business activity and would have a stimulating effect on the economy.

A relatively similar perspective is offered by those who support the so-called "profit-squeeze" hypothesis (Boddy and Crotty 1975; Boldrin and Horvath 1995; Bhaduri and Marglin 1990) in which high wages lead to recession through the demand side. The causal pathway here would be from high wages to low profits, and from low profits to falling investment and the lack of effective demand with unsold goods that characterizes recessions. Some authors who support the profit-squeeze hypothesis also seem to hold underconsumptionist views, since they de-emphasize the role of investment in business cycles by claiming that, with a "relatively weak response of investment to profitability . . . consumption necessarily assumes the dominant role in effective demand" (Bhaduri and Marglin 1990). In a purely underconsumptionist view, too-low wages generating too-low purchasing power for consumer goods reduce aggregate demand and cause recession, so that an increase in wages during a slump would tend to stimulate recovery. Indeed, this was Michał Kalecki's (1984) view that was later taken up by many radical authors, for instance by David Harvey (2010). Kalecki's views will be examined in more detail in the context of a review of theories in which investment is the leading variable of the business cycle.

3. Investment Leading the Cycle: Kalecki and Keynes

It is a common view today that Michał Kalecki independently discovered many elements of what later would be called Keynesian theory. Many would even agree that Kalecki's construct is superior to that of Keynes in crucial aspects. At any rate, as we will see, for both Keynes and Kalecki, and for the whole Keynesian school, investment is the key variable explaining macroeconomic dynamics, and thus leads the cycle.

In the early years of the Great Depression, Kalecki published several articles in *Przegląd Socjalistyczny*, an independent Polish "socialist review." Kalecki had no academic degree, since he had never finished his engineering studies. He had been earning his living as an economic journalist and working as an analyst for the Polish Institute for the Study of Business Cycles and Prices (ISBCP). This probably explains why he published in the socialist review under a pseudonym. Signing as Henryk Braun, Kalecki (1990, pp. 37–53) commented in the early 1930s on different aspects of the world depression. In one of the articles, he referred to Keynes as "a representative of British imperialism" and "possibly the leading bourgeois economist" (Kalecki 1990, 45–47). In "Is a 'capitalist' overcoming of the crisis possible?" (1932), Kalecki argued that during a crisis, investment shrinks and that

> it is precisely here that one should seek the starting-point of processes that will bring an upswing of the business cycle. Owing to the fact that during a crisis investment activity is at a lower level than that required for simple reproduction (maintenance) of the existing capital equipment, thus equipment is also gradually depleted. Unused and outdated machines are sold for scrap and new ones are not purchased to replace them. Besides, a considerable number of machines – and equipment in general – still kept in factories has not been reconditioned nor maintained properly, and may have become obsolete as well (due to technological progress), and is therefore only partially usable. On the other hand, since in a certain phase of the crisis the output of consumer goods generally starts declining more slowly than the rate of this contraction of capital equipment, there is a real need to employ

the existing equipment more fully, which in turn requires investment. There is then a better chance of intensifying investment activity, which is the basic foundation for overcoming the crisis. . . . In the final analysis . . . of those components of the mechanism of the capitalist economy which could form a foundation for overcoming the crisis, the contraction of capital equipment caused by the decline of investments (and also by the running down of stocks) should be put in first place. . . . Finally, we should mention yet another possibility, namely a certain form of inflation consisting of individual states, or groups of states, starting up major public-investment schemes, such as construction of canals or roads, and financing them with government loans floated on the financial market, or with special government credits drawn on their banks of issue. This kind of operation could temporarily increase employment, though on the other hand it would retard automatic, "natural" adjustment processes which might lead to overcoming the crisis. (Kalecki 1990, pp. 51–53)

This quotation shows that Kalecki had already developed a highly elaborated theory of the business cycle in 1932. Kalecki's theoretical scheme was further developed in a booklet titled *Próba teorii koniunktury* (Essay on the theory of the economic conjuncture), that was published by the ISBCP in 1933, when Kalecki also presented his views on the business cycle in the Econometric Society. In 1935 abbreviated translations of his booklet were published in *Econometrica* and *Revue d'économie politique*. In 1936 Kalecki was planning to write a general exposition of his macroeconomic ideas in a book, until he read Keynes's *General Theory*. It was the book Kalecki was planning to write, and he felt deeply disappointed by having been beaten to it by Keynes (Shackle 1967, p. 127).

In contrast to the humble economic origins of Kalecki, who was almost completely unknown in the 1930s in his native Poland and abroad, Keynes was, at the time he published *The General Theory,* a prestigious economist. He was the editor of the *Economic Journal* and had occupied important positions in the administration of the British government. In his *General Theory* Keynes considered the business cycle "as being occasioned by a cyclical change in the marginal efficiency of capital, though complicated, and often aggravated by associated changes in the other significant short-period variables of the economic system" (Keynes 1936, p. 313). For Keynes the marginal efficiency of capital is the expected rate of return of capital. In terms of nineteenth-century political economy, it is the expected rate of profit, and for Keynes it depends "not only on the existing abundance or scarcity of capital-goods and the current cost of production of capital-goods, but also on current expectations as to the future yield of capital-goods" (Keynes 1936, p. 315).

Considering the view that the crisis—"the substitution of a downward for an upward movement tendency that often takes place suddenly and violently"—may be due to too-high levels of the rate of interest, Keynes claimed that "a more typical, and often the predominant, explanation of the crisis is, not primarily a rise in the rate of interest, but a sudden collapse in the marginal efficiency of capital." But why would the marginal efficiency of capital—the expected profitability—fall suddenly after it had been steadily rising or at least remaining stable during the boom? What Keynes thought is that as long as the boom "was continuing, much of the new investment showed a not unsatisfactory current yield. The disillusion comes because doubts suddenly arise concerning the reliability of the prospective yield, perhaps because the current yield shows signs of falling off. . . . Once doubt begins it spreads rapidly" (p. 317).

Keynes suggests that the fall in expectations about profitability may be perhaps caused by the declining current yield. He does not seem to put much faith in that explanation, however, because during the crisis

> it is not so easy to revive the marginal efficiency of capital, *determined, as it is, by the uncontrollable and disobedient psychology of the business world*. It is the return of confidence, to speak in ordinary language, which is so insusceptible to control in an economy of individualistic capitalism. This is the aspect of the slump which bankers and businessmen have been right in emphasising, and which the economists who have put their faith in a "purely monetary" remedy have underestimated. (p. 317, emphasis added)

From the dependence of the trade cycle on the psychology of investors, Keynes concluded that in conditions "of laissez-faire the avoidance of wide fluctuations in employment may, therefore, prove impossible without a far-reaching change in the psychology of investment markets such as there is no reason to expect" (p. 320).

One year after the publication of *The General Theory*, Keynes clarified in the *Quarterly Journal of Economics* some of the issues that had been raised by the book. For Keynes his theory could be summed up "by saying that, given the psychology of the public, *the level of output and employment as a whole depends on the amount of investment*" (emphasis added). Keynes was explaining his theory this way, focusing on investment, "not because this is the only factor on which aggregate output depends, but because it is usual in a complex system to regard as the *causa causans* that factor which is most prone to sudden and wide fluctuation" (Keynes 1937).

Kalecki reviewed *The General Theory* in the Polish journal *Ekonomista* in 1936, praising it as "a turning point in the history of economics." The book had, in Kalecki's view, two main components: one discussing the mechanisms determining a short-period equilibrium once the level of investment was given, and the other dealing with the determination of the level of investment. Keynes, Kalecki said, had reasonably succeeded in the former, but had failed in the latter. Kalecki agreed that "investment is the factor which decides the short-period equilibrium, and hence, at a certain moment, the size of employment and of social income. In fact the volume of investment will decide the amount of the labor force which will be absorbed by the existing production apparatus" (Kalecki 1990, p. 228).

Kalecki saw serious deficiencies in Keynes's belief that the level of investment would be determined by the equalization of expected profitability and the rate of interest. This would not lead to equilibrium, but to a continuous process in which higher investment led to a never-ending process of higher expected profitability, which in turn raises investment:

> Keynes's concept . . . meets a serious difficulty along this path also. In fact, the growth of investment in no way results in a process leading the system toward equilibrium. Thus it is difficult to consider Keynes's solution of the investment problem to be satisfactory. The reason for this failure lies in an approach which is basically static to a matter which is by its nature dynamic. Keynes takes as given the state of the expectations of returns, and from this he derives a certain definite level of investment, overlooking the effects that investment will in turn have on expectations. It is here that one can glimpse the road one must follow in order to build a realistic theory of investment. Its starting point should be the solution of the problem of investment decisions, of *ex ante* investment. Let us suppose there to be, at a given moment, a certain state of expectations as to future incomes, a given price level of investment goods, and, finally, a given rate of interest. How great then will be the investment that entrepreneurs intend to undertake in a unit of time? Let us suppose that this problem has been solved (despite the fact that it seems impossible to do this without introducing some special assumptions on the psychology of entrepreneurs or on money market imperfections). A further development of the theory of investment could be as follows. The investment decisions corresponding to the initial state will not generally be equal to the actual volume of investment. Therefore, in the next period the volume of investment will generally be different and the short-period equilibrium will change together with it. Hence we should now deal with a state of expectations that in general will be different from that of the initial period, different prices of investment goods, and a different rate of interest. From these a new level of investment decisions will result — and so on. . . . Keynes did not explain precisely what causes changes in

investment, but, on the other hand, he has fully examined the close link between these changes and global employment, production, and income movements. (Kalecki 1990, pp. 230–32)

Keynes likely never knew about this review, which was only translated into English in the 1980s. But in the late 1930s Kalecki went to England and forged an awkward intellectual relationship with Keynes, eventually gaining his respect.

According to Steindl (1991, p. 597), Kalecki published three versions of his theory of the business cycle, corresponding roughly to his 1933 booklet, his 1954 *Theory of Economic Dynamics*, and his late works. Though the relation between profitability and investment is explained in slightly different terms in each version of the theory, it remained substantially unchanged in its main aspects. In his 1933 booklet, Kalecki presented profitability as the variable "that stimulates the desire to invest. This is entirely consistent with reality, since the incentive to invest is expected profitability, which is estimated on the basis of the profitability of existing plants" (Kalecki 1990, p. 68). However, investment or consumption of some capitalists creates profit for others and, as a class, capitalists "gain exactly as much as they invest or consume" so that capitalists "determine their own profits by the extent of their investment and personal consumption" (p. 79). In his *Theory of Economic Dynamics* (1954) Kalecki wrote that capitalists "can decide to consume and invest more in a given period than in the preceding period, but they cannot decide to earn more. It, is therefore, their investment and consumption decisions which determine profits, and not vice versa" (Kalecki 1991, p. 240). Profits "in a given period are the direct outcome of capitalist consumption and investment in that period" (p. 244). More formally, profits at a time t are a linear function of investment at time t and previous times $t - \lambda$; profits "will thus be a function both of current investment and of investment in the near past; or roughly speaking, profits follow investment with a time lag" (p. 247). In turn, "investment at a given time is determined by the level and rate of change in the level of investment at some earlier time" (p. 292).

The final version of the Kaleckian theory of the business cycle would be the one presented in his publications of the late 1960s. In "The Marxian equations of reproduction and modern economics" (1968), Kalecki again presented investment and capitalist consumption as the independent variables that determine the levels of national income and profits (Kalecki 1991, p. 461). In the introduction to *Selected Essays on the Dynamics of the Capitalist Economy 1933–70*, published posthumously in 1971, Kalecki explained that the theory of economic demand that he had formulated in the 1930s had remained unchanged; however, "there is a continuous search for new solutions in the theory of investment decisions." But he included in the book his theory of profits of 1954, restating his view that it is "investment and consumption decisions which determine profits, and not vice versa" (Kalecki 1971, p. 79).

According to Asimakopulos (1977, p. 329), Kalecki "emphasized a double-sided relation between investment and profits." It is true that in a number of places Kalecki argues that investment depends on profits, or that profitability stimulates investment. He argues for instance that the rate of investment decisions is influenced by the increase in profits per unit of time, so that rising profits "from the beginning to the end of the period considered renders attractive certain projects which were previously considered unprofitable, and thus permits an extension of the boundaries of investment plans in the course of the period" (Kalecki 1991, p. 282). For Asimakopulos (1977, p. 339) Kalecki poses current investment as predetermined by past decisions, and through its effects on sales and profits contributing to determine expected profitability. In turn, this expected rate of profit influences, along with other factors, the investment decisions made in this period for implementation in future time periods. Even in this presentation, however, investment is the *causa causans* (the cause of the cause), while profits are just an intermediate link in the causal chain. Considering the major works in which Kalecki presented his macroeconomic theory, it is difficult to disagree with the way Targetti and Kinda-Hass (1982, p. 254) summarize it: "[T]he level of profits at a certain date is entirely and solely determined by past decisions to invest." Even allowing for subtleties, in Kalecki the determination is from rising investment to rising profits, and in the relation there is little room, if any, for reverse causation.

4. Investment Leading the Cycle: The Keynesian School

For Joan Robinson (1979) Keynes had presented in *The General Theory* a scheme of comparative statics, though containing key elements to develop a dynamic theory. It was left for economists following Keynes's tradition to develop such a theory, that is, a Keynesian theory of the business cycle. Leaving aside Kalecki, *The Trade Cycle* by Robin C. O. Matthews, published in England in 1959 and republished in the United States as *The Business Cycle*, can arguably be considered one of the first systematic examinations of business-cycle theory from an explicitly Keynesian point of view.[5] Judging by the authors cited and the ideas discussed, it seemed that Matthews was open minded toward recent ideas of Paul Samuelson, J. R. Hicks, Milton Friedman, and others who were making powerful inroads in economics in the 1950s. The general perspective of the book, however, is plainly Keynesian. Matthews repeatedly also cited Michal Kalecki's *Theory of Economic Dynamics*, at that time the most recent presentation of Kalecki's macrodynamic ideas.

Matthews opened his book with a discussion of the variables that may produce an imbalance between aggregate demand and aggregate supply. When briefly mentioning Slutsky's views on recessions being the consequence of the economy responding to random shocks of a diverse character, Matthews commented that statistical data indicate "that economic fluctuations are not due *solely* to random factors, and it is also clear both from an *a priori* reasoning and from our more detailed knowledge of history that certain forces do operate which are in principle capable of causing fluctuations of a systematic character" (p. 202, emphasis in the original). This was shrewdly suggesting that the business cycle is a rather endogenous economic phenomenon, in which random factors may indeed have some influence—which probably would be agreed by any author espousing an endogenous theory of the business cycle.

According to Matthews, "The doctrine that consumption expenditure depends principally on the level of national income is one of the foundations of Keynesian economics. It is because of this doctrine that the other main component of national income, investment, is regarded as the prime mover in fluctuations in national income, the role of consumption being a passive one" (p. 113). To discuss the basic determinants of investment must therefore be a key aspect of the theory of the business cycle. In this respect, the major consideration "affecting the inducement to do investment is profitability. Investment will be done if the expected profits represent an adequate return on the sum spent. The physical relation between output and capital is important only in so far as it influences the expected rate of return on investment" (p. 34). In other words, "the basic postulate is that the amount of investment done is a function of the expected rate of return. If conditions are such as to promise a high rate of return, much investment will be done, and conversely. There will be a certain critical level of expected returns at which zero net investment is done" (p. 36).

Matthews meticulously considered the relation of investment with competition, technical progress, animal spirits, finance, inventories, and home construction. His conclusion was that "the chief reason for the waves of high and low investment that are the essence of the cycle is the existence of a cumulative effect by which if investment in any period is high relative to its long-run trend value, it encourages investment in the next period to stay high or to rise further, up to a point, while if investment is low it likewise discourages investment in the next period" (p. 82). This means that with appropriate investment the economy would grow without interruption, and slumps would be avoided: "If entrepreneurs can only screw themselves up to do enough investment, it will eventually justify itself, since the income generated will absorb the excess capacity" (p. 178).

A comparison of the theories of the business cycle in Matthews's *Trade Cycle* and in Hyman Minsky's *Stabilizing an Unstable Economy*, written and published three decades later, reveals many common views but also some major differences in emphasis and even in conception. Both Matthews and Minsky were self-professed Keynesians, but Minsky's view of economic fluctuations emphasized the financial factors creating economic disturbances and leading to financial crises and recessions, while Matthews was quite adamant that business cycles are phenomena mostly related to the real economy, in which their causes need to be examined. For Matthews it was an outdated view

> that the causes of fluctuations lay wholly or largely in the sphere of money and finance. The trend of opinion has now swung in the opposite direction. Most modern theoretical treatments of the cycle are based on an analysis of real forces, and it is implicitly assumed that secondary importance, at most, attaches to any effects that may be brought about by changes in the cost and availability of finance. (Matthews 1959, p. 128)

After a detailed discussion of factors leading to speculation and bubbles in different markets, Matthews had concluded that financial crises generally occur after the downturn in the real economy has already started, so that the financial crisis may aggravate the downturn but does not cause it. The contrast is patent with the main thrust of *Stabilizing an Unstable Economy*, where Minsky emphasizes the role of financial factors and criticizes the neoclassical synthesis for its inability to recognize that "the instability so evident in our economy is due to the behavior of financial markets, asset prices, and profit flows" (Minsky 2008, p. 156).

According to Minsky, a basic aspect of modern capitalism is that past financing of investment leaves a legacy of payment commitments, and for these commitments to be fulfilled the income of indebted investors must be sufficient. The price system must therefore "generate cash flows ... which simultaneously free resources for investment, lead to high enough prices for capital assets so that investment is induced, and validate business debts. For a capitalist system to function well, *prices must carry profits*" (p. 158, original emphasis).

What are the determinants of profits is thus a key question, and Minsky concludes that "[i]*nvestment and government spending call the tune for our economy because they are not determined by how the economy is now working. They are determined either from outside by policy (government spending) or* by today's views about the future (private investment)" (p. 184, original emphasis). Causality, then, "runs from investment and government spending to taxes and profits," and in recessions "Big Government, with all its inefficiencies, stabilizes income and profits. It decreases the downside risks inherent in a capital-intensive economy that has a multitude of heavily indebted firms" (p. 186).

Investment is therefore the basic determinant of the dynamic status of the economy. To look for economic factors causing investment to rise or fall is beside the point, since the present level of investment determines the present level of income and the future level of profits and investment. In the colorful words of Minsky, government spending and investment "call the tune." Only the psychological sphere of expectations remains as the source of investment fluctuations. Given adequate investment, profits will rise and the economy will grow.

It is investment, then, which in the view of Kalecki, Keynes, and the Keynesians "calls the tune" by determining profits and thus leading the business cycle.

5. Profits Leading the Cycle: Marx and Mitchell

Karl Marx and Wesley Mitchell are infrequently cited in modern discussions on macroeconomic issues, perhaps because compared with predominant neoclassical or Keynesian views they provide quite a different perspective on how our economy works. Marx and Mitchell share with the Keynesian school the view that investment, or capital accumulation in Marx's terminology, is a key variable in economic dynamics.[6] However, neither Marx nor Mitchell attributes to investment the major causal role in business cycles, because they see investment as depending itself on profitability.

Marx's analysis of the business cycle has been considered an unwritten chapter, and "no coherent picture of it has emerged, or is likely to emerge, that would command the approval of all Marxologists." This opinion of Schumpeter (1954, p. 747) still looks true, as proven by recent controversies already cited. However, some particular elements of Marx's theory of crises are not controversial. What Marx called the industrial cycle, or cycle of crises—in which periods of capital accumulation alternate with crises—is mostly discussed in manuscripts that were posthumously published by Engels or others. In one of them, Marx wrote that the rate at which the capital is valorized, that is the rate of profit, "is the spur to capitalist production (in the same way as the valorization of capital is its sole purpose)," so that a decline in this rate "slows down the formation of new, independent capitals and thus appears as a threat to the development of the capitalist production process; it promotes overproduction, speculation and crises" (Marx 1981b, pp. 348–49). In his notebooks published as *Theories of Surplus Value*, Marx asserted that accumulation is determined "by the ratio of surplus-value to the total capital outlay, that is, by the rate of profit, *and even more by the total amount of profit*" (Marx 1968, p. 542, emphasis added).

Explicit insights on crisis theory are also given in the only volume of *Capital* that Marx published himself, in 1867. There, in the chapter on "the general law of capitalist accumulation," Marx stated that the characteristic evolution of modern economies is typically a ten-year cycle in which periods of average activity are followed by production at high pressure, crisis, and finally stagnation (Marx 1977, p. 785). In the manuscripts written in the late 1870s, published by Engels as volume 2 of *Capital,* Marx speculated that the crisis cycle is a periodic phenomenon, related with an average period of ten years for the renovation of fixed capital, though the precise periodicity "is not important" (Marx 1981a, p. 264).

Marx rejected Say's law, as he saw absolute overproduction— overproduction affecting all fields of production and not only a few important spheres of production—as typical of periods of economic crisis in which there is insufficient surplus value, that is, profits, to valorize capital. In these periods profits decline "at a point . . . when the increased capital produced just as much, or even less, surplus-value than it did before its increase . . . i.e., the increased capital $C + \Delta C$ would produce no more, or even less, profit than capital C before its expansion by ΔC" (Marx 1981b, pp. 359–60). In no place did Marx describe economic crises as being long periods of stagnation; indeed he emphasized them as being short phenomena, and he rejected in plain terms Ricardo's idea of a permanent crisis (Marx 1968, p. 497).

In multiple publications on economic issues in the 1840s, the 1850s, and the early 1860s, Marx paid attention to the concrete timing and periodicity of economic crises in England and other countries. He hesitantly referred to the recurrence of crisis by citing periods of about five, six, or seven years. However, in the first volume of *Capital* he proposed that crises had a decennial periodicity (Marx 1977, p. 790). We can compare Marx's view of what he usually called the industrial crisis cycle with Burns and Mitchell's definition of the business cycle, which describes the recorded facts of about two centuries of capitalism by establishing a varying length of the recurrent phenomenon:

> Business cycles are a type of fluctuation found in the aggregate economic activity of nations that organize their work mainly in business enterprises: a cycle consists of expansions occurring at about the same time in many economic activities, followed by similarly general recessions, contractions, and revivals which merge into the expansion phase of the next cycle; in duration, business cycles vary from more

than one year to ten or twelve years; they are not divisible into shorter cycles of similar characteristics. (Burns and Mitchell 1946, p. 3)

In *Capital* Marx presented the periods of capital accumulation—that is, economic expansions with high levels of investment—as characterized by an increased demand for labor power, such that during the cycle there is a constant formation, absorption, and reformation of a mass of unemployed workers—the "industrial reserve army." This mass of unemployed workers, "during the periods of stagnation and average prosperity, weighs down the active army of workers; during the periods of overproduction and feverish activity, it puts a curb on their pretensions" (Marx 1977, p. 792).

Periods of capital accumulation are the most favorable for workers in terms of income because "a larger part of the mass of profits, which is increasing and is continually transformed into additional capital, comes back to them in the shape of means of payment, so that they can extend the circle of their enjoyments, make additions to their consumption fund of clothes, furniture, etc. and lay by a small reserve fund of money" (Marx 1977, p. 796).

The tightness of the labor market during periods of expansion will likely produce a rise in wages, and then two things can happen:

Either the price of labour keeps on rising, because its rise does not interfere with the progress of accumulation.... Or, the other alternative, accumulation slackens as a result of the rise in the price of labour, because the stimulus of gain is blunted. The rate of accumulation lessens; but this means that the primary cause of that lessening itself vanishes. . . . The mechanism of the process of capitalist production removes the very obstacles that it temporarily creates. (p. 770)

Marx portrays the level of investment as a function of profitability, as it is shown by his reference to accumulation slackening "because the stimulus of gain is blunted." On the other hand, a profit-squeeze mechanism is also suggested, since Marx admits that rising wages might cut profits and in this way induce a fall in the rate of investment that triggers a downturn. This is offered as a possibility, but in the same paragraph Marx rejects the implied causal pathway as an important one. He emphatically explains it by using a mathematical terminology that is uncommon in his writings: "To put it mathematically: the rate of accumulation is the independent, not the dependent, variable; the rate of wages, the dependent, not the independent, variable." In causal language this means that a rising or falling rate of accumulation is the cause of respectively rising or falling wages, not the other way around.

Profit is for Marx the monetary translation of surplus value, unpaid labor supplied by the working class to the owners of capital. When profit "accumulated by the capitalist class increases so rapidly that its transformation into capital requires an extraordinary addition of paid labour, then wages rise, and, all other circumstances remaining equal," profit diminishes. But as soon as this diminution reaches the point at which profit that nourishes capital "is no longer supplied in normal quantity, a reaction sets in: a smaller part of revenue is capitalized, accumulation slows down, and the rising movement of wages comes up against an obstacle. The rise of wages therefore is confined within limits that not only leave intact the foundations of the capitalist system, but also secure its reproduction on an increasing scale" (Marx 1977, p. 771). Marx emphasized the idea that accumulation depends on profitability by quoting in *Capital* the opinion of the English trade unionist Thomas Dunning, who had written that capital

> eschews no profit, or very small profit, just as Nature was formerly said to abhor a vacuum. With adequate profit, capital is very bold. A certain 10% will ensure its employment anywhere; 20% certain will produce eagerness; 50%, positive audacity; 100% will make it ready to trample on all human laws; 300%, and there is not a crime at which it will scruple, nor a risk it will not run, even to the chance of its owner being hanged. If turbulence and strife will bring a profit, it will freely encourage both. (cited in Marx 1977, p. 926)

Marx took a critical stance on underconsumptionism in one of his late manuscripts, apparently written in 1878, and published by Friedrich Engels in 1885 as volume 2 of *Capital*. In a passage in chapter 20 of Engels's edition, Marx made explicit his stance against underconsumption views:

> It is a pure tautology to say that crises are provoked by a lack of effective demand or effective consumption. The capitalist system does not recognize any forms of consumer other than those who can pay, if we exclude the consumption of paupers and swindlers. The fact that commodities are unsaleable means no more than that no effective buyers have been found for them, i.e. no consumers (no matter whether the commodities are ultimately sold to meet the needs of productive or individual consumption). If the attempt is made to give this tautology the semblance of greater profundity, by the statement that the working class receives too small a portion of its own product, and that the evil would be remedied if it received a bigger share, i.e. if its wages rose, *we need only note that crises are always prepared by a period in which wages generally rise, and the working class actually does receive a greater share in the part of the annual product destined for consumption.* From the standpoint of these advocates of sound and "simple" (!) common sense, such periods should rather avert the crisis. It thus appears that capitalist production involves certain conditions independent of people's good or bad intentions, which permit the relative prosperity of the working

class only temporarily, and moreover always as a harbinger of crisis. (Marx 1981, pp. 486–7, emphasis added)

Is this passage an anomaly in Marx's theory? For many Marxists who maintain underconsumptionist views, it would be, as a frequently cited passage of the third volume of *Capital* states that "[t]he ultimate reason for all real crises always remains the poverty and restricted consumption of the masses as opposed to the drive of capitalist production to develop the productive forces as though only the absolute consuming power of society constituted their limit" (Marx 1981b, p. 615). This is in the manuscript that Engels edited as volume 3 of *Capital*. It had been written by Marx in the mid-1860s, that is, some twenty years before he wrote his mocking remarks on the idea that crises are caused by low wages. So he could have changed his views. Whatever the case, what is important is that the lack of consumption because of low wages is a very poor explanation of the economic slumps that we observe in reality. Marx saw it in his time, and data on downturns of recent years also prove it, as will be shown in section 6 of this chapter.

As economic thinkers and public personalities, Mitchell and Marx are obviously quite different cases. Marx rejected from his first intellectual contributions what he called the bourgeois views of political economy, persistently titled his books as critiques of such discipline, and was paid in kind by being mostly ignored and later plainly rejected by those who claimed to be developing such science. Contrarily Mitchell was throughout his long life a highly respected member of the economic profession who taught economics at leading universities, served in many government committees even in wartime, was once president of the American Economic Association, and was a founding member and for decades director of research of the prestigious NBER. However, in the 1950s his views on the business cycle were trashed as atheoretical, and soon after his death his work disappeared into oblivion.

As already mentioned, the criticism addressed against Mitchell that his contributions lacked theory contrasts with the reality that he had presented quite elaborate views on the causes of expansions and recessions—that is, a theory of the business cycle—as early as 1913. In his unfinished *What Happens during Business Cycles*, which was published in 1951 after his death, Mitchell briefly restated his ideas—which had changed remarkably little since 1913— on the causes of the business cycle. He still viewed the cycle as a continuous endogenous development, with recession processes leading to expansion, and expansion processes leading to recession. Investment played a key role in the transitions from expansion to recession and vice versa. Though capital goods, Mitchell noted, "form less than 18% of the gross national product, their output is subject to such violent alternations . . . that this minor segment of the economy contributes 44% of the total cyclical fluctuation in output, and nearly half of the cyclical declines" (Mitchell 1951, p. 153).

For Mitchell profits had a major role in economics in general, and in business cycles in particular. This was probably the result of both his empirical studies of business and economic life and his acquaintance with Thorstein Veblen, one of the proponents, according to Mitchell himself, of the theory that profit is the key variable explaining economic fluctuations (Mitchell 1927, pp. 42–44). The Veblenian influence seems clear in Mitchell's view of what he called "the money economy," the organization of the modern industrial society in which the bulk of economic activity takes place through the activities of enterprises that perform with the purpose of producing money profit. For Mitchell, in economic circumstances where the money economy predominates, that is, where economic activity takes the form of making and spending money incomes, "natural resources are not developed, mechanical equipment is not provided, industrial skill is not exercised, unless conditions are such as to promise a money profit to those who direct production" (Mitchell 1913, pp. 21–22).

In one of his late contributions, Mitchell insisted on the centrality of money profits for understanding business cycles:

> Since the quest for money profits by business enterprises is the controlling factor among the economic activities of men who live in a money economy, the whole discussion [of expansions and recessions] must center about the prospects of profits. On occasion, indeed, this central interest is eclipsed by a yet more vital issue – the avoidance of bankruptcy. But to make profits and to avoid bankruptcy are merely two sides of a single issue – one side concerns the well-being of business enterprises under ordinary circumstances, the other side concerns the life or death of the same enterprises under circumstances of acute strain. (Mitchell 1941, p. xii)

In Mitchell's endogenous theory of the business cycle during the phase of prosperity, the very conditions "which make business profitable gradually evolve conditions which threaten a reduction in profits" (Mitchell 1913, p. 502). Though economic downturns often start with a financial crisis in which banks, insurance companies, and other financial firms go bankrupt, these financial phenomena are preceded by processes that encroach profits in the real economy, at least in a score of major enterprises or industrial sectors. The various stresses rising costs and putting caps on revenue, and thus limiting profits,

> become more severe the longer prosperity lasts and the more intense it becomes, and since a setback suffered by any industry necessarily aggravates the stress among others by reducing the market for their

products, *a reduction in the rate of profits* [emphasis added] must infallibly occur . . . if an average rate of profits could be computed for a whole country, it would not be surprising to find it reaching its climax just before the crisis breaks out. But this result would not mean that there had been no serious encroachment upon profits. On the contrary, it would mean that the critical point is reached and a crisis is precipitated as soon as a decline of present or prospective profits has occurred in a few leading branches of business and *before that decline has become general* [original emphasis]. (Mitchell 1913, p. 503)

Rejecting underconsumptionist explanations that view insufficient demand for consumption goods as the trigger of downturns, Mitchell explained that in the late phases of prosperity, "the impossibility of defending profits against the encroachments of costs is experienced earlier by enterprises which handle raw materials and producers goods. . . . The technical journals usually report that the factories and wholesale houses are restricting their orders some weeks, if not months, before they report that retail sales are flagging" (Mitchell 1913, p. 502).

The decline in profitability in some parts of the economy creates financial strain and reduces sales in other industries, all of which in turn reduce the incentive to maintain or increase inventories. Investment in wages, raw materials, and new machines or production facilities also falls, which eventually reduces the level of business activity, since business failures and reduction of business activity cut both wages and investment, the two basic sources of demand. This vicious cycle would then operate for months or years, sending the economy into a minor or major recession or depression. Eventually the "very conditions of business depression beget a revival of activity," favorable conditions for investment are newly created and the economy starts expanding again (Mitchell 1913, p. 452). This is so because immediately after a depression "within large groups of enterprises or industries, the rate [of profit] rises promptly with the tide of prosperity. . . . Indeed it is certain in particular cases and probable on the average *that profits begin to pick up before the period of depression is over*" (Mitchell 1913, p. 469, emphasis added). This will increase the volume of investment because in such a situation of business revival, "the prospect of good profits leads not only to greater activity among the old enterprises, but also to extensions of their size and to the creation of new enterprises. This expansion of business undertakings is the more important because for a time at least it imparts new energy to the very causes which produced it" (Mitchell 1913, p. 471).

In spite of all their differences, Marx and Mitchell coincide in asserting an important economic regularity: that rising profitability is the key determinant, via expanding investment, of business prosperity; and that falling profitability is the key determinant, via falling investment, of depression.

6. Empirical Evidence

Richard Goodwin once explained that the first attempts to subject business cycles to econometric analysis were those of Jan Tinbergen in the two monographs published in 1939 for the League of Nations. At that time, on the basis of general agreement among economists, Tinbergen selected investment "as the crucial cycle variable to be explained" (Goodwin 1964).

Now, in terms of causation, from the Keynesian-Kaleckian perspective investment is the key variable that determines profits, while for Marx and Mitchell the direction of causality is the opposite, with investment determined by profits. An additional issue that will be examined here is whether lack of consumption and low wages show any ability to explain recessions, as many authors claim. Does the empirical evidence support these views?

Descriptive statistics

It has been known since long ago that the main element of aggregate demand fluctuating upward during expansions and downward during recessions is investment, while consumption varies little between expansion and recession (Mitchell 1951; Sherman and Kolk 1997). In the US national income and product accounts (NIPA) for the years 1929–2013, the mean shares in the gross national product (GNP) are 63.8 percent for consumption, 32.0 percent for government expenditure, 15.4 percent for gross investment, 10.8 percent for business investment, 8.2 percent for profits before taxes, and 5.9 percent for profits after taxes. This shows that the "big bills" in "the economy" are consumption and government spending, but these two variables are much less volatile than the others, as for these shares in GNP the coefficients of variation (the ratio of the standard variation to the mean) are 9.3 percent for consumption, 23.0 percent for government expenditure, 23.7 percent for business investment, 28.4 percent for profits before taxes, and 29.3 percent for profits after taxes. Thus, measuring the macroeconomic variables as shares of GNP, the variability of investment is much greater than the variability of consumption, but profits are much more volatile than any other variable.

Table 3.1. Annual growth of wages and salaries (W&S), unemployment rate (U), government expenditure (G, computed as current expenditure plus gross government investment), gross private domestic investment (I), personal consumption expenditure (C), and corporate profits (before taxes) of domestic industries (P), 1970–2014. Source: BEA, NIPA, author's calculations.

Year	W&S	U	G	I	C	P
1970	1.1	1.4	4.5	-1.4	1.8	-18.2
1971	0.9	1.1	3.6	-0.4	3.0	11.6
1972	4.8	-0.4	4.2	7.8	5.2	11.2
1973	5.2	-0.7	2.4	11.7	4.9	4.4
1974	0.0	0.7	3.6	1.6	0.5	-16.2
1975	-3.5	2.9	5.5	-5.8	1.4	5.0
1976	4.7	-0.8	1.4	5.6	5.6	20.4
1977	4.1	-0.6	1.4	11.3	4.5	11.4
1978	5.3	-1.0	3.0	13.5	4.4	8.0
1979	3.3	-0.3	2.5	9.8	3.0	-8.2
1980	0.5	1.3	5.2	-0.2	1.2	-19.5
1981	0.6	0.5	3.3	6.2	0.9	5.8
1982	-1.0	2.1	4.1	-3.3	0.9	-14.6
1983	1.7	-0.1	4.5	-4.4	6.1	19.3
1984	6.2	-2.1	3.8	13.0	5.5	18.9
1985	4.1	-0.3	5.6	4.4	5.6	1.8
1986	4.0	-0.2	4.7	-2.0	4.3	-11.7
1987	4.7	-0.8	2.7	-1.2	4.1	9.0
1988	4.4	-0.7	1.6	4.0	4.6	8.7
1989	1.9	-0.2	3.6	4.1	3.3	-6.6
1990	2.4	0.3	3.9	-0.5	2.7	-5.2
1991	-0.6	1.2	1.9	-5.3	0.2	6.4
1992	3.0	0.7	5.6	0.2	4.1	4.9
1993	1.4	-0.6	0.7	5.2	3.6	8.1
1994	2.9	-0.8	0.9	6.5	3.8	19.7
1995	3.4	-0.5	2.7	8.5	3.0	9.9
1996	3.9	-0.2	1.5	6.5	3.8	10.1
1997	5.4	-0.4	1.2	8.3	3.8	9.0
1998	6.7	-0.5	1.5	7.9	5.0	-8.5
1999	5.2	-0.3	3.1	7.2	5.3	-0.4
2000	5.8	-0.2	2.7	7.3	5.3	-12.3
2001	0.4	0.7	4.3	-4.8	2.2	-10.1
2002	-0.7	1.1	4.5	-8.6	2.4	26.3
2003	0.8	0.2	4.0	-0.3	3.1	16.6
2004	2.7	-0.5	2.8	3.8	3.5	18.0
2005	1.7	-0.4	3.4	6.7	3.1	11.3
2006	3.2	-0.5	2.8	6.9	2.6	8.9
2007	2.8	0.0	3.7	5.3	2.1	-17.6
2008	0.2	1.2	4.7	-0.9	0.8	-26.7
2009	-5.1	3.5	6.1	-16.5	-2.4	17.4
2010	0.8	0.3	2.9	0.3	2.4	28.4
2011	1.9	-0.7	-0.9	7.1	2.7	1.1
2012	2.6	-0.8	-0.9	6.9	1.9	14.2
2013	1.2	-0.7	-1.0	2.6	2.1	3.6
2014	3.6	-1.2	0.8	6.0	2.4	-1.9

The figure for the monetary variables is the percent rate of growth, computed from nominal NIPA data transformed into 2009 dollars by using the GDP deflator, also from NIPA. The figure for the unemployment rate is the annual variation in percentage points, computed from statistics of the Department of Labor.

Basically the same is shown by the rates of growth of the components of the national product measured in real terms. Table 3.1 presents the annual change of wages, unemployment, government expenditure, investment, consumption, and profits in the forty-five years between 1970 and 2014. Just a general examination of the table attending to the signs of the figures indicates that consumption has the lowest volatility: except in one year, 2009, in which its rate of growth is negative, consumption always grows at a rate of a few percentage points (3.1 percent per year is the mean rate of growth for the 45-year sample). Profits reveal the highest volatility, as they often increase or decrease at two-digit rates; thus they decreased 17.6 percent in 2007 and 26.7 percent in 2008, immediately before the Great Recession, but then they grew 17.4 percent and 28.4 percent in 2009 and 2010. The volatility of the annual changes of these series as quantified by the coefficient of variation for the years 1970–2014 is 56.0 percent for consumption, 102.2 percent for wages, 194.4 percent for investment, and 344.9 percent for profits. While during this period of forty-five years real consumption only decreased once, in 2009, wages and salaries decreased in each period of recession, that is, in 1975, 1982, 1991, 2002, and 2009 (table 3.1). The year 2009, in which profits increased 17.4 percent and wages and salaries shrank 5.1 percent, saw the greatest annual contraction of consumption (–2.4 percent) and wages (–5.1 percent) in the whole period. The correlation of consumption with wages and salaries—with both series in annual rate of growth—is very strong and positive, 0.82, revealing that most consumption comes from wages and salaries, so that the two series basically rise or fall at the same time.

The unemployment rate rises when there is a recession. Table 3.1 shows that in 2009 during the Great Recession, the rate of unemployment rose 3.5 percentage points, the greatest annual increase in the sample 1970–2014. Since recessions are the periods in which wages and salaries typically decrease, the annual change in unemployment has a very strong and negative correlation (–0.84) with the change in wages and salaries, and also with the annual change in consumption (–0.80). The correlations of consumption and wages with investment are respectively 0.58 and 0.79, indicating that all these variables tend to increase in expansions and to decrease in recessions, though the movements are less synchronized between them than those of consumption with wages. Finally the annual growth of profits correlates weakly (just 0.24) with consumption and has almost zero correlation (0.03) with the rates of growth of both investment and wages, which indicates that profit moves almost without any synchronization with investment and wages during the business cycle. As we will see, this is because profits rise (or fall) *before* investment and wages rise (or fall). Thus profits are a leading variable with respect to investment and wages, which are lagging variables with respect to profits.

The annual change in unemployment has a strong and negative correlation (−0.81) with the annual growth in investment. This is because a recession is precisely characterized by falling investment, which immediately causes rising unemployment, while an expansion is characterized by rising investment, which implies hiring of workers and falling unemployment.

Rates of growth of income flows along the phases of the business cycle and in the vicinity of its turning points provide major insights to ascertain what is going on during business cycles and what the most likely directions of causation are. But to examine what happens in the vicinity of turning points of the business cycle, quarterly data are needed, as annual data are too gross to reveal important details.

Rates of growth of income flows

Table 3.2 is computed using NIPA data corresponding to 275 quarters of the US economy between 1947 and 2015. I use the NBER chronology to date business cycles, assuming that a recession starts in the peak quarter and ends in the next trough quarter, with both peak and trough quarters considered as part of the recession (this is an arbitrary choice; any other would do). All rates of growth were computed with variables adjusted for inflation by transforming nominal figures from NIPA into 2009 dollars. The second and third lines of the table present the mean rate of growth of the variables for the quarters classified by pertaining either to an expansion (225 quarters) or a recession (50 quarters). Then the expansion quarters and the recession quarters are further classified by the proximity to the turning points of the cycle. Thus "peak −7" refers to the sample that includes all *expansion* quarters that preceded the next recession by seven quarters; "trough +1" refers to the expansion quarters immediately following the end of the recession, and so forth. According to the NBER chronology in the period 1947–2015, there were eleven recessions in the US economy; therefore table 3.2 presents the mean rate of growth of profits, investment, and so on in the eleven quarters that were peak quarters, in the eleven quarters that were trough quarters, and the eleven expansionary quarters that were immediately following the trough (trough +1). However, not all eleven recessions in the sample were preceded by five quarters of expansion; for that reason the table presents classified as "peak −5" the average rates of growth of the variables for only ten quarters. Since several recessions lasted only three quarters, only seven cases are available to compute the mean rates of growth in the third recession quarter after the peak (peak +3).

Period	Profits		Investment	Wages & Sal.		N
	Before T.	After T.		Without Sup.	With Sup.	
All quarters	0.8	0.9	1.6	0.7	0.8	275
Expansion	1.8	1.7	2.2	1.0	1.0	225
Recession	−3.7	−2.6	−1.1	−0.4	−0.3	50
Peak −7	3.1	3.2	2.8	1.5	1.5	10
Peak −6	1.5	2.2	1.7	0.9	0.9	10
Peak −5	0.0	0.4	2.8	1.3	1.2	10
Peak −4	−0.9	−1.0	3.5	1.0	0.9	10
Peak −3	−0.7	−1.1	1.6	1.1	1.1	11
Peak −2	0.0	0.1	2.2	0.7	0.8	11
Peak −1	−1.9	−0.8	1.3	0.9	0.9	11
Peak	−2.7	−4.2	0.1	0.4	0.5	11
Peak +1	−7.0	−5.2	−1.5	−0.4	−0.3	11
Peak +2	−5.1	−3.0	−1.2	−0.7	−0.6	11
Peak +3	0.7	0.2	−0.7	−0.4	−0.3	7
Trough −2	−6.7	−7.8	−1.0	−0.3	−0.2	11
Trough −1	−0.1	3.4	−2.2	−1.1	−0.9	11
Trough	−2.4	−0.7	−0.9	−0.8	−0.6	11
Trough +1	9.5	10.4	1.9	0.5	0.7	11
Trough +2	7.1	6.1	2.9	1.2	1.3	11
Trough +3	5.0	5.0	3.4	0.9	1.0	11
Trough +4	4.9	5.9	3.1	1.6	1.7	10

Table 3.2. Mean quarterly rates of growth (%) of profits (domestic industries, before and after taxes), fixed private domestic investment, and wages and salaries (with and without supplements) during the recessions and expansions of 275 quarters of the US economy. Shaded areas correspond to figures for recession quarters, 1947–2015. Source: NIPA quarterly data 1947:II to 2015:IV. For definitions and explanations see text.

On average, in the 275 quarters included in the sample, profits before and after taxes increased, respectively, 0.8 percent and 0.9 percent per quarter, while wages and salaries with or without supplements increased, respectively, 0.8 percent and 0.7 percent (table 3.2, line 1). This shows that inequality of income is steadily increasing in the long run, as on average capital income (profits) is increasing slightly faster than labor income (wages).[7] During expansions, profits before taxes increased on average 1.8 percent per quarter, while during recessions they dropped on average 3.7 percent per quarter.

Profits increasing during expansions more than wages and decreasing during recessions more than wages also show that income inequality is procyclical, that is, it grows during expansions and decreases during recessions. This is a fact that many left-wing authors find puzzling, but data not only for the United States but for other countries show it very clearly (Piketty 2014, pp. 288, 296).

Profits after taxes have lower volatility than profits before taxes. Thus profits before taxes grow at a mean rate of 1.8 percent per quarter in expansions and −3.7 percent per quarter in recessions, while profits after taxes grow at 1.7 percent per quarter in expansions and −2.6 percent per quarter in recessions (table 3.2, lines 2 and 3). This suggests that taxation laws are set to facilitate a steady flow of profits and that they dampen to some extent the effects of the economy. Wages and salaries without supplements rise on average 1.0 percent per quarter and drop 0.4 percent per quarter in recessions. Capital income represented by profits (either before or after taxes) is much more volatile than labor income represented by wages and salaries (either with or without supplements). Investment on average grew 2.2 percent per quarter in expansions, and dropped 1.1 percent per quarter in recessions, so that it is more volatile than wages and salaries, but less volatile than profits.

More interesting is to examine the evolution of income flows in the vicinity of the turning points of the business cycle. *Data show that profits stop growing, stagnate, and then start falling a few quarters before the recession, when investment and wages start falling.* Table 3.2 shows that profits before taxes on average grew 3.1 percent in the seventh quarter before the recession started, but then the rate of growth declined as the recession approached, so that in the fifth quarter before the start of the recession they stopped growing and in successive quarters they shrank, and that in the quarter immediately before the peak they shrank 1.9 percent. During the recession, profits before taxes on average contracted 3.7 percent per quarter, but in the peak quarter they contracted only 2.7 percent; they contracted much more (7.0 percent) in peak +1, that is, the quarter following the peak. As the end of the recession gets closer, profits stop falling and profits before taxes basically remain at the same level (−0.1 percent) in the quarter previous to the end of the recession, in which profits after taxes increase by 3.4 percent. Though profits both before and after taxes still decrease in the trough quarter, they quickly recover in the following quarters so that, for instance, profits after taxes increase 10.4 percent in trough +1, the quarter following the end of the recession. The general pattern for profits before and after taxes is that they start decreasing about a year before the recession, have their greatest fall in the first quarters of the recession and stabilize at the end of the recession, to grow quickly immediately after the end of the recession.

Table 3.2 shows that investment starts declining one quarter after the recession started, that is in peak +1, when it decreases 1.5 percent. As shown, profits had started declining about two years before the start of the recession. The largest decrease in investment is at almost the end of the recession, in the quarter trough −1, when investment decreases on average 2.2 percent. Following the end of the recession, investment grows, for example, 1.9 percent in the quarter immediately following the end of the recession, trough +1.

Wages and salaries continue growing even in the quarter in which the recession starts—when they grow 0.4 percent and 0.5 percent without and with supplements respectively—so that they start shrinking in peak +1, when profits have already been falling for several quarters.

Overall, the rates of growth of profits, investment, and wages in the quarters leading up to the recession and during the recession itself show that investment starts falling several quarters after profitability does. A drop in investment because of animal spirits, or any other reason that would trigger a decline in profits à la Keynes and Kalecki, is not consistent with the sequence of events. A fall in wages that triggers a decline in investment and profits, as the underconsumptionist view maintains, is also at odds with the sequence of facts.

Table 3.2 shows that once the recession ends, the recovery of profits is quick, with a quarterly increase close to 10 percent—considering profits either before or after taxes—in the quarters immediately following the end of the recession. In that same quarter, however, wages grow at a very low rate, well below 1 percent, while investment grows at a rate of 1.2 percent. This is quite inconsistent with the view that an autonomous rise in wages, consumption, or investment would cause the end of the recession.

Are the observed rates of growth of profits, wages, and investment consistent with a profit-squeeze explanation? According to that explanation, wage growth would reduce profits and that would lead to falling investment. Now, table 3.2 shows that profits grow on average at a rate of 1.7 percent or 1.8 percent per quarter during the expansion, while wages and salaries increase at 1 percent per quarter. In the quarters immediately preceding the recession, the growth of wages is faster than the growth of profits, but that is not because wages started growing faster (as the profit-squeeze scheme would imply), but, contrarily, it is because the growth of profits ended and then profits started to decrease. In the previous quarters, profits had been growing at faster rates than wages, for instance, in the seventh expansion quarter before the recession (peak +7) wages had increased 1.5 percent per quarter, while profits before or after taxes had been growing at much greater rates (3.1 percent and 3.2 percent, respectively).

The general pattern inferred from the statistics on 275 quarters of the US economy presented in table 3.2 is on profits falling before investment (at the end of the expansion) and recovering before investment (at the end of the recession). This is also what has happened in recent recessions. For instance, profits were falling in 2007 and 2008 at two-digit rates, while investment still grew at 5.3 percent in 2007 (table 3.1) and only dropped in 2008, by 0.9 percent. During the expansion of the 1990s, profits started declining long before investment dropped in the recession. Thus profits peaked in 1997:III while investment peaked in 2000:IV, as shown by data in real dollars (fig. 3.1, *top panel*) or as shares of GDP (fig. 3.1, *bottom panel*). In 1998, 1999, and 2000 profits dropped while investment was growing (table 3.1), and only in 2001 did both profits and investment drop. In the recession of the early 1990s, investment dropped in 1990 and 1991, and profits had dropped in 1989 and 1990. In the early 1980s, investment decreased in 1980, 1982, and 1983; profits had negative growth in 1979, 1980, and 1982. In the recession of the mid-1970s, the drop in investment in 1975 was preceded by the fall in profits in 1974. The evidence is quite overwhelming that profits peak several quarters before the recession, while investment peaks immediately before the recession. Then profits recover before investment does, as illustrated by the investment trough that occurs around the end of the recession or the start of the expansion but following the profit trough for at least a few quarters (fig. 3.1). In data for the late decades of the nineteenth century and early twentieth, Wesley Mitchell found that "the rate [of profit] rises promptly with the tide of prosperity" so that "it is certain in particular cases and probable on the average that profits begin to pick up before the period of depression is over" (Mitchell 1913, p. 469). A century later the same can be observed in the recessions of the mid-1970s, 1991, and 2001, and in the Great Recession—in all of which, profits (both before and after taxes) pick up before the recession has ended, when investment is still falling (fig. 3.1). Profits recovered in 2009, 2002, 1991, 1983, and 1975 (table 3.1), while investment only recovered positive growth in 2010, 2004, 1992, 1984, and 1976.

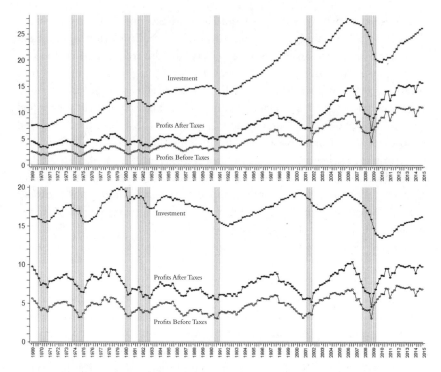

Figure 3.1. Corporate profits and investment, in billion real dollars
(top) and as shares of GDP (bottom), from 1969 to the Great Recession.
Dark areas are recessions according to the NBER chronology.
Source: author's elaboration from quarterly data in NIPA tables
5.1 and 5.3.5, seasonally adjusted at an annual rate (SAAR).

Because of the generally accepted principle that the cause precedes its
effect in time (Pearl 2000, p. 42), data in table 3.2 support the hypothesis
of causality from rising or falling profits to respectively rising or falling
investment. But they do not support causality in the opposite direction,
from rising (or falling) investment to rising (or falling) profits, because
investment is generally rising in the late quarters of the expansion when
profits start falling, and then investment is falling in the late quarters of the
recession when profits start growing again. Data, however, support negative
causality from investment to profits, that is, rising investment leading to
falling profits or falling investment leading to rising profits.

A recovery of profits after a slump that were dependent, à la Keynes-
Kalecki-Minsky, on a recovery of investment would imply some lag for
investment spending to be translated into increased profits for firms selling
either capital goods to other firms, or consumer goods to wage workers
hired as the result of new investment. But the data (fig. 3.1, tables 3.1 and
3.2) do not indicate the existence of that lag. Contrarily, what they show

is a lag in the other direction, that is, changes in profits being followed by changes in investment. As will be seen in the next section, the regression analysis provides further evidence that changes in profits are followed by changes in investment *in the same direction*. However, it also provides evidence of movements in investment being followed by movements in profits *in the opposite direction*, a fact that is completely at odds with the expected causal link implied by the Keynesian scheme.

Regression analysis: profits and investment

Regression models provide a way to explore the potential causal links between profits and investment by testing how changes in investment predict changes in profits, and vice versa. I have investigated these relations by regressing the rates of growth of a variable on present and lagged values of the rate of growth of the other variable. I tried this method using both quarterly rates of growth (Tapia 2013) and annual rates of growth of profits and investment (Tapia 2015). Vector auto regression (VAR) models including both variables, or a larger set of variables, indicate similar effects.

In regression models using quarterly rates of growth, profits—particularly profits before taxes—predict significantly investment, while the change in investment does not predict significantly the change in profits (Tapia 2013, table 3.2, panels I and III). Considering the model with the best fit, the rates of growth of profits before taxes during the present quarter and the five former quarters have a very significant and positive effect on the rate of growth of investment, with 44 percent of the variation in the rate of growth of investment explained by the variation in profits (Tapia 2013, table 3.2, panel I, model F). Profits after taxes during the present quarter and previous quarters also have a noticeable effect on investment, but the effect is much weaker, and, compared with profits before taxes, the proportion of change in investment explained is considerably reduced, just 32 percent. In the other potential direction of causation, lag regressions do not provide evidence of investment growth predicting the rate of growth of future profits (Tapia 2013, table 3.2, panel III). The effect at lag zero is very strong and positive, but obviously in a regression model the lag-zero effect is consistent with causality in any direction. But in these models computed with quarterly rates of growth, lagged effects of investment on profits are not statistically significant, and they even have "the wrong sign"—that is, past investment had a *negative* effect on present profits.

In regression models using annual data from 1934–2014, I found similar results with some important differences. Rates of growth of profits and investment significantly predict the other variable with a lag of one or two years, but rising profits predict rising investment while falling investment predicts falling profits (Tapia 2015). In regressions using data for the years 1991–2013, in the models with the best fit (i.e., the lowest Akaike Information Criterion [AIC], that which produces a probability distribution with the smallest discrepancy), investment at year $t - 1$ has a negative significant effect (-0.77, $P < 0.05$) on profits after taxes at year t, while profits at years $t - 1$ and $t - 2$ have positive significant effects (0.26, $P < 0.05$, and 0.32, $P < 0.001$, respectively) on investment.

Thus I find a negative statistical effect of investment on profits in regressions with both annual and quarterly data, but the effect is statistically significant in the annual analysis only. The lack of statistical significance in the quarterly analysis may be explained by the fact that quarterly data are noisier than annual data, so that the signal is buried in the noise. Whatever the case, if past investment were determining present profits in the Keynesian way, we would expect significant *positive* lagged effects of investment on profits. However, in regression using either quarterly or annual data, the observed lagged effects of investment on profits are *negative,* though not always significant, while lagged effects of profits on investment are always statistically significant and *positive*. These results are consistent with profits determining investment, à la Marx and Mitchell, but they are inconsistent with investment determining profits, à la Keynes, Kalecki, and Minsky.

Granger-causality tests: profits and investment

The results of tests to assess Granger causality between profits and investment are sensitive to the number of lags included in the test. When many lags are included in the test regression, bidirectional Granger causality usually appears, with past profits helping to predict investment and past investment helping to predict profits. However, the null hypothesis that profits before or after taxes do not help to predict investment is rejected at very high levels of significance in all lag specifications I tried, while the hypothesis that investment does not help to predict profits often could not be rejected even at the 5 percent level of significance (Tapia 2013, table 2.3, panels A and C). Overall, causality from profits to investment is strongly supported by Granger tests at all lags, while that is not the case for causality from investment to profits.

7. Discussion

Explanations of recessions as being caused by lack of purchasing power due to a declining share of labor in national income do not match the data. As I have shown, consumption as well as wages and salaries have a quite stable rate of growth through the business cycle and, particularly, immediately before recessions. Statistical models in which investment is a lagged function of profits show that the change in present investment is strongly dependent on the change in past profits, so that increasing profits are followed several quarters later by increasing investment and, symmetrically, falling profits are followed a few quarters later by falling investment. The statistical evidence in favor of these patterns is strong, and Granger-causality tests also support causation from profits to investment. In the other potential direction of causation, models in which profits are a lagged function of investment show a negative effect, so that an increase in the rate of growth of investment tends to be followed by a decrease in profits and, symmetrically, a decline in the rate of growth of investment tends to be followed by an increase in profits. The evidence provided by regression models and Granger-causality tests in support of this negative causality from investment to profits is weaker than the evidence that changes in profits are followed by changes in investment in the same direction, but it is still considerable. Overall I interpret all this as meaning (1) that there is strong evidence for a positive causal link between past profits and present investment; (2) that weaker evidence supports a negative causal link between past investment and present profits; and (3) that quarterly data are noisier than annual data, so that the identification of the signal is more difficult, which maybe the reason why the negative effect of investment on profits only appears significant in the annual analysis.

To summarize the implications of the empirical analyses presented in the former section, it could be said that the profit-squeeze scheme (high wages leading to low profits, this in turn leading to falling investment and recession), the underconsumptionist theory (low wages leading to low consumption, this in turn leading to low profits and low investment), and the Keynesian exogeneity of investment (as prime mover of the economy, determined by psychological factors and not by other economic variables) are hypotheses that do not have empirical support. The results of tests for Granger causality and of regression models, and the leads and lags apparent in the data are inconsistent with these three hypotheses. Furthermore, the likelihood of these three hypotheses is reduced by the fact that profits are more volatile than investment, and investment is more volatile than wages. But under the hypotheses of profit squeeze, underconsumption, or exogenous investment, the movements in profits are caused by movements in another variable. For the movement of a more volatile variable causing the dampened movement of a more stable one, friction in the transmission is an easy explanation. However, for the movement of a more volatile variable being caused by the movements of a more stable one, some magnification mechanism should exist. What this mechanism might be, it is not easy to figure out. But, of course, unknown factors can always be claimed as explanations; we are all prone to look for them when we dislike a simpler explanation consistent with the observed facts and the known variables. However, the principle of parsimony (Occam's razor) favors the simplest explanation (Pearl 2000, p. 45).

A bidirectional causal relation between profits and investment, with both effects having different signs, is consistent with the fact that there are oscillations of both variables, as in a predator-prey model in which, for instance, investment represents wolves and profits represent rabbits. An increasing number of rabbits (rising profits) raises the number of wolves (rising investment), which in turn reduces the number of rabbits (falling profits), so that the number of wolves declines (falling investment) and that of rabbits increases again (rising profits), starting a new cycle.

Positive effects in both directions would imply a circle of positive feedback and absolute instability, leading to explosive growth of both variables. Such bidirectional causation of profits–investment, with different signs in each direction, provides some stability to the economy, though it is just a relative stability at the cost of recurrent periods of economic disarray in which a strong drop in investment restarts the growth of profits. Thus crises appear as Marx saw them: as temporary circumstances restoring, for a while, the normal conditions for the accumulation of capital, which, in turn, will lead to another crisis. Rising unemployment during crises reduces wages and favors the deterioration of work conditions, thus facilitating the increase in the rate of exploitation. At the same time, crises destroy thousands of small business and may also slash savings, all of which raises misery for large sections of the population. But they open the door to a new wave of expansion, in which different kinds of misery are generated. Mass unemployment and low wages are the consequences of crisis and economic stagnation; escalating social inequality and a faster destruction of the environment are the consequences of a booming economy (Tapia et al. 2013; Tanuro 2014).

In the Keynesian-Kaleckian tradition, investment and government expenditure are the key variables to explain the economy; as Minsky said, they "call the tune." In this view, with appropriate investment the economy will prosper. As Matthews put it, with entrepreneurs screwing themselves up to do enough investment, profits would eventually rise. This is as if entrepreneurs and owners of money in general were able, like Baron Munchausen, to pull themselves up by their bootstraps. In a sense, if this were true, supply—in the form of investment—would create its own demand, and Say's law, supposedly tossed out the door by Keynes and his followers, would come back in through the window. At any rate, data show that increasing investment is followed by falling profits, so the reasoning of Matthews is faulty. Entrepreneurs "screwing themselves up" to do enough investment would just lead to the usual outcome: decreasing profits and a recession.

A further consideration is that in the Keynesian-Kaleckian scheme, fluctuations of the economy occur because entrepreneurs change the level of investment due to psychological factors outside of the economic realm. Were it not for rich people's whims determining investment, and ruling political forces determining government spending, there would be no recessions. Then the Keynesian-Kaleckian perspective looks like an exogenous theory of the cycle.[8]

Whatever the endogenous or exogenous character of the business-cycle theory of the Keynesian school, what is clear is that a basic component of that theory, the *positive* dependence of profits on investment, is inconsistent with the data, which contrarily show substantial evidence of a *negative* causal dependence of present profits on past investment, as well as very strong evidence of a *positive* causal dependence of investment on past profits. Furthermore Keynes himself said that it is usual in a complex system to regard "as the *causa causans* that factor which is most prone to sudden and wide fluctuation" (Keynes 1937). But profits are precisely the most volatile macroeconomic variable. With strong statistical evidence showing a strong determination of investment by profits, and two centuries of philosophizing and actual business practice demonstrating that money profits are the engine of the free market system, is not all that sufficient to consider profits as the determinant factor, the *causa causans* of the business cycle?

Significant hoards of money pile up during recessions (Wilson 2009; Dash and Schwartz 2011). This issue has not been examined in this chapter, but macroeconomists are aware that "money" leads economic growth; that is, it can be proved by statistical procedures that the mass of money as defined in specific ways tends to start growing before investment and consumption start growing during the expansion. Indeed that regularity observed in the data of the US economy was used by Milton Friedman to elaborate a theory of the business cycle in which money is the leading factor explaining the business cycle. This is the essence of monetarism that has extended its influence to almost all schools of economics and supposedly provides a technique for dampening or eliminating the business cycle by keeping steady the growth of money. But economists following the monetarist theory are oblivious to the fact that the conversion of money hoards into revenue-producing investment is a key element for getting the economy out of a slump. For the mobilization of money hoards into investment, the rise in profitability is the key issue, not monetary policy or low interest rates. At least in passing, it can be said here that the explanatory power of money in statistical regressions in which economic growth is the dependent variable is null when the model is computed with data for recent decades; it also disappears when other variables are included in the model.

To conclude this discussion of theories and facts on the variables determining the dynamic conditions of the economy, it may be worth citing the views of Howard Sherman, who, after publishing many interesting contributions on macroeconomic dynamics, presented in 2010 a theory of the business cycle that, pretending to be progressive, is purely incoherent.

Sherman asserts that the macroeconomic theory that is currently dominant is incorrect and shall be replaced by a complete theory whose foundations were laid by Keynes and the post-Keynesian Mitchell, by the institutionalists, and by Kalecki and the radical or neo-Marxist tradition. This attempt to put together Kalecki, Mitchell, Keynes, and Marx would generate a highly incoherent theory that could only be a poor substitute for mainstream macroeconomics. Unfortunately Sherman's views are paradigmatic of what is often presented as progressive or even radical economics.

8. Concluding Remarks

In 1873 Marx wrote to Friedrich Engels that he had been "racking his brains" for some time about analyzing "those graphs in which the movements of prices, discount rates, etc., etc., over the year, etc., are shown in rising and falling zigzags." Marx thought that by studying those curves he "might be able to determine mathematically the principal laws governing crises." But he had talked about it with his mathematical consultant, Samuel Moore, who had the opinion that "it cannot be done at present." Marx resolved "to give it up *for the time being*" (Marx and Engels 1966, p. 82).

The available "graphs" to be analyzed and the statistical methods to analyze them have improved very much since Marx was racking his brains. This chapter has presented evidence showing that the recessions of the US economy as dated by mainstream economics have essentially the characteristics of economic crises as Marx conceptualized them. These recessions, depressions, or crises are characterized by an interruption of the accumulation of capital, which in national statistics appears as a drop in private investment. As Marx thought, crises appear when profits start contracting, such that the valorization becomes difficult for the social capital at large and impossible for many individual capitals. Thus recessions are preceded by a drop in profits several quarters before, but profits recover in the last quarters of the recession and quickly rise immediately after. The fall of investment during the recession follows the fall of profits, and investment recovers during the expansions following the upturns in profits. During the recession, labor income falls and the total amount of capital is reduced by cancellation of debts, destruction of inventories of perishable commodities, liquidation of other inventories at firesale prices, general devaluation of capital assets, and so forth—all of which often leads to an associated financial crisis. All this is consistent with Marx's view of economic crises as momentary interruptions of the accumulation of capital. By reducing the total amount of capital and increasing the rate of exploitation, recessions allow for the recovery of profitability. I have shown data on many of these processes, though others—like the financial crises and the destruction of capital associated with recessions—are outside of the scope of this chapter.

Elsewhere I have argued that the NBER recessions of the past half century—that is, those dated 1973–75, 1980–82, 1990–91, 2001, and 2007–2009—are actually the manifestations in the United Stated of five general crises of the world economy (Tapia 2014). The recent IMF book by Kose and Terrones (*Collapse and Revival*, 2015) provides abundant evidence to date global recessions in the years 1975, 1982, 1991, and 2009. However, by using a scholastic procedure to date the recessions, Kose and Terrones reject the existence of a worldwide crisis at the turn of the century, and they say that the global economy experienced two separated downturns in 1998 and 2001 that "fall short of qualifying as a global recession" (Kose and Terrones 2015, p. 99).

The role of profitability as the major determinant of investment was statistically shown by Tinbergen already in 1939 and then "rediscovered" much later by other authors (Bhaskar and Glyn 1995; Blanchard et al. 1993). Several investigators have concluded in recent years that the United States is a profit-led economy (Barbosa-Filho and Taylor 2006; Rada and Taylor 2006; Mohun and Veneziani 2008), which amounts more or less to the same. All that is consistent with the results presented in this chapter. As mentioned above, Mitchell had described already in 1913 the decline of enterprise earnings—what he described as the encroachment of profits by costs—as a late-prosperity phenomenon leading to recession. However, Tinbergen was the first who used statistical procedures to show more formally a relation between profits and investment that could be conceptualized as a causal effect (Tinbergen 1939; 1950; 1952). This result was unsound according to the high priests of the economic science. It was trashed by Keynes and Friedman, and many joined the chorus. Richard Goodwin, usually considered a major theorist of business cycles, joined the critical clique, saying that "if we reverse the·direction of causality and say that investment determines profits through the multiplier and income, we rob one of Tinbergen's chief results of much of its significance." For Goodwin this could be done because in business cycles "most things go up and down together, and hence the danger of spurious correlation is very great" (Goodwin 1964, p. 433).

Goodwin's critical comments against Tinbergen are based on faulty reasoning, as spurious correlations take place when series trend up together or trend down together, or trend in opposite directions—not when they oscillate following each other or mirroring each other repeatedly. For instance, both at the level of national economies and the global economy, CO_2 emissions and economic activity go up and down together, and this does not represent a spurious correlation but a causal link (Tapia et al. 2012). Certainly, as Goodwin said, many things swing up and down "together" in the business cycle, but observed lags and statistical analysis can be exploited to provide evidence on which signs and directions of causation have empirical support. The evidence presented in this chapter is strongly at odds with the views of the Keynesian school of which Richard Goodwin was an outstanding member. The evidence, however, is strong in favor of an endogenous theory of the business cycle in which profitability has the leading role. From the point of view of such a theory of economic crises that seems supported by solid theoretical considerations as well as empirical data, data of recent years suggest it is very likely there will be a new recession in the global economy (Tapia 2016b).

Both mainstream economists and radical authors often maintain that different economic crises have different causes, and that it is therefore nonsensical to look for common patterns or common explanations (Mankiw 2009; 2010; Duménil and Lévy 2011; Harvey 2011, pp. 213–24). Robert Lucas, probably the most typical representative of classical views in macroeconomics, declared in 2012 that he had changed his ideas on how important "financial shocks" and "real shocks" are in each recession since the 1930s to the present. "Of course, this means I have to renounce the view that business cycles are all alike!" (cited in Kose and Terrones 2015, p. 172). Now, in pure or applied science it is a well-accepted principle that when studying the causes that determine a phenomenon (let's think about earthquakes, tides, the yield point of a material, lung cancer, or puerperal fever), rather than looking for the particularities that always exist in a specific case or a particular experiment, the proper strategy is to examine multiple occurrences of the phenomenon and from that multiplicity to try to grasp its essential features and determinants. But in present-day economics, to look for common patterns of economic crises is rather a rarity. Interestingly, the tendency to think that each crisis is different coexists in economics with an ahistorical approach that assumes that business cycles—like markets, credits, and capital—have existed forever, so that any kind of economic disturbance, even one that happened many centuries ago, is to be included when the purpose is to study economic crises (Reinhart and Rogoff 2009).

In the field of heterodox economics, crises are often conceptualized as long periods of stagnation. For most radical economists and commentators, American capitalism only has had two crises after the Second World War: the one that took place more or less in the 1970s–1980s, and the worldwide crisis that started in 2007. This point of view implies that the business-cycle recessions of the United States dated by the NBER in 1991 and 2001, or the global recession identified by IMF authors in 1991 are not economic crises in any sense. For instance Shaikh (2016, p. 733) refers to 1982–2007 as a boom period of the US economy. Interestingly the idea of a period of "Great Moderation," with steady economic growth, was advanced in mainstream economics precisely for those years. But how can 1982–2007 be a boom period when IMF authors refer to a worldwide recession at the start of the 1990s and in US economic data all the typical elements of a crisis are present? There was a major contraction of profits, followed by falling investment and wages and rising unemployment (table 3.1). The same applies to 2000–2001.[9]

Contrasting with the view of radical economists who see only two crises of capitalism after the Second World War—one in the 1970s–1980s and other starting in 2008—is the notion of historians working in the context of world-systems theory, who claim that economic crises may last more than a century (Arrighi 2003, pp. 527–39; Wallerstein 2001, p. 23; 2011). The Marxologist geographer David Harvey (2014) believes that crises in capitalism are never solved, but they are just moved around. In the view of all these authors, capitalism has been in a kind of permanent crisis for quite a while, perhaps since the time—one century ago—when Lenin claimed that imperialism was the highest and final stage of capitalism.[10]

To maintain these views implies an extreme unwillingness to use the available data that, with all their imperfections, provide the only possible insight into the real world of economic phenomena. Data from multiple sources show, for instance, that the global economy had a crisis in the early 1990s and then a strong expansion in the following years, only to return to crisis conditions around the end of the century.

To develop scientific knowledge is to advance concepts that are useful to describe reality, to make testable predictions, and to be ready to assess any hypothesis by contrasting it with empirical data. Economic crises lasting decades or centuries, or just being "moved around," are no less fantastic than the "Great Moderation" of mainstream economics, or a 25-year expansion of the US economy between 1982 and 2007. Phlogiston did not have a place in chemistry, and economic crises of a fuzzy character shall not have a place in social science.

Parts of this chapter were previously published in 2013 as "Does Investment Call the Tune? Empirical Evidence and Endogenous Theories of the Business Cycle," in Research in Political Economy, *vol. 28, pp. 229–59.*

Notes

1   References in which these disagreements can be found are Duménil and Lévy (2011), Roberts (2009), Mattick Jr. (2008), Harvey (2011), Kliman (2012), Heinrich (2013), and Carchedi and Roberts (2016). Anwar Shaikh's entry on "economic crises" in Bottomore's *Dictionary of Marxist Thought* has interesting material on modern interpretations of Marx's theory, but not much about Marx's theory of crisis itself. For those interested in a general review of Marx's theory of

crisis, the best presentations in my view are those of Mattick (1981) and Clarke (1994).

2   I have examined the role of oil in causing downturns of the global economy in Tapia (2016a).

3   For a modern survey of theories of the business cycle, see Knoop (2004). The encyclopedia edited by Glasner and Cooley (1997) is a wealth of information.

4   For the sake of the record, I must say that the Great Recession did not catch me "flat-footed." I had mentioned the possibility of "a major depression that, because of unsustainable processes in the world economy, may appear at any moment as a world crash" in my book review of Duncan Foley's *Adam's Fallacy: A Guide to Economic Theology*. I wrote that book review in 2007. It was published in *Challenge*, vol. 51, no. 2 (March 2008), pp. 110–20.

5   *Business Cycles and National Income* (Hansen 1964, first published in 1959), could also lay claim to that distinction.

6   For Marx capital accumulation takes place when money profits are spent in purchasing capital goods (constant capital in Marxian parlance) or paying wages (variable capital) to expand production. In that respect the Marxian concept of capital accumulation is wider than the concept of "investment" in national accounts and mainstream economics, which usually refers to purchase of capital goods.

7   Kalecki pointed out that salaries in national income accounts include both salaries of government officials—which are paid from tax-revenues—and salaries of top-level executives—which should be rather classified as profits (Kalecki 1991, p. 237 n17). That observation is even more relevant nowadays, as profits are increasingly presented as salary compensation for the high-level managers who are often also owners of significant shares of the corporation. Piketty (2014) supplies data that abundantly illustrate this trend. However, these issues will be ignored in this chapter. For the sake of simplicity, it will be assumed here that NIPA "wages and salaries" correspond to labor income.

8   Whether Kalecki has an exogenous or an endogenous theory of the business cycle is not an easy question. The editor of Kalecki's *Collected Works*, Jerzy Osiatyński, says that in Kalecki's *Theory of Economic Dynamics* "the long-run development of the capitalist economy, and even its passage to the phase of the business upswing, *was only possible under the influence of exogenous factors*" (Kalecki 1991, p. 551, emphasis added). This sharply contrasts with assertions by Minsky, who, claiming to follow Kalecki's views on economic dynamics, argued that cycles and crises "are not the result of shocks to the system or of policy errors . . . they are endogenous" (Minsky 1991).

9   In *Capitalism,* Anwar Shaikh shows his skepticism on the building cycle of fifteen to twenty-five years that was proposed by Kutznets (Shaikh 2016, footnote 26, p. 107), but he maintains the existence of long waves. Consistent with the idea of long waves is Shaikh's chronology of crises (which Shaikh calls great depressions) in the years 1873–94, 1929–39, 1969–82, and 2008– (for this crisis no ending year is given). The evidence for the existence of long waves provided in the book seems to me very weak and unconvincing. Shaikh mentions on page 726 the views of Kondratieff, but he presents his own evidence based on wholesale prices in gold terms, which would show the long waves in the evolution of capitalism. In figure 2.10 of the book, Shaikh presents wholesale prices in gold; in figure 16.1 the same data are presented as deviations from a cubic trend; in

figure 17.1 Hodrick-Prescott trends (the smoothing parameter is not indicated) are presented. If all that is useful for anything, it is to support the assertion that wholesale prices in gold have a long-term fluctuation. Why should the basic dynamics of the accumulation of capital be linked with these long waves of prices in gold? On page 197 of *Capitalism*, there are some theoretical considerations on inventories and replacement of fixed capital that perhaps are plausible from a merely theoretical point of view, but they seem rather useless for the purpose of analyzing crises because there is no way to find a correlate for them in economic statistics. Referring to 2008–2011 Shaikh says, apparently surprised, that "it is striking that in the midst of a major global crisis profit rates have risen," attributing it to falling wages but also to governments over the world infusing "staggeringly large sums of newly created money into the coffers of banks and businesses" (p. 736). That does not seem a good explanation, since the profit data Shaikh is using (apparently NIPA data, though that is not clear as the appendix 6.8.II.7 that is given as data source can be found neither in the book nor online) would not be affected by government actions to save banks. On the other hand, as I have explained in this chapter, for both Marx and Mitchell it is to be expected that profits and profit rates *rise before the crisis ends*, and that is indeed what data show.

10   The case of Mattick Jr. is a special one. His *Business as Usual: The Economic Crisis and the Failure of Capitalism* (Mattick 2011) is a superb presentation, following Marx's views, of the general processes that lead to crisis in capitalism and the particular processes that had a major role in the development of the Great Recession. However, Mattick never provides in the book a chronology for the crisis or crises he is talking about. He does so in an interview (Clegg and Benavav 2011) in which he asserts that the crisis that started in 2008 is just a continuation of the crisis of the 1970s. Thus, in his view capitalism has been in a permanent crisis since many decades ago. As I already mentioned, Marx plainly rejected the view that crises can be permanent (Marx 1968, p. 497). Recurrent crises have a key role in Marx's theory of capitalism. For Schumpeter, crises are like the beat of the heart of capitalism, and Marx probably would have agreed with that metaphor. That capitalism has been in cardiac arrest since the 1970s seems to me quite an optimistic view. I rather think that the beast, though decrepit and rundown, is still alive and kicking.

References

Acemoglu, D. et al. (2012) "The Network Origins of Aggregate Fluctuations," *Econometrica*, Vol 80, No 5, pp. 1977–2010.

Adelman, I. (1960) "Business cycles—Endogenous or Stochastic?" *Economic Journal*, Vol 70, pp. 783–96.

Arrighi, G. (2003) "Spatial and Other 'Fixes' of Historical Capitalism," *Journal of World-Systems Research*, Vol 10, No 2, pp. 527–39.

Asimakopulos, A. (1977) "Profits and Investment: A Kaleckian Approach," in Harcourt, G. C., ed., *The Microeconomic Foundations of Macroeconomics: Proceedings of a Conference held by the IEA*, Macmillan.

Barbosa-Filho, N. H. and L. Taylor (2006) "Distributive and Demand Cycles in the US Economy: A Structuralist Goodwin Model," *Metroeconomica*, Vol 57, No 3, pp. 389–411.

Besomi, D. (2005) "Clément Juglar and the Transition from Crises Theory to Business Cycle Theories," paper for ninth annual conference of the European Society for the History of Economic Thought, University of Stirling, June 9-12, 2005, Paris, available at www.unil.ch/webdav/site/cwp/users/neyguesi/public/D._Besomi_.

Bhaduri, A. and S. Marglin (1990) "Unemployment and the Real Wage: The Economic Basis for Contesting Political Ideologies," *Cambridge Journal of Economics*, Vol 14, No 4, pp. 375–393.

Bhaskar, V. and A. Glyn (1995) "Expectations and Investment: An Econometric Defense of Animal Spirits," in G. A. Epstein and H. Gintis, eds., *Macroeconomic Policy after the Conservative Era: Studies in Investment, Saving and Finance*, Cambridge University Press.

Blanchard, O., C. Rhee, and L. Summers (1993) "The Stock Market, Profit, and Investment," *Quarterly Journal of Economics*, Vol 108, No 1, pp. 115–36.

Bloom, N. (2014) "Fluctuations in Uncertainty," *Journal of Economic Perspectives*, Vol 28, No 2, pp. 153–76. ·

Boddy, R. and J. Crotty (1975) "Class Conflict and Macro-Policy: The Political Business Cycle," *Review of Radical Political Economics*, Vol 7, No 1, pp. 1–19.

Boldrin, M. and M. Horvath (1995) "Labor Contracts and Business Cycles," *Journal of Political Economy*, Vol 103, No 5, pp. 972–1004.

Bowles, S. and R. Edwards (1985) *Understanding Capitalism: Competition, Command, and Change in the US Economy*, Harper & Row.

Burns, A. F. and W. C. Mitchell (1946) *Measuring Business Cycles*, NBER.

Butler, E. (2010) "The Financial Crisis: Blame Governments, Not Bankers," in P. Booth, ed., *Verdict on the Crash: Causes and Policy Implications*, Institute of Economic Affairs.

Cámara, S. (2013). "The Cyclical Decline of the Profit Rate as the Cause of Crises in the United States, 1947–2011," *Review of Radical Political Economics* Vol 45, No 4, pp. 463–71.

Carchedi, G. and M. Roberts (2013) "A Critique of Heinrich's 'Crisis Theory, the Law of the Tendency of the Profit Rate to Fall, and Marx's Studies in the 1870s,'" *Monthly Review*, December 1.

Cassidy, J. (2010) "Interview with Eugene Fama," *New Yorker*, January 13.

Clarke, S. (1994) *Marx's Theory of Crisis*, St. Martin's Press.

Clegg, J. and A. Benanav (2011) "The Economic Crisis in Fact and Fiction: Interview with Paul Mattick," *Brooklyn Rail*, June, http://www.brooklynrail.org/2011/06/express/the-economic-crisis-in-fact-and-fictionpaul-mattick-with-john-clegg-and-aaron-benanav.

Dash, E. and N. D. Schwartz (2011) "Banks Flooded with Cash They Can't Profitably Use," *New York Times*, October 24, Business, p. 1.

Devine, J. N. (1986) "Empirical Studies in Marxian Crisis Theory: Introduction," *Review of Radical Political Economics*, Vol 18, pp. 1–12.

Duménil, G. and D. Lévy (2011) *The Crisis of Neoliberalism*, Harvard University Press.

Foley, D. (2012) "The Political Economy of Post-crisis Global Capitalism," *South Atlantic Quarterly*, Vol 111, No 2, pp. 251–63.

Friedman, M. (1940) "Review of Tinbergen's 'Business cycles in the United States,'" *American Economic Review*, Vol 30, No 4, pp. 657–60.

Frisch, R. (1933) *Propagation Problems and Impulse Problems in Dynamic Economics*, Universitetets Økonomische Institutt.

Gabaix, X. (2011) "The Granular Origins of Aggregate Fluctuations," *Econometrica*, Vol 79, No 3, pp. 733–72.

Glasner, D. and T. F. Cooley, eds., (1997) *Business Cycles and Depressions: An Encyclopedia*, Garland.

Goodwin, R. M. (1964) "Econometrics in Business-Cycle Analysis," in Hansen (1964), pp. 417–68.

Gordon, R. A (1961) *Business Fluctuations*, 2nd ed., Harper.

Haberler, G. (1960) *Prosperity and Depression: A Theoretical Analysis of Cyclical Movements*, 4th ed., Harvard University Press.

Hall, T. E. (1990) *Business Cycles: The Nature and Causes of Economic Fluctuations*, Praeger.

Hamilton, J. D. (1988) "A Neoclassical Model of Unemployment and the Business Cycle," *Journal of Political Economy*, Vol 96, No 3, pp. 593–617.

———. (2009) "Causes and Consequences of the Oil Shock of 2007–08," *Brookings Papers on Economic Activity*, spring, pp. 215–67

———. (2011) "Historical Oil Shocks," NBER working paper, No 16790.

Hansen, A. H. (1949) "Wesley Mitchell, Social Scientist and Social Counselor," *Review of Economics and Statistics*, Vol 31, p. 245.

———. (1964) *Business Cycles and National Income*, 2nd ed., George Allen & Unwin.

Harvey, D. (2010) *The Enigma of Capital and the Crises of Capitalism*, Oxford University Press.

———. (2011) "The Enigma of Capital & the Crisis This Time," in C. Calhoun and G. Derluguian, eds., *Business As Usual: The Roots of the Global Financial Meltdown*, New York University Press.

———. (2014) "A Commentary on the Falling Rate of Profit in Marx's Crisis Theory," lecture, available at https://www.youtube.com/watch?v=-ZJrNgb-iiY&spfreload=10.

Heinrich, M. (2013) "Crisis Theory, the Law of the Tendency of the Profit Rate to Fall, and Marx's Studies in the 1870s," *Monthly Review*, Vol 64, No 11.

Huntington, E. (1920) *World-Power and Evolution*, Yale University Press.

Kalecki, M. (1954) *Theory of Economic Dynamics: An Essay on Cyclical and Long-Run Changes in Capitalist Economy*, George Allen & Unwin.

———. (1971) *Selected Essays on the Dynamics of the Capitalist Economy 1933–1970*, Cambridge University Press.

———. (1984) "The Mechanism of the Business Upswing," in Foster, J. B. and Szlajter, H., eds, *The Faltering Economy: The Problem of Accumulation under Monopoly Capitalism*, MR Press.

———. (1990) *Collected Works*, Vol 1, *Business Cycles and Full Employment*, J. Osiatinsky, ed., C. A. Kisiels, trans., Clarendon Press.

———. (1991) *Collected Works*, Vol 2, *Capitalism, Economic Dynamics*, J. Osiatinsky, ed., C. A. Kisiels, trans., Clarendon Press.

Keynes, J. M. (1936) *The General Theory of Employment, Interest, and Money*, Macmillan.

———. (1937) "The General Theory of Employment," *Quarterly Journal of Economics*, Vol 51, No 2, pp. 209–23.

———. (1939) "Professor Tinbergen's Method," *Economic Journal*, Vol 49, No 195, pp. 558–68.

Kliman, A. (2012) *The Failure of Capitalist Production: Underlying Causes of the Great Recession*, Pluto Press.

Knoop, T. A. (2004) *Recessions and Depressions: Understanding Business Cycles*, Praeger.

Koopmans, T. C. (1947) "Measurement without Theory," *Review of Economic Statistics*, Vol 29, pp. 161–72.

Kose, M. A. and M. E. Terrones (2015) *Collapse and Revival: Understanding Global Recessions and Recoveries*, International Monetary Fund.

Krugman, P. (2009) "How Did Economists Get It So Wrong?," *New York Times Magazine*, September 2.

Leamer, E. E. (2010) "Tantalus on the Road to Asymptopia," *Journal of Economic Perspectives*, Vol 24, No 2, pp. 31–46.

Mankiw, N. G. (2009) *Principles of Macroeconomics*, 5th ed., Southwestern.

———. (2010) "Economic View: A Call for Humility—Trying to Tame the Unknowable," *New York Times*, March 26, p. BU6.

Marx, K. (1873) "Letter to Friedrich Engels, May 31, 1873," *Marx and Engels Collected Works*, Vol 44, p. 504.

———. (1968) *Theories of Surplus-Value*, part 2, Progress.

———. (1977) *Capital,* Vol 1, B. Fowkes, trans., Vintage.

———. (1981a) *Capital,* Vol 2, F. Engels, ed., D. Fernbach, trans., Vintage.

———. (1981b) *Capital,* Vol 3, F. Engels, ed., D. Fernbach, trans., Vintage.

Marx, K. and F. Engels (1966) *Collected Works*, Vol 3, Dietz.

Matthews, R. C. O. (1959) *The Business Cycle*, University of Chicago Press.

Mattick, P., Jr. (1981) *Economic Crisis and Crisis Theory*, M. E. Sharpe.

———. (2008) "Review of 'The Limits to Capital' by David Harvey," *Historical Materialism*, Vol 16, No 4, pp. 213–24.

———. (2011) *Business as Usual—The Economic Crisis and the Failure of Capitalism,* Reaktion Books.

McNally, D. (2010) *Global Slump: The Economics and Politics of Crisis and Resistance*, PM Press.

Minsky, H. P. (1991) "The Financial Instability Hypothesis: A Clarification," in M. Feldstein, ed., *The Risk of Economic Crisis*, University of Chicago Press.

———. (2008) *Stabilizing an Unstable Economy*, McGraw-Hill.

Mitchell, W. C. (1913) *Business Cycles*, University of California Press.

———. (1927) *Business Cycles: The Problem and Its Setting*, NBER.

———. (1941) *Business Cycles and Their Causes: A New Edition o' Mitchell's Business Cycles,* part 3, University of California Press.

———. (1944) "Test of Free Enterprise: Depression-Proof Economy Is Sought," *New York Times*, September 18, p. 22.

———. (1951) *What Happens during Business Cycles: A Progress Report*, NBER.

Mohun, S. and R. Veneziani (2008) "Goodwin Cycles and the U.S. Economy, 1948–2004," in P. Flaschel and M. Landesmann, eds., *Mathematical Economics and the Dynamics of Capitalism: Godwin's Legacy Continued*, Routledge.

Morgan, M. S. (1990) *The History of Econometric Ideas*, Cambridge University Press.

Ohanian, L. E. (2008) "Back to the Future with Keynes," *Federal Reserve Bank of Minneapolis Quarterly Review*, Vol 32, No 1.

Panitch, L. (2013) "Crisis of What?," *Journal of World-Systems Research*, Vol 19, No 2, pp. 129–35.

Pearl, J. (2000). *Causality – Models, Reasoning, and Inference*, Cambridge University Press.

Perlo, V. (1973) *The Unstable Economy: Booms and Recessions in the United States since 1945*, International Publishers.

Picketty, T. (2014) *Capital in the Twenty-First Century*, A. Goldhammer, trans., Belknap Press/Harvard University Press.

Pigou, A. C. (1927) "Wage Policy and Unemployment," *Economic Journal*, Vol 37, No 147, p. 355.

Rada, C. and Taylor, L. (2006) "Empty Sources of Growth Accounting, and Empirical Replacements à la Kaldor with Some Beef," *Structural Change and Economic Dynamics*, Vol 17, pp. 487–500.

Reinhart, C. and K. S. Rogoff (2009) *This Time Is Different: Eight Centuries of Financial Folly*, Princeton University Press.

Roberts, M. (2009) *The Great Recession: Profit Cycles, Economic Crises—A Marxist View*, author's edition.

Robinson, J. (1979) *The Generalisation of the General Theory, and Other Essays*, Macmillan.

Schumpeter, J. A. (1939) *Business Cycles: A Theoretical, Historical, and Statistical Analysis of the Capitalist Process*, McGraw-Hill.

———. (1954) *History of Economic Analysis*, George Allen & Unwin.

Schwartz, A. J. (2010) "Origins of the Financial Market Crisis of 2008," in P. Booth, ed., *Verdict on the Crash: Causes and Policy Implications*, Institute of Economic Affairs.

Shackle, G. L. S. (1967) *The Years of High Theory: Invention and Tradition in Economic Thought 1926–1939*, Cambridge University Press.

Shaikh, A. (1983) "Economic Crises," in T. Bottomore et al., eds., *A Dictionary of Marxist Thought*, Harvard University Press.

———. (2016) *Capitalism: Competition, Conflict, Crises*, Oxford University Press.

Sherman, H. J. (2010) "Toward a Progressive Macroeconomic Explanation of the Recession," *Challenge*, Vol 53, No 4, pp. 68–85.

Sherman, H. J. and D. X. Kolk (1997) *Business Cycles and Forecasting*, Addison-Wesley.

Steindl, J. (1991) "Some Comments on the Three Versions of Kalecki's Theory of the Trade Cycle," in Kalecki (1991), pp. 597–604.

Tanuro, D. (2014) *Green Capitalism—Why It Can't Work*, Fernwood Publishing.

Tapia, J. A. (2012) "Statistical Evidence of Falling Profits as a Cause of Recession: A Short Note," *Review of Radical Political Economics*, Vol 44, No 4, pp. 484–93.

———. (2013) "Does Investment Call the Tune? Empirical Evidence and Endogenous Theories of the Business Cycle," *Research in Political Economy*, Vol 28, pp. 229–59, reprinted in this volume as chapter 3, "Investment, Profit and Crises: Theories and Evidence."

———. (2014) "From the Oil Crisis to the Great Recession: Five Crises of the World Economy," paper presented at the ASSA-AEA 2014 Meeting, Philadelphia. Available at http://www.drexel.edu/coas/faculty-research/faculty-directory/JoseTapia/.

———. (2015) "Profits Encourage Investment, Investment Dampens Profits, Government Spending Does Not Prime the Pump: A DAG Investigation of Business-Cycle Dynamics," available at http://www.mpra.ub.uni-muenchen.de/64698/.

———. (2016a) "Oil Prices and the World Business Cycle: A Causal Investigation," available at https://ideas.repec.org/p/pra/mprapa/68978.html.

———. (2016b) "Toward a New Global Recession? Economic Perspectives for 2016 and Beyond," *Brooklyn Rail*, February, http://www.brooklynrail.org/2016/02/field-notes/toward-a-new-global-recession-economic-perspectives-for-2016-and-beyond.

Tapia, J. A., E. L. Ionides, and O. Carpintero (2012) "Climate Change and the World Economy: Short-Run Determinants of Atmospheric CO2," *Environmental Science and Policy*, Vol 21, pp. 50–62.

Targetti, F. and B. Kinda-Hass (1982) "Kalecki's Review of Keynes's General Theory," *Australian Economic Papers*, Vol 21, No 38, pp. 244–60.

Tinbergen, J. (1939) *Statistical Testing of Business-Cycle Theories*, Vol 2, *Business Cycles in the United States of America 1919–1932*, League of Nations.

———. (1950) *The Dynamics of Business Cycles: A Study in Economic Fluctuations*, J. J. Polak, ed. and trans., University of Chicago Press.

———. (1952) "Comments on Orcutt's 'Toward Partial Redirection of Econometrics,'" *Review of Economics and Statistics*, Vol 34, No 3, pp. 205–6.

Wallerstein, I. (2001) *Unthinking Social Science: The Limits of Nineteenth-Century Paradigms*, 2nd ed., Temple University Press.

———. (2011) *Modern World-System III: The Second Era of Great Expansion of the Capitalist World-Economy, 1730s-1840s*, University of California Press.

Wilson, M. (2009) "Sales of Safes Boom as the Economy Falters: Looking for Security in a Cube of Steel," *New York Times*, March 6.

PART II

THE INTERNATIONAL DIMENSION

THE TENDENCY OF THE RATE OF PROFIT TO FALL SINCE THE NINETEENTH CENTURY AND A WORLD RATE OF PROFIT

Esteban Ezequiel Maito

1. Introduction

In classical political economy, there was a concern about the downward trend in the rate of profit. Adam Smith and David Ricardo, among others, noted that there was such a trend.[1] The systemic tendency to crisis and insufficient profits generation has also been discerned by exponents of other economic schools (like Schumpeter or Keynes). All accepted the immanently real nature of this trend, despite the theoretical particularities of each of these economic schools.

Ricardo argued that this trend was due to the increase of labor costs caused by decreasing agricultural productivity, as agricultural production expanded on "badlands." For Ricardo, the rate of profit of capital was similar to the rate of surplus value because in the denominator of the profitability equation, he identified only the variable capital component (paid wages), ignoring the constant capital component. But it's precisely the relative increase in constant capital that is the main determination of the law of the tendency of the rate of profit to fall. Moreover, the Ricardian assumption of diminishing marginal productivity in agriculture has proved unrealistic. The rate of profit shows a downward trend, not because productivity decreases, but precisely because it increases in historical terms.

Marx established, as the most important law of political economy, the law of the tendency of the rate of profit to fall. Capitalist production consists of a valorization process (M–M') through the exploitation of the labor force (M–C . . . –P . . . –C'–M'). The capital advanced in the form of money (M) is exchanged for commodities (C)—means of production, raw materials (constant capital or CC) and the labor force (variable capital or VC). The secret of capitalist production is that the labor force is able to generate more than its reproduction value: namely, a surplus value. For this reason, the capital advanced for the labor force is variable capital (VC), while capital advanced for the means of production (machinery, infrastructure) and raw materials is constant capital (CC).

So the production process (P) occurs when the labor force, using the means of production, transforms inputs, which are then realized in a mass of commodities of a greater value (C') than the original money advanced (M). The final product includes the value of constant capital consumed, plus an additional amount generated by the labor force, equal to variable capital (the reproduction value of the labor force) exchanged with the capitalist, and a surplus value. Thus capital transmutes from money capital to commodity capital, then productive capital, finally returning to the form of commodity capital along with money capital of a greater value. This last step is the one that involves the sale on the market ($C'-M'$), that is, the realization of the profit and the completion of the valorization process.

There is continual pressure for each capitalist to sell at a lower price than competitors, thus raising their market share. This implies a constantly increasing expenditure, mainly on fixed capital—equipment and infrastructure—that enables the productivity of labor to rise, or the labor time necessary to produce commodities to be reduced, thus reducing the individual value, including that of the cost of reproduction of the labor force. But to do this, there will be a relative rise in the value of constant capital compared to that of variable capital (for the reproduction of the labor force).

Capital's sole purpose is to increase the surplus value extracted from the labor force, but its only means of doing so is by increasing constant capital relative to variable capital, the latter being the only source of profits. So capital finds its own internal limit: "The means – unconditional development of the productive forces of society – comes continually into conflict with the limited purpose, the self-expansion of the existing capital" (Marx 1999b, ch. 15).

For Marx, this downward trend in the rate of profit would occur regardless of a decline or stagnation in wages relative to profits; that is, a constant or rising rate of surplus value (expressed as profits / variable capital):

> This continual relative decrease of the variable capital vis-à-vis the constant, and consequently the total, capital is identical with the progressively higher organic composition of the social capital in its average. It is likewise just another expression for the progressive development of the social productivity of labour, which is demonstrated precisely by the fact that the same number of labourers, in the same time

– i.e. with less labor – convert an ever-increasing quantity of raw and auxiliary materials into products, thanks to the growing application of machinery and fixed capital in general. . . . This mode of production produces a progressive relative decrease of the variable capital as compared to the constant capital, and consequently a continuously rising organic composition of the total capital. The immediate result of this is that the rate of surplus value, at the same, or even a rising, degree of labour exploitation, is represented by a continually falling general rate of profit. (Marx 1999b, ch. 13)

This does not deny the fact that the rate of profit may show periods of growth, but these exist precisely because the countervailing forces manage to reverse this downward pressure for a time. This gives Marx's law the character of a tendency:

We have thus seen in a general way that the same influences which produce a tendency in the general rate of profit to fall also call forth counter-effects, which hamper, retard and partly paralyse this fall. The latter do not do away with the law, but impair its effect. Otherwise, it would not be the fall of the general rate of profit, but rather its relative slowness, that would be incomprehensible. Thus, the law acts only as a tendency. And it is only under certain circumstances and only after long periods that its effects become strikingly pronounced. (Marx 1999b, ch. 14)

The tendency of the rate of profit to fall is an *inherent* aspect of the capitalist mode of production. It is the logical conclusion of the Marxian law of value, and it is his explanation of technological change, competition and the formation of a general rate of profit (debunkers have usually applied lazy revisionism in these matters, too). Marx himself states this obvious connection between his theory of value and the downward trend, which appears expressed in the value of any particular commodity as the "economic cell of bourgeois society":

Since the development of the productiveness and the correspondingly higher composition of capital sets in motion an ever-increasing quantity of means of production through a constantly decreasing quantity of labour, every aliquot part of the total product i.e. every single commodity, or each particular lot of commodities in the total mass of products – absorbs less living labour, and also contains less materialised labour, both in the depreciation of the fixed capital applied and in the raw and auxiliary materials consumed. Hence every single commodity contains a smaller sum of labour materialised in · means of production and of labour newly added during production.

This causes the price of the individual commodity to fall. But the mass of profits contained in the individual commodities may nevertheless increase if the rate of the absolute or relative surplus value grows. The commodity contains less newly added labour, but its unpaid portion grows in relation to its paid portion. However, this is the case only within certain limits. With the absolute amount of living labour newly incorporated in individual commodities decreasing enormously as production develops, the absolute mass of unpaid labour contained in them will likewise decrease, however much it may have grown as compared to the paid portion. (Marx 1999b, ch. 13)

The law of the tendency of the rate of profit to fall expresses the very simple fact that, as the mode of production expands in time, the value composition of social production changes in a specific way, increasing the relative share of dead labor or constant capital with respect to living labor. These changes are based in the commodity itself and in the law of value that determines not only the reduction of the individual value (social necessary labor time) of commodities with the development of productive forces, but also the relative reduction of living labor compared to dead labor in the value of commodities (fig. 4.1).[2]

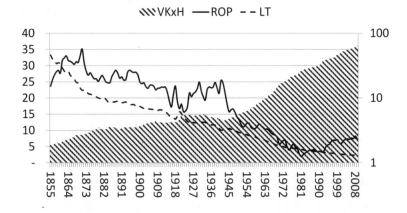

Figure 4.1. Labor time to produce one pound at 2006 prices (LT, in minutes, LHS), volume of fixed capital per hour of work (VK × H, RHS) and rate of profit (%)—United Kingdom, 1855–2009. Source: see appendix B.

As can be seen in the last quote, there is a clear connection in Marx's arguments about the value components in commodities and the tendency of the rate of profit to fall. Both refer to the same reality from two different angles. In both cases, the increase in the rate of surplus value has clear limits in offsetting the relative increase in objectified labor (constant capital) and in determining both the value of commodities and the rate of profit. This connection between the law of the tendency of the rate of profit to fall and the law of value is first practically established in volume 1 of *Capital*—for instance in the "General law of capitalist accumulation": "The accumulation of capital, though originally appearing as its quantitative extension only, is effected, as we have seen, under a progressive qualitative change in its composition, under a constant increase of its constant, at the expense of its variable, constituent" (1999a, ch. 24). It is the same principle. The tendency of capital to increase constant capital (fixed and circulating, but mostly fixed) compared to the variable establishes the downward trend in the rate of profit. So Marx makes clear both the validity of the law of profitability and its foundation in the law of value. In chapter 24 of volume 3, he writes,

> As demonstrated in part 3 of this book, the rate of profit decreases in proportion to the mounting accumulation of capital and the correspondingly increasing productivity of social labour, which is expressed precisely in the relative and progressive decrease of the variable as compared to the constant portion of capital. To produce the same rate of profit after the constant capital set in motion by one labourer increases tenfold, the surplus labour-time would have to increase tenfold, and soon the total labour-time, and finally the entire 24 hours of a day, would not suffice, even if wholly appropriated by capital. (1999b, ch. 24)

The tendency of the rate of profit to fall is not necessarily expressed in a steady downward trend, nor exempt from recovery periods. There are factors counteracting the trend, some of which have been identified by Marx (1999b, pp. 159–64) and Grossman (2005, ch. 2); namely, the cheapening of constant capital, the payment of the labor force below its value, an increasing turnover speed of circulating capital, capital exports, and foreign trade to expand markets, among others. Grossman concludes that these countertendencies introduce cyclical movements within the long-term trend: "The operation of these countertendencies transforms the breakdown into a temporary crisis, so that the accumulation process is not something continuous but takes the form of periodic cycles" (2005, ch. 2).

These counteracting factors alleviate only in a relative way the decrease in the rate of profit over the long run. They initially tend to increase profitability, but then they get diluted or reversed in the opposite direction. For instance, if the cheapening of the elements of constant capital reduces its relative value to variable capital, raising profitability, this cheapening will also promote increased spending on constant capital in the context of capitalist competition. In the case of capital exports, when capital flows to a new area, despite its initial better accumulation conditions, it eventually tends to develop the same tendencies. So, although initially this export of capital prevents its accumulation in the source area from depressing the profit rate, even allowing a rise in the global profitability by increasing the rate in the new area, the accumulation trend continues to develop and is now expressed in both areas, generating a fall in the rate of profit in global terms.[3]

Authors who deny the law often argue that by increasing productivity and the rate of surplus value, capital compensates for the increase of the composition and the previous fall of the rate of profit; and this results in a general indetermination that is intertwined with a characterization of economic cycles as detached from any general long-term trend, and instead occurring on a flat, linear, eternal trend. Capitalism then would be on an eternal repetition of mutually compensatory increases and decreases.[4]

Rosdolsky asserted that those authors "overlook that the increase in the rate of profit secured by raising the intensity of the exploitation of labour is no abstract procedure or arithmetical operation; . . . the surplus labour which a worker can perform has definite limits. On the one hand, the length of the working day, and on the other, the part of the working day necessary for the reproduction of the workers themselves" (1977, p. 408).[5]

Some authors like Reuten or Heinrich pretend to install a very questionable interpretation: that the law of the tendency of the rate of profit to fall was abandoned by Marx in *Capital*. So chapters 13 to 15 of *Capital,* volume 3 were just the result of misrepresentative editing by Engels. So the tendency to collapse of the capitalist mode of production that Marx recognized in the *Grundrisse* would appear in *Capital* only as an explanation of cyclical crises.

But this argument is weak in several aspects. First, it is a dubious interpretation according to the textual evidence itself, and to the work of Marx. As we explained before, there is an immanent relation between the law of value and the tendency of the rate of profit to fall.

Second, this argument establishes a false division between the tendency of the rate of profit to fall and accumulation cycles, but these are bound together. Indeed, the tendency of the rate of profit to fall develops its own trend simultaneously with and through accumulation cycles. Cyclical ups and downs are not compensated for mutually over the long term like symmetric fluctuations in a flat trend line. The reasons are precisely those argued by Marx in *Capital,* related to the law of value, technological change and the relative increase in constant capital related to variable capital or living labor.

Third, statistical evidence shows that there is no relevant increase in the rate of surplus value that checks or compensates for the increase in constant capital. National accounts in all countries studied here show a clear increase in wage share at least until the last years of the 1970s. In the last decades of the twentieth century, there were increases in the net profit share in GDP in several countries. But over the long run, net taxes and consumption of fixed capital (which is an indirect expression of the capital composition) showed a relative increase in their share of GDP. So net profits over the long term suffered a fall in the share of GDP.

This is true even when we look at the corporate sector alone, as data from the United States and from the work of Piketty (2013) show. The US corporate sector has had a higher profit share compared to the national economy in the latter decades of the twentieth century, but the downward trend in share is still similar over the long term. So, not only did the change in surplus value fail to check the tendency for the rate of profit to fall, but it actually strengthened it.

Increases in productivity or the rate of surplus value have not shown a development that could counteract the downward trend in the rate of profit, contrary to the assertions of many authors. We might define the rate of profit as

$$(1) \; ROP = P/K = (Y/K) \times (P/Y)$$

$$\text{or} \; (2) \; ROP = P/(K + VC) = (P/VC)/(VCC + 1)$$

$$\text{or} \; (3) \; ROP = P/K = (P/Y)/(K/Y).$$

In equation 1, the rate of profit is the result of the combined influence of the maximum rate of profit (Y/K) and the share of profits in net output (P/Y); in equation 2 it is the result of dividing profits, constant capital and variable capital by variable capital (obtaining then the rate of surplus value in the numerator and value composition in the denominator); and in equation 3 it is the result of dividing the share of profits (P/Y) by the composition of capital as the relation of dead and living labor (K/Y).

The main interest in this chapter is to focus on the concrete historical expression of the law of the tendency of the rate of profit to fall, rather than on the law's relationship with "theories of crisis." Our concern is therefore whether there was such a tendency in the real world that would ultimately express the historical limitation of capital as the hegemonic mode of production of social life (fig. 4.2).[6]

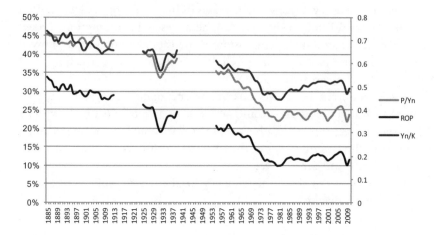

Figure 4.2. Net output–capital ratio (Yn/K), rate of profit, % (ROP; LHS) and profit share (P/Yn) in core countries (simple means, 1885–2010). Source: author's calculations.

But the downward trend in profitability may be countervailed not only by increasing the rate of surplus value, but also by increasing the value added relative to fixed productive capital. Even if there is a stable or even falling rate of surplus value over the long term, larger increases in value added than those in fixed capital could counterweight the tendency. This would be expressed in the output–capital ratio, that is, the maximum rate of profit (the rate for the extreme case in which the time required for reproduction of the labor force has been reduced to zero and all the value added becomes profit).

Thus the law of the tendency of the rate of profit to fall is based on what the output–capital ratio, or the maximum rate of profit, reflects: namely, the inherent trend of capital to overaccumulation: "A fall in the rate of profit and accelerated accumulation are different expressions of the same process only in so far as both reflect the development of productiveness. Accumulation, in turn, hastens the fall of the rate of profit, inasmuch as it implies concentration of labour on a large scale, and thus a higher composition of capital" (Marx 1999b, ch. 15). The tendency of the rate of profit to fall is just another expression of the increased accumulation and social productivity of labor *under capitalist relations of production*. As stated above, this tendency is an *inherent* aspect of the mode of production and, thus, of Marxian political economy. Paul Mattick points out:

> Although it first appears in the process of circulation, the real crisis cannot be understood as a problem of circulation or of realisation, but only as a disruption of the process of reproduction as a whole, which is constituted by production and circulation together. And, as

the process of reproduction depends on the accumulation of capital, and therefore on the mass of surplus value that makes accumulation possible, it is within the sphere of production that the decisive factors (though not the only factors) of the passage from the possibility of crisis to an actual crisis are to be found. . . . The crisis characteristic of capital thus originates neither in production nor in circulation taken separately, but in the difficulties that arise from the tendency of the profit rate to fall inherent in accumulation and governed by the law of value. (1974, ch. 2)

The tendency of the rate of profit to fall is derived from the contradictions that constitute the mode of production and the commodity itself as a product of social labor under its particular relations of production. Marxist scientific analysis, which differs from all the previous socialist political traditions and all previous forms of bourgeois economics, has clarified that it ultimately expresses something as obvious as it is elemental: capitalism is a historically bounded system.[7]

If the system tends toward lower returns, it gradually exhausts its own sustenance. But is there empirical evidence of this trend? The rest of this chapter will attempt to consider the evidence for this immanent tendency of the capitalist mode of production to liquidate its own base.

2. The Rate of Profit

In Marxian terms, the rate of profit is calculated from the ratio of profits on one side and, on the other side, capital advanced in machinery, infrastructure (fixed constant capital, FCC), inputs (circulating constant capital, CCC) and wages (variable capital, VC). Fixed constant capital transfers its value to the product over several years. The constant and variable circulating capital is transferred to the final product after every production process and gets recovered by the capitalist once the commodities are sold, to be newly relaunched for production and revalorized.

However, given the difficulty of calculating the constant and variable circulating capital, the rate of return on fixed constant capital is sufficient to analyze the evolution of profitability in any country. Anyway, the rate of profit on fixed capital tends to converge with the Marxian rate of profit in the long run. The reason for this is simple: the growth in turnover speed of circulating capital steadily reduces the proportion of circulating capital in the total capital advanced.

The rate of profit on fixed capital has been, by far, the most commonly used measure in studies on capital profitability. Chan-Lee and Sutch (1985), in one of the first comparative analyses, studied the profit rates of countries in the Organisation for Economic Co-operation and Development (OECD) for the period 1960–80 and confirmed the decline in profitability in the '70s. Li et al. (2007) conducted a study that considered the long-term profitability for the UK, United States, Japan, and the Eurozone since the '60s in the context of a historical analysis of the global hegemony of successive states in the world system. Duménil and Lévy (2005) also compared the profit rate levels for these countries, although in a more limited temporal range. Zachariah (2009) performed a similar exercise, adding China and India. However, he does not estimate the return on reproductive fixed capital, but includes dwellings, which are not part of the fixed capital and the process of capitalist production itself.

In this chapter we present estimates for fourteen countries, covering, in some cases, more than a century of history, and representing more than half of world production in the last seventy years (62 percent of world GDP in 2010). In relation to the work of Li et al. (2007), we incorporated over the longer term (in a time series of more than a century) estimates for Germany, Argentina, Sweden, and the Netherlands. The inclusion of Argentina in the early twentieth century, as well as Korea and China in recent decades, allowed a better analysis of the most dynamic peripheral areas of global accumulation and their relation to the general trend of profitability.

In all cases, the rate of profit is measured as the ratio of net operating surplus to fixed constant capital (net reproductive capital stock) of the whole economy, valued at current reproduction prices. Finally, statistical and methodological appendixes for each country are included, specifying the estimates' sources.

3. Movement of Capital and Rate of Profit

In volume 3 of *Capital*, the general process of capitalist production is founded on the existence of different individual capitals. Profitability spreads between different areas (between branches or national spaces), fostering an influx of capital to the most profitable branches or countries. This influx intensifies competition, resulting in a general decline of profitability in that industry or national space.[8] The action of individual capitals to increase their own productivity is what finally erodes the general rate of profit. These continual movements involve a tendency to equalization and a fall in the rate of profit.[9]

A conclusion that emerges from this chapter is that in historical terms, profitability in the "core countries" is lower than elsewhere due to higher relative levels of fixed capital accumulation. In the core countries, production processes require a higher minimum initial capital. However, the peripheral countries have seen a greater relative decline in profitability in recent decades compared to the core countries, reflecting the higher rates of accumulation and growth in the former in the recent period.

The historical development of capital promotes the entry of peripheral countries into the world market, with particular dominance in certain agricultural and mining branches; this primacy is driven by cheap and mass production of means of production, including transport in the core countries and favorable international relative prices of agriculture products and raw materials (Collins and Williamson 2001; Oribe Stemmer 1989). The decades of nineteenth century were divided by the great 1871–73 general crisis, after which there was a steady decline in the rate of profit in the core countries and a major boost to capital in the peripheral countries. The consolidation of imperialism in the last decades of the century can be viewed as the result of counteracting elements to the downward tendency (the export of capital, the cheapening of constant capital, and inputs produced more easily in the periphery, etc.).

The decline in the rate of profit in the 1870s clearly shows that a growing mass of capital was overaccumulated. The export of capital to the periphery allowed a significant portion of that mass to be valorized, usually at higher profitability levels, based on the production of commodities bearing land rent and related activities (infrastructure, etc.). In the first two decades of the twentieth century, the downward trend in profitability is less pronounced compared to the years after the general crisis of 1871–73.

The export of capital was a factor counteracting the tendency of the rate of profit to fall. But it was also a limited factor over the long term, as it finally deepened capital accumulation in peripheral countries, and the tendency to collapse now operated on a global scale, including the peripheral countries. This is supported by the downward and converging trend in the rates of profit in the core and peripheral countries.

Although Grossman (1929), unlike Lenin, had already integrated the export of capital into Marxist economic theory in a more formal and systematic way, Harman (1981) showed that the export of capital was a counteracting mechanism that, back in Grossman's time, still retained a significant role in the periphery (in areas of infrastructure, finance or marketing, and to a lesser extent in industrial production itself).

The industrialization of the periphery only really deepened in the post-1945 period, through the development of transnational companies from the United States and Europe. This method for the export of capital now used mainly industrial or productive capital, originating in the core countries after the recovery in profitability after World War II.

It was during this postwar period that the entry into the world market by new geographical areas was most dynamic. It was based not on the production of commodities bearing land rent, but on the production of industrial goods—first, those related to the textile industry, but subsequently in higher value-added sectors of industry, as in the Korean case.

The movement of capital in search of higher profits is not only international, but also national. In the new areas, capital increasingly exploited its own labor force and reinvested there. This was an important aspect of the postwar capitalist development of East Asia although, strictly speaking, it is a general process of historical development of capital. Indeed, the contribution of foreign capital in Asia through inflows of direct investment by multinational enterprises has been relatively minor, at least compared with Latin America.

However, the growth of accumulation and the trend in declining profitability—whether checked by controls or restrictions on international capital mobility, or boosted by increased profitability in new areas of exploitation (the economic fundamentals described by Marx)—continued to operate. Regardless of the more developed capitals prevailing in a particular nation or the specific characteristics of a particular national capitalist class, Marx's law of profitability has remained valid. Indeed, Japan and Korea have probably experienced the largest decreases in profitability during the postwar period.

4. The Rate of Profit from the Mid-nineteenth Century

The rate of profit over the long run shows a clear downward trend, shared by both the core and the peripheral countries.[10]

The core countries

For core countries, our series starts in the second half of the nineteenth century, marked by the general crisis of 1871–73 that, as noted earlier, shows a sharp fall in profitability (see table 4.2 in appendix A), followed by some stability in the early decades of the twentieth century. The series begins with three national spaces that were the core of capitalist system for several centuries (Netherlands, United Kingdom, and United States), together with two countries that posed strong economic competition to American hegemony in the twentieth century (Germany and Japan) and Sweden (fig. 4.3).

The rate of profit shows a sharp decline in the general crisis of 1930 (14.9 percent in 1932 from 22.1 percent in 1929 for the weighted rate of profit) and a subsequent recovery whose highest point is reached during World War II. After the war, the rate drops and eventually returns to the previous trend line.

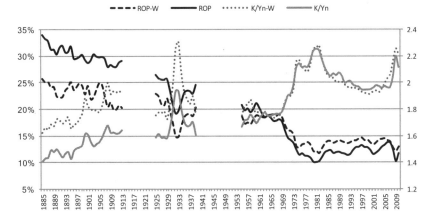

Figure 4.3. Rate of profit (%, LHS), and organic composition
(RHS) in core countries, simple and weighted (–W)
mean, 1885–2010. Source: author's calculations.

From the nineteenth century to the 1970s, there was, except for the period
1930–44, a very regular downward trend, which was then interrupted by a
sharp decline during the period 1970–82. The subsequent partial recovery
has been very limited, from a 10.6 percent average rate in core countries
in 1980–84 to a 12.9 percent average rate in 1995–99, below even the
1970–74 level. The last decades clearly appear as those with lower levels of
profitability, with 2009 almost repeating the historic trough of 1982, and
thus reversing the cycle of very limited recovery started in the 1980s.

Capital's inability to restore profitability is revealed not only by the
smaller rise, but also by the longer period of time involved in reaching a
new peak. This is especially so, considering that in the latter decades, capital
applied many counteracting factors (increased "free" trade, financial and
investment liberalization, and worsening labor conditions). The last decades
clearly appear as those with lower levels of profitability, with 2009 almost
repeating the historic trough of 1982 and thus reversing the cycle of very
limited recovery started in the 1980s.

The United States was the successor to the Netherlands and the United
Kingdom in the global hegemony. Its profit rate dropped significantly from
1880 to 1890, showing lower levels than the rest and expressing the greater
development of the productive forces and corporations in the United States
during those years, as well as its consolidation as a major exporter of capital
and foreign investor since the early twentieth century. After the crisis of
1930, there was a sustained recovery in the US rate of profit, mainly after
the US entry into World War II in 1941, from 9.4 percent in 1933 to 21.0
percent in 1944.

Within the European context, there were higher rates of profit in Germany, Netherlands, and Sweden during the nineteenth century compared to in the United Kingdom. From the early twentieth century, these differentials disappeared. Due to higher capital accumulation rates in Germany and the lower rate of profit since then, just as in the case of the United States, Germany has become a major capital exporter, with an increasing amount of foreign investment by German companies (as was the case of Japan and the UK). The end of British hegemony coincided with a sharp decline in the UK rate of profit after World War I.

The postwar period was characterized by a higher economic expansion in European countries that nevertheless resulted in a greater rate of decline in the rate of profit than in the United States, which exported capital to a larger extent as a counteracting factor to the tendency of the rate of profit to fall (figs. 4.4 and 4.5).

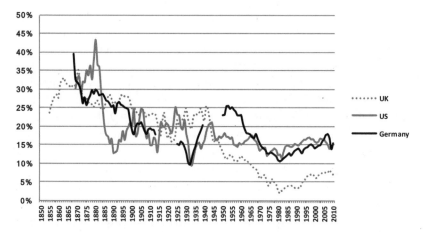

Figure 4.4. Rate of profit in Germany, United Kingdom and United States (%), 1855–2010. Source: see appendix B.

Japan experienced a remarkable economic dynamism during the postwar period, which allowed it to become a major capitalist power, gaining positions in the world market in productive branches or phases, whereas countries like the United States, the United Kingdom, and Germany lost competitiveness. However, this profitability differential relative to the rest of the core derived precisely from a high rate of capital accumulation that finally drove down the rate of profit, pushing the Japanese economy into a chronic crisis during the last decades of the twentieth century.

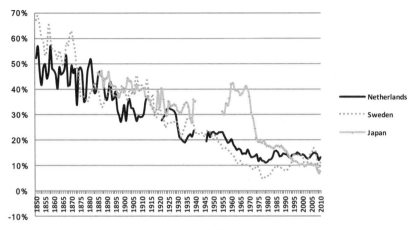

Figure 4.5. Rate of profit in Netherlands, Sweden and Japan (%), 1850–2010. Source: see appendix B.

The peripheral countries

The most dynamic periods for the peripheral countries in terms of production and trade were expressed in significant profitability differentials over the core countries. These differentials have decreased or converged toward the levels of the core, but they still remain. After a certain point, profitability in peripheral countries has fallen more markedly (from much higher levels) and has converged toward the general trend expressed by the core countries. Probably the most obvious cases are Argentina and Korea, countries that, at different historical moments, were among the most dynamic in the periphery (fig 4.6).

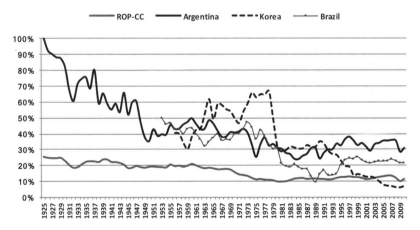

Figure 4.6. Rate of profit in core countries (ROP-CC), Argentina, Korea, and Brazil (%), 1925–2010. Source: see appendix B.

The core countries express the general trend of the profitability of capital because they show a higher development of productive forces and greater relative contribution to world production, due to a greater accumulation of capital. In this sense, the profitability differentials enjoyed in many peripheral countries, accompanied by periods of strong devalorization processes and devaluation crises, have less effect in counteracting the general downward trend—despite their higher profitability—because of their lower share in the world aggregate output. The higher levels of profitability in the periphery are countered by their lower contribution to the global mass of profits. This applies, for example, to the growth in profitability in Chile during the '70s and '80s, in Argentina for several periods after crises and devaluations, or in the United Kingdom in the interwar period.

The opposite is true for Korea in the postwar period. Korea's strong development of the productive forces and its contribution to global output coincided with an exacerbated decline in profitability. This exemplifies, again, Marx's assertion that the tendency of the rate of profit to fall expresses the development of the productive forces under the capitalist mode of production.

In recent decades, however, the relative contribution of the core countries to the world economy has declined, and peripheral Asian countries like China and Korea have gained relatively.

The world rate of profit (1955–2010)

Figure 4.7 shows the average rate of profit in fourteen countries and the average rate in the core and peripherals. As noted above, profitability in the peripheral countries has fallen more sharply than in the core. Any recovery since 1982 has been mainly in core countries, although even there it has been very slight.

The world or global rate of profit arising from these series can be measured as either a simple average or a weighted average of the different national rates. The weighted rate of profit is closer to the Marxian rate in the sense that it expresses the return on total social capital (here reduced to fourteen countries that from 1955 to 2010 accounted for 57.3 percent of the world economy). The individual rates are weighted by the share of each country in the fourteen countries' aggregate production as a whole. So the overall profitability in the national rates is adjusted by the size of the individual economies.[11]

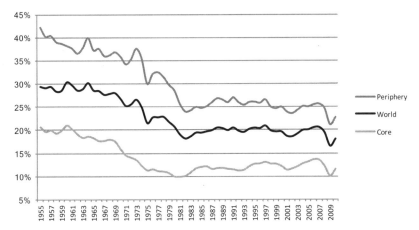

Figure 4.7. World rate of profit and rates of profit in core and peripheral countries (simple means, %), 1955–2010. Source: author's calculations.

The simple average rate has a stronger tendency to decline than the weighted one, largely due to a fall in national profitability differentials in the peripheral countries. This is shown in the remarkable fall of the simple average rate and the standard deviation of the core and peripheral rates during the '70s and early '80s, as well as in the inability to recover to previous levels. The higher relative capital expansion during the postwar period in Japan, Korea, Mexico, and Argentina, which had higher rates of profit, has been eroding (by its own action in these national spaces) those differentials. So the increasing competition between national spaces, including peripherals, in world markets lowered the differentials in profit rate, so that there have been very similar trajectories in both the simple average rate (*RoPM*) and the weighted rate without China (*RoP − Ch*).

The main dynamic element of the first decade of this twenty-first century has been the increase of capital in China. China's higher growth rate between 2001 and 2008 has boosted the weighted rate of profit including China (*RoPW*) compared to the rate excluding China (*RoP − Ch*). The behavior of the rate of profit in China has a growing influence in global capital accumulation.

China's rate of profit has been boosted by many counteracting factors to the tendency of the rate of profit to fall: the payment of the labor force below its value, the cheapening of constant capital elements, capital export, and foreign trade. But the world rate shows a peak, in 1997, in the recovery in profitability since the trough of 1982. In the period 1998–2001, rates show a steady decrease.[12] The deepening of the capitalist transformation of China since 2001 has been a focal point for capital in its attempt to break from this new downward global trend, from which China itself was not free (fig 4.8).

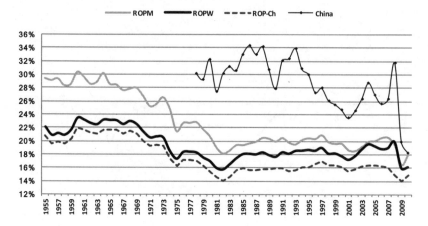

Figure 4.8. World rate of profit as simple mean (ROPM), weighted (RPOW) including and excluding China (ROP–Ch), and rate of profit in China (%), 1955–2010. Source: author's calculations.

The widening gap between the two weighted rates (with and without China) for 2002–2008 is explained by the growing contribution of China to world profitability. In 2008, the weighted rate (19.9 percent)—the closest measure to the actually existing rate—exceeds the simple average rate (19.3 percent) and the weighted rate without China (15.0 percent).[13] In that year, China's profitability rose 4.9 percentage points within the global weighted rate. (In 2001, it rose just 1.6 points.) The weighted world rate of profit including China (*RoPW*) exceeded, unlike the global measures, its 1997 peak.

China's rate of profit after the cyclical trough of 2001 reached a peak in 2008 and then collapsed in 2009, from 31.8 percent to 20.0 percent. The current crisis places the rate, both in China and globally, more or less near the trend mark of the 1998–2001 period. So the China recovery cycle of 2002–2008 seems to have ended. The same can be said about the long cycle of recovery in the global rate of profit started in 1983. The profitability crisis and China's rising tensions are thus an expression of the general crisis and the depletion of capital's ability to counteract the global trend of profitability.[14]

5. Concluding Remarks

The empirical confirmation of the tendency of the rate of profit to fall highlights the historically limited nature of capitalist production. If the rate of profit measures the vitality of the capitalist system, the logical conclusion is that it is getting closer to its end point.

There are many ways that capital can attempt to overcome crises and regenerate constantly. Periodic crises are specific to the capitalist mode of production and allow, ultimately, a partial recovery of profitability. This is a characteristic aspect of capital, and the cyclical nature of the capitalist economy. But the periodic nature of these crises has not stopped the downward trend of the rate of profit over the long term. So the arguments claiming that there is an inexhaustible capacity of capital to restore the rate of profit and its own vitality—and which therefore consider the capitalist mode of production as a natural and ahistorical phenomenon—are refuted by the empirical evidence (fig. 4.9).

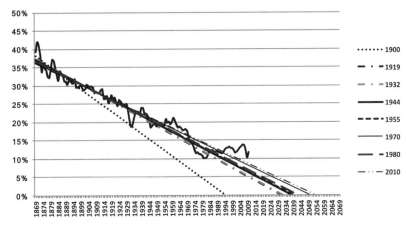

Figure 4.9. Core countries rate of profit current trend line in selected years (simple mean, %), 1869–2069. Source: author's calculations.

Obviously, there is no specific date on which to place the end point. The move toward the "end point" should be understood, rather, as a particular historical period that poses significant political challenges for the working class. But we can make projections from the linear trend of the average rate of profit in the core countries.

Two points can be highlighted from these projection exercises. As noted earlier, the trend does not develop in a steady way, but changes its slope according to the historical moment and the counteracting factors. So by 2010, the projected limit in 1900 had moved sixty-six years, from 1994 to 2053. However, the downward trend continues, increasingly reducing the number of years with respect to the projected limit. It now seems to remain fixed to the middle of this century. The inability of capital and the counteracting factors to reverse the downward tendency in recent decades is reflected in this hypothetical limit.

Appendix A: Statistics

Year	RoPM	RoPW	RoP – CH	Year	RoPM	RoPW	RoP – CH
1955	29.4%	22.1%	20.7%	1983	18.5%	16.5%	14.7%
1956	29.1%	20.9%	19.6%	1984	19.3%	17.4%	15.6%
1957	29.3%	21.2%	19.8%	1985	19.3%	18.0%	15.9%
1958	28.3%	20.9%	19.6%	1986	19.6%	18.1%	15.7%
1959	28.5%	21.7%	20.3%	1987	19.9%	18.0%	15.7%
1960	30.3%	23.5%	22.0%	1988	20.4%	18.3%	15.8%
1961	29.6%	23.2%	21.7%	1989	20.3%	17.9%	15.9%
1962	28.5%	22.7%	21.3%	1990	19.9%	17.6%	16.0%
1963	28.8%	22.5%	21.1%	1991	20.4%	18.3%	16.0%
1964	30.1%	23.2%	21.8%	1992	19.7%	18.1%	15.6%
1965	28.5%	23.2%	21.7%	1993	19.5%	18.6%	15.6%
1966	28.4%	23.2%	21.7%	1994	20.1%	18.6%	16.1%
1967	27.6%	22.6%	21.1%	1995	20.4%	18.7%	16.1%
1968	27.8%	23.0%	21.6%	1996	20.3%	18.6%	16.6%
1969	27.9%	22.6%	21.1%	1997	20.8%	19.0%	17.0%
1970	26.7%	21.4%	20.1%	1998	19.8%	18.2%	16.4%
1971	25.2%	20.5%	19.2%	1999	19.6%	18.2%	16.5%
1972	25.5%	20.7%	19.4%	2000	19.6%	17.8%	16.1%
1973	26.5%	20.5%	19.2%	2001	18.6%	17.2%	15.6%
1974	24.8%	18.5%	17.3%	2002	18.5%	17.8%	15.8%
1975	21.4%	17.3%	16.2%	2003	19.1%	18.8%	16.2%
1976	22.6%	18.3%	17.2%	2004	19.9%	19.6%	16.4%
1977	22.7%	18.4%	17.2%	2005	20.0%	19.3%	16.4%
1978	22.8%	18.3%	17.1%	2006	20.5%	18.9%	16.2%
1979	21.7%	17.5%	16.3%	2007	20.5%	19.0%	16.1%
1980	20.6%	17.0%	15.4%	2008	19.3%	19.9%	15.0%
1981	19.0%	15.9%	14.7%	2009	16.4%	16.0%	14.1%
1982	18.1%	15.7%	14.0%	2010	18.0%	16.1%	15.0%

Table 4.1. World rate of profit, simple mean (RoPM), weighted (RoPW), and weighted without China (RoP – CH), 1955–2010. Source: author's calculations.

Years	Core Countries	Germany	USA	Netherl.	Japan	UK	Sweden	Argentina
1850-54				49.2%			64.0%	
1855-59	44.6%			49.2%		26.6%	57.9%	
1860-64	43.6%			45.5%		31.3%	53.9%	
1865-69	42.9%	36.0%	30.0%	46.1%		31.0%	55.2%	
1870-74	38.2%	29.2%	31.6%	44.9%		30.9%	54.6%	
1875-79	33.7%	27.8%	35.1%	42.6%		26.3%	36.5%	
1880-84	34.6%	28.9%	33.9%	44.8%		25.8%	39.5%	
1885-89	32.5%	26.4%	17.2%	43.5%	44.6%	27.1%	35.9%	
1890-94	31.0%	25.4%	14.3%	38.2%	43.0%	26.4%	38.8%	
1895-99	30.2%	24.3%	18.9%	31.5%	39.0%	27.9%	39.3%	
1900-04	29.4%	19.5%	20.3%	32.7%	41.8%	24.1%	38.2%	
1905-09	29.0%	19.3%	20.7%	29.6%	39.6%	23.4%	41.6%	
1910-14	28.0%	18.8%	15.1%	32.9%	38.0%	23.0%	40.1%	93.3%
1915-19	26.4%		19.8%		33.7%	20.0%	32.3%	83.0%
1920-24	25.7%		20.7%	29.6%	33.8%	16.7%	28.3%	95.1%
1925-29	25.1%	15.1%	21.3%	31.5%	33.9%	21.7%	26.8%	91.8%
1930-34	20.5%	11.4%	13.0%	20.9%	32.0%	21.9%	23.7%	71.2%
1935-39	22.9%	17.5%	14.8%	21.8%	31.8%	23.6%	27.8%	69.7%
1940-44	22.2%		19.4%		35.2%	22.3%	22.6%	58.4%
1945-49	19.0%		17.0%	21.6%		15.7%	22.5%	51.4%
1950-54	19.2%	24.3%	17.2%	22.8%		12.0%	19.8%	39.0%
1955-59	20.0%	23.8%	15.3%	20.5%	33.0%	11.1%	16.2%	44.8%
1960-64	19.5%	19.8%	15.8%	17.6%	40.4%	11.0%	12.5%	45.9%
1965-69	17.9%	17.2%	16.4%	15.2%	39.4%	8.8%	10.5%	41.0%
1970-74	14.1%	14.0%	13.5%	13.7%	28.3%	6.1%	9.1%	39.7%
1975-79	11.3%	12.5%	13.4%	11.8%	19.0%	4.8%	6.1%	32.1%
1980-84	10.6%	11.0%	12.8%	12.9%	17.1%	2.7%	7.1%	27.9%
1985-89	12.0%	12.6%	14.7%	14.5%	17.4%	3.8%	8.9%	27.6%
1990-94	11.7%	13.5%	15.5%	13.7%	14.1%	4.1%	9.3%	28.9%
1995-99	12.9%	14.6%	16.6%	14.4%	11.0%	6.7%	14.1%	34.9%
2000-04	12.1%	14.8%	16.1%	13.3%	10.2%	6.7%	11.8%	32.2%
2005-09	12.6%	16.5%	15.1%	14.0%	9.2%	7.6%	13.3%	34.0%

Table 4.2. Rate of profit in core countries and Argentina, five-year averages (%), 1850–2009. Source: author's calculations.

Period	Periph. Countr.	Australia	Brazil	Chile	China	Korea	Spain	Mexico
1950–54							45.4%	32.6%
1955–59	40.1%		43.1%			36.2%	45.2%	30.1%
1960–64	38.0%	27.3%	37.4%	35.7%		47.7%	40.2%	31.8%
1965–69	36.8%	22.5%	37.0%	36.1%		55.1%	34.6%	31.1%
1970–74	35.7%	19.7%	42.8%	29.7%		55.0%	32.9%	30.1%
1975–79	31.2%	13.7%	36.2%	23.4%	29.7%	61.5%	25.1%	26.4%
1980–84	25.5%	13.3%	22.3%	26.8%	30.3%	30.5%	24.9%	27.9%
1985–89	25.8%	14.0%	15.5%	28.3%	33.1%	31.4%	31.2%	25.7%
1990–94	26.1%	15.5%	14.7%	31.9%	31.4%	30.2%	26.5%	29.5%
1995–99	25.6%	17.0%	23.5%	29.2%	27.4%	18.0%	28.1%	27.0%
2000–04	24.4%	18.5%	22.3%	24.7%	25.6%	12.3%	29.1%	30.2%
2005–09	24.4%	18.9%	22.7%	30.3%	26.2%	6.8%	26.0%	30.3%

Table 4.3. Rate of profit in peripheral countries, five-year averages (%), 1950–2009. Source: author's calculations.

Appendix B: Methodology

Argentina. Rate of profit series from Maito (2013).

Australia. Australian Bureau of Statistics (ABS), tables 34 (Income) and 56 (Capital Stock) for 1960–2011, available at www.abs.gov.au.

Brazil. Series of fixed reproductive capital and net operating surplus from chart C2 (p. 466) in Grinberg (2011) for 1953–2005, and net operating surplus and fixed reproductive capital nominal variations from IPEADATA (www.ipeadata.gov.br) for the last years.

Chile. Official capital stock series from Banco Central de Chile for 1985–2010, available at www.bcentral.cl. For previous years, capital stock from Souza and Feu (2005), investment prices from Braun et al. (2000), and reproductive construction participation from Aguilar and Collinao (2001). The resulting series were linked with the official. Net operating surplus available on CEPALSTAT.

China. Rate of profit on fixed reproductive capital from Bai et al. (2006) for 1978–2005, linked with series from Hongbin et al. (2013) for the last years.

Germany. Tables DE1C (1850–1950), DE1, and DE2b (1950–2010) from Piketty and Zucman (2013) database, available at http://piketty.pse.ens.fr/files/capitalisback/Germany.xls.

For the period 1868–1939, in which there are no data for subperiods 1914–24 and 1940–49, fixed reproductive capital at current prices is obtained from columns BX, CJ, and CN, ("Business Assets," "Public Railways," "Public Construction," excluding dwellings), of which the original source is the work of Walther Hoffmann.

For net profits as the expenditure (Column H) and income (Column W) approach, estimates of the national income series from Hoffmann differ for the first decades, so it was decided to keep income series as a base for those decades' estimates, mostly because the wage share implied with this series was more related to that estimated by official institutions covering 1925 and onward (Statistisches Bundesamt, Statistisches Jahrbuch 2012). Like the graph shows, if we had applied income shares to the national income from expenditure approach, the wage share would be lower.

The series for capital income including self-employment and labor income excluding self-employment (columns AG and AH) only covers 1925–39. For previous years, capital income excludes self-employment (column X). Thus for those years, capital income is subtracted from national income and a wage share is estimated by multiplying that result (a labor income including self-employment) by the share of salaried workers in labor force (column BP). The same operation is applied with the share of self-employment (column BQ) and the result added to total capital income. It is assumed that employees and self-employees get the same individual money income. This delivers a harmonized series of net profits including self-employment and a wage bill excluding self-employment.

For 1950–2010, data on fixed reproductive capital ("Other buildings and structures" and "Machinery and equipment") comes from table DE2b and net profits using table DE1 by substracting to GDP (column G) the amounts from depreciation (column H), net taxes on production (column I) and wages (column DG).

Japan. For 1885–1940, official series available at Hayashi and Prescott (2008) and Moriguchi and Saez (2008). We use real reproductive capital stock series from Hayashi and Prescott database (machinery, reproductive buildings, and structures—series ID O37, O38, O40) deflated by an investment price index that we build using nominal and real capital formation series (nominal gross capital formation [O73] / real gross capital formation [O52, O53, O54, O55]).

For profits, from nominal GNP (O62) the amounts of depreciation (O63), imputed net taxes on production (from 4.4 percent of GNP in 1885 to 7.7 percent in 1940) and the wage bill. The latter has been estimated taking real wage bill from Moriguchi and Saez for 1929–40 (table C1) and previous years' (1886–1928) growth rates of labor force and average income (table A0 4 and 8). As this is a wage bill deflated by a CPI index, the wage bill at current prices is estimated applying that index.

Series of fixed reproductive capital and net profits (1955–2010) are from Statistics Bureau of Japan (SBJ), available at www.stat.go.jp/english/.

Korea. Series of fixed reproductive capital and net operating surplus from chart C15 (p. 471) in Grinberg (2011) for 1956–2005, and net operating surplus and fixed reproductive capital nominal variations from KOSTAT (www.kostat.go.kr/eng) for the last years.

Mexico. Rate of profit from Mariña and Cámara (2016).

Netherlands. Income (pp. 172–74) and fixed reproductive capital series from Smits et al. (2000) for 1850–1913. Profit series from Centraal Bureau voor de Statistiek (CBS) (www.cbs.nl) and fixed reproductive capital from Groote et al. (1996) and CBS (for the period 1921–2010) using perpetual inventory method with linear depreciation and nineteen years for machinery and forty years for reproductive buildings and structures. Real fixed reproductive capital in reproductive buildings and structure has been deflated by CBS building costs. For the period 1921–69, we assumed machinery prices variations as 70–75 percent of the rate of variation in CPI.

Spain. Rate of profit over fixed reproductive capital from Izquierdo (2006) for 1954–2002, and net operating surplus and fixed reproductive capital nominal variations from Instituto Nacional de Estadística (INE) (www.ine.es) for the last years.

Sweden. Series of fixed reproductive capital and net operating surplus from Edvinsson (2005) for 1850–2000, and net operating surplus and fixed reproductive capital nominal variations from Statistiska Centralbyrån (SCB) (www.scb.se) for the last years.

United Kingdom. Fixed reproductive capital as real fixed reproductive capital deflated by investment prices from Bank of England, "Three Centuries of Data" series (http://www.bankofengland.co.uk), and net operating surplus from Piketty and Zucman (2013) for 1855–2010, available at http://piketty.pse.ens.fr/files/capitalisback/UK.xls.

United States. Fixed reproductive capital from section 1, table 1.1 and lines 5–6 and 11–12 from BEA official estimates of capital stock. Net operating surplus estimated as GDP (section 1, table 1.1.5, line 1) minus compensation of employees (section 6, tables 6.2.A and 6.2.B, lines 1), net taxes on production (section 3, tables 3.5 and 3.13, lines 1), and consumption of fixed capital (section 1, table 1.3, lines 4–10) for 1929–2010. Linked according to variation in the rate of profit from Duménil and Lévy database for period 1869–1928, available at www.jourdan.ens.fr/levy/uslt4x.txt.

Core countries weighted rate of profit and composition of capital / weighted world rate of profit. The rates were weighted by GDP from Maddison tables. For 2009–2010, series were expanded using UNSTAT real GDP growth rates, according to the share on the aggregated GDP of the fourteen countries.

Each country share on the weighted rate of profit is given by its rate of profit multiplied by its share in the sample GDP. The sum of all is equal to the weighted world rate of profit.

Figure 4.1. Labor time to produce one pound (of 2006) in minutes was estimated as (1/*real net value added per hour*) × 60. Total worked hours as totally employment multiplied by weekly worked hours (both available in "Supply side data" sheet of the Bank of England's "Three Centuries of Data" series) and fifty weeks imputed. Volume of fixed capital per hour was estimated as *real fixed reproductive capital / total worked hours*.

Note that the reduction in this labor time did not consider some qualitative aspects. For instance, as real GDP evolution had mostly covered quantitative growth, if in some year one computer were produced with a processing capacity of one megahertz, and the next year three computers were produced with double this processing capacity, statistics tended to measure mostly the increase from one to three computers, rather than the increase from one megahertz to six megahertz of processing capacity. In this regard our measure clearly underestimates the reduction of labor time, which would be much more pronounced.

Notes

1   "When the stocks of many rich merchants are turned into the same trade, their mutual competition naturally tends to lower its profit; and when there is a like

increase of stock in all the different trades carried on in the same society, the same competition must produce the same effect in them all" (Smith 2005, p. 77). "The natural tendency of profits is to fall; for in the progress of society and wealth, the additional quantity of food required is obtained by the sacrifice of more and more labour" (Ricardo 2001, pp. 78–79).

2   In this sense, only Marxian theory could establish a proper explanation of this historical tendency of the mode of production that other schools recognized but failed to explain because the Marxian theory was the one to define in a scientific way not only the determinations of value, but a proper definition of constant and variable capital, which until Marx were always confused.

3   Harman (1981) explained it in the following terms: "In the period 1880 to 1913 something like 15% of the British national product went into overseas investment. If invested in Britain, this would have had to increase the pressure for capital intensive investment domestically and to have reduced the rate of profit. . . .This 'outside' existed when capitalism was still restricted to the Western edge of the Eurasian land mass and to part of North America, with precapitalist forms of exploitation dominating even in those parts of the rest of the world which were integrated into the capitalist world market. But once imperialism had done its work, and capitalist forms of exploitation dominated more or less everywhere the "outside" no longer existed. In a world of multinational corporations, surplus value which flows away from one area reducing the upward pressure on the organic composition of capital, merely serves to increase the upward pressure elsewhere. The average *world* rate of profit falls. The world system is driven to stagnation just as the national economy was in Marx's time."

4   See for instance Sweezy (1946, pp. 96–108), Robinson (1942, pp. 35–42), and more recently Heinrich (2013) and Reuten and Thomas (2011). Heinrich suggested that even with decreasing surplus value rate or profit share, in order to confirm the law, the capital value or composition should not decrease at a higher rate than surplus value rate.

5   "If the normal working day amounts to 8 hours, no increase in productive power can squeeze more surplus labour out of the worker than 8 minus as many hours as correspond to the production of the wage. If the technique of production succeeded in reducing the necessary labour-time from e.g. 4 hours to half an hour, then surplus labour would still not come to more than 15/16 of the working day (with an 8-hour day); it would increase from 4 to 7; i.e. not even double. At the same time the productivity of labour would have to grow enormously. . . . The larger the surplus-value of capital before the increase of productive force, the larger the amount of presupposed surplus labour, or surplus-value of capital; or the smaller the fractional part of the working day which forms the equivalent of the worker, which expresses necessary labour, the smaller is the increase in surplus-value which capital obtains from the increase of productive force. Its surplus-value rises, but in an ever smaller relation to the development of the productive forces" (Rosdolsky 1977, pp. 408–9).

6   The assertion that Marx did not propose a "breakdown theory" is primarily attributable to the revisionist interpretation of Marx before and after World War I. Rosa Luxemburg and Henryk Grossman both rendered inestimable theoretical services by insisting, as against the revisionists, on the breakdown theory" (Rosdolsky 1977, p. 382).

7   To affirm the existence of the tendency of the rate of profit to fall in no way implies the existence of a "permanent crisis" or that the rate of profit falls always. That crises may be preceded by a period of growth in the rate of profit does not deny the validity of the tendency. Nor does any increase in output necessarily imply a growth in the rate of profit. The postwar decades showed high economic growth in most economies, but over that particular period the rate of profit declined steadily, mainly due to the very basic reason that the share of investment in GDP increased more than GDP rose. Recent decades have shown a partial recovery of profitability in conjunction with lower GDP growth rates compared to postwar decades.

8   Although this process intensifies the equalization of the rates of profit, the determination of the general rate of profit is dependent not on competition but on the movement of capital in general.

9   There are, however, performance differences related to technical characteristics of production in certain branches. For example, the production and distribution of electricity and other services requires significant amounts of fixed capital relative to variable capital. Thus, in general, branches of this type of industry have had historically lower rates than the rest. The trend toward the equalization of the rate of profit between such branches and others is slower than between manufacturing branches. However, this tendency to equalization does take place over the long term. It happens not so much by a sustained increase in branches with high fixed capital requirements in infrastructure, but by the relative decline in the rate of profit in the other branches, as Duménil and Lévy (2002) have found in the American case.

10   Germany, the United States, the Netherlands, Japan, the United Kingdom, and Sweden are considered core countries, while Argentina, Australia, Brazil, Chile, China, Korea, Spain, and Mexico are considered peripheral.

11   "Since the general rate of profit is not only determined by the average rate of profit in each sphere, but also by the distribution of the total social capital among the different individual spheres, and since this distribution is continually changing, it becomes another constant cause of change in the general rate of profit" (Marx 1999b, ch. 9).

12   Usually, explanations of the crisis in the peripheral countries during this period (Southeast Asia, Russia, Brazil, Argentina) have not even suggested a relationship with the cycle of declining profitability, but have concentrated on characterizing it as a crisis caused by purely financial or economic policy issues. This is the same reading that has prevailed as an explanation for the current global crisis.

13   The China series starts in 1978. So for earlier years (1955–77), the weighted global rate excludes China; however, China was marginal in global capital before 1978. Also, the expansion of capital in China before the 1990s was relatively minor. Thus it is only since the 1990s that China was a factor in the global rate.

14   Although many analyses recognize that China's economy presents new issues, most underestimate the growing problems facing capital accumulation in that country, since China still has high GDP growth rates. But this only refers to the expansion of physical production. It does not capture the abrupt decline in the rate of profit. China's investment rate is around 46 percent of GDP, according to the World Bank. So in the coming years, a further decline in the rate of profit in China can be expected, most likely in a similar way to what happened in Japan and Korea.

References

Aguilar, X. and M. P. Collinao (2001) "Cálculo del stock de capital para Chile 1985–2000," *DT*, No 133, Banco Central de Chile.

Bai, C. E., C. T. Hsieh, and Y. Qian (2006) "The Return to Capital in China," NBER Working Paper, No 12.755.

Braun, J., et al. (2000) "Economía chilena 1810–1995. Estadísticas históricas," *DT*, No 187, Instituto de Economía, Universidad Católica de Chile.

Chan-Lee, J. and H. Sutch (1985) "Profits and Rates of Return in OECD Countries," OECD Economic and Statistics Department Working Paper, No 20.

Collins, W. and J. Williamson (2001) "Capital-Goods Prices and Investment 1870–1950," *Journal of Economic History*, Vol 61, No 1.

Duménil, G. and D. Lévy (2002) "The Profit Rate: Where and How Much Did It Fall, USA 1948–2000," available at http://www.jourdan.ens.fr/levy/.

———. (2005) "From Prosperity to Neoliberalism: Europe Before and After the Structural Crisis of the 1970s," available at http://www.jourdan.ens.fr/levy/.

Edvinsson, R. (2005) "Historical National Accounts for Sweden 1800–2000," Stockholm University.

Grinberg, N. (2011) "Transformations in the Korean and Brazilian Processes of Capitalist Development Between the mid-1950s and the mid-2000s: The Political Economy of Late Industrialisation," PhD thesis, London School of Economics and Political Science (LSE).

Groote, P., R. Albers, and H. De Jong (1996) "A Standardized Time Series of the Stock of Fixed Capital in the Netherlands, 1900–1995," GGDC Working Paper, No 25.

Grossman, H. (2005) *The Law of Accumulation and Breakdown of the Capitalist System*, available at https://www.marxists.org/archive/grossman/1929/breakdown.

Harman, C. (1981) "Marx's Theory of Crisis and its Critics," *International Socialism*, Vol 2. No 11.

Hayashi, F. and Prescott, E. (2008) "The Depressing Effect of Agricultural Institutions on the Prewar Japanese Economy," *Journal of Political Economy*, Vol 116, No 4.

Hongbin, Q., J. Wang, and S. Junwel (2013) "Return on Capital: Perception vs Reality," *HSBC Global Research*.

Li, M., F. Xiao, and A. Zhu (2007) "Long Waves, Institutional Changes and Historical Trends: A Study of the Long Term Movement of the Profit Rate in the Capitalist World-Economy," *Journal of World-System Research*, Vol 13, No 1.

Maito, E. E. (2013) "La Argentina y la tendencia descendente de la tasa de ganancia 1910–2011," *Revista Realidad Económica*, No 275.

Mariña F., A. (2006) "La onda larga capitalista en España (1954–2002)," *Revista Sociedad Brasileña de Economía Política*.

Mariña F., A. and S. Cámara (2016) "The Structural Causes of the Severity of the World Crisis in Mexico," in J. Santarcángelo, ed., *Latin America after the Financial Crisis*, Palgrave Macmillan.

Marquetti, A., E. M. Filho, and V. Lautert (2010) "The Rate of Profit in Brazil 1953–2003," *Review of Radical Political Economics*, Vol 42, No 4.

Marx, K. (1999a) *Capital*, Vol 1, available at http://www.marxists.org/archive/marx/works/1867-c1.

———. (1999b) *Capital*, Vol 3, available at http://www.marxists.org/archive/marx/works/1894-c3.

Mattick, P. (1974) *Economic Crisis and Crisis Theory*, available at https://www.marxists.org/archive/mattick-paul/1974/crisis.

Moriguchi, C. and E. Saez (2008) "The Evolution of Income Concentration in Japan 1886–2005: Evidence from Income Tax Statistics," *Review of Economics and Statistics*, Vol 90, No 4.

Oribe Stemmer, J. (1989) "Freight Rates in the Trade between Europe and South America 1840–1914," *Journal of Latin American Studies*, Vol 21, No 1.

Piketty, T. (2014) *Capital in the 21st Century*, Harvard University Press.

Piketty, T. and G. Zucman (2013) *Capital Is Back: Wealth-Income Ratios in Rich Countries 1700–2010*, available at http://piketty.pse.ens.fr/files/PikettyZucman2013WP.pdf.

Reuten, G. and P. Thomas (2011) "From the 'fall of the rate of profit' in the *Grundrisse* to the cyclical development of the profit rate in *Capital*," *Science and Society*, Vol 75, No 1.

Ricardo, D. (2001) *On the Principles of Political Economy and Taxation*, Batoche Books.

Robinson, J. (1942) *An Essay on Marxian Economics*, Macmillan.

Rosdolsky, R. (1977) "The Making of Marx's *Capital*," Pluto Press.

Smith, A. (2005) "An Inquiry into the Nature and Causes of the Wealth of Nations," Pennsylvania State University Electronic Classic Series.

Smits, J. P., E. Horlings, and J. L. van Zanden (2000) "Dutch GNP and its Components, 1800–1913," GGDC Monograph Series, No 5.

Souza, M. and A. Feu (2005) "Capital Stock in Latin America: 1950–2000," *E&E*, No 50.

Sun, W., X. Chang and G. Xiao (2011) "Understanding China's High Investment Rate and FDI Levels: A Comparative Analysis of the Return to Capital in China, the United States and Japan," *USITC Journal of International Commerce and Economics*.

Sweezy, P. (1946) *The Theory of Capitalist Development*, Dobson Books.

Timmer, M. and B. V. Ark (2002) "Capital Formation and Foreign Direct Investment in Korea and Japan: Copying with Diminishing Returns?," in J. Lindblad, ed., Asian Growth and Foreign Capital: Case Studies for Eastern Asia, Aksant.

Zachariah, D. (2009) "Determinants of the Average Profit Rate and the Trajectory of Capitalist Economies," *Bulletin of Political Economy*, Vol 3, No 1.

CHAPTER 5

JAPAN'S "LOST" TWO DECADES: A MARXIST ANALYSIS OF PROLONGED CAPITALIST STAGNATION

Takuya Sato

1. Introduction[1]

According to official government statements, the Japanese economy, the third largest in the world, has definitively emerged from the severe recession triggered by the 2007–2008 global financial crisis. The Economic and Social Research Institute, linked to the Japanese Cabinet Office, reports that in Japan the "trough" of the long recession was experienced in March 2009. Furthermore, the Nikkei Stock Average price soared to ¥20,000 in April 2015, a high point not reached in fifteen years. Largely on the strength of the Nikkei's performance, the country is now regarded as having achieved an "expansion" of over five years' duration.

Despite the upbeat assessments by Japanese politicians and business elites, however, the reality is that Japan's crisis of severely depressed growth rates—a crisis which is now over two decades old—is far from over. Figure 5.1 shows that the average real growth rate of gross domestic product has long been and remains very low, averaging between 0 and 2 percent from 1992 to 2013, depending on the measure used. The only significant annual exceptions were the severe *contractions* of 1998 and of 2008–2009. In fact, the value of Japan's GDP has stagnated at around ¥500 trillion for two decades, and there is no sign of this stagnation being overcome.

Figure 5.1 also reveals that the *nominal* growth rate of Japan's economy is actually lower than the *real* growth rate for almost every year across these two decades. A price index that has often been negative suggests a protracted problem of "deflation." In response, the Bank of Japan (the Japanese central bank) has pursued long-term monetary policies intended to stimulate inflation and economic growth, particularly since 2000. During the preceding decade, in response to the country's recession of the early 1990s, the Bank of Japan had pioneered the policy of "quantitative easing," later adopted by central banks in several Western countries—above all the US Federal Reserve—in response to the "Great Recession" of 2008–2009.

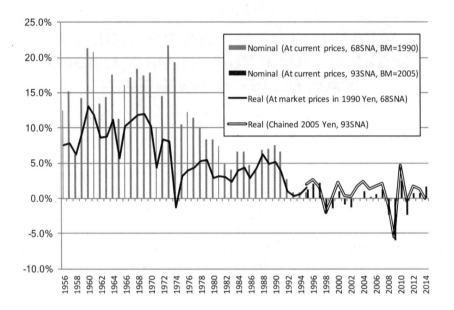

Figure 5.1. Annual growth rate of real and nominal GDP (%), 1956–2014. Sources: from 1956 to 1995, the Cabinet Office, national accounts for 1998 (68SNA, benchmark year = 1990); from 1995 on, national accounts for 2014 (93SNA, benchmark year =2005), http://www.esri.cao.go.jp/en/sna/data/kakuhou/files/kako_top.html.

In contrast to most other G7 countries, the crisis of 2007–2008 in Japan followed an extremely weak expansion, not an actual economic "boom." This expansion featured an annual average growth rate of real GDP of just 2.1 percent (see fig. 5.2), despite being the "longest" phase of expansion since World War II. According to official "business-cycle dating" by the Japanese Cabinet Office, this (weak) "expansion" had a duration of no less than six years.

These facts demonstrate that the Japanese economy has suffered extraordinary stagnation since the beginning of the 1990s—indeed, they suggest that stagnation has become the "new normal" for Japan. At the same time, they suggest that the fundamental issue requiring serious analysis is not the conjunctural collapse of 2007–2008, but the *prolonged structural crisis* afflicting Japanese capitalism, which is itself a manifestation of a larger global crisis.

Despite the long-term lackluster condition of the Japanese economy, the nominal profit rate has nevertheless risen since the late 1990s (see fig. 5.5). The profit rate in 2014 was about 26 percent, a level higher than that in the booming 1980s. It is altogether remarkable that profit rates under conditions of such protracted stagnation could reach levels comparable to those of one of the biggest economic booms in Japan's history, the bubble economy of 1986–91, which registered an annual average GDP growth rate of 5.6 percent.

The glaring contradiction between the apparent recovery of the rate of profit and unprecedentedly prolonged economic stagnation requires explanation. In particular, it is necessary to give a coherent answer to the following two questions: On the one hand, why has Japan's economy suffered from such prolonged stagnation? On the other, why has the average profit rate nevertheless recovered, despite such poor economic conditions?

In my view, these questions should by no means warrant an abandonment of Marx's law of the tendency of the rate of profit to fall. On the contrary, the conceptual framework of the LTRPF and Marx's labor-value theory is indispensable to an adequate explanation of the *recovery* of the rate of profit, which is a feature not only of the financial sector but of non-financial (productive) sectors as well.[2] In addition, once we understand the structure of the law we can more adequately explain why the vicissitudes of the rate of profit have caused such persistent economic malaise in Japan, and why its recovery has been associated with *worsening stagnation*. Accordingly, this chapter will seek to show that the fundamental cause of the Japanese economy's prolonged stagnation has been capitalist behavior involving the pursuit of higher profits through a strategy of *restrained investment* in the "real," productive economy.

In section 2, I show how restrained productive investment over the past two decades has weakened the Japanese economy. In section 3, I discuss how this restrained productive investment also led to a recovery in profitability (consistent with Marx's theory). These discussions will serve to reveal the *mechanisms* that brought about the rise in the rate of profit and prolonged stagnation. In section 4, some theoretical and empirical issues pertaining to these mechanisms will be discussed. Finally, in section 5, I will conclude with some considerations about the most "fundamental" contradiction of Japanese capitalism and the actuality of Marx's LTRPF.

2. Low Growth in Investment Leading to Prolonged Stagnation

As previously noted, a peculiar feature of the expansion period (January 2002–October 2007) leading up to the 2007–2008 crisis was that this expansion was too weak to be defined as a "real expansion," much less a "boom." Figure 5.2 indicates that the annual growth rate of GDP was no more than 2.1 percent and that the growth rate of consumption was extremely low at just 1.1 percent.

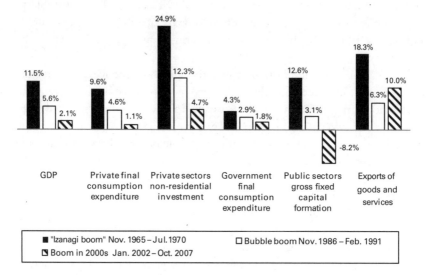

Figure 5.2. Annual average growth rate of real GDP (%) for three booms. Sources: for the "Izanagi boom," the Cabinet Office, national accounts for 1998 (68SNA, benchmark year = 1990); for the other booms, national accounts for 2007 (93 SNA, benchmark year = 2000), http://www.esri.cao.go.jp/en/sna/kakuhou/kakuhou_top.html.

A frequently cited reason for the weak consumption growth has been that employee compensation failed to grow from 2002 to 2006. While accepting this point, the restrained growth rate of investment (in particular, private nonresidential investment) during the economic expansion period must be emphasized. The growth rate of investment in that period was only 4.7 percent, while the rate was 24.9 percent during the "Izanagi boom" from October 1965 to July 1970, and 12.3 percent during the bubble economy from November 1986 to February 1991.

Let us consider some of the features of this restrained investment. According to figure 5.3, gross capital formation has been stagnant since 1992. Such low investment reflects low growth in aggregate demand, and in particular low demand for "capital goods" (the means of production). In addition, low levels of investment involved low demand for labor power, leading to low levels of consumption. Because investment and consumption are the major components of GDP on the demand side, their low growth rates must result in low overall GDP growth.

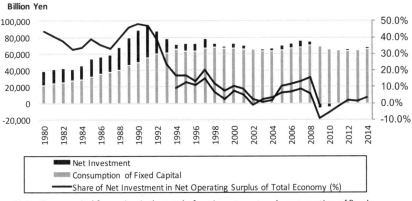

Note: Gross capital formation is the total of net investment and consumption of fixed capital.

Figure 5.3. Gross capital formation and net investment (private nonresidential investment), bn yen, 1980–2014. Sources: from 1980 to 1993 (and from 1980 to 2009 of the share of net investment in net operating surplus of total economy), the Cabinet Office, national accounts for 2009 (benchmark year = 2000); from 1994 on, national accounts for 2013 (benchmark year = 2005).

Furthermore, the volume of net investment dropped dramatically after the collapse of the bubble economy at the beginning of 1990s. Between 1998 and 2006, the level of net investment was much lower than before, and almost zero for 2002–2004 and 2009–2014. This means that recent investment is only for replacement of fixed assets due to capital consumption, and that it does not involve any net addition to existing assets.

The ratio of net investment to the net operating surplus in figure 5.3 was also around 0 percent in 2002–2004, and it stood at only 15 percent at the peak of the last expansion in 2008—not more than during the prolonged period of stagnation in the 1990s. This underscores that capitalists did not expend the operating surplus on expansion of plant and equipment. The net operating surplus is calculated by subtracting fixed capital consumption from gross operating surplus, which is one of the major components of the "value added" produced within a country. Although the net operating surplus is not synonymous with the category of surplus value in Marxist economics, these circumstances suggest that there has been little or no real capital accumulation over the course of these two decades.

Marx defines accumulation as the addition of a part of currently produced surplus value to existing capital—that is to say, the use of a part of surplus value to purchase additional means of production and/or labor power for the next production period. Through the process of accumulation, the overall level of production expands—a dynamic known as "expanded reproduction." If no true accumulation occurs in Marx's sense, then we can only speak of "simple," not "expanded," reproduction. Figure 5.3 implies that simple reproduction was a frequent feature of Japan's economy between 1997 and 2014 (for example, in 1999, 2002–2004, and 2009–2014). Such economic conditions are highly abnormal because the capitalist mode of production is historically associated with expanded reproduction.

Figure 5.4 serves to illuminate the reasons for the restrained investment and consequent lack of accumulation. First, the level of production capacity was very high throughout the 1990s, even after the collapse of the bubble economy at the beginning of that decade. If this collapse had been a "normal" cyclical crisis, it would have destroyed the excess production capacity, and this forcible destruction would have prepared an ensuing economic expansion. However, the high level of excess capacity persisted for a decade! Consequently, capacity utilization dropped steeply from an index of over 120 to around 105 at the beginning of the 1990s, and this low level persisted through the 1990s. Technically, these indices are not the "actual" utilization rates. If the actual utilization rate is calculated by using the figures referenced by the Ministry of Economy, Trade and Industry, which is 76.7 percent in the manufacturing sector in 2010, the actual rate of capacity utilization dropped from over 92 percent to around 80 percent.

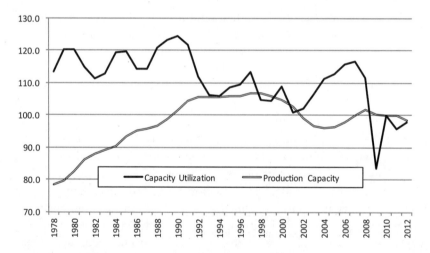

Figure 5.4. Indices of production capacity and capacity utilization in manufacturing (2010 = 100), 1978–2012. Source: Ministry of Economy, Trade and Industry—linked indices of production capacity and capacity utilization, seasonally unadjusted data, from January 1978 to December 2012. The figure is changed into an annual figure by weighted averaging for every twelve months. http://www.meti.go.jp/statistics/tyo/iip/b2010_result-2.html.

Such a fall in the level of capacity utilization leads to a fall in so-called "capital productivity" and profitability, as will be described in section 3. Excess capacity and the low level of capacity utilization of the 1990s thereby produced a very low level of net investment (see fig. 5.3).

Second, economic conditions changed greatly in the 2000s. The rate of capacity utilization rose from 100 in 2001 to nearly 120 in 2007, accompanied by an expansion of production, during the longest economic "boom" since World War II. However, this expansion failed to induce an increase in investment or an expansion of production capacity. On the contrary, the overall level of production capacity actually decreased in the 2000s. The index of production capacity went down from around 105 to around 95 at the beginning of the 2000s, and it was unable to recover to more than 100 even at the peak of the economic "boom" in 2007.

For production capacity to decrease in absolute terms during an economic boom is a very unusual situation in a capitalist economy. However, the parallel rise in utilization had a positive impact on capital efficiency and profitability. Under conditions of no growth in net investment, the growth in production naturally led to a rise in profitability, and *that* is the fundamental reason that Japanese capitalists restrained their investments even as the level of production went up. (I will discuss the relationship between restrained investment and rising profitability further in the next section.)

To summarize, capitalists restrained their productive investment in the 1990s and the 2000s, and this restrained investment brought about a low-growth economy. There was no net investment, and thus there was no significant accumulation. Consequently, the reproduction of capital in Japan during this period took the form of "simple reproduction." This provides the general background to Japan's two decades of stagnation.[3]

3. Restrained Investment Brings About Recovery in the Rate of Profit

Although restrained investment exerted downward pressure on the Japanese national economy, it also brought about a recovery in the non-financial rate of profit after the end of the 1990s (see fig. 5.5). While the rate of profit trended downward overall between the mid-1960s and 2014, after hitting a low point of 10 percent in 1998–99, it rose to almost 20 percent in 2006 and to 26 percent in 2014. The rate of profit in 2014 was higher than its highest point during Japan's bubble economy of the late 1980s. This is quite remarkable, as the annual average growth rate of GDP was 5.6 percent during the bubble economy, compared to 2.1 percent during the boom of 2002–2006 (see fig. 5.2) and less than 2 percent in 2014 (see fig. 5.1).[4]

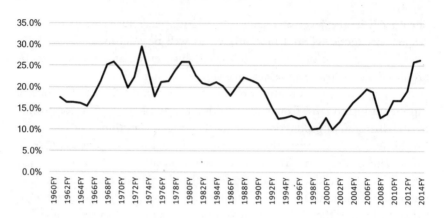

Figure 5.5. Non-financial rate of profit (S/C),
1960–2014. Source: see appendix.

Why did the rate of profit rise despite the persistence of stagnation in the 2000s? The most important reason was the restrained investment in the "real economy" during this period. Two processes were crucially involved. The first process was a rise in the ratio of new value (N, the sum of variable capital and surplus value) to constant capital stock (C) brought about by the lower growth of C compared to N, alongside the increase in capacity utilization. The second was a rise in the rate of surplus value (S/V), and in the share of surplus value in relation to total new value (S/N), by a fall in real wages resulting from weak demand for labor power.

According to Marx's theory, the rate of profit (RP, expressed as S/C)[5] is co-determined by the organic composition of capital (OCC, expressed as C/N)[6] and the rate of surplus value (RS, expressed as S/V) or the share of surplus value in new value (S/N).

Consider the following formula:

$$S/C = N/C \times S/N$$

Here, C is constant capital stock, S is surplus value, and N is new value (the sum of variable capital—the wage bill of *productive* workers—and surplus value). On the one hand, if N/C (the ratio of new value to constant capital) increases, the rate of profit S/C also increases. N/C is the inverse of OCC (C/N). Therefore, if the OCC decreases, the rate of profit S/C increases. On the other hand, if S/N (the share of surplus value) increases, then S/C also increases.

These two determinants of the rate of profit, N/C and S/N, shall now be explored empirically in relation to the Japanese economy.

The N/C ratio (the inverse of the OCC)

Figure 5.6 shows that the ratio of "new value to constant capital" (*N/C*)—the inverse of the OCC—has recovered since the beginning of the 2000s, after a long period of decline.

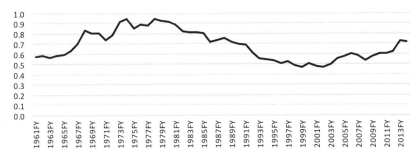

Figure 5.6. Ratio of new value to constant capital stock (N/C), 1961–2013. Source: see appendix.

Figure 5.7, which compares the annual growth rates of constant capital stock and new value, indicates that a low level of investment is the basic cause of the rise in *N/C*. While the trend lines for both variables decline dramatically from 1961 to 2014, the growth rate of *C* has been lower than the growth rate of *N* in almost every year since the end of the 1990s. This means that capitalist corporations have restrained their investment in constant capital stock (fixed capital assets), allowing the *N/C* ratio to rise in the 2000s, even though this was a period of modest growth in new value.

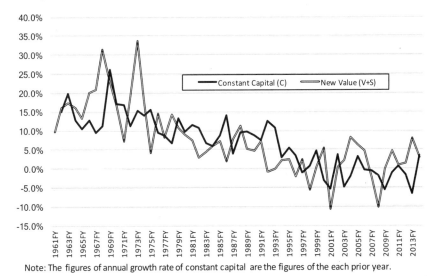

Note: The figures of annual growth rate of constant capital are the figures of the each prior year.

Figure 5.7. Annual growth rates of constant capital and new value (%), 1961–2013. Source: see appendix.

Figure 5.6 reveals two periods of a rise in the ratio of new value to constant capital. One is in the 1960s, and the other is from 2002 to 2014. However, these two periods are otherwise very different. In the 1960s, the growth rate of constant capital was very high, fluctuating between 10 and 25 percent for almost every year. Even so, the ratio of new value to constant capital rose because the annual growth rate in new value was much higher than that of constant capital. By contrast, the 2000s saw a flat trend in the annual growth rate of constant capital stock, allowing for a rise in N/C.

I will consider N/C to be an index of "capital productivity" here. To be sure, this expression is unacceptable from the standpoint of the labor theory of value because the latter holds that new value is created solely by living labor, not by "capital." However, this expression has the advantage of allowing us to see that a rise in "capital productivity" (defined as N/C) can produce a rise in the rate of profit. In a "healthy" capitalist economy, productivity can rise with the introduction of new technology alongside investments to replace or expand existing fixed capital assets. But during the 2000s, a strategy of highly restrained investment brought about a recovery in "capital productivity" by *decreasing* the denominator of N/C. Such a strategy reflected the negative attitude of capitalists toward investment in constant capital stock while making possible a recovery in productivity (N/C) and with it the rate of profit (S/C).

When N/C rises, capacity utilization also rises, as new value is now being produced with smaller capacity.[7] As mentioned above, capital utilization went down in the 1990s and up in the 2000s (see fig. 5.4). This movement of capital utilization is in fact parallel to that of N/C. Because N/C is one of the determinants of the rate of profit, both capital utilization and the rate of profit went down in the 1990s and then up in the 2000s.

Thus, despite the continuing lethargic growth of the national economy (as measured in GDP), Japanese capitalists are now enjoying higher rates of profit—around 20 percent in 2006–2007 and 26 percent in 2014—than they did during the bubble economy of the 1980s.

Share of surplus value (or the rate of surplus value)

Figure 5.8 indicates the trend for the share of surplus value in relation to total new value (S/N), which is the second determinant of the rate of profit. The figure shows that the surplus-value share of new value has gone up since the end of the 1990s.[8] It peaks in 2006 at around 33 percent, and at 36 percent in 2014—figures *higher* than during the booming 1960s.

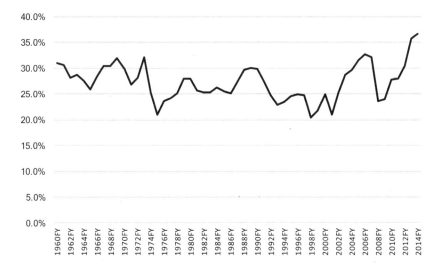

Figure 5.8. Share of surplus value in new value (S/N, %), 1960–2014. Source: see appendix.

What accounts for the recovery in *S/N*? Once again, it was the climate of restrained investment. Restrained investment inhibited employment growth, and this exerted a downward pressure on wages. When demand for labor power is weak, the working class has little choice but to accept a decline in wages. Moreover, large numbers of workers are employed precariously, that is to say, they are "underemployed." An increase in underemployment, in turn, exerts a downward pressure on the wage level of regular workers. This is one of the effects of what Marx calls relative surplus population.

Figure 5.9 shows that the level of employment has gone down since 1998. Declining demand for labor power must produce a downward pressure on real wage rates. Accordingly, real wage indices also started to decrease from 1998 onward. Wage reductions raise the share of surplus value in new value (*S/N*), and thus the rate of profit (*S/C*). This is the second contribution of restrained investment to a rising profit rate.

With regard to the rate of surplus value, two additional issues should be mentioned. The first is the relationship between Marx's concepts of the "technical composition of capital" (TCC) and "relative surplus population." The second is the relationship of labor productivity to both the real wage rate and the rate of surplus value.

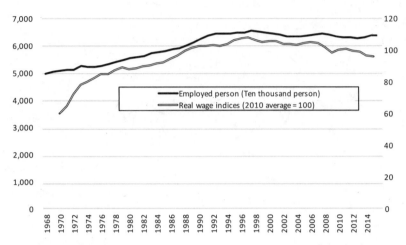

Note. Real wage indices are for establishments with 30 employees or more and based on total cash earnings. Employed person includes employees, self-employed workers and family workers of all industries.

Figure 5.9. Employed persons (× 10,000, LHS) and real wages (%, 2010 average = 100, RHS), 1968–2014. Sources: (1) for real wage indices, Ministry of Health, Labor and Welfare (2016), monthly labor survey, historical data, http://www.e-stat.go.jp/SG1/estat/List.do?lid=000001150075; (2) for employed persons, Ministry of Internal Affairs and Communications, labor force survey, historical data, annual average figures, results of whole Japan for employed person and employment rate by age, five-year group, since 1968, http://www.stat.go.jp/english/data/roudou/lngindex.htm.

First, the TCC as defined by Marx is the ratio of capital assets (dead labor) to productive living labor (conceived in terms of physical magnitudes). If capitalists replace living labor with means of production (for example, machinery and other equipment), the TCC will rise, and with it the OCC. Therefore, the TCC's level is a significant indicator of technical progress in production processes. I will represent the TCC here as the ratio of fixed assets to employed persons.

Figure 5.10 shows that the trend of the TCC (in terms of its absolute *level*) has been rising since 1980. However, it also shows that the rising trend of the TCC has slowed down since around 1990. In order to highlight this slowdown in the rising trend of the TCC and consider its implications, the annual growth *rate* of the TCC is presented in figure 5.11.

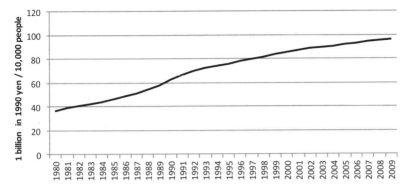

Note: TCC is calculated based on net fixed assets of financial and non-financial corporations. Employed person includes employees, self-employed workers and family workers of all industries.

Figure 5.10. Technical composition of capital (TCC: net fixed assets / employed person), 1980–2009. Sources: for fixed assets, national accounts for 2009; for employed person, labor force survey.

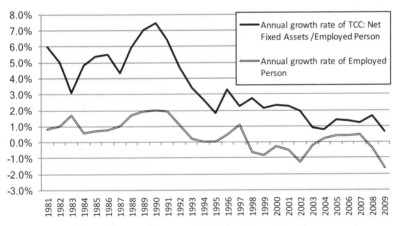

Figure 5.11. Annual growth rates of TCC and employed persons (net fixed assets / employed person, %), 1981–2009. Source: see figure 5.10.

Figure 5.11 shows that Japanese corporations invested more in fixed assets than labor power until around 1990. Between 1981 and 1990, the TCC grew between 3 and 8 percent annually. However, after 1990 the annual growth rate of the TCC declined considerably, dropping to an average of under 2 percent between 2001 and 2009. Such a decline in the growth rate of the TCC is historically associated with an increase in employment, since a fall in the growth rate of the TCC involves a rise in the ratio of employed persons to means of production. However, that is not what happened during this period in Japan. On the contrary, the growth rate of employment has stagnated or fallen since the early 1990s. Thus, the decline in the annual growth rate of the TCC has not entailed an increase in employment in Japan.

According to Marx's theory of relative surplus population (aka the "industrial reserve army"), if the TCC rises then relative surplus population should also increase, placing downward pressure on wage rates as capital accumulation proceeds. This is what one might call the "normal" effect of a growing relative surplus population on a "healthy" capitalist economy.

However, in today's Japanese economy, despite the slow growth of the TCC, there has been an expansion of the relative surplus population (encompassing both unemployed and underemployed people). Figure 5.11 reveals that the annual growth rate in employed persons has actually been negative for many years since 1998, suggesting that the relative surplus population increased during this period.

A key aspect to Marx's theory of relative surplus population is that even under conditions of strong growth and capital accumulation, a relative surplus population is generated by a rising TCC. However, the current Japanese situation is actually much worse for the working class than anything Marx imagined. Since the mid-1990s, the Japanese economy has been characterized by very weak accumulation accompanied by a TCC that is nevertheless rising, albeit modestly. Under conditions of a gradually rising TCC and weak accumulation, the relative surplus population can easily increase.

Second, the decline in the growth rate of the TCC implies that technological progress has slowed down. As mentioned in the previous section, restrained investment in means of production can raise so-called "capital productivity" by reducing the denominator in the formula N/C. However, such a slowdown in investment in production processes should also bring about a slowdown in the growth of labor productivity. Of course, one of the major reasons for low growth of labor productivity is the low rate of growth of GDP since the 1990s. For even if productivity in production process is high and rising owing to technological advances, a low level of demand for products depresses aggregate productivity, as calculated on the basis of GDP data. In other words, there is a gap between actual and potential GDP. Nevertheless, low growth in the TCC will tend to dampen progress in labor productivity insofar as this progress is dependent upon technological innovation.

Figure 5.12 shows that the annual growth rate of labor productivity has been around 0 to 2 percent since 1990. Before that, it was very high, registering between 2 and 11 percent for most years. On the other hand, the growth rate of the "relative wage"—the share of wages within GDP or the "labor share"—was negative in almost every year between 1975 and 2014. This suggests that the rate of surplus value rose overall during this period.[9]

If labor productivity is high, both the growth rate of the real wage and the trend for the rate of surplus value could be positive. However, as mentioned above, an increase in relative surplus population produces a downward pressure on the real wage rate, which can easily result in a rise in the rate of surplus value, regardless of any slowdown in labor productivity.

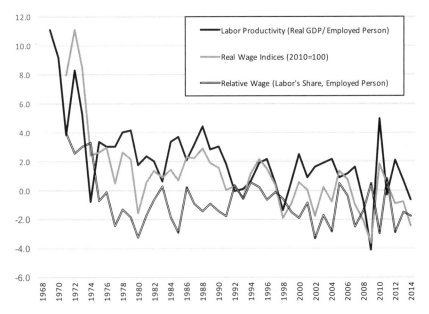

Note: Relative Wage (Labor's Share) is calculated by dividing the growth rate of real wage indices by the growth rate of labor productivity. Real GDP up to 1993 is based on 63SNA, and from 1994 on it is based on 93SNA.

Figure 5.12. Annual growth rate of wage and productivity with labor's share (%), 1968–2014. Sources: for real wage indices and for employed persons, see figure 5.9; for real GDP, see figure 5.1.

4. The Contradictions of Japanese Capitalism

Before proceeding to a more theoretical discussion of the issues raised in this study, a preliminary summary of the empirical evidence is in order. In the 1990s, Japanese capitalists faced huge excess capacity and a drop in capacity utilization. The fall in utilization signified a fall in N/C (and therefore a rise in the OCC or C/N), which produced a negative impact on the rate of profit. The 1990s were thus a period of steep decline in the rate of profit, and capitalists responded by restraining productive investment in order to avoid greater losses in profitability.

In the 2000s, capitalists restrained their investment still more, which led to a reduction in production capacity and a rise in capacity utilization. At the same time, however, restrained investment boosted the rate of profit via rising "capital productivity" (N/C) and a spike in the rate of the surplus value (S/V). However, in the process of this recovery of the rate of profit, capital accumulation weakened, the growth in labor productivity slowed, the employed labor force shrank, and real wages declined.

This is the context for the stark contradiction between the recovery in the rate of profit and the persistent growth stagnation of the past two decades—a long-term depression that encompassed the longest-lasting but also weakest economic "boom" (that between 2002 and 2007) in postwar Japanese history. The upshot is that Japanese capitalists are now enjoying much higher profitability than they did in the 1990s, despite the still-depressed condition of the economy.

The peculiar dynamics that have brought about a recovery of profitability in the midst of prolonged stagnation present some theoretical and empirical problems that require further exploration.

The role of crises in capitalism

From the standpoint of Marx's theory, *cyclical* crises play an indispensable role in restoring a semblance of equilibrium to a capitalist economy and bringing about a subsequent expansion of production. Marx writes in *Capital,* volume 3:

> Crises are never more than momentary, violent solutions for the existing contradictions, violent eruptions that re-establish the disturbed balance for the time being. (p. 357)
>
> [. . .] Under all circumstances, however, the balance will be restored by capital's lying idle or even by its destruction, to a greater or lesser extent. This will also extend in part to the material substance of capital; i.e. part of the means of production, fixed and circulating capital, will not function and operate as capital, and a part of the productive effort that was begun will come to a halt. (p. 362)
>
> [. . .] The stagnation in production that has intervened prepares the ground for a later expansion of production – within the capitalist limits. (pp. 363–64)

As a capitalist economy enters into crisis, the price level and the profit rate go down. Therefore, some production capacity has to be forcefully devalued or even destroyed, with capitalists seeking to replace older means of production with more productive ones. These processes encourage new investment and pave the way for subsequent economic recovery and expansion. In this sense, the capitalist mode of production has a built-in "self-recovery" mechanism.

Capitalism survives as a system of socioeconomic reproduction, not in spite of, but precisely because of its cyclical crises.

However, in contemporary capitalism and particularly in Japan, the cyclical self-recovery mechanism, originally described by Marx in an epoch of capitalist ascent, has broken down. In the 1990s, Japanese capitalists did *not* reduce their excess capacity, even though this was clearly a period of crisis and stagnation after the collapse of the bubble economy. In addition, in the 2000s, although productive capacity declined, capitalists did *not* ratchet up new investment, despite a higher rate of profit. It would seem, then, that in contemporary capitalism (and above all in the case of Japan) cyclical crises and the ensuing rising profitability are playing little role in inducing new investment, in bringing about a "later expansion of production," or in "reestablishing the disturbed balance."

Strong state intervention in the era of neoliberalism

The apparent "uselessness" of contemporary cyclical crises, as mechanisms for restoring the disturbed equilibrium, explains why strong state intervention is increasingly required. Capitalist states intervene in the capitalist economic process in order to reduce excess capacity and to stimulate new investment. Consider the following examples.

First, one of the most significant interventions by the Japanese state from the late 1990s to the mid-2000s involved disposing of nonperforming loans. The Japanese government injected huge amounts of money into banks. The central public bank (the Bank of Japan) also helped the private banks to raise their profit margins by lowering interest rates through a super-easy monetary policy—the so-called "zero-interest rate policy," "Quantitative Easing" (QE), and "Quantitative and Qualitative Easing" (QQE). Thanks to these initiatives of the state, banks were able to dispose of huge quantities of nonperforming loans. The disposal of bad debt caused many bankruptcies of small companies, and a rapid restructuring and downsizing of larger corporations. Such bankruptcies, restructuring, and downsizing contributed to a reduction in production capacity for the whole economy following the end of the 1990s, as seen in figure 5.4.

Second, the deregulation of legislated employment practices and standards, which enabled corporations to "legally" lay off personnel more easily, was another important intervention by the state in this period. Some employment-related statutes, for example the Worker Dispatch Act and the Labor Standards Act, have been overhauled to the detriment of labor since the 1990s. These acts have dramatically expanded the number of temporary and contract workers. The "Act on the Succession to Labor Contracts upon Company Split" also gave companies a useful means to downsize their workforces through cuts to unprofitable departments or branches.

Backed by these extraordinary pro-business state interventions, capitalists succeeded in raising their profitability by reducing their production capacities and workforces, and thereby cutting wage costs. Thus, strong state intervention in the economy has been a defining feature of so-called neoliberal policy since the 1990s. This is ironic, of course, because neoliberalism is usually understood—by most on the right and the left alike—to involve a pro-"free market" policy of "less government." However, the reality is precisely the opposite. State intervention in the economy in the era of neoliberalism has increased, not lessened; but this intervention has also been almost entirely oriented toward strengthening the profitability and prerogatives of big corporations and financial institutions, and weakening the position of labor (in contrast to the ostensibly more "class-neutral" Keynesian policies that prevailed in the postwar period up until the 1970s).

Ineffectiveness of current economic policies

Although the neoliberal state interventions described above helped capitalists to achieve higher profit rates, they contributed little to improving investment and employment, and therefore to an improvement in the Japanese macroeconomy.

In particular, Japan's "super-easy" monetary policies could not increase the "money stock" (MS),[10] although they did allow the "monetary base" (MB) to skyrocket (see fig. 5.13). Roughly speaking, MS is defined as banknotes, coins and deposits, and so on held by non-financial corporations and households. MS includes deposits created by bank-extended credit, but banks and other financial institutions hold no MS, according to the definition. This means that MS is money used by non-financial corporations and households in the "real" economy, not the "financial economy." On the other hand, MB consists of all banknotes and coins in circulation and the "current account deposits in the Bank of Japan," that is, deposits held by financial institutions. Accordingly, when the Bank of Japan purchases bonds from financial markets, the "current account deposit" increases. However, an increase in MB does not necessarily mean an increase in MS. Only when financial institutions extend credit to non-financial corporations or to households—"deposits held by non-financial corporations and households," which are the major components of MS—would MS increase. However, if non-financial corporations have no need to borrow money from financial institutions, the expansion of such credit-based MS is limited. As discussed earlier in this chapter, Japan's non-financial corporations are earning a higher rate of profit by restraining their investment, and therefore they have at their disposal a huge amount of idle money capital, which reduces their dependency on bank credit. This is why the easy monetary policy has not worked to stimulate growth for over two decades, even though the policy makes Japan the country with *the highest public ratio of debt to GDP in the world*, sometimes causes depreciations in the yen, and often plays a crucial role in supporting prices on the Tokyo Stock Exchange.

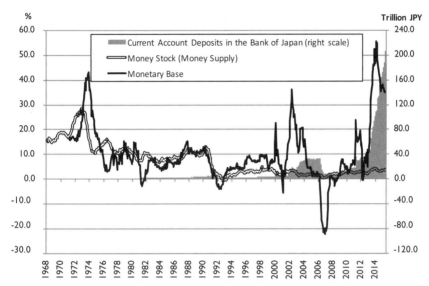

Figure 5.13. Money stock and monetary base (year-on-year % change by month), 1968–2014. Source: Bank of Japan, BOJ time-series data search, https://www.stat-search.boj.or.jp/index_en.html.

A "virtuous cycle" for big capitalists

Figure 5.14 shows that in the 2000s, the total assets of the largest-scale non-financial corporations were increasing while their "operating assets" were decreasing.[11] For relatively small corporations, total assets as well as operating assets decreased since the mid-1990s (fig. 5.15).

From these facts, we can deduce the following conclusions. First, the difference between total assets and operating assets includes many kinds of financial assets. Although some shares are held in order to retain ownership of other related companies, and some cash and deposits are held for daily business operations, it is obvious that big non-financial corporations are increasingly committed to financial activities in pursuit of financial profits. Such a change in the structure of the assets of large "non-financial" companies is one of the important sources of the rapid expansion of financial activities, providing financial institutions and financial markets with larger volumes of money capital. The expansion and development of financial markets have in turn placed pressure on companies to increase their profit rates. For example, in order to heighten the return on assets (ROA) or the return on equity (ROE), which are standard indices used in financial markets to evaluate firms, companies must use their fixed and financial assets as efficiently as possible. Thus, the recent expansion of financial activities increasingly forces companies to restrain investment in fixed assets, cut wage costs, and improve profitability.

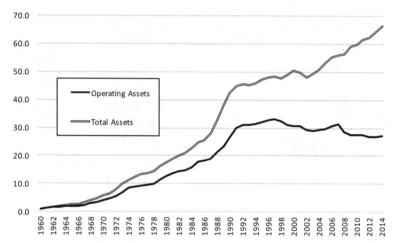

Note: Operating Assets are the total of products and commodities, goods in progress, raw materials and stocks, construction in progress, other tangible fixed assets and software.

Figure 5.14. Operating assets and total assets; non-financial corporations, capital stock of 1 billion yen and over (1960 FY = 1.0). Source: Ministry of Finance, corporation statistics.

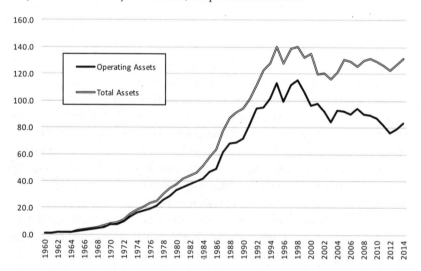

Figure 5.15. Operating assets and total assets: non-financial corporations, capital stock of 10 million to less than 100 million yen (1960 FY = 1.0). Source: Ministry of Finance, corporation statistics.

Second, the difference in the asset structure between large and small corporations reflects the difference in their rates of profit. Large-scale corporations have made a rapid recovery in their rate of profit, which reached nearly 15 percent in 2005–2007 and 20 percent in 2014 (fig. 5.16)— a level higher than that in the bubble economy. The recovery in profitability of large-scale corporations looks altogether extraordinary in light of the historically weak economic "boom" of the 2000s (see fig. 5.1). On the other hand, the rate of profit of small corporations has remained at a historically very low level, around 5 to 10 percent, throughout the 2000s.

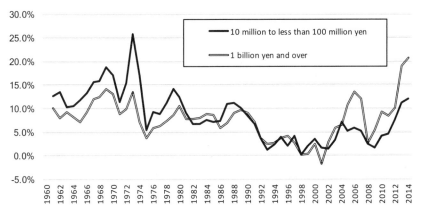

Note: For constant capital and surplus value, see appendix. Surplus value of this figure excludes salary and bonus for directors.

Figure 5.16. Profit rate by size of capital stock (excluding salary and bonus for directors). Source: Ministry of Finance, corporation statistics.

Third, according to Japanese accounting rules, when corporations reduce their fixed assets, they have to book "extraordinary losses" in their corporate accounts. These extraordinary losses are not the ordinary costs or losses associated with the normal operations of corporations, but rather temporary costs or losses associated with restructuring and downsizing. Therefore, figure 5.17 implies that since the end of the 1990s, large-scale companies (with capital stocks valued at ¥1 billion or more) have pursued restructuring and downsizing much more aggressively than have small companies.

Only the big corporations can book extraordinary losses because they possess huge idle assets resulting from higher rates of profit. Only they can withstand temporary losses or deficits. In addition, once they succeed in restructuring and downsizing, at the cost of temporary but often huge losses, they can enjoy much higher productivity and profitability, once again due to reductions in fixed assets and personnel. A higher rate of profit then contributes to the regeneration of assets. Thus, only the strongest and largest companies are in a position to expand. This is a "virtuous circle" for them and a key reason for the concentration of profits in the hands of large corporations. All the same, although these corporations continue to enjoy higher rates of profit, continuous restructuring and downsizing serves to erode "corporate competitiveness," even from the capitalist viewpoint. Capitalists are undermining the foundations on which they stand.

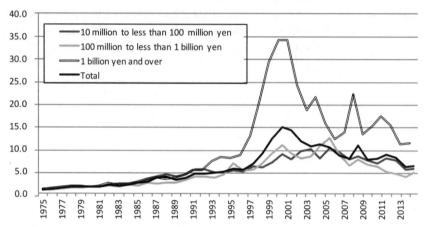

Figure 5.17. Extraordinary losses by size of capital stock (non-financial corporations, 1975 FY = 1.0, %) 1975–2014.
Source: Ministry of Finance, corporation statistics.

5. Concluding Remarks: The Fundamental Contradiction and the LTRPF

This study reveals that after a long period of declining profitability, Japanese capitalists have succeeded in raising the average rate of profit through strong state interventions, based on neoliberal policies. However, such interventions have reinforced the trend toward prolonged stagnation and actually deepened the structural crisis of the Japanese economy.

These same policies, I contend, will soon produce downward pressure on *profitability*. Capitalists can continue to raise profitability by decreasing constant-capital investment, the process that boosted "capital productivity" (N/C) and a rise in the rate of surplus value (S/V). However, since only *productive labor* can create new value and therefore surplus value, reductions in productive investment—in particular, reductions leading to a diminution in the contribution of productive living labor to the economy—will inevitably undermine the average rate of profit. The production of inadequate quantities of surplus value in relation to total capital investment remains the most fundamental contradiction confronting the Japanese economy—and indeed the global capitalist economy as a whole. And this problem can be mitigated or masked for only so long by generating money profits based on an expansion of debt, rather than on commodity production.

By affirming the actuality of Marx's LTRPF, we are able to understand the precise mechanisms of the recent, and undoubtedly transient, recovery in the Japanese rate of the profit and the structural crisis associated with it. As long as the rise in the TCC and OCC (C/N) is effectively restrained, a rise in the rate of profit is to be expected, given the fundamental premises of the LTRPF. But if this restraint is decisively dependent upon the generation of "profits" through non-productive and even parasitical means, the barriers to a rising OCC and a fall in the rate of profit will be flimsy and insubstantial.

Related to this latter point, Kliman et al. (2013) have noted that Heinrich's (2013) claim "that Marx failed to prove the [LTRPF] is rooted in his mistaken belief that the law is an assertion that the rate of profit *must, under all circumstances, fall in the long run*. In fact, however, the law is not a prediction of what must inevitably happen, but an *explanation* of what does happen; it explains why the rate of profit does tend to fall *in the long run*" (p. 3, emphasis added). As these proponents of Marx's law emphasize, it is not at all necessary to demonstrate that the rate of profit falls "under all circumstances" in order to affirm the actuality of the LTRPF and the central role it plays in capital accumulation and crises.[12]

In order to overcome stagnation, the Japanese economy clearly needs an increase in wages and employment—one capable of stimulating consumption and productive investment. A redistribution of revenues through more equitable taxation and social security policies is also needed and could have positive effects for working people. Government policies that have hitherto supported capitalists' efforts to raise profitability must be rejected in favor of pro-labor policies in order to make the economy work for the great majority. That said, however, as long as economic life remains dominated by the capitalist law of value, the *governing* macroeconomic indicator (and regulator of growth) will always be the average rate of profit. Furthermore, given the stage of structural crisis that capitalism has reached, in Japan and globally, capitalists will continue to restrain *productive* investment in favor of short-term profitability—however shaky the foundations of that profitability might be. Accordingly, unless working people themselves act to transform fundamentally the current economic system—a system in which a small group of big capitalists enjoys a monopoly of economic decision making—there is no prospect that productive capacity and the increasingly powerful means of production it contains will be utilized in their interests and to achieve real social progress. To take the LTRPF seriously, then, is to affirm, with Marx, an urgent need to "expropriate the expropriators."

Appendix: Sources

In figures 5.5, 5.6, 5.7, and 5.8, the categories of constant capital, variable capital, surplus value, and new value were calculated from official statistics using the same basic methodology as Smith and Butovsky (2012) (see the appendix to chapter 14 in this volume). However, because of certain limitations of Japan's national accounts, and in particular because these accounts only go back to 1980 for data series of fixed assets, I have been obliged to use the "Financial Statements and Statistics of Corporations by Industry" issued by the Ministry of Finance, Policy Research Institute.

Constant Capital (C). The value of tangible fixed assets, excluding land, construction in progress, and software (for the previous year) in all non-financial industries.

Variable Capital (V). Salaries, bonuses, and benefits for employees in all non-financial industries minus those in "unproductive" industries (including wholesale and retail trade, eating and drinking services, real estate, goods rental and leasing, advertising, scientific research, professional and technical services, and employment and worker-dispatching services).

Surplus Value (S). Net profits (after tax), plus salaries and bonuses for directors of all non-financial industries.

New Value (N). N is the sum of V and S.

Notes

1   This chapter is based on Sato (2011, in Japanese), as well as two presentations at Brock University, Ontario, in 2013 and 2014. My original article in Japanese has been extensively revised here, thanks to Murray E. G. Smith's valuable discussions and suggestions while I was a visiting international scholar at Brock University from March 2012 to March 2014. I'd like to express my special thanks to Dr. Smith for assisting with the English-language composition of this chapter, as well as to Guglielmo Carchedi and Michael Roberts for providing me with an opportunity to contribute to this volume.

2   In contrast to the United States and other advanced capitalist countries, the recovery of profitability in Japan over the past two decades has not been mainly confined to financial firms. To facilitate the analysis of Japan's unique economic history and to sidestep theoretical and empirical problems related to the growing weight of "fictitious profits" in the financial sector (see Smith and Butovsky 2012; Smith 2014; and chapter 14 in this book), the rate of profit calculated here is only a *non-financial rate of profit.* Abstracting from the financial sector, with its anomalously high rate of profit, may well get us closer to a true "Marxian rate of profit" for the Japanese economy than would the traditional method of including financial profits that may or may not be legitimate elements of social surplus value.

3   In a few exceptional industries, for example, electronics parts and devices, including crystal panels for TV, PCs, and cell phones, investment was increased by "the coercive laws of competition" (Marx 1976, p. 433) operating in the global market. It is true that corporations in these industries increased investment in order to maintain a lead over competitors through rapid technological progress, thereby promoting prosperity in the short run, and contributing to macroeconomic growth at the same time. However, after such a short boom, they faced much more severe conditions. Many corporations, even gigantic

monopolistic or oligopolistic corporations, went into actual bankruptcy, and were merged and acquired by other companies or investors under circumstances of excess capacity.

4   As for the United States and other Western countries, many studies indicate a similar recovery in the rate of profit. For example, as part of his reply to Husson's (2009) dismissal of the LTRPF, Harman (2010) surveys many studies that point to a recovery in the rate of profit since the mid-1980s. For a discussion of the peculiarities of this recovery, see Smith and Butovsky, chapter 14 in the present volume.

5   Marx's original definition of the rate of profit was $S/(C + V)$. However, making reasonable estimates of variable capital from official statistics is very difficult. That is because official statistics give only the total annual wage *flow*. If we tried to calculate V as a *stock* variable from this data, we would need to estimate turnover time and then divide the "flow" of wage data by the turnover time. This would substantially reduce the magnitude of V, which is why many studies of the LTRPF simply assume that the stock of variable capital is zero and define the rate of profit as the ratio of surplus value to the constant capital stock (S/C). Marx himself defines the denominator of the rate of profit as the "capital advanced," but the magnitude of variable capital actually advanced is small and unlikely to affect trends in the rate of profit in significant ways. See Smith and Butovsky, chapter 14 in this volume, for further discussion of this issue.

6   There is also a controversy surrounding the definition of the organic composition of capital. Is it C/V or C/N? Marx writes: "I call the value-composition of capital, in so far as it is determined by its technical composition and mirrors the changes in the latter, the organic composition of capital" (1976, p. 762). Fine and Saad-Filho (2010, pp. 89–92) consider C/V to be the organic composition of capital. On the other hand, Mage (1963, pp. 68–74), Moseley (1991, p. 4), and Smith and Butovsky (2012, p. 67, n76) define it as C/N. I will follow the latter definition because, in my view, C/N allows for a focus on the role of living productive labor in the creation of new value generally and surplus value in particular more clearly than does C/V.

7   In addition, modest expansion of production capacity could help to support the price level of commodities under contemporary conditions of global capitalist "competition." This has a positive impact on sales and thus on "productivity," at least in terms of nominal prices.

8   The rate of surplus value (S/V) has also gone up during the same period.

9   In figure 5.10 and 5.11, I use the number of employees, self-employed workers and family workers for "all industries" as the denominator of the TCC, instead of using the number of workers employed only in "productive" sectors of the economy. (This means that my measure of the TCC is not strictly comparable to my measure of the OCC, the denominator of which includes the earnings of productive workers only. However, the main point of the discussion here, which pertains to the relationship of the TCC to relative surplus population, is not affected by those considerations.) In addition, the data I use in figure 5.12 is based on official GDP figures, not on "new value" defined in Marxist terms. Hence, it refers to a measure of gross labor productivity, rather than net productivity.

10 Bank of Japan changed its definition of money supply into money stock in 2008.

11 In Ministry of Finance statistics for corporations, corporations are classified by size. The biggest classification in terms of capital stock is ¥1 billion and over.

12   Freeman (2012, p. 167) tries to demonstrate that "there is a consistent long-run fall in the UK and US rate of profit which, contrary to the figures widely used by Marxists, have both fallen almost monotonically since 1968." In order to demonstrate this "long-run fall," however, he changes the definition of the Marxian average rate of profit (ARP) by including financial securities in the *denominator* of the ARP. For a detailed critical assessment of this approach, see Sato (2015). Having noted Freeman's error in this regard, it should be recognized that his correct criticism of Heinrich in no way requires a demonstration of a "long-run fall in the UK and US rate of profit" in order to affirm the actuality of the LTRPF. Even if profitability recovers during some periods, the law remains essential to explaining the movements of the rate of profit and the ever-changing tactics deployed by capitalists to counteract its fall.

References

Fine, B. and A. Saad-Filho (2010) *Marx's* Capital, 5th ed., Pluto Press.

Freeman, A. (2012) "The Profit Rate in the Presence of Financial Markets: A Necessary Correction," *Journal of Australian Political Economy*, No 70.

Harman, C. (2010), "Not All Marxism Is Dogmatism: A Reply to Husson," *International Socialism*, No 125.

Heinrich, M. (2013) "Crisis Theory, the Law of the Tendency of the Profit Rate to Fall, and Marx's Studies in the 1870s," *Monthly Review*, Vol 64, No 11.

Kliman, A. et al. (2013) "The Unmaking of Marx's Capital: Heinrich's Attempt to Eliminate Marx's Crisis Theory," Social Science Research Network.

Mage, S. (1963) "The 'Law of the Falling Tendency of the Rate of Profit': Its Place in the Marxian Theoretical System and Relevance to the U.S. Economy," PhD thesis, Columbia University.

Marx, K. (1976), *Capital*, Vol 1, Penguin Books.

———. (1981) *Capital*, Vol 3, Penguin Books.

Ministry of Economy, Trade and Industry (METI), available at http://www.meti.go.jp/statistics/tyo/iip/qa.html.

Ministry of Finance, Policy Research Institute, "Financial Statements Statistics of Corporations by Industry," available at http://www.e-stat.go.jp/SG1/estat/GL08020101.do?_toGL08020101_&tstatCode=000001047744&requestSender=dsearch.

Moseley, F. (1991) *The Falling Rate of Profit in the Postwar United States Economy*, St. Martin's Press.

Sato, T. (2011) "The Prolonged Stagnation of Japanese Capitalism: Focusing on Restrained Investment and Increasing in Profit' (published in Japanese as "Nihon Shihonshugi no Chouki Teitai: Toushi no Yokusei to Rijun no Kakudai wo Chushin ni"), *Keizai*, Vol 189.

———. (2015) "On Freeman's New Approach to Calculating the Rate of Profit," *Journal of Australian Political Economy*, Vol 75.

Smith, M. E. G. (2014) *Marxist Phoenix: Studies in Historical Materialism and Marxist Socialism*, Canadian Scholars Press International.

Smith, M. E. G. and J. Butovsky (2012) "Profitability and the Roots of the Global Crisis: Marx's 'Law of the Tendency of the Rate of Profit to Fall' and the US Economy, 1950–2007," *Historical Materialism*, Vol 20, No 4.

CHAPTER 6

THE UK RATE OF PROFIT AND BRITISH ECONOMIC HISTORY

Michael Roberts

1. Marx's Law

Why is a study of the movement in the rate of profit or return (to use the mainstream economics term) on capital invested in an economy important? Mainstream economics, on the whole, does not bother to look at this category. It concentrates on output growth, incomes, consumer expenditure, capital formation, prices, and for the longer term, on population and productivity growth.

In the Marxist view, an analysis of the rate of profit in an economy is important, moreover essential, because Marxist economics starts from the (realistic) assumption that all value created comes from the labor expended by human beings to produce commodities (both objective and mental), namely, use values with an (exchange) value. The problem with the modern economy is that production is interrupted and reversed by regular and recurrent crises and breakdown. And this is because the modern economy is not a harmonious process of accumulation, production, and consumption, but is riven by a key contradiction between the drive to increase productivity and the tendency for the surplus value relative to the capital invested to fall. When the contradiction reaches a crisis point, accumulation and production are interrupted until profitability is restored—only for the whole thing to go round again.

Mainstream economics ignores or denies the existence of this contradiction. It also disputes, or derides, the labor theory of value (that all value comes from labor). It thus dismisses any measures of the health of a capitalist economy that are evaluated by the rate of profit that capitalists obtain from their ownership of the means of production and their employment of labor.

Marxist economics argues that, by assuming the labor theory of value and by making some realistic assumptions based on the law of value, a compelling explanation of why capitalism has recurrent and regular breakdowns and crises can be provided.[1] The essence of this explanation is Marx's law of the tendency of the rate of profit to fall. The "law as such" is simple. It is based on two realistic assumptions: (1) that all value is created by labor alone; and (2) that in order to raise the profitability of capital, capitalists continually resort to replacing labor with machines and other technology. As a result, over time, the amount (and value) of the means of production will increase relatively to the employment (and cost) of labor. This development Marx called "a rising organic composition of capital."

Based on these two assumptions, Marx's law of profitability says that there will be a tendency for the rate of profit on the capital (both in means of production and in labor power or wages) invested by capitalists to fall.

The simple formula for the rate of profit is $s/(c + v)$, where s is the surplus value appropriated by the owners of the means of production from the total value created by labor, c is the value of the means of production accumulated by the owners, and v is the cost of employing the labor force to produce value. Marx's law (as such) of the tendency of the rate of profit to fall follows: if c/v rises, and the rate of exploitation, s/v, is unchanged, the rate of profit, $s/(c + v)$, must fall.

There are countertendencies to the tendency for the rate of profit to fall. That is why the law is a tendency. Marx lists several factors that could lead to a period of rising profitability. The two most important ones are (1) when the organic composition of capital, c/v, *rises* but at a slower pace than the rise in the rate of exploitation, s/v; and (2) when c/v *falls* because the value of the new means of production falls as a result of a greater productivity of labor.

Marx argues cogently that these countertendencies cannot predominate indefinitely or even for a long time, that is, not more than several years, or a decade or so—a short period in the history of capitalism. Eventually, in the long run, the organic composition of capital will rise more than the rate of exploitation rises, and the rate of profit will resume its fall.

Crises and breakdowns come about because a falling rate of profit eventually reaches a point where there is a fall in the new value created by labor, and/or a fall in the mass of profit. The rate of profit is an average across all sectors of production. Some capitalists may actually experience a fall in profits, or even outright losses, well before the more efficient and stronger ones do. The weaker capitalists will go bust or reduce investment spending first, causing a cascade effect across other sectors. Once investment starts falling, employment and incomes will follow. A slump ensues. This is the mechanism of crises that begins with Marx's law.[2]

2. The Evidence for the United Kingdom

This chapter looks at the movement of the rate of profit in the United Kingdom since 1855 using several data sources and makes some observations on the changes in the development of the UK economy (imperialism) that flow from the results.

The major periods of decline in the UK rate of profit were the late-nineteenth-century depression of 1871–84, the immediate postwar period of 1914–22, and the postwar profitability crisis of 1954–75. The major periods of rising profitability are found in 1871–85, 1920–38, and 1975–98. For the last ten years we have been in a global depressionary period that began in 2008.

The secular decline from 1855

The whole period covered here is from 1855 to 2009, ending in the Great Recession. For the full period, there are two sources of data: (1) the data from the UK's Office for National Statistics and other series compiled by the Bank of England (2016); and (2) the work of Esteban Maito on the UK from his recent papers (2014). All sources and the methods of calculation used in this chapter can be found in the appendix. The ONS-BOE calculations of the UK rate of profit are compared with Maito's results. Figure 6.1 shows the results from (1) and (2).

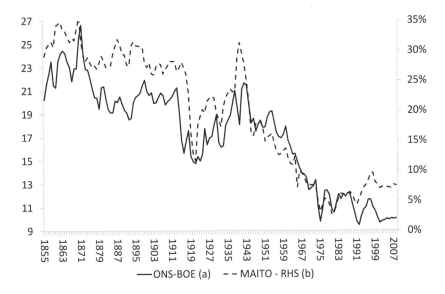

Figure 6.1. The UK rate of profit (%), 1855–2009. Bank of England (ONS-BOE), left; Maito, right. Sources: Bank of England; Maito (2014); author's calculations.

There are differences in the actual levels of the rate of profit calculated in the two series. This is due to slightly different source data used and also to a different categorization of s (surplus value) and c (constant capital) for calculation. Also, the ONS-BOE data include variable capital as part of the denominator for the rate of profit, while Maito's do not, following the consensus view among Marxist economists.[3]

Although the rates of profit differ between a and b, the trend and turns for the 150 years are much the same. This is an important confirmation of the robust nature of the results in both. And the results could not be clearer: the rate of profit on UK capital since 1855 has been in secular decline: in a, from around 25 percent in the 1850s to about 10 percent in 2009; and in b from about 30 percent to 5 percent. In a, the rate of profit has fallen to 39 percent of its level in the 1850s, and in b it has fallen to 26 percent. Thus Marx's forecast or prediction that the rate of profit would fall under capitalism is confirmed. Of course, there could be a different explanation of that fall that is not based on Marx's law. We shall deal with that point later.

Four counteracting periods

Within the secular decline, there have been periods when the UK rate of profit on capital has risen, sometimes for decades. Table 6.1 shows the movement of the rate of profit in percentage terms for different periods from 1855 to 2009.

Period	MAITO (b)	ONS-BOE (a)
1855–71	8.1	31.7
1871–84	−12.6	−28.2
1884–1901	2.0	7.7
1901–14	−3.0	−6.6
1914–21	−57.1	−23.4
1922–42	138.5	46.7
1942–46	−43.0	−14.0
1946–54	2.1	3.4
1954–75	−80.7	−49.3
1975–97	203.7	19.3
1998–2008	−20.8	−13.8

Table 6.1. Change in the rate of profit (%), 1855–2008. See text for details. Source: author's calculations from ONS-BOE data.

There was a rise in the rate profit from 1855 to 1871 of about 8–30 percent, a similarly sized fall between 1871 and 1884, a rise of 2–7 percent from

1884 to 1901, and a similarly sized fall up to World War I in 1914. There was massive drop in profitability during and immediately after the war, up to 1922, of 23–57 percent. Then there was a huge rise in the 1920s, partly sustained in the 1930s. Profitability peaked during the 1939–45 world war, held up briefly after the war ended, and then UK profitability entered a sharp downward trend from the mid-1950s to a trough in the mid-1970s (–20–50 percent). Then there was reversal and a significant rise up to 1997. Since 1997, the UK rate of profit has declined, by 13–21 percent.

From the results, it is clear that the UK rate of profit has not fallen in a straight line. Indeed, there have been periods when the rate of profit has risen, even for decades. We can discern four periods since 1855 when the rate of profit rises on a reasonably sustained basis. They are 1855–71, 1884–1901, 1922–42, and 1975–97.

These periods can be recognized in the economic history of British capitalism. The 1855–71 period was the "long boom" that worried Marx and Engels so much that they thought another crisis would never come.[4] The 1884–1901 period was the recovery from what would be called the "Long Depression" of 1871–84 in the UK and the United States. This recovery period was the "Belle Époque," which was only partially sustained in the early 1900s. The 1922–42 period followed a calamitous fall in profitability immediately after World War I that annihilated much of Britain's old heavy industry (more on this period later). And the 1975–97 period has been characterized as the "neoliberal" period starting after the classic "profitability crisis," which began early in the UK from the mid-1950s and led to the further "financialization" of the UK economy.

Depression of the 1880s

We can look closer at the rate of profit in the late nineteenth century using another set of data provided by Arnold and McCartney (2002), to calculate the UK rate of profit from 1855–1914.[5] The results are in figure 6.2.

Figure 6.2 reveals that the UK rate of profit rose sharply from 1855 to 1871 (30 percent) then fell sharply during the Long Depression to a low in the mid-1880s (–22 percent), which was not really overcome until the mid-1890s (17 percent). In the 1900s, profitability showed a (mild) fall up to World War I (see table 6.2).

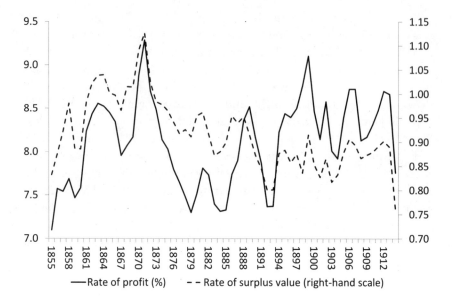

Figure 6.2. UK rate of profit and the rate of surplus value
(ratio), 1855–1912. Source: author's calculations.

Period	% Change in RoP
1855–71	30.8
1871–84	−21.3
1884–1901	17.3
1901–08	−5.3
1908–14	−4.6

Table 6.2. Percent change in rate of profit, 1855–1914 . Source: Arnold and
McCartney 2002.

Figure 6.3 combines the results from the three sources used so far for the
period 1855–1914: the ONS-BOE data, the Maito data, and the Arnold
and McCartney data. The change in profitability can be subdivided into
four periods: a period of boom (rising profitability), a period of depression
(falling profitability), a period of recovery (rising profitability), and renewed
crisis (stagnant/falling profitability). All four subperiods of the changing
movement in profitability match important changes in the economic history
of British capitalism.

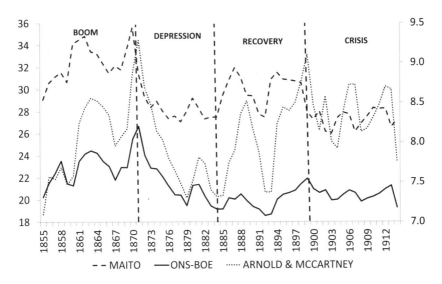

Figure 6.3. The UK rate of profit (three measures), 1855–1914. Sources: see figures. 6.1 and 6.2.

In the 1850s (following the 1851 Great Exhibition), British imperialism was at its height. It was the hegemonic capitalist power, with dominance in industry, trade, finance, imperial incomes/colonies, and armed forces. But by the end of the long boom up to the early 1870s, British imperialism began to give ground (relatively) to the rising economic powers of the United States (now united after a civil war) and Germany (also now united), and to some extent France after the defeat of the Paris Commune in 1870.

During the Long Depression of the 1880s (and 1890s), Britain's hegemonic position was further undermined by the rise of Bismarckian Germany and America's growing industrial population. The period of economic recovery from the 1890s was weaker in the United Kingdom than it was in Germany or the United States (Lewis 1967). Profitability did not rise in the 1900s, and by the time of World War I, both Germany and the United States could rival the United Kingdom's position.

The 1914–21 industrial collapse

The weakness of British industry and imperialism was exposed immediately after World War I. As the profitability data from figure 6.1 and table 6.1 show, the UK rate of profit plummeted by 30–60 percent between 1914 and 1921. Britain entered a depression that was sharp and catastrophic to its aging industry. The government tried to restore and preserve its hegemonic position globally in trade and finance by sticking to the gold standard. But this only weakened the position of British industry in global markets further, especially once France and Germany recovered from the war and Germany was relieved of the draconian reparations imposed under the Versailles treaty. To restore profitability, British capital then set about closing down old industries and reducing, in a big way, the share of value going to labor. This policy was cemented by the defeat of the transport unions in 1921 and the defeat of the 1926 general strike: The government came off the gold standard in 1925 (see Norfield 2012a). This laid the basis for a sustained rise in UK profitability that even the Great Depression of the 1930s did not stop (in contrast to the US). Britain had its depression first. The data from the ONS-BOE series (a) and the Maito series (b) confirm this analysis, as figure 6.4 shows. Under (a) the rate of profit rose from 15 percent to 21 percent from 1921 to 1938, and in (b) it rose from 12 percent to 24 percent. Profitability did fall during the worst years of the Great Depression (1930–32), but it remained above its early-1920s level and recovered significantly in the mid-1930s.

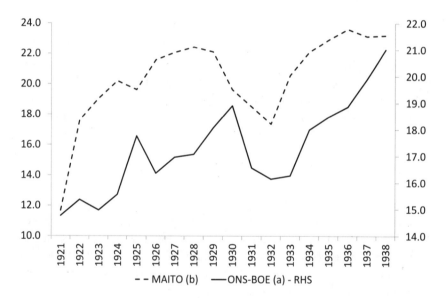

Figure 6.4. The UK rate of profit (two measures), % 1921–38. Source: see figure 6.1.

These results can also be supplemented by another study from Vincent Brown and Simon Mohun for the interwar period. Brown and Mohun (2011) find that the "the UK rate of profit rose considerably over the interwar period and hence this period was one of significant recovery for capital, albeit with some volatility." Figure 6.5 compares the movement in the rate of profit between 1921–38 from all three sources/calculations. On the Maito series, UK profitability nearly doubles; on ONS-BOE, it rises over 40 percent; and from the Brown-Mohun series, it rises 80 percent. In the Brown-Mohun study, they also quote from another study done by Paul Cockshott et al. They find that UK profitability in the same period rose 90 percent.[6]

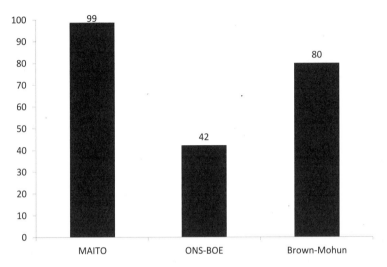

Figure 6.5. Change in UK rate of profit (three measures), 1921–38 (%, indexed 100 = 1921). Sources: Maito (2014); ONS-BOE; Brown and Mohun (2011).

The economic history of the period would suggest that UK profitability was restored by the counteracting factor of an increased rate of exploitation of labor exceeding any rise in the organic composition of capital. Figure 6.6 from the ONS-BOE data series confirms that. In the 1920s, the rate of surplus value (exploitation) rose nearly 26 percent, while the organic composition of capital fell (as old means of production were disposed of). In the 1930s, the impact of the Great Depression was to drive down the organic composition of capital even further, while the rate of surplus value stabilized.

Brown and Mohun (2011) reach similar conclusions: "A Marxian decomposition shows that the 1920s were characterized by a rising rate of surplus-value and a falling composition of capital; and the 1930s by a constant rate of surplus-value and a falling composition of capital" (p. 1047). This was a perfect combination for the restoration of profitability. As Brown and Mohun put it, "From the end of the First World War to the mid-1920s, capital was very successful in reimposing its prerogatives over labour: real output per hour increased much faster than the real hourly wage rate, so that the rate of surplus-value increased sharply and correspondingly the value of labour-power fell sharply." In the 1930s, however,

[i]n terms of the balance of class forces, while labour was severely weakened by mass unemployment, capital could not take advantage because of the collapse in world markets. The comfortable corporatism engendered by the shelter of protectionist tariffs was not a period of intense class struggle. Indeed, for capital, the adverse effects of a return to gold at an overvalued exchange rate and the collapse of the international economy into a protectionist, semi-autarky just about counterbalanced the positive effects of the General Strike victory and the rapid rise of unemployment. Apart then from the first half of the 1920s, the rise in the rate of profit did not have as a contributory factor a rise in the rate of surplus-value. Rather, the rate of profit was driven up by the maintenance of productivity growth while capital intensity fell. (Brown and Mohun 2011)

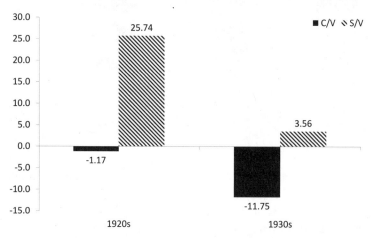

Figure 6.6. Change in organic composition of capital and rate of surplus value (%), 1920s and 1930s. Source: ONS–BOE, author's calculations.

The postwar period

The profitability of capital in the UK (and in the US) reached peaks during World War II. This was partly the product of new profits from arms production, such that investment in productive "civilian" assets fell, reducing the organic composition of capital. But it was also because the wages of labor were diverted into "savings" (war bonds) that were utilized by the governments to pay for arms and for the war machine. The rate of surplus value rose accordingly.

But after the war, British capitalism was in an exceedingly weak position, obviously compared to the United States, but also compared to France and Germany (and even Japan)—where American credit and capital was plowed in to exploit millions of cheap laborers and the latest technology was available to boost productivity and lower unit costs to compete (with weaker currencies) on world markets. As at the end of World War I, the UK had aging capital stock, and while it had some new technologies to exploit, it had a small workforce unwilling to be exploited at low rates after being "winners" in the war.

· So it was not long before UK profitability began to fall sharply. All the major capitalist economies began to experience a "classic profitability" crisis from about the mid-1960s. But the profitability crisis came earlier for the UK. As a result, it was also the first major capitalist economy to try and reverse the decline with policies of "neoliberalism" designed to raise profitability by increasing the rate of exploitation and privatization of state assets, which had been expanded in the immediate postwar period. Neoliberalism in the UK began as early as the end of the first simultaneous global recession of 1974–75, when the then-Labour government called on IMF emergency funding and dispensed with so-called Keynesian government spending policies.

Figure 6.7 shows three periods of change in profitability in the UK: the profitability crisis of 1951–75, the neoliberal recovery period of 1975–97, and the current crisis period of falling profitability from 1997. Figure 6.7 also incorporates new series of data and calculations for comparison. In addition to the Maito series and the ONS-BOE series, there are series based on the PENN world tables, the extended Penn world tables, and the EU AMECO database. On top of these, there are series calculated by Simon Mouatt (2013), as well as the official series on the net rate of return on the capital stock (NRC) on UK non-financial companies compiled by the UK's ONS (see appendix for sources). That is a total of seven sources/studies.

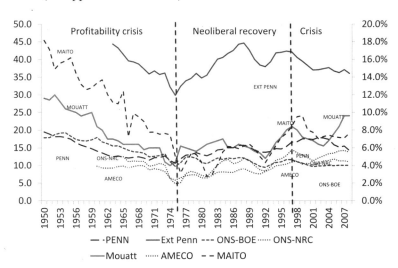

Figure 6.7. The UK rate of profit (seven measures, %), 1950–2008. Source: see appendix.

What figure 6.7 confirms is that (1) UK profitability fell from 1950 through to 2008; (2) most of this fall was from 1950; and (3) six sources reckon that the rate troughed in 1975 (only the Maito series has a later trough). Of those series that cover 1950–75, Maito records a 72 percent fall in the UK rate of profit; the PENN tables find a 45 percent fall; the long-term ONS-BOE series records a similar 45 percent fall; while the Mouatt series, based on the corporate sector only and using historic cost measures, sees a 62 percent fall.

For the neoliberal period, 1975 to 1997, all sources agree that there was a rise: from just 19 percent on the ONS-BOE series to a tripling from the official ONS-NRC series. The only series based on the corporate sector and on historic costs (Mouatt) still finds a rise of over 90 percent.

Finally, in the current profitability downturn since 1997, all sources except Mouatt (up 14 percent) and AMECO (remaining flat) confirm a fall between 6 and 14 percent up to the beginning of the Great Recession. Profitability was falling well before the Great Recession hit the UK (see table 6.3).

Period	Maito	PENN	Ext. Penn	ONS-BOE	ONS-NRC	Mouatt	AMECO
1950–75	−72.3	−45.4		−45.3		−62.1	
1975–97	67.4	56.1	40.9	19.3	202.1	90.9	88.4
1997–2008	−9.3	−14.3	−14.4	−13.8	−5.5	14.3	0.0
1950–2008	−58.0	−27.0		−43.8		−17.2	

Table 6.3. Change in rate of profit (seven measures, %), 1950–2008. Source: see appendix.

So UK profitability data from several sources have broadly similar trends, supporting the robustness of the results. In particular, the Mouatt series based on the historic measure confirms the fall in profitability from the 1950s to the mid-1970s, but also the rise in the neoliberal period from the mid-1970s (fig. 6.8).[7] As Mouatt puts it: "[A] *clear* secular decline, a 29.4% reduction, is identified between 1948 and 2007. . . . There have been times of partial restoration for the profit rate, however, notably the mid 1970s and early 1990s, but this has not been sustained." (p. 13) Mouatt's results show a rise in profitability of 91 percent in the period from 1975 to 1997, and then a further rise from 10 percent in 1975 to 24 percent in 2009. For the period 1950–2009, in applying a similar historic cost measure as that used by Mouatt to the ONS-BOE data, the results show a similar rise in the rate of profit in the neoliberal period (fig. 6.9).

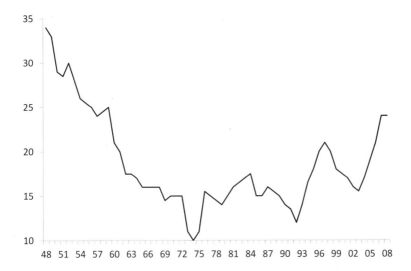

Figure 6.8. UK corporate profit rate based on historical costs (%), 1948–2008. Source: Mouatt (2013).

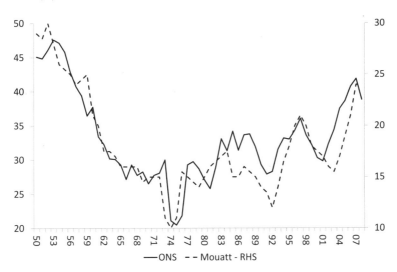

Figure 6.9. UK corporate rate of profit since 1950 on historic cost basis (two measures, %), 1950–2007. Source: Mouatt (2013), author's calculations.

Decomposing the rate of profit

What was the main reason for the secular decline in UK profitability in the last 160 years and for the periods of rising profitability within the secular decline? If Marx's law of the tendency of the rate of profit to fall is a compelling explanation, then there should be a high inverse correlation between a rising organic composition of capital and the rate of profit, and conversely there should be a relatively low positive correlation between the rate of surplus value and the rate of profit.

Moreover, during periods when the organic composition of capital rises faster than the rate of surplus value, the rate of profit should be falling—and vice versa. Was that the case for the UK?

The evidence on correlation for the postwar period (which has the most number of sources with the data decomposed) is clear. There is an inverse correlation between the rate of profit and the organic composition of capital of −0.57 for the AMECO series, and of −0.91 for the ONS-BOE series. There is a positive correlation between the rate of profit and the rate of surplus value of 0.91 for the AMECO series and of 0.22 for the ONS-BOE series. What is also significant is that the UK rate of profit fell on all those series beginning in 1950 (Maito by 58 percent, PENN by 27 percent, ONS-BOE by 44 percent, and Mouatt by 17 percent), and yet the rate of surplus value rose. On the ONS-BOE series, the rate of surplus value rose from 1950 to 2008 by 8 percent, but the rate of profit fell by 46 percent. This suggests that it was the rising organic composition of capital that drove the UK rate of profit down, according to Marx's "law as such."

Indeed, following the ONS-BOE data, whenever the organic composition of capital rose faster than the rate of surplus value, the rate of profit fell, as in 1946–75 (table 6.4). Whenever the reverse was true, the rate of profit rose, as in 1975–97. Overall, there was a secular fall from 1946 to 2008, when the organic composition of capital nearly doubled, while the rate of surplus value rose by only 7 percent. All this tends to confirm that Marx's law can explain changes in the UK rate of profit.

Period	C/V	S/V	ROP
1946–2008	182	8	−46
1946–75	54	−13	−33
1975–96	46	56	20
1996–2008	15	−4	−14

Table 6.4. Changes in the organic composition of capital (C/V), the rate of surplus value (S/V) and the rate of profit (%), 1946–2008. Source: ONS-BOE.

British capitalism: from workshop to financial center

The data for measuring the UK rate of profit start around 1850, when British capitalism was at its global zenith as "the workshop of the world." They end in 2009, when Britain had replaced its dominance in industry and trade with a new role as a major financial center (Norfield 2012b). British capitalism is increasingly a "rentier" economy, which sucks up the surplus value appropriated by other manufacturing economies and circulates and redistributes capital looking for a higher profit in return for a "cut"— through interest rates, commissions, and fees.[8]

British capitalism has always been a financial power, but this role has become dominant within the economy as the manufacturing and industrial base has weakened and declined in world markets. This change was accelerated during the neoliberal period from 1975 onward. In particular, the relaxation of all financial regulations and restrictions, and the influx of foreign financial institutions in the "Big Bang" of the 1980s changed the structure of British capitalism decisively.

Mouatt finds that the UK financial sector profit rate rose about 45 percent from 1975 to 2008, while the non–financial sector rate rose only 18 percent. From 1997, financial profits as a share of total UK corporate profits were about 10 percent. The rate of profit fell in the UK from that date (on nearly all measures), but the share of total profits going to the financial sector reached nearly 25 percent (fig. 6.10).

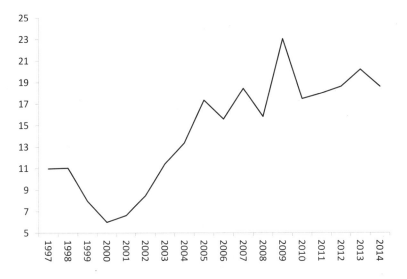

Figure 6.10. UK financial sector gross operating profits as share of total corporate profits (%), 1997–2014. Source: Mouatt (2013).

Tony Norfield points out that

> Britain's status as an imperialist power rests on two economic foundations: huge foreign direct investments and the UK-based banking system that acts as a broker for the global capitalist economy.... The financial system based in Britain is now a key factor in Britain's

global economic status. It generates important trading revenues and is
a mechanism to provide cheap funds for British capital. (2012b)

Norfield presents an index of imperialism based on the relative weight
of GDP, military firepower, financial investment, the size of the banking
system and the level of foreign exchange (FX) trading. On these criteria,
British capitalism lies second only to that of the United States.

3. Conclusion

Marx's law of the tendency of the rate of profit to fall helps to explain the
development of British capitalism since it became the hegemonic capitalist
power in the mid-nineteenth century—at the time Marx himself was writing
Capital, his fully fledged analysis of the capitalist mode of production, based
on the reality of the UK economy.

From the analysis of the movement in the rate of profit from various
sources, it is clear that there was a secular decline in the UK rate of profit over
the last 150 years, supporting the predictions of Marx's law and paralleling
the decline of British imperialism. The periods of steepest decline in the
rate of profit matched the most difficult times for British capitalism: the
Long Depression of the 1880s, the collapse of British industry after 1918,
and the long profitability crisis after 1946. But there were also periods
when profitability rose: the recovery after the 1880s in the late Victorian
era; the substantial recovery in the 1920s and 1930s after the defeat of the
British labor movement and demolition of old industries during the Great
Depression; and the neoliberal revival based on further dismantling of the
welfare state, the privatization of state assets, the defeat of labor struggles,
and, most important, the switch to reliance on financial sectors as Britain
increasingly adopted rentier capitalism.[9]

The UK economy now lives, or dies, with the health of the global
financial sector and its associated business, legal, and commercial services.

Appendix: Sources and Methods

For the period 1855–2008, the following sources have been used, and where the
author has used the database to calculate the rate of profit, the method and categories
are specified below. Excel sheets with workings are available on request.

AMECO. From EU Commission AMECO database, available at http://ec.europa
.eu/economy_finance/ameco/user/serie/SelectSerie.cfm. Formula: *Net national
income (UKAUVNN) − employee compensation (UKAUWCD)/net capital stock
(UKAOKND); inflated by GDP price deflator (UKAPIGT) + employee compensation
= rate of profit.*

Extended PENN world tables. Extended PENN world table v4.0, compiled by
Adalmir Marquetti, available at http://homepage.newschool.edu/~foleyd/epwt/.
Formula: *GDP (X) − labor compensation (N × w)/K + N × w = rate of profit.*

Maito. Fixed reproductive capital from Office for National Statistics (ONS), available at www.ons.gov.uk. Net profits from Piketty and Zucman (1855–2010), available at http://piketty.pse.ens.fr/files/capitalisback/UK.xls.

Office for National Statistics. Profitability of UK non-financial companies, available at http://www.ons.gov.uk/ons/rel/pnfc2/profitability-of-uk-companies/q1–2015/dst-profitability-of-uk-companies-q1–2015.html.

ONS-BOE. Bank of England, "Three centuries of data," available at http://www.bankofengland.co.uk/research/Documents/onebank/threecenturies_v2.2.xlsx. Formula: real GDP—column B170–323; labor share—supply-side data F9–162; fixed capital stock—supply-side data E9–162. *real GDP – labor compensation (real GDP × labor share)/fixed capital stock + labor compensation = rate of profit.*

ONS-Historic Cost. From the UK ONS series. Formula: *gross operating surplus (UKNRJKA + UKNQNVA)/net capital stock (UKCIXI + UKCIXH)* deflated by historic cost depreciation (as measured from US data).

PENN world tables. Available at http://www.rug.nl/research/ggdc/data/pwt/pwt-8.1. Formula: GDP *(cgdpo)*; capital stock *(ck)*; labor share *(labsh)*. *GDP – labor compensation (cgdpo × labsh)/ck + labor compensation = rate of profit.*

Notes

1 For a much fuller account and defense of Marx's law from its realistic assumptions, see Carchedi and Roberts (2013).
2 For the fuller account of the mechanism of crises, see Carchedi (2011).
3 For an explanation of why variable capital can be calculated and included, see Carchedi and Roberts, "The Rate of Profit and Circulating Capital," unpublished manuscript.
4 "Permanent crises do not exist"—Marx and Engels (1990, p. 128n).
5 See Arnold and McCartney (2002). The author has calculated the rate of profit from the raw data provided from Arnold and McCartney in Roberts (2009).
6 The data for Cockshott and colleagues are taken from Brown and Mohun (2011), table 3.2 (Cockshott et al. 1995, p. 121).
7 For more on the debate on whether to use historic cost or current cost measures for fixed capital and depreciation, see Roberts (2011).
8 To quote Tony Norfield (2012b), "Marx once famously summed up capital as 'dead labour, that, vampire-like, only lives by sucking living labour, and lives the more, the more labour it sucks.' To continue the metaphor, British imperialism has developed a financial system that acts like a blood bank for the value produced worldwide, one that takes a sip of every value flowing through it."
9 Financial services now account for almost half of total FDI flows into the UK—£21.3 billion out of £43.7 billion—and the UK dominates mergers and acquisitions in Europe for fully 41 percent (US$75 billion) of total European deal value of US$185 billion. In terms of international listings, the London Stock Exchange is second only to New York; the LSE had 298 international listings, compared with 523 on the NYSE, 357 on the NASDAQ OMX, and 123 on Euronext (see Norfield, "The City UK," 2015).

References

Arnold, A. J. and S. McCartney (2002) "National Income and Sectoral Rates of Return on UK Risk-Bearing Capital 1855–1914," University of Exeter.

Bank of England (2016) "Three Centuries of Data," available at http://www.bankofengland.co.uk/research/Pages/onebank/threecenturies.aspx.

Brown, V. and S. Mohun (2011) "The Rate of Profit in the UK, 1920–1938," *Cambridge Journal of Economics*, Vol 35, No 6.

Carchedi, G. (2011) *Behind the Crisis*, Brill.

Carchedi, G. and M. Roberts (2013) "Marx's Law of Profitability: Answering Old and New Misconceptions," *Critique: Journal of Socialist Theory*, Vol 42, No 4.

———. (Unpublished) "The Rate of Profit and Circulating Capital," available at www.marx2010.weebly.com.

TheCityUK (2015) "UK's Competitiveness as a Global Financial Centre—August 2015," https://www.thecityuk.com/research/annual-report-201516/.

Cockshott et al. (1995) "Does Marx Need to Transform," in R. Bellofiore, ed. (1998) *Marxian Economics: A Reappraisal*, Vol 2, Macmillan and St. Martin's.

Lewis, W. A. (1967) "The Deceleration of British Growth 1873–1913," available at http://www.princeton.edu/rpds/papers/WP_003.pdf.

Maito, E. E. (2014) "The Historical Transience of Capital: The Downward Trend in the Rate of Profit since XIX Century," reprinted in ths volume as chapter 4, "The Tendency of the Rate of Profit to Fall since the Nineteenth Century and a World Rate of Profit.

Marx, K. and F. Engels (1990) *Collected Works*, Vol 32, International Publishers.

Mouatt, S. (2013) "The Dissolution of the Financial State," paper presented at AHE Conference, London and Southampton Solent University.

Norfield, T. (2012a) "Churchill, Keynes, Gold & Empire—A Historical Vignette," *Economics of Imperialism* (blog).

———. (2012b) "The Rate of Profit, Finance and Imperialism," paper presented at conference of the AHE/FAPE/IIPPE in Paris, available at http://economicsofimperialism.blogspot.co.uk/2012/07/the-rate-of-profit-finance-imperialism.html.

Roberts, M. (2009) *The Great Recession*, Lulu.

———. (2011) "Measuring the Rate of Profit: Profit Cycles and the Next Recession," paper presented at AHE Conference, available at http://gesd.free.fr/mrobprof.pdf.

CHAPTER 7

THE LONG DEPRESSION IN THE SPANISH ECONOMY: BUBBLE, PROFITS, AND DEBT

Juan Pablo Mateo

1. Introduction

In this chapter I analyze the crisis of the Spanish economy using a Marxist approach. The basic reference period is the long wave of growth beginning after the crisis of 1992–93 and ending in 2008.[1] From the second half of that year, Spain was plunged into a Long Depression in which there was a close relationship between the housing bubble, profits, and debt.

There are deep controversies among Marxists over the theory of crisis, and in particular over the causes of the recent Great Recession. The idea here is that crises are due to a problem of insufficient capacity to generate surplus, the logical outcome of the labor theory of value (LTV). This means a crisis of capital valorization, manifested as a drop in profitability. Based on this initial hypothesis, the purpose is to elucidate *how* (and not *if*) the general laws of capital accumulation manifested themselves in Spain. In other words, what are the particular features of the law of the falling tendency of the rate of profit (RoP, *r*) in Spain—that is, the specific traits that have enabled the law to reveal itself in a particular way (see Tapia and Astarita 2011)?

Why is this study of the economic crisis in Spain interesting for the Marxist approach? Several elements can be enumerated to justify its relevance:

The center–periphery dichotomy. First, Spain is a developed country belonging to the Organisation for Economic Co-operation and Development (OECD) club. But at the same time, it belongs to the periphery of a currency area, the Eurozone, the core of which has a higher level of productive development. This duality comes with some specific factors, such as the importance of the foreign trade and the type of productive specialization.

The distortions of the accumulation process. The growth phase referred to in Spain was characterized by a sectoral restructuring and, above all, by a speculative boom associated with the construction sector, mainly residential.

The latter requires applying a theory of rent and finance (fictitious capital) to a phenomenon in which many different aspects converge.[2]

Difficulties in estimating the surplus in Spain's System of National Accounts (SNA). There are several reasons for this:

(1) (There was a large increase in credit availability, supported by a huge net inflow of foreign capital, which has generated high indebtedness in Spanish corporations and households. This greatly increased the surplus in circulation with respect to that internally generated.

(2) Valorization and the inflation of asset prices diverged, with banks playing a central role. This implies a certain "fictitious" component in the surplus recorded in SNA.

(3) The rescue of banks by the European Central Bank (ECB) and the Spanish government socialized losses in various ways, so the crisis of profitability was reflected in public debt, falling wages, and so forth.

There is another set of reasons of a different kind to justify the relevance of this study: the almost complete absence of research employing the Marxian approach or any focusing on the central role of valorization to characterize the Spanish crisis. López et al. (2013) estimate business profits using the Levy-Kalecki equation. In their work, they pinpoint the need to include extra profits (capital gains), "profits derived from the change in the valuation of assets" (p. 37), which are not incorporated in the Levy-Kalecki equation. From a Marxist approach, Boundi (2014) addresses the profit rate and its determinants, but from a long-term perspective (1964–2012). This study is not focused on the current crisis, but it does show that the RoP has not recovered in recent decades, and that "the collapse of housing demand created a large surplus that could not be realized as profit, all of which led to the collapse of prices in 2008" (López et al., p. 96). From an orthodox view, the BBVA Foundation (FBBVA) has published several reports on the process of capital accumulation in Spain. Although not prioritizing the central role of the RoP, Mas et al. (2013) point out an issue that we share (and this is probably not very coherent with the marginalist theory of value): that "the rhythm of Spanish accumulation during the last stage of the boom was not accompanied by a sufficient improvement in the capacity to generate value. It was probably because the profitability of investments did not actually depend on productivity, but rather on the revaluation of assets" (p. 43). This idea is followed by Perez (2013) in analyzing the conventional indicators of profitability. While not characterizing the crisis as originating from a fall in the rate of profit, Perez still attributes its decline to the falling of both demand and profit per unit sold, which in his view "reflects one of the characteristics of the Spanish economy: the rigidity of the productive and cost structure" (p. 175), emphasizing those (so-called) "rigidities" related to wages.

This chapter presents both theoretical aspects (section 2), and empirical results (section 3), in which the profitability and evolution of the main macroeconomic categories of Marxian approach are included. In order to shed light on the specifics outlined in the previous section, section 4 subsequently addresses the internal restructuring of the Spanish economy by both sectors and assets.

2. Theoretical Elements of the Analysis
The theory of crisis

This section considers aspects of the theory of crisis that are particularly relevant to developments in the Spanish economy.[3]

The ultimate cause of crises in Spain, like in any other capitalist economy, is an insufficient capacity to generate surplus that increases the value of the stock of capital. Profits, however, may not only be generated from production; it is also possible to receive foreign savings or to create internal debt, given the endogenous capacity to create means of payment by the financial sector, leading to a gap between profits appropriated and surplus generated. Although through credit, extra surplus can be expanded and maintained over time (especially with favorable conditions in the Eurozone), it is ultimately the internal productive development, expressed within capitalism as production of surplus value, that must sustain accumulation. In this sense, we can speak of certain *underlying conditions of profitability.*

The outbreak of a crisis occurs when investment collapses. However, the way that the link between profitability and accumulation materializes depends on several elements: existing alternatives for profit in other sectors or countries, funding opportunities, the institutional framework (property rights, free movement of capital, potential restrictions, etc.), the type of investment (degree of obsolescence of assets, expectations of demand, risks, etc.), and economic conditions (inflation or deflation, etc.).

The profit rate is a ratio that does not indicate the level at which the crisis is generated; therefore the general idea of profitability must be approached from different angles and using different measures.[4] In the first instance, the RoP constitutes the basic indicator of the ability to generate surplus, so it can be considered as a cause of the crisis, as long as capitalist production is seen as the production of surplus value. At the same time, this ratio can be expressed from its determinants of production and distribution. In this sense, it would be a consequence, for it can be characterized as a "surface variable" (Tapia and Astarita 2011). This duality does not negate the need to distinguish causes from consequences, nor to establish a logical order of causality levels to characterize the crisis.

Thus, although the origin of crises is found in the area of value production, their manifestation substantially differs. Crises are perceived as imbalances in the *commercial* sphere, that is, between production and demand (whether it be excessive production or impossibility to sell on the part of businesses); in *finance*, because of the effect of the banking collapse on the rest of the branches; in *indebtedness*, from the inability to repay debts incurred by companies, the state, and/or households; in excessive volatility of the *exchange rate* (usually a depreciation of the domestic currency); or in *state intervention*, in terms of the so-called "rigidities" against the free market. So crises generate a corresponding *specific theory of the crisis*, depending on the dominant element in each situation.

What is important is to define the underlying phenomenon of these imbalances. In other words, we must integrate the essence and appearance, not through a multiplicity of theories of crisis elaborated from their outward appearance, but on the contrary, by following the method of Marx. The aim is to reveal how the fundamental laws of capital accumulation are manifested in the Spanish economy and how they generate crises. And that must follow the underlying cause: an insufficient capacity to generate surplus.[5] This is the only way to provide an explanatory framework for the recurrence of crises as necessary, inevitable, and indispensable moments in the process of capitalist accumulation.

Real estate speculation

A model of accumulation that is based largely on a speculative process associated with residential-asset inflation poses certain challenges for the labor theory of value and the theory of crisis. In capitalism, the land becomes a commodity that, although not a product of labor, does have a price. As such, it fluctuates for different reasons, but its main aspect is its relation to a future income. The investor acquires land by paying a high price because it gives him the possibility to receive an annual rent. The existence of this permanent flow of income can be considered as an interest from a fictitious capital (Marx 1894).

> The land becomes a form of fictitious capital, and the land market functions simply as a particular branch – albeit with some particular characteristics – of the circulation of interest-bearing capital. Under such conditions the land is treated as a pure financial asset which is bought and sold according to the rent it yields. Like all such forms of fictitious capital, what is traded is a claim upon future revenues. (Harvey 1982, p. 347)

The rent is surplus value, product of the surplus labor of the worker. Therefore, it is the existence of a ground rent susceptible to appropriation that generates the stimulus to speculate, not the asset (building/house) itself.

These characteristics of land, as happens with housing, push higher the price of securities in times of low interest rates and a plethora of capital. This may generate speculative phenomena characterized by a disconnection between prices and their fundamentals, that is, conditions of production according to the socially necessary labor time. Thus, capital is attracted by the possibility of achieving higher profits in real estate. As investment increases, both prices and profits continue to rise. On the demand side, houses are acquired not only for use by a great part of the population, but also as an asset to generate profit.

In this way, profitability is actually linked to monetary price, so it is possible to allude to it as a "price effect" because fictitious capital can itself create forms of (fictitious) profit without creating surplus value (Jones 2013). This dynamic is manifested as a demand phenomenon because house prices, and thus profits, depend on the ability to capture a flow of income from buyers. But this "primacy of demand" is merely apparent, since it is not independent of the conditions of surplus production. Therefore, in this context the rate of profit of the Spanish national accounts contains a fictitious component, so it is necessary to include the indebtedness in the analysis of profitability.

3. Profitability and Accumulation in Spain

After signing the Treaty on European Union in Maastricht in February 1992, an economic program of neoliberal inspiration began with the purpose of joining the European Economic and Monetary Union (EMU). The fixed exchange rates were established in 1999, and from January 2002, a new currency began to circulate: the euro.

Spain was incorporated into a monetary area that had an overall higher level of productive development.[6] Economic growth between 1994 and 2007 was great than 3 percent annually (OECD 2016), above the average of the OECD member countries and, in particular, the European Union and the Eurozone average, as well as other advanced economies such as the United Kingdom and the United States. The recession that emerged in 2008, however, had a bigger impact in Spain compared to other economies. In 2015, the Spanish GDP at current prices was still 3.65 percent below the level of 2008 (INE 2016), so only after eight years, in 2016, could the Spanish economy reach the peak of 2008 at current prices. A recovery is currently under way, but the crisis of profitability is still not solved, so

more destruction of capital (in price terms)—of means of production and/
or labor—is required.

Profitability of capital

In this section I address the question of profitability using various estimates.
Inasmuch as the business surplus has been largely linked to housing (the
core of the real estate speculative process), a reference to different price
deflators should be the starting point. As shown in figure 7.1, there are two
striking gaps. First, that between the housing price (*PH*) index and those
of both the GDP (*PY*) and capital stock (*PK*). According to the Ministry of
Public Works (2016), the price per square meter of private housing rose from
€670.8 in 1995Q1 to €2101.4 in 2008Q1, when it reached its maximum—
that is, three times the initial value. *PH* grew during the boom years, with
annual rates of increase of 16–18 percent from 2002 until mid-2005. The
contrast is evident with *PY*, which "only" increased by slightly more than
50 percent in 1995–2008. From 2008 onward, the trend of housing prices
reverses, with a decline of −30 percent between March of that year and the
last quarter of 2014 (MPW 2016).

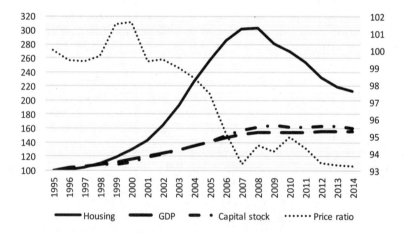

Figure 7.1. Comparative path of housing, GDP and capital stock price
indexes (%, 1995 = 100), 1995–2014. Price indexes of housing, GDP
and the total net non-residential capital stock in the left axis. Price
ratio (PY/PK) in the right axis (excluding finances and real estate
activities). Sources: BoS (2016a), FBBVA (2015), MPW (2016).

There is a kind of divergence between *PY* and *PK* from 2000 to 2007. On
the one hand, the relative rate of inflation in Spain has been 20 percent
higher than in the Eurozone (eighteen countries) in 1995–2007 (AMECO
2017), therefore leading to the appreciation of the real exchange rate, in a

context in which the euro has appreciated by 78 percent with the US dollar from 2002 to 2008 (BoS 2016a). On the other, the ratio PY/PK decreased by 8 percent between 2000 and 2007, so the relative cost of the capital stock in relation to the general deflator increased, thus contributing to the fall in profitability.

Therefore, the mass of profit (excluding finances and real estate, "FIRE") deflated by the capital stock price index (as claimed by Shaikh 2016) reached a maximum of €327 billion (at 2006 prices) two years before the outbreak of the crisis, in 2006, and also prior to the collapse of the housing prices and investment, as shown in figure 7.2. Between 1995 and 2000, the generation of surplus increased intensely, to an annual average of 3.3 percent; but between 2000 and 2006 it slows down to just 1.1 percent annually. During 2006–2009, three years after the peak, the annual drop reaches –1.9 percent, following a mere partial recovery, and still in 2014 the mass of profit was 6.3 percent below the 2006 level. But if compared with the mass of surplus using the GDP deflator, figure 7.2 shows another decisive gap. As a consequence of the relative increasing cost of the capital stock, the general purchasing power (using PY) of the surplus generated kept rising until 2007, up to a total of 16 percent in 2000–2007, which in fact is misleading when it comes to the analysis of the capital accumulation process. In this sense, first, there is indeed a near stagnation of the mass of profit in relation to the capacity to dispose of capital assets, with barely a 6.9 percent increase between 2000 and 2006; and second, it begins to descend one year before of the fall in investment and the housing price index, in 2006.[7]

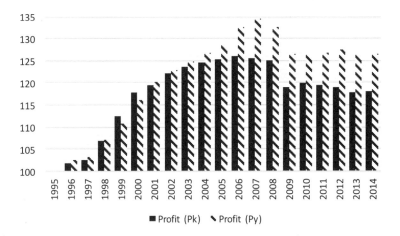

Figure 7.2. The mass of profit (%, 1995 = 100), 1995–2014. Mass of profit in real terms, using the capital stock deflator (Pk) and the GDP deflator (Py). Sources: FBBVA (2015), INE (2015b).

The second variable is the rate of profit, a fundamental category that indicates the extent to which capital achieves its goal of valorization. It expresses business profit (p) in relation to the outlay, materialized in a net nonresidential fixed stock of capital (K), so $r = p/K$. Figure 7.3 shows three measures, depending on the surplus used: (1) gross profit from all the branches, (2) excluding FIRE, and (3) also excluding government activity. FIRE and government are excluded because they can be considered as unproductive (Shaikh and Tonak 1994. It is clear that there was a huge fall in these measures of profitability in the period of intense economic growth (1995–2008), ranging from 20.5 percent to 32.5 percent, which finally reaches 30–42 percent until 2014. Moreover; once FIRE is excluded from the analysis, the profit rate falls 10–12 percentage points more, while the government activity only affects the absolute level of the profit rate, not its evolution. Along the path of the profit rate, the fall is more intense from 2000 to 2008, as it reaches an annual average of –3.8 percent—higher than during both the crisis period (2008–2014), when it amounted to –2.5 percent, or during the second half of the '90s, when it was barely –1 percent per year. However, if mixed income is excluded from the total profit (but the amount of capital is kept the same), the fall of the profit rate in 1995–2014 is limited to –25.8 percent, reaching –45 percent if depreciation is taken out from the surplus and gross capital stock is used (instead of "net"), and even –60 percent in the case of net profit (without depreciation, but including mixed income) in relation to gross capital stock (FBBVA 2015, INE 2015b, OECD 2016).

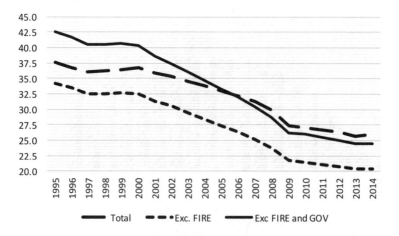

Figure 7.3. The gross rate of profit in Spain before and after the Great Recession (%), 1995–2014. Measures of the profit rate using the whole gross profit recorded in the SNA (total), excluding finance, insurance and real estate (exc. FIRE), and additionally with government activities

(exc. FIRE and GOV). Capital stock: net nonresidential stock of capital of the year before (t − 1). Sources: INE (2015b), FBBVA (2015).

In historical perspective, it has to be considered that the profit rate excluding FIRE in 1995 is 31 percent lower than the average of the period 1970–77, which would be 40 percent lower in relation to the peak of profitability reached in 1974 (EU-Klems 2014; FBBVA 2015). Thus, there is both an absolute low level of profitability at the beginning of the boom and then a deep fall, characterizing the underlying profitability crisis.[8]

The conventional indexes of profitability of non-financial corporations (NFCs) also have to be taken into account in the light of the speculative boom and its "capital gains." They reveal a relatively constant level (or a slight increase) until the second half of 2006, when the maximum rate of profit is reached, with the exception of the net profit over fixed assets (BACH 2015), which rose by 64 percent. Then, a sharp decline begins, before the outbreak of the crisis. The fall of different ratios from the BoS between 2006 and the average of 2011–14 reaches −42/−54 percent, while that of measures of the BACH database shows an even higher drop in 2006–13, which in the case of the above-mentioned net profit over fixed assets amounts to −67 percent in relation to the average of the last three years (fig. 7.4).

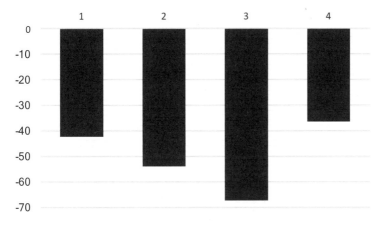

Figure 7.4. Rate of change of conventional measures of profitability (%). (1) Ordinary return of net assets; (2) ordinary return on equity; (3) net profit or loss of the period / fixed assets; (4) net operating profit / total balance sheet. Variation from 2006 to 2011–14 average (ratios 1 and 2) and 2011–13 (ratios 3 and 4). Sources: 1 and 2: BoS (2016b); 3 and 4: BACH (2015).

Along with this path, a growing divergence occurs in profitability based on the size of corporations. In general, the absolute level of profitability in relation to total assets is higher for larger corporations from 2001/2005

(BACH/BoS, respectively), and the subsequent fall is higher the smaller the corporation. Thus, the net return on total assets of large corporations falls by −39 percent between 2006 and 2011–14, but it reaches −43 percent and −69 percent for medium and small ones, respectively (BoS 2016b), and −62/−65 percent and −93 percent for large/medium-sized and small corporations, respectively, following BACH (2015) until 2012.

Finally, the stock market also reflects the same trends, but in a more pronounced way. Both the general index of the Madrid Stock Exchange and the IBEX 35 grew substantially between the last quarter of 2002 and the third and fourth quarters of 2007, peaking in October of that year with a cumulative increase of 192–199 percent.[9] From then until mid-2012, the fall exceeded 60 percent (BoS 2016c).

Thus, it has been shown that the sharp decline in profitability prior to the crisis appears in a clearer way in conventional indexes of NFC due to the asset-inflation model that has led the valorization cycle. For its part, the closest expression to the Marxian approach (p/K) also shows a huge fall, but also an absolute level substantially lower than the one existing decades ago. This low level of profit rate, an index of the capacity to generate surplus, is in any case essential for understanding the housing boom because it "makes the economy less stable, more prone to crises and serious slumps," so that "many phenomena that are sometimes regarded as effects of a *decline* in the rate of profit are actually effects of a *low* rate" (Kliman 2011, p. 18). In addition, the proliferation in Spain of small-sized companies has brought a very unequal incidence of crisis, as SMEs suffered a more acute problem of profitability.

Debt and socialization of losses

One of the specific features of the asset-inflation model of capital accumulation has been the extraordinary growth of credit. Consequently, the Spanish economy has shown a high level of indebtedness in recent years, exacerbated by the crisis and fed by the neoliberal context. Thus, the possibility of achieving significant gains in the real estate business also attracted many foreign funds, largely channeled through the banks. Real estate came to represent 7–10 percent of GDP in the first quarter of 2005 and 2009 (BoS 2016a).

The total debt of institutional agents doubled in relation to GDP. It represented 135 percent in 1995, but in 2012 it reached 270 percent. However, its composition has substantially changed. General government debt declined from 65 percent of GDP in 1996 to 35 percent in 2007, representing only 15 percent of the total debt stock in 2007. Meanwhile, households and NFC debt increased significantly. NFC increased their rhythm of indebtedness from 1999, with an average annual growth of 23 percent from mid-year until the end of 2007. In 1995, the stock of debt was only 43 percent of GDP, but it reached 115 percent of GDP in 2009–2010, which represented 44–45 percent of total debt in these years (fig. 7.5).

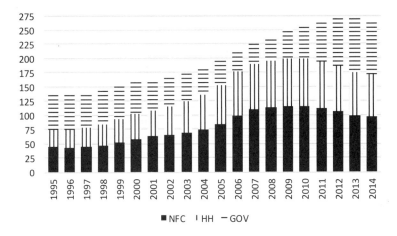

Figure 7.5. Debt of government (GOV), households (HH), and non-financial corporations (NFC) (% of GDP), 1995–2014. Source: BoS (2016c).

The rising debt of NFCs was due to the issuance of bonds, as NFCs did not have their own resources for investment. In the case of households, and mainly working-class households (the majority), it was driven by the rise in house prices in a context of stagnant wages.[10] The household debt-to-GDP ratio rose from 30 percent in 1995 to over 44 percent in 2000, with a similar rise in NFC debt. The banks lent to both the supply (NFC) and the demand (households) side of this credit expansion, thus receiving significant profits from their intermediation activity. Out of total bank loans, those related to the real estate bubble (construction and housing) increased from 38 percent to 60 percent of the total between 1995 and 2006–2008, and since then continue to account for 58–59 percent of the total (BoS 2016a).

For capital, however, rising housing prices were a source of enrichment, while for working-class households it was impoverishment, as to have access to a house meant reducing their spending on other necessaries (see Mateo 2016, Mateo and Montanyà 2018). But if sales are not fully achieved, the market cannot validate the concrete labor embodied as socially necessary labor, so no value or surplus is generated.[11] Then the amount of money in circulation, as well as profits, are not supported by a corresponding creation of value. This imbalance requires a devaluation of the currency or of goods. In this situation, it is clear that the existence of the euro implies the need to implement policies to reduce costs by cutting wages and rising interest rates (risk premium) to protect the value of the euro, hence the monetarist logic of the European Central Bank (ECB).

A holistically based Marxist approach takes the whole valorization process as the starting point for the analysis of indebtedness. Thus, it is the level of the profit rate that ultimately led to a problem of high debt (Roberts 2012). So, the debt of different agents, private or public, has to be addressed as being part of the same whole process, interconnected and related to the capitalist production process. In these terms, the Spanish crisis was expressed as a problem of excessive debt, and so of a banking character, because when profitability starts falling, the interest burden appears as the cause of the crisis. In fact, there has been a deep increase in the amount of profits destined to interest payments after 2006, together with a plunge of the spread of profitability in relation to the cost of debt (–94 percent in 2006–12) (fig. 7.6).

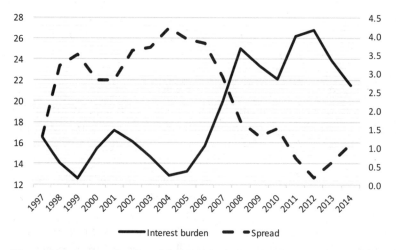

Figure 7.6. Interest burden (%, LHS) and spread return on investment and debt cost (RHS), 1997–2014. Interest burden = interests on borrowed funds/(gross operating profit + financial revenue). Source: BoS (2016b).

The rise in the interest burden expresses the recomposition of the conditions of valorization after the distortion introduced by the appreciation of the real exchange rate in the growth period. In this sense, there was another consequence. After the outbreak of the crisis, a process of deleveraging of NFC and households began, along with a bailout of the banking system. The result was the corresponding increase in government debt between 2006 and 2014, from less than 40 percent to 94 percent of GDP. In the last instance, the aims of the economic policy were to avoid further losses for the private sector and to reduce the different expression of the wage (also social spending and pensions). This strategy explains the extraordinary length of the recession, because the rise in the government debt expresses the underlying profitability problem of the private sector (Norfield 2012).

Until 2012, the Spanish government had spent €164.3 billion, without counting more than €900 billion in collateral (for banking debt emission and implicitly to bank deposits) (Mato 2013), as well as the deferred-tax assets, out of a GDP of €1,042 billion in 2012 (INE 2015b). However, it was the ECB that served as the main provider of funds to save the Spanish banking system, lending €357.3 billion (Mato 2013), that is, nearly a third of the liquidity injections to banks carried out by this institution, at an interest cost between 0 and 1 percent, generally for three years.

These injections were not to fund investments, because around one-third of the amount served to meet the liquidity needs of banks, while the rest went to purchasing government debt at 3.5–4.5 percent interest (Lorenta and Capella 2014). This spending did not boost the profit rate—except in a predatory way, through indirect transfer to private banks—and the underlying profitability crisis remains. Profitability has not fallen further during the years of crisis because of two added and interrelated reasons (Pérez 2012): (1) incomes of financial and extraordinary character resulting from inflows of subsidiaries of the group abroad, given the rise in foreign direct investments outflows since the '90s, in turn favored by the financial support of the state; and (2) the corresponding tax cuts, which emerge as the public sector deficit. In short, the rise in debt has a class character, and it is another manifestation of the crisis of profitability, showing the further need to wipe out excess capital.

Technical change, productivity, and distributional pattern

The process of capital accumulation has been very intense in Spain. Investment (I, or GFCF) grew by 6.3 percent annually between 1995 and 2007, accounting for 31 percent of GDP in this last year. The consumption by both households and the public sector has grown less, 3.6 percent and 4.2 percent, respectively (INE 2015b). Between 1995 and 2007, the rate of accumulation (k) averaged 4.6 percent per year, with a smooth cyclical path: it peaked in the late '90s (1999) and, after a slight slowdown, it began again to rise until 2007.[12]

Despite this high level in the rate of accumulation, one of the particular outcomes has been the extraordinary capacity to create jobs. In fact, Spain was responsible for more than a third of the jobs created in the Eurozone during this growth period (Estrada et al. 2009). After ranging 20–24 percent from 1992Q4 to 1997Q4, the rate of unemployment fell to 8 percent in 2006–2007 (BoS 2016a). Waged employment grew at an annual average rate of 4 percent, continuing the tendency toward an increase of the salaried workers within the occupied population, from 79 percent in 1995 to around

86 percent since 2006. This evolution happened in two phases: one where wage employment grew at an average of 4.6 percent between 1995 and 2000, and the other where it did so at "only" 3.7 percent between 2000 and 2007 (fig. 7.7).

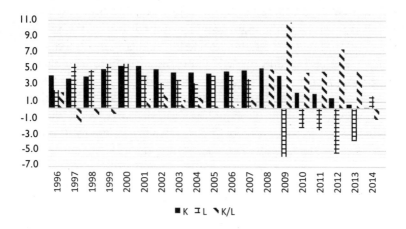

Figure 7.7. Annual rates of change of the stock of capital at constant prices, (K), waged labor (L), and mechanization (K/L, %), 1996–2014. Sources: INE (2015b), FBBVA (2015).

The K/L ratio is an indicator of the degree of mechanization of the production process because it represents the monetary value at constant prices of the stock of capital per waged employee. So it can be considered as an approximation of the technical composition of capital (TCC). Contrary to what would be expected from an expansion phase, between 1995 and 2007 the K/L ratio showed only a slight increase, just 5.4 percent. Beginning in 2007 the growth in the ratio is higher, explained by an increase in unemployment, along with rising idle capacity in corporations. Indeed, the trajectory of the TCC was determined more by the dynamics of employment, for in the second half of the '90s TCC fell by an average of −0.32 percent per year, while growing at 0.99 percent in 2000–2007.

This peculiar behavior of the TCC reflects the distorted nature of capital accumulation and the important sectoral reconfiguration of the Spanish economy (see section 4). This is shown in figure 7.8, in which TCC is related to labor productivity and real wages, both determining the rate of profit. Consider the following equation:

$$r = \frac{Y - W}{K} = \frac{Y^*P_Y - W^*P_Y}{K^*P_K} = \frac{\pi - w}{TCC}$$

where π is the product (value added) at constant prices ($Y^{\star}$) per waged worker, the index of labor productivity, and w is the wage per worker (W/L) in real terms.[13] Therefore, the profit rate depends on the profit margin ($\pi -$ w) reached by capital with mechanization (TCC), as adjusted by the price deflators of GDP and the stock of capital (PY and PK, respectively). For thirteen years labor productivity did not increase. Indeed, when deflated by the capital stock index price, it fell by 14.3 percent between 1995 and 2007, and 8.2 percent in relation to the GDP price index. However, productivity recovered after 2007, along with the recession.[14] Thus, the Spanish economy was unable to increase the value produced per employee, or to raise the capacity to generate surplus during the long boom.

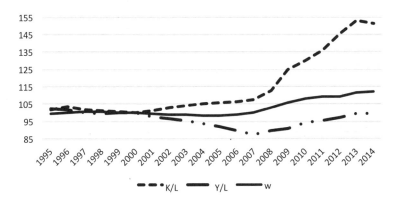

Figure 7.8. Technical composition (K/L), labor productivity (Y/L; capital stock deflator) and real wage (per worker, w) (%, 2000 = 100). Sources: INE (2015b), FBBVA (2015).

The contradictory path of TCC and π has its corollary in what can be denominated as "capital productivity" (PK). This category shows the ability of capital, understood as a social relationship, to increase output, although only its fixed constant part of the stock is used to measure this:

$$PK = \frac{Y}{K} = \frac{\pi}{TCC} \cdot \frac{P_Y}{P_K}$$

The PK ratio relates the productive efficiency of technical change (π/TCC) with the relative increase or cheapening of the assets of capital stock (PY/PK).[15] In the growing phase, PK fell by 18 percent, a trend that intensified after the crisis. After 2008–2009, it fell by more than 3 percent per year, so that in 2014 it was 34 percent lower than in 1995. Before 2000 it remained almost constant due to a relative cheapening of the fixed capital stock (small increase of PY/PK). Since 2000, however, it began a decline derived primarily from the negative contribution of the productive efficiency of investment, which fell by 11.1 percent until 2007, but also because of the above-mentioned relative increase in the capital stock prices (fall of PY/PK). This ratio (Y/K) is important because it is a key determinant of the RoP, together with the profit-share (p/Y), and it expresses the maximum rate of profit:

$$r = \frac{B}{Y} \cdot \frac{Y}{K}$$

The path of profitability coincides with that of PK if p/Y remains constant. In fact, the profit share in Spain was 45 percent in 1995, and 5 percentage points smaller in 2008–2011, excluding net taxes (INE 2015b), but in a context of an increase in the number of salaried workers within total employment. Therefore, as can be seen in figure 7.9, PK fell by only 2.7 points, less than it did between 2000 and 2014. This shows that the technology composition is the major contributor to the behavior of profitability.

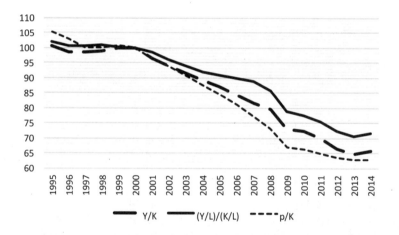

Figure 7.9. Capital productivity, productivity efficiency of investment and prices (%, 1999 = 100), 1995–2014. Y/K: output–capital ratio, current prices; (Y/L)/TCC: ratio of labor productivity and mechanization (productivity efficiency of investment), constant prices, using the GDP and capital stock price indexes, respectively; p/K: rate of profit. Sources: INE (2015b), FBBVA (2015).

In short, the intense process of capital accumulation in Spain that led to the long boom from 1995 to 2007–2008 was also able to generate more employment. But more concrete labor does not involve a greater capacity to generate value. Therefore, in order to explain this paradox, the distortion of investment is addressed in the next section in terms of the housing bubble and the productive specialization.

4. Internal Restructuring of the Spanish Economy

In this section I analyze distortions within the accumulation process in relation to the type of assets in which investment was made, and the sectoral reconfiguration experienced by the Spanish economy.

The distribution of total investment in Spain has been biased toward construction-related assets (fig. 7.10), which represented 68.6 percent of the total in 1995 and 71–72 percent between 2004 and 2007. Residential investment stands out within this category, rising from 29.8 percent to 39–40 percent between 2003 and 2006.

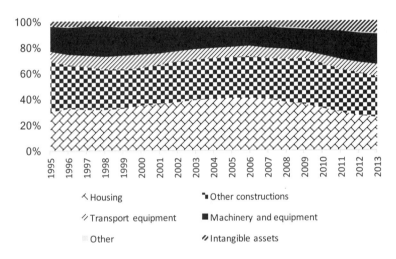

Figure 7.10. Composition of investment by type of asset (%), 1995–2013. Gross investment of "intangible assets"; "machinery, equipment and other assets"; "transportation equipment"; "other constructions"; and "other" (cultivated assets). Source: FBBVA (2015).

The "price effect" of this accumulation process is reflected first in the price deflators of different types of assets of investment flows. There is a divergence between the movement in prices of "other constructions" and "housing," on the one hand, and "transportation equipment" and "machinery, equipment and other assets," on the other. Figure 7.11 shows the average annual rates of change, which led to different corresponding, huge accumulated variations. In the first group, prices increased by 69 percent (other constructions) and 201 percent (housing, from MPW 2016), respectively, between 1995 and 2007, but prices increased by only 10–26 percent in transportation and machinery.

This asymmetry deepened in the subperiod 1999–2006, when the price deflators of residential assets and the rest of construction grew by 139 percent and 45 percent, respectively, compared to 9–16 percent of the others.

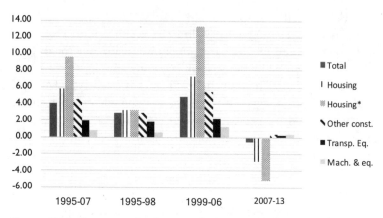

Figure 7.11. Average price increase in investment by type of asset (%), 1995–2013. Annual rates of change of investment assets price as an index of housing, other constructions, transport equipment, and machinery and equipment. "Housing*" refers to housing prices as consumption goods, recorded by MPW (2016), from the price index used by FBBVA (2015) to elaborate the stock capital database, which does not incorporate the revalorization. Sources: FBBVA (2015), MPW (2016).

This asymmetry by type of asset was also reflected in the economic structure. The most dynamic sectors were the non-tradable and/or those directly or indirectly related to the housing bubble (table 7.1). More than a third of total investment on average, including that of residential type, went into construction and real estate, reaching 45.7 percent between 2004 and 2007. In the last four years of the boom, construction received the same percentage of investment as all the other branches of industry put together, including not only the entire manufacturing industry, but also energy and mines. Even during the long depression, investment in construction matched that destined to manufacturing, which was falling within industry. In addition, trade, transport, and hotels received 17.5 percent of total investment, while general government and social services got 13.6 percent, but with a downward trend. If residential investment is excluded, we see that investment was concentrated in these above-mentioned areas.

| | Investment | | | | | | | GDP | | | |
| | Total | | | | | Non residential | | Structure | | | Growth |
	1995–2007	1995–99	2000–03	2004–07	2008–13	1995	2007	1995	2007	2014	1995–2007
TOTAL	100	100	100	100	100	100	100	100	100	100	3.78
AGR	2.14	2.50	2.09	1.75	2.18	3.14	2.41	4.21	2.71	2.52	2.99
INDUS	16.31	20.19	15.58	12.18	16.90	25.19	18.10	21.38	18.18	16.99	3.23
CONST	8.17	5.09	7.32	12.87	6.42	5.49	15.46	9.29	11.22	5.42	2.76
T-TR-HO	17.52	19.53	18.24	14.28	17.12	22.87	20.32	24.87	22.08	24.12	2.60
INF-COM	4.24	3.90	5.44	3.45	4.00	4.46	4.82	3.79	4.38	4.26	5.78
FIN	1.96	2.46	1.62	1.67	3.68	5.06	1.43	4.79	5.31	4.15	8.08
R.E.	28.14	24.23	28.30	32.87	26.21	1.92	4.96	5.45	8.91	12.03	5.05
PRO-SER	5.02	5.28	5.06	4.67	3.02	6.39	6.01	5.42	7.17	7.38	5.00
GOV-SER	13.60	14.79	12.99	12.73	15.30	22.92	21.08	16.77	16.31	18.81	3.30
OTH SER	2.91	2.03	3.36	3.55	5.18	2.55	5.42	4.03	3.72	4.33	4.51

Table 7.1. Composition of investment and GDP by sector of activity (%). AGR: agricultural activities; INDUS: industry (manufacture, energy and mines); T-TR-HO: trade, transport and hotels; CONST: construction; INF-COM: information and communication; FIN: finance; R.E.: real estate; PRO-SER: professional services; GOV-SER: general government and social services; OTH-SER: other services. Data at current prices except the average rate of growth in 1995–2007. Source: FBBVA (2015), INE (2015b).

These distortions in investment affected the structure of GDP growth. The hypertrophy of construction is reflected in its increased share in total GDP, from 9.3 percent to over 11 percent in 2004–2008, along with the increase of real estate, even during the depression. The counterpart has been the fall in the contribution of agriculture and, above all, industry, while there was an expansion of the financial sector, professional services, information and communications.

Sectoral accumulation rates can help the analysis of the structure of investment flows to give a clear idea of the disequilibria of Spanish capitalism (table 7.2). The most dynamic sectors in terms of the "rate of increase" in K were (1) "other services," a group of low-tech activities; (2) "construction"; (3) "information and communication"; and (4) "professional services." However, these last two have a downward trend, since their rates of accumulation fell in the subperiod 2003–2007, while other services and construction intensified their level of accumulation.

Job creation between 1995 and 2007 evidenced a profound asymmetry. Sixty-seven percent of wage employment was created in the activities of trade, transport, and hotels; as well as in construction and professional services, to which we can add the 14 percent from government and social services. However, only around 30 percent of total investment and 40 percent of nonresidential investment went to these branches, revealing a contrast between the distribution of investment and the creation of wage employment. Thus the increase in wage employment was concentrated on activities with a lower relative level of mechanization (table 7.2, columns 2 and 3). There is, therefore, a dichotomy between the sectoral accumulation rates and K/L ratios. Only construction, information and communications, along with other services, are able to make their growth rate of K materialize in a corresponding increase in the degree of mechanization (columns 3 and 4), although in the first case this is limited to the phase after 2001, and in the second that beginning in 1999.

TCC and labor productivity are found to have a contradictory relationship (table 7.2, column 4). Construction, information and communications, and other services, increased their K/L ratio, especially the latter (7.5 percent per year). But productivity growth was different from that which theoretically would have been expected. With the exception of "other services," productivity was nearly stagnant (information and communications), or fell (construction and professional services by −3.82 percent and −3.84 percent annually, respectively). The "most efficient" activity was finance, which managed to increase its level of "productivity" by 7.1 percent per year.[16]

	(1) $\Delta K/K$		(2) % L	(3) K/L: Relative Level		(4) Average Increase	
	1995–07	2003–07	95–07	1995	2007	K/L	Y/L
TOTAL	4.54	4.68	100	100	100	7.51	−0.29
AGR	1.12	1.41	1.36	194.28	167.08	0.05	1.01
INDUS	2.65	1.90	6.63	133.63	146.78	−0.82	1.80
CONST	8.27	12.71	19.72	60.80	67.69	1.22	−3.82
T-TR-HO	5.44	4.09	31.71	83.75	79.68	1.34	−2.67
INF-COM	8.93	6.09	2.96	114.04	161.40	0.02	0.40
FIN	1.19	1.41	0.57	74.45	73.35	3.39	7.14
RE	5.07	9.83	1.64			0.31	−5.93
PRO-SER	8.35	7.44	15.89	54.38	47.01	−5.92	−3.84
GOV-SER	3.93	4.10	14.45	109.51	120.78	−0.78	0.64
OTH-SER	10.80	11.87	5.06	27.63	62.54	1.26	1.41

Table 7.2. Dynamics and level of capital accumulation by sector, 1995–2007. AGR: agricultural activities; INDUS: industry (manufacture, energy and mines); T-TR-HO: trade, transport and hotels; CONST: construction; INF-COM: information and communication; FIN: finance; R.E.: real estate; PRO-SER: professional services; GOV-SER: general government and social services; OTH-SER: other services. (1) and (4) annual change (%), at constant prices; (2): sectoral contribution (%) to the total change in labour; (3) sectoral index of K/L ratio in relation to the average level (%). Sources: INE (2015b), FBBVA (2015).

There are two conclusions from this. First, due to incorporation into the European common market, Spanish industry has been undergoing a restructuring process since the 1980s by specializing in low- and medium-technology activities.[17] Second, the banking sector has played a leading role in the construction bubble, so its profits have largely depended on rising housing prices and infrastructure works. As a consequence, the data do not reflect the underlying reality.[18] In addition, state intervention has also helped in offering projects to benefit the private sector, hence the role of the general government sector.

The most dynamic sectors in terms of rate of growth of the capital stock have also shown the biggest price increases (fig 7.12). The price deflator for construction, trade, transport, hotels, and professional services rose by 3.4 to 5.9 percent per year while labor productivity went down 2.6–3.8 percent annually.

Theoretically, competition among capitals should be expressed in the continuous revolution of production processes through technological change, which can reduce costs by increasing the productive capacity of the labor force. So we should expect a certain relationship between the dynamism of sectors in terms of accumulation rates, the cheapening of commodities and levels of RoP. But in the Spanish "real estate capitalism," the most inflationary sectors have been those which have experienced a greater increase in the capital stock (with the exception of information and communications); the same sectors have also been the most labor-intensive and had low relative levels of TCC, below 80 percent of national average (table 7.2, column 3). Valorization has been achieved by asset price inflation, along with a productive specialization in sectors with low technological dynamism, which is expressed in a lower capacity to create value.[19]

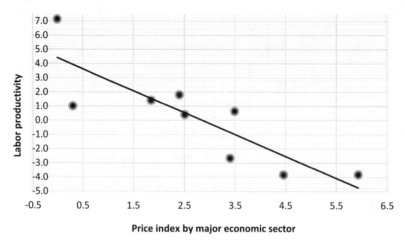

Figure 7.12. Annual average rates of labor productivity and price deflators by economic sector (%), 1995–2007. Source: INE (2015b).

After deducting all payments (interest, dividends, etc.) and correcting for mixed income, it is worth briefly noting two aspects about the absolute level and the evolution of sectoral profit rates over the period. On gross measures, the most dynamic sectors in terms of accumulation had the highest profit rates at the beginning of the growth phase, but they experienced the deepest falls along the boom. That was also the case with construction, trade and hotels, and professional and other services, with profit rates above the average but then falls of 50–75 percent between 1995 and 2014.

5. Conclusions

This analysis of the crisis of the Spanish economy from a Marxian approach has looked at certain theoretical aspects of Marx's law of profitability, and also at empirical evidence of profitability, capital accumulation, and sectoral restructuring.

The approach adopted tried to place the crisis starting in late 2008 in Spain within the framework of the most important law of political economy, the law of the falling tendency of the rate of profit. This law expresses the consequences of the law of value on the process of capitalist accumulation and makes up the basis of the Marxist theory of crisis. As such, it does not imply the need for the RoP to fall continuously; indeed, it is verified by how intensively capitalism tries to activate the "counteracting forces." And this is precisely what the accumulation process in Spain from 1995 to 2014 shows, with the speculative bubble in construction.

There is, however, a distinction between essence and appearance. The labor theory of value refers to the process underlying the visible phenomena and provides an understanding of certain basic laws of operation of the system. But we also need to understand the phenomena as they appear on the surface. Crises are necessary moments in the accumulation process by which a warning to the process of accumulation is given; that is, they occur whenever any surplus in money must be reconciled with the fundamentals of socially necessary labor time. That is precisely what took place in Spain beginning in 2008.

In this chapter I have explained the crisis of the Spanish economy as one arising from an insufficient capacity to generate surplus value, an unavoidable outcome of the functioning of the capitalist system. The Spanish case, however, provides some features that do not contradict the theoretical framework, but require extensive work to link the abstract with the concrete. They can be summed up as follows:

(1) The boom in Spain generated a particular distortion in the way the factors of crisis have been expressed. The rise in the price of housing continued as long as there was sufficient demand. Real wages, however, showed a relative decline during the economic upswing, but this was precisely because the most dynamic sectors did not develop the productive forces by increasing the TCC and by reducing production costs. Instead, investment went into construction assets—particularly residential ones, commercial trade (transport and hotels), and services—all of them with low technological content, along with information and communications. Therefore, the falling rate of profit first appeared as a problem of both demand and income distribution, and then with a financial content, that is, around the limit imposed by the gap between housing prices and wages, that banking lending could manage. This was the demand side of the crisis.

(2) The classic rate of profit, p/K, is not a complete indicator of a degree of valorization, because of the rise in the price of real estate assets. However, it shows a drop of 30 percent between 1995 and 2008, and 40 percent up to 2014, although the underlying problem of valorization is much deeper. Thus, conventional measures of profitability for non-financial corporations, the returns on both net assets and equity, did show a decrease of −42 percent and −54 percent between 2006 before the outbreak of the crisis and during the last four years of the depression, respectively, according to the BoS.

Following BACH, the drop is −67 percent and −36 percent for fixed and total assets respectively, while the stock exchange showed a fall of more than 60 percent from October 2007 until 2012. The mass of profit peaked in 2006 after a weak period of increase in 2000–2006 (with an average of only 1.1 percent per year), and then it decreased during the next three years by −5.7 percent. After this fall, from 2009 there was a weak recovery, but growth was below the rate of the pre-crisis level. Residential investment began to fall in 2007Q4, while in early 2008 house prices peaked and in the second quarter the fall in total GFCF and imports began, followed by productive investment.

(3) Debt cannot be considered as separate from the movement in profitability. The "price effect" of the housing boom in Spain brought an extension of credit, both for companies that invest in this activity, and for house buyers. In addition, debt emerged as a mechanism for the transference of losses from the private sector in the crisis to the public sector, which in turn led to the reduction in the labor and wage conditions of workers. This was the socialization of the crisis of profitability. To sum up, the increase of debt not only reveals the fictitious level of profitability of the Spanish economy but has also popularized a series of heterodox analyses of the current crisis in terms of neoliberalism and financialization.

This chapter has sought to contribute to filling an important gap in the studies of the Spanish economy from the Marxist approach. Although it does not answer all questions, at least it does try to ask the right ones and, in this sense, to encourage further research on the subject.

Appendix: Key

The following variables are net of finances and the real-estate sector (FIRE), unless otherwise specified.

Y: GDP

p: Profit, gross surplus without net taxes

K: Net nonresidential fixed stock of capital, at constant prices for the K/L ratio, and current prices for the Y/K ratio

r: Rate of profit

L: Equivalent waged workers

w: Compensation of employees per L, deflated by GDP prices

Labor productivity: GDP at constant prices per L

Notes

1   For reasons of availability of a homogeneous statistical series by the Spanish Statistical Office (INE), 1995 will generally be taken as a starting point, considering 2007–2008 as the end of the expansion.

2   From the particularly attractive orography, together with climatic conditions, the relationship between state intervention, social conflict and European superstructure as well as the central role of banks in the Spanish economic history (see Taifa 2008; BoS 2009; Mateo and Montanyà 2018), and even the laundering of "black money," estimated at over €50 billion in the late 1990s, before the arrival of the euro (Puig 2011).

3   For a more detailed discussion of my interpretation of Marxist crisis theory and its theoretical controversies, see Mateo (2007, chs. 3, 4, and 5).

4   Marx (1894, ch. 6) argued that accumulation of capital is linked more to the amount of surplus value, rather than to the rate of profit. This idea was rescued by H. Grossman, and subsequently by A. Shaikh (see Mateo 2007). But even so, the influence of the amount of the mass of profit on investment depends on the conditions of the concrete situation.

5   As opposed to a multicausal theory of crisis—not because this denies the existence of different causal factors, but because it is considered that they do not operate in a vacuum, they can be logically structured from the foundation of the LTV (see Mateo 2007, section 5.3).

6   GDP per hour worked in Spain was 76 percent of the US level in 1999, compared to an average of 85 percent of the Eurozone or 93 percent of Germany (OECD 2016).

7   Another question is the exclusion of FIRE sectors, even using the same capital stock deflator. In this case, the divergence starts in 2000—curiously, right after the year when the fixed exchange rates were established. The total profit rises by 14.9 percent in 2000–2006, eight points more than the narrower expression (without FIRE).

8   From an international comparison, the study of Pérez (2013) reveals that the profitability of Spanish corporations was lower than those of France and Germany in all sectors except construction. In section 4 the highest RoP in this sector is shown.

9   It is a market capitalization weighted index comprising the thirty-five most liquid Spanish stocks traded in the Madrid Stock Exchange General Index.

10   According to BoS (2008), 40 percent of indebted households with less income had spent 73.4 percent of the debt to purchase their own house, while the richest 10 percent did the same with only 42.2 percent of the debt. In turn, 40 percent of the poorer households had only used 11 percent of their debt to buy other than the main residence, facing 42.8 percent of the 10 percent of households with more income.

11   Including the impossibility of households to pay the whole price of their houses, which means a fictitious flow of income.

12   Indicating the rate of increase of the capital stock in real terms ($K^\star$), so $k = \Delta K^\star / K^\star$, expressed in a percentage.

13   From the perspective of the analysis of capital accumulation, the deflator of the capital stock (PK) should be used for both productivity and the real wage in order to measure the purchasing power in terms of capital assets. For this reason, in figure 7.8 productivity with PK is shown, while in figure 7.9 the GDP price index is used to put Y/L in relation with K/L. However, the GDP deflator is taken for the real wage, justified due to the implications of housing prices.

14   Although explained by the fall of both L and the type of worker (less qualified), and also by the sector in which unemployment increases, since the construction

has generated more than half of the loss of jobs between 2007 and 2012 (INE 2015b).

15 In this expression the GDP deflator is used in order to make a comparison, instead of *PK*, as was shown in figure 7.8.

16 It should be noted that this measure of productivity for finance is misleading, as it is a consequence of a housing boom, thus reflecting the distorted path of the capital accumulation in Spain.

17 In terms of both $I + D$ (innovation and development) and qualification of labor, as classified by the OECD. In fact, Spain, Portugal and Greece are the countries with the lowest weight of industries with more advanced technology (Álvarez et al. 2013).

18 As confirmed by a study of the very Bank of Spain, in which it is asserted that "the high growth rates of raw productivity estimated for the banking industry during the years prior to the crisis were not an indicator of efficiency and technical progress . . . cannot be attributed to a higher growth rate in technical progress" (Martín-Oliver et al. 2012, p. 27). Rather, "the proportion of real estate and mortgages in the loans portfolio of banks is positively correlated with productivity" (p. 24).

19 It is not possible to explain the underlying interpretation of the LTV, for which we refer to Astarita (2015).

References

Álvarez, I., F. Luengo, and J. Uxó (2013) *Fracturas y crisis en Europa*, Clave Intelectual.

AMECO (2017) "Annual Macro-Economic Database," European Commission, Economic and Financial Affairs.

Astarita, R. (2015) "Trabajo potenciado y la 'tesis transferencia,'" *Rolando Astarita blog*, https://rolandoastarita.wordpress.com/2015/06/02/trabajo-potenciado-y-la-tesis-transferencia/.

BACH (2015) "Annual Accounts of the Non-financial Corporations," Bank for the Accounts of Companies Harmonised, Banque de France.

BoS (2008) *Survey of Household Finances (EFF) 2008*, Bank of Spain.

———. (2009) *Annual Report*, Bank of Spain.

———. (2016a) *Statistical Bulletin*, Bank of Spain.

———. (2016b) *Central Balance Sheet Data: Non Financial Corporations*, Bank of Spain.

———. (2016c). *Economic Indicators*, Bank of Spain.

Boundi, F. (2014) "Tasa de beneficio y distribución del ingreso en la economía española (1964–2012)," *Ensayos de Economía*, Vol 23, No 44.

Estrada, Á., J. F. Jimeno, and J. L. Malo (2009) "La economía española en la UEM: los diez primeros años," *Documentos Ocasionales*, No 0901, Bank of Spain.

EU-KLEMS (2012) "EU KLEMS Growth and Productivity Accounts: Data in the ISIC Rev. 4 Industry Classification, 'ESP Basic 2012,'" Groningen Growth and Development Centre.

Fundación BBVA/Ivie (2015) "El stock y los servicios del capital en España y su distribución territorial y sectorial (1964–2013)," FBBVA, available at https://www.fbbva.es/.

Harvey, D. (1982) *The Limits to Capital*, Verso.

Instituto Nacionalde Estadistica (INE) (2015a) "Quarterly Spanish National Accounts, Base 2010," Spanish Statistical Office.

―――. (2015b) "Spanish National Accounts, Base 2010, Series 1995–2014," Spanish Statistical Office.

―――. (2016) "Spanish National Accounts, Base 2010, Series 1995–2015," Spanish Statistical Office.

Jones, P. (2013) "The Falling Rate of Profit Explains Falling US Growth," paper to the 12th Australian Society of Heterodox Economists Conference.

Kliman, A. (2011) *The Failure of Capitalist Production: Underlying Causes of the Great Recession*, Pluto.

López, F., L. Dávila, and J. López (2013) "Profits and Extraordinary Profits in the Spanish Economy during the 2000's," *Aestimatio*, Vol 7.

Lorente, M. A. and J. R. Capella (2014) "El coste del rescate bancario: las cifras reales. De 'ni un euro' a 130.000 millones," *Mientras Tanto*, Vol 122.

Martín-Oliver, A., S. Ruano, and V. Salas-Fumás (2012) "Why Did High Productivity Growth of Banks Precede the Financial Crisis?," working paper 1239, Bank of Spain.

Marx, K. (1894) *Capital,* Vol 3, available at http://www.marxists.org/.

Mas, M., F. Pérez, and E. Uriel (2013) *Inversión y stock de capital en España (1964–2011): evolución y perspectivas del patrón de acumulación*, Fundación BBVA, Economy and Society Report.

Mateo, J. P. (2007) "La Tasa de ganancia en México, 1970–2003: Análisis de la crisis de rentabilidad a partir de la composición del capital y la distribución del ingreso," PhD thesis, Complutense University of Madrid.

―――. (2016) "The Great Recession in the US from the Perspective of the World Economy," *World Review of Political Economy*, Vol 7, No 2.

Mateo, J. P. and M. Montanyà (2018) "The Accumulation Model of the Spanish Economy: Profitability, the Real Estate Bubble and Sectoral Embalances," in L. Buendía and R. Molero, eds., *The Political Economy of Modern Spain: From Miracle to Mirage*. Routledge.

Mato, C. S. (2013) "Las ayudas públicas al sector bancario (diciembre 2012)," *Economia para críticos e indignados*, available at http://matoeconomia.blogspot.com/2013/09/las-ayudas-publicas-al-sector-bancario.html.

Minstry of Public Works (2016) Statistical information, Ministry of Public Works, Spain.

Norfield, T. (2012) "Finance, the Rate of Profit and Imperialism," paper to the WAPE/AHE/IIPPE conference, Paris.

Organisation for Economic Co-operation and Development (OECD) (2016) "OECD. Stat. Statistical Databases," OECD.

Pérez, F. (2012) *Crecimiento y competitividad. Motores y frenos de la economía española,* Fundación BBVA-Ivie report.

Puig, A. A. (2011) "El modelo productivo español en el período expansivo de 1997–2007: insostenibilidad y ausencia de políticas de cambio," *Revista de Economía Crítica*, Vol 12.

Roberts, M. (2012) "Debt Matters," *The Next Recession*, reprinted in this volume as chapter 11.

Shaikh, A. (2016) *Capitalism: Competition, Conflict, Crises*, Oxford University Press.

Shaikh, A. and A. Tonak (1994) *Measuring the Wealth of Nations: The Political Economy of National Accounts*, Cambridge University Press.

TAIFA (2008) *Auge y crisis de la vivienda en España*, economy report 5, Seminario de Economía Crítica TAIFA.

Tapia, J. A. and R. Astarita (2011) *La Gran Recesión y el capitalismo del siglo XXI*, La Catarata.

CHAPTER 8

SURPLUS VALUE, PROFIT, AND UNPRODUCTIVE LABOR IN THE GREEK ECONOMY, 1958–2013

Thanasis Maniatis and Costas Passas

1. Introduction

It is well known that the Greek economic crisis has reached proportions similar to those of the Great Depression for the advanced capitalist countries of that era. Despite the recent political change and the formation of a new coalition government dominated by the center-left party of Syriza, economic and social conditions have not changed at all. Thus, it is still necessary to focus on the details involved in explaining the origins and nature of the current economic crisis, in the same way that the recent world economic crisis sparked a new round of debates around the different Marxist theories of crisis. In this chapter we examine from a classical Marxian perspective this latest crisis episode, not isolated historically, but as an integral part of the long-term evolution of the postwar Greek economy.

Three important issues have emerged in the recent discussion about the different aspects of the current crisis. The first regards the question of which radical or Marxist theory explains the crisis in a better way: those based on (low, insufficient) profitability and the Marxian law of the falling rate of profit in particular; or those approaches that claim that capitalist crises are caused by different factors each time, with the recent one, especially, being a multicausal type of crisis. Marxists who oppose the validity of the law of the falling rate of profit have resorted to one of the following causes (or a combination of them): (a) some version of a paradigm failure in the form of a failed neoliberal regime with low wages and insufficient effective demand (Harvey 2010; Kotz 2008, 2010; and Laskos and Tsakalotos 2013, for the Greek case), where overconsumption and underaccumulation characterize the unstable trajectory of the US economy after the stagflation crisis of the

1970s (Duménil and Lévy 2011); or (b) the excesses and disproportionalities associated with the financialization process and the transformation of capitalism in this direction, during the same period (Gowan 2009; Palley 2009; Lapavitsas et al. 2010).

Second, in many ways the above discussion has been closely connected with the evaluation of the economic record of the neoliberal period; was it a boom period or one of relative stagnation? More concretely, was there a full, or at least a partial, recovery of profitability, capital accumulation and growth compared to the corresponding economic performance of the "Golden Age" period? In this respect, of particular significance were the contributions of Brenner (1998, 2006), who insisted (while neoliberalism was still going on at full force) that the economic record of the neoliberal period was mediocre at best, due to the partial, incomplete or insufficient recovery of the rate of profit. During the period in which the crisis was unfolding, Brenner (2009) repeated and summarized his argument.[1] An exchange between McNally (2011) and Choonara (2012) clarified further that the opponents of the Marxian law of the falling rate of profit objected to the particular view that there was a continuous, uninterrupted crisis since the 1970s, including the neoliberal period. For those authors, the neoliberal record was one of a strong economic expansion that was abruptly stopped by the development of certain disproportionalities and other conjunctoral reasons in 2007–2008. In fact, though, for most of the proponents of the Marxian law and the thesis that insufficient profitability was the source of the crisis, neoliberalism was a period of *low, inadequate*, even if not continuously decreasing, rates of profit and relative stagnation before the eruption of crisis, which surfaced when the various "bubbles" generated during the period burst. Again, the examination of the behavior of the rate of profit and its constituents is very important for the evaluation of those opposing claims.

Third, in the same way as it did in the previous crisis—the stagflation crisis of the 1970s—the use of the theoretical distinction between productive and unproductive labor plays a major role in the construction of the appropriate Marxian categories on the basis of which we evaluate the course of development of a typical capitalist economy.[2] The relationship between the rate of surplus value and the profit share or the profit–wage ratio, the relationship between the Marxian general rate of profit and the net rate of profit, the proper measurement of the level and the rate of growth of labor productivity, and in general the importance of the growth of unproductive activities on the evolution of the structure of the system, all hinge on the implementation of this distinction.

Our study uses the methodological framework of Shaikh and Tonak (1994) in constructing the crucial Marxian variables. In general, our approach falls within the classical Marxian approach in the following ways:

(1) We use the distinction between productive labor and unproductive labor in estimating the level and fluctuations, as well as the constituent elements, of variables such as the rate of surplus value, the organic composition of capital, the productivity of labor, the Marxian general rate of profit, and the net rate of profit.

(2) The profitability of capital as expressed either by the Marxian general rate of profit or the net rate of profit plays the most significant role in evaluating the state and development of the postwar Greek economy in its different phases.

(3) Our study emphasizes not only the importance of the Marxian law of the tendency of the rate of profit to fall, but also the importance of the growth of unproductive activities in curtailing further net profitability and making the crisis even more severe than what could have happened through the operation of the law in its classic form alone.

This approach follows closely the analysis of a lot of Marxists for whom this crisis is not just a conjunctural event or the outcome of some policy mistakes,[3] but rather a product of the normal functioning of the capitalist economy, which suffers from time to time from a serious breakdown of the accumulation process. Crisis is a periodic result of the inherent mechanisms at work in a capitalist economy, not the result of wrong, misguided policies or of exogenous shocks. Even though the characteristics of the neoliberal institutional structure usually blamed as the cause of the crisis are not disputed, a more thorough analysis of the behavior of a capitalist economy requires their integration into an analytic scheme that should include, at a minimum, the explicit consideration of the profit rate and its constituent elements, and their evolution over time. Thus, leaving the sphere of circulation and distribution and looking at the deeper structure of the economy, a different picture emerges from the examination of the trajectory of profitability and the capital accumulation process. As Shaikh (2011) notes, despite radically changing institutions, regulations, and balance of class forces, structural systemic crises reappear every thirty to forty years in the terrain of the world capitalist economy. The recurrence of crises has to be traced to a more or less common cause. Those recurrent accumulation crises are inevitable as long as the system runs on the profit motive. Accumulation is based on profitability, and the determinants of profitability have to be examined carefully in order to understand the different phases of accumulation and growth.

Thus, a number of Marxist authors—Shaikh (2011), Laibman (2010), Brenner (1998, 2006, 2009), Moseley (1991, 1997), Mohun (2006), Bakir and Campbell (2009, 2010), Maniatis (2012), Roberts (2013), Kliman

(2011), Paitaridis and Tsoulfidis (2012)—despite their differences, base their discussion of the entire postwar period, including the neoliberal period and the explanation of the current crisis, on the detailed examination of the profit rate in the US economy. In their work, a crucial common element emerges: the incomplete recovery of the profit rate during the neoliberal years and the fact that even this partial recovery was caused almost exclusively by the attack on wages and on labor costs in general. Paitaridis and Tsoulfidis (2012), in particular, place emphasis on the importance of the growth in unproductive activities in generating the latest crisis, in a manner reminiscent of Shaikh and Tonak's (1994) analysis of the stagflation crisis of the 1970s. The present study also shares this approach, even though the available data for the Greek economy do not allow a similarly detailed mode of empirical investigation.

In sum, this chapter claims that inadequate profitability remains the fundamental cause of crisis, regardless of the proximate cause each time, and that this holds true for the case of the Greek economy as well. We argue, in particular, that the Greek economic crisis is the combined result of the operation of the Marxian law of the falling rate of profit (Marx 1894, ch. 15) and the growth of unproductive activities and unproductive labor in particular. Estimating the main Marxian variables in the manner discussed in the next section provides us with a powerful way to trace and discuss the trajectory of the postwar Greek economy based on the trend and fluctuations of the profitability of capital and the contours of the capital accumulation process.

2. Productive Labor, Unproductive Labor, and Marxian Categories

According to Marx, productive labor is labor that produces surplus value. Its magnitude is of paramount importance in the Marxian theoretical scheme because it is the sole provider of the fuel on which a capitalist economy runs. It finances investment, capitalist consumption, and partially some state functions. More concretely, in order to distinguish between productive and unproductive labor in the context of the economic sector classification used by the official national accounts, it is more intuitive and analytically helpful (1) to start from the distinction between production sectors/activities (agriculture, mining, manufacturing, construction, transportation, health, education, etc.) and non-production activities/sectors (wholesale and retail trade, financial activities, real estate, public sector administrative activities, advertising, etc.); and (2) to take into account non-production labor within each production sector (mostly supervisory labor), thus distinguishing between production labor and non-production labor first. Then, we can define productive labor, that is, labor productive of surplus value, as wage labor (possibly adjusted for self-employment in the production sectors) employed by capital in production activities as a specific subset of production labor.

Unproductive labor could be defined as all other types of labor. Since in the classical and Marxian traditions of political economy the argument that identifies unproductive labor with social consumption is very prominent, it should be noted that even though it does not produce surplus value and strictly speaking should be classified as unproductive labor, such labor for social consumption does, however, create new wealth (albeit at the margin of the dominant social relations); and it certainly does not consume already-existing use values without providing other use values with greater value. That is, production of use values for own consumption, production of value by simple commodity producers, and most importantly production of use values by the state (health, education, culture, recreation, etc.) may involve unproductive labor (no surplus value is produced), but they are not a net cost for the system. This last case underlines the importance of the drive for privatization of state provided services for the health of the system, which depends to a great extent on the available mass of surplus value and profits.

Shaikh and Tonak (1994) have presented a complete account of the correspondence between Marxian categories and the categories of national income and product accounts and input-output tables. The distinction between productive and unproductive labor lies at the base of this construction and underlines the major differences that arise between those two sets of categories. In Shaikh and Tonak's scheme, the use of the distinction between productive and unproductive labor creates four major differences between the main variables of the two theoretical approaches, the orthodox and the Marxian one.

First, Marxian (gross or net) value added (MVA) defined in the way shown below is greater than, less than, or equal to (gross or net) value added in the orthodox national accounts according to whether materials and depreciation in the trade sector plus royalties paid by the primary (production and trade) sectors to the royalties sector are greater than, less than, or equal to the wages of the government employees (the imputed contribution of the state to the annual product) and other imputations, for instance owner-occupied rent of households that are arbitrarily added to the orthodox measure of market value added in the national accounts methodology:

$$MVA = VAp + VAt + IIt + royalties\ paid\ from\ p\ \text{(production) and}$$
$$t\ \text{(trade) sectors to } R\ \text{(royalties sector)}\ (\approx VAfire) + IBT$$

$$S = MVA - V$$

$$s' = S/V$$

where VA = value added; II_t = intermediate inputs in the trade sector; p = production; t = trade; *fire* = finance, insurance, real estate; IBT = indirect business taxes; V = variable capital or the compensation of productive laborers; S = surplus value; and s' = rate of surplus value.

Second, productivity (y) measured in the Marxian sense is necessarily different than the conventional measure because it compares Marxian value added to hours worked by productive labor alone, and not national accounts aggregate value added to hours worked by all employees in the entire private economy. (It is noteworthy that even in the mainstream studies the productivity measure derived from the orthodox national accounts usually excludes the government sector from both the numerator and the denominator of productivity.)

$$y_{mainstream} = \frac{Real\ Gross\ Value\ Added}{Total\ Labor\ Hours}$$

$$y_{marxian} = \frac{Real\ Gross\ Marxian\ Value\ Added}{Productive\ Labor\ Hours}$$

Third, the main measures of interclass income distribution, that is, the rate of surplus value (surplus value over variable capital, S/V) and the profit–wage ratio (II/W) differ necessarily in magnitude, and possibly in their trend. The rate of surplus value is greater than the profit–wage ratio because *surplus value* includes *profits* plus other components like wages of unproductive labor, the costs of circulation and other non-production activities, and indirect business taxes; and *variable capital* is only one portion of *total wages*. In addition, if the wages of unproductive labor and other costs of non-production activities (U) rise sufficiently relative to variable capital, the two measures may exhibit opposing trends, with the rate of surplus value increasing at the same time that the profit–wage ratio is falling:

$$\frac{II}{W} = \frac{S-U}{V+U} = \frac{\frac{S}{V} - \frac{U}{V}}{1 + \frac{U}{V}}$$

Fourth, the distinction between productive and unproductive labor, and therefore between total surplus value and profits, allows for the estimation of two different measures of profitability in Marxian theory. The first is the broad one, the Marxian general rate of profit, where R is defined as total surplus value over the total fixed capital stock; the other is the net rate of profit, where r is defined as profits over the fixed capital stock. The first denotes the growth potential of the system if no unproductive activities existed, whereas the second is the major determinant of investment since it is the measure of profitability that becomes known to capitalists and influences their behavior. Marx derives the law of the falling rate of profit in the third volume of *Capital* in terms of the general rate of profit at a relatively high level of abstraction. A rising C/L (capital–output ratio, or K/Y, the materialized composition of capital; see Shaikh 1987) is the sufficient condition for the rate of profit to start falling at some point, even with a rising rate of surplus value (the normal course of events regarding distribution between capital and productive labor in the Marxian approach). Thus, the intertemporal trend of the net rate of profit will also depend on the behavior of the ratio of non-production costs (for wages, materials, and depreciation) over fixed capital. If this ratio (U/K) decreases over time, the net rate of profit will (1) fall less than the general rate of profit, (2) stay constant, or (3) even rise as profits become a bigger portion of the total mass of surplus value. If this ratio (U/K) increases over time, the net rate of profit will fall more than the general Marxian rate of profit; and if the ratio stays constant, the net rate of profit will fall in parallel fashion with the general rate of profit:

$$R = \frac{S}{K}$$

$$r = \frac{\Pi}{K} = \frac{S - U}{K} = \frac{\frac{S}{V} - \frac{U}{V}}{K/V} = R - U/K$$

Now, in all studies (mostly for the US economy) that distinguish between productive and unproductive labor (Shaikh and Tonak 1994; Mohun 2005; Moseley 1991, 1997) this ratio has been found to increase especially during the "Golden Age." In Moseley's studies in particular, it is the fundamental cause for the fall in the net rate of profit in the 1960s and '70s since the general Marxian rate of profit was found to be roughly constant until 1977. The same is true in the more recent study by Paitaridis and Tsoulfidis (2012), who emphasize the role of the growth of unproductive activities in investigating the phase changes of the postwar US economy. From all the above, it follows that our investigation and graphical presentation should focus on the following variables and their interconnection expressing the inner structure of a capitalist economy in a Marxian theoretical framework:

(1) *Interclass income distribution*

    (a) Rate of surplus value ($s' = S/V$) and profit share (Π/Y), profit–wage ratio (Π/W)

    (b) Productivity of (productive) labor (y)

    (c) Growth of productivity of (productive) labor and real wage growth (y, ω)

(2) *Technical change*

    (a) Organic composition of capital (C/V) and materialized composition of capital or capital–output ratio (C/L or K/Y)

(3) *Profitability*

    (a) General Marxian rate of profit (R) and net rate of profit (r)

    (b) Profitability and output growth

    (c) Profitability (net rate of profit, r, and rate of profit of enterprise, PE) and investment (capital accumulation, $I/K\text{-}1$)

(4) *Mass of real profits and outbreak of the crisis*

(5) *Structural change*

    (a) The ratio of unproductive labor to productive labor compensation (U/V)

    (b) The ratio of the mass profits to the mass of surplus value (Π/S)

    (c) The share of investment in the total mass of surplus value (I/S)

(6) *Relationship between unproductive labor and productivity of labor*

We should note also that we do not apply any adjustment for changes in the degree of capacity utilization for lack of adequate data. However, this adjustment is relevant mostly for short-run variations in profitability and it could not possibly affect the clear secular fall in all rates of profit (Marxian general rate of profit, net rate of profit, rate of profit of enterprise) observed in our data.

3. Empirical Results: The Law of the Falling Rate of Profit in the Greek Economy, 1958–2013

As we noted above, the most crucial element distinguishing the Marxist approach from the other heterodox analyses has to do with the importance of the profit rate[4] in the examination of the structure of the capitalist economy in the Marxist tradition.

Figures 8.1 to 8.7 depict the story of the postwar Greek economic development in terms of the main Marxian ratios, namely the general Marxian rate of profit ($R = S/K$); the net rate of profit ($r = \Pi/K$); the rate of surplus value ($s' = S/V$); and the value and organic (materialized) composition of capital ($k = K/V$ and $k' = K/Y$), where S = surplus value, V = variable capital, K = private capital stock, Π = profits or property type income, $U = S - \Pi$ = wages of unproductive labor and other costs of unproductive activities, and Y = net output or net income.

The general Marxian profit rate (R), which is the one for which Marx derives the law of the falling rate of profit in volume 3 of *Capital*, and the net profit rate (r)—which depends like R on the composition of capital and the rate of surplus value but also on the ratio of the unproductive labor and unproductive costs in general to either productive labor or the stock of fixed capital—are depicted in figures 8.1 and 8.2. The movement of the net profit rate (*r*), in particular, delineates three broad phases of profitability, capital accumulation, and growth in the postwar Greek economy before the onset of the current crisis. Those are similar to the ones observed in all advanced capitalist economies in the postwar period, namely the "Golden Age" of capital accumulation, the stagflation crisis of the 1970s, the period of neoliberalism and the current crisis. In figure 8.1 we observe that the general Marxian rate of profit (*R*) even though it was falling from the beginning of the "Golden Age" of capital accumulation, remained on average at a very high level for the entire period expressing the enormous growth potential of the Greek economy at the time. Then, it fell considerably from 1973 until 1987, roughly the period of the "stagflation crisis" for the Greek economy. During the years of the period of neoliberalism, the Marxian general rate of profit rose somewhat compared to its lows in the mid-1980s, but it did not even reach the higher rates of profit of the stagflation period before it started to fall again rapidly, especially during the years of the recent crisis.

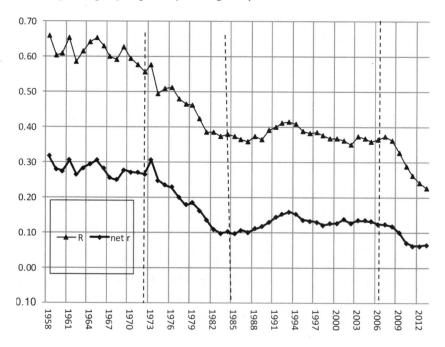

Figure 8.1. The general Marxian (R) and the net profit rate (r), Greece 1958–2013. Source: authors' calculations.

The general Marxian rate of profit forms the upper bound of the net rate of profit. According to the development of the net rate of profit (*r*), we distinguish in a precise way the four different phases of the postwar Greek economy; "Golden Age" (1958–73), stagflation crisis (1974–85), neoliberalism (1986–2009), and current crisis (2009–present). Overall, the net profit rate (*r*) followed closely the movement of the general Marxian profit rate but fell much more than *R*, from one-half of *R* at the beginning of the period 1958–2013 to one-third at its end. The reason for this divergence was the fact that unproductive labor wages and other expenses in the non-production sectors (like costs for circulation and financial activities) rose significantly in relation to productive labor and the stock of fixed capital.

Figure 8.2. The net rate of profit in Greece, 1958–2013. Source: authors' calculations.

In figure 8.3, the development of the ratio between unproductive labor and productive labor compensation is presented in three different forms: *UL/PL* is the ratio of unproductive labor wages over productive labor wages; *ul/pl* is the same ratio adjusted for self-employment, that is, adding an estimated wage equivalent for self-employed persons to the wages of both categories; and *UL/W* is the ratio of unproductive labor compensation to total wages, also adjusted for the wage equivalent of self-employed persons. All three ratios increase almost continuously, indicating that the increase in the importance of unproductive labor is a structural element and almost an irreversible trend in current capitalism.

Figure 8.3. Ratio of unproductive labor to productive labor compensation, 1958–2013. UL/W, right. Source: authors' calculations.

The other way to describe this type of structural change that took place in the postwar Greek economy is through the depiction of the share of profits or property type income as a share of surplus value; as shown in figure 8.4, this share exhibited a clear downward trend over the entire period, broadening the difference between r and R. It is obvious that the process of development of the postwar Greek economy was characterized by a squeeze of surplus value from unproductive activities that eventually resulted in an insufficient (for the normal functioning of the system) mass of profits.

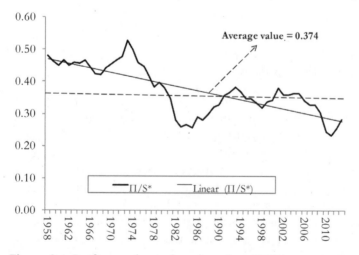

Figure 8.4. Profits as a share of surplus value, 1958–2013. Source: authors' calculations.

Returning to the different phases of the postwar experience of the Greek economy, the first one, which lasts from the beginning of the period examined here until about the middle of the decade of the 1970s, could be characterized as the "Golden Age" of Greek capitalism in similar fashion to what happened in all advanced capitalist countries after the end of World War II as they embarked on the process of reconstructing their economies. High profit rates, despite a slightly falling trend, caused exceptionally high rates of output growth (see fig. 8.5) and capital accumulation (see fig. 8.6) that in turn stimulated labor productivity growth and allowed increases in the real wage for productive workers and workers in general, despite a rising rate of surplus value (see fig. 8.7).

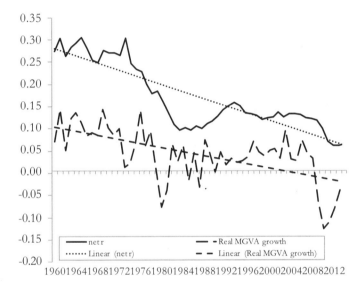

Figure 8.5. Real output growth (Marxian gross value added) and net rate of profit, 1960–2012. Source: authors' calculations.

The second period is that of the stagflation crisis, starting in Greece around 1973–74—almost half a decade later than the beginning of the crisis in other advanced capitalist economies, which occurred in the late 1960s. The significant increase in the organic or materialized composition of capital, C/L (or capital–output ratio, K/Y, in mainstream terms), during the "Golden Age" (the sufficient condition for the profit rate to fall), combined with the fall in the rate of surplus value (see fig. 8.7) and the profit share (as a result of the increased strength of the working class and the successful labor struggles conducted after the fall of the military dictatorship), produced a sharp fall in net profitability. This fall lasted until 1985 (while the general Marxian rate of profit bottomed down in 1987), affecting in a negative way investment and output growth, and resulting also in stagnating or slightly falling productivity, real wage growth (see fig. 8.8) and employment.

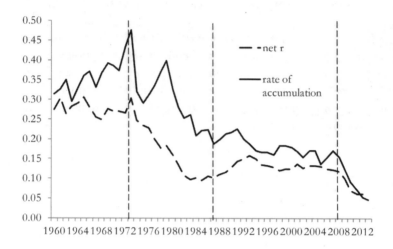

Figure 8.6. Net rate of profit and rate of capital accumulation (%), 1960–2012. Source: authors' calculations.

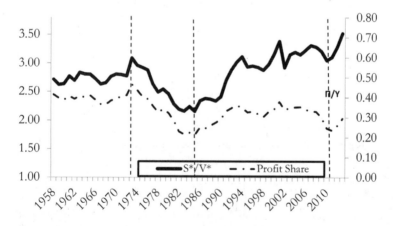

Figure 8.7. The rate of surplus-value (S/V) and the profit share (Π/Y), 1958–2013. Source: authors' calculations.

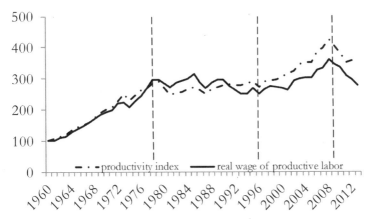

Figure 8.8. Productivity growth and real wage growth, 1960–2013. Source: authors' calculations.

The third phase, that of neoliberalism, started in the Greek economy after 1986 and entered full force after 1991, again with a time lag of about one-half to one decade after this policy regime was established in all advanced capitalist economies. It is well known that the neoliberal experience meant everywhere the dramatic increase in the exploitation of workers (see fig. 8.7) in an effort to raise sufficiently the profit rate and restore the conditions for a new "Golden Age" of capital accumulation. However, this recovery in profitability did not, and could not, happen without a massive devaluation or destruction of the capital stock and a significant decrease of unproductive labor and other similar costs. This scenario was not politically feasible at the time, because it would imply a rise in the unemployment rate at levels similar to those of the Great Depression. Hence, the neoliberal period brought about only a partial recovery of the profit rate, which resulted in a relatively low rate of investment activity. This is shown in figure 8.6, as well as in figure 8.9, where the investment share in total output is related to the rate of profit of enterprise—that is, the net rate of profit minus the real interest rate—following the recent argument advanced by Shaikh (2011). Low profitability and slow capital accumulation resulted in low output growth and, most importantly, slower productivity growth than that of the "Golden Age" period. But nevertheless it once again outpaced real wage growth, raising the rate of surplus value.

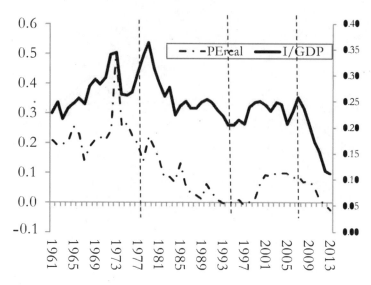

Figure 8.9. Rate of profit of enterprise (PE real) and investment share (I/GDP) (%), 1961–2013. Source: authors' calculations.

Even the modest output growth of the period, especially after 1995 (when the initial boost of neoliberal arrangements and institutions had lost steam, and profitability during the neoliberal period had already peaked), was achieved through the indirect impact of the financial bubbles created mostly by the expansive monetary policy of that period. Those bubbles, first in the stock exchange market in the late 1990s and then in the real estate sector, created significant "wealth effects" for households, stimulating consumption demand, the only source of growth during the neoliberal period as low profitability held investment activity down. Meanwhile, the value composition of capital ($k = K/V$), and most importantly the materialized composition of capital ($k' = C/L$ or K/Y, the capital-output ratio), kept increasing (see fig. 8.10), putting downward pressure on all measures of profitability and offsetting the positive effect of the increases in the rate of surplus value.

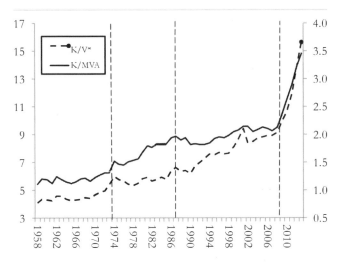

Figure 8.10. Value (k = K/V), left, and materialized (k' = K/Y) composition of capital, right, 1958–2013. Source: authors' calculations.

In figure 8.11 we observe the movement of the three crucial Marxian variables in the four different phases of the postwar period. During the "Golden Age" the capital–output ratio (and much more so the value composition of capital) rose, and even though the rate of surplus value was also rising, the net rate of profit was falling. Starting in 1974 the rising trend of the composition of capital was supplemented by a falling rate of exploitation (and profit share), therefore producing a sharp fall in the rate of profit that lasted until 1985. Then, during the first decade of the neoliberal period, only one of the three requirements for a meaningful recovery of profitability and growth was fulfilled. The capitulation of the social democratic government to the market forces and the resurgence of the neoliberal spirit resulted in a significant increase of the rate of surplus value. However, the capital–output ratio remained more or less constant as the massive destruction or devaluation of fixed capital failed to materialize, and the importance of unproductive labor and non-production activities in general continued to increase (see fig. 8.3). In the second decade of the neoliberal period, the value composition of capital increased sharply, the capital–output ratio resumed its upward trend, establishing a slightly falling tendency for the net rate of profit, even though the rate of surplus value continued to increase.

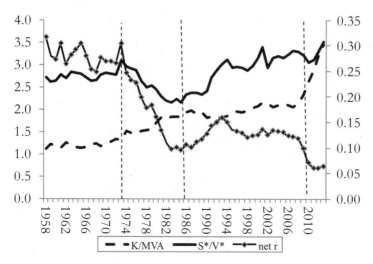

Figure 8.11. The rate of surplus-value (S/V) the capital–output (K/Y) ratio and the net rate of profit (r), 1958–2013. Source: authors' calculations.

As is well known, the law of the falling rate of profit does not imply that any fall in the rate of profit will produce a crisis. This happens, rather, when after a long-enough period of low and falling profit rates, the mass of profits stagnates or even falls from one period to the next (the "point of absolute overaccumulation of capital" according to Marx). At that point in time, capitalists realize that the investment they undertook in the previous period did not increase profits at all, and they cut investment sharply with all the crisis phenomena (increase in unemployment, bankruptcies, falling real wages, etc.) following. In figure 8.12, where the mass of real profits and its rate of change are depicted, we observe that in both cases of postwar crises, at the points of eruption of the crisis (namely in 1974 and 2007–2008), the mass of real profits stagnated, with a sharp fall ensuing during the period of crisis per se.

Figure 8.13 provides one way to look at the importance of the "financialization" process of the Greek economy during the neoliberal period. While in 1985 and in 1990 the profit rate in the non-financial sector was very close to the profit rate of the financial sector, the latter exploded after 1990, remaining at very high levels even one year before the beginning of the crisis.

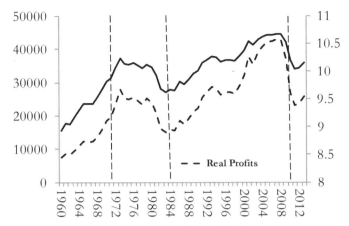

Figure 8.12. Mass of real profits, €bn, 1960–2013. Source: authors' calculations.

The mass of profits of the financial sector was 2 percent of total profits in 1985 and 1990, and it had increased to 9 percent of total profits by 2000, remaining at this percentage in 2008. This compares to a rise in the share of financial profits in total profits from 10 percent in 1980 to 40 percent in 2007 for the US economy.[5] It is generally accepted that the process of financialization in Greece had not gone as far as in the major advanced capitalist economies. Financial rates of profit were quite high, but the recent failure of the Greek economy was caused by the fall in overall profitability and its low level, and not by some overexpansion of the financial sector.

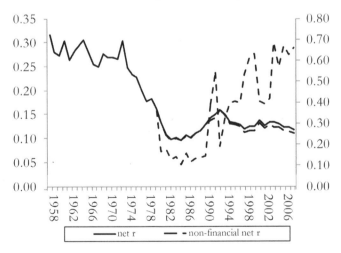

Figure 8.13. The net profit rate, financial (right) and non-financial profit rate (left), % Greece 1958–2008. Source: authors' calculations.

In figure 8.14 we can see another expression or consequence of the process of growth of unproductive activities and financialization in particular. The share of investment in the total mass of surplus value peaked in 1979, and it has been declining ever since, with the exception of a slight increase on average during the second half of the neoliberal period (1995–2007), which again never even approached the accumulation rates of the "Golden Age" period. In other words, the picture of stumbling accumulation and growth processes over a long period of time that we have seen above has been brought about for two reasons: (1) long-term falling profitability caused mainly by the capitalization of production; and (2) a shift from production to non-production activities for structural reasons, and possibly also influenced by low and falling profitability.

Figure 8.14. Gross investment as a share of surplus value, 1960–2013. Source: authors' calculations.

An additional point related to the new structural characteristics of the late neoliberal period, and to financialization in particular, has to do with the increase in personal debt, as financial firms took advantage of deregulation and pursued profits aggressively, lending to middle- and low-income people who were not considered creditworthy even as recently as the late 1990s. In figure 8.15 we observe that consumer debt was still quite low as a percentage of total national income in the mid-1990s, rising rapidly especially after 2002—the year the euro was adopted and a regime of low interest rates was established. Mortgage debt was always higher than consumer debt as a percentage of national income, and it rose even more sharply in the 2000s, bringing the total personal debt as a percentage of national income close to 90 percent in the beginning of the crisis, though it remained lower than that in most advanced capitalist economies. Obviously, much of the modest growth that occurred during the late neoliberal period was the result of stimulation in aggregate demand stemming from increased household demand for consumer goods and real estate, and this growth was based on easy credit and "wealth effects" that do not exist anymore.

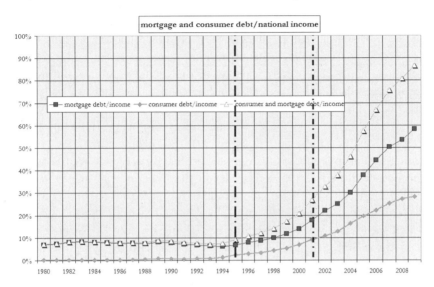

Figure 8.15. Personal debt as a percentage of national income, 1980–2009. Source: authors' calculations.

It is also interesting to note that in recent studies of the Greek and the US economy, the rate of profit appears to have the same behavior over the entire postwar period. First, a "Golden Age" period of high profit rates, strong capital accumulation and output growth; then a crisis period of sharply falling profit rates; and after that, a *partial, limited* recovery of profitability during the neoliberal era determined mostly by the movement of the capital–output ratio or the materialized composition of capital. Thus, it could be argued that both the stagflation crisis of the 1970s and the current crisis are results and expressions of the workings of the law of the falling rate of profit, due to the rising organic composition of capital, despite a generally rising rate of surplus value.

In the literature regarding the nature of the current crisis, the arguments blaming high wages and/or social benefits (supposedly causing the large public deficits of the period) for workers, along with those blaming insufficient demand, have dominated the discussion about the fundamental cause of the crisis. Our empirical analysis has shown that none of these arguments is valid;[6] the crisis has to do with the deeper dynamics and the current phase of development of all capitalist economies, which is the result of the operation of certain laws of capitalist development.

4. Conclusions

In analyzing the development of the postwar Greek economy and tracing the roots of its current crisis, the examination of the behavior of the profit rate and other Marxian variables is of the utmost importance. This study examines these variables in detail over the entire postwar history of the Greek economy. The different phases of the capital accumulation process are distinguished and analyzed according to the movement of the profit rate. The "Golden Age" of the 1958–74 period of high profitability and strong growth was followed by the stagflation crisis of the 1970s and early 1980s. After 1985 and especially after 1991, the "neoliberal solution" to the crisis resulted in a modest recovery of profitability, capital accumulation, and output growth based exclusively on the huge increase in the rate of exploitation of labor. When the stimulus to aggregate demand provided from personal consumption—driven by debt and "wealth effects" and state deficit spending—was removed, the underlying structural crisis in the real economy manifested itself fully from 2009 until today. The insufficient recovery of profitability during the neoliberal era appears to lie at the core of the economic difficulties currently encountered by the Greek economy. Evidence for that is provided by the strongly negative trend of both the general Marxian and the net profit rates over the entire postwar period.

Thus, the claims of certain Marxists that the present crisis is not a crisis of profitability seem to be unfounded. Low profitability persisted during the neoliberal era and especially in the years before the onset of the crisis. This happened because two of the factors of the classical scenario of a definite recovery from a serious crisis were absent. Those are (1) the massive destruction, depreciation, and restructuring of capital; and (2) a technological revolution that would (possibly) raise productivity growth significantly and lower the value and materialized compositions of capital, as well as decrease the importance of unproductive activities. It is evident that this solution could not be politically accepted at that time, because it would create economic and social conditions similar to those of the Great Depression. The unprecedented political strengthening of the Left and the social and political upheaval of the last five years, once those drastic measures were gradually introduced, testify to this.

It is also evident that capital and the state in the last years of the crisis have been attempting to achieve the much-needed increase in profitability at all costs, even if those include halving the standard of living, and ruining the lives of workers and the vast majority of the population. This attack has been implemented by all governments of the period, and the Syriza government has been no exception to this trend (contrary to its simplistic Keynesian illusions), illustrating the deep structural problems of the system.

In addition, taking into account the net fiscal position of the working class (see note 6) in Greece and in other countries, it appears that the term "welfare state" is a misnomer for the actual role played by the capitalist state in the redistribution of income as far as labor is concerned.[7] This is so because the already negative net social wage is consistently negative; that is, it is actually a net tax on labor. As Shaikh and Tonak (1987) noted in the 1980s, the welfare state and the social wage were a "myth," and they remain so three decades later.

This fact does not imply that labor should not fight against attempts for cutbacks in social spending, increases in retirement age, and increases in labor taxes, all of which will lower even further the net social wage. Those attempts by the state and capital do not stem exclusively from the fiscal difficulties encountered by governments all over the world. The reduction in the market income share and the post-fiscal income share of labor is even more necessary nowadays for the system. That is so because the performance of capitalist economies during the neoliberal period, and especially during the current crisis, lags seriously behind the experience of the "Golden Age" period, allowing no wage or social wage concessions.

On the contrary, the survival of the system in this era of diminished productive potential requires further attacks on the income and the standard of living of a class that was already losing ground in the distributive battle against its main enemy, capital. The fight against neoliberal capitalism has been ineffective so far because the first round of neoliberalism was treated by its opponents and radicals, in particular, as an inefficient policy regime, rather than as the only form that current capitalism can assume given its productive capabilities. The fight against neoliberalism can only be effective if it is a fight against the system as a whole, and not against some presumably erroneous or unjust economic and social policies. The answer on the part of the dominated classes can only be a direct challenge and overthrow of the profit system itself, and not the search for some "appropriate" policy that will benefit both workers and capital.

Notes

1   In Brenner, it is the persistence of overcapacity and over-competition that explains the incomplete recovery of profitability, whereas in our account it is mostly the absence of fixed capital destruction or devaluation, and the persistence of unproductive labor, which does so.

2   See, among others, Moseley (1988, 1991) and Shaikh and Tonak (1994).

3   Laibman (2010, p. 382), commenting on the arguments put forth by Palley
     (2009) and Kotz (2009), states that "the obvious problem with this analysis from a
     Marxist point of view is its unstated implication: the crisis was a crisis of a policy,
     neoliberalism (despite the use of the word "systemic" by Kotz and others)."

4   For a detailed account of the method followed in estimating the Marxian
     categories in the context of the Greek national accounts and their categories, see
     Maniatis (2005) and Maniatis and Passas (2013).

5   See Maniatis (2012) and Roberts (2013).

6   We have argued elsewhere that there are three main dimensions in the current
     Greek economic crisis. The first has to do with the world economic recession
     that started in 2007–2008, and especially with the US case that we analyze in
     Maniatis (2012), and determines the (stagnationist) international context in which
     the Greek economy operates. The second has to do with the overaccumulation
     crisis of the Greek economy that we analyze here. Both are the results of the
     workings of the law of the falling rate of profit. The third dimension is discussed
     in Maniatis (2015), and it has to do with the fiscal crisis of the Greek state that
     was exacerbated by the accumulation crisis of the real economy; it is argued
     there that the net fiscal position of the Greek working class vis-à-vis the state is
     negative—that is, the net social wage (i.e., the difference between labor benefits
     received from the state minus labor taxes) for Greek workers was systematically
     negative over the entire postwar period. This finding addresses the arguments that
     a generous welfare state was the cause of the crisis and provides the basis for a
     workers' government to deny the repayment of the public debt.

7   See Maniatis (2014) for the estimation and comparison of the net social wage in
     a number of advanced capitalist economies.

References

Bakir, E. and A. Campbell (2009) "The Bush Business Cycle Profit Rate: Support in
    a Theoretical Debate and Implications for the Future," *Review of Radical Political
    Economics*, Vol 41, No 3.

———. (2010) "Neoliberalism, the Rate of Profit and the Rate of Accumulation,"
    Science and Society, Vol 74, No 3.

Bowles, S., D. Gordon, and T. Weisskopf (1983) *Beyond the Wasteland: Democratic
    Alternatives to Economic Decline*, Doubleday.

———. (1986) "Power and Profits: The Social Structure of Accumulation and the
    Profitability of the Post-war US Economy," *Review of Radical Political Economics*, Vol
    18, Nos 1 and 2.

Brenner, R. (1998) "The Economics of Global Turbulence: A Special Report of the
    World Economy, 1950–98," *New Left Review*, No 229.

———. (2006) *The Economics of Global Turbulence*, Verso.

———. (2009) "What is Good for Goldman Sachs is Good for America: The Origins
    of the Current Crisis," Prologue to the Spanish edition of *The Economics of Global
    Turbulence*, Akal.

Cámara, S. (2007) "The Dynamics of the Profit Rate in Spain," *Review of Radical Political
    Economics*, Vol 39, No 4.

Crotty, J. (2000) "Structural Contradictions of the Global Neoliberal Regime," *Review
    of Radical Political Economics*, Vol 32, No 3.

Duménil, G. and D. Lévy (2011) *The Crisis of Neoliberalism*, Harvard University Press.

Glyn, A. and B. Sutcliffe (1972) *Capitalism in Crisis: British Capitalism, Workers and the Profit Squeeze*, Penguin Press.

Gowan, P. (2009) "Crisis in the Heartland," *New Left Review*, No 55.

Harvey, D. (2010) *The Enigma of Capital*, Profile Books.

Kliman, A. (2011) *The Failure of Capitalist Production: Underlying Causes of the Great Recession*, Pluto Press.

Kotz, D. (2003) "Neoliberalism and the SSA Theory of Long-Run Capital Accumulation," *Review of Radical Political Economics*, Vol 35, No 3.

———. (2008) "Contradictions of Economic Growth in the Neoliberal Era: Accumulation and Crisis in the Contemporary U.S. Economy," *Review of Radical Political Economics*, Vol 40, No 2.

———. (2009) "The Financial and Economic Crisis of 2008: A Systemic Crisis of Neoliberal Capitalism," *Review of Radical Political Economics*, Vol 41, No 3.

———. (2010) "The Final Conflict: What Can Cause a System-Threatening Crisis of Capitalism?," *Science and Society*, Vol 74, No 3.

Laibman, D. (2010) "Capitalism, Crisis, Renewal: Some Conceptual Excavations," *Science and Society*, Vol 74, No 3.

Lapavitsas, C. et al. (2010) "Eurozone in Crisis: Beggar Thyself and Thy Neighbour," *Research on Money and Finance*, Occasional Report.

Laskos, C. and E. Tsakalotos (2013) *Crucible of Resistance: Greece, the Eurozone, and the World Economic Crisis*, Pluto Press.

MacNally, D. (2011) "Global Slump: The Economics and Politics of Crisis and Resistance, Spectre, PM Press.

Maniatis, T. (1996) "Testing Marx: A Note," *Capital and Class*, Vol 59.

———. (2005) "Marxian Macroeconomic Categories in the Greek Economy," *Review of Radical Political Economics*, Vol 37, No 4.

———. (2012) "Marxist Theories of Crisis and the Current Economic Crisis," *Forum for Social Economics*, Vol 41, No 1.

———. (2014) "Does the State Benefit Labor? A Cross-Country Comparison of the Net Social Wage," *Review of Radical Political Economics*, Vol 46, No 1.

———. (2015) "The Fiscal Crisis in Greece: Whose Fault?," in S. Mavroudeas, ed., *Greek Capitalism in Crisis: Marxist Analyses*, Routledge.

Maniatis, T. and Passas, C. (2013) "Profitability, Capital Accumulation and Crisis in the Greek Economy, 1958–2009: A Marxist Analysis," *Review of Political Economy*, Vol 25, No 4.

Marx, K. (1981) *Capital,* Vol 3, Penguin.

Mohun, S. (2005) "On Measuring the Wealth of Nations: The US economy, 1964–2001," *Cambridge Journal of Economics*, Vol 29, No 5.

Moseley, F. (1988) "The Rate of Surplus-Value, the Organic Composition and the General Rate of Profit in the US Economy, 1947–1967: A Critique and Update of Wolff's Estimates," *American Economic Review*, Vol 78, No 1.

———. (1991) *The Falling Rate of Profit in the Post-war United States Economy*, St. Martin's Press.

———. (1997) "The Rate of Profit and Economic Stagnation in the US Economy," *Historical Materialism*, Vol 1, No 1.

Palley, T. (2009) "America's Exhausted Paradigm: Macroeconomic Causes of the Financial Crisis and Great Recession," New American Contract policy paper, available at http://www.newamerica.net/publications/policy.

Roberts, M. (2013) "From Global Slump to Long Depression," *International Socialism*, No 140.

Shaikh, A. (1983) "Economic Crises," in T. Bottomore et al., eds., *A Dictionary of Marxist Thought*, Harvard University Press.

————. (1987) "The Falling Rate of Profit and the Economic Crisis in the US," in *The Imperiled Economy*, URPE.

————. (2011) "The First Great Depression of the 21st Century," in L. Panitch, G. Albo, and V. Chibbert, eds., *The Crisis This Time: Socialist Register 2011*.

Shaikh, A. and E. A. Tonak (1987) "The Welfare State and the Myth of the Social Wage," in R. Cherry et al., eds, *The Imperiled Economy*, Book 1, URPE.

————. (1994) *Measuring the Wealth of Nations: The Political Economy of National Accounts*, Cambridge University Press.

CHAPTER 9

THE PROFIT RATE IN BRAZIL, 1953–2008

*Adalmir Marquetti, Eduardo Maldonado Filho
and Vladimir Lautert*

1. Introduction

The Great Depression of the 1930s was seen as the failure of economic liberalism as an organizing principle of modern societies. The understanding that the role of the markets in allocating resources should be restricted superseded the conception that free markets were the foundation for economic progress. Then, the conception became prevalent that capitalism had to be organized not according to the principles of liberalism but rather by some sort of regulated capitalism or "embedded capitalism."

After World War II, domestic markets emerged as regulated capitalism. Labor market regulations, coupled with high economic growth (Maddison 1995) and reduced rates of unemployment, conferred more power to the working class in its bargain with capitalists. As a consequence, the working classes in the advanced capitalist countries experienced an unheard-of improvement in their standards of living (Glyn et al. 1991).

Nevertheless, by the late 1960s there were signs that the model of regulated capitalism was not working properly: a structural crisis was underway. What caused this crisis? Marxian analyses of the "Golden Age" pointed to the fall of the profit rate due to the decline in capital productivity and the rise of wages in parallel with gains in labor productivity (Duménil and Lévy 2003).

The regulatory framework was restricting the ability of the capitalist class to overcome the profitability crisis. It was necessary to embark on a process of neoliberal reforms that would restore free markets as the central mechanism for the allocation of resources in order for the capitalist class to regain its strength. Neoliberalism was successfully imposed within advanced capitalist countries by the late 1970s and early 1980s. The empirical evidence shows that after the restoration of capitalist class power, there was a rise in the profit rate in developed capitalist economies (Duménil and Lévy 2002).

For many developing capitalist countries, the turning point was the debt crisis in the 1980s. From then on, developing countries began a process of reforming their institutional framework in order to build up the neoliberal one. The International Monetary Fund and the World Bank played an important role in this process.

The changes in the institutional framework of the world economy and its dominant economic ideology, as briefly stated above, are fundamental for analyzing the evolution of the Brazilian economy and the movements of its structural and economic variables. The international context gave the economic and ideological constraints and incentives for the building up of two Brazilian economic models: the import substitution industrialization model (ISI) during the Golden Age of capitalism, and the neoliberal model. The crisis and rupture of the ISI extended from the mid-1970s to the late 1980s. After 2003, in a favorable international context, elements of both models were combined with a redistributive policy.

During 1953–2008, there were two phases of economic growth in Brazil. The economy was very dynamic during the Golden Age, growing at 7.3 percent per year between 1953 and 1980. Then, there was a sharp decline in growth during the neoliberal years; Brazilian GDP expanded at only 2 percent between 1980 and 2003, while in the period 2003–2008, GDP expanded at 4.7 percent per year.

The aim of this chapter is to explain, from a Marxian perspective and taking into account the changes in the world economic and ideological frameworks, the evolution of the profit rate and its decomposition in Brazil during the 1953–2008 period. Behind this goal is the conception "that the profit rate is crucial to the functioning of . . . capitalist economies" (Duménil and Lévy 1993, p. xi).

This is a first and necessary step toward a more ambitious objective, which is to employ the Marxian analytic framework to explain the process of accumulation of capital in Brazil since the beginning of the 1950s—in particular, to explain the decline of GDP growth after 1980. This is a major task, which is left for future research.

In accordance with Marx's conception, there was a declining tendency of the profit rate during the period in analysis that was determined by technological change, reflecting the rapid mechanization of the economy after World War II. The evolution of the profit rate displayed three phases that are consistent with institutional changes in Brazil, as well as with international capitalist transformations.

The chapter is organized as follows: Section 2 presents a brief delineation of the Brazilian economy's growth for the 1953–2008 period. Section 3 addresses the Marxian theory of the profit rate and its decomposition, while section 4 describes the evolution of the profit rate and its components for the

Brazilian economy. Finally, the last section concludes with a brief review on the results and implications for further research.

2. Brazilian Economic Growth, 1953–2008

The difference in the historical record in terms of economic growth between the Golden Age and neoliberalism is remarkable in both advanced and developing countries. In relation to the latter, Easterly (2001, p. 21)— among many others—has "documented a significant puzzle in empirical growth research: the stagnation of the typical developing country in the '80s and '90s, despite policy reforms that according to growth regressions should have led to accelerating, not falling, growth."

In few countries is the difference in economic performance as striking as in Brazil. The Brazilian economic growth during the period 1953–2003, as stated above, was characterized by two phases. In the Golden Age of capitalist development, the country was one of the most dynamic economies worldwide. The GDP rose at 7.3 percent per year between 1953 and 1980, but this rate collapsed to 2 percent in the 1980–2003 phase.[1] During 2003–2008, the GDP growth rate accelerated to 4.7 percent.

Between 1953 and 1980, economic growth was led by the industrial sector in a process of import substitution industrialization. The industrial share increased from 26.3 percent in 1953 to 44.1 percent in 1980, while the agricultural share declined from 24.4 percent to 10.9 percent. In the 1980–2003 period, the share of industry dropped to 38.8 percent and of agriculture to 9.9 percent. The deindustrialization process continued between 2003 and 2008.

During the Golden Age of ISI (1953–73), there were two economic booms in the Brazilian economy. The first was in the 1950s, when Brazil went through a very rapid industrialization process, led by the rapid expansion of the consumer durable and capital goods sectors. This expansion was especially fast during the "Plano de Metas" (target program) between 1956 and 1960, and Brazilian GDP expanded at an annual compound growth rate of 7.7 percent between 1953 and 1962.[2]

In the beginning of the 1960s, the growth rates declined, inflation accelerated and the class struggle intensified. In 1964, a military coup overthrew the left-wing government, restoring capitalist class power, carrying out institutional reforms and launching a stabilization program to control inflation. Insofar as the reforms are concerned, the most important ones were implemented in the years 1964–65, reshaping the financial markets, the tax system, and the labor markets. Labor market reform, plus the repression against labor unions and the left-wing political parties, led to the increase in the rate of surplus value.

Despite the market-oriented flavor of the reforms, they did not redirect the Brazilian development strategy. In fact, the ISI model was strengthened, and coordination and planning by the central government continued to be pivotal for the economic policy. The reforms and economic policies implemented by the military dictatorship consolidated the industrialization of the Brazilian economy, reaching their economic apex in the 1968–1973 years. The so-called "Milagre Econômico" (economic miracle), as this period is known, was marked by an impressive annual compound growth rate of 10.8 percent in GDP and 14 percent in manufacturing.

After 1973, the Brazilian ISI model started to show its limits as the international economy entered into a period of stagflation. The answer to the international crisis by the military dictatorship was not only to keep its commitment to the industrialization model, but also to implement a new and ambitious plan—the Second National Development Plan—that aimed to extend ISI to intermediate goods and to greatly expand energy production. The investment boom was led by state enterprises and was mainly financed by massive foreign loans. The public enterprises raised their share of gross fixed capital formation from 12.9 percent in the 1969–1973 period to 23.1 percent during 1974–1979, while the external debt rose from US$14.9 billion in 1973 to US$55.8 billion in 1980 (Ipeadata 2009).

Although the Brazilian average rate of growth declined after 1973, its performance was still strong. For the 1973–1980 period, the GDP annual average rate of growth was 6.6 percent. Perhaps the most obvious manifestation of the crisis was the acceleration of inflation that, measured by the GPD deflator, rose from 29.6 percent in 1973 to 92.1 percent in 1980 (IBGE 2003).

The period of reduced economic growth between 1980 and 2003 can be divided into two subperiods: first, the 1980–89 years, when the Brazilian economy was characterized by stagnation and accelerating inflation but had not yet adopted a new development strategy; and second, the 1989–2003 years, when the Brazilian economy embraced the neoliberal model.

Brazil, which had adopted a risky strategy of rapid growth within a context of stagflation of the advanced capitalist economy, was severely hit by the external debt crisis, and the country had one of its worst recessions in the early 1980s. During the 1970s, it was becoming increasingly clear that the Brazilian economic model had structural problems, but it was the global debt crisis and its aftermath that raised the possibility of adopting a new economic model.

As the next sections show, the profit rate and the growth rate of labor productivity declined markedly during the Second National Development Plan. The country was not able to generate a current account surplus to service and pay the foreign debt. The answer of the military dictatorship to the international crisis expanded the external debt, placing Brazil in a position of high financial fragility.

In the early 1980s, there were lively and illuminating discussions among Brazilian economists about the causes of the economic crisis and the alternatives for returning to the path of economic growth. Several economic plans, combining orthodox with heterodox measures, were implemented, but all of them failed to control inflation or to spur growth. After 1986, the plans were known as "heterodox plans" because their central economic measure was a freeze on prices and wages. These failures increasingly gave political support for the implementation of a program of neoliberal reforms that the IMF and the international and national financial capitals were advocating as the only model for organizing the economy and society.

The 1980s were thus characterized by persistent economic crisis, and from ideological and practical standpoints, the decade marks the transition from ISI toward neoliberal capitalism. The annual GDP growth rate declined to 2.2 percent between 1980 and 1989, and for this reason the 1980s are known as the "lost decade"; the inflation rate reached 1,034 percent in 1989.

It is important to emphasize that it took a long transitional phase for the Brazilian economy to move from ISI to the neoliberal model. Brazil was one of the last countries in Latin America to adhere to the neoliberal paradigm, and this is partially explained by the success of the ISI and the long process of political transition between the dictatorship and the democratic order. Neoliberalism represented the adoption of a market-led growth model. This new model implied the reduction in the role of the state in the economy, privatization of public enterprises, more flexible capital and labor markets, and greater international integration. According to its proponents, after these reforms the Brazilian economy would benefit from the globalization process, receiving a new flux of international investment (Franco 1998). From a political perspective, it represented the turnover of hegemony within the bourgeoisie from industrial to financial capitalists.

From 1989 onward the Brazilian economy went through a series of neoliberal reforms. Among them was the adoption of a new form of international integration through commercial and financial liberalization (Cysne 1998). The national program of destatization started in 1990, and the public enterprises in petrochemical and metal sectors were the first to be sold.

The renegotiation of external debt within the context of the Brady Plan allowed the return of Brazil into the international financial markets, which established the basis for launching the Real Plan in 1994.[3] This new plan was composed of two parts: the first was a set of short-term macroeconomic policies to control inflation, and the second consisted of neoliberal reforms to spur growth. High interest rates, coupled with the return of Brazil to international capital markets, led to an overvalued exchange rate—the main factor in reducing the inflation rate from 1,996.2 percent per year in 1993 to 8.3 percent in 1997. After 1994, destatization in the public services began as well, with the sale of enterprises in the telecommunication, electrical, and financial sectors.

With the Real Plan, Brazil fully adopted the neoliberal agenda. Even though these reforms and the macroeconomic policies implemented succeeded in bringing down inflation, they failed to revive the former dynamism of the Brazilian economy. The GDP expanded just 1.8 percent per year between 1989 and 2003, lower than during the so-called "lost decade," but the economic structure changed significantly as a result of the adoption of the neoliberal model, the industrial share in GDP declining from 46.3 percent in 1989 to 35.5 percent in 1997 (IBGE 2003).

Even from the standpoint of the neoliberal model, one of the major shortcomings of the Real Plan was the strong expansion of the Brazilian external debt. It rose from US$124 billion in 1991, the year of the intensification in the opening of the capital account (Cysne 1998), to US$241.5 billion in 1998. The export share of GDP declined from 8.9 percent in 1989 to 7.5 percent in 1997, while imports expanded from 5.5 percent to 9.9 percent. The increase in external financial fragility associated with the volatility of international capital drove the devaluation of the real in the beginning of 1999. The Brazilian external financial problems followed a sequence of international financial crises, initiated by Mexico in 1994, and followed by Asia in 1997 and Russia in 1998.

The Brazilian economic authorities answered the 1999 crisis by adopting an economic policy that combined an inflation target program, primary fiscal surplus, and a floating exchange rate. Monetary policy based on a high interest rate played a central role in this economic arrangement to keep inflation under control and to attract international capital. The result was the continuation of the reduced economic growth between 1997 and 2003, with the GDP expanding at 1.5 percent per year. This growth was led by the increase in exports, whose share in GDP rose to 16.4 percent in 2003.

In the 2003–2008 period, there was an expansion in capital accumulation in Brazil. The question is whether it represents a cyclical movement, or a rupture with the period of reduced economic growth. Initially, the Brazilian economy raised its commodity exports to China. Then, there was a strong rise in investments with the "Programa de Aceleração do Crescimento" (Growth Acceleration Program) in 2005. The goal of this program was to stimulate economic growth, with the state acting to promote the investment of public and private enterprises. Another characteristic of this period was the increase in the real minimum wage and income transfer programs, raising the income of the poor population.

Table 9.1 summarizes the evolution of Brazilian GDP over the 1953–2008 period. Between 1953 and 1973, there was the Golden Age of the ISI; from 1973 to 1989, there was the erosion and crisis of ISI; and between 1989 and 2003 there were the neoliberal years. The economic policy in the 2003–2008 period combined elements of both models with a policy of income redistribution.

Period	GDP Annual Growth Rate
1953–2008	4.8
1953–1973	7.6
1953–1962	7.7
1962–1973	7.5
1973–1989	3.9
1973–1980	6.4
1980–1989	2.0
1989–2003	1.7
1989–1997	1.4
1997–2003	2.0
2003–2008	4.7

Table 9.1: GDP growth rates (%), Brazil, 1953–2008. Source: see appendix.

3. Analytic Framework and Definition of Variables

From the standpoint of Marxian theory, profit—and not self-interest or welfare maximization—is the overriding driving force of capitalism. Money capital is advanced in order to make more money, that is, profit. The profit rate measures the degree of valorization of the total capital advanced. It is central for the dynamics of the capitalist system, regulating the macroeconomic processes of accumulation, the competition among capitals, and the degree of capacity utilization with which firms operate. The profit motive provides the rationale for the capitalists' defense of free markets, resistance to wage increases, and compulsion to increase productivity.

According to Marx's theory, profit—the apparent form of the surplus value—is created in the process of production, but its appropriation is realized in the markets. Competition is one of the main mechanisms that redistributes profit among industrial, commercial, and financial capitalists, as well as among landlords. The state also plays an important role in the process of redistribution of surplus value.

The profit rate is measured by the ratio between the total profits created during a period of time and the total advanced capital. This is the broadest measure of the degree of valorization of the total productive capital in operation. The profit rate is the most relevant variable for analyzing long-run tendencies of capitalism such as accumulation and crises—that is to say, it is the crucial variable for analyzing the dynamism of the economy as a whole. It is also clear that this variable does not provide the necessary information for analyzing the dynamics of competition and its effects. In other words, according to a Marxian approach, it is the time profile of the profit rate that ultimately underlies the visible ups and downs of the process of capital accumulation, and the attendant class struggle.

It is important to remember, however, that only one part of the total profit created is really appropriated by capitalists and rentiers—capitalist classes for short. Part of the total surplus value created is appropriated by unproductive workers, for example, by commercial workers and the state, not to mention the international transfer of surplus value. Moreover, from that part of the total profit that is in fact appropriated by the capitalist classes, competition and property rights operate to redistribute it further as industrial profit, commercial profit, interest, and rent. It is therefore theoretically possible that a rising profit rate does not necessarily generate an acceleration of capital accumulation.

The following analysis of the time profile of the profit rate in Brazil is based on a model that is informed by the Marxian approach. However, it must be made clear that due to limitations of the data base, the empirical measurements must be seen as a first approximation of the theoretical categories. For a better approximation of the traditional Marxian measurements of profit rate, it would be necessary to have information on the amount of productive and unproductive labor and on total capital advanced in production.

The computation of the profit rate is based on national income accounts, a procedure similar to that employed by Weisskopf (1979), Duménil and Lévy (2002), and Wolff (2003), among others. The profit rate is defined as

$$(1)\ r = Z/K$$

where Z is the total profits and K is a measure of the nonresidential fixed capital stock, both expressed in current prices. The appendix presents the source and basic methodological procedure employed in the organization of the data set and in the computation of the variables.

In order to better understand its determinants, it is useful to decompose the profit rate as follows:

$$(2)\ r = (Z/Y) \times (Y/K)$$

where Y is output at current prices.

The profit share (Z/Y) reflects the effects of distribution between capital and labor on the profit rate, whereas capital productivity reflects the effects of technology. This conception resembles Marx's analysis of the profit rate in terms of distribution and technology.

Initially, this is based on the decomposition of the profit share. It is expressed by

$$(3)\ (Z/Y) = (Y - W)/Y$$

where W is the total nominal wage. It can be written as the product between nominal average wage (w) and number of workers (L). The output can be expressed as the multiplication between real output (YR) and the output deflator (PY). Thus, it is possible to rewrite equation 3 as

$$(4)\ (Z/Y) = (PYYR - wL)/(PYYR) = 1 - [(w/PY)/(YR/L)] = 1 - (wR/yR)$$

where wR is the real average product wage and yR is real labor productivity. The evolution of the profit share is thus determined by the difference between the growth rates of real labor productivity and real product average wage. The latter expresses the real cost of the employee from the capitalist's perspective. It is different from the nominal wage deflated by the consumer price index, which reflects the command of workers over consumption goods. The profit share will increase—and consequently the profit rate—if the real product wage rises at lower rates than the real productivity of labor.

Capital productivity, in its turn, can be decomposed into relative prices and real output capital ratio:

$$(5)\ (Y/K) = (PYYR)/(PKKR) = (PY/PK) \times (YR/KR)$$

where PK is price index of net capital stock and KR is the real net capital stock, that is, $K = PKKR$. The real capital productivity can be written as the ratio between real labor productivity and the real capital–labor ratio. Thus, it is possible to express equation 5 as

$$(6)\ (Y/K) = (PY/PK) \times [(YR/L)/(KR/L)] = (PY/PK) \times (yR/kR)$$

where kR is the real capital–labor ratio.

Therefore, capital productivity rises—and as a consequence, the profit rate increases—whenever (1) the price of fixed capital in relation to the price of output declines; (2) labor productivity in real terms increases; and finally, (3) the real capital–labor ratio decreases.

4. The Evolution of the Profit Rate and Its Determinants
Empirical results
The profit rate over the period 1953–2008 is shown in figure 9.1. In a long-run perspective, the profit rate declined substantially; in 2008 it represented

44 percent of its peak level in 1953.[4] However, the downward trend extended from 1953 to the early 1990s, when the profit rate started to increase.

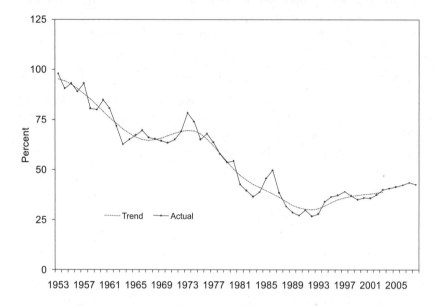

Figure 9.1. Brazil rate of profit (%), 1953–2008. Source: see appendix.

The time profile of the profit rate has three main phases. First, the profit rate declined at 2.2 percent per year during the Golden Age of the ISI (see table 9.2). Brazil's industrialization in the 1950s and political turmoil in the early 1960s were followed by the military coup in 1964 and the economic boom in the 1968–73 period. The political change and the rapid economic growth may explain the expansion in the actual profit rate from the mid-1960s to the early 1970s. Second, the profit rate fell markedly between 1973 and 1989. From a Marxian perspective, this decline represents one of the central determinants of the structural crisis of the Brazilian economy.[5] This phase is marked by the Second National Development Plan and the accumulation of external debt in the 1970s, followed by the combination of the debt crisis, high inflation rate, and low growth rates of the 1980s. Finally, in the third phase, between 1989 and 2003, there was an increase in the profit rate. This later phase corresponds to the neoliberal years in the Brazilian economy. Despite its recovery, the profit rate in 2003 was somewhere between its 1983 and 1984 levels, although between 2003 and 2008, owing to rising capital productivity, the profit rate continued its mild increase. The phases of the profit rate were correlated to the institutional changes and the economic growth in the Brazilian economy.

Period	r	Y/K	chg Y
1953–2003	−1.51	−1.53	0.02
1953–1973	−1.11	−1.39	0.28
1953–1962	−3.45	−3.72	0.27
1962–1973	0.81	0.52	0.28
1973–1989	−6.30	−5.51	−0.79
1973–1980	−5.24	−4.81	−0.43
1980–1989	−7.13	−6.05	−1.08
1989–2003	2.39	1.44	0.95
1989–1997	3.92	3.25	0.67
1997–2003	0.36	−0.96	1.32
2003–2008	1.32	2.30	−0.98

Table 9.2. Decomposition of the profit rate determinants, Brazil, 1953–2008. Source: see appendix.

It is relevant to ask whether it is distribution or technology that is the main determinant of movements of the profit rate in the Brazilian economy. Examining the decomposition of the profit rate allows us to answer this question.

There are three interesting features on the time profile of the profit share, displayed in figure 9.2. First, the profit share remained relatively stable in the long term, with an average of 52.1 percent. Second, between 1953 and the early 1990s, the graph reveals a cyclical pattern. The profit share increased during the economic boom of the late 1950s and then declined during the 1960s, in the period of sluggish growth. Its fall in the early 1960s is also associated with the rising of the working-class and peasants' movements and the central government's pursuit of left-wing reforms and economic policies. Among the reforms were the statute of the rural worker (regulating the rural labor market) and the law that restricted profit remittances by multinationals. The profit share stabilized under military rule, when pro-capital reforms and economic policies were implemented, and it rose during the 1968–73 economic boom. The military dictatorship ended the job tenure in the private sector, introduced a new wage policy that restricted wage increase, and removed the restriction to profit remittances. From the mid-'70s to the late 1980s, the profit share fell once again. Economic stagnation—combined with the indexation of the wages in a period of accelerating inflation as well as the reawakening of working-class militancy in the late 1970s—played an important role that helps explain this decline.[6]

Third, during the neoliberal years the profit share rose steadily from 43 percent in 1990 to 56 percent in 2003, which departs from the previous experience, when its behavior was positively associated with economic growth. This upward movement seems to be related with the impact of the neoliberal reforms and macroeconomic policies upon the rate of surplus value. Neoliberalism represented a major institutional change that reinforced the political power of the capitalist class.

After 2004 the profit share returned to its procyclical pattern, declining due to the higher economic growth and the adoption of redistributive policies by the Workers' Party. The real minimal wage rose 6.5 percent annually between 2003 and 2008.

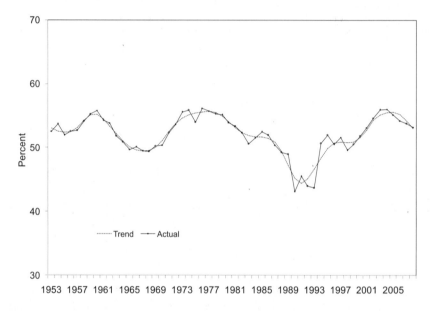

Figure 9.2. The profit share (%), Brazil, 1953–2008. Source: see appendix.

Figure 9.3 presents the productivity of capital. There were three phases in its movements, quite similar to those observed for the profit rate. During the first phase, between 1953 and 1973, capital productivity declined at 1.4 percent per year. In the second phase, between 1973 and 1989, there was a steep fall of 5.5 percent per year. It is important to point out that Brazil was going through a particularly intense process of industrialization in the 1950s and 1970s with the Target Program and the Second National Development Plan. In the third phase, from 1989 to 2008, there was a mild rise in the productivity of capital. In 2008 it was close to its early-1980s level. The third phase represents a change in the long-term behavior of capital productivity in Brazil.[7] The increase may reflect the incorporation of the technological innovations associated with the third industrial revolution. The effects of the business cycle on the productivity of capital are less apparent than in the case of the profit share; therefore, *the long-term behavior of the profit rate in the Brazilian economy was mainly determined by technology*, as it is reflected in capital productivity. This result is consistent with the Marxian analysis of the tendency for profit rate to fall in volume 3 of *Capital*.

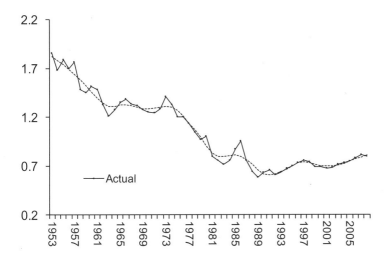

Figure 9.3. The productivity of capital, Y/K Brazil, 1953–2008. Source: see appendix.

Explaining the behavior of the profit share

The decomposition of the determinants of the profit share demonstrates that the evolution of the profit share depends positively on the growth of labor productivity and negatively on the growth of the real product wage. Figure 9.4 displays both labor productivity and the real product wage for Brazil over the 1953–2003 period. It is possible to identify three phases, perhaps a fourth one, in the real product wage.

First, between 1953 and the late 1970s, when the real product increased markedly, it was during a period of high capital accumulation and rising demand for labor in urban and industrializing regions. Brazil had a large reserve army of labor in the rural sector, and this demand was mainly attended by rural migration. Moreover, from 1964 to the mid-1970s, the political repression by the military dictatorship played an important role in restraining wage increases and maintaining strict control over the workers' movement.

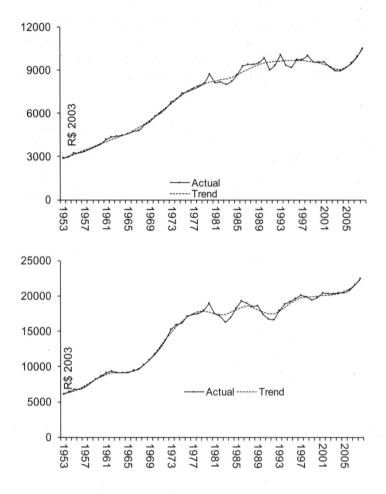

Figure 9.4. Real product wage (top) and real labor productivity (bottom), Brazil, 1953–2008. Source: see appendix.

Second, during the late 1970s, and particularly in the 1980s, there was a strong decline in the growth rate of the real wage. During this phase the labor movement underwent a reorganization, forming the "Partido dos Trabalhadores" (Workers' Party) in 1980 and the "Central Única dos Trabalhadores" (Unified Workers' Central) in 1983. The reorganization of the labor unions and the process of redemocratization played a key role in the ability of the wage to keep pace with high inflation.[8]

Third, from the late 1980s to 2003, the real product wage declined 0.4 percent per year, and in 2003 it was somewhere between its 1985 and 1986 levels. This had never happened before, even under the high political repression of the military dictatorship or during the period of high inflation. This decline may be explained by a combination of slack labor markets (due to reduced capital accumulation) and neoliberal reforms in the economy and in the labor market itself.

Fourth, between 2003 and 2008 the real product wage expanded at 3.2 percent per year, its highest growth rate since 1980. Following their victory in the national elections in 2002, the Workers' Party instituted an economic policy that combined elements of a development model (expansion in investment of the public sector and of public enterprises) with a neoliberal one (high interest rate). The higher economic growth, in turn, improved the bargaining power of workers.

The productivity of labor also presents three, or maybe four phases: first, between 1953 and the mid-1970s, when productivity rose; second, from 1976 to the late 1980s, when it was basically constant; and third, from the early 1990s to 2003, when there was a moderate increase in labor productivity. Labor productivity subsequently expanded at 2 percent between 2003 and 2008, reflecting a rise in capital accumulation.

Both of the first two phases were fundamentally different from the period of the early 1990s to 2003. In the former years, the real product wage and labor productivity grew at similar rates, while in neoliberalism, real labor productivity rose at higher rates than the real product wage (see table 9.3). The increase in the profit share in the neoliberal years was one of the factors behind the expansion in the profit rate. In the 2003–2008 period, there was the largest annual growth rate of the labor share, indicating a possible decline in the rate of surplus value. From this perspective, the 2003–2008 years represent a shift from the neoliberal years.

Period	$(1 - \pi)$	w_R	y_R
1953–2008	−0.03	2.35	2.38
1953–1973	−0.33	4.28	4.6
1953–1962	−0.31	4.52	4.83
1962–1973	−0.34	4.07	4.42
1973–1989	0.87	2.12	1.25
1973–1980	0.52	3.58	3.06
1980–1989	1.14	0.99	−0.16
1989–2003	−1.05	−0.45	0.6
1989–1997	−0.68	0.24	0.92
1997–2003	−1.54	−1.37	0.18
2003–2008	1.18	3.23	2.05

Table 9.3. Decomposition of the wage share, Brazil, 1953–2008, wage share (w), labor productivity (y), growth rates (%). Source: see appendix.

Explaining the behavior of the productivity of capital

The above analysis showed that the fall in capital productivity was the main cause behind the declining profit rate in Brazil. Here we discuss the evolution of the productivity of capital and its main determinants: the price of output relative to the price of fixed capital, the real productivity of labor, and the real capital–labor ratio.

Figure 9.5 displays the price of output relative to the price of fixed capital. It has a general downward trend, indicating that the price of capital goods became relatively costly. As table 9.4 shows, it declined at 0.85 percent per year in the 1953–2008 period. The time profile of the relative price also displays three phases. In the first phase, from 1953 to early 1970s, the effect of relative price on the productivity of capital was negative, declining 0.56 percent per year between 1953 and 1973. During the second phase, from 1973 to late 1989, the relative price of output relative to the price of fixed capital declined 3.84 percent per year. This was the major event responsible for the fall in capital productivity.

Critics of the ISI model, such as Bacha and Bonelli (2004), have pointed out that it resulted in a highly concentrated industry of capital goods, with lower productivity than that of international competitors. An environment of expanding inflation combined with commercial protection allowed these oligopolistic firms to raise prices in order to maintain their high profitability. In Bacha and Bonelli's view, the ISI model resulted in an inefficient industry, mainly in the capital goods sector.

Another line of research considers that the rising prices of capital goods after the mid-1970s resulted from the high cost of implementing the projects associated with the Second National Development Plan, combined with reduced capacity utilization in the 1980s (Marquetti 2002). Segments of the capital goods sector were industrialized during this period. However, the projects associated with the ISI were less successful in raising labor productivity than they had been in the past.

In the third phase, between late 1989 and 2003, the price of output relative to the price of capital goods expanded at 1.7 percent per year, contributing to the rise in capital productivity. However, the trend of the relative prices was practically constant from the early 1990s to 2003. It indicates that there was no significant reduction in the relative price of capital goods after the adoption of neoliberalism by the Brazilian economy. From 2003 to 2008, there was no change in the trend of relative prices.

Figure 9.5. Price of output relative to price of capital, Brazil (%), 2003 = 100), 1953–2008. Source: see appendix.

The time behavior of the real capital productivity is displayed in figure 9.6. It declined at 0.68 percent per year between 1953 and 2008. The phases of real capital productivity are less apparent in the data; its trend shows two, or maybe three phases. During the first phase, it declined at 0.8 percent per year between 1953 and 1973. From 1973 to 1980, real capital productivity fell at 2.8 percent per year, its strongest decline during the whole analyzed period. Then, in the second phase from the early 1980s to 2003, it fluctuated according to the business cycle around a slowly declining trend. In 2003, it was close to its level in 1984 and 1985, while in the 2003–2008 period, it expanded at 2 percent. However, this high growth rate may be a result of the expansionary phase of the business cycle.

The real productivity of capital declined during the process of industrialization and higher economic growth from the 1950s to the late 1970s. It was relatively constant after 1980, the period of lower capital accumulation and economic growth. From the mid-1980s on, the investments in information and computer technology may have had some positive effects on the real productivity of capital.

The drop in capital productivity is explained by a combination of the rising relative cost of capital goods and declining real capital productivity. Each one explicates approximately half of the fall in capital productivity.

The movements of real capital productivity can be further decomposed into the growth rates of real labor productivity and the real capital–labor ratio. As table 9.4 shows, the growth rate of the real capital–labor ratio was superior to that of real labor productivity, except during the 2003–2008 period. The path of real capital productivity in the Brazilian economy was determined by the evolution of the real capital–labor ratio.

As regards the real capital–labor ratio, two phases are apparent in figure 9.6. From 1953 to 1980, the real capital–labor ratio grew at 5.6 percent per year. Then, from 1980 to 2008 its growth dropped to less than 1.0 percent per year. There was a sharp transition between these phases.

The growth rate of the real capital–labor ratio is a measure of capital accumulation, and it is one of the main determinants of labor productivity growth.[9] Table 9.4 indicates that capital accumulation during the 1953–80 period was much higher than in the 1980–2008 years. The reduced economic growth of the Brazilian economy after 1980 originates from the fall in capital accumulation. This latter is explained by a combination of a declining profit rate and falling investment due to the payments of external debt in the 1980s.

Period	Y/K	P_Y/P_K	y_R/k_R	y_R	k_R
1953–2008	−1.53	−0.85	−0.68	2.38	3.05
1953–1973	−1.39	−0.56	−0.83	4.6	5.43
1953–1962	−3.72	−2.77	−0.95	4.83	5.78
1962–1973	0.52	1.26	−0.73	4.42	5.15
1973–1989	−5.51	−3.84	−1.67	1.25	2.92
1973–1980	−4.81	−1.97	−2.84	3.06	5.91
1980–1989	−6.05	−5.3	−0.76	−0.16	0.6
1989–2003	1.44	1.73	−0.29	0.6	0.89
1989–1997	3.25	3.38	−0.14	0.92	1.06
1997–2003	−0.96	−0.47	−0.49	0.18	0.67
2003–2008	2.3	0.28	2.02	2.05	0.03

Table 9.4. Decomposition of capital productivity, Brazil (compound annual growth rate, %), 1953–2008. Source: see appendix.

After the adoption of neoliberalism, there was no increase in capital accumulation. In the 1989–2003 period, the rate of growth rate of the capital–labor ratio was just 1.0 percent per year. The expansion of the growth rate of labor productivity from 0.1 percent in the 1980s to 0.8 percent in the 1989–2003 years might be explained by the technical change associated with the investments in the information and computer technologies. Hence, during neoliberalism the Brazilian economy did not accelerate the growth rates of either the real capital–labor ratio or real labor productivity. It contradicted the prediction of many neoliberal economists.

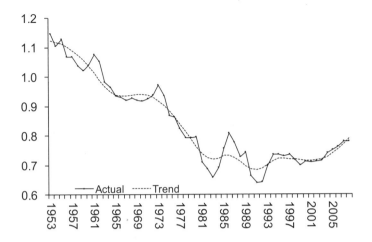

Figure 9.6. Real capital productivity ratio, Brazil, 1953–2008. Source: see appendix.

The decline in the growth rate of the real capital–labor ratio in the 2003–2008 years may indicate that the higher capital accumulation was accompanied by the expansion in employment. The unemployment rate declined from 12.3 percent in 2003 to 7.9 percent in 2008.

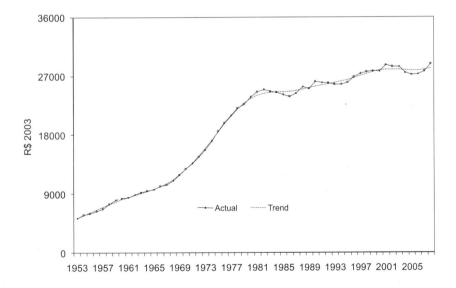

Figure 9.7. Real capital–labor ratio, R$ per employee, Brazil, 1953–2008. Source: see appendix.

5. Conclusion

The growth performance of the Brazilian economy between 1980 and 2003 was poor: the annual average growth rate, which had been 7.3 percent during the period of the ISI model, collapsed to a meager 2.0 percent. From the standpoint of mainstream economics, this collapse of growth performance is seen as a "mystery," especially after the adoption of neoliberal reforms in the late 1980s and early 1990s. However, this performance is not a phenomenon peculiar to Brazil, as Easterly (2001) has shown this to be the case among many developing countries. From 2003 to 2008, the annual growth rate expanded to 4.7 percent. It may represent a new period of higher economic growth or may reflect the expansionary phase of the business cycle.

Although this chapter did not tackle the reasons for the collapse of growth in Brazil, the analysis of the time behavior of the profit rate, and its determinant factors, is a preliminary and necessary step toward that end. It is well known that from the Marxian analytic perspective, the overriding force of capitalism is the profit motive, and consequently that the movement of the profit rate is central to understanding real GDP growth performance in capitalism.

Section 2 outlined the main characteristics of Brazilian economic growth over the 1953–2008 period. Whereas Brazil was one of the most dynamic economies during the Golden Age, it became one of the laggards during neoliberalism. This empirical characterization set the background scenario for the study of the profit rate in Brazil.

Informed by the Marxian theory of the profit rate, the profit rate was decomposed into profit share and capital productivity. Each one of these was further decomposed. The main empirical results can be summarized as follows:

(1) The profit rate presented a downward trend from 1953 to the very beginning of the 1990s; from then on, its trend was slightly upwards, but its 2008 level was similar to that in the early 1980s.

(2) The main determinant of the falling profit rate was declining capital productivity, which is a proxy for technology. This evidence is consistent with Marx's theory of the falling tendency of the profit rate. The profit share presented a cyclical pattern, but its trend was relatively stable, around 52.1 percent for the whole period. Neoliberal reforms and macroeconomic policies led to an increase of the profit share.

(3) There were three phases in the evolution of the profit rate and in most of its determinants. The third phase represented a structural crisis of the ISI model of development. These phases were consistent with the institutional changes and growth of the Brazilian economy.

(4) The fall in capital productivity was explained by the rising cost of capital goods and declining real capital productivity. The growth rate of the real capital-labor ratio was the main determinant in the evolution of real capital productivity.

(5) Neoliberalism was not capable of significantly expanding the profit rate, despite the sharp decline in the wage share during this period. It failed in reducing the cost of capital goods and providing a significant rise in capital and labor productivities; the 2003–2008 period displayed a change in the functional income distribution, the wage share expanded, and there was a higher growth rate in labor productivity.

These results answer some questions and open up others, of which further investigation might explain the collapse of economic growth in Brazil since 1980. From a Marxian perspective, the strong decline in the profit rate during the 1973–89 period, followed by a slim expansion in the 1990s, is certainly a part of the explanation for this apparent puzzle. As for the links between the profit rate, capital accumulation and institutional arrangements in Brazil, these are questions that are not yet answered. The answers, however, will almost certainly solve the so-called "mystery" of the performance of the Brazilian economy.

This chapter was previously published as Marquetti, A., Maldonado Filho, E., Lautert, V. (2010) "The Profit Rate in Brazil, 1953–2003," Review of Radical Political Economics, vol. 42, pp. 485–504. The authors have expanded the data set and the analysis until 2008. Financial support was partially provided by CNPq.

Appendix: Sources and Methods

This appendix presents the data sources and the basic procedure employed to organize and construct the data set. One of the major problems in writing this chapter was to collect and organize a consistent data set over a relatively large time frame for the Brazilian economy. The country started to publish data on national accounts in 1947. However, just after the last major methodological change in the Brazilian national accounts (BNA) in 1990, it started to contain the necessary information for computing the profit rate, except for the capital stock. For the period 1953–89, the BNA is available on IBGE (2003) and IBGE (1990). The BNA between 1990 and 2003 is available on IBGE (2003, 2004).

The profit rate is defined as the ratio between total profits at current prices and the net nonresidential fixed capital stock at current prices. The total profits at current prices are computed as the value added at current prices minus total wages at current prices. The value added at current prices is measured as the GDP minus depreciation minus imputed rent. The data on GDP and the GDP deflator was obtained in IBGE (2003) for the 1953–98 period and in IBGE (2004) for the 1999–2003 period.

For the 1990–2003 period, there is information on real and imputed rents. The latter oscillates from 64 percent to 70 percent of the total rents. For the 1953–89 period, imputed rents were computed by the multiplication between its average share during 1990–2003 and the total rent. The data source for these pieces of information is IBGE (1990, 2003, 2004).

There is information on wages and employee compensation at current prices in the BNA for the period 1990–2003. The income of the self-employed and employers is divided in two parts: one summed with wages, another with profits. This procedure is employed to facilitate the wage computation in the 1953–89 period. There is data on wages available for 1953, 1954, 1955, 1956, 1957, 1958, 1959, 1960, 1970, 1975, 1980, and 1985. The data source for this information is IBGE (1990, 2003). For the years without this information, the wage was estimated employing an econometric exercise.

The profit rate is computed employing the net nonresidential fixed capital stock. The data on inventories is not available for the whole period in study, thus it is not considered in the analysis. Brazil has no official measurement of capital stock and depreciation. Mesquita and Marquetti (2005) computed the net nonresidential fixed capital stock and depreciation for Brazil between 1950 and 2003 through a perpetual inventory method (PIM). It was calculated in constant prices and then converted to current prices using the price indexes for gross fixed capital formation.

The PIM procedure employed is similar to the methodology followed by the Bureau of Economic Analysis (BEA). The depreciation rate is calculated by R/T where R is the factor that defines the degree of declining balance due to depreciation, and T is the average asset life. However, there are two main differences in relation to BEA methodology. First, in PIM, it is assumed that there is a double declined balance where R is equal to two. Second, in PIM, the assets are retired when they reach their average life. Three kinds of assets were considered in the computation of the net nonresidential capital stock: nonresidential structures, machinery and equipment, and others. The asset life was forty years for nonresidential structures, fourteen years for machinery and equipment, and eight years for others. It is assumed that new assets are placed in service in the middle of the year. The series on gross capital formation and price deflators for the 1910–98 period was obtained in IBGE (2003) and for 1999–2003 in IBGE (2004). The consumption of fixed capital is measured as the capital stock at the beginning of the year plus investment less the capital stock at the end of the year.

Hofman (2000) also employs PIM to compute the gross and net fixed capital stocks for seven Latin American countries, including Brazil, in the 1950–94 period. He calculates the gross fixed capital stock employing a simultaneous exit mortality function, then he considers a straight-line depreciation function to calculate the consumption of fixed capital to obtain the net fixed capital stock. The asset life for nonresidential structure was forty years, and for machinery and equipment it was fifteen years.

Morandi and Reis (2004) compute the gross and net stock of fixed capital for the 1950–2002 period. They employ an asset life of forty years for nonresidential structure and twenty years for machines and equipments. The gross capital formation in the category "other" is summed with the gross capital formation in machines and equipments. The retirement of the assets follows a simultaneous exit mortality function, and depreciation is computed using a geometric function. The depreciation rate is calculated employing the results estimated for R to the

US economy by Hulten and Wykoff (1981). The value of R is 1.65 for equipment categories and 0.91 for structure categories.

Table 9.5 displays the real productivity of capital for some years in the 1953–2002 period for the three estimates. Hofman (2000) and Morandi and Reis (2004) did not compute the stock of capital in current prices. The estimated real productivity of capital by Mesquita and Marquetti (2005) is higher than that of Morandi and Reis (2004) and lower than that of Hofman (2000) for the 1953–89 years. From 1990 on, Mesquita and Marquetti (2005) present the highest estimated real capital productivity. The trends of the three estimates were similar; there was a decline from the early 1950s to late 1980s, followed by a rise.

The sources of difference between the analyses of Mesquita and Marquetti (2005) and Morandi and Reis (2004) are the employment of distinct average asset life and depreciation rates. The employment of higher asset lives and lower depreciation rates results in a greater net capital stock. The differences between Mesquita and Marquetti (2005) and Hofman (2000) are due to variations in the PIM procedure. The former follows closely the BEA methodology, while the latter employs the traditional approach that computes the gross stock of capital as a step to compute the depreciation and net capital stock. OECD (2001) presents both procedures and discusses their peculiarities.

Year	Hofman (2000)[a]	Morandi and Reis (2004)[b]	Mesquita and Marquetti (2005)[c]
1953	1.45	0.82	1.15
1960	1.25	0.75	1.04
1973	1.07	0.69	0.97
1980	0.82	0.57	0.8
1990	0.66	0.49	0.66
1994	0.68	0.52	0.73
2002		0.54	0.71

Table 9.5. A comparison of the real capital productivity estimates in Brazil, Y/K, 1953–2002. (a) Results computed at 1980 international dollars; (b) Results computed at 2000 Brazilian real; (c) Results computed at 2003 Brazilian real. Sources: Hofman (2000), Morandi and Reis (2004) and Mesquita and Marquetti (2005).

The quality of the capital stock in Brazil depends on the capacity of the deflators of gross fixed capital formation to capture the price changes in an inflationary environment. Inflation in the Brazilian economy accelerated in the second half of the 1970s. The inflation measured by the GDP deflator rose from 33.4 percent in 1975 to 149.6 percent in 1986. The period of high inflation started during 1987, when inflation went from 206.2 percent to 1996.2 percent in 1993. However, in the 1987–93 period, real capital productivity and nominal capital productivity moved closer to each other. This is also observed in the 1995–2003 years, when the inflation rate was less than two digits per year. It is significant that the deflators of the capital goods were capable of measuring accurately the changes in price in the high-inflation period. Therefore, the quality of the net capital stock estimate is not negatively influenced by the employment of incorrect price deflators.

The number of workers for the 1990–2003 period was obtained in IBGE (2003, 2004). This data was collected from the Brazilian census for 1959, 1970, 1975, 1980, and 1985. The data source for the missing observations is Summer and Heston (1991). The data obtained in this publication was adjusted to fit in the existing series. The difference between the figures in Summer and Heston (1991) and in IBGE (2003) was only 2 percent for 1990.

The average real product wage was calculated as the ratio between the total wages deflated by the GDP deflator and the number of workers.

Real labor productivity is the ratio between the real value added and the number of workers.

The real capital–labor ratio is the ratio between the net nonresidential fixed capital stock in constant price and the number of workers.

The productivity of capital is the ratio between the value added and the net nonresidential fixed capital stock. It was computed at current and real prices.

The data set was expanded to the 2004–2008 years using the growth rates of the variables obtained in Marquetti and Porsse (2014).

Notes

1   From the standpoint of Brazilian orthodox economists, this dismal performance is a mysterious one. According to Bacha and Bonelli (2004, p. 1), a "mystery surrounds Brazil's long-term growth experience. Why is it that this country's GDP collapsed since 1980 after expanding at some 7% per year from 1940 through 1980?"

2   The 1962, 1973, 1980, 1989, and 1997 years are at or close to the peak of the business cycle. Estimates of the GDP time trend display 1953 on the time trend and 2003 on the bottom of the business cycle.

3   Although some market-oriented reforms were introduced previously, it was the Collor Plan in 1990 that initiated a deliberate transformation of the institutional framework of Brazil toward neoliberalism. The Real Plan broadened and deepened the process of transformation. For a critical assessment of the Real Plan see Saad-Filho and Maldonado-Filho (1999).

4   The high profit rate in Brazil is a result of the high productivity of capital. Underdeveloped countries tend to have higher capital productivity than the developed economies (Marquetti 2003). The appendix describes the data set and makes a comparison between three estimates of the fixed capital stock in the Brazilian economy.

5   In the US economy, the fall in the profit rate started in the 1960s (Wolff 2003).

6   The Workers' Party was founded in 1980, following the strikes of 1979.

7   Capital productivity started to rise in the United States in the early 1980s (Duménil and Lévy 2002).

8   Redemocratization was the process of moving from military dictatorship to democracy. It started in the second half of the 1970s and extended to late 1980s. In 1979, the law of political parties and the amnesty law were passed, opening the possibility of organizing new political parties and the return of the exiled Brazilians. The Workers' Party was established in 1980. In 1983, there was the movement *Diretas Já* (direct elections now), which demanded direct presidential elections for 1984. Although the proposal was not approved, the movement had enormous relevance. After this immense social mobilization, some political sectors

that support the military dictatorship made a deal with the opposition parties, electing a civilian government. In 1988, the new constitution was approved, and, finally, in 1989 there was a direct presidential election.

9   The estimate of the elasticity of real labor productivity in relation to the real capital–labor ratio was 0.79 in the 1953–73 and 1989–2003 phases. It declined to 0.41 in the 1973–89 phase, as there was a slowdown in the growth rate of real labor productivity in relation to the capital accumulation in this period.

References

Bacha, E., and R. Bonelli, (2004) "Accounting for Brazil's Growth Experience – 1940–2002," *Texto para Discussão*, No 1018, IPEA.

Cysne, R. (1998) "Aspectos macro e microeconômicos das reformas brasileiras," *Ensaios Econômicos da EPGE*, No 328, Fundação Getúlio Vargas, available at http://www.fgv.br/.

Duménil, G. and D. Lévy (1993) *The Economics of the Profit Rate—Competition, Crises and Historical Tendencies in Capitalism*, Edward Elgar.

———. (2000) "Sortie de crise, manaces de crises et nouveau capitalisme," in F. Chesnais et al., eds., *Une nouvelle phase du capitalisme?*, Syllepse.

———. (2002) "The Profit Rate: Where and How Much Did It fall? Did it Recover? (USA 1948–2000)," *Review of Radical Political Economy*, Vol 34.

———. (2003) Économie marxiste du capitalisme, La Découverte.

Easterly, W. (2001) *The Elusive Quest for Growth: Economists' Adventures and Misadventures in the Tropics*, MIT Press.

Franco, G. (1998) "A inserção externa e o desenvolvimento," *Revista de Economia Política*, Vol 18.

Glyn, A. et al. (1991) "The Rise and Fall of the Golden Age," in S. Marglin and J. Schor, eds., *The Golden Age of Capitalism*, Clarendon Press.

Hofman, A. (2000) "Standardised Capital Stock Estimates in Latin America: A 1950–94 Update," *Cambridge Journal of Economics*, Vol 24.

Hulton, C. and F. Wycoff (1981) "The Measurement of Economic Depreciation," in C. Hulten, ed., *Depreciation, Inflation, and the Taxation of Income from Capital*, Urban Institute Books.

Instituto Brasileiro de Geografica e Estatística (1990) *Estatísticas Históricas do Brasil: séries econômicas, demográficas e sociais de 1550 a 1988*, IBGE.

———. (2003) *Estatísticas do Século XX*, IBGE, CD-ROM.

———. (2004) *Sistema de Contas Nacionais: Brasil 2003*, IBGE.

IpeaData (2009) *Ipeadata*, available at http://www.ipeadata.gov.br/.

Maddison, A. (1995) *Monitoring the World Economy*, OECD.

Marquetti, A. (2002) "Progresso técnico, distribuição e crescimento na economia brasileira: 1955–1998," *Estudos Econômicos*, Vol 32.

———. (2003) "Analyzing Historical and Regional Patterns of Technical Change from a Classical-Marxian Perspective," *Journal of Economic Behavior and Organization*, Vol 52.

Mesquita, R. and A. Marquetti (2005) "Estimativa do Estoque de Capital Fixo na Economia Brasileira: 1950–2003," Texto para discussão PPGE, Pontifícia Universidade Católica do Rio Grande do Sul.

Marquetti, A. and M. Porsse (2014) "Patterns of Technical Progress in the Brazilian Economy, 1952–2008," *CEPAL Review*, Vol 113.

Morandi, L. and E. Reis (2004) "Estoque de capital fixo no Brasil, 1950–2002," *Anais do XXXII Encontro Nacional de Economia*, João Pessoa, available at http://www.anpec.org.br/encontro2004/artigos/A04A042.pdf.

OECD (2001) *Measuring Capital: A Manual on the Measurement of Capital Stocks, Consumption of Fixed Capital and Capital Services*, OECD.

Pinheiro, A., R. Bonelli, and B. Schneider (2004) "Pragmatic Policy in Brazil: The Political Economy of Incomplete Market Reform," Texto para discussão, No 1035, IPEA.

Saad-Filho, A. and E. Maldonado Filho (1998) "Políticas Econômicas no Brasil: da heterodoxia ao neomonetarismo," *Indicadores Econômicos FEE*, Vol 26.

Summers, R. and A. Heston (1991) "The Penn World Table (Mark 5): An Expanded set of International Comparisons, 1950–1988," *Quarterly Journal of Economics*, Vol 106.

Weisskopf, T. (1979) "Marxian Crisis Theory and the Rate of Profit in the Postwar US Economy," *Cambridge Journal of Economics*, Vol 3.

Wolff, E. (2003) "What's Behind the Rise in Profitability in the US in the 1980s and 1990s?," *Cambridge Journal of Economics*, Vol 27.

CHAPTER 10

THE CHINESE ECONOMIC CRISIS: A MARXIST APPROACH

Mylène Gaulard

1. Introduction

With real GDP growth at 6.9 percent in 2015, its lowest growth rate since 1991, China has undeniably been slowing down since the end of the 2000s (see fig. 10.1). This slowdown is often attributed to the international economic crisis, the dependence on trade and, above all, on the weak global demand that may partially explain the fall in the export-to-GDP ratio. According to some economists, China's investment rate is too strong and threatens future accumulation; however, in order to understand the impact on accumulation, the evolution of the rate of profit must be studied.

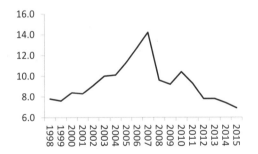

Figure 10.1. Annual growth rate in China (%), 1998–2015. Source: National Statistics.

In this chapter, we refer to the analytic tools provided by the theory of the falling rate of profit. Indeed, this theory, introduced more than a century ago by Karl Marx, can best explain the situation now confronting the Asian economic giant.

2. An Analysis of the Chinese Investment Rate: A Too-Strong Investment

A productivity problem

In China, the investment rate reached 47 percent of the GDP in 2014, a world record. However, rather than congratulating themselves, Chinese authorities were worried about it. According to the National Development and Reform Commission, "[I]f the investment scale is too important, if the investment growth is too fast, and if the investment composition is irrational, so solidity and the growth rhythm of the Chinese economy can be upset" (NDRC 2016). On what are the authorities basing this claim? This is what we will try to explain here.

For many economists, "rising savings and investment rates, for a growth rate that is stable at around 8 percent by year, are symptomatic of the difficulties for China in allocating efficiently its resources" (Cieniewski and Benaroya 2004, p. 9). As Krugman (2000, pp. 39–57) has analyzed it for the Asian newly industrialized countries (NICs) before the 1997 crisis, Chinese economic growth has relied only on the accumulation of factors of production and not on productivity growth. In the same way, Young and Lau showed that between 1960 and 1994, total factor productivity explained only 20–30 percent of the growth rate of the Asian NICs (South Korea, Taiwan, Singapore, and Hong Kong),[1] while the capital accumulation explained 50–70 percent. So, according to Yanrui Wu (1996), Chinese growth would also be the result of factor accumulation (capital and labor). For example, at the beginning of the 1980s, in Shanghai, while the state enterprise output increased by 6.1 percent a year, total factor productivity increased by only 0.8 percent. For this reason (the lack of productivity growth), Chinese economic growth is unsustainable and the world position of China could be put into question in future years. Indeed, we will see that factor accumulation without real productivity gains threatens returns on investment.

However, in 2006, French economists Diana Hochraich and Benjamin Delozier claimed that Chinese investment was not excessive. It would be so if we found a decline in the return on capital and a slowdown in total factor productivity growth in Chinese enterprises; but, according to these economists, this is only observed in state-owned enterprises, and apart from SOEs there has not been excessive investment. State-owned enterprises show debt rates higher than 50 percent of their total assets, although their output performance is weaker than the national average. For a long time, these enterprises were protected against international competition and received many subsidies from the government. As a result, managers didn't try to increase productivity; this explains inefficiency nowadays. Bad debts still increase in these enterprises, although the government regularly takes measures to restrain debt growth and has created entities designed to eliminate bad debts accumulated since the beginning of the 1990s. However, Moody (2005) reckoned that $620 billion (25 percent of 2006 Chinese GDP) were still necessary to recapitalize the banking system in 2005. Finally, except for these state enterprises, total factor productivity growth slowed during the 1990s but increased, according to Hochraich and Delozier, by 4 percent between 2002 and 2004. Capital productivity has fallen since the end of the 1980s, but this was due to a labor productivity increase (capital–labor substitution) and not to excessive capital accumulation.

The essential social side of public investment in China

Public investment represents 40 percent of Chinese investment, while 17 percent of the enterprises established in China are state-owned. Weak profits in these state enterprises are often explained by a social aspect: wages are higher than the national average, and huge sums are spent to give employees "decent" conditions of life (we will see that this is less and less true). It is usual that Chinese workers still receive wages from the state enterprise when they have been laid off (World Bank 1997, p. 47). In the same way, it is assumed that about 20 percent of employees are unnecessary (Perotti and Sun 1998, p. 13). So state enterprises cannot be considered as like others: the search for profit is not (and overall, was not) their main objective. It was estimated that 40 percent of the difference in profitability between state enterprises and township and village enterprises (TVEs) could be put down to the cost of social protection. Among Chinese peasants, it was frequently claimed that socialism was only established in urban areas and in state enterprises. State enterprises are also established in sectors where prices are kept very low, in order to make national accumulation easier. Thus 80 percent of energy production is provided by SOEs (Eyraud 1999, p. 154), and sales are often at loss. Far from giving priority to profitability, state enterprises have played a social role that was, for a long time, necessary for the continuation of capital accumulation. Furthermore, until the beginning of the 1980s, state enterprises had to transfer all their profits to the Chinese state, and reinvestment was allowed only a few times, for the most efficient ones. So there were no incentives for the managers to improve their economic performance (Eyraud 1999, p. 249).

Hochraich and Delozier's work leads to conclusions contrary to those claimed by various studies on Chinese productivity. According to Eichengreen, Park, and Shin (2011), the stagnation of the total factor productivity (TFP) related to a decline in capital productivity would account for 85 percent of the economic slowdown that occurred over recent years. Since the middle of the 2000s, capital productivity growth keeps on slowing (Zheng and Bigsten 2008; Anand et al. 2014). While it accounted for 30–58 percent of China's growth between 1978 and 1995, it only accounted for 7.8 percent of China's GDP growth in 2008 (Zheng and Bigsten 2008).

Moreover, the two authors forget a main element: public investment represents 40 percent of China's GDP. It is therefore necessary to take into account the results of public sector to measure the evolution of Chinese productivity. Furthermore, as figure 10.2 shows, private enterprises seem to make losses, too, which will be important to explain below.

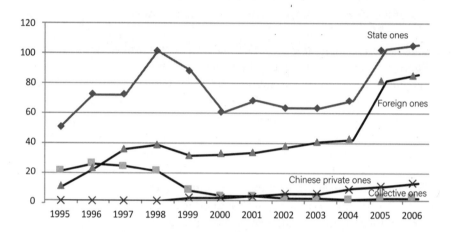

Figure 10.2. Chinese enterprises losses (in billions of yuans), 1995–2006. Source: National Statistics.

An overproduction problem

Since 1949, Chinese labor productivity has risen. For a long time, this was stimulated by the strong accumulation in state enterprises. In 1949, just before the Chinese Communist Party came to power, industry only represented 10 percent of GDP against 35 percent in 1978 (just before the "economic opening"). This industrialization was made possible by an intensive use of fixed capital. Although China has the advantage of an abundant workforce, the state enterprises have delivered, since the 1950s, a very strong capital intensity. From 1952 to 1995, the value-added of heavy industry doubled against only 15 percent for the value-added of light industry (Maddison 1998, p. 89). In 1999, state enterprises used 53 percent of national fixed capital stock but only 41 percent of national workforce (Chang 2001, p. 54). Chinese enterprises—and, overall, state ones—used far more capital than labor. Justin Lin (et al., 2001, 2007) still reproaches the Chinese mode of accumulation of being too capital biased. According to him, this mode of accumulation develops itself at the expense of employment, thus creating bottlenecks in basic industries (energy, transports, and raw materials) (Lin et al. 2001, p. 151).

In addition, the strong capital intensity of state enterprises was also responsible for very large-scale production inappropriate to the level of national consumption. In 1978, the average Chinese industrial enterprise employed eleven times more workers than the average Japanese one (Maddison 1998, p. 16), leading to idle capacity due to insufficient demand. In 1980, only 66 percent of the production capacity was utilized (Boutillier and Uzinidis 1989, p. 19). Investment expansion is still responsible for huge overproduction. Chinese investment stays at extremely high levels, essentially because of a proliferation of very capital-intense industrial enterprises. For example, there are 200 car manufacturers in the country, producing only a few thousand cars each per year, and 8,000 cement factories (against only 110 in the United States, 51 in Russia, 58 in Brazil, and 106 in India). Competition between many sectors leads enterprises to lower their prices and sometimes to have recourse to mafia networks in order to get rid of their more dangerous rivals and excess output (He 1999). As surplus production increases, it weighs on profit margins. For example, in the steel industry, there is an estimated excess of 120 million tons (more than the whole production of the second-largest world producer, Japan) (Lardy 2006). It is undeniable that China has excessive investment.

As has been shown above, the excess of capital has led to a decrease of capital productivity and to a slowdown of TFP growth. It is also responsible for huge unemployment, leading to the formation of a growing surplus workforce. Because of this surplus, the private consumption demand grows slowly, thus strengthening overproduction. So strong Chinese growth can be explained by capital overaccumulation rather than by technical progress. This high level of investment brings overproduction and is thus excessive.

3. Reasons for This Huge Investment, and Solutions
The role of regional bureaucracy
Regulation is necessary in order to reestablish a high profitability, to curb the capital productivity decrease, and to stop overproduction. Why cannot China's economic system regulate and decrease its excessive investment rate?

In 1979, when Chinese executives decided to liberalize the economy, state enterprises began to face competition with private firms, and their weight in the Chinese economy fell. SOEs were responsible for 80 percent of industrial production in 1979, but this share fell to only 40 percent in 2009. This doesn't mean they are now profitable: in 2008, it was estimated that 40 percent of them were loss making. Many reasons can explain the survival of these inefficient firms. First, the central government as well as the regional ones receive more than two-thirds of their incomes from these state enterprises (Eyraud 1999, p. 154). Indeed, their tax rate is higher than the other enterprises because they cannot pressure and negotiate with national authorities by threatening to leave the state sector (Perotti 1998, pp. 13–14). In spite of their low productivity, state enterprises continue to bring in money to the Chinese government, so it is not encouraged to close them. With his image of the bird and the cage, the conservative CCP Central Committee member Chen Yun claimed in 1992 that the state had to maintain its influence on the Chinese industry and on the whole economy: "We have to stimulate the economy with economic planning. It is like the relation between the bird and the cage. You cannot simply keep the bird in your hands, otherwise it dies. You have to let it fly, but you can only let it fly inside a cage. Without cage, the bird flies away." In spite of the privatization of many public enterprises since the mid-1990s, the state does not want to get rid of every public firm. Low-productivity enterprises are also retained in order to limit social dissent engendered by the economic liberalization (World Bank 1997, p. 29).

Moreover, these enterprises benefit from a positive image among local populations. So local governments maintain many low-productivity enterprises in order to justify their power, without interesting themselves in improving profitability. In the same way, new investment projects are regularly undertaken at the expense of the improvement of existing investments. This behavior also contributes to increasing overproduction. Finally, managers often are high party officials, and their responsibility is never called into question in case of financial losses. This does not encourage them to improve the profitability of the firms of which they are in charge. Indeed, local authorities want to increase their power by investing, and in this way, they also have more chance to get advantageous loans.

Until 1979, such investments were all the more attractive because the Chinese market was closed to international competition, and state enterprises enjoyed a monopoly status. Indeed, Chinese provinces introduced many customs barriers to impede some products from being imported or exported. Even now, enterprises established on Chinese territory still have to face barriers decided by local authorities. In spite of the economic opening of the country and its entry into the World Trade Organization in 2001, liberalization of regional borders has not followed that of China's national borders. These "feudal" aspects of the Chinese production apparatus, which are actually elements from the Asiatic mode of production (Gaulard 2014), explain a part of the superabundance of investment projects, as well as the imbalance between investment and national demand.

The necessity to lower the interest rates and
to expand the national market

These "feudal" aspects of the Chinese production apparatus do not discourage capitalists from investing, in spite of a relatively small national market and overproduction. That's because government expenditure is continuously increasing to help investors who are in trouble. Very low interest rates allow them to get some advantageous loans (the state enterprises represent 75 percent of bank loans, while other enterprises essentially depend on self-financing or shadow banking). It is undeniable that the compulsory reserve rate is very high (more than 15 percent, against 2 percent for the Eurozone), but the borrowing rate stays at low levels (lower than 8 percent) in spite of this bank constraint. This is due essentially to abundant savings (higher than 50 percent of the GDP) coming from the Chinese households and from the national enterprises.

To solve the Chinese overinvestment problem, Nicholas Lardy (2006) proposed to increase private consumption, essentially by reducing the savings rate. According to him, it was necessary to fight overproduction and overinvestment by acting directly on consumer demand. To do so, it would be essential to reduce the savings rate by cutting taxes (above all for the rural Chinese population, who are the most affected by taxes), and by increasing wages and social expenditure (to limit precautionary savings).

In recent years, health expenditure has increased from 1.8 percent of GDP in 2004 to a bit more than 3 percent in 2011 (in the same year, expenditure in India, Brazil, and France reached 4 percent, 9 percent, and 12 percent, respectively). With his project of "harmonious society," former president Hu Jintao had been trying since the beginning of the 2000s to improve China's social security system, with the aim of covering the whole of its population by the year 2025, particularly in the areas of health and pensions. This program is being pursued by Xi Jinping with the same objective: the reduction of precautionary saving and the increase of household consumption.

This new growth "orientation" toward a balance of power that is beneficial to workers is still viewed as a positive move by most economists, who over the last ten years have been calling for a better distribution of the value-added toward the workers and a higher household consumption. However, we should not forget that any increase in unit labor costs can also damage the profitability of Chinese and foreign enterprises. In March 2010, a survey conducted by the American Chamber of Commerce in Shanghai stated that 28 percent of American firms settled in China viewed labor costs as too high in the coastal regions, and that 8 percent of them were planning to relocate their production to Vietnam, India, Thailand, or Indonesia. In 2012, General Electric even decided to move its production of fridges and washing machines back to Kentucky. So the move toward a more "harmonious" society raises new difficulties.

Much more than wage rises, the decline in capital productivity is dangerously hampering the profitability of Chinese companies. Only the Marxist analysis can explain this issue as inherent in the capitalist mode of production: the accumulation process is affected not only by overproduction, but by a falling rate of profit.

4. The Falling Rate of Profit in China
The capital productivity evolution[2]

The analysis of the profit rate in China will help us to understand better the problems encountered in the accumulation process. It is important to stress the link existing between the Marxist theory of the falling rate of profit and the problems encountered by China's investment nowadays. The data given by the Chinese statistics offices are controversial, and any results obtained are only approximations. But on this question, only the trends matter. First, it will be shown that the organic composition of capital has been rising for two decades. Under certain conditions (more particularly, if the organic composition increase is higher than the exploitation rate increase), that rise will weigh on the profit rate—corresponding to $(s/v)/[(c/v) + 1]$, where s/v is the exploitation rate and c/v is the organic composition of capital.

Calculating the rate of profit

To calculate the rate of profit that, according to Marx, corresponds to the expression $s/(c + v)$, we have to use the data given by the Chinese official statistics. For Marx, the profit rate is calculated with values, not prices. It is pointless here to come back to the Marxian value/price debate, launched in the beginning of the twentieth century; for this calculation, I therefore set aside the debate on the transformation of values into prices and employ the working hypothesis that the sum of prices is equal to the sum of values on a national scale.

Using official data, we assume that GDP (reduced by wages) corresponds most closely to the Marxist surplus value (for Marx, the production value corresponds to $s + v + c$). GDP, the sum of value-added, does not take into account intermediate consumption, which can be likened to c but includes wages, which consequently must be subtracted in order to obtain the surplus value. For constant capital (s), we take the stock of fixed capital used during the process, from which residential investment is subtracted. Finally, variable capital (v) corresponds to the stock of wages. According to Marx, variable capital corresponds to productive workers only, but this distinction will not be made here because it is extremely difficult from a statistical perspective to differentiate productive and unproductive workers. Moreover, the stock of wages is so weak compared to the stock of fixed capital that subtracting the wages of unproductive workers would not change the results much.

The falling rate of profit cannot be analyzed without studying capital and labor productivity. For the needs of this analysis, it is considered that the organic composition of capital corresponds to what it is known as "capital intensity." If the labor productivity increase is higher than the capital productivity one, then the organic composition of capital is rising, and vice versa. To sum up, if the s/v increase is higher than the s/c increase, this implies that the c increase is higher than the v increase and that c/v is rising. It has been shown that China is still confronted with an overinvestment problem. This overinvestment manifests itself when the total factor productivity (TFP) increase begins to slow down and when the very strong labor productivity increase (observed since 1991) is essentially obtained by a capital productivity decrease (and thus by an increase of the organic composition of capital). Here, it is essential to stress the fact that the capital productivity has been decreasing since 1991 and that this is responsible for the strong rise of the organic composition of capital. The capital productivity decrease is often seen as a direct consequence of the overproduction. For example, according to Cieniewsky (2006), such an evolution is due to the existence of many small enterprises that stay alive thanks to social pressures. This weak concentration leads to a price war and huge production growth, and since 2004–2005, a rise of non-profitable enterprises.

Also, rising inequality of wealth allows the upper classes to mobilize a lot of capital, as well as a very cheap workforce, meaning that production often exceeds consumer demand. Although exports can help to absorb a part of that production, they cannot replace a whole national market. As we saw earlier, a large number of enterprises are working with less than 60 percent of their capacity. In such a situation, the stock of fixed capital can appear excessively high (because of the difficulty of matching this stock with economic fluctuations), compared to what is produced. This weighs on capital productivity. On the other hand, it is easier to reduce the employed workforce, so that labor productivity does not decrease; on the contrary, it is now rising (figs. 10.3 to 10.5).

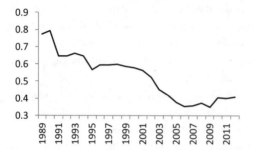

Figure 10.3. Chinese capital productivity ratio, 1989–2012. Source: author's calculations.

Figure 10.4. Chinese labor productivity ratio, 1978–2012. Source: author's calculations.

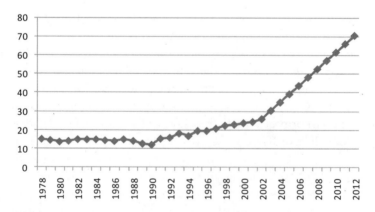

Figure 10.5. Chinese organic composition of capital, 1978–2012. Source: author's calculations.

The labor productivity increase and the falling rate of profit

The strong increase in labor productivity in China during the 1990s can be explained, essentially, by the disappearance of the economic protection given in the past to many workers by state enterprises. Nowadays, these enterprises are disappearing from the economic landscape, as well as from "the iron rice bowl." The exploitation rate is strongly increasing in order to respond to China's economic expansion and to world competition. It is essential for China to adapt to new production techniques and to progressively replace variable capital with constant capital. This drive manifests itself in a very weak elasticity of the ratio of employment to GDP growth. According to the Organisation for Economic Co-operation and Development (OECD), this elasticity was only 0.1 in the 1990s, against 1.0 for Brazil. Thus, China produces more and more goods with relatively less and less employment, which considerably increases labor productivity. This increase is obtained not only by work intensification, but also by an increased use of equipment goods. But with real technical progress absent, this weighs on capital productivity. While in 1980 two or three dollars of investment was necessary to obtain one dollar of economic growth, in 2000 China's industry needed four dollars of investment to get the same result. The ratio of investment to growth is therefore excessively high (a ratio of four-to-one against three-to-one for India) (Plantade 2006, p. 181).

So it is the accumulation process that explains the decrease in capital productivity and the rise of the organic composition of capital. A study by Xiaoqin Fan (2005) compared the different economic performances of China and India. In contrast to India, which had far-weaker investment and capital productivity increases, the falling rate of profit in China could be explained by a capital productivity decrease (Xiaoqin Fan 2005). So, following Marx, a rise of the organic composition of capital from a capital productivity decrease (while labor productivity is increasing) will reduce the profit rate. From 1960 to 1972, the profit rate in Japan was about 30 percent, and for the United States and Germany, it was higher than 20 percent. In China now, according to Xiaoqin Fan, this rate is about 8.5 percent.

These results are slightly different from ours because Fan uses another method to calculate the profit rate—one that differs from Marx's analysis (in the denominator, Xiaoqin's equation takes the whole fixed capital into account, including the residential one; in the numerator, taxes are subtracted from the surplus value, while in Marx, the taxes are part of this surplus value). However, I reach the same conclusions as Xiaoqin Fan with regard to the importance of the organic composition of capital in determining the profit rate.

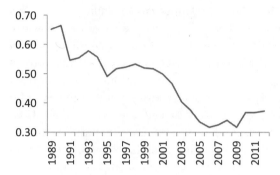

Figure 10.6. The Chinese rate of profit, 1989–
2012. Source: author's calculations.

According to Marx, the organic composition of capital weighs on the profit rate. Figures 10.5 and 10.6 show that since 1991, an increase in the organic composition of capital goes with a falling rate of profit (in the 1980s, the profit rate stagnates while the organic composition stays stable).

Chinese overproduction is more and more important because of a rising gap between supply and demand. Indeed, in order to offset the falling rate of profit, managers are encouraged to boost their mass of profit by producing more. In this way, "the capitalist gladly reduces his profit on each good, but these losses are offset by producing more" (Marx 1972, p. 1014).

One of the current debates on the Chinese economy concerns this rise in the mass of profit while the profit rate is decreasing. For some authors (Hofman and Kujis 2006), such a situation is rather beneficial because only the mass of profit matters (according to these authors). Between 1999 and 2005, the mass increased by 36 percent, which is not insignificant. However, this increase in the mass of profit was obtained at the same time as the idle capacity was rocketing and the decrease of the profit rate was making uncertain the further pursuit of accumulation (Shan 2006b), as enterprises obtained less and less surplus value relative to constant and variable capital used—a situation that might induce financing difficulties for both state enterprises (which depend on bank loans) and the others. Uncertainty about repayment of loans could then drive up interest rates, curbing investment (because of financing difficulties, but also because of exports plummeting). Therefore, it is wrong to expect an increase in the mass of profit to permanently offset the falling rate of profit. On the contrary, this "compensation" is responsible for huge overproduction and may impede the accumulation process.

However, figure 10.6 shows that the rate of profit enjoyed a slight improvement since 2006. Elsewhere, I have offered an explanation for this evolution, namely, the creation of a fictitious surplus value in speculative property and financial sectors (Gaulard 2014) as well as a slowdown in accumulation in the productive sectors that was precisely caused by the expansion of these unproductive sectors. Grossman's (1992) theory provided the same explanation for the booming of the financial sector in the United States in the 1920s, viewed as a countertrend to the decline in the rate of profit in the productive apparatus. However, the upward trend of this rate of profit is quite hazardous for China's economic growth. The problems generated by the decline in capital productivity and speculation that are used to counter this decline are really early signs of China's entry into the middle-income trap, indicating a forthcoming growth deceleration (Gaulard 2014).

It is important to note that, according to Marx, surplus value can only be created within the productive apparatus. Any deceleration in the accumulation process—although it may in the short run help to slow down, or even thwart, the decline in the rate of profit through the creation of a fictitious surplus value in sectors that are partly speculative—will thus in the long run be responsible for a decline in the mass of profits. For this reason, the starting point of an economic crisis might be directly linked to a decrease in the mass of surplus value, that is, to a burst of the speculative bubble created in the property and financial sectors. Furthermore, this trend in the accumulation process reduces the incentives to invest in research, thus preventing any effective technological catch-up, a process that would have helped China to reduce its unit labor costs via an increase in productivity that would outdo the hike in labor costs.

Indeed, an increasing number of bank crises might well reveal the freeze in the productive apparatus that will eventually make it impossible for speculative revenues to keep on booming in a sustainable manner. In February 2014, the losses suffered by the Industrial and Commercial Bank of China through its investment fund China Trust seemed to strengthen that theory. In 2015 there was an increase in bad debts that went along with the booming of approved bank credit and an underestimation of risks linked to the extraordinary rise in informal financing, better known as "shadow banking," leading to a real estate and financial bubble bust.

5. Conclusion

This analysis seems to go against the current view of the unprecedented nature China's economic growth. The falling rate of profit that China is facing will be harmful for continued high accumulation. In order to fight the overproduction problem, many solutions are proposed by China specialists. However, the slowdown in investment that would be obtained by these solutions risks revealing other weaknesses, apart from idle capacity. In China, as in the rest of the world, it is the whole capitalist system that bears the responsibility for the problems encountered by the accumulation process. Accumulation is the main characteristic of, and reason for, capitalism, but the system carries the conditions of its own destruction. This analysis of China could be extended to all the countries integrated into the capitalist system.

Notes

1   Total factor productivity (TFP) is the wealth growth that is not explained by an increased use of production factors, capital and labor. The main determinant of TFP is technical progress that, supported with a given combination of production factors, allows the creation of more wealth. Of course, the calculation of TFP raises divergences, not only because of the obtained results, but also because from a Marxist point of view, it is not really pertinent to make such a calculation. Although we share this perspective, we wanted to present here the most important analysis made on this TFP because we think that these studies effectively introduce our analysis on the rate of profit. Indeed, studies about China's TFP often stress the decrease of Chinese capital productivity, which is very important for explaining the falling rate of profit.

2   It could be said that using the term "capital productivity" is not really pertinent, because from a Marxist approach, only workforce can create surplus value, and thus only work is productive. However, for the purpose of our analysis (and keeping in mind potential limitations), this criticism will be disregarded here. Moreover, while in Marx's work, constant capital corresponds to equipment goods and to raw materials (elements able to transmit their own value without creating value by their own), only the fixed capital will be taken into account here (that is to say, the means of production that are not destroyed during the production process, and for which life duration is higher than one year). Taking into account raw materials would not change the results very much, because this cost is insignificant compared to the equipment goods costs; furthermore, this would only strengthen our results because it would increase even more the organic composition of capital. Indeed, our calculations of the profit rate and of the organic composition of capital are approximations; only their evolution matters.

References

Anand, R. et al. (2014) "Potential Growth in Emerging Asia," IMF Working Paper.
Anderson, J. (2007) "China Should Speed Up the Yuan's Rise," *Far Eastern Economic Review*, Vol 170, No 6, pp. 14–20.
Artus, P. (2008) *La Chine, Le Cercle des Economistes*, Presses Universitaires de France.
Barnett, S. and R. Brooks (2006) "What's Driving Investment in China," IMF Working Paper, No 265.
Boutillier, D. (1989) *Chine, Questions sur l'ouverture aux multinationales*, L'Harmattan.
Chang, G. (2001) *The Coming Collapse of China*, Random House.
Cieniewski, S. and F. Benaroya (2004) "Chine: la longue marche vers la société de prospérité moyenne," *DREE dossiers*, Ambassade de France à Pékin.

————. (2005) "Les entreprises chinoises, Forces et faiblesses, Défis et perspectives," *Article DREE*, Ambassade de France à Pékin.

————. (2006) "La profitabilité des entreprises chinoises," *Fiches de Synthèse DREE*, Ambassade de France à Pékin.

Delozier, B. and D. Hochraich (2006) "L'investissement en Chine est-il excessif?," *Economie et Prévisions*, No 173.

Eichengreen, B., D. Park, and K. Shin (2011) "When Fast Economies Slow Down: International Evidence and Implications for China," *NBER Working Paper*, No 16919.

Eyraud, C. (1999) *L'entreprise d'Etat chinoise, De l'institution sociale totale vers l'entité économique*, L'Harmattan.

Felipe, J., E. Xiaoqin Fan (2005) "The Diverging Patterns of Profitability, Investment and Growth of China and India, 1980–2003," CAMA Working Paper Series, No 22, The Australian National University.

Gaulard, M. (2014) *Karl Marx à Pékin*, Editions Demopolis.

Grossman, H. (1992) *The Law of Accumulation and Breakdown of the Capitalist System*, Pluto Press.

Hay, F. and Y. Shi (2006) *La Chine: forces et faiblesses d'une économie en expansion*, Presses Universitaires de Rennes.

He, Q. (1999) "China's Latent Economic Crisis and Potential Risks," *Modern China Studies*, Vol 65, No 2.

Hofman, B. and L. Kujis (2006) "Profits Drive China's Boom," *Far Eastern Economic Review*.

Krugman, P. (2000) *Pourquoi les crises reviennent toujours*, Seuil.

Kujis, L. and T. Wang (2005) "China's Pattern of Growth: Moving to Sustainability and Reducing Inequality," *China and the World Economy*, Vol 14, No 1.

Lardy, N. (2006) "China: Toward a Consumption-Driven Growth Path," Institute for International Economics, Washington.

Li, M. (2003) "Aggregate Demand, Productivity, and Disguised Unemployment in the Chinese Industrial Sector," *World Development*, Vol 32, No 3.

Lin, J., F. Cai, Z. Li (2001) *Le miracle chinois: Stratégie de développement et réforme économique Paru en mars*, Economica.

————. (2007) "The Lessons of China's Transition to a Market Economy," *CATO Journal*, Vol 16, No 2.

Lindbeck, A. (2006) "An Essay on Economic Reforms and Social Change in China," World Bank Policy Research Working Paper, No 4057.

Maddison, A. (1998) *L'économie chinoise, une perspective historique*, OECD.

Marx, K. (1972) *Le Capital, Livre III*, La Pléiade.

Moody's Investors Service (2005) "Reform of China's State Banks: Moving Beyond IPOs," available at www.kiep.go.kr/.

National Development Reform Commission (2016) "Positive Rating Actions Likely," NDRC, official website, http://en.ndrc.gov.cn/policyrelease/201612/P020161207645766966662.pdf.

Ngo, N. N. (2006) "Chine: bilan social contrasté d'un formidable essor," BNP Paribas, *Conjoncture*, http://hussonet.free.fr/c0607a1.pdf.

Palley, T. L. (2006) "External Contradictions of the Chinese Development Model: Export-Led Growth and the Dangers of Global Economic Contraction," *Journal of Contemporary China*, Vol 15, No 46.

Perotti, E. C. and S. Laixiang (1998) "State-Owned versus Township and Village Enterprises in China," World Institute for Development Economics Research Working Paper, No 150, United Nations University.

Plantade, J. M. and Y. Plantade (2006) *La Face cachée de la Chine*, Bourin Editeur.

Shan, W. (2006a) "The World Bank's China Delusions," *Far Eastern Economic Review*, Vol 166, No 29.

———. (2006b) "China's Low-Profit Growth Model," *Far Eastern Economic Review*, Vol 169, No 9.

World Bank (1997) *China 2020*, World Bank, Washington.

Wu, Y. (1996) *Productive Performance in Chinese Enterprises*, Macmillan Press.

Zheng, J. and A. Bigsten (2008) "Can China's Growth Be Sustained? A Productivity Perspective," *World Development*, Vol 34, No 4.

PART III

CREDIT, FICTITIOUS CAPITAL AND CRISES

CHAPTER 11

DEBT MATTERS

Michael Roberts

Since one unit's liability is another unit's asset, changes in leverage represent no more than a redistribution for one group (debtors) to another (creditors) . . . and should have no significant macroeconomic effects.

—Ben Bernanke (*Essays on the Great Depression*, 2000)

1. Introduction

The expansion of global liquidity in all its forms (bank loans, securitized debt, and derivatives) during the last thirty-five years has been unprecedented. The Marxist view is that credit (debt) can help capitalist production take advantage of prospective profit opportunities, but that eventually speculation takes over and financial capital becomes fictitious. It becomes fictitious because its price loses connection with value and profitability in capitalist production. This leads eventually to a bursting of the credit bubble, intensifying any economic slump.

Before the crash of 2008, there had been a massive buildup of private sector credit in the United States, reaching over 300 percent of gross domestic product (GDP), if financial sector debt is included. The graph of the rise in US private credit was described by Steve Keen (2011) as a hockey stick, in an allusion to the graph of the rise in global temperature in the last century that first alerted scientists to the dangers of global warming (fig. 11.1). The experience of the United States was repeated, more or less, in all the major advanced economies.

Throughout the neoliberal period, debt rose—and not just mortgage debt, but also corporate debt (fig. 11.2). The boom in credit went into residential property in the United States and other economies. By mid-2006, the US residential property boom had reached mega proportions (fig. 11.3).

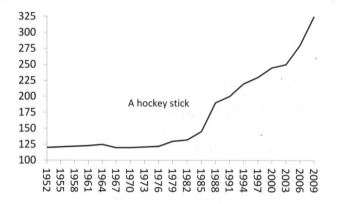

Figure 11.1. US private credit to GDP (%), 1952–2009.
Source: Bank for International Settlements (BIS).

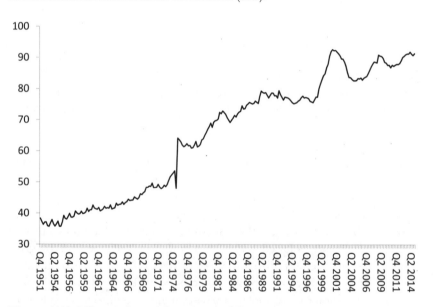

Figure 11.2. US non-financial corporate debt to
GDP (%), 1951–2014. Source: BIS.

Global liquidity expanded at an unprecedented rate beginning in the early 1990s. Liquidity here is defined as bank loans, securitized debt (both public and private), and derivatives; derivatives are made up of interest-rate hedges, commodities, equities, and foreign exchange. Interest-rate derivatives play the most important role in hedging the cost of borrowing. The notional value of derivatives rocketed from the early 1990s, reaching over $600 trillion, or ten times global GDP, by 2007.

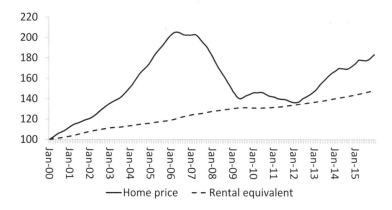

Figure 11.3. US home prices and rents (%, indexed 2000 = 100), 2000–2015. Source: Case Shiller.

In effect, global liquidity is a measure of what Marx called "fictitious" capital.[1] Global liquidity rose from 150 percent of world GDP in 1990 to 350 percent in 2011. The pace of growth accelerated during the late 1990s, and after a pause in the mild recession of 2001, liquidity took off again until the start of the global credit crunch in mid-2007.

If we exclude derivatives and look only at global credit (bank loans and debt), we can identify four credit bubbles and crunches from the early 1990s onward. First, there was the credit bubble of late 1980s and early 1990s, which was mainly visible in Japan, where it ended in the Japanese banking crisis. The second bubble was the high-tech dot-com bubble of the late 1990s that ended in the equity crash of 2000 and the recession of 2001. Then there was very fast credit bubble based on new forms of money (namely, shadow banking and derivatives) in the mid-2000s, culminating in the credit crunch of 2007 and subsequent Great Recession of 2008–2009.

2. It's Private Sector Debt

The rise in credit—or debt—took place in the private sector, not the public sector. US non-financial business and household debt rose to postwar record levels by 2007. In the US between 1950 and 1980, the ratio of non-financial debt (household, corporate, and government) was quite stable at 130 percent of GDP, but after 1980 it nearly doubled, to more than 250 percent, while for advanced economies, the average weighted mean ratio rose 80 percent. Only about one-third of the increase in overall debt was due to government borrowing, and business and household debt was consistently higher than government debt. Indeed, in the United States, gross public sector debt in

2012 stood at $14.11 trillion, but non-financial business and household debt
stood at just under $25 trillion.

US non-financial business debt is now higher than in any period since
World War II, and well above its level in 1929 (90 percent of GDP today,
compared with 56 percent in 1929). It is only below the 1933 peak because
GDP fell 43 percent beginning in 1929, which was a lot faster than the speed
at which companies could reduce their 1929 debt. The Great Recession
was marked by this sheer size of the debt accrued by companies before
the crash. Non-financial corporate (NFC) debt, in 2011, remained the
largest component of overall debt in the advanced capitalist economies at
113 percent of GDP, compared to 104 percent for government debt and 90
percent for household debt (fig. 11.4).

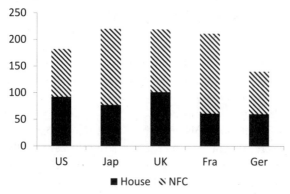

Figure 11.4. G5 private sector debt to GDP (%), 2011. Source: IMF GFS report.

Household debt expanded rapidly during the so-called neoliberal era as
a result of falling interest rates that reduced the cost of borrowing. The
resulting property boom in many advanced capitalist economies in the last
fifteen years expanded the debt. The creditors were the banks and other
money lenders. Their assets (home values) eventually collapsed, placing a
severe burden of deleveraging on the financial sector.

Corporate debt was even higher in other major economies, and the
underlying position was worse than the debt figures show because companies
shifted much of their debt off balance sheet. "Shadow banking"—or non-
bank credit institutions—covered money mutual funds, investment funds
other than mutual funds, structured financial vehicles, and hedge funds.
According to the Basel-3 BIS-IMF Financial Stability Task Force, so-
called "shadow banking" grew rapidly from $27 trillion in 2002 to $60
trillion in 2007. After the 2008 Great Recession, shadow banking assets fell
back but were still $45 trillion in 2017—over 15 percent of the total global
financial system, or half the size of traditional banking assets globally. The

United States had the largest shadow banking sector, with 31 percent of that $45 trillion.[2]

Marxist theory agrees with Keen that private credit can become excessive. Indeed, this flows from the Marxist view that money is not neutral in the capitalist economy, but central to it. Credit can and will get out of line with the capitalist production.[3] "Fictitious capital" is money capital advanced for the titles of ownership of productive and unproductive capital, namely, shares, bonds, derivatives, and so forth. The prices of such assets anticipate future returns on investment in real and financial assets. But the realization of these returns depends ultimately on the creation of new value and surplus value in the productive capitalist sector. So much of this money capital can easily turn out to be fictitious.

For Marx, the capitalist economy is a monetary economy; and it is an economy with credit as a key constituent. Capital exists either in liquid form, that is, as money, or in tangible form as means and materials of production or as commodities. In the general circulation of capital and commodities, credit in all its forms increasingly substitutes for money. This "fictitious capital" is "a kind of imaginary wealth which is not only an important part of the fortune of individuals," but also "a substantial proportion of bankers' capital" (Marx 1959). For Marx, financial instruments—both credit and equity—are entitlements to present or future value of capital: "The paper serves as title of ownership which represents the capital. The stocks of railways, mines, navigation companies, and the like, represent actual capital" (Marx 1959, ch. 29).

The existence of these fictitious capitals imparts flexibility to the economy, but over time they become an impediment to its health.[4] The drive for profit in the capitalist sector is behind the expansion of credit, while a fall in the rate of profit in the productive sectors promotes speculation. If the capitalists cannot make enough profit producing commodities, they will try making money by betting on the stock exchange or by buying various other financial instruments. Capitalists all experience the falling rate of profit almost simultaneously, so they all start to buy these stocks and assets at the same time, driving prices up. When stocks and assets prices are rising, everybody wants to buy them—this is the beginning of a bubble on exactly the lines we have seen them, again and again since the tulip crisis of 1637.[5]

Even some mainstream economists recognize this propensity; as Irving Fisher (1933, p. 348) wrote, "[O]verindebtedness must have had its starters. It may be started by many causes, of which the most common appears to be new opportunities to invest at a big prospective profit, as compared with ordinary profits and interest." But prospective profit eventually gives way to "an expansion of 'the speculative element' and enterprises keep up an appearance of prosperity by accumulating debts, increasing from day to day their capital account."

Fictitious values accumulate during extended boom periods and are subsequently shed in the course of the bust. This shakeout "unsettle[s] all existing relations." (Marx 1959, ch. 20). As Paul Mattick (1971) put it, "[S]peculation may enhance crisis situations by permitting the fictitious overvaluation of capital, which cannot satisfy the profit claims bound up with it."[6] So a debt or credit crisis is really a product of a failure of the capitalist mode of production as a monetary economy.[7]

Can we show more directly the relationship between debt and the profitability of capital? One way of measuring the impact of fictitious capital on profitability is to measure profit against the net worth of companies, not just against their tangible assets. This allows us to encompass profits from unproductive investments (loans, bonds, and shares). Such a measure for US companies shows that from 1966 to 1982, profitability against net worth falls at a slower pace than profitability measured conventionally against tangible fixed assets. This measure also shows that it recovered more quickly in the neoliberal era, 1982–97, so that profitability against net worth was higher than conventional profitability. In the period 1997–2011, conventional profitability was broadly flat, but against net worth, profitability has dropped significantly.

Against net worth, US corporate profitability nearly halved between 1997 and 2000. And after 2000, the rate of profit based on net worth remained below the rate of profit against tangible assets for the first time on record, suggesting that the "financial" part of the non-financial capitalist sector became a significant obstacle to any recovery in capital accumulation (fig. 11.5). If we decompose the components of US corporate net worth, we find that US capitalists increased their borrowing to buy back their shares, and that this was exponential after the early 1990s. Companies used the extra debt to buy back their own company shares in order to boost the share price. UK companies bought back equity at an annual rate of 3 percent of GDP, while those in the United States did so at 2.3 percent. Up to 1985, US companies issued shares (i.e., they were sellers). But since then, they have become the most important buyers in the stock market by far.

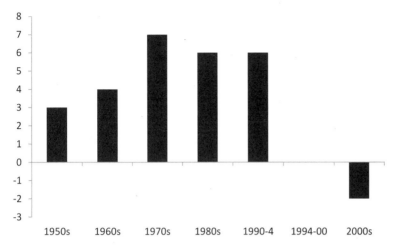

Figure 11.5. Difference in rate of profit for tangible assets and corporate net worth (%), 1950s–2000s. Source: US Federal Reserve, author's calculations.

3. The Leap in Sovereign Debt as a Result of the Great Recession

Although public debt ratios climbed from the late 1970s until the mid-1990s, they declined toward their historical peacetime average prior to the global financial crisis of 2008. Private credit maintained a fairly stable relationship with GDP until the 1970s and then surged to unprecedented levels in the decades that followed, right up to the outbreak of the crisis (fig. 11.6). By the 1970s, private sector debt in the advanced capitalist economies was larger than sovereign debt for the first time since the early 1900s (Jordà et al. 2013).[8]

In the United States, after the credit binge of 2002–2007, private sector debt (households, businesses, and banks) had reached $40.8 trillion in 2008. These sectors subsequently deleveraged to $38.6 trillion by 2012, a decrease of 8 percent, mainly because banks shrank and households defaulted on their mortgages. But this private sector deleveraging was countered by a huge rise in public sector debt, up over 70 percent from around $8 trillion in 2007 to $13.7 trillion in 2010—and still rising, if more slowly.

The public sector debt rose in order to finance the bailout of the banking system, as well as to fund widening budget deficits as tax revenues collapsed and unemployment and other benefit payouts rocketed. As a result, the overall debt burden (public and private) in the United States is still rising and at a rate that more than matches nominal GDP growth. So the overall debt-to-GDP ratio was still not falling in 2017.

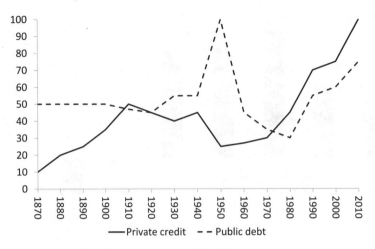

Figure **11.6**. OECD private and public debt to
GDP (%), 1870–2010. Source: BIS.

This explains why the apologists for capitalism want to reduce the public
sector debt or at least shift the burden of financing it onto labor and away
from capital. Tax struggles are class struggles in disguise. In this sense, the
rise in public sector debt becomes part of the overall crisis induced by falling
profitability and excessive private sector debt.

4. Debt Matters

Keynesians sometimes argue that debt does not matter and that more
(public) borrowing is not a problem, at least not for now. Krugman (2011,
p. 4) seems to recognize that there could be "debt-driven slumps," arguing
that an "overhang of debt on the part of some agents who are forced into
deleveraging is depressing demand." From that (Fisher-style) debt deflation,
the liquidity trap and the Keynesian multiplier emerge.

Contradictorily, Krugman also denied the role of debt in crises, suggesting
that it does not matter in a "closed economy," that is, one where one person's
debt is another's asset;[9] it's only a problem if you owe it to foreigners. The
IMF (2012, p. 155) disagrees: "[R]ecessions preceded by economy-wide
credit booms tend to be deeper and more protracted than other recessions,"
and "housing busts preceded by larger run-ups in gross household debt are
associated with deeper slumps, weaker recoveries and more pronounced
household deleveraging."

The debt historians Carmen Reinhart and Kenneth Rogoff (2010)
confirm the relationship between debt and growth under capitalism. They
looked at twenty-six episodes of public debt overhangs (defined as where
the public debt ratio was above 90 percent) and found that on twenty-three

occasions, real GDP growth was lowered by an average of 1.2 percent points a year. And GDP was about 25 percent lower in 2010 than it would have been at the end of the period of overhang.[10]

Studies by McKinsey (Roxburgh et al. 2011) and the IMF (Cottarelli et al. 2010) also found that GDP declines by an average of 1.3 percent points for two to three years after a financial crash, and that the ratio of debt to GDP must fall by up to 25 percent to complete deleveraging. There are a host of other studies that reveal basically the same thing. The IMF found that when public sector debt levels are above 100 percent of GDP, economies typically experience lower GDP growth than the advanced country average. Most important, the IMF found that where debt levels were between 90 and 100 percent and were decreasing over the fifteen years following the peak, economic growth was faster than for countries, even those below the 100 percent threshold. Thus, deleveraging is crucial to recovery, whatever the level of debt reached.

The correlation between high debt and low growth seems strong, but the causation is not clear. Is it a recession that causes high debt, meaning the only way to get debt down is to boost growth (Keynesian)? Or does high debt cause recessions, so that the only way to restore growth is to cut debt (Austerian)? The Marxist alternative is that a contraction of profitability leads to a collapse in investment and the economy, which then drives up private debt. If the state has to bail out the capitalist sector (finance), then public debt explodes.[11]

What is important is that if the capitalist sector is burdened with heavy debt, it will be more difficult to launch an economic recovery.[12] The Great Recession was triggered by a massive expansion in debt used by households to buy homes in the United States, and by companies to support share prices. Wage growth was restricted, and profitability had been falling since the late 1990s. Extra credit was needed to sustain investment in unproductive sectors like property and financial speculation. Eventually, that credit toppled over.

Since 2008, total national debt (financial, household, non-financial, and government) relative to GDP has not fallen in the major advanced economies. The financial sector has deleveraged the most, not surprisingly, as this sector suffered a meltdown in 2008. However, even in this sector, only the United Kingdom and the United States managed a significant cleansing of debt liabilities relative to GDP. Eurozone banks took on more debt since 2008, although they did start to reduce this last year. Japanese financials also took on more debt, at home and abroad, and they remain the most leveraged in developed markets.

Households in the countries where the property burst was greatest deleveraged, mainly through mortgage defaults, downsizing, and refinancing—that is, within the locus of the property boom in the United

States and the United Kingdom. But households in the Eurozone as a whole have not done so at all, except with a small decline following a peak in 2010.

The non-financial corporate sector deleveraged even less than households did. Companies took advantage of low interest rates and plentiful liquidity to take on more debt, in order to buy back equity to support share prices, pay larger dividends and hoard cash. In the United States, corporations expanded their debt relative to GDP by 14 percent. Elsewhere, corporate debt-to-GDP levels in 2012 were much the same as in 2008, or some 15–20 percent higher than they were at the start of the credit boom in 2003.

The Bank for International Settlements found that in 2012, out of thirty-three advanced and emerging economies, twenty-seven had non-financial debt-to-GDP levels above 130 percent. Two of those had ratios above 400 percent, and four between 300 and 400 percent. Only six had ratios below 130 percent, and only three below 100 percent of GDP—namely Turkey, Mexico, and Indonesia. Of the thirty-three economies, eighteen had rising debt ratios, eleven were flat, and only four had falling debt ratios. Of those four, three were in International Monetary Fund or "Troika" bailout programs (Greece, Ireland, and Hungary). Only Norway reduced its overall non-financial debt ratio "voluntarily," while only Mexico and Thailand reduced their overall debt levels between 1997 and 2012. Household debt ratios fell in some developed markets, including the United Kingdom and the United States, as well as in some peripheral Economic and Monetary Union (EMU) countries. But twenty-seven economies experienced a rise in private-debt-to-GDP ratios following the global financial crisis.

5. Awash with Cash?

We now see an apparent conundrum: in the United States and some other major economies, there were rising/record profits, with corporations apparently "awash with cash," but these countries were still not investing enough in the "real economy" to achieve a sustained recovery.

In the United States, the level of corporate fixed investment as a share of corporate cash flow was at 25-year lows in 2013 (fig. 11.7) and there has been no pickup since. Much was made in the financial media of the huge cash reserves built up by the likes of Apple or Google, although most of this cash was held overseas in tax havens like Luxembourg. But it is true that cash reserves in US companies reached record levels, at just under $2 trillion.

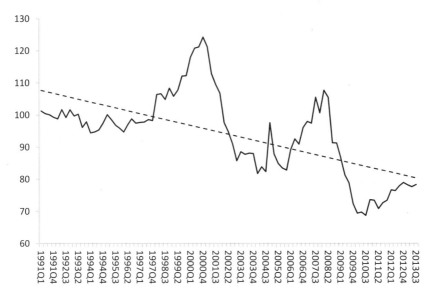

Figure 11.7. US fixed investment as share of internal cash flow (%), 1991–2013. Source: US Federal Reserve.

Comparing US corporate fixed capital formation to corporate operating surplus, Michael Burke (2013, p. 2) found that

> the increase in profits has not been matched by an increase in nominal investment. In 1971 the investment ratio (GFCF/GoS) was 62%. It peaked in 1979 at 69% but even by 2000 it was still over 61%. It declined steadily to 56% in 2008. But in 2012 it had declined to just 46%. If US firms investment ratio were simply to return to its level of 1979 the nominal increase in investment compared to 2012 levels would be over US$1.5 trillion, approaching 10% of GDP. This would be enough to resolve the current crisis.

Burke reckons that US companies used their rising profits either to increase dividends to shareholders or to purchase financial assets (stocks): "[O]ne estimate of the former shows the dividend payout to shareholders doubling in the 8 years to 2012, an increase of US$320 billion per annum." Burke goes on to point out that cash hoarding has been happening in other economies, too. Over in Canada, Michal Rozworski (2013) noted the same phenomenon, as has Jim Stanford (2013) at Unifor.[13]

Burke noted that this hoarding began well before the Great Recession and that this is significant. Since the mid-1980s, firms have been increasingly unwilling to make productive investments, preferring to hold financial assets like bonds and stock and even cash, which has limited returns in interest. Why is this? Well, it seems that companies have become convinced that the returns on productive investment are too low relative to the risk of making a loss. This is particularly the case for investment in new technology or in research and development, which requires considerable upfront funding with no certainty of eventual success.

Some scholars found that there was "a dramatic increase from 1980 through 2006 in the average cash ratio for U.S. firms." The "main reasons for the increase in the cash ratio are that inventories have fallen, cash flow risk for firms has increased, capital expenditures have fallen, and R&D expenditures have increased" (Bates, Kahle, and Stulz 2009). In order to compete, companies increasingly must invest in new and untried technology, rather than just increase investment in existing equipment. That's riskier.[14] So companies have to build up cash reserves as a sinking fund to cover likely losses on research and development.

In the 1980s, average capital expenditures as a percentage of assets were more than double average R&D expenditures as a percentage of assets (8.9 percent vs. 3.2 percent). In contrast, in the 2000s, R&D exceeded capital expenditures (6.7 percent vs. 5.4 percent).[15] Rising cash is more a sign that investments are perceived as riskier than it is of corporate health.

The same story as for the United States is also repeated in the United Kingdom. Ben Broadbent (2012) from the Bank of England noted that UK companies were setting very high hurdles for profitability before they would invest because they perceived that new investment was too risky.[16] The current net rate of return on UK capital is well below pre-crisis rates.

6. Not Really . . .

Liquid assets (cash and those assets that can be quickly converted into cash) may have risen in total. But US companies were also expanding *all* their financial assets (stocks, bonds, insurance, etc.). When we compare the ratio of liquid assets to total financial assets, we see a different story (fig. 11.8).

US companies reduced their liquidity ratios in the "Golden Age" of the 1950s and 1960s, in order to invest more or to buy more stocks. That stopped during the neoliberal period, but there was still no big rise in cash reserves compared to other financial holdings. The ratio of liquid assets to total financial assets was about the same as it was in the early 1980s. That tells us that corporate profits may have been diverted from real investment into financial assets, but not particularly into cash. And those cash reserves are very concentrated. The notion of US corporates being awash with cash does not hold up to scrutiny as a general market characteristic (Galbraith 2014). If we strip out financials, corporate net debt per share has ascended to new highs since the Great Recession ended.

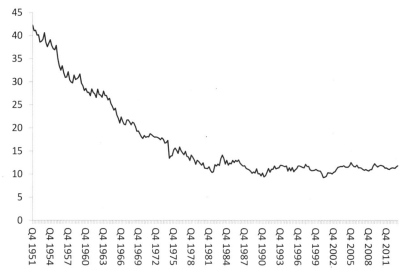

Figure 11.8. Ratio of cash to total financial assets in US corporates (%), 1951–2011. Source: US Federal Reserve, author's calculations.

There was a rise in the ratio of cash to investment between the early 1980s and 2012. But that ratio was still below where it was at the beginning of the 1950s (fig. 11.9).

Figure 11.9. Ratio of cash holdings to fixed investment in US corporates (%), 1951–2012. Source: US Federal Reserve, author's calculations.

Why did the cash-to-investment ratio rise after the 1980s? Well, it was not because of a fast rise in cash holdings; rather, it was because the growth of investment in the real economy slowed during the neoliberal period. The average growth in cash reserves from the 1980s to 2012 was 7.8 percent a year, which was actually slower than the growth rate of *all* financial assets at 8.6 percent a year. But business investment increased at only 5.3 percent a year, so the ratio of cash to investment rose.

If we compare the growth rate of corporate cash reserves to that of all financial assets in the five years after the start of the Great Recession in 2008, we find that corporate cash rose at a much slower pace of 3.9 percent year-over-year (yoy). That's slightly faster than the rise in total financial assets—3.3 percent yoy. But investment has risen at just 1.5 percent a year, so consequently, the ratio of investment to cash has slumped from an average of two-thirds since the 1980s to just two-fifths.

Thus, companies are not really "awash with cash" any more than they were thirty years ago. What has happened is that US corporations have used more and more of their profits to invest in financial assets, rather than in productive investment. Their cash ratios are pretty much unchanged, suggesting that there is not a "wall of money" out there waiting to be invested in the real economy.

Corporate debt remains the issue. Sure, interest rates on debt have fallen sharply over the last thirty years, so debt-servicing costs are down. But corporate debt levels have also risen in the same period, increasing the burden of risk on companies if there is any sign of a downturn in profitability or rise in interest rates.

Corporate sector debt in the United States expanded at a rapid pace after 2008, with gross issuance reaching a record in 2013. So whereas net debt to assets rose from around 16 percent in 2007 to 22 percent at the depth of the financial crisis, it only fell back to 20 percent by 2011 and was back above 21 percent in 2013. The US corporate sector was much more indebted than it has been at this point (five years after recession) in previous business cycles (fig. 11.10), and corporate debt in other major economies remains high, as well.[17] This increase in debt means that companies must raise profitability or be forced to reduce investment in productive capacity to service rising debt. The private sector in the major economies has been trying to "deleverage"—reduce its debt burden—at the expense of spending more (in the case of households) or investing more (in the case of companies).

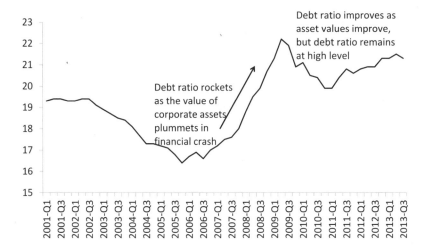

Figure 11.10. Ratio of net debt to total assets in US corporates (%), 2001–2013. Source: US Federal Reserve.

Deleveraging has gone further in the United States,[18] while the UK private sector has not been so successful at reducing its debt burden. Strip out the government sector, and the UK has the highest private sector debt ratio (and this does not include the banks), although that is mainly due to its very high household debt ratio. Indeed, even in the United States things have not been looking quite so rosy. If we compare the level of cash reserves to overall corporate debt in the United States, while it is at still at high levels compared to fifteen years ago, the ratio of cash to debt is falling steadily.

Small companies have neither cash reserves nor banks willing to lend to them at sustainable rates. So they are not investing in new equipment or buildings at all. There are thousands of heavily indebted small companies that are barely keeping their heads above water, despite low interest rates (Société Générale 2013). According to research by the "free market" Adam Smith Institute (2013), 108,000 so-called zombie businesses in the UK were only able to service the interest on their debt, preventing them from restructuring. This held back a recovery in overall profitability and new investment.[19] In other words, these zombie companies slowed the "creative destruction" of capital that requires the liquidation of the weak for the strong.

As a result, the capitalist sector did not invest in sufficient new productive capacity to engender much in the way of higher employment or pre-crisis trend growth, and the alternative of public investment was shunned. Public investment in the US was at its lowest level since 1945, and gross capital investment by the public sector dropped to just 3.6 percent of US output compared with a postwar average of 5.0 percent.

7. Deleveraging and the Depression

As I have shown above, the longer the necessary period of deleveraging, the longer these cash hoards will be held and accumulated.[20] Deleveraging excessive debt is part of the task of recovery from depression. Restoring profitability so that companies will start a period of sustained investment in employment, technology, and plant also depends on reducing the debt burden built up in the period before the crash of 2008. This adds to the duration of the depression.

Some capitalist economies have made more progress in this than others. But there has been no fall in corporate debt in the United States, where many corporations continue to raise cheap debt in order support their share prices through buybacks. As a result, corporate leverage (the ratio of net debt to GDP) was higher at this point of business cycle than it was in recoveries from previous recessions. That does not bode well for a quick escape from the depression if interest rates on debt start to rise.

As the IMF (2014, p. 6) summed it up: "[I]ncreased borrowing has not yet translated into higher investment by non-financial corporations whose depressed capital expenditures are taking up a smaller share of internal cash flows than in previous cycles. . . . Firms are more vulnerable to downside risk to growth than in a normal credit cycle." Debt matters and there is still a way to go in getting it manageable.

Notes

1   Marx made it clear that credit and fictitious capital are not the same, but the rise in the measure of global liquidity is a good indicator of the expansion of fictitious capital, too.

2   See FSB *Global Shadow Banking Monitoring Report* (2018).

3   "Credit accelerates the violent eruptions of this contradiction – crises – and thereby the elements of the disintegration of the old mode of production" (Marx 1967, ch. 27).

4   "At low levels, debt is good. It is a source of economic growth and stability. But at high levels, public and private debts are bad, increasing volatility and retarding growth. It is in this sense that borrowing can first be beneficial. So long as it is modest. But beyond a certain point, debt becomes dangerous and excessive" (Cecchetti et al. 2011, p. 2).

5   Tulipmania was a futures manipulation and options scheme (credit with leverage), accompanied by futures rules changes enacted by the Dutch legislature in 1636. Daniel Gross (2004) writes: "The classic description of Tulipmania appeared in Clarence Mackay's 1841 classic *Memoirs of Extraordinary Popular Delusions and the Madness of Crowds*: 'In 1634, the rage among the Dutch to possess them was so great that the ordinary industry of the country was neglected, and the population, even to its lowest dregs, embarked in the tulip trade.' The normally sane Dutch bourgeoisie got carried away and bid up prices of tulip bulbs spectacularly in winter 1637, only to see them crash in spring. One bulb was reportedly sold in

February 1637 for 6,700 guilders, 'as much as a house on Amsterdam's smartest canal, including coach and garden,' and many times the 150-guilder average income. As Earl A. Thompson, an economist at the University of California at Los Angeles, and Jonathan Treussard, a graduate student at Boston University, note in a working paper, 'the contract price of tulips in early February 1637 reached a level that was about 20 times higher than in both early November 1636 and early May 1637.'" So it was with the banks and property investors in the 2000s.

6   Marx put it similarly: "The credit system appears as the main lever of overproduction and overspeculation in commerce solely because the reproduction process, which is elastic by nature, is here forced to its extreme limits, and so is forced because a large part of the social capital is employed by people who do not own it and who consequently tackle things quite differently than the owner, who anxiously weighs the limitations of his private capital in so far as he handles it himself. This simply demonstrates the fact that the self-expansion of capital based on the contradictory nature of capitalist production permits the free development only up to a certain point, so that it constitutes an imminent fetter and barrier to production, which are continually broken through by the credit system. Hence, the system accelerates the material development of the productive forces and the establishment of the world market. It is the historical mission of the capitalist system of production to raise these material foundations. At the same time credit accelerates the violent eruptions of this contradiction – crises – and thereby the elements of the disintegration of the old mode of production" (1959, p. 441).

7   Mattick continues: "In a system of production, where the entire control of the reproduction process rests on credit, a crisis must obviously occur when credit suddenly ceases and cash payments have validity. At first glance therefore, the whole crisis seems to be merely a credit and money crisis." But, "what appears to be a crisis on the money market is in reality an expression of abnormal conditions in the very process of production and reproduction" (Mattick 1971, p. 51).

8   Private credit is aggregate private bank loans to the non-financial sector. Public debt is general consolidated government debt. The average is for seventeen advanced economies: Australia, Belgium, Canada, Denmark, Finland, France, Germany, Italy, Japan, the Netherlands, Norway, Portugal, Spain, Sweden, Switzerland, the United Kingdom, and the United States.

9   "The debt we create is basically money we owe to ourselves and the burden it imposes does not involve a real transfer of resources" (Krugman 2011, p. 2).

10   These divisions in macroeconomics were highlighted by the recent terrible scandal of the "two RRs" (see Roberts 2013) over the errors and distortions in their famous paper that suggested that once public debt-to-GDP gets above 90 percent in any economy, subsequent economic growth is likely to be 2 percent lower than if the debt ratio is lower than 90 percent. Carmen Reinhart and Kenneth Rogoff published an errata to their 2010 paper on public debt and growth, acknowledging more errors in the figures, but leaving their basic conclusion unchanged. In the errata (2013), the two RRs correct the mean averages for growth from 1946 to 2009 that were originally criticized by Robert Pollin and his coauthors at the University of Massachusetts, Amherst. But they also argue that the corrections do not affect their most up-to-date work (2012), which still shows a slowdown in growth when debt hits 90 percent of GDP. "The point is, whichever way you slice it you have lower growth rates by about 1 percentage point," Carmen Reinhart said (note: not "2 percent" any more).

Their latest set of data, which includes more countries and more years of data, still finds a drop in median growth from 2.8 percent to 1.8 percent when debt hits the 90 percent threshold. In response, the critics wrote a new criticism to point out that these median figures were also affected by the same error (Ash and Pollin 2013). Pollin says he accepts that there are different ways to weight the numbers but a conclusion should be robust. "The two RRs results are entirely dependent on using their particular methodology." And so it goes on. You can see why this debate has become so intense. The Austerians have used the two RRs data to "prove" that austerity is necessary to get debt down and restore economic growth. Now the Keynesians are triumphant that the evidence has been "proved" false.

11   As John Cochrane put it in his blog (2012), "[W]hen I read the review of the 'studies,' they are the usual sort of growth regressions or instruments, hardly decisive of causality." In other words, the studies show a correlation between high debt, big budget deficits, and recessions, but not the causal direction.

12   "Debt is the central problem. When debt to income or debt-to-GDP doubles, triples or quadruples, you have doubled, tripled or quadrupled the amount of future earnings you are using today. That necessarily means you will have less to spend in the future. It's not rocket science" (White 2010, p. 10).

13   "Because corporations are taking in so much more than they are spending, liquid cash assets in the non-financial corporate sector continue to swell, and now total almost $600 billion" (Stanford 2013, p. 4).

14   "The greater importance of R&D relative to capital expenditures also has a permanent effect on the cash ratio. Because of lower asset tangibility, R&D investment opportunities are costlier to finance than capital using external capital expenditures. Consequently, greater R&D intensity relative to capital expenditures requires firms to hold a greater cash buffer against future shocks to internally generated cash flow" (Bates et al. 2009, p. 4).

15   "R&D intensive firms require a greater cash buffer against future shocks to internally generated cash flow. In contrast, capital expenditures are more likely to generate assets that can be used as collateral and hence are easier to finance. As a result, capital expenditures may mostly consume cash, which would be consistent with their negative relation with the cash ratio" (Bates et al. 2009, p. 5).

16   As Broadbent (2012, p. 12) put it, "Yet on a recent Agency visit, many companies told me that their hurdle rates of return had risen. Prior to the crisis finance directors would approve new investments that looked likely to pay for themselves (not including depreciation) over a period of six years – equivalent to an expected net rate of return of around 9%. Now, it seems, the payback period has shortened to around four years, a required net rate of return of 14%." Broadbent continued: "the investments most vulnerable to such a shift – where you'd expect to find the sharpest increase in required returns – are those that have some element of irreversibility. This will include many projects (spending on intangibles, for example) that are necessary to improve productivity. Thus high risk premia may be inhibiting not just demand but the economy's supply capacity as well. . . . *Even if the crisis originated in the banking system there is now a higher hurdle for risky investment – a rise in the perceived probability of an extremely bad economic outcome.* . . . In reality, many investments involve sunk costs. Big FDI projects, in-firm training, R&D, the adoption of new technologies, even

simple managerial reorganizations – these are all things that can improve productivity but have risky returns and cannot be easily reversed after the event."

17   The Bank of England (2013, p. 2) explains, "Global debt levels increased rapidly before the global financial crisis. In the decade before 2007, non-financial sector debt to GDP ratios in advanced economies rose by an average of 40 percentage points. Since then, low interest rates have reduced borrowing costs and supported the values of financial and physical assets. Some borrowers have used this period to delever. But low interest rates have also encouraged some private sector borrowers to increase their debt levels. And government debt levels have increased materially. As a result, non-financial sector debt to GDP ratios in advanced economies have risen since 2007, by 55 percentage points on average."

18   "Deleveraging in the United States has occurred more quickly than in Europe. Since 2007, the US household debt to GDP ratio has fallen by 15 percentage points, to less than 80 percent. And while the US PNFC debt to GDP ratio has risen, it remains lower than in most other advanced economies" (Bank of England 2013, p. 3).

19   Because "Zombie firms stop workers and money being redeployed to more productive uses, they prevent new, better firms entering the market, they undermine competitiveness, reduce productivity and slow the growth of the whole economy" (Adam Smith Institute 2013, p. 2).

20   Sam Williams (2014) recently expounded reasons for this so-called conundrum between profits, the stock market and investment in production. Williams wrote, "When a crisis strikes, the capitalists in order to minimize the risk of a loss of all or a part of their capital are forced to attempt to convert all their accounts receivable into cash as quickly as they can. They therefore demand immediate payment on accounts that are only slightly overdue, become very reluctant to sell commodities for anything but cash, and demand payment on all 'callable' loans. Similarly, the capitalists are faced with demands for immediate payment of any payables that have fallen even slightly behind their due dates or are in any sense 'callable.' The whole chain of credit suddenly contracts." Such is the description of the credit crunch and the "financial panic": "For the capitalists, the means of defense against such a situation is a large cash hoard. With profits low if not negative, the 'opportunity cost' of holding cash is not nearly as great as it would be in times of prosperity. And unlike real capital (factory buildings, machines, raw materials and so on), cash can be used to pay off any debts they owe to their fellow capitalists. Therefore, during periods of credit contraction – 'deleveraging' – that begin with the crisis and extend through the post-crisis stagnation, the capitalists do all they can to build up their cash hoards. As a result of this process, the jerry-built structure of credit is replaced with a system based far more on solid cash. The economy reverts to a much 'sounder' cash economy but at the price of a more or less extended period of economic stagnation."

References

Adam Smith Institute (2013) "Zombie Firms Threaten to Cause a Lost Decade of Economic Stagnation," available at http://www.adamsmith.org/news/zombie-firms-threaten-to-cause-a-lost-decade-of-economic-stagnation/.

Ash, M. and R. Pollin (2013) "Supplemental Technical Critique of Reinhart and Rogoff, 'Growth in a Time of Debt,'" *Political Economy Research Institute*, University of Massachusetts.

Bank of England (2013) "Financial Stability Report," available at http://www .bankofengland.co.uk/publications/Documents/fsr/2013/fsr34sec2.pdf.

Bates, T., K. Kahle, and R. Stulz, (2009) "Why Do US Firms Hold So Much More Cash than They Used To?," *Journal of Finance*, Vol LXIV, No 5, October.

Bernanke, B. (2000) *Essays on the Great Depression*, Princeton University Press.

Broadbent, B. (2012) "Deconstruction," Bank of England speech given at Lancaster University Management School, available at http://www.bankofengland.co.uk/ archive/Documents/historicpubs/speeches/2012/speech618.pdf.

Burke, M. (2013) "The Cash Hoard of Western Companies," *Socialist Economic Bulletin*, No 21.

Cecchetti, S., M. R. King, and J. Yetman (2011) "Weathering the Financial Crisis: Good Policy or Good Luck?," available at https://frbatlanta.org/-/media/Documents/ news/conferences/2011/financial-markets-conference/papers/cecchetti.pdf.

Cochrane, J. (2012) "Two Views of Debt and Stagnation," *Grumpy Economist* (blog), September 20, https://johnhcochrane.blogspot.co.uk/2012/09/two-views-of-debt- and-stagnation.html.

Cottarelli, C. et al. (2010) "Default in Today's Advanced Economies," IMF staff position note, September 1, https://www.imf.org/external/pubs/ft/spn/2010/spn1012.pdf.

Financial Stability Board (2018) *Global Shadow Banking Monitoring Report*, March 5, FSB.

Fisher, I. (1933) "The Debt Deflation Theory of Great Depressions," *Econometrica*, Vol 1, No 4.

Galbraith, J. K. (2014) "The Big Disconnect between Leverage and Spreads," *Alpha. Sources.CV* (blog).

Gross, D. (2004) "Bulb Bubble Trouble," MoneyBox, *Slate*.

International Monetary Fund (2012) *World Economic Outlook, April 2012*, International Monetary Fund.

———. (2014) *Global Financial Stability Report, April 2014*, International Monetary Fund.

Jordà, O., M. H. P. Schularick, and A. M. Taylor (2013) "Sovereigns versus Banks: Credit, Crises, and Consequences," NBER Working Paper, No 19506.

Keen, S. (2011) *Debunking Economics*, Zed Books.

Krugman, P. (2011) "A Thought on Debt History," Conscience of a Liberal, *New York Times*, December 31, https://krugman.blogs.nytimes.com/2011/12/31/a-thought- on-debt-history/.

Marx, K. (1959) *Capital,* Vol 3, Progress Publishers.

Mattick, P. (1971) *The Limits of the Mixed Economy*, Merlin Press.

Reinhart, C. M. and K. S. Rogoff (2010) "Growth in a Time of Debt," *American Economic Review*, No 100.

———. (2013) "Errata: 'Growth in A Time of Debt,'" Harvard University, May 5, http://www.carmenreinhart.com/user_uploads/data/36_data.pdf.

Reinhart, C. M., V. R. Reinhart, and K. S. Rogoff (2012) "Public Debt Overhangs: Advanced-Economy Episodes since 1800," *Journal of Economic Perspectives*, Vol 26, No 3.

Roberts, M. (2013) "Revising the Two RRs," *The Next Recession*, April 17, https:// thenextrecession.wordpress.com/2013/04/17/revising-the-two-rrs/.

Rosworski, M. (2013) "Canada's Profitability Puzzle," *Political Eh-conomy,* December 13, http://rozworski.org/political-eh-conomy/2013/12/03/canadas-profitability-puzzle/.

Roxburgh, C. et al. (2011) "Debt and Deleveraging: The Global Credit Bubble," McKinsey Global Institute.

Société Générale (2013) "UK Lending to SMEs," *Economics,* October 30, available at https://thenextrecession.files.wordpress.com/2013/11/uk-lending-to-smes.pdf.

Stanford, J. (2013) "Good Time to Rethink Corporate Tax Cuts," *Progressive Economic Forum,* November 14.

White, W. (2010) "The Origins of the Next Crisis," speech to the Inaugural Institute of New Economic Thinking.

Williams, S. (2014) "Change of Guard at the Fed, the Specter of 'Secular Stagnation,' and Some Questions of Monetary Theory," *A Critique of Crisis Theory,* May 24, https://critiqueofcrisistheory.wordpress.com/2015/05/24/capitalist-economists-debate-secular-stagnation/.

CHAPTER 12

THE NEOLIBERAL FINANCIALIZATION OF THE US ECONOMY

Sergio Cámara Izquierdo and Abelardo Mariña Flores

Marxist economic theory characterizes the economic process as a process of capital accumulation. Capitalism is a social order that abstracts from the subjective dimension of the process of human reproduction; the reproduction of the capitalist social relation of production is based on the unlimited self-expansion of capital as a quantitative magnitude of value, that is, on the logic of valorization. Therefore, capital constitutes the subject of the economic process and subsumes every aspect of human life.[1]

The unlimited self-expansive nature of capital is inherently contradictory and leads to structural crises of the process of capitalist accumulation. This is certainly the case behind the well-known law of the tendency of the rate of profit to fall. The relentless competition among capitals impels them to accumulate productive capital by introducing new forms of technical progress that involve larger masses of fixed capital in relation to living labor, which are not completely offset by the consequent increases in labor productivity. It is widely accepted in the Marxist literature that this was the underlying mechanism that was at play during the postwar "long boom," the crisis of the 1970s being characterized as a structural crisis of overaccumulation related to the law of the falling rate of profit.[2]

The new structural crisis that manifested violently in the 2008–2009 world recession, often labeled as the "Great Recession," has logically opened a new debate within the Marxist literature about its nature. Among the wide range of explanations proposed, two broad positions can be highlighted. A first position sticks to the falling rate of profit as the main direct or indirect explanation of the structural crisis. A second position, discarding the profitability thesis, points to the contradictory nature of world capitalism in the period since the 1980s, labeled as "neoliberalism" and/ or "financialization."[3] The debate has predominantly taken place in terms of the ability of Marxist economics to provide a thorough account of the crisis. A prominent advocate of the falling rate of profit explanation argues against the view that "the latest financial crisis has exploded in a period of rising profitability so that the productive sphere cannot be the cause of the financial crisis, *contrary to Marx*" (Carchedi 2011, emphasis added). Equally significantly, an adherent of the second position states that the "current crisis is more of a Minsky crisis than a Marx crisis. I am not saying that we should throw away Marx (obviously), but rather that we should supplement Marx with Minsky, especially for analysis of the modern capitalist financial system" (Moseley 2008).

The main objective of this chapter is to show that the current structural crisis relates to the basic mechanisms of the process of capitalist accumulation described by Marx. In other words, it is argued that the boundless, expansive nature of capital—the contradictory logic of capital valorization and accumulation—is also at the root of neoliberalism, financialization, the Great Recession, and the current structural crisis.[4]

Neoliberal financialization is a historically specific renewed hegemony of the financial forms of capital valorization, set forth by the structural profitability crisis of the world in the 1970s and early 1980s as a consequence of the materialization of the tendency of the rate of profit to fall in the previous decades. The subsequent structural transformations of the world economy were labeled as "neoliberalism": a period of a multidimensional restructuring of the world economy in order to recompose the conditions of valorization of capital through processes oriented to the recovery of the general rate of profit, and to counteract its fall by activating alternative mechanisms and spaces of valorization. Neoliberal financialization must be accounted as a key feature of these transformations, and one that relates heavily with the other major neoliberal transformations.

Neoliberalism can be depicted in relation to three valorization spaces involved in structural transformations (Cámara and Mariña 2010; Cámara 2012). The recovery of the general rate of profit of the traditional "active capital"—industrial and commercial capital—spaces of valorization was pursued mainly by anti-labor policies and the devalorization of the labor force. A favorable technical change based on the investment in information and communication technologies also contributed to an ephemeral restoration of profitability broadly restricted to the 1990s. Nonetheless, the reduction of the tax burden on capitalist profits had the larger effect on capital's profitability. On the other hand, a recovery of the rate of profit was pursued through the opening of new economic and geographical spaces of productive valorization of capital. This was accomplished by means of the privatization of public companies, the destruction of non-capitalist forms of production, and, for the most part, the deregulation of the mobility of productive and commodity capital at the international level, to the benefit of transnational corporations. This latter transformation has given way to neoliberal globalization, another key feature of neoliberalism.

Finally, the low profitability of active capital was counteracted by the reactivation of the financial mechanisms and spaces of valorization, highly restricted during the previous Keynesian period (Mariña and Torres 2010). Therefore, the neoliberal financialization is essentially conceived as an attempt to counteract the fall in the rate of profit of active capital through a renewed hegemony of the financial and speculative forms of capital valorization. This pursuit was achieved by several different means with diverse complexities and origins, though they all can be linked to the structural profitability crisis. In broad terms, we can identify three intertwined mechanisms leading to the neoliberal financialization: (1) the deregulation of national and international financial markets, and the consequent liberalization of the international mobility of money capital; (2) the steep increase in nominal and real interest rates since the 1979 coup; and (3) the managerial revolution in favor of the interest of the shareholders.

The first mechanism is related to the development of a new international finance beginning in the 1960s. This movement is rooted in the internationalization of production as transnational companies transcend national barriers as a consequence of declining profitability at home. This new international economic activity had to be accompanied by the internationalization of financial institutions. Additionally, the structural crisis brought about deep changes in the international money markets beginning in the late 1960s, which led to the expansion of international dollar markets (the Euromarkets), later reinforced by the breaking of the Bretton Woods system and the oil price hikes. Both events empowered the international financial system and pressed for the deregulation and liberalization, on a world scale, of financial activities, instruments, institutions, and markets. Concurrently, the development of information and communication technologies boosted the expansion of financial innovations (McNally 2010; Duménil and Lévy 2005, pp. 24–25; Orhangazi 2008, pp. 32–34; Lapavitsas 2009a, p. 104; Isaacs 2011, pp. 12–15).

The second mechanism relates to the high levels of inflation caused by supply constraints related to the structural profitability crisis and by the enhanced demand boosted by the Keynesian-oriented anti-cyclical policies. During the 1960s, the ensuing increase in the nominal interest rates started to create trouble in the banking sector. However, the rise of the rate of inflation during the 1970s kept the real interest rates at very low levels, raising the profitability of the financial sector. This monetary situation implied huge income transfers from the lenders (money capital) to the borrowers (mainly the non-financial sector), a situation that became unacceptable for the empowered "finance." The terrific surge in the nominal and interest rates in order to fight inflation in the benefit of money capital has been labeled as the 1979 coup. Beyond the financial crises detonated by the monetary contraction, the maintenance of high real interest rates during the 1980s and 1990s boosted the profitability of "capital property"—financing capital, as well as loans and equity—in relation to active capital. (Duménil and Lévy 2004, pp. 69–73; 2005, p. 25; 2011, pp. 60–62; Orhangazi 2008, pp. 30–31.)

The third mechanism was detonated by the hostile takeover movement of the 1980s, which was itself fueled by the creation of money markets for corporate control and the rise of institutional investors. This context was complemented by low stock prices, as a consequence both of the strategy of retaining and reinvesting earnings (prevalent until the 1970s) and of the structural crisis itself. Many corporations confronted hostile takeover bids, while most of them were threatened by the movement. The defensive strategy of the corporations consisted in maximizing the stock prices by means of increasing the dividend payments, the leveraged buybacks of stocks, and the implementation of stock options as a method of paying the managers. On the whole, a new corporate governance, oriented to the interests of the profitability of the shareholders—capital property—was implemented, jeopardizing the prospects of active-capital accumulation (Orhangazi 2008, 34–39; Erturk et al. 2008).

Neoliberal financialization has radically changed the hegemonic structure of the forms of valorization, having effects on the class structure and class power relations, as well as on the nature of economics institutions and their management. It has also manifested at different levels: those of individual capitals and agents; of sectors and intersectoral relations; and of capital in general and international relations. We can briefly sketch the nature of financialization by summarizing the major transformations of behavior of non-financial firms, of banks and the whole financial sector, of workers' and household income, of the national states, and of the international institutions.

Non-financial firms have turned to self-finance through retained earnings, and they have also developed financial skills and direct access to financial markets; nonetheless, this access has not been used to finance their productive investment, but rather their financial activities—especially buybacks of their own shares. Both circumstances have enhanced their independence from the banking system. They have also become more involved in financial and speculative forms of valorization through the lending of idle capital, the development of consumer credit, and the participation in financial and derivative assets markets. Moreover, they have gone through a revolution in their corporate governance, based on the "downsize and distribute" motto, reasserting the power of the stockholders (capital property) (Lapavitsas 2009a, 2009b; 2011, p. 620; Dos Santos 2009; Isaacs 2011, pp. 17–21; Duménil and Lévy 2004, pp. 73–75, 77, 121; 2011, pp. 62–64).

Consequently, banking firms have shifted their business financial intermediation for productive investment toward money-dealing and capital-dealing forms of valorization, that is, toward investment banking, fund management, and direct involvement in financial and derivative assets markets. They also have focused their financing operation toward final consumption through consumer credit and mortgages. Moreover, a new financial sector has grown, founded on the new financial "engineering" and risk-management techniques, promoted by innovations in information technology. Beyond an increase in the relative weight of the financial sector (financial corporations and investment funds) and profits, financial institutions such as government-sponsored enterprises, private asset-backed securities issuers, and broker-dealers have proliferated; also, derivative markets have surged heavily. Major features of this new financial sector are its high level of indebtedness and the extensive use of levering as the basis of its profitability (Lapavitsas 2011, pp. 620–22; Orhangazi 2008, pp. 11–14; Duménil and Lévy 2004, pp. 110–12; 2011, pp. 101–8).

Other economic sectors have also been shaken by neoliberal financialization. Workers and households have experienced a steep increase of their debts in order to finance greater proportions of their consumption. This indebtedness is related with neoliberal wage compression and the precarization of labor, and the subsequent requirement to finance the consumption of education, medical services, and, above all, housing. But it is fundamentally based on the predatory lending practices of the banking sector in their search for profits, especially to low-income and marginalized households, in a relation that is asymmetric. The privatization of pension funds has also financialized the households' income (Dos Santos 2009; Dymsky 2009; Isaacs 2011, pp. 22–25). The national states have also financialized their monetary policy based on inflation targeting and central bank independence, along with their state finances, through involvement in speculative debt markets. Finally, there has been a financialization of international relationships by means of an expansion of world money markets and of international banking, financial, and speculative activities.

This chapter now analyzes empirically the process of neoliberal financialization in the US economy by comparing empirical estimations of the profitability of active capital and capital property. As a first approximation, we employ the real long-term interest rate of the US ten-year Treasury bond as a proxy to the profitability of capital property. Then, the *profitably* of active capital is calculated as the difference between the general rate of profit of the non-financial corporate sector (which includes all the sectors and does not correct for productive and unproductive labor) and this rate. Two considerations must be made here: First, the only form of financial profit considered here is interest; consequently, profits of capital-dealing-capital and speculative profits are excluded. Second, one would expect that this proxy underestimates the general profitability of financing capital, given that the Treasury bonds tend to pay lower interest rates than the rest of the financing capital.

Figure 12.1 shows the comparison of both rates of profit.[5] The rate of return of active capital was considerably higher during the 1950s, 1960s, and 1970s (broadly the Keynesian expansive "long wave"), but the situation reversed with the increment in the rates of interest in 1979. During the neoliberal "long wave," the rate of return of capital property was significantly higher during the 1980s, and slightly higher in the 1990s, but then lower in the 2000s, a situation that will deserve further attention below.

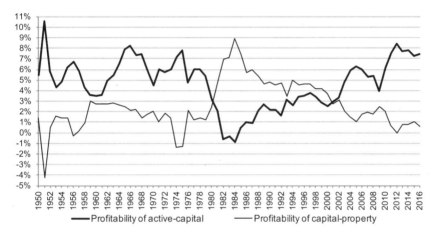

Figure 12.1. Profitability of active capital versus capital property (%); first approximation, United States, 1950–2016. Source: BEA, authors' calculations.

Next, we calculate the profitability of specific financial assets. Given the available data, corporate equities are relevant for our analysis because they are priced in market value terms. Therefore, their rate of return includes both its financial profit (dividends) and the speculative profit (holding gains on assets).[6] Also, an adjustment for the depreciation for inflation is applied.

Figure 12.2 shows three different measures of the profitability of corporate equities: profitability excluding speculative profits, showing a rather flat behavior; profitability including speculative profits, which shows sharp fluctuations; and the latter series smoothed with a conventional Hodrick-Prescott filter in order to better appreciate the series trend.

In figure 12.3, we present the profitability of different forms of financing capital: government debt, households' and non-profit organizations' debt, and non-financial corporate debt,[7] along with the smoothed profitability on corporate equities. It is observed that the profitability of these capital-property forms of valorization was rather low during the Keynesian expansive long

wave—except for the profitability on equities during the 1950s and mid-
1960s—but it increased to much higher values during the neoliberal long
wave. Nonetheless, their profitability started to deteriorate with the 2000–
2001 crisis, the burst of the dot-com bubble, and the ensuing fall in interest
rates. Therefore, this cyclical crisis can be considered the starting point of
the crisis of neoliberalism. Significantly, the profitability of the credit forms
of valorization only recovered very slightly in the recovery phase of the
2000s and continued to diminish as a consequence of the Great Recession.
In contrast, the profitability on corporate equities strongly recovered after
the last US cyclical crisis, up to its maximum historical levels.

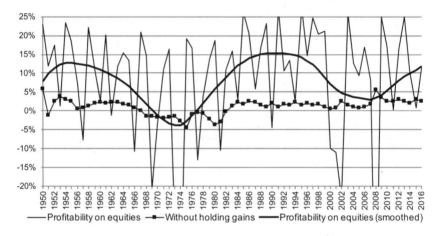

Figure 12.2. Profitability on corporate equities, United States
(%), 1950–2016. Source: BEA, authors' calculations.

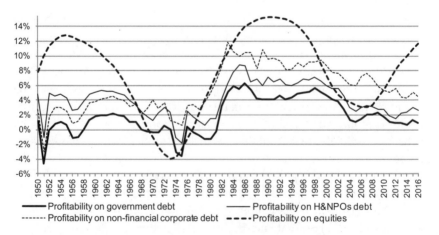

Figure 12.3. Profitability of different forms of financing capital,
United States (%), 1950–2016. Source: authors' calculations.

Finally, we show a second approximation to the calculation of the profitability of active capital and capital property (fig. 12.4), where the profitability of capital property is the weighted average of the rates of return of figure 12.3, while the profitably of active capital is calculated in the same way as in figure 12.1.

Again, it is evident that the profitability of active capital was relatively high during the Keynesian period, and that it fell dramatically to very low levels during the neoliberal period. In contrast, the profitability of capital property was relatively low during the Keynesian period and increased to very high levels during the neoliberal financialization. Consequently, the profitability of active capital was higher during most of the Keynesian expansive long wave, but the profitability of capital property was significantly higher during the neoliberal long wave. Therefore, neoliberalism can be characterized as a period of hegemony of the financial and speculative forms of valorization.

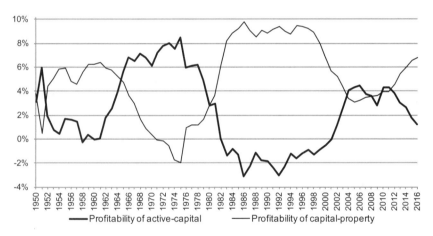

Figure 12.4. Profitability of active capital versus capital property; second approximation, United States (%), 1950–2016. Source: authors' calculations.

A last word must be said about the dynamics of both rates since the 2000–2001 cyclical crisis. As stated above, this crisis can be seen as a turning point in the process of financialization as a consequence of the deterioration of the profitability of credit and equity capital-property forms. The 2007–2009 deep cyclical crisis meant a further challenge to the financial hegemony of the neoliberal period. Indeed, the perpetuation of very low interest rates, far beyond the cyclical recovery, has entailed an ongoing relatively low profitability of the credit forms. Even so, the huge recovery of the profitability on corporate equities has implied a significant recovery of the general profitability of the capital-property forms. Consequently, it can be affirmed that financial hegemony has been renewed in the post-crisis period.

We have presented an empirical analysis of the neoliberal financialization in the US economy, where the profitability of active capital and of capital property have been estimated by two different approximations. It has been shown that the rate of return of the latter was consistently higher during the neoliberal period, contrary to what was the case during the Keynesian long wave. Therefore, the hegemony of the financial and speculative forms of valorization is illustrated by the higher profitability of these forms. Nonetheless, the empirical calculations have not encompassed every capital-property form of valorization; further research in order to comprise more forms is still needed. Also, the analysis has been restricted to long-run trends; it is our contention that a cyclical analysis of the process of financialization is also enlightening.

Neoliberal financialization has been portrayed as an inherently contradictory process, both on theoretical and empirical grounds. The logic of valorization of individual capitals clashes with the logic of valorization of capital in general. This contradictory process is helpful to derive a concise characterization of the economic performance of the last decades of the US economy. The expansion of the financial forms of valorization has appropriated and attracted a significant portion of the surplus value away from active-capital investment, which has tended to slow down productivity growth and, therefore, the dynamics of relative-surplus-value production mechanism. Therefore, neoliberal financialization has hindered a greater long-run recovery of the general rate of profit in United States. The cyclical crises of 2000–2001 and 2007–2009 and the current structural situation are external manifestations of the unsustainability of neoliberal restructuring, with financialization as one of its prominent characteristics; and these crises seem to lay the foundation for a new restructuring of the conditions of valorization of capital, one that has not yet taken definite shape.

Notes

1 An analysis of capital as the subject of the economic process can be found in Robles (2011).
2 Duménil et al. (1987), Shaikh (1992), and Moseley (1991) jump to this conclusion in their analysis of the US economy; Mariña and Moseley (2001), Cámara Izquierdo (2008, pp. 55–62), Freeman (1991), Li et al. (2007), and Marquetti et al. (2010), among others, arrive at the same conclusion for other countries of the world economy.
3 Cámara Izquierdo (2014) provides a literature review of both positions, as well as an empirical and analytic examination of the role of the rate of profit in the origination of the crisis in the US economy.
4 Neoliberal capitalism is not an exception, contrary to Duménil and Lévy's (2011) consideration that neoliberalism is dominated by the logic of income and consumption of luxury commodities of the upper fraction of the capitalist class.

5   The sources of data of the series presented correspond to national income and products accounts and fixed assets sccounts from the Bureau of Economic Analysis, and to financial accounts of the United States, from the board of governors of the Federal Reserve System. For reasons of space, the methodology employed in the calculations cannot be detailed here.
6   As stated above, it will also include founder's profit.
7   Holding gains on these assets are rare or null in the available data, so their profit is mainly interest.

References

Cámara Izquierdo, S. (2012) "Génesis, naturaleza y crisis del capitalismo neoliberal: Una perspectiva estructural," *Revista ECA, Estudios Centroamericanos*, Vol 67, No 729.

———. (2014) "The Role of Long-Term and Short-Term Dynamics of the US Rate of Profit in the Current Crisis," *International Journal of Management Concepts and Philosophy*, Vol 8, No 1.

Cámara Izquierdo, S. and A. Mariña Flores (2010), "Naturaleza y perspectivas de la actual crisis: una caracterización marxista de largo plazo," *Política y Cultura*, Vol 34.

Carchedi, G. (2011) "Behind and Beyond the Crisis," *International Socialism*, Vol 123.

Dos Santos, P. (2009) "On the Content of Banking in Contemporary Capitalism," *Historical Materialism*, Vol 17, No 2.

Duménil, G., M. Glick, and J. Rangel (1987) "The Rate of Profit in the United States," *Cambridge Journal of Economics*, Vol 11, No 4.

Duménil, G. and D. Lévy (2004) *Capital Resurgent: Roots of the Neoliberal Revolution*, Harvard University Press.

———. (2005) "Costs and Benefits of Neoliberalism: A Class Analysis," in G. Epstein, ed., *Financialization and the World Economy*, Edward Elgar.

———. (2011) *The Crisis of Neoliberalism*, Harvard University Press.

Dymsky, G. (2009) "Racial Exclusion and the Political Economy of the Subprime Crisis," *Historical Materialism*, Vol 17, No 2.

Erturk, I. et al. (2008) "General Introduction: Financialization, Coupon Pool and Conjuncture," in I. Erturk et al., eds., *Financialization at Work: Key Texts and Commentary*, Routledge.

Freeman, A. (1991) "National Accounts in Value Terms: The Social Wage and the Rate of profit in Britain, 1950–1986," in P. Dunne, ed., *Quantitative Marxism*, Polity Press.

Isaacs, G. (2011) "Contemporary Financialization: A Marxian Analysis," *Journal of Political Inquiry*, No 4, Department of Politics, New York University.

Lapavitsas, C. (2009a) "Financialization, or The Search for Profits in the Sphere of Circulation," *Ekomomiaz*, Vol 72.

———. (2009b), "Financialised Capitalism: Crisis and Financial Expropriation," *Historical Materialism*, Vol 17, No 2.

———. (2010) "Financialization and Capitalist Accumulation: Structural Accounts of the Crisis of 2007–9," *Research on Money and Finance Discussion Paper*, No 16.

———. (2011) "Theorizing Financialization," *Work, Employment and Society*, Vol 25, No 4.

Li, M., F. Xiao, and A. Zhu (2007) "Long Waves, Institutional Changes, and Historical Trends: A Study of the Long-Term Movement of the Rate of profit in the Capitalist World-Economy," *Journal of World-Systems Research*, Vol 13, No 1.

Mariña Flores, A. and F. Moseley (2001) "La tasa general de ganancia en Mexico: 1950–1999," *Economía: teoría y freepráctica*, Vol 15.

Mariña Flores, A. and G. N. Torres (2010) "Gestación y desarrollo de la hegemonía de las formas y mecanismos de valorización financieros y especulativos: desde la década de 1970 hasta la crisis actual," *Ensayos de Economía*, Vol 37.

Marquetti, A., E. Maldonado-Filho, and V. Lautert (2010) "The Rate of Profit in Brazil, 1953–2003," *Review of Radical Political Economics*, Vol 42, No 4.

McNally, D. (2010) *Global Slump: The Economics and Politics of Crisis and Resistance*, PM Press/Spectre.

Moseley, F. (1991) *The Falling Rate of Profit in the Post-War United States Economy*, Macmillan Press.

———. (2008) "Some Notes on The Crunch and the Crisis," *International Socialism*, Vol 119.

Orhangazi, Ö. (2008) *Financialization and the US Economy*, Edward Elgar.

Robles, M. (2011) "Marx: lógica y capital. La dialéctica de la tasa de ganancia de la forma-precio," *Colección Teoría y Análisis*, Universidad Autónoma Metropolitana-Xochimilco.

Shaikh, A. (1992) "The Falling Rate of Profit as the Cause of Long Waves: Theory and Evidence," in A. Kleinknecht et al., eds. *New Findings in Long Wave Research*, St. Martin's Press.

CHAPTER 13

THE ROOTS OF THE GLOBAL CRISIS: MARX'S LAW OF FALLING PROFITABILITY AND THE US ECONOMY, 1950–2013

Murray E. G. Smith and Jonah Butovsky

1. Introduction[1]

The aim of this chapter is to establish why a satisfactory account of the current malaise of global capitalism must involve centrally the "law of the tendency of the rate of profit to fall" (LTRPF), considered by Karl Marx to be "the most important law of modern political economy" (Marx 1973, p. 748). In concert with this goal, and building upon our previous work, it also reports our most recent attempt to chart the average rate of profit, the composition of capital, and the rate of surplus value for the US economy between 1950 and 2013. The disclosed trends for these "fundamental Marxian ratios" support three central propositions of our earlier work:

(1) The global capitalist slump, manifested most acutely in the financial crisis and Great Recession of 2007–2009, has its deepest roots in the persistent profitability problems of *productive capital* on a world scale.

(2) These problems are an expression of Marx's LTRPF in an era that has been marked by persistently high "organic" and "value" compositions of capital (reflecting technological innovations that have displaced living labor from production), as well as by the growing weight of "unproductive capital" and "socially necessary unproductive labor" in the richest capitalist countries.

(3) The profitability problems of productive capital, the hypertrophy of unproductive capital and the capitalist state, and the unprecedented growth of global debt in the opening decades of the new century are interrelated expressions of a "historical-structural crisis" of the capitalist mode of production (CMP).

The root cause of this systemic malaise, in our view, is an intensifying problem of *valorization*—a system-wide crisis in the creation of adequate volumes of aggregate surplus value, the "social substance" uniquely extracted from living labor by productive capital. Tables 13.1 and 13.2 depict a significant consequence of this fundamental problem: long-term declining growth rates in the global economy and in the advanced capitalist economies alike.

1960s	1970s	1980s	1990s	2000–09
4.9%	3.93%	2.95%	2.70%	2.58%

Table 13.1. Average annual growth rates of global GDP by decade (%), 1960s–2000s. Source: World Bank.

1980–89	1990–99	2000–09
3.09%	2.64%	1.75%

Table 13.2. Average annual growth rates of combined GDPs of top thirty-five "advanced (capitalist) economies" by decade (%), 1980s–2000s. Source: International Monetary Fund, World Economic Outlook Database.

Our itinerary is as follows. In section 2, we discuss the main elements of Marx's LTRPF, the theoretical controversy surrounding it, and some of the major problems involved in empirically evaluating the actuality of the law. We then outline our own approach to theoretically specifying the value categories that comprise the Marxian ratios and discuss some of the controversial issues posed by this specification. In section 3, we consider these issues in greater depth and explore their implications for an analysis of the current slump that traces the roots of the financial crisis of 2007–2008 to the longer-term crisis of profitability and valorization of the advanced capitalist world. In section 4, we present the findings of our empirical study of the US economy, concluding in section 5 with some observations concerning the political-programmatic implications of our findings.

2. The Rate of Profit and the Crisis of Global Capitalism
Marx's law of the tendency of the rate of profit to fall (LTRPF)
Capitalism is dominated by historically specific laws that are rooted in its fundamental social relations of production—relations that are at once class-exploitative, competitive, and formally egalitarian. The capitalist law of value regulates socioeconomic reproduction by allocating resources in accordance with the principle that only living, commodity-producing labor can create new value. This new value finds expression in the wages of *productive* wage laborers (in Marx's terminology, variable capital, v) and in the surplus value

(*s*) appropriated by the class of capitalist property owners. As the competitive dynamics of capitalist accumulation assert themselves, individual capitalist enterprises seek to improve their productivity and lower their costs of production / doing business by reducing their dependency on living wage labor and relying on labor-saving technologies. The result is an increase in the technical composition of capital (TCC)—the ratio of "capital stock"[2] to living, productive labor (measured as "physical magnitudes")—as well as a probable increase in the rate of surplus value (*s/v*, the rate of exploitation of productive labor).[3] To the extent that the increase in the former ratio finds expression in value/money terms, the consequence will be increases in the "value composition of capital" (VCC, measured as *C/v*) and the "organic composition of capital" (OCC, measured as *C/s + v*), where *C* is defined, in value-theoretic terms, as "*constant capital* stock."

An increase in *C/v* will only lead to a fall in the average rate of profit (measured as *s/C*) if it rises faster than the rate of surplus value (*s/v*). However, inasmuch as any change in *C/s + v* already manifests changes in *s/v*, an increasing organic composition of capital (OCC) *must* be associated with a falling rate of profit.[4] This is the essence of Marx's LTRPF.

The capitalist law of value and the LTRPF are understood by Marx to involve and reflect a deepening structural contradiction between the development of the productive forces and the reproduction of capitalist social relations. Indeed, they inform and give expression to a growing incompatibility between the "technical-natural" and "social" dimensions of capitalism as a historical mode of production (Marx 1859; Smith 2010). Thus, while playing an important (though not always central) role in periodic crises of the capitalist economy, the LTRPF also finds long-term, "secular" expressions and can be viewed as integral to an unfolding historical-structural crisis in the valorization of capital.

Marx's value categories, the temporal modes of value, and the LTRPF

The theoretical presupposition of Marx's argument is that economic value originates in social labor and must be conceptualized both in terms of the *class dynamics* of capitalism and *temporally*. For Marx, value is above all a *social relation*, the substance of which is abstract labor, the measure of which is socially necessary labor time, and the form of appearance of which is money. His fundamental value categories of constant capital, variable capital, and surplus value are vital to conceptualizing the specifically capitalist mode of class exploitation, the process of capital accumulation, and the distribution of value in national income and gross output. But the Marxian theory of capitalist crisis—and especially any Marxian theory of the historical-structural crisis of the CMP premised on the LTRPF—must also distinguish between three *temporal modes* of value: previously existing value (PEV), new or currently produced value (NV), and anticipated future (not-yet-existing) value (AFV).

In Marx's theory, the concept of constant capital corresponds to PEV, while variable capital and surplus value are two forms of NV whose relative magnitudes are, within certain limits, determined by class struggle. The concept of AFV is not fully developed by Marx but is nevertheless implicit in his discussions of the credit system and "fictitious capital." Stocks, bonds, and debt obligations, together with more recent innovations in fictitious capital such as credit default swaps, constitute claims on current and previously existing value (NV and PEV), but also wagers on AFV—value that has yet to be, and that may never be, produced.[5]

Fictitious capital has long played an important role in the operations of capitalist economies and should not be viewed as purely parasitic or predatory. Fundamentally, however, it is money capital seeking to enlarge itself through speculative claims on future income, signifying an attempt on the part of a fraction of the social capital (centered in the financial sector but involving other sectors as well) to liberate itself from the problems of the "productive economy" and the constraints of the law of value—above all, the tendency of the rate of profit to fall.

All in all, Marx's LTRPF provides a simple and remarkably compelling foundation for the argument that capitalism's capacity to develop the productive forces and promote human progress runs up against definite and insurmountable historical limits. Indeed, precisely because it stands opposed to any notion that capitalism can enjoy a progressive, crisis-free evolution, theoretical formulations of this law have been the target of repeated criticism from both defenders of the capitalist order and reformist leftists who envision and propose a gradual, incremental transition to socialism. Having noted this important dialectic of program and theory, we are nevertheless obliged to consider the scientific merit of the major theoretical objections to the LTRPF, since no empirical demonstration can establish its veracity so long as significant doubts about it at the theoretical level remain.[6]

The controversy surrounding the LTRPF[7]

The most important objections to Marx's exposition of the LTRPF are to be found in four (somewhat overlapping) arguments: (1) the argument that the tendencies that Marx himself identifies as "counteracting" the fall in the rate of profit are sufficient to effectively negate the "law as such"; (2) the "neutral technological progress" argument, according to which technological innovation under capitalism can evince a "capital-saving" bias just as easily as it can a "labor-saving" one; (3) the "rising technical composition / stable organic composition" argument, according to which the displacement of living labor from production and any concomitant increase in the TCC need not be reflected in a rising OCC; and (4) the "choice of technique" argument, according to which Marx's theory fails to establish why individual capitalist firms would adopt techniques of production that lower the average rate of profit. Let's consider each of these in turn.

The "counteracting tendencies" argument. In evaluating what Marx cites as counteracting tendencies to a falling rate of profit, those factors that contribute to an increase in the rate of surplus value should first of all be distinguished from those that pertain directly to the OCC. With respect to the former we can identify (1) "increases in the intensity of exploitation," (2) "reduction of wages below their value," and (3) "relative overpopulation." With respect to the latter we can identify (4) "the cheapening of the elements of constant capital" and (5) "foreign trade" (Marx 1981, ch. 14).

"Increasing the intensity of exploitation" encompasses two distinguishable modes of increasing exploitation, only one of which can counter a fall in the rate of profit. In this connection, Marx points to methods employed by capitalists to increase labor productivity that do *not* involve investments in labor-saving technology conducive to a rising OCC. Such methods are generally associated with the production of "absolute surplus-value" and include speedup and a prolongation of the working day—methods that run up against physiological limits, worker resistance, and associated pressures to increase wages. Marx also mentions productivity-enhancing technical innovations, as these are applied by individual capitalists "before they are universally applied" and, presumably, before they have an impact on the economy-wide OCC.

As with the methods employed to increase the intensity of labor exploitation, "the reduction of wages below their value" is generally an *ephemeral* factor in countering the fall in the rate of profit, for any permanent reduction would amount to a lowering of the value of the commodity labor power, thereby compromising workers' performance within the labor process and eventually inciting serious worker resistance. Thus, a long-term reduction of wages below their value can be envisioned only under conditions of severe anti-labor repression.

"Relative overpopulation" can also have a positive impact on the rate of exploitation by pushing down wages, but it encounters a significant barrier in the limited size of the working population. Only where capitalism is in the process of uprooting non-capitalist modes of production and constantly replenishing a massive "reserve army" of the unemployed is "relative overpopulation" likely to have anything more than a short-term impact as a counteracting factor.

Conjuncturally, all three of the above factors can play a role in increasing the rate of surplus value without inducing a rise in the OCC. Even so, Marx's apparent expectation that the rate of surplus value will show a *secular* tendency to rise is inseparable from his view that it will rise mainly due to an increased TCC. And such an increase, Marx assumed, will find a value expression in a rising OCC. Only if a rising TCC occurs without a concomitant increase in the OCC can this lead to a situation of rising productivity and exploitation with no falling rate of profit.

It is in just this connection that "the cheapening of the elements of constant capital" assumes its exceptional significance as a counteracting factor. Marx writes:

> [The] same development that raises the mass of constant capital in comparison with variable reduces the value of its elements, as a result of a higher productivity of labor, and hence prevents the value of the constant capital, even though this grows steadily, from growing in the same degree as its material volume, i.e. the material volume of the means of production that are set in motion by the same amount of labor-power. (Marx 1981, ch. 14)

Marx insists that the OCC will rise less impetuously than will the TCC, but he does *not* assert that a rise in the OCC will be prevented by "a higher productivity of labor." For a rise in the OCC to be fully blocked, the elements of constant capital must "increase [in mass] while their total value remains the same or even falls" (Marx 1981, p. 343). Although he does not specify well the limitations of "constant capital saving" as a factor inhibiting the fall in the profit rate, one can reasonably assume that Marx considered labor-saving innovation a *greater priority* for capitalists. The drive by capitalist enterprises toward labor-saving innovation is deeply rooted, after all, in the *totality* of social production relations in which they are enmeshed—relations that impel them not only to cut costs per unit of output in order to meet the challenges of competition, but to cut them in ways that simultaneously strengthen capital's hand in relation to labor.

Marx's fifth counteracting factor is "foreign trade and investment"—a factor that is clearly germane to the performance of *national* rates of profit, but much less so to an increasingly internationalized rate of profit. Even so, this factor can play a role in elevating the average rate of profit of particular national economies only to the extent that the terms of trade *continue* to improve, and/or the rate of return on capital invested abroad *continues* to rise from the standpoint of a given "national" social capital. Accordingly, the results of foreign trade and investment need to be viewed as a two-edged sword, capable of depressing as well as raising national rates of profit.

This survey of the tendencies counteracting the LTRPF suggests that "the law as such" and the counteracting tendencies to the law are *not coequal* "tendential laws," as some have suggested.[8] While the "countertendencies" are unquestionably key components of capitalist dynamics, all of the counteracting tendencies cited by Marx—with the possible exception of the cheapening of the elements of constant capital—have clearly defined *limits* as means to stemming a fall in the average rate of profit. On the other hand, the "law as such"—a rising OCC, accompanied by a falling rate of profit—finds its limit only in economic crises that bring about a devaluation of capital assets. In Marx's theory, then, it is *capitalist crisis* that creates the conditions for a recovery of the profit rate and resumed accumulation. Moreover, it is precisely the *recurrence* of capitalist crises that induces the capitalist class to deploy ever-changing "tactics" to increase the rate of profit, ensure the conditions of accumulation, and mitigate the destabilizing influences of severe economic dislocations on capitalist society's "class equilibrium."

The "neutral technological progress" argument. Marx's LTRPF postulates that technological progress under capitalism has an inherently *labor-saving bias*. Against this, several of his critics argue that, *given a constant real wage*, there are no good reasons to believe that capitalists will economize more on labor than on constant capital. But a constant real wage is by no means a "given" in the real world, and it is precisely the real-world possibility of wage increases outstripping the growth of labor productivity that ensures that technological progress must exhibit a labor-saving bias.

What needs to be emphasized here is that the labor-saving bias of capitalist innovation has its most fundamental roots in the "real subsumption of labor by capital."[9] Labor-saving technical innovation—the utility of which is to increase "relative surplus value"—strengthens capital's hand by rendering it as independent as possible of living labor in general and of skilled labor in particular. This is the first "functional" benefit accruing to capital from a rising TCC.

The second benefit of labor-saving innovation is more straightforward and was alluded to earlier. Since the limited size of the working population is an obvious barrier to the accumulation process, capitalists must find ways to increase output in the face of labor shortages. Labor-saving technological innovation is by far the most effective solution to this problem. If technical change were to exhibit instead a neutral tendency or a constant capital-saving bias, capital's dependence on the available working population would become ever greater, depleting the reserve army of labor and forcing up wages.

If Marx's TCC refers to "what modern economists call 'capital intensity,' the quantity of capital goods in real terms co-operating with each worker at some 'normal' level of full employment" (Mage 1963, p. 72), then the TCC can be defined as the ratio of means of production (expressed in "constant dollars") to the number of production workers, or, better still, as the constant-dollar value of capital stock employed per hour worked. All theoretical speculation aside, several empirical studies establish unmistakably that technological change does indeed exhibit a pronounced labor-saving bias in the long term, and furthermore that this tendency entails a marked increase in the TCC.[10]

The "rising TCC / stable OCC" argument. The most frequently encountered theoretical objection to the LTRPF concerns Marx's expectation that a rise in the TCC (a ratio of "use-value" magnitudes) will be accompanied by a rise in the OCC (a ratio of value magnitudes). As noted above, Marx acknowledges that the rise in the OCC will not be as pronounced as the rise in the TCC, owing to productivity increases associated with the latter. His critics go further, however, arguing that productivity increases in industries producing means of production have the effect of reducing the value of constant capital, in this way deflating the value of the constant capital stock, which is the numerator of the OCC.

It can be demonstrated, however, that productivity increases are unable to *completely* negate the tendency of the OCC to rise along with the TCC. As already noted, the rise in the TCC is attributable to a labor-saving bias in capitalist technical innovation—a proposition rooted in Marx's explicit recognition of the capital–labor relation as *antagonistic*. Such a notion is completely absent from the neoclassical theory of technical progress, and for just this reason it is difficult to see from the latter perspective that the use value of a "capital good" is a function not only of its "capacity-increasing effect" but of its "labor-saving effect" as well (Mage 1963, p. 159). All the same, once this *dual* function of capitalist means of production is recognized, it is evident that the TCC is neither proportional to nor quantitatively coextensive with labor productivity.

Labor productivity is the ratio of *the mass of use values produced* (as output or capacity) to the number of hours worked. The TCC, on the other hand, refers to the ratio of *the use value of the means of production* in relation to the number of hours worked. Accordingly, the use value of the numerator of the TCC (the capital stock) encompasses *both* output/capacity-expanding and labor-saving effects. If technical innovation displays a labor-saving bias, for all the reasons pointed to by Marx, then the numerator of the TCC should increase at a *faster* rate than the numerator of labor productivity—because all positive changes in the latter will be reflected in the former, but not all positive changes in the former will find expression in the latter. Since the OCC is the value expression of the TCC, it follows that a rise in the OCC will be restrained by increased labor productivity, but not entirely blocked.[11]

The "choice of technique" argument. If a rising OCC is compatible with a stable or rising rate of profit *for particular capitals*,[12] the precise "micro-economic" criteria by which individual capitalist firms choose different techniques of production need to be established. The much-cited "Okishio theorem" attempts to show that the criteria actually employed by capitalists would rule out a fall in the *general* rate of profit (Okishio 1961).

Under competitive conditions, a capitalist enterprise will only adopt a specific technique of production if it lowers per-unit production costs or increases per-unit profits at prevailing prices. Such innovation enables the firm to achieve a "transitional" rate of profit higher than the prevailing "general" rate. Consistent with the dubious "neo-Ricardian" presupposition of an absolute tendency toward profit rate uniformity, the Okishio theorem assumes that "the new average rate will be higher than the old average, due solely to the introduction of a cheaper technique (real wages being given)" (Shaikh 1978b, p. 242).

In his response to this "choice of technique" argument, Shaikh suggests that Okishio's theorem merely underscores Marx's own thesis that "the battle of competition is fought by the cheapening of commodities" and that "the cheapest method of production will win out in the wars among capitals" (Shaikh 1978b, p. 245). But there is a crucial difference between the "cheapest method of production" *per unit of output* and the "cheapest method" from the standpoint of *capital invested*. In order to grasp this, the distinction between *flows* and *stocks* must be appreciated. The cheapening of commodities is predicated on the lowering of unit cost-price—that is, a reduction in the *flow* of capital used up in producing each unit of output. Marx's argument is precisely that this reduction is generally accomplished through increased investment in the fixed-capital *stock*. The "increase in the productive powers [of laborers]" (Marx 1973, pp. 776–77)—which brings about the lowering of unit costs—is paid for through an increased "roundaboutness" of production. Elaborating on Marx's point, Shaikh argues,

> Once the difference between production costs and investment costs is grasped, it immediately follows that there in fact exist two different measures of profitability; profits in relation to capital used up in production . . . which I shall call profit-margin on costs, and profits in relation to capital advanced, or the profit rate. The former is a ratio of two flows, the latter a ratio of flow to stock. (Shaikh 1978b, pp. 242–3)

Since the Marxian rate of profit is a ratio of the surplus-value flow to the constant-capital stock, the increased fixed capital needed to cheapen commodities "will lower not only the maximum but also the actual rate of profit – precisely because this cheapening 'necessitates a costly and expensive apparatus' [Marx]."[13]

Theoretical issues in empirical measurement

The preceding discussion establishes that the major theoretical objections to the LTRPF are by no means conclusive and that substantial grounds exist for affirming that this law has a real and significant impact on the macroeconomic dynamics of capitalist economies, and on the actual history of capitalism. Nevertheless, significant theoretical problems still confront those seeking to empirically test the major hypotheses suggested by the LTRPF.

The first problem concerns the value-theoretic rectitude of measuring the value categories and the Marxian ratios in magnitudes of money. Some readings of Marx posit a *dualism* of labor values and money prices, which enjoins the theorist either to reject in principle *any* empirical measurement of "value" (a stance common to many "value form" theorists) or to insist upon the measurement of value in units of labor (a stance associated with Ricardian, neo-Ricardian and Sraffa-based interpretations of Marx's theory, but also with some "fundamentalist" Marxist ones). In counterpoint to such readings, we affirm our general agreement with Moseley that Marx's concepts of constant capital, variable capital, and surplus value "can be defined in terms of sums of money which function as capital. In principle, these concepts correspond to entries in the income statements and balance sheets of capitalist firms" (Moseley 1991, p. 30).

A second problem has to do with the appropriate theoretical specification of the value categories of Marx's system and the empirical translation of these categories using conventional data sets (as furnished by capitalist states)—data sets that tend to be recalcitrant to Marxist concepts and especially to the critical distinction between productive and unproductive labor. As this problem is central to our concerns in the rest of this chapter, we will not dwell on it at this point.

The third problem concerns the appropriate "unit of analysis" for disclosing the real trends of the fundamental Marxian ratios. Can meaningful results be achieved by analyzing *national* capitalist economies, or must the analysis be conducted at the level of the world economy—a postulated "international rate of profit"?

Certainly, as the internationalization of capital proceeds, manifested through increased international capital mobility, the formation of international "prices of production" and more pronounced tendencies toward profit rate equalization across national lines, one must acknowledge that processes of international surplus-value redistribution and "unequal exchange" will play an increasingly important role in the realization of profits within individual capitalist nation-states. Such processes will necessarily obscure *the transnational origin* of *some* of the surplus value that appears as "domestic profit"—and, to a certain extent, "delink" the (increasingly "internationalized") category of surplus value from the "nationally measured" value categories of constant capital stock and variable capital.[14]

However, the globalization of the capitalist economy has not reached a point where one can speak of a "general" or "uniform" international rate of profit, and it is impossible, in any case, to measure an average rate of profit on an international scale. What's more, it can be assumed—to the extent that processes involving transfers of surplus value through unequal exchange are operative on a world scale—that these would tend to favor the national capitalist economies exhibiting the highest rates of labor productivity and the highest organic compositions of capital. Therefore, if the LTRPF can be measured and recognized as operative in the most powerful and productive national capitalist economy, the United States, there can be little doubt that it is also operative on a world scale.[15]

Transfers of surplus value across national lines do not occur entirely, or even mainly, through processes of unequal exchange. They also occur through foreign direct investment and the "repatriation" of corporate profits earned abroad. Over the past twenty-five years, US corporate profit earned "in the rest of the world" has increased considerably as a percentage of total corporate profit. This, too, complicates any empirical test of Marx's LTRPF because the capital investments "standing behind" these profits are not easily measured. This issue will be returned to later, but we note here that the greatest share of these foreign investments was made in high-wage countries exhibiting high compositions of capital.[16]

The foregoing considerations suggest that empirical measurements of the Marxian ratios in any national framework, even that of the United States, must always be scrutinized carefully and with many caveats in mind. That said, we think the exercise is still well worth doing.

The LTRPF and the historical-structural crisis of capitalism

The burden of the present study is to defend, on the basis of a value-theoretic analysis of the laws of motion of capital in the US economy, the thesis that the current malaise "should be viewed against the backdrop of a historical-structural crisis of capitalism − as an extreme conjunctural expression of the decay of the profit system."[17] To support this thesis, we have elsewhere explored four issues pertaining to the "deepening structural contradiction between the development of the productive forces and the reproduction of capitalist social relations."[18]

The first is the negative impact on profitability of a rising, or persistently high, organic composition of capital in the capitalist core—the issue highlighted in Marx's original formulation of the LTRPF, and the central issue under investigation in this study.

The second is the impact of the growing specific weight of unproductive capital and of "socially necessary unproductive labor" in the advanced capitalist economies—an issue that not only enormously complicates any empirical evaluation of the LTRPF, but also points to a certain corruption or *adulteration* of Marx's law, and to the declining dynamism of the capitalist mode of production:

> If capitalism's tendency to promote the "objective socialization" of labor and of production once reflected its historically progressive role in developing the forces of production, it now *also* reflects a hypertrophy of the capitalist state and the sphere of circulation – a hypertrophy which impedes the advance of the productive forces by diverting enormous economic resources *away from* production. (Smith 2010, p. 90)

The third issue is that the *systemic costs* associated with the expansion of unproductive capital relative to productive capital—involving a concomitant expansion of the wage bill of socially (or "systemically") necessary unproductive labor (SNUL)—constitute elements of *a rapidly growing constant capital flow*: "[If] the growth of constant capital in relation to newly created value once signified a growth in the productivity of labor, it now *also* signifies a relative diminution of productive labor in relation to socially-necessary unproductive labor" (Smith 1994, p. 181). As a manifestation of a historical-structural crisis of capitalism, this phenomenon reveals that a growing share of economic resources is being used to sustain and perpetuate the distinctive institutional and class-antagonistic structures of capitalism. It signifies, in other words, that the social relations of capitalist production and reproduction are standing more and more as *an obstacle to the progressive development of human productive capacities*.

These considerations lead directly to a fourth issue: the massive growth of fictitious capital and fictitious profits. The downward pressure on the rate of profit of productive capital, associated with a rising composition of capital and an enormous expansion of the constant capital flow, has brought about a deepening, systemic *crisis of valorization*. Inadequate levels of surplus-value production (relative to overall systemic costs) have compelled dominant fractions of the social capital in the richest capitalist countries to resort to investment strategies predicated on speculation, the extraordinary expansion of credit and debt, criminal parasitism, and, more recently, central-bank money printing ("quantitative easing"), rather than on the production of commodities embodying surplus value.[19] Hence, money profits, particularly in the financial sector, are less and less likely to represent "redistributed" shares of surplus value originating in capitalist production, and more and more likely to represent aliquot shares of "anticipated new value" (AFV) circulating as paper assets in an increasingly debt-burdened economy.

Our claim is that *the proliferation of forms of fictitious capital whose "temporal value composition" is weighted more and more toward AFV has emerged as a hallmark of the historical-structural crisis of capitalism in the neoliberal era.*

As the flow of constant capital (PEV) grows relative to the flow of NV (due to the declining role of productive wage labor in the capitalist economy), there is a corresponding tendency for representations of AFV to acquire increased importance. This process is manifested in the proliferation of *increasingly fictitious* forms of financial capital and a malignant growth of unsustainable debt. Consequently, the true extent of the "valorization crisis" of late capitalism is concealed by the false appearance of (some) AFV as part of the "profit" component of currently produced surplus value. Booked profits, as these appear in conventional national-income accounts, reflect not only a determinate share of the new value produced by productive living labor, but also "fictitious profits" that have no substantial foundation in the value-creation process.

To be sure, some profits that do not arise from the current exploitation of living labor represent *transfers* within the circuits of capitalist revenue (NV) or from certain streams of constant capital (for example, PEV flows originally earmarked for state expenditures). Such profits can be conceptualized as "profit upon alienation" or "profit through dispossession." But alongside such (non-NV) profits exists a growing mass of fictitious profits (above all in the financial sector) that constitutes claims on AFV in the form of debt obligations—and therefore claims on income whose actualization depends on the future performance of productive labor.[20]

The mechanisms whereby booked profit is bolstered by transfers involving one or another form of AFV are myriad and cannot be examined in detail here. Nevertheless, theoretical acknowledgement of this reality is vitally important to registering the significance of the long-term divergence between the rate of profit on productive capital and the rate of profit on financial capital. The more robust performance of the latter compared to the former has been one of the most striking features of capitalism in the neoliberal era.[21] At the same time, however, it can be seen as constituting a new and rather significant "adulteration" of Marx's LTRPF—one that further complicates the already-daunting task of evaluating this law through empirical analysis.

Notwithstanding these difficulties, Marxist analysis of the historical dynamics of the capitalist world economy ought not to dispense with serious attempts to measure such fundamental Marxian (value-theoretic) ratios as the average rate of profit, the rate of surplus value, and the organic composition of capital. To be sure, such attempts can never offer much more than rough approximations. Even so, they are vitally important to charting and comprehending essential *trends* in the CMP—trends that can usefully inform, if only in a very general sense, the political-programmatic perspectives and tasks of Marxist socialists in relation to the broader working-class movement.

Several of these issues are considered further in the next section, which addresses the problem of the empirical specification of Marx's value categories in relation to conventional macroeconomic data sets.

3. The Specification of Marx's Value Categories and the Origins of the Current Malaise

Originally proposed by Shane Mage, the value-theoretical specification of the unproductive "overhead costs" of the capitalist system as elements of constant capital is controversial and stands opposed to an entrenched convention to treat such costs (that is to say, tax revenues and the wages of unproductive workers in general) as non-profit elements of social surplus value and/or as part of variable capital (if the relevance of the productive/unproductive distinction is denied).[22] In a series of publications, we have documented the uncertain status of these costs in Marx's own writings and defended a constant-capital specification of SNUL and tax revenues.[23] Table 13.3 provides a schematic representation of how productive labor is defined in Marxist theory along with three alternative ways of specifying SNUL.[24]

Productive Labor (PL)	
PL and PL wage costs as value	As variable capital
Does PL produce surplus-value?	Yes
Does PL produce new value?	Yes
Does PL preserve previously existing value?	Yes
Does PL function as variable capital?	Yes
Are PL wages a component of social-surplus value?	No
Are PL wages a component of constant capital flow?	No

Socially Necessary Unproductive Labor (SNUL)			
SNUL and SNUL wage costs as value (alternative conceptions)	As variable capital (denies u/p distinction)	As surplus value (upholds u/p distinction)	As constant capital (upholds u/p distinction)
Does SNUL produce surplus-value?	Yes	No	No
Does SNUL produce new value?	Yes	No	No
Does SNUL preserve previously existing value?	Yes	Unclear	Yes

Does SNUL function as variable capital?	Yes	No	No
Are SNUL wages a component of social surplus value?	No	Yes	No
Are SNUL wages a component of constant-capital flow?	No	No	Yes

Table 13.3. Conceptualizing productive labor and socially necessary unproductive labor in relation to Marx's value categories (variable capital, surplus value and constant capital).

Without exploring the finer points of this debate, it is sufficient to note here that the Mage-Smith approach allows us to agree with the critics of the productive/unproductive distinction that such costs are indeed *systemically necessary* from the point of view of the social capital (and are therefore *not* elements of surplus value readily "convertible" to profits),[25] while also agreeing with our fellow defenders of the productive/unproductive distinction that it is incorrect to treat the wages of workers employed in supervisory activity, bookkeeping, finance, trade, and many service industries as part of variable capital—that is, as capital that is exchanged with *productive labor.*[26] In dialectical fashion, the constant-capital specification of these systemic overhead costs allows us to recognize that unproductive capital and SNUL are at once *necessary* to overall capitalist profitability and *hazardous* to it. But to theoretically sustain this specification, we are obliged to conceptualize the category of constant capital as the value expression not only of physical means of production (its definition at the level of abstraction of the first volume of *Capital*) but of *all* the expenses and investments implicated in the total process of capitalist production and reproduction, *with the singular exception of living, productive labor,* which is the sole creator of the *new value* that enters into profit-of-enterprise, interest and rent (the principal components of surplus value) as well as the productive-labor wage bill.

Such a conceptualization of constant capital has enormous implications for empirical Marxist analysis, for it suggests that the *flow* of constant capital represents a much-larger share of the total value of gross output than is usually thought—and this is especially true for the most developed capitalist economies with expansive state, commercial, service, and financial sectors. Other things being equal, real growth in the SNUL wage bill and in tax revenues must produce an increase in what Smith calls the "value composition of output"—$Cf/(Cf + Vf + Sf)$—that is, the ratio of the annual flow of constant capital to the total value of gross product—an increase "likely to be associated with a declining average rate of profit."[27]

In defending Marx's account of a rising OCC leading to a falling rate of profit, Smith refers to the results of his empirical study of the Canadian economy from 1947 to 1991 (Smith and Taylor 1996). This study, based on the specification of Marx's value categories outlined above, produced an almost "ultra-Marxist" set of conclusions regarding the long-term dynamics of capitalist development between 1947 and 1975: a falling rate of profit, a gradually increasing rate of surplus value, and an impetuously rising OCC. In the ensuing 1976–91 period of capitalist restructuring in response to the profitability crisis (one marked by a determined mobilization of the "counteracting tendencies" to the LTRPF), the trend lines for the rate of profit and the OCC stabilized, and the rate of surplus value rose sharply.

These empirical findings were in many respects unique compared to those of other participants in Marxist debates on post–World War II profitability trends. It was distinctive, above all, because Smith rejected a measure of "gross surplus value" that included tax revenues and/or SNUL wages, while also postulating that the LTRPF expresses itself in an "adulterated" form in what he considers an epoch of capitalist decline.

How, then, does this analysis assist us in understanding the process of financialization and the proximate causes of the financial crisis of 2007–2008? In brief, the profitability crisis of the 1970s, particularly as it afflicted productive capital in the core capitalist countries, was never fully resolved, due to the determination of capital and capitalist states to (1) avoid the kind of deep global depression that would involve widespread bankruptcies and a significant devaluation of capital stocks; and (2) restore profitability through a *gradual* increase in the rate of exploitation, but in ways that would not provoke a major politico-ideological crisis for world capitalism in the era of the Cold War. Furthermore, to sustain effective demand and to mitigate crises of overproduction, the credit system was overhauled and extended in ways that allowed for the accumulation of dramatically larger volumes of debt across the world economy. Along with the globalization of capitalist production and the creation of significant new sites of surplus value production in Asia and Latin America, the expansion of the debt bubble helped restore profitability and conferred upon financial capital a much-enhanced role in maintaining the conditions of capital accumulation and economic growth, even as the rate of new capital formation and the growth rate of global GDP slowed in the 1980s and the 1990s.[28] Under these circumstances, fictitious capital and profits became much more significant phenomenons within the global circuits of capital.

The proliferation of fictitious capital and the buildup of ever-greater debt between 2001 and 2007 stimulated an anomalously high rate of profit in the United States and robust global economic growth. But the escalating financial panic of 2007–2008 signaled a growing recognition that the rising value of an array of dubious financial assets (collateralized debt obligations and other derivatives) was wildly out of line with the "economic fundamentals" (the precarious realities of the US subprime mortgage market, the profitability problems of productive capital, the stagnancy of real wage growth, etc.). In the end, the capitalist law of value asserted itself as a kind of gravitational force, pulling down the financial house of cards and precipitating the worst global recession since the 1930s.

This analysis suggests that the global slump that began in 2008 is by no means a typical periodic crisis of capitalism, but rather an extreme manifestation of a longer-term crisis of capitalist profitability rooted in a persistently high organic composition of capital in the "advanced capitalist" core of the world economy. Short of a complete collapse of the latter into deep depression, the immediate prospect is for a major escalation of the offensive by capital against labor on a world scale in order to both boost surplus-value production and reduce systemic overhead costs, all with a view to restoring the conditions of profitability and arresting the burgeoning debt crisis.[29]

While a conjunctural fall in US profitability was not the exclusive, or even the main, "trigger" for the crisis of 2007–2008, we argue that the factors contributing to the profitability crisis of the 1970s and 1980s (above all, a high organic composition of capital) forced the average rate of profit in the US economy into *a relatively low range* for an extended period. The lackluster profitability of productive capital set the stage for "financialization" and related processes that made both the US and global economies increasingly susceptible to a steep debt buildup, a proliferation of dubious forms of financial capital, and, in the upshot, a financial panic—the global sell-off of mortgage-backed securities and other exotic debt instruments sparked by the collapse of the Lehman Brothers investment bank.

Some radical political economists have argued that by the early 2000s, the average rate of profit in the US economy had been restored to much healthier levels—with the possible implication that reform of the "global financial architecture" might be all that is needed to set the world capitalist economy back on a reasonably stable path of robust growth. In our view, however, these commentators have underestimated the degree to which the heightened profitability of the period 2002–2007 (and to a lesser extent much of the 1990s) was *anomalous*, and critically dependent on an explosion of fictitious capital and profits associated with an orgy of unrestrained "financial innovation" and double-dealing.

This last consideration invites a final caveat concerning any attempt, including our own, to empirically test Marx's LTRPF. In the neoliberal era of "financialized capitalism," the growing weight of fictitious profits calls for considerable skepticism regarding the *composition* of "total corporate profits" as represented in conventional national income accounts.[30] Not only are the figures for these "booked profits" more and more *disconnected* from real magnitudes of currently produced surplus value; they are also, to an increasing extent, an index of the growing reliance of contemporary capitalism on measuring wealth in terms of *future labor time*—in particular the labor time required to service the debt accumulated by working people and by the capitalist state. Any nominal "improvement" in the rate of profit that is substantially based on profits deriving from "relations of debt/credit," rather than the creation of surplus value, must be regarded as fundamentally spurious—a fiction masking an underlying pathology that is hardly recognized by the policy doyens of capital, not to mention by the myriad of left-reformist proponents of income and wealth redistribution.

In line with our argument in section 2, it is also worth emphasizing that "fictitious capital" and "fictitious profits" can evince *varying degrees of "fictitiousness."* To the extent that the specific weight of fictitious capital and profits in relation to total capital and profits increased significantly over the past thirty years, and especially in the 2002–2007 period and beyond, this could only have skewed official data in such a way as to suggest both a higher rate of profit and a lower organic composition of capital than was actually the case. And since the statistical category of "total corporate profits"— inclusive of fictitious profits—is a major component of overall GDP, there is also good reason to believe that real GDP growth, in the United States as elsewhere, has actually been somewhat lower than suggested by the official data reported (see fig. 13.1).

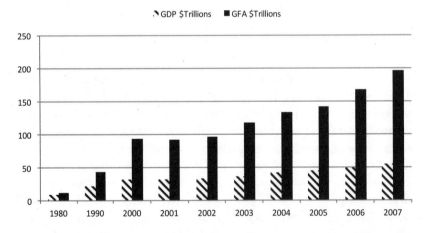

Figure 13.1. "Real" GDP wealth and global financial assets ($trn), 1980, 1990, and 2000–2007. Sources: BIS, IMF.

4. The Rate of Profit, the Rate of Surplus Value, and the Composition of Capital in the US Economy, 1950–2013

In this section, we apply the theoretical perspectives outlined in sections 2 and 3 to an empirical analysis of the US economy from 1950 to 2013. We attempt, in particular, to "test" Marx's LTRPF for the US economy in a way consistent with the constant-capital specification of tax revenues and SNUL advocated by Mage in his pioneering study of 1963. We caution, however, that our results are somewhat inconclusive, owing to numerous technical problems associated with the translation of official economic data into the Marxian value categories. This translation problem is especially evident in our calculations of surplus value (after-tax profits and elite salaries) and variable capital (after-tax wages of productive workers).

The national income and product accounts (NIPA) tables published by the US Bureau of Economic Analysis (BEA) include no data for *after-tax* wages or the *corporate-officer share* of "wage and salary accruals" (an income stream that properly belongs to surplus value), rendering the calculation of after-tax wages of productive workers ("variable capital," or V) problematic. Nor do these data sets allow us to easily discriminate between productive and unproductive labor, either within economic sectors/industries or between them.

In addressing these problems, we have been obliged to apply a crude "average tax rate on personal income" in order to derive our estimates of variable capital (V). In addition, we have derived a rough estimate of corporate-officer compensation by defining the top 1 percent of wage and salary earners as recipients of such compensation for every year from 1950 to 2013. This estimate, based on figures provided by Saez (2015), was subtracted from after-tax wage and salary incomes and added to after-tax corporate profits to obtain our measure of surplus value (S). Inasmuch as the proportion of total wage and salary accruals received by the top 1 percent increased considerably between the 1960s and the 2000s, the growth of this (revenue) component of surplus value contributed to the upturn in the rate of profit over the past thirty years while doing little to improve the rate of capital accumulation.[31]

In distinguishing between productive and unproductive labor, we have followed the classification system suggested by Shaikh and Tonak (1994) and Mohun (2005), defining as entirely unproductive the following divisions represented in the BEA/NIPA tables: wholesale trade, retail trade, finance, insurance and real estate, business services, legal services, miscellaneous professional services, other services, private households, and general government. All other divisions, including construction, manufacturing, transportation, and several service industries, were defined as *entirely* productive.[32] This compromise procedure—that is to say, the treatment of *all* labor employed by productive capital as productive—may skew our results for the rate of surplus value and the composition of capital to the extent that the ratio of supervisory to nonsupervisory labor and, more generally, the ratio of unproductive to productive labor in these productive divisions vary over time. Nevertheless, we think it is reasonable to assume that the basic long-term *trends* revealed for these ratios would not be affected substantially by more exact measurements that captured such changing ratios within the productive divisions.

Notwithstanding these difficulties and compromises, our estimates should be of considerable interest to those who recognize the importance of empirically operationalizing the productive/unproductive distinction in the analysis of the fundamental Marxian ratios, and particularly to those persuaded of the need for a constant-capital specification of taxes and SNUL wages—a specification that effectively *removes* these flows from the calculation of the rate of profit, the rate of surplus value, and the OCC. A detailed account of our methods and sources for calculating the basic variables of this study is provided in the appendix at the end of the chapter.

The principal findings of our study can be summarized concisely and are presented in a series of charts below. First, with respect to the rate of profit (ROP), the current-cost ROP displays a slight upward trend over the entire period from 1950 to 2013 (see fig. 13.2). As one might expect, it falls rather dramatically between 1950 and the 1980s, but then it begins to climb sharply from 1990 to 2007, the eve of the Great Recession.[33] Furthermore, a truly remarkable increase is observable following the recession of 2001; indeed, the ROP reaches a postwar peak of 16.5 percent in 2006.[34]

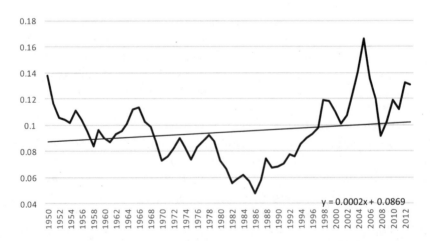

Figure 13.2. The current-cost rate of profit (%), 1950–2012. Source: BEA, authors' calculations.

As previously noted, however, there are compelling grounds for regarding the exceptionally strong performance of the ROP between 2002 and 2007 (and beyond) as *anomalous*, and based to a considerable extent on "fictitious profits" booked in the finance, insurance, and real estate sectors, and perhaps also by many firms operating in the productive economy (as indicated in note 20). This suspicion is reinforced by the performance of the before-tax "non-financial" ROP calculated by Shaikh, which showed a steep rise between 2002 and 2006, but only to a peak of 12 percent—a level about one-third below its postwar high in 1966. Our own *after-tax* non-financial ROP (presented in fig. 13.3) reaches a peak during this period of just under 7 percent in 2006, fully *half* its postwar highs in 1950 and 1965–66. Moreover, the unprecedented growth in the mass of profits during this period was accompanied by rates of new capital formation that were unusually sluggish in the context of an allegedly booming economy,[35] as well as by a relatively low taxation rate on corporate profits.[36] As investment in capital stocks stagnated, already-high levels of public and private debt soared under the combined impact of the costly Iraq War and the expanding housing bubble. And so, of course, did profits. The conclusion is obvious: the anomalously high mass and rate of profit during the "era of financialization"—and most obviously during the 2002–2007 period—was made possible only by the accumulation of an enormous volume of debt obligations—that is to say, of fictitious capital understood as claims on future income.

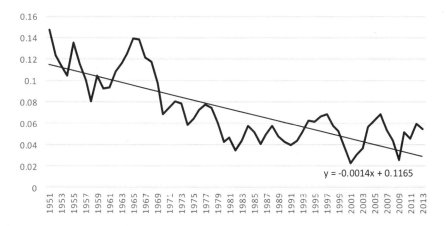

Figure 13.3. Non-financial corporate rate of profit (after tax %), United States, 1950–2013. Source: BEA, authors' calculations.

The anomalous 2002–2007 ROP was, then, both illusory and unsustainable. The ROP was bound to fall dramatically, and this was duly accomplished in 2008. With slightly higher profits in 2009, the ROP returned to a level closer to its long-term trend line. Overall corporate revenues remained low, however, suggesting that enterprise cost-cutting (and some devaluation of capital stock resulting from the recession) was responsible for the improved profit rate. The NIPA estimates for after-tax domestic corporate profits of $666 billion in 2008 and $845 billion in 2009 stood well below the record $1.12 trillion registered in 2006. However, a sharp spike to an estimated $1.07 trillion in 2010, followed by $1.00 trillion in 2011, $1.28 trillion in 2012, and $1.36 trillion in 2013, suggested continuing volatility in the mass of profits, the ratio of financial to non-financial profits, and the nominal ROP. Indeed, this spike was due in good part to the remarkable recovery of financial profits made possible by the government-funded bailout of the big banks, as well as by the massive infusion of liquidity into the banking system by the US Federal Reserve at 0 percent interest. The Fed's continuing "quantitative easing" policy beyond 2010 explains a major part of the continuing recovery of profitability over the 2011–2013 period. While the ROP of this period undoubtedly benefited from some real gains in the rate of exploitation of productive labor (S/V), it is entirely reasonable to think that, due to the continuing presence of massive fictitious profits generated in the financial sector and beyond, the nominal ROP, as reported, remains considerably inflated relative to the "real" (Marxian) ROP.

Second, with respect to the rate of surplus value (S/V), we find that it averaged 38 percent in the 1950s, 38 percent in the 1960s, 42 percent in the 1970s, 34 percent in the 1980s, 46 percent in the 1990s, and 62 percent from 2000 to 2013 (see fig. 13.4). While the trend for S/V is essentially flat between 1950 and the 1970s, it falls after 1978, reaching its lowest point in 1986. It then embarks on a strongly upward trend between 1986 and 2007. Its trajectory over this latter period, as well as between 2008 and 2013, is very similar to that of the (anomalous) ROP. These findings support the proposition that the decline in the ROP was arrested in good part due to a significant increase in the rate of exploitation of productive labor (S/V), with a long-term decline in corporate taxation playing a supplementary role. This increased exploitation is reflected in the widening gap between the growth of labor productivity and the growth of hourly real compensation,[37] which itself must be explained in terms of changes in the labor process, on the one hand, and falling or stagnant real wages, on the other. Again, however, to the extent that it reflects a massive growth of fictitious financial profits, the sharp spikes in S/V between 2002 and 2007, and again between 2010 and 2013 should be viewed as anomalous.[38] That said, it is important to note that while the ROP's trend line increased only slightly over the 63-year period examined, the trend line for S/V nearly doubled. The large discrepancy between these two trends is, of course, attributable to the effect of a rising value and organic composition of capital.

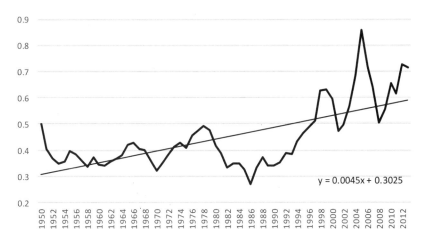

Figure 13.4. The rate of surplus value, United States, 1950–2013 (S/V). Source: authors' calculations.

Finally then, with respect to the organic composition of capital (OCC), which Marx understood to be the *value expression* of the ratio of "dead to living labor in production,"[39] we find that the current-cost OCC displays a strong upward trend between 1950 and 2007, reaching a peak of 4.54 in 1982 compared to a postwar low of 2.42 in 1950 (see fig. 13.5).[40] Much of this increase occurs after the onset of the profitability crisis of the 1970s. However, the OCC exhibits a very gradual long-term declining trend between 1982 and 2007. The stabilization of the OCC during this period (in a range that is nevertheless well above that of 1950–74) suggests that the major underlying cause of the profitability malaise of the past thirty to forty years continues to assert itself. This conclusion is reinforced by the even stronger upward trend of the value composition of capital (C/V), a ratio that effectively removes both actual and fictitious profits from the picture (see fig. 13.6 for the current-cost C/V).[41]

The steep fall in the OCC in the early 2000s coincides with comparably steep rises in the ROP and S/V. We think that this fall is associated with the proliferation of fictitious capital and profit, the super-profits realized by US "defense" contractors following the invasions of Afghanistan and Iraq, and the anomalously slow pace of new capital formation during the Bush-era "boom." In light of all this, it is reasonable to think that the path of the "real" OCC may be returning to its historic (upward) trend line, even as our reported OCC for 2009–2013 remains below it, owing to the inflationary effect of fictitious profits on its denominator.

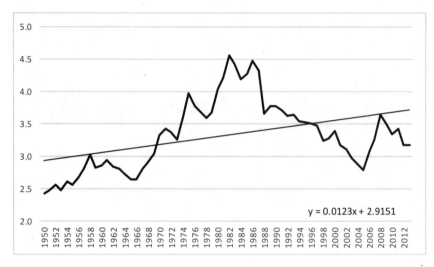

Figure 13.5. The organic composition of capital, United States, 1950–2013 (C/S + V). Source: authors' calculations.

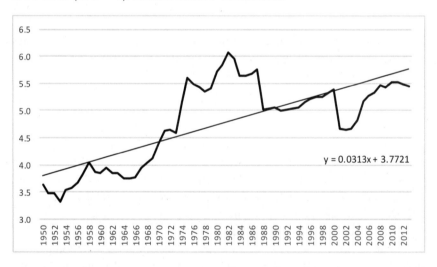

Figure 13.6. The value composition of capital, United States, 1950–2013 (C/V). Source: author's calculations.

5. Concluding Remarks

The results of this study of the US economy lend considerable support to the thesis that the crisis of global capitalism that erupted in 2007–2008 is due to the persistent profitability problems of productive capital, and that these problems are at the root of the "financialization" phenomenon and of debt crises that are now destabilizing the world system. Furthermore, our findings reinforce the argument that the global capitalist slump is unlikely to be overcome without much more savage attacks on labor by capital than those that characterized the pre-2008 neoliberal era, and without a quite-significant devaluation of capital stocks involving widespread bankruptcies and persistently high levels of unemployment. In some significant measure, the super-profits reaped by Wall Street and European banks in the wake of the government bailouts of 2009 must also be seen as having been purchased through an increase in state debt obligations—a form of fictitious capital. To stem this rising tide of debt, draconian austerity measures and increased levels of exploitation are now being imposed on the international working class.[42]

The period we are entering marks a critical turning point within (or beyond) the neoliberal era. In the absence of concerted and effective working-class resistance, which would require the emergence of a consciously anti-capitalist labor movement, a major restructuring of capital values and class relations is well underway—one that may augur well for "real" profitability in the long term but that will also produce devastating results for the working class of the developed capitalist world.

This new period—one that might be dubbed "neoliberalism with a vengeance"—is clearly fraught with great perils, including the likelihood of intensified rivalry among the major economic powers, the rise of right-wing populism, and an accelerated assault on the rights and living standards that working people took for granted in the liberal-democratic West for decades following World War II—and even well into the neoliberal era.

Taken as a whole, our analysis suggests that, for the working-class majority of the United States and other advanced capitalist countries, improved living standards will *not* be achieved through increased taxes on the rich or other modes of "progressive" income redistribution. To be sure, the capitalist class is hoarding—and in many cases hiding—vast amounts of money profit. But much of this profit has a purely "fictitious" character, deriving from a growing volume of debt borne by capitalist governments and the working class. The function of this hoarded profit is to lubricate a financial system that increasingly resembles a gigantic Ponzi scheme. Under the rule of capital, this paper wealth—consisting more and more of claims on "anticipated future value" (AFV)—cannot be made available for investment in the "real" (productive) economy, nor will it be transferred to workers with a view to stimulating "aggregate demand." The reason is simple: such reallocations of AFV would amount to using existing debt to finance activities that risk increasing the OCC and/or lowering the rate of exploitation, thereby exacerbating the crisis of valorization and lowering the (real) rate of profit. In short, any strategic project predicated on the "progressive reform of capitalism" is little more than a utopian-reformist pipe dream—and far more unrealistic than Marx's own revolutionary-transformative project of effecting "the expropriation of a few usurpers by the mass of the people" (Marx 1977, p. 929).

The conclusion is unavoidable. Now, more than ever, socialists must declare boldly and without equivocation that the time has arrived to replace a socioeconomic order geared toward generating profits for the few with a socialist system of production to meet the needs of the many.

Appendix: Sources and Methods

The following data sources and methods were used for figures 13.1 to 13.5:

Constant capital stock (C). Value of the net stock of private assets measured according to both current-cost (C) and historic-cost $(C2)$ criteria. C = current-cost net stock of private fixed assets, year-end estimates (BEA fixed assets, table 6.1, line 2). Our charts refer only to C as calculated in our spreadsheet. $C2$ = historic-cost net stock of private assets, year-end estimates (BEA fixed assets, table 6.3, line 2) and are referred to in endnotes based on our spreadsheet data. $C2$ figures in our spreadsheet, for each year, correspond to the historic-cost figure at the beginning of the year, i.e., to the end of the prior year. (For example, the 1980 figure in the BEA table is our spreadsheet figure for 1981. This is the procedure also followed by Kliman 2010.)

Surplus value (S). Corporate profits after tax, for domestic industries, taken from BEA NIPA table 6.19B, line 2 plus the after-tax earnings of the top 1 percent of the recipients of "wage and salary accruals" = S. The proportion of earnings represented by the top 1 percent of wage and salary earners was obtained from Saez (2015).

Variable capital (V). Total wages and salary accruals (NIPA table 6.3B, line 1) *minus* line 50 (wholesale trade), line 51 (retail trade), line 52 (finance, insurance, and real estate), line 63 (business services), line 69 (legal services), line 74 (miscellaneous professional services / other services), line 74 (private household services), and lines 72 and 83 (general government services, federal, state, and local) = before-tax wage bill of productive labor. V = before-tax wage bill of productive labor *minus* estimated tax deductions calculated by multiplying the "effective tax rate on income" by the productive-labor wage bill. The effective tax rate was calculated as the ratio of personal current taxes (NIPA table 3.1, line 3) to personal income (NIPA table 2.1, line 1).

After-tax, non-financial ROP. The procedure for calculating the after-tax, non-financial ROP (fig. 13.3) follows Shaikh (2010) exactly, with the exception that we used after-tax profit figures whereas Shaikh used before-tax figures. "Corporate profit as listed in NIPA is net of actual net monetary interest paid, so we need to add the latter item back in order to get profits before interest" (Shaikh 2010, p. 58, appendix).

Notes

1   This chapter is a revised and updated version of a study originally published in the journal *Historical Materialism* (Smith and Butovsky 2012) and subsequently reprinted as components of chapters 1 and 2 of Smith's 2014 book *Marxist*

Phoenix, published by Canadian Scholars' Press International. The authors thank *HM*'s editors, especially Adam Hanieh, as well as the CSPI editors for their earlier contributions to the study and its presentation. Thanks are also due to Guglielmo Carchedi and Michael Roberts for their invitation to contribute to this collection and for their helpful suggestions for abridgments and revisions. The authors are solely responsible for all remaining weaknesses.

2   The capital stock encompasses not only "means of production" but also the "means of circulation" within a capitalist economy—i.e., the fixed capital assets of industrial, commercial, and financial capital.

3   We refer to a merely "probable" increase in the rate of surplus value because labor-saving innovation will not automatically produce an increase in the rate of exploitation of productive labor. If the real wages of productive workers rise in tandem with gains in labor productivity, a rising composition of capital can be accompanied by a more-or-less constant rate of surplus value. Indeed, Marx's theoretical model for the LTRPF explicitly allows for just this possibility.

4   This conceptualization of the relationship between the fundamental Marxian ratios follows the approach suggested by Mage (1963) and differs from the influential treatment by Sweezy (1968). Smith summarizes the approach as follows: "The rate of surplus-value is the ratio of two *flows* of living labour (L), which together constitute the 'net value' of the commodity product: surplus value and variable capital. Hence, s'=s/v. It follows from this that s=L-v=L-(s/s') = L/(1+1/s')=L(s'/1+s'). Now, if the OCC is Q and this equals C/s+v, then Q=C/L, and the capital stock C equals LxQ (C=LQ). If the rate of profit is the ratio of surplus value to the capital stock (s/C), then through substitution we arrive at r = L(s'/1=s')/LQ=s'/(Q(1+s'). In this formula, changes in the rate of surplus value will impact on both the rate of profit and the OCC, so that if the OCC increases, this must mean a fall in the rate of profit. An increase in the rate of surplus value contributes to maintaining or increasing the rate of profit only if it occurs without an increase in the OCC defined as C/s+v" (1994, p. 149). Marx's own representation of the relationships between these ratios in *Capital* fails to distinguish between stock and flow expressions of constant capital. He also treats variable capital as part of the "capital advanced," despite his observation that wages are paid out only after the value that they represent has been produced. On the latter point, see Mage (1963) and Reuten (2006). For further discussion, see note 41 below. For alternative definitions of the technical, organic, and value compositions of capital, see Reuten and Williams (1989), Carchedi (1991), and Saad-Filho (2002).

5   In *Capital*, vol. 3, Marx writes: "With the development of interest-bearing capital and the credit system, all capital seems to be duplicated, and at some points triplicated, by the various ways in which the same capital, or even the same claim, appears in various hands in different guises. The greater part of this 'money capital' is purely fictitious" (1981, p. 601). An obvious instance of this in the lead-up to the most recent financial crisis is the appearance of "money capital" at first as a mortgage and subsequently as a mortgage-backed security. Further on, Marx observes that "commodity capital largely loses its capacity to represent *potential* money capital in time of crisis, and generally when business stagnates. The same is true of fictitious capital, *interest-bearing paper*, in as much as this itself circulates as money capital on the stock exchange. As the interest rate rises, its price falls. It falls further, owing to the general lack of credit, which compels the owners of this

paper to unload it onto the market on a massive scale in order to obtain money" (1981, pp. 624–25, emphasis added). Carchedi observes, "Titles of credit/debt have no intrinsic value. However, they have a price. Take a bond. Its price is given by the capitalization of future earnings and thus depends on the rate of interest. Marx refers to this as the 'most fetish-like form' of capital because it seems that it is capital that creates surplus value, not labour. . . . If loan capital is fictitious, loan (financial) profits are fictitious too. They are fictitious not because they do not exist (as in some fraudulent accounting practices). They are the appropriation of a representation of value (money), and in this sense they are real. But they are fictitious because this appropriation is based upon a relation of debt/credit rather than of production. Financial capital sells valueless titles of debt for money" (2011, pp. 5–6). See also Carchedi (2012).

6   Reuten and Williams (1989, p. 118, addenda a). The widely discussed critique by Michael Heinrich (2013) of Marx's LTRPF, which draws on many traditional objections, has been effectively answered by Carchedi and Roberts (2013), among others. This latest iteration of the controversy will not be reviewed here.

7   The following discussion borrows heavily, though incompletely, from Smith (1994, ch. 7). The collections edited by Bellofiore (1998) and Campbell and Reuten (2002) also provide useful surveys of many of the controversial issues surrounding Marx's LTRPF, as does Carchedi (2012).

8   See for example, Albo, Gindin, and Panitch (2010, p. 39).

9   See "The Results of the Immediate Process of Production," appendix to Marx (1977).

10   See Leontieff (1982), Shaikh and Tonak (1994), and Webber and Rigby (1996).

11   A more detailed development of this argument can be found in Smith (1984, pp. 144–48).

12   High-OCC firms are able to achieve higher-than-average rates of profit due to their ability to capture surplus value produced by other firms. Capitalists tend to realize as profit a share of socially produced surplus value commensurate with their share of the total economy-wide capital investment. But individual capitals may realize above-average shares due to their superior competitive performance in the market—and this may be due to a higher TCC (and therefore OCC).

13   Shaikh (1978b, p. 244). For insightful critiques of the choice of technique argument that are complementary but not identical to Shaikh's, see Freeman (1998), and Reuten and Williams (1989). The latter argues that "[o]nce the theory is cast in dynamic terms, conditions of existence (or, appropriate 'mircoeconomic foundations') for the TRPF can indeed be provided, and the analysis of the Okishians reduced to a special case" (p. 117). Reuten and Williams seek to provide such microfoundations inter alia by emphasizing the issue of "capital stratification" and centralization as contributing to a rising composition of capital. They write, "[W]hilst the average rate of profit decreases, profit is 'redistributed' from the bottom to the top of the stratification" (1989, p. 134). See also Kliman (2007) for a critique of the Okishio theorem that relies on the controversial "temporal single system" interpretation of Marx's value theory.

14   For extended discussions of these issues, see Smith (1994, ch. 9) on "international and inter-regional value transfers," and Carchedi (1991, ch. 7) on "production and distribution as worldwide processes."

15   In this regard, Moseley has argued that the "most likely source of bias resulting from [estimating the Marxian variables more narrowly in terms of the US

economy] is that the composition of capital may have increased slower in the U.S. than in the world capitalist economy" (1991, p. 182).

16 According to one analyst, "Typically, U.S. firms have placed the largest share of their annual investments in developed countries, primarily in Western Europe, but this tendency has increased since the mid-1990s. In the last half of the 1990s, U.S. direct investment abroad experienced a dramatic shift from developing countries to the richest developed economies: the share of U.S. direct investment going to developing countries fell from 37% in 1996 to 21% in 2000. [In 2009] Developed countries received nearly 70% of the investment funds of U.S. multinational firms, while developing countries received about 30%" (Jackson 2011, p. 4).

17 Smith (2010, p. x). The discussion on the next few pages borrows from Smith (2011).

18 Smith (2010, p. 6). See also Smith and Butovsky (2012) and Smith (2014).

19 The financialization phenomenon that led up to the financial crisis of 2007–2009 was summarized by Smith (2010) as "significantly increased investment in financial activity, the appearance of new financial instruments like derivatives and hedge funds, frenzied speculation surrounding a growing volume of fictitious capital, a massive overloading of the credit system and a generalized 'irrational exuberance,' to borrow Alan Greenspan's famous phrase" (p. 15).

20 Harman notes, "The shock of the financial crisis . . . is now leading some bourgeois economic commentators to recognize that there were 'fictitious profits' – and with them 'fictitious economic growth' – in the mid-2000s, if not earlier. Most calculations of profitability try to circumvent this problem by restricting themselves to non-financial corporations (or, sometimes, the non-financial business sector). But many major non-financial corporations . . . became increasingly dependent on financial operations from the 1990s onwards" (2009b, p. 3). Lapavitsas and Levina (2010) suggest that "financial profit remains redistributed loanable capital, hence, a part of the existing flows of value."

21 See Duménil and Lévy (2004), Brenner (2006), Shaikh (2010).

22 Mage (1963) argues that all costs associated with unproductive labor in the spheres of production, circulation, and the state should be treated as part of constant capital, noting that the "difference between variable capital and constant capital is founded on their differing modes of transferring value to the commodity-product; and in the case of constant capital this characteristic mode is precisely *the addition of previously existing values*." An elaboration of this argument is to be found in Smith (2010).

23 See Smith (1993, 1994, 1996, 2010, 2014); Smith and Butovsky (2012).

24 Note that this table incorporates a correction to an earlier version that appeared in Smith (2014, p. 63), which erroneously suggested that the constant-capital specification treats SNUL wages as a component not only of the constant-capital flow but of social surplus value as well.

25 See, for example, Laibman (1992).

26 See Moseley (1991), Shaikh and Tonak (1994), Shaikh (1999), and Mohun 1996. It should be noted that some recent defenders of the LTRPF (notably Kliman 2010 and 2012) have undertaken empirical analyses in support of it that treat SNUL wages as part of variable capital. This has the effect of skewing the trend for the rate of profit downward (when defined as $s/C + v$), while also misrepresenting the real trends for the rate of surplus value (s/v) and the composition of capital ($c/s + v$ or c/v). On this, see also Carchedi (2012, p. 139 n12).

27   Smith (2010, p. 89); see also Smith (1984). It should be noted that massive amounts of constant capital, understood as PEV, are also stored up in physical assets whose value is not represented in annually measured gross output.

28   "Between the fourth quarter of 1981 and that of 2008, credit market debt in the U.S. mushroomed from 164 percent to 370 percent of GDP" (Smith 2010, p. 9).

29   "Confidence" must not only be restored in the ability of the system to generate adequate profits but also in its ability to "make good" on the Anticipated Future Value (AFV) represented by a mountain of debt—estimated in 2010 at over $40 trillion for the OECD countries alone. It is in this light that the hard line of the "Troika" (the European Commission, IMF, and European Central Bank) regarding Greece's debt crisis must be understood.

30   See Sato (2015, p. 66), who correctly observes: "In the context of a dramatic increase in the volume and variety of financial securities, our best strategy for improving the calculation of the Marxian ARP [average rate of profit] must be one that focuses on disaggregating the various elements of financial and corporate profits in ways that would reduce to a minimum the fictitious elements included in its numerator." Since the current study does not attempt such a disaggregation, it must be acknowledged that the "average ROP" reported in the next section of this study cannot be considered a truly Marxian ROP. What's more, from the mid-1980s onward, the trend for our reported ROP will deviate more and more from that of the Marxian ROP, as the weight of fictitious profits increases in the statistical category "total corporate profits."

31   Just as not all corporate profits should be regarded as surplus value, neither should all of the after-tax income of the top 1 percent. An indeterminate but growing share of this income actually derives from fictitious profits.

32   Integrating estimates of the ratio of productive to unproductive labor in different sectors and industries is a notoriously difficult and arduous task. Clearly, the financial, insurance, and real estate (FIRE) sector is reasonably regarded as unproductive in Marxist terms, as are retail and wholesale trade, whose workers are involved essentially in "changing titles of ownership" to commodities that have already been produced. But it is certainly true that many "personal service" firms produce "useful effects" that assume the commodity form and represent surplus value. At the same time, however, many workers employed by productive capital (from bookkeepers and marketing specialists to supervisory personnel) are clearly not involved directly in producing commodities or surplus value and should therefore be treated as SNUL. Among the NIPA divisions producing "service commodities" that we have defined as productive and as employing productive labor are hotels, personal services, auto repairs, motion pictures, amusement and recreational services, miscellaneous repair services, health services, educational services, and social services. This classification system represents an advance over the system used by Smith and Taylor (1996) and reported in Smith (1999 and 2010), which involved the treatment of all Canadian service divisions as entirely unproductive.

33   In Smith and Butovsky (2012), we reported that the trend line for the current-cost rate of profit (S/C) between 1950 and 2007 fell slightly, while the historic-cost rate of profit ($S/C2$) registered a marginally steeper decline. Distinguishing between two phases of this 57-year period, we found that in the first, longer phase (1950–82) the unstandardized regression coefficient for S/C was 0.002, a statistically significant result. In the second, shorter phase (1983–2007), this

coefficient is 0.003. The results of the current study reflect some changes in official data measurement, as well as the extension of the time series to 2013. The period from 2007 to 2013 saw the current-cost rate of profit fall below the trend line in only one year: 2008. In Smith and Butovsky (2012), we reported results for the ROP and other ratios when "profits from the rest of the world" were added to the domestic corporate profit estimates to obtain S. The charts indicated that these additional profits had a positive impact on the ROP trend line, and that this was particularly so for the neoliberal period. As we noted, however, the difficulty with adding these "repatriated" profits to the numerator was that the value of the capital stocks standing behind them in "the rest of the world" also needed to be added to the denominator of the revised ROP. This proved impossible, however, due to the unavailability of reliable data pertaining to these stocks.

34   Chart 2 displays our modified version of Shaikh's (2010, p. 48) "profit-of-enterprise" ROP—the rate of profit for US non-financial corporations measured as the ratio of *after-tax* profits to the beginning of year current cost of their plant and equipment. It should be noted that this ROP is not the rate of profit of "productive capital" alone, as it includes profits realized by commercial capital and unproductive capital operating in the service sector, as well.

35   See Bakir and Campbell (2010).

36   See McIntyre and Nguyen (2004).

37   See Shaikh (2010, pp. 49–50).

38   The trend line for S/V is flat in the 1950–82 phase but registers a strong, statistically significant rise in the 1983–2013 phase (its unstandardized regression coefficient in the latter phase is 0.014).

39   In *Capital*, vol. 1, Marx writes, "I call the value composition of capital, in so far as it is determined by its technical composition and mirrors the changes in the latter, the *organic composition* of capital. Wherever I refer to the composition of capital, without further qualification, its organic composition is always understood" (Marx 1977, p. 762, emphasis added). For the OCC to mirror changes in the TCC in value terms, it needs to be conceived as the value ratio of "the mass of the means of production employed" to "the mass of labor necessary for their employment"—that is, as the value of the constant capital stock in relation to the total new value ($s + v$) produced by living labor. Means of production include circulating constant capital as well as fixed capital—but it is the tendency for the value of the fixed constant capital to rise in relation to the living labor performed that is the cornerstone of the LTRPF. Smith (1984) found that a calculation of the capital stock that included circulating constant capital did not produce *trends* for the rate of profit or the OCC between 1947 and 1980 in Canada that were different from a calculation that included only fixed capital. In the present study of the US economy, as in Smith and Taylor (1996), only a fixed-capital measure of the capital stock was employed.

40   In Smith and Butovsky (2012), we noted that the "upward trend for the historical-cost OCC is even more pronounced, with the latter reaching a peak of 2.43 in 2000 compared to 1.16 in 1950."

41   For the first (1950–82) phase, the regression coefficients for the OCC and the VCC are 0.04 and 0.05 respectively, while for the second (1983–2013) phase it is −0.03 for the OCC. In the second phase, the VCC registers a flat trend.

42   After fluctuating between 69 and 76 percent between 1993 and 2005, the total financial liabilities of OECD governments as a percentage of the OECD's

combined GDP rose rapidly between 2006 and 2011, from 74.5 to 102.4 percent. The total deficit for OECD countries saw a sixfold increase as a percentage of combined GDP between 2006 and 2010 (–1.3 percent to 7.7 percent) (OECD 2011).

References

Albo, G., S. Gindin, and L. Panitch (2010) *In and Out of Crisis*, PM Press.

Bakir, E. and A. Campbell (2010) "Neoliberalism, the Rate of Profit and the Rate of Accumulation," *Science and Society*, Vol 74, No 3.

Bellofiore, R., ed. (1998) *Marxian Economics: A Reappraisal—Essays on Volume III of Capital, Volume 2: Profits, Prices and Dynamics*, Macmillan Press.

Brenner, R. (2006) *The Economics of Global Turbulence: The Advanced Capitalist Economies from Long Boom to Long Downturn, 1945–2005*, Verso.

Campbell, M. and G. Reuten, eds., (2002) *The Culmination of Capital—Essays on Volume III of Marx's Capital*, Palgrave.

Carchedi, G. (1991) *Frontiers of Political Economy*, Verso.

———. (2011) *Behind and Beyond the Crisis*, unpublished manuscript, available at http://gesd.free.fr/carchedib.pdf.

———. (2012) *Behind the Crisis: Marx's Dialectics of Value and Knowledge*, Haymarket.

Carchedi, G. and M. Roberts (2013) "A Critique of Heinrich's 'Crisis Theory, the Law of the Tendency of the Rate of Profit to Fall, and Marx's Studies in the 1870s,'" *Monthly Review*, December 1.

Duménil, G. and D. Lévy (2004) *Capital Resurgent: Roots of the Neoliberal Revolution*, Harvard University Press.

Freeman, A. (1998) "A General Refutation of Okishio's Theorem and a Proof of the Falling Rate of Profit," in R. Bellofiore, ed., *Marxian Economics*, MacMillan.

Heinrich, M. (2013) "Crisis Theory, the Law of the Tendency of the Rate of Profit to Fall, and Marx's Studies in the 1870s," *Monthly Review*, Vol 64, No 11.

Jackson, J. K. (2011) "U.S. Direct Investment Abroad: Trends and Current Issues," Congressional Research Service, http://www.crs.gov/.

Kliman, A. (2007) *Reclaiming "Marx's Capital": A Refutation of the Myth of Inconsistency*, Lexington Books.

———. (2010) *The Persistent Fall in Profitability Underlying the Current Crisis*, Marxist-Humanist Initiative.

———. (2012) *The Failure of Capitalist Production: Underlying Causes of the Great Recession*, Pluto Press.

Laibman, D. (1992) *Value, Technical Change and Crisis*, M. E. Sharpe.

Lapavitsas, C. and I. Levina (2010) "Financial Profit: Profit from Production and Profit upon Alienation," *Research on Money and Finance*, Discussion Papers, No 24.

Leontieff, W. (1982) "The Distribution of Work and Income," *Scientific American*, Vol 247, No 3.

Mage, S. (1963) "The 'Law of the Falling Tendency of the Rate of Profit': Its Place in the Marxian Theoretical System and Relevance to the U.S. Economy," PhD thesis, Columbia University.

Marx, K. (1859) "Preface," *A Contribution to the Critique of Political Economy*, available at http://www.marxists.org/.

———. (1973) *Grundrisse*, M. Nicolaus, trans., Penguin.

———. (1977) *Capital*, Vol 1, B. Fowkes, trans., Vintage.

————. (1978) *Capital*, Vol 3, Progress Publishers.

————. (1981) *Capital*, Vol 2, D. Fernbach, trans., Vintage.

McIntyre, R. S. and T. D. Coo Nguyen (2004) *Corporate Taxes in the Bush Years*, joint publication of Citizens for Tax Justice and the Institute on Taxation and Economic Policy.

Mohun, S. (1996) "Productive and Unproductive Labor in the Labor Theory of Value," *Review of Radical Political Economics*, Vol 28, No 4.

————. (2005) "On Measuring the Wealth of Nations: The U.S. Economy, 1964–2001," *Cambridge Journal of Economics*, Vol 29.

Moseley, F. (1991) *The Falling Rate of Profit in the Postwar United States Economy*, St. Martin's Press.

Organisation for Economic Co-operation and Development (2011) *Economic Outlook*, Vol 2011, No 89.

Okishio, N. (1961) "Technical Changes and the Rate of Profit," *Kobe University Economic Review*, Vol 7.

Reuten, G. (2006) "On the Quantitative Homology between Circulating Capital and Capital Value—The Problem of Marx's and the Marxian Notion of 'Variable Capital,'" Paper for *Historical Materialism* Annual Conference 2006, "New Directions in Marxist Theory."

Reuten, G. and M. Williams (1989) *Value Form and the State*, Routledge.

Saad-Filho, A. (2002) *The Value of Marx: Political Economy for Contemporary Capitalism*, Routledge.

Saez, E. and T. Piketty (2015) "Income Inequality in the United States, 1913–1998," Excel spreadsheet updated to 2013, available at http://elsa.berkeley.edu/~saez/.

Sato, T. (2015) "On Freeman's New Approach to Calculating the Rate of Profit," *Journal of Australian Political Economy*, No 74.

Shaikh, A. (1978) "Political Economy and Capitalism: Notes on Dobb's Theory of Crisis," *Cambridge Journal of Economics*, Vol 2.

————. (1999) "Explaining the Global Economic Crisis," *Historical Materialism*, Vol 5.

————. (2010) "The First Great Depression of the 21st Century," in L. Panitch, G. Albo, and V. Chibber, eds., *Socialist Register 2011*, Merlin Press.

Shaikh, A. and A. E. Tonak, (1994) *Measuring the Wealth of Nations: The Political Economy of National Accounts*, Cambridge University Press.

Smith, M. E. G. (1984) "The Falling Rate of Profit," MA thesis, University of Manitoba.

————. (1993) "Productivity, Valorization and Crisis: Socially Necessary Unproductive Labor in Contemporary Capitalism," *Science and Society*, Vol 57, No 3.

————. (1994) *Invisible Leviathan: The Marxist Critique of Market Despotism beyond Postmodernism*, University of Toronto Press.

————. (2010) *Global Capitalism in Crisis: Karl Marx and the Decay of the Profit System*, Fernwood Publishing.

————. (2011) "Author's Reply to Reviews of 'Global Capitalism in Crisis: Karl Marx and the Decay of the Profit System,'" *Global Discourse*, Vol 2, No 1, available at http://global-discourse.com/contents.

————. (2014) *Marxist Phoenix: Studies in Historical Materialism and Marxist Socialism*, Canadian Scholars Press International.

Smith, M. E. G. and J. Butovsky (2012) "Profitability and the Roots of the Global Crisis: Marx's 'Law of the Tendency of the Rate of Profit to Fall' and the US Economy, 1950–2007," *Historical Materialism*, Vol 20, No 4.

Smith, M. E. G. and K. W. Taylor (1996) "Profitability Crisis and the Erosion of Popular Prosperity: The Canadian Economy, 1947–1991," *Studies in Political Economy*, Vol 49.

Sweezy, P. (1968) *The Theory of Capitalist Development*, Monthly Review Press.

Webber, M. and D. Rigby (1996) *The Golden Age Illusion: Rethinking Postwar Capitalism*, Guilford Press.

CHAPTER 14

DERIVATIVES AND CAPITALIST MARKETS: THE SPECULATIVE HEART OF CAPITAL

Tony Norfield

1. Introduction

More than ten years after the world crisis broke in 2008, many countries continue to be plagued by high unemployment and stagnant economic activity. Even in the United States, chronic problems remain. Surely, it is a little odd for a supposedly vibrant capitalist economy to be one where the US central bank, the Federal Reserve, is still holding more than $1,700 billion of mortgage-backed securities it bought from stricken private sector financial companies. The central bank is cautious about raising official interest rates, even though they remain below the rate of inflation. There is clearly something wrong with the capitalist system. But because many symptoms of the crisis were financial—a huge growth of borrowing, lending, and financial trading in the years leading up to 2008—many people believe that the cause of the trouble was also "financial" in some sense. So, problems could be resolved, or at least new ones avoided, by fixing "finance." This perspective avoids asking awkward questions about whether the source of the crisis lies in some more fundamental features of the capitalist economy, ones that might also lie behind the expansion of the financial system. It is nevertheless a convenient view for the ruling elites, helping to focus debate on forms of regulation to make sure that banks do not trade "excessively" or lend too much compared to their capital, rather than on how capitalism is a dysfunctional and destructive system.

One part of the financial system figured large in the years leading up to 2008, and also later: financial derivatives. The huge scale of derivatives trading made them easy to single out as examples of finance gone wild, which should be brought back to sensible proportions to restore order to capitalist markets. For example, in 2013 the annual turnover of interest rate derivatives alone was almost thirty times the value of world GDP.[1] Derivatives trading would appear to be as distant from "real" economic activity as making bets on how many goals are scored in a soccer match is from actually playing in the match. However, derivatives are a natural development of capitalist markets, not an unfortunate, destabilizing anomaly, and they are far from being the source of today's economic problems. Instead, the difficulties faced by capitalists in making a profit from their business operations were what spurred the growth of derivatives. Derivatives, and other forms of financial dealing, are best seen as tools used by capital in the major powers—especially in the United States and the United Kingdom, the major banking giants—to try and overcome weak profitability.

This chapter begins by explaining how to understand the origin of derivatives, showing how they develop as a hedging tool within the capitalist market system. After looking at the extent to which it is possible to distinguish speculation from hedging, I then put the growth of derivatives trading in the context of declining profitability. Examples of the role of derivatives in commodity speculation, the mortgage debt fiasco and the sovereign debt crises illustrate these points. These observations are based on the experience I gained from some twenty years of working in bank dealing rooms in the City of London, running research teams. During that time, I took positions in interest rate swaps and futures, forward currency values, "non-deliverable forwards" and a variety of "vanilla" and "exotic" currency options. Working with dealers and bank clients (non-financial corporations, pension funds, hedge funds, central banks, etc.) gave me insight into the role of financial derivatives in the capitalist economy.

2. What Are Derivatives?

The simple definition of a derivative is deceptively straightforward. It is a financial contract whose value is derived from something else. However, the capitalist market throws up a confusing array of "somethings." The value of the derivative contract could depend on anything from the price of copper, to the price of a particular financial security (a government bond or a company's share price), to the temperature, to the risk of a default on a debt payment, to the price of *another* derivative contract (as in the case of an option on a futures contract). Or the derivative contract's value may reflect the price of many other financial assets (in the case of the FTSE-100 Index), or it may have other features that will affect its value.[2] Whatever else it is, the derivative is *not* the underlying asset or security; it is not a bond, a company share, a bank loan or deposit.

For example, the owner of a futures contract to buy a tonne of copper at a particular price does not actually own the copper. He or she will only do so when the contract expires, for example in December 2018, and only if the money is advanced to buy the relevant number of tonnes of the metal. Ahead of that time, the buyer of the futures contract is only exposed to moves in the price of copper. The contract may be sold and a profit or a loss realized, given the difference between the price of copper stipulated in the contract and the latest market price. A similar thing is true of all futures contracts, whether on commodities or financial instruments or anything else. For options derivatives, the owner of an option to buy a financial security at a particular price in December 2018 does not gain any dividend or accrued interest from ownership before the option is exercized, because he or she *does not own the actual security.* All that is owned is a contract to buy the security at a particular price up to the expiry date (and the option would not be exercized if the relevant market price was lower than the option strike price). For interest rate swap (IRS) derivatives, the counterparties to a deal agree to exchange one sequence of interest payments for another. For example, one might pay the other a fixed rate of 2 percent every six months for the next five years on a sum of $100 million, while the other agrees to receive this in exchange for paying in return whatever was the six-month money market interest rate on the same sum of $100 million. The $100 million is not exchanged, only the different *interest payments* on it.

Given these features of derivatives, it is quite misleading for Bryan and Rafferty (2006a, p. 90) to argue that derivatives are "commodities that play multiple monetary functions" and that their "commodified commensuration is what makes financial derivatives fundamentally different from other paper titles, such as fiat money." This "commensuration" is simply the calculated value of the derivative, which is almost exclusively expressed in terms of a major currency, most often US dollars. There is no "derivative currency" money, with units of account measured in pages of contract terms, or with denominations determined by how far it is from the underlying asset value. The commensuration comes through the fiat money value of the derivative that they claim derivatives have somehow transcended.[3]

This so-called commensuration via derivatives is also particularly *unstable* because of the typically complex relationship between the value of the derivative and the price of the underlying security. In the case of bonds or equities, the underlying security's price is *already* the capitalized value of expected future revenues—what Marx called "fictitious capital." Here the "money or capital value represents either no capital at all, as in the case of state debts, or is regulated independently of the value of real capital [in the case of equities, for example] which it represents" (Marx 1974, ch. 29, p. 468). A *derivative* on fictitious capital, as with bond or equity futures and options, has a value that is regulated in yet another independent manner, even further removed from the underlying capital or commodity on which it is ultimately based.

Take the example of call options, although similar arguments apply to all derivatives. After it is bought, the value of a call option to buy a commodity or security at a particular fixed price will range from zero to an unlimited positive number of dollars, euros, sterling, or other currency. Another call option with the *same* expiry date and the *same* strike price for the *same* security might have a "barrier" condition attached to it. The condition may be that the second call option is only valid if the security's price *falls* to a certain level over the next two weeks (a "knock in" barrier). They are both derivatives on the same security, but each derivative's value will be calculated very differently. This calls into question the validity of both the commensuration and the claim that derivatives are a form of money.

Furthermore, there is only a limited time during which a derivative is valid. It is no good if the underlying security's price means the derivative does not "make money" up to expiry, but would have made 10 percent the day after. The derivative did not generate a profit, because the bet is one day wrong. Even depreciating dollar bills do not have an expiry date! These features of derivatives are hardly ones that can mark them out as "distinctly global money" (Bryan and Rafferty 2006a, p. 93) or as "distinctively capitalist money" (p. 77). That opinion loses sight of some key roles of money: derivatives give a quite unstable "measure of value," as well as a very unsatisfactory "store of value."

Bryan and Rafferty are correct that derivatives are an "integral expression of capitalism" (2006b, p. 214). But their notion of derivatives seems to have been influenced more by the huge volume and diversity of derivatives trading, and its explosive growth in recent decades, than by an examination of what has driven these developments. Writing two years before the crisis struck, the authors do allow for the risk that a financial crisis would have a "pervasive and speedy impact" because of the global spread of derivatives. Yet they can also argue that the global financial system is "regulated, in the sense of being kept orderly [*sic*], by processes and conventions in which derivatives play a central role" (pp. 208–9). Implicitly, they allow for the role that derivatives play in helping spur capital accumulation, but they ignore the problems of capital accumulation and falling profitability, and how these factors explain the context for the growth of derivatives in the first place.

3. Market Risk and Capitalism's Need for Price Insurance

The market-based origin of derivatives is found by considering the simplest form of the purchase and sale of commodities. The sale of a commodity for money and the purchase of another commodity with this money bring a number of risks. If producers of the first commodity cannot sell their output, they are stuck with a use value that has no exchange value. If they *can* sell it, then they may receive less cash than bargained for. With that cash, they may not be able to buy another commodity, either because the price is too high, or because there is none on the market at any price. Or they may decide to hold on to the cash and not purchase anything, so that another commodity seller will be disappointed.

There are two broad areas of risk for any capitalist company. Firstly, that the demand for particular commodities may collapse or the supply of particular commodities dries up; secondly, that the price received by the seller of a commodity is "too low" or the price demanded by the seller of another, needed commodity is "too high." Companies attempt to cover the first area of risk with various forms of supply contract to deliver the products needed. Derivatives are based on the *second* area of risk, one focused on price levels.

If the prices paid for commodities bought and sold are such that a company can make no profit, then there is no point in producing them. So the reality of the capitalist market creates a demand for some form of price insurance to cover against unexpected losses. Outside of commodity prices, there are clearly other areas of commercial risk faced by companies in their business operations. Levels of interest rates and exchange rates are the most important; the more volatile these are, the more they might damage profitability. And this is where derivatives come in.

The scale and scope of derivatives markets have exploded in recent decades, although there are historical examples of derivatives trading dating back to the mid-nineteenth century, and even to before the emergence of capitalism.[4] Derivatives were initially developed for important agricultural and industrial commodities that had volatile prices. A much-later development was in *financial* derivatives. These came to prominence from the early 1970s, with the break up of the Bretton Woods financial system. Chicago futures exchanges began trading currencies in 1972 and Treasury bonds in 1975. Several important futures and derivatives exchanges were also set up in Europe (in the UK, Germany, and France) after the dramatic moves in currencies, interest rates, oil prices and other commodities in the 1970s. Derivatives emerge from the instability of capitalist market exchange.

4. The "Real World" Demand for Derivatives

Derivatives are often seen as a tool that speculators use to make bets on prices. This view would appear to be supported by the fact that the largest share of trading in derivatives is done by financial companies, rather than by non-financial companies who might need to hedge their commercial price risks. For example, data from the Bank for International Settlements show that non-financial companies transacted less than 20 percent of different derivatives contracts.[5] However, just because financial companies do most of the derivatives trading does not imply that derivatives exist only to satisfy the demands of speculators. Financial companies themselves may also be using derivatives to hedge their risks, rather than simply to make a bet on price movements. Banks and other financial companies—not just industrial and commercial companies—are exposed to changes in interest rates and exchange rates that will impact the cost of their funding or the value of their future revenues. So it is a mistake to identify all financial trading with speculation.[6]

Furthermore, even if "pure" speculators make up the bulk of derivatives trading, this does not mean that the *underlying demand* for derivatives originates with them. This point can be seen from the following observations: Firstly, there are no significant markets for derivatives where there is a complete absence of commercial hedgers. This suggests that commercial hedging is a critical factor in such markets. Secondly, the history of derivatives exchanges shows that trading will not develop if the contract that is traded fails to reflect the price risk faced by a wide range of commercial companies. When the derivative contract fails to do this, it will fail as a derivative because companies cannot use it to hedge their risks. This is so, even if the contract is easy to trade and thus suitable for speculators. So this epitome of exchange value, the derivative, must have a commercial use value![7] The core demand for derivatives comes from those in the economy who have to hedge a commercial risk. It does not come from speculators.

5. Speculation and Hedging

If "non-speculative" demand is necessary to support derivatives trading, why do trading volumes seem to be dominated by speculators? The answer is found by considering the risk-management decisions of those doing the trading.

In the case of a company *hedging* its price risk with derivatives, the position taken will offset the risk of a change in the price of the underlying asset or liability. Assuming that the contract is a precise hedge—in other words, the maturity and payout from the derivatives contract offsets the price risk exactly—there is no need for the hedging company to trade again. It holds the derivatives contract to maturity. On maturity, the company will have a gain (or loss) from the derivative that matches the loss (or gain) on the underlying asset or liability. In these circumstances, a hedger would not have to trade frequently, or even more than once. Additional trades by the hedging company are only needed where the hedge needs to be altered due to a change in the value of the asset or liability that is being hedged (for example, when an order gets revised). The volume of trading by hedgers is limited by the scope of their regular business operations.

The case of a *speculator* trading in derivatives is quite different. If a speculator buys or sells a derivatives contract, there is no "underlying position" of an owned asset or a liability that is being hedged. The change in price of the derivative represents a change in the speculator's profit and loss account, and there is no offsetting of loss/gain from a separate asset. The speculator is managing a trading book and will therefore change his or her trading positions in derivatives to fit the risk profile that is required. If the positions are losing value, the speculator may want to place bets in the opposite direction to close out the exposure. Or there may simply be a change of mind about the direction of prices, for example, becoming "bullish" on a market that was previously thought to be going down. Or profits could be taken on contracts previously sold, and which went down in price, through buying them back.

The gap between the prices at which a professional trader agrees to buy and sell (the bid-offer spread) is an important part of gaining a trading profit, aside from betting correctly on the movement of the derivatives price. For this reason, only a small net exposure to price moves might still make significant profits. Also for this reason, the scale of trading undertaken by speculators is not directly related to the amount of their risk exposure. Making ten bets that the price will go up is more risky than making fifty that they will go up and another fifty offsetting bets that they will go down, even if the latter volume of deals is ten times larger.[8]

Trading-book risk management makes it likely that the speculator (or "non-commercial" trader) side of the market will engage in a higher volume of trading than will the company-hedger side of the market. This is an inevitable and pervasive feature of derivatives markets. It is also important for speculators to be present in the market for such hedging to take place, and the history of derivatives markets shows that speculators are necessary for their effective operation. It is bound to be difficult for a non-financial company to find other hedgers with exactly offsetting risks. Here is where activity by "market makers" or speculative dealers is critical. In derivatives exchanges, dealers have commitments to provide such prices as part of their membership rules if they are designated as market makers. In over-the-counter (OTC) markets, outside the official exchanges, banks usually act as market makers for their clients. This market making is speculative, but without it the market will remain illiquid and will not function.[9]

It is a mistake to identify *all* the trading of financial companies as the trading of "speculators," since this will also include deals done to hedge their business risks. By the same token, the so-called "commercial" or "non-financial" companies will also do speculative deals rather than simply hedge. Accounting rules attempt to determine whether a company's deal enters its "trading book" or whether it can be classed as a "hedge." Yet there are many ambiguities here.

Firstly, note that a company that does *not* have any hedges for its market price exposure is effectively gambling ("speculating") that future price moves will not damage its business. Companies thus tend to hedge their risks with derivatives; the alternatives to hedging are either to take whatever the market delivers, or not to do any business at all! The fact that access to hedging is easier and cheaper for the larger companies is also one element in the process of monopolization.

However, a company that has hedged its business risks may decide to take the hedges off again. For example, it may have thought that there was a risk of a fall in the value of a currency that would damage its revenues. That fall may have taken place, so the hedge turned out to be profitable (offsetting the implicit loss on its commercial business). But the company may then unwind the hedge at a profit, believing no further fall, or even a rise in the currency, is now likely. Even if a company plans to be fully hedged, it will have some timing leeway (intra-day, intra-week, or over the period to end-month, etc.) to pick the best levels of market prices from which to buy or sell when conducting the hedge. This kind of small-scale speculation when dealing in derivatives is very common in corporate treasury departments. As I know from my observations of company behavior when working in banks, big corporations are also active traders in derivatives, competing with the banks and other dealers, and they usually have to meet profit targets on their dealings.

Companies may also make a policy decision to hold out for better prices at which to hedge. They will then aggressively hedge when prices go to the desired levels. If that bet does not work, they might change their minds and panic to hedge if prices continue to move in the "wrong" direction. Dramatic moves in market prices can therefore result from *hedging* as much as from speculation. For example, Japanese life insurance companies, owners of a huge volume of US financial assets, have caused sharp moves in the dollar–yen exchange rate as a result of changes in the currency "hedging ratio" for their holdings of US bonds.

One cannot distinguish "speculation" from "hedging" by looking at the data for derivatives trading from the BIS or from individual commodity exchanges. Distinguishing "financial" dealers from "non-financial," or "commercial" dealers from "non-commercial" does not capture the motives for the transaction.[10] *But the problem goes beyond how to define or measure speculation.* The real issue is that price uncertainty and risk confront all businesses in the capitalist market system. Each must act in a way that will protect and expand company profitability; all speculators will be hedgers and all hedgers will be speculators to some degree. A US Senate report into speculation correctly made the point that the line between speculation and hedging is "exceedingly difficult to draw" (US Senate 2009, p. 54).

6. Profitability and the Financial Form of the Crisis

The immediate phase of the crisis after 2007 took on a dramatic financial form. Major banks and other institutions became insolvent, money markets seized up, and governments and central banks abandoned "free market" rhetoric and tried to rescue the financial system. Speculative bubbles, banking crises, and crashes have characterized the history of capitalism, but the incidence of banking crises has risen since the 1970s. The authors of one study of these remarked that "the tally of crises is particularly high for the world's financial centers: the United Kingdom, the United States, and France" (Rogoff and Reinhart 2008). This fact implies that something *systematic* is going on.

What can appear to be a purely *financial* crisis is really the end result of developments that emanate from problems capitalism has in producing enough profit. The origins of the financial *form* of the crisis we see today lie in the promotion of financial business, particularly by American and British imperialism, and especially beginning in the late 1970s.[11] The policy decisions of the US and UK governments to liberalize financial markets were based upon them seeing these as a key area of the global economy in which they had a competitive advantage. This advantage is based upon the British and US imperialist role in the world economy, and it was an important option for them, especially given how difficult it was for them to try and regain industrial competitiveness.[12] The fact that the policies have persisted under administration after administration, Republican or Democrat (in the US) and Conservative or Labour (in the UK)—with versions of these in other countries—shows the degree to which the financial policies are *embedded in the core of the system*. The origin of these systematic policies can only be properly explained by capitalism's crisis of profitability.

Many things complicate measures of the rate of profit on capitalist investment—not simply companies hiding or boosting profits by accounting tricks. Even the location of the investment that brought the profit is difficult to pin down when giant corporations supply their own global network, or when they get cheap inputs from other companies in low-wage countries who must bow to their every whim. Also, a key distinction of Marxist value theory, that between activities that are productive and unproductive, cannot be determined easily when using economic data: many companies have both kinds of operation, which are not distinguished in the numbers. Furthermore, a company might be able to register a large profit on financial investments that have nothing to do with any actual production at all.

From the data available, I do not think it is possible to get a good approximation for the rate of profit on capitalist production, as understood by Marx.[13] But that is not to say nothing can be done to take the profit pulse of the capitalist system. One method is to see what the profitability data imply at first sight, and then to examine if other evidence would argue for a different perspective.

The United States has the most comprehensive, detailed, and easily available numbers, and this is why most analysts looking at the question of profitability focus on US data. Almost all measures of the rate of profit for major countries show a trend decline from the 1950s into the early 1970s (Armstrong et al. 1984). As a result, there is little dispute about falling profitability as the underlying cause of the 1970s economic and financial turmoil, at least among those who base their views on some version of Marxist theory.[14] For example, figure 14.1 shows one measure of the US corporate rate of profit, in which there is a clear downtrend in both pre-tax and post-tax measures from the late 1940s into the early 1980s. Pre-tax profits are obviously higher than post-tax profits because, despite their best efforts, US governments have never managed to make the overall corporate tax rate zero or negative.

For the subsequent period, from the 1980s into the mid-2000s, most writers argue that the rate of profit was on a rising trend, at least the one for US capitalists. There is far from universal agreement that this is correct, since a number of reasonable adjustments to the data could be made, but as the plain data stand they do show an uptrend from the mid-1980s to 2013, although one severely punctuated by a slump in the late 1990s (which witnessed the crises centered on Russia and Asia) and another drop in the 2007–2008 market seizure. Many people argue from this that the crisis starting in 2007 in the rich countries was a result of financial excess, rather than having any relationship to a capitalist profitability crisis. The financial form of the latest crisis—a massive buildup of debts, speculation, fraudulent deals, and so forth—has encouraged this view.

It would be odd if there were a major crisis and the evidence showed that the rate of profit in the years ahead of the crisis had been relatively high. The data in figure 14.1 do indeed show relatively high rates of profit ahead of 2007, which would appear to give support to a "financial malfunction" thesis. However, one does not need to accept the available data uncritically, especially that for the United States.

There are four factors that cast different light on the calculations of rising US profitability beginning in the 1980s. The first was the attack on working-class living standards by the US government and business, including the use of migrant labor and the marginalization of labor unions. To some extent, this effect can be measured, although there are debates regarding which productivity, price, wage, and benefits data to use; nevertheless, this would have had an impact. Yet it was likely to have been more of a one-off factor in the 1980s, and most measures of US rates of profit show lower rates into the end of the 1990s.

A second factor has been, arguably, more important, but it does not directly appear in any US data: the impact of low-cost products available to US capital through trading relationships with low-wage countries, particularly China. US data do show the profits from foreign investment (these are not included in fig. 14.1, which covers domestic profitability), but there is no accounting for how the low cost of imported cheap labor products boosted the recorded profits of US corporations. If the goods are supplied cheaply, then that is judged to be what they are worth, and the huge profit margins made on the sale to final consumers are then supposedly due to "value added" after they are unloaded at the port. The domestic profits of US companies (such as Walmart and Apple) appear to come from their domestic operations, but in reality part will depend upon these products of super-exploited labor (Smith 2012). This would help explain the apparent paradox that while US domestic corporate profits might be high, domestic US investment remains weak. Fans of the imperial system applauded these events, which in the United States were summed up as the "Great Moderation," with a lower cost of living for most US workers coinciding with cheap inputs for business, resulting in reasonably steady growth and lower inflation. They did not look into the stratification of global production between rich and poor countries on which this development was based. Immigration controls in rich countries, with strong popular support for these, have prevented an equalization of rates of exploitation globally.

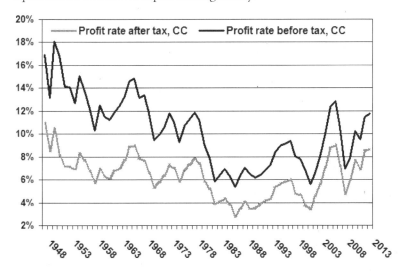

Figure 14.1. US corporate rate of profit (%), 1948–2013. The rate of profit is calculated by dividing current year domestic corporate profits by an average of the domestic fixed assets for the current end-year and the previous end-year. CC means the "current cost" measure of fixed assets is used. Source: BEA NIPA, Table 6.1, line 2; Table 6.17, line 2; Table 6.19, line 2.

Of course, this point is also relevant beyond the United States. In the United Kingdom, to give one example, there was an unprecedented period of uninterrupted quarter-on-quarter GDP growth from 1991 to early 2008. This entrenched an unrealistic optimism about the capitalist economy: things could only get better! It led both ordinary people and financial analysts to discount the possibility of any potential setback, leading to high levels of borrowing and little regard for risk.

Cheap foreign labor was a significant boost to global profitability, but its incremental impact is now likely to be much less. It is getting more difficult for major corporations to find the extra tens of millions of ultra-cheap productive workers, and wages have begun to rise in China, India, Bangladesh, and elsewhere.

The third factor boosting US corporate profitability for industrial and commercial capitalists was progressively lower nominal and inflation-adjusted interest rates. This development was based on an unwinding of the previous, very high rates that followed the tightening of Federal Reserve policy by Fed Chairman Paul Volcker in the early 1980s, on the success of capital in attacking the US working class, on the low cost of imports, and on Asian countries accumulating huge foreign exchange reserves (buying US securities and so reducing their yields) as an insurance against financial trouble after the crisis of 1997–98. The end result was a sharp rise in US consumer borrowing that gave more credit-fueled demand for the products of industry and commerce, as well as a rise in the price of securities and a boom in financial trading, which helped boost profitability in the financial sector, too. These influences reinforced each other to raise the recorded rate of profit in the years leading up to 2007. As we know, that credit bubble burst.

A final element missing from the data in figure 14.1 is the financial rescue operation mounted by the US Federal Reserve from 2007. What is one to think about buoyant private sector profitability that has been sustained by aggressive action—otherwise known as a bailout—from the central bank? After 2008, the US Fed bought many hundreds of billions of dollars of both US Treasury securities and private mortgage-backed securities in its "quantitative easing" programs. As of early 2017, the Fed had some $2,460 billion of Treasury bonds and $1,770 billion of mortgage securities on its books, roughly 25 percent of US GDP. Buying Treasuries pushed all borrowing rates lower in the US economy, despite banks still being unwilling to lend to what were now more risky projects. Buying mortgage-backed securities also took unsaleable "assets" from crisis-hit US financial companies. Many American citizens making payments on their mortgages might be surprised to learn that the recipient is actually the US government! Still, you can't keep an innovative capitalist system down. When the US

Treasury pays interest on its bonds and notes to the US Fed, the Fed ends up giving most of the money back again. The wonders of imperial finance!

During the initial phase of the crisis, in 2007–2008, the Fed boosted its lending to financial companies dramatically and undertook a series of rescue operations. These were largely reversed as what remained of the US financial system was put back on its feet by ultra-low funding rates and mergers. What was not reversed, at least up to mid-2017, were the Fed's purchases of US Treasuries and mortgage securities, even though the US government had long declared the crisis over.[15]

This is the real-world backdrop for the US data on profitability. As these summary points indicate, international and national financial developments are multifaceted, and their relationship to the data on the rate of profit is complex. But my argument is that one should not look upon any figures showing credit-fueled profit rates for the period up to 2007, still less the more-recent data, as a sign that there was no problem with profitability.

Financial derivatives were another dimension of the developments just discussed. The role of derivatives was to help extend the speculative boom, and in that sense they made the crisis worse than it might have otherwise been, especially since the deals spread far beyond the United States, overcoming any more-local barriers. However, derivatives did not cause the crisis; they merely helped to give it a peculiar intensity and financial form. Low growth and low profitability were the reasons for the boom in derivatives trading and other forms of "financial innovation." Alongside other aspects of the credit system, derivatives can give the impression that risks are lower than reality, and they help to continue the flow of recorded profits and extra business based on speculation-driven demand.[16] A blip in the system, for instance a loan that does not get repaid as expected, can then trigger a financial collapse as it calls into question the assumptions behind a myriad of other deals. This is what is really meant by a "lack of confidence" in financial markets: a fear that the expected values are *illusory*. The financial collapse impacts the "real" economy, as credit is withdrawn and the funds lent by banks dry up, even those to previously viable companies. The end result is a worse crisis, when it finally occurs.

7. Finance, Derivatives and Crises

Derivatives can play a part in financial debacles, but not always. It is important to examine the circumstances surrounding crisis events, especially since financial dealing can translate a more hidden, underlying problem into something that looks like the cause was a financial one. Three examples follow.

Pension funds and commodity markets

When the oil price moved up from $90 to $150 in the first half of 2008 and then slumped down to $40 by year-end, even the most anti-regulation, free-market US lawmaker was concerned about market instability and the potential for damage to the economy from speculation. What gained particular attention was the influx of investment funds into commodity markets, along with accompanying signs of increased price volatility. Commodity derivatives markets are much smaller than the markets for financial derivatives. This means that the impact on prices of $1 billion invested in commodity derivatives is large compared to the impact it would have in foreign-exchange or interest-rate markets.

One witness testifying to a US Senate committee noted that there had been a "new category of participant in the commodities futures markets: Institutional Investors" (Masters 2008).[17] These included company and government pension funds, university endowments, sovereign wealth funds, and other institutional investors. This challenges the popular picture of speculators as outrageous gamblers after a fast buck. However, he called these funds "speculators" because they bought futures contracts hoping for price increases, rather than using futures as a hedge. This is technically correct, but the fact that the funds are long-term investors in commodities does not sit well with the usual understanding of a speculator.

A large number of global pension funds and other institutional investors bought into commodities from the early 2000s because the returns on regular financial investments that had been their core assets (especially equities, but also bonds) were poor. Major equity markets had plunged in value by some 50 percent or more between 2000 and early 2003, and long-term bond yields had fallen to levels significantly below those prevailing in the 1990s—certainly in nominal terms, but also in real, inflation-adjusted terms. While the lower bond yields delivered capital gains on existing bond holdings, they meant that new bond investments were progressively less attractive. These factors made commodities look compelling as an alternative "asset class." This decision to move into commodities was also a classic portfolio-management strategy: look for a new asset that has good potential returns and whose price has a low correlation with existing assets. This improves the risk–reward profile of the total portfolio. The scope for future commodity price increases was seen in the predictions of extra demand coming from Asian countries, especially China, as growth raised living standards.

So pension funds and other long-term investment funds moved into commodities. From a relatively small $13 billion at the end of 2003, the assets allocated to commodity index trading strategies rose by a factor of twenty to $260 billion by March 2008.

These institutions only allocated a small proportion of their assets (generally less than 5 percent) to commodities. This was far from a case of "betting the ranch," and it tallied with their conservative investment approach. However, a small share of a huge asset value nevertheless adds up to a very large sum of capital. The funds also bought futures contracts rather than the commodity itself. Instead of going to the trouble of storing barrels of oil, bushels of wheat and live cattle in the company car park, they could simply "roll over" the futures contracts into the next period before they expired, rather than accepting physical delivery of the goods.[18]

One of the major global pension funds is Stichting Pensioenfonds ABP, based in the Netherlands and responsible for the pensions of 2.8 million government and education workers. Its objective in the early 2000s was to deliver an annual return of 7 percent on investments—not easy when government bond yields were much lower (ABP Investment Objectives n.d.). It moved into commodities in the early 2000s, and by end-2009 was investing almost 3 percent of its €260 billion funds—close to €7 billion—in this "asset class." Another major fund, CalPERS, the California Public Employees' Retirement System, had investment assets of close to $200 billion at end-2009. It manages retirement benefits for some 1.6 million people, and it also began investing in commodity derivatives in 2007. Its 2008 board meeting expressed the long-term aim of allocating up to 3 percent in commodities (CalPERS 2007; Kishan 2008). The Ontario Teachers' Pension Plan, which manages pension for 289,000 active and retired teachers in Canada, also got involved in commodities and had C$1.9 billion, nearly 2 percent of its net assets, invested in commodities at end-2009 (Ontario 2009, p. 108).

The move into commodity derivatives by pension and other investment funds was the result of low returns on their financial investments, not some sudden desire to gamble on commodity prices. Those low financial returns stemmed from declining profitability in the system as a whole. It is clearly unsustainable for capitalism to have high real rates of interest when the system's profitability is low. The rate of profit for capitalist companies in the productive sector of the economy, the yields on bonds, and the dividends paid from company shares are different things, with different drivers. However, the productive sector is the originator of the surplus value that is redistributed via the financial markets to enable the payment of interest and dividends. The trend to lower financial yields was based on the underlying fall in the rate of profit, but the impact was to drive many commodity prices higher and to exacerbate market volatility. The pension funds' aim was to maximize the profitability of their investments, limit their member's contributions and generate returns to pay pensions and other income.[19]

Bank profitability, CDOs and CDS

The US mortgage debt crisis and its spread around the globe, helped by derivatives, has been discussed extensively (Dos Santos 2009; McNally 2009). Here it is worth covering only the aspects that relate to my arguments about derivatives trading. From the 1970s, US banks created securities from the payments they received from holders of mortgage debt. By the late 1980s, other forms of loans and debts to banks were also securitized, resulting in collateralized debt obligations, or CDOs. The advantage for banks was that this was a mechanism to boost their earnings and profit potential. They could sell the securities to investors, receive cash, and have fresh capital with which to fund a new round of business. Essentially, this was how banks used derivatives to shorten the period of circulation of capital, in order to boost profitability by not having to wait until the mortgages were fully repaid. From an estimated \$68 billion in 2000, global CDO issuance increased nearly sevenfold to a massive \$456 billion in 2006.[20] Alongside this, financial sector profits more than doubled over the same period.[21]

The new securities were designed to take advantage of laws on taxation and rules for bank capital adequacy set by government regulators. This was done in a way that minimized the banks' use of capital and maximized potential returns on capital. This might involve setting up a special purpose vehicle that becomes the owner of the loans, issues the CDO and pays the bank from the revenues it receives. The result was a massive issuance of such securities by US banks and their sale all around the world. This made the US subprime mortgage debt crisis a global event.

Compared to the low yields on equity and bond markets, the securities based on US mortgage debt looked attractive to a wide range of investors, both in the United States and beyond, yielding some 2 to 3 percentage points of interest above similarly rated corporate bonds. The fact that the US banks had a far better idea of the actual (*worse*) credit risk of the new securities than did the ratings agencies, or their investors, was another way that the former profited from the transactions. There have been many reports of how the credit ratings of such securities were inflated before being sold to investors, and there was no doubt a large element of fraud in this business. Perhaps the most infamous example was where the US Securities and Exchange Commission (SEC) sued Goldman Sachs for allowing one of its hedge fund clients to choose the mortgages in a CDO that were then sold to other investors. The hedge fund made \$1 billion by betting that the credit rating of the CDO would slump (Gallu 2010). However, the investors were enticed into the new market by its offer of an escape from the low-yield environment that threatened their businesses.

The collapse in value of the CDOs had nothing directly to do with the derivatives market. Neither can CDOs really be considered as a derivative.

Instead, they are a form of bond security, even if the CDO is based on a number of different payments. It was rising mortgage defaults, as the economic crisis unfolded and real estate prices fell, that prompted a drastic downgrade of credit ratings of CDOs. Where the derivatives market *did* play a role in this, however, was through the medium of another acronym: CDS.

Credit default swaps (CDSs) started life in the early 1990s, but the easing of US bank regulations after 1996 led to a boom in the growth of this financial derivative. They are a form of insurance contract, where the CDS buyer pays an annual premium and receives compensation from the seller if there is a default on payments. The payments may be for a company's bonds, for local and national government debts, or for CDO securities. Data on CDS derivatives show that in mid-2001 the notional amounts outstanding were $631.5 billion, but this multiplied by a factor of ninety-two by the end of 2007, to an astonishing $58,244 billion (ISDA 2001; BIS 2010c). Following the crisis in 2007–2008, the scale of this market slumped by nearly half to "only" $30,261 billion by June 2010.

The reason behind the extraordinary growth in CDS contracts was the same as for CDOs: they enabled banks to expand their profitability. But they did so in a different way. If banks were selling CDSs, they would earn fees. More importantly, their purchase of CDSs would enable them to save capital.[22] The debt securities on their books that had a weak credit rating demanded significant capital reserves to offset the risk that the debtors might default. With that default risk reduced by the CDS insurance contract, the required capital reserves could be cut, and the funds were then "set free" to use for further business expansion. Much of the credit risk reduced in this way was the risk from CDOs.

This mechanism accelerated the growth of the US banks' mortgage business alongside the growth in volume of CDO and CDS deals. They were very closely intertwined. What also helped spur this dramatic growth was the delusion of low credit risk, with the US economic recovery after 2001, steady growth and continued low interest rates. The growth recovery appeared to make mortgages less risky, and low interest rates made them more affordable. This opened up the route into subprime lending. One study has shown that by 2006 the banks had run out of borrowers with much ability to pay back loans, so they delved ever more deeply into the subprime risks (Barnett-Hart 2009).

CDSs were catalysts in the growth of banking and finance. The demand for them was both for financial insurance and as a way for banks to adjust their credit exposure to customers. But this demand grew dramatically because it was also a means to expand profitability at a time when low interest rates were threatening to damage financial investment revenues.

Sovereign debt crises and derivatives

Credit default swaps had also been written on the risk of countries defaulting on their debts since the late 1990s. However, in the early period, the CDSs related to countries like Indonesia, Thailand, South Korea, Russia, Mexico, and Brazil. The only major capitalist power with any significant volume of CDSs written on it was Japan, given the financial market's worries about the country's prolonged stagnation and its large and rising public sector debt. When a crisis loomed, as in a number of Asian countries and in Russia in 1997–98, speculators would of course be attracted to buy the CDSs. However, this kind of financial market activity did not cause a stir in official policy circles. The most significant thing that happened on this score was that the industry group, the International Swaps and Derivatives Association (ISDA), changed the rules on sovereign CDS contracts in 1999 and thereafter, in order to clarify the terms of default and payment details (Das 2006, pp. 279–81).[23] The real worries about financial markets betting on sovereign default only began after 2008, when attention turned to the economic plight of countries much closer to one of the centers of global power: Europe.

The shockwaves from the US subprime crisis after 2007 spread around the globe and into Europe, both because many European banks and financial institutions had bought into the related "toxic assets" from the United States, and because of the vulnerability each country already had from its own version of the financial and credit bubble of the previous years. High and rising levels of consumer credit card debt, property-market speculation, and easily available cheap bank loans were common throughout the euro-area countries and beyond, especially in the UK. The credit crunch put economic growth into reverse, while the drop in tax revenues and huge bailouts for the banking system led to a sovereign debt crisis for the weaker euro states.

Given this course of events, it makes little sense to judge that CDSs were the cause of the sovereign debt crisis. The CDS market's signals that there was a higher risk of a country defaulting on its debt were reflections of reality. In the case of Greece, the country first in the default firing line, ISDA noted that the volume of positions on Greek sovereign CDSs had barely risen from 2009 to early 2010. In any case, the $9 billion volume of positions was barely 2 percent of the value of the Greek government bond market (in excess of $400 billion), and it could not reasonably be argued that the CDS market was driving Greek government bond market prices.[24]

Neither is it valid to argue that so-called "naked" CDSs should be blamed (i.e., CDS contracts held by those who do not hold government bonds). These are part of the total of contracts registered, and these CDS buyers could well have *other* claims on the government (e.g., through profitable valuations on interest rate swaps) or claims on the private sector that would be at risk if the government defaulted. They may not have been speculating. Even if it were found, contrary to the evidence, that there had been a huge buildup of speculative CDS positions, that would still simply be a response to a crisis that was plain for all to see.

All the evidence shows that the Greek debt crisis was long in the making. The root causes were a mixture of widespread tax evasion, the misuse (since the 1980s) of EU development funds to finance current government spending, a private sector credit boom based on borrowing rates not far above Germany's after joining the Economic and Monetary Union in 2001, and declining competitiveness.[25] The Greek government used derivatives to hide its weak finances, although it is not clear whether these or other, more usual, accounting tricks, were used ahead of Greece joining the EMU in 2001; it is certain, however, that they were used afterward (Dunbar 2012). Derivatives were one of Greece's means to cover up, temporarily, its failure to develop as a successful capitalist economy. This was a result of the nature of capitalism today (and economic and political corruption in Greece), not of the excesses of the derivatives markets.

8. Derivative Dynamics and Regulation

Derivatives trading exploded in the 2000s. Measured by the notional values of contracts outstanding, the sum of all derivatives on and off exchanges rose from less than $100 trillion in 1998 to nearly $670 trillion in 2007, increasing by an average of some 25 percent per annum. While the circumstances behind this lie in the economic and profitability background, it is also important to note the official policy stance, especially in the United States, that helped fuel the boom. There were five key issues:[26]

(1) Official regulators did not respond to clear signs in the early 2000s that the major credit ratings agencies were profiting a great deal from "greasing the flow of structured products with optimistic ratings" (Levine 2010).

(2) In 1996, the US Federal Reserve allowed banks to use CDS contracts to reduce their required reserves of capital; it then did nothing to regulate the market as the volume of CDS derivatives jumped·and there was a concentration of risk. For example, insurance company AIG had exposure to some $500 billion of CDS and other derivatives, compared to its capital of just $100 billion.

(3) The US Fed, Treasury, and SEC blocked calls for more "transparency" in the OTC derivatives market and backed legislation to keep this market unregulated. The US Congress passed the Commodity

Futures Modernization Act of 2000, one consequence of which was the so-called "Enron loophole" that allowed energy commodities to be traded on nonregulated exchanges.

(4) In 2004, the US SEC allowed investment banks to use their own models of market risk to compute how much capital they needed to hold against risky securities they held as assets. Guess whether the banks over- or under-estimated the capital needed!

(5) The US Commodity Futures Trading Commission (CFTC), in charge of regulating futures markets, allowed investment banks a "swaps loophole" whereby they could use futures to "hedge" their positions with clients. This enabled hedge funds, pension funds, and so forth to accumulate market positions, via the investment banks, that were well above the regular position limits allowed for speculators.

Such criticisms of government policy come from people who would be far from considering themselves anti-capitalist. Their focus is on what they consider either to be policy mistakes, reasonable policies with unintended consequences, or even policies that they suspect were deliberate concessions to political supporters. The point of their critiques is to try to correct the "mistakes" and prevent a recurrence of similar crises.[27]

The regulation changes *were* critical in the growth of derivatives markets, and they helped generate both the scale and the global breadth of the financial crisis that broke in 2007–2008. However, this leaves an important question unanswered: Why were the rules changed?

The previous policy stance made sense for the dominant section of US capital. For the US Federal Reserve, the Treasury, and the Securities and Exchange Commission to back a particular policy, and for that policy to be supported in the US Congress, surely implies that the policy has the backing of a powerful section of the ruling class, even if there are some dissident voices. Just because the policy ends in tears is no proof that it was a gamble to benefit only a narrow stratum of financiers. More broadly, the rationale for the US authorities to "back the bankers" rests on the key role that finance plays for the US's imperial position in the global economy. New York is the world's biggest capital market, in terms of raising debt and equity funds for companies, and the United States is the second biggest foreign exchange market (after the UK). Consider also the tool of financial sanctions, which US imperialism can implement through its influence over global banking against countries, like Iran, that step out of line![28]

UK governments have taken a similar stance, although they do not have as much power to lead key changes in policy or much ability to work outside of cooperation with the United States.[29] The UK financial sector accounts for only around 1 million jobs (some 3–4 percent of the workforce), but some 7 percent of GDP and 11–12 percent of total tax revenues: in other words, it is a "high value" sector of the UK economy according to official data. The United Kingdom houses the world's biggest center for foreign exchange dealing and the largest international banking center, and it accounts for nearly half of all global trading in "over-the-counter" (OTC) interest-rate derivatives. The repeated policies favoring finance that come from the *centers of global finance*—the United States and the United Kingdom—are a deliberate and conscious strategy of the ruling class that is based on a considered assessment of their interests.

That is why there is no sign of either the United States or United Kingdom changing course, and why the UK government has defended the UK financial sector from any encroachments by policy proposals from the European Commission and elsewhere, although it has accepted some measures in an effort to limit the risk of future trouble, given the political and economic shock the crisis produced.[30] Agreed reforms for derivatives are based on putting OTC trading through a central clearing system, so that ownership and volumes can be monitored and made "more transparent." But the UK's compliance with financial reform does not extend to the proposals—from European politicians and "think tanks"—for a tax on financial transactions.

The proponents of this tax hope that it will limit both the size of the financial sector and the risk of further crises. Again, such policies are based on a belief that curbing the more financial forms of capitalist excess will help to patch up the system. As a bonus, taxes on finance are also seen as easily available revenues to fund more government spending or to finance worthy causes. For example, Oxfam believes that what it and others call a "Robin Hood" tax "would raise billions to fight poverty and tackle climate change around the world" (Oxfam 2014). It seems that there is nothing a curb on finance could not achieve—while still keeping capitalism intact, of course.

If there were new taxes on equity, bond and derivatives transactions, or other measures to constrain financial trading, this would probably curb the growth of the financial sector in the countries to which the measures apply. But these measures address only one of the symptoms of the serious crisis that capital accumulation faces, and there is only a small probability that any government of any country would do much to restrict the activities of their major corporations, banks and other financial institutions. Amendments to limit the impact of the tax will probably be made before any final (potential) implementation, and it has already been watered down from the initial proposals.

For critics of the capitalist system, there is no reason to get involved in this debate about the details of financial reform—a debate that will at best only address the symptoms of a fundamentally dysfunctional imperialist system of exploitation and oppression. As former US president Barack Obama once said in a different context, "You can put lipstick on a pig, but it is still a pig."

9. Conclusions

The growth of derivatives trading in the past two decades or so was facilitated by changes in government regulation. But the fundamental reasons why derivatives trading exploded have more to do with the attempts by banks, other financial companies, and also non-financial corporations to boost their flagging profitability and revenues. "Financial innovation" was an easier way to make money than productive investment. In this context, derivatives helped to postpone the crisis by adding fuel to a speculative boom, but they made the crisis worse. Government policymakers are now planning reforms to guard against another debacle, but reforms are unlikely to make much difference to the crisis-prone system, and there are already concerns about new kinds of financial trouble—ones more focused on levels of outstanding debt, which has increased despite the austerity measures enacted in recent years. One report notes that from 2007 to 2014, "global debt has grown by \$57 trillion, raising the ratio of debt to GDP by 17 percentage points" (McKinsey 2015, p. viii).

It is surely a sign of the decrepitude of modern capitalism, particularly in the United States and United Kingdom, when it has to rely on the leverage for profits that is provided by rules on taxation, derivative financial products and other such mechanisms. It is not a question of the banks (or finance in general) versus the "real economy." The real capitalist economy is one of value expansion, irrespective of its use-value form. That is why it is easy for "industrial" corporations to mold part of their operations into purely financial activities. This is especially easy when the lines between financial services, manufacturing operations, and commercial activities are blurred for the major corporations. The origins of banking and financial profits are not the same as for industrial or commercial capital, but each division of capital is closely linked, providing business for the others. Simply to oppose finance, banks, or derivatives is to miss the point that this is a single, integrated system of exploitation. In the United States and the United Kingdom, furthermore, the financial sector is a key dimension of their economic power as imperialist countries.[31] If this means that financial companies have been favored by Anglo–American policy, then that can hardly be a surprise.

Notes

1   Interest rate derivatives are the biggest part of the market, a category that also includes foreign exchange, commodity, and other derivatives. Data are taken from the regular Bank for International Settlements surveys of exchange traded and over-the-counter derivatives.

2   For a comprehensive textbook on options, futures, swaps, and other derivatives, see Hull (2009).

3   See my fuller critique of their arguments in Norfield (2013).

4   The Dōjima Rice Exchange in Osaka, Japan, is considered to have been the first official futures exchange market, beginning futures trading in 1730. The Chicago Board of Trade traded the first standardized futures contract in 1864. The London Metal Market and Exchange Company was founded in 1877. As another sign of the real-world basis of futures trading, the metal exchange's initial three-month forward limit for futures trading originated with the length of time it took a steam ship to arrive in London from Chile, bringing copper (LME 2011).

5   Calculations from BIS data (BIS 2010a) on over-the-counter (OTC) derivatives. For exchange-traded derivatives (ETD), the distinction made by US exchanges is usually between "non-commercial" and "commercial" transactions. Deals that are undertaken by companies with an exposure to hedge are designated commercial. Noncommercial deals tend to predominate in ETD trading as well. It is often assumed, though not justifiably so, that "commercial" deals are hedge related, while "noncommercial" deals are more, or completely, speculative in nature.

6   The BIS distinguishes between financial companies, separating them into "reporting dealers," the professional market makers, and "other financial institutions." All trades are done with "reporting dealers," but in most categories of derivatives trading the "other financial" category has a greater volume of derivatives outstanding than the dealers have between themselves (BIS 2010c).

7   Pennings and Meulenberg (1999) give details of failed contracts for commodity derivatives on commodity and futures exchanges, and a fuller discussion of the essential features of a derivatives contract. By definition, the "over-the-counter" (OTC) contracts between banks and their clients are also highly likely to be determined according to a bank's customer demand. This is not to deny that banks want to sell products that are profitable for them and that may be bad for their clients, but there has to be a demand for the product from the bank's clients.

8   The commonly used BIS data for the volume of derivatives trading show huge numbers, in the many trillions of dollars. However, the BIS notes that the scale of market trading is not a good indicator of the scale of market risks (see BIS 2010c, p. 9). For example, as of June 2010, the total notional amount of derivatives outstanding in the OTC market amounted to $582,655 billion. But this was nearly twenty-four times the estimated $24,673 billion "gross market value" that is a closer estimate of the market risk. For example, an option to buy $1 million of a currency might have a market value of $5,000 or less, given the maturity and strike price of the option. The $5,000 is the gross market value, but the $1 million is the notional amount of the option. Similarly, an interest rate swap deal could be based on a notional $100 million, but the current levels of interest rates in the market might result in the market value of that swap being close to zero.

9   A market's liquidity is reflected in how much a price has to move to get a deal transacted. It is also true that banks sell derivatives ideas to their customers from

the point of view of earning fees, and that the deal may not be in the best interests of the customer.

10   These are the standard definitions of different classes of trader that are commonly used as a proxy for distinguishing the speculators from the others.

11   A rejection of previous so-called "Keynesian" economic policies and the promotion of finance started *before* the Thatcher and Reagan years, though it accelerated after 1979. Examples for the US, the UK and other powers are given in Norfield (2016, chapter 3).

12   Helleiner (1996) has a useful review of this topic, although he tends to see policy developments as the drivers of events, rather than policy being driven by changes in the global economy.

13   Many valiant efforts have been made, mostly using US economic data and making adjustments as the writer sees necessary. See, for example, Freeman (2009), Kliman (2012), and Moseley (1991). Michael Roberts has also done much work on this, including some further interesting work on trying to produce a *world* rate of profit, using international data (Roberts 2012).

14   However, I have to note that a common, and to my mind wrong, perspective was that the fall in profit rates for most analysts, including the authors of the Armstrong et al. book, was due to wage militancy, rather than a rising organic composition of capital.

15   Of course, the Fed was not alone in taking such measures; other central banks have done similar things, including the Bank of Japan, the Bank of England, and the European Central Bank.

16   Derivatives and financial system trading is not necessarily a "zero sum game" for capitalism, despite operating in the sphere of circulation. Consider a simple non-derivatives example: If a company issues shares whose price then rises, buyers have made a capital gain. But the company's "loss" (it could have sold at a higher price) is also a gain because its market capitalization is higher. This can become collateral for investment loans from banks or for other forms of borrowing from financial markets.

17   I would disagree with a number of the assertions made by Masters in this article, but the overall picture of institutional involvement in commodities is correct, and there are some useful estimates of the quantity of fund assets involved in these markets that I cite below.

18   Market observers were baffled by the fact that higher demand did not draw down the level of futures exchange stocks. This was because the rolled-over long futures positions meant there was no actual delivery of commodities. So prices had increased without the higher demand-versus-supply showing up in lower stocks.

19   Many pension and endowment funds have investments in assets other than in bond and equity holdings. Apart from commodities, they include investments in real estate, timber, infrastructure, private equity funds, and hedge funds.

20   See SIFMA (2011).

21   In 2000, profits of the US financial corporate sector were $206.1 billion, rising to $427.6 billion in 2006. US non-financial corporate profits also rose sharply, nearly doubling to $923.9 billion, helped by the reduction of interest payments as rates fell and by credit-fueled economic growth.

22   AIG, the large US insurance company, rescued by the US government in 2008, was also a huge seller of CDS "insurance," helped by its former AAA (top-rank)

credit rating. A high credit rating is necessary for your insurance to be valuable to a CDS buyer.

23 The other significant thing at this time was the financial crisis (mainly limited to the US) caused by the collapse of the major US hedge fund Long-Term Capital Management in 1998. LTCM had started out by arbitrage trading between similar securities and made strong returns, but it grew larger and found that higher profits depended on hugely leveraged trades using derivatives in a wider range of securities. The Russian credit default caused only a minor panic in markets, but it made previously strong statistical relationships break down. This destroyed LTCM's trading strategy and led to its demise. The 1997 Asian crisis, by contrast, had little relation to derivatives. It was triggered by a slowdown in capital accumulation, rampant speculation and then a reversal of short-term inflows of funds that had been attracted by high local interest rates.

24 See ISDA (2010). The ISDA press release is also correct in noting that if speculators drove up the credit risk on Greek bonds beyond the yields seen in the cash market, then arbitrage activity would lead to the spread falling back again. There are debates about whether the transparency of the derivatives market, despite its small scale, means that it can drive cash market prices. But for Greece there is no case for arguing that CDSs caused the crisis.

25 See Norfield (2011b), where it is noted that a large proportion of foreign debt to banks is owed by the Greek private sector.

26 See Levine (2010) for points 1 to 4; Greenberger (2008) for point 3; and Masters (2008) for point 5.

27 Following his blistering critique of regulatory failures, Levine (2010) proposes establishing a "sentinel" with powers to gather information. This is a nonstarter, but other policies to restrict the amount of bank "leverage" and increase the amount of capital that banks must hold for their operations (e.g., Basel III) are being implemented.

28 US and UK financial centers dominate the global markets in virtually all financial products. International Labour Organization data for 2006 indicate that 5 percent of the US workforce was employed in "financial intermediation."

29 UK statistics indicate that PricewaterhouseCoopers (PwC) produces a regular report on financial tax revenues for the City of London that gives the tax information (see City of London 2010). London is the world's most diversified banking center, with the largest foreign exchange market.

30 Examples of new financial regulation include new Basel rules for the required levels of bank capital, and proposals from the UK's Vickers Commission on banking to "ring-fence" retail banking from what were considered more risky wholesale market activities, among others (BIS 2010b; Jenkins 2013; Edmonds 2013).

31 This economic and political status factor is something that both the US and UK will fight to maintain, though the going will get much tougher for them in the coming years with the rise of economies that are seeking more political and economic independence, and of those that are seeing the growth of their own financial sectors, such as China.

References

ABP Investment Objectives, n.d., "About," ABP official website, http://www.abp.nl/abp/abp/english/about_abp/investments/about_investments/01objectives.asp.

Barnett-Hart, A. K. (2009) "The Story of the CDO Market Meltdown: An Empirical Analysis," Harvard University, BA degree essay, available at http://www.hks.harvard.edu/m-rcbg/students/dunlop/2009-CDOmeltdown.pdf.

Bureau of Economic Analysis, National Income and Product Accounts Tables (n.d.) available at http://www.bea.gov/iTable/iTable.cfm?ReqID=9&step=1 - reqid=9&step=1&isuri=1.

Bank for International Settlements (2010a) "Quarterly Review," Statistical Annex.

———. (2010b) "The Basel III Capital Framework: A Decisive Breakthrough," speech by Hervé Hannoun, deputy general manager of the BIS, in Hong Kong.

———. (2010c) "Triennial and Semi-annual Surveys: Positions in Global Over-the-Counter (OTC) Derivatives Markets at end-June 2010."

Bryan, D. and M. Rafferty (2006a) "Money in Capitalism or Capitalist Money?" *Historical Materialism*, Vol 14, No 1.

———. (2006b) *Capitalism with Derivatives: A Political Economy of Financial Derivatives*, *Capital and Class*, Palgrave Macmillan.

CalPERS (2007) "Fixed Income Overview," with a section on commodity investments, available at http://www.calpers.ca.gov/index.jsp?bc=/investments/assets/fixed-income/fixedoverview.xml.

City of London (2010) *The Total Tax Contribution of UK Financial Services*, PWC report for City of London Corporation.

Das, S. (2006) *Traders, Guns and Money: Knowns and Unknowns in the Dazzling World of Derivatives*, Pearson Education Limited.

Dos Santos, P. L. (2009) "On the Content of Banking in Contemporary Capitalism," *Historical Materialism*, Vol 17.

Dunbar, N. and E. Martinuzzi (2012) "Goldman Secret Greece Loan Shows Two Sinners as Client Unravels," *Bloomberg News*, March 5.

Edmonds, T. (2013), "The Independent Commission on Banking: The Vickers Report," House of Commons Library, SNBT 6171, January 3.

Freeman, A. (2009) "What Makes the US Profit Rate Fall?," *Munich Personal RePEc Archive*, available at http://mpra.ub.uni-muenchen.de/14147/.

Gallu, J. and C. Harper (2010) "Goldman Sachs Sued by SEC for Fraud Tied to CDOs," *Bloomberg*, March 5.

Greenberger, M. (2008) Testimony before the Committee on Homeland Security and Governmental Affairs, on "Financial Speculation in Commodity Markets: Are Institutional Investors and Hedge Funds Contributing to Food and Energy Price Inflation?," May 20.

Helleiner, E. (1996) *States and the Re-Emergence of Global Finance: From Bretton Woods to the 1990s*, Cornell University Press.

Hull, J. C. (2009) *Options, Futures and Other Derivatives*, 7th ed., Pearson Prentice Hall.

International Swaps and Derivatives Association (2001) "Summaries of Market Survey Results," 2001 Year End Market Survey, available at http://www.isda.org/statistics/recent.html - 2000_MID.

———. (2010) "ISDA Comments on Sovereign CDS," Press release, March 15.

Jenkins, P. (2013a) "HSBC Prepares to Leap the Vickers Ringfence," *Financial Times*, December 8.

Kishan, S. (2008) "Calpers to Boost Commodity Investments Through 2010," *Bloomberg*, February 28.

Kliman, A. (2012) *The Failure of Capitalist Production: Underlying Causes of the Great Recession*, Pluto Press.

Levine, R. (2010) "The Governance of Financial Regulation: Reform Lessons from the Recent Crisis," BIS Working Papers, No 329.

London Metal Exchange (2011) "History of the LME," available at http://www.lme .com/who_ourhistory.asp.

Marx, K. (1974) *Capital,* Vol 3, Lawrence & Wishart.

Masters, M. (2008) Testimony before the Committee on Homeland Security and Governmental Affairs, on "Financial Speculation in Commodity Markets: Are Institutional Investors and Hedge Funds Contributing to Food and Energy Price Inflation?," May 20.

McKinsey (2015) *Debt and Not Much Deleveraging*, McKinsey Global Institute.

McNally, D. (2009) "From Financial Crisis to World-Slump: Accumulation, Financialisation, and the Global Slowdown," *Historical Materialism*, Vol 17, No 2.

Moseley, F. (1991) *The Falling Rate of Profit in the Post-War United States Economy*, Macmillan.

Norfield, T. (2011a) "The Economics of British Imperialism," *Economics of Imperialism* (blog), May 22, https://economicsofimperialism.blogspot.co.uk/.

————. (2011b) "Origins of the Greek Crisis," *Economics of Imperialism* (blog), June 24.

————. (2013) "Derivatives, Money, Finance and Imperialism: A Response to Bryan and Rafferty," *Historical Materialism*, Vol 21, No 2.

————. (2016) *The City: London and the Global Power of Finance*, Verso.

Ontario Teachers' Pension Plan (2009) *Annual Report, 2009.*

Oxfam (2014) "Financial Transaction Tax," Oxfam International, available at http:// www.oxfam.org/en/tags/financial-transaction-tax.

Pennings, J. M. E. and M. T. G. Muelenberg (1999) "The Financial Industry's Challenge of Developing Commodity Derivatives," Office for Futures and Options Research at the University of Illinois at Urbana-Champaign, paper No 99–01.

Roberts, M. (2012) "A World Rate of Profit: Globalisation and the World Economy," *The Next Recession*, September, https://thenextrecession.files.wordpress.com/2012/09/ a-world-rate-of-profit.pdf.

Rogoff, K. and C. Reinhart (2008) "Banking Crises: An Equal Opportunity Menace," NBER paper.

Securities Industry and Financial Markets Association (2011) "Global CDO Issuance," SIFMA, official website, http://www.sifma.org/research/statistics.aspx.

Smith, J. (2012) "The GDP Illusion: Value Added versus Value Capture," *Monthly Review*, Vol 64, No 3.

UK Financial Services Authority and HM Treasury (2009) "Reforming OTC Derivative Markets: A UK perspective."

US Senate (2009) *Excessive Speculation in the Wheat Market*, majority and minority staff report, Permanent Subcommittee on Investigations.

CHAPTER 15

HIGH-FREQUENCY TRADING: THE UNFOLDING HISTORY OF SPECULATIVE CAPITAL

Steve Nash

1. Introduction

In investigating high-frequency trading (HFT), one cannot go beyond the "it is good / it is bad" platitudes without understanding what the practice entails and how it came about. Only then will it be possible to understand the implications and consequences of this ultra-rapid form of trading. We must therefore approach the subject historically, tracing the practice to its origin. Such going back in time allows us to see the subject's genesis, and therefore its fundamental, defining characteristics that are at present concealed by layers of cosmetic and incidental features added throughout the years.

This point is clearer if we look at the example of an early "car." Because the "car" is primitive—it could also be a "train"; it makes no difference for the purpose of our example—we can readily see its main components: (1) an engine that produces power; (2) a mechanism to transfer the power to wheels; and (3) the wheels that do the work (of moving). These are the three main components of all the vehicles in the world, past and present. But in a modern car, one would be hard pressed to recognize them because the evolution of cars in the past hundred and odd years has resulted in a facade that hides these components.

In a similar fashion, there is little to say about the practice of buying and selling stock rapidly and through computers. One is hard pressed to explain how HFT is different from "ordinary" trading except for the speed. In tracing the historical evolution of HFT, the purpose of the practice and its consequences become clear, including the fact that speed, which appears to be the defining characteristic of HFT, in fact conceals a more critical attribute of the practice.

Broadly, HFT is the final stage of the evolution of technical trading, in which stocks are bought and sold not on the basis of their "fundamentals" (i.e., the financial prospects of the company that they represent), but on that of "technical" factors such as daily supply/demand, news reports, the pattern of change in the stock price, and the like. The logic behind technical trading is that the markets absorb all the information, public and private—which is another way of saying that the prices reflect everything "out there" about a company.

Technical trading is inherently short term. The "buy" and "sell" signals from the market change within days, hours and even minutes: a stock that was ho-hum for months suddenly breaks the price resistance and must be bought—or its price falls below the ten-day moving average and must be sold. So unlike the fundamental traders who buy and hold the stock for months and years, technical traders hold a stock for only a couple of days— or hours. In HFT, that window is compressed to its physical limits: high-frequency traders buy and sell within a millisecond. Naturally, their profit margin is correspondingly small, in the order of a fraction of a penny in each trade. To compensate for that drawback, high-frequency traders buy and sell millions of times within a second. The sum of small profit over billions of shares adds up to a profit that is large enough to make HFT a going concern.

The defining characteristic of HFT is "risklessness"; in HFT one can have what Western economists throughout the ages claimed one could not have: profit without risk. That, at any rate, is what HFT appears to deliver: the time between buying and selling the stock is so short that there is literally no time left for an adverse change in the stock price (which could then result in a loss). Before examining this point, let us do away with an important misconception surrounding HFT with which it is intricately linked, namely, speed.

Much has been made of the role of speed and computers in the rise of HFT. No doubt a practice that depends on light-speed execution of trades could not exist without computers. But the technical base of a practice that makes it possible is an entirely different thing from the social and economic factors that give rise to the practice. It is misleading, at best, to say that speed *created* HFT. Starting from that false premise, one is led down the path of faux ethical questions of the "HFT is good / HFT is bad" variety—and the main issue is hopelessly lost. A historical anecdote will help see this point.

Legend has it that Nathan Rothschild, head of the celebrated family's London branch, had an agent in the Battle of Waterloo. Upon seeing that the tide of the war was turning against Napoleon, the agent rode to nearby Brussels and hired a sailor for the unheard sum of 2,000 francs to take him across a stormy Channel to England and his boss. With valuable intelligence at hand, Nathan rushed to the London Stock Exchange and feigned selling.

The crowd followed, on the belief that Wellington had lost. After the share prices had collapsed during the selling frenzy, Nathan Rothschild began buying, making millions.

How would we judge the agent if he had used a mule instead of a horse, or if he had waited for a scheduled ferry and calmer seas? Why, that would amount to the willful sabotage of his mission, treason, a crime punishable by death at wartime.

Imagine now, if you will, that the Rothschilds had an equally sharp rival family, the Rosenzweigs. The Rosenzweigs, too, considered war a man-sent opportunity for making handsome profits, but they could not place an agent in Waterloo. What they did, instead, was to place a jockey with a fast Arabian horse at the ferry stop on the English side. They instructed their jockey to take a peek at the open message that the Rothschild agent was carrying and rush to the Rosenzweigs with that information ahead of Rothschild's man.

The scenario is a bit contrived (for a *truly* contrived scenario you would have to read Friedman's "government helicopter" dropping money on the consumers), but you can see where I am going with it. Would the ethical dimension of the story change if the Rothschild agent had used a steamboat instead of a sailboat, or if the Rosenzweig man had used a car instead of horse, or if one of them had used a cell phone to pass the message along or traveled with the speed of electrons?

To ask these questions is to give the answer: "getting there first" is a technical matter unrelated to "fairness" in the context that is being discussed. Nor is it an end in itself, as it is in a race. For capital to bother traveling, there must be a profit opportunity in the destination. In the United States, one could always use Western Union to send money anywhere in the country in fifteen minutes. But in the 1970s, there was no reason for anyone to rush money from, say, New York to Dallas, in the absence of a profit-making opportunity. That is why the Western Union service remained a mere lifeline for friends and family members in immediate need of cash and never morphed into a trading platform.

So, the critics of HFT who make an issue of the fairness of the speed cannot maintain a logical position, especially in light of the indisputable effects of HFT in reducing trading costs.[1] Long before the rise of HFT, brokerage firms touted their fast execution capabilities as a competitive advantage and selling point, in the same way that many news organizations now tout their speed in covering "breaking news." In a free enterprise system, such advantages will be exploited until their logical or physical limits are reached, which is why the story of Nathan Rothschild and the Waterloo is told approvingly, as an admiration of the acumen of an ear-to-the-ground businessman. In terms of speed, HFT is simply the latest stage of this incessant push toward a faster way of getting there. It is not logical, then, to pick an arbitrary speed threshold as the ethical turning point of a historical evolution; this is why these critics have been dismissed as parties trying to protect their own interests in the face of more agile competition.[2]

The second line of criticism directed at HFT has to do with destabilizing the markets. The critics point to the so-called "Flash Crash" of May 2010 and a few similar near-crashes as evidence that HFT distorts the markets and causes unexplained crashes. But there, too, the arguments are impoverished, and charges and counter-charges are made in general terms and without explanation or specifics:

> Automated dealing could "trigger a number of risks for orderly trading and financial stability," the European Central Bank has warned. . . . The ECB said automated trading, in particular high-frequency trading (HFT), had experienced "strong growth" in recent years. But it added: "Such a development may trigger a number of risks for orderly trading and for financial stability. First, the existence of players with very short horizons may lead to the prices in the market being driven by short-term objectives and may therefore reflect fundamentals less efficiently." (Financial Times 2011a, p. 22)

The problem is that the "short-termism" of Western, and especially US, business has a long history; it was always a point of concern and subject of criticism. So, it is not clear how and why HFT represents a particularly worrisome step up in that department.

But the flash crashes are real and must be explained; that is our purpose in this chapter. The question before us is this: Does HFT present a new paradigm of market instability and distortion, and if so, how and in what way?

The starting point of that investigation is the realization that the impetus for the appearance of HFT is not speed, but *speculative capital*. Speculative capital is a historical and a logical phenomenon. To understand it we must follow its evolution—one that directly leads to HFT. Nasser Saber has studied the phenomenon in the three volumes of his *Speculative Capital* series. Here, we offer only a general outline.

Speculative capital is the latest and most advanced form of finance capital. Logically and historically, it develops from commercial capital— that is, capital earmarked for the circulation (as opposed to production) of commodities. It generates profit by buying the commodity low in one place and selling it high in another. Thus, it is capital in the hand of the merchant, the banker, and the usurer.

The cycle of buying and selling exposes the capital to risk of loss: once a commodity is purchased, there is no guarantee that it can be sold at a higher price. Therefore, every merchant in the market is a "price taker," to use an expression of textbook economics, meaning that he or she has little control over the forces that shape the prices. The prices change in response to a great many socioeconomic variables, from supply glut to political instability. After any purchase, a merchant might be forced to sell at a loss. If the loss is sufficiently severe, it could wipe out his capital and bankrupt him. The commonness of bankruptcies throughout the ages—an "occupational hazard" for the merchants and lenders—was always a reminder that risk was an integral part of commercial activity. Naturally, then, they gave a lot of thought to schemes for reducing the risk, which they associated with time. Saber explains:

> After any purchase, the speculator faces the risk that what he has just bought will fall in price. That can only happen with the passage of time. It is through time that the price of widgets drops, and it is through time that the speculator fails to find a buyer. Time is the medium through which the risk – and everything else – materializes. To the uncritical, yet practical, mind of the speculator, time appears as the source of the risk. He concludes that if the time between his purchase and sale is shortened, the risks of the transaction must proportionally diminish. In the extreme case, when the time between the two is zero, the risk would completely disappear. In that case, he could earn a risk-free profit. That is because no purchase is made unless a sale is already in hand. When the time between purchase and sale is reduced to zero, the two acts become simultaneous. A simultaneous "buy-low, sell-high" results in a risk free profit. That is arbitrage. The speculator has found the Holy Grail of finance: making money without risking money. (Saber 1999, pp. 70–71)

This holy grail of capital remained a dream until the conditions for its realization began to emerge with the collapse of the Bretton Woods system in 1971.[3]

The post–World War II Bretton Woods Agreement had fixed the exchange rates between the currencies. The relation between the US dollar and Japanese yen, for example, was fixed at $1 = ¥360. While many economic factors were considered in setting this relation, the decision itself was primarily a political one, agreed to by the foreign ministers and finance ministers.

The collapse of Bretton Woods put an end to the governments' role in regulating currencies. In their absence, "freedom" in economic relations, about which the likes of Milton Friedman had been sounding off for a while, had a chance to be realized. The currencies were set free to float and find their (price) equilibrium level based on supply and demand. In this way private capital stepped in to fill the vacuum created by the exit of governments from the economic arena.

Prior to the collapse of the fixed-exchange-rate regime, a company such as Toyota exporting cars to the United States could confidently gauge the profitability of its export markets. If the cost of a particular model of car it produced was ¥3,600,000, which included a profit margin of ¥400,000, it was clear that the US price of the car would be $10,000.[4]

After these exchange relations were thrown into turmoil, that calculus became impossible. In response to higher demand for yen, for example, the currency could strengthen to ¥320 per dollar. In that case, the company would have to raise the US price of the car to $11,125.[5] Or, if it decided to protect the market share and keep the US price unchanged, it would have to suffer a ¥400,000 loss, which would wipe out its profit.[6] This situation was not sustainable, and a solution had to be found.

The solution that private capital offered was *hedging*. It came, naturally, from the large international banks and their privileged position of access to various national markets and currencies. This is how hedging worked:

Imagine that you were IBM and you were negotiating with a Japanese customer to sell mainframe computers for ¥3.2 billion. The delivery was due in one month. At the current exchange rate of $1= ¥320, that translated to $10 million, which included a $600,000 profit. But in the environment of floating rates, the yen could weaken to, say, ¥340 per dollar. In that case, the agreed-upon price of ¥3.2 billion would be worth only $9.4 million.[7] That would wipe out the entire profit of the deal. So you went to an international bank like JP Morgan for advice and a solution.

Let us assume that JP Morgan also had a private-equity client in the United States that wanted to buy a Japanese property for ¥3.2 billion. With the current dollar–yen exchange rate, that would translate to $10 million, which is the amount the fund had budgeted for the deal.[8] But if the yen strengthened to, say, $1 = ¥300, then $10 million would only be ¥300 billion, falling ¥200 million short of the price. Naturally, the fund wanted to protect itself against this unpleasant eventuality, so it, too, went to JP Morgan for advice.

The bank was in an ideal position to offer such advice. By virtue of having knowledge of the upcoming transactions, it could see the solution, which is almost self-suggesting.

The bank entered into a contract with IBM to buy ¥3.2 billion from it for $10 million in one month. It also entered into a contract with the fund to sell ¥3.2 billion for $10 million. On the delivery date, IBM received ¥3.2 billion from its customer, which it paid to JP Morgan, which then passed it to the fund investing in Japan. In return, the banks received $10 million from the fund, which it paid IBM in return for the ¥3.2 billion it had received.

The three-way contract insulated parties from the market. IBM and the fund exchanged $1 for ¥320, no matter what the market exchange rate between the two currencies. This was hedging, or protection against market fluctuation.

Our focus in this example was on the mechanics of the transaction, so we said nothing about the bank's commission. But no bank would facilitate such a transaction for free; it could not afford to. An intermediary bank must recoup its costs and make a profit in the process, so it will work the cost of the transaction into the deal. As an example, in this case JP Morgan would buy the dollar from the fund for slightly less than ¥320, say, ¥318, and sell the dollars to IBM for slightly higher than ¥320, say, ¥323. That would translate to a ¥5 profit per dollar, or ¥50 million in the transaction—equal to about $156,000.

The critical point here is that the position of the bank is *riskless*. Even though it buys and sells US dollars and Japanese yen, it is insulated against currency fluctuations because the yen it has agreed to buy from IBM are already sold to the fund. More accurately, it has agreed to buy yen because it already sold them to the fund. Still, as a "one-off" trade, this position is unremarkable and no different from any transaction involving an intermediary. Keep in mind only that IBM and the fund do not directly deal with each other. Nay, they do not even know of the other's Japan plans.

In the post–Bretton Woods volatility of exchange rates, such situations became quite common. In fact, all the large- and medium-sized US and Japanese corporations faced similar problems and wanted similar solutions. For JP Morgan, the commercial purposes behind the corporations' need mattered little. It saw in these deals opportunities for making a riskless profit through simultaneous purchase and sale of currencies. Naturally, it made no difference whether the currency in question was Japanese yen, Swiss franc, or British pound. Any currency and, for that matter, any financial instrument would do. All it took was surveying the landscape of financial data to find buyers and sellers whose needs it could fulfill simultaneously for a riskless profit.[9]

If you now imagine hundreds of companies like IBM expecting to "sell" yen in return for dollars on one hand, and hundreds of companies such as the fund expecting to "buy" yen for dollars, the intermediary banks were in a position to earn riskless profits many times over. It was precisely the increase in the number of buyers and sellers of (in this case) currency that transformed conservative hedging, initiated to insulate a producer or an investor from the market fluctuation, to aggressive arbitrage, initiated to lock in a riskless profit. Saber again:

The purpose of hedging is to insulate the parties from the adverse changes in the markets. The purpose of arbitrage, by contrast, is profit. In arbitrage, the focus shift from the producers and even investors to the middleman. The arbitrageur has neither an asset nor a liability. He zeros on *any two* positions that will enable him to "lock in" a spread. Hedging and arbitrage as indistinguishable on an after-the-fact basis. What *logically* separates them is the purpose of each act that translates itself to the *sequence* of execution of trades. When done sequentially, the act is defensive hedging. When done simultaneously, it is aggressive arbitrage. Otherwise, the transformation of one to the other is seamless. The capital earmarked for arbitrage is speculative capital. . . .

Speculative capital is "opportunistic." It is constantly on the lookout for "inefficiencies" across markets that it can exploit. The opportunities arise suddenly and at random points in time, so the capital that hopes to exploit them must always be available; it cannot afford to be locked into long-term commitments and investments. The requirement to be opportunistic translates into the need to be mobile, to be nomadic and interested in short-term ventures. Capital that has such characteristics is *speculative capital*. Indeed, speculation is defined precisely in terms of short-term engagement of capital in arbitrage trades. (Saber 1999, original emphasis)

Simultaneous buying and selling is the hallmark of speculative capital and defines it. We must only bear in mind that "simultaneous" in finance is less restrictive than it is in mathematics or physics. It is "practically simultaneous" or "near simultaneous," meaning that within the constraints of buying and selling across financial markets, the interval between buying and selling is the shortest practicable.

2. The Intellectual Underpinning of HFT

The rise of speculative capital impressed itself on the minds of academics and scholars of finance, who proceeded to create a "theory" to explain it.

Those academics and scholars had no training in finance. As the idea of the use of mathematics in finance appeared, they were drawn to the discipline from the mathematics and physics department of the universities in quest of creating an "objective," "value-free" finance. Naturally, they knew nothing about speculative capital or other forms of capital, or the laws of capital's growth and movement: "Today's financial markets are the result of a recent but obscure revolution that took root in the groves of ivy rather than in the canyons of lower Manhattan. Its heroes were a tiny contingent of scholars, most at the very beginning of their careers, who had no direct interest in the stock market and whose analysis of the economics of finance began at high levels of abstraction" (Bernstein 2005, p. 1). Against their immense theoretical poverty, mathematically oriented academics set out to create a theory for the events they were witnessing.

The most striking feature of the new regime was the frequency of trading that was driven by the speculative capital–induced arbitrage activities. Simultaneously buying and selling to lock in a riskless profit is the *idea* behind arbitrage. In practice, in modern markets, such easy opportunities rarely exist, and when they do, they are rapidly arbitraged away. Speed, always important in trading, becomes even more critical because the opportunities pop up and disappear fast. A trader must thus react accordingly.

Rapid, frequent trading meant that it took place without pause; one could say that it was *continuous*. Something continuous is continuous *in time*. Time continuity is the fundamental feature of natural phenomena as formulated by Newtonian mechanics. Starting from that observation, the mathematically inclined newcomers to the discipline proceeded to create *continuous-time finance* (CTF) or modern finance.[10]

Newtonian mechanics revolves around key terms like *instantaneous speed* and *constant acceleration*. These are not intuitive concepts. In fact, they are mathematical, and their discovery came about at the end of a long and torturous road precisely because they are not intuitive. CTF is the adaptation and importation of this system to finance. It is finance in a world in which prices change continuously and instantaneously—exactly the way distance traveled by a falling body changes, except that prices are bidirectional, and unlike a falling object, they can go up *and* down.

CTF is an inconsistent combination of disparate theories, yet finance professors consider it the crown jewel of their discipline. There are practical and ideological reasons for the boast.

On the practical side, CTF solved some of the most bedeviling problems of finance, such as option valuation. The explosion in option trading that followed the publication of the Black-Scholes formula in 1973 was the high watermark of the discipline. It showed that the esoteric mathematics of modern finance had practical use. Paul Samuelson picked up on this point when, in the introduction to Robert Merton's *Continuous-Time Finance*, he wrote, "When today's associate professor of security analysis is asked, 'Young man, if you are so smart, why ain't you rich?' he replies by laughing all the way to the bank or to his appointment to a high-paid consultant to Wall Street" (Samuelson 1994, p. xi). Ideologically, mathematics is the language of nature. If finance, a social science, could be expressed in that language, it followed that its structural relations resembled nature, with all the implications that followed. The most important implication was the matter of stability and permanence. The *way* heat dissipates in a solid body does not change from day to day. If the "dissipation" of the price of stock in the Black-Scholes model had a similar structure, it followed that the stock price movement, and from there, the financial system in which that price movement took pace, was as stable as physical relations. That was another way of saying that the financial relations of capitalism were as stable as those of nature. "Capitalism forever," then, was no longer a slogan but a mathematically derived conclusion in conformity with nature.

And all that was thanks to the "markets." The premise was that the markets worked themselves toward a state in which everything was in equilibrium—supply and demand, buyers and sellers, bids and asked prices. In these markets, all the information was reflected in prices, and no one had an advantage over others; everyone could buy or sell with ease, quickly, and with minimum expense. It followed, then, that the longer and harder markets worked, the faster they became efficient; hence, the critical role of continuous-time trading. The incessant, round-the-clock trading appeared as the logical means for taking society toward a financial nirvana, a Norman Rockwellian society in which everyone happily traded all the time for both their own and the common good.

In reality, speculative capital is self-destructive; it eliminates the opportunities that give rise to it. Although it then seeks new opportunities, its self-destructive tendency never goes away. That is why the turn of events driven by speculative capital turned out to be different from what the best and brightest of modern finance had envisioned.

3. Arbitraging "Equivalent Positions": Rise of Program Trading

Because speculative capital eliminates the opportunities that give rise to it, it must constantly find new opportunities. The search, on one hand, leads to the expansion beyond national boundaries that has created "globalization." At the same time, beginning with the local markets, speculative capital discovers "equivalent" positions.

The idea of equivalent positions comes from geometry. A triangle and a square whose areas are each 100 square feet are called equivalents. The definition highlights the critical unity-in-difference: a triangle is a different shape than a square, but their area is same. Suppose now you are asked to find an equivalent rectangular. For that, you will need some mathematical knowledge, namely, that the area of a rectangular is the product of its length and width. Assuming an arbitrary length of 20, the width turns out to be 5. But there are other possibilities; rectangles with the following dimensions all qualify: 1×100, 2×50, 4×25, 8×12.5. And there are many more—infinitely more, in fact.

In finance, as well, two positions are said to be equivalent if they are two qualitatively different securities (like a rectangle and a triangle) but have (or must have) the same price. If they do not, that is, if their prices are different, one can buy the lower-priced equivalent position and sell the higher-priced position for a riskless profit.

And in finance, too, like geometry, finding the equivalent positions requires mathematical calculations. It was the rise of speculative capital in search of arbitrage opportunities that brought mathematics, and with it, computers, to finance. Before the beginning of the current millennia, arbitrage trading was firmly in place.

> At BNP/Cooper Neff, stocks aren't companies in the industry sector. They are "mathematical objects." . . . [The company's president] thinks studying news and financial reports . . . is a waste of time. . . . And the only way to beat the market . . . is to trade thousands of stocks, by the millions of shares, in search of tiny inefficiencies. . . . [H]e sees the world as 7,000 stocks to trade against one another in one gigantic hedge fund. (Wall Street Journal 1997a, p. A1)

But the most significant form of equivalent trading had come earlier, from option valuation.

Let us assume that you want to sell a stock that is currently trading at fifty dollars, but because of some legal limits, you must wait for three months. What is the price of a *right* that would allow you to sell the stock at fifty dollars in three months, *no matter what the stock price at that time?*

Recall that this is the old currency problem, where JP Morgan stepped in to create a *riskless* position to all involved, including itself, regardless of the future price of the two currencies. Can we similarly create a riskless position here, where we would have a certain profit no matter what happens to the stock price? We assume that in three months, the stock price could rise to sixty dollars, or drop to forty dollars.

If you do not do anything—that is, if you keep your position "naked," as they call it in the trading room—you will profit if stock rises to $60. You could sell it at that price for a profit of $10. But the price might fall to $40, in which case you will lose $10.

A *right* to sell the stock at $50 will allow you to sell the stock at $60 and realize $10 profit if the stock rises. This is an important point to keep in mind because your right is that: a right. It is not an obligation. You are not obligated to sell your stock at $50 if the market price is $60. So the upside profit is defined by the stock price.

The critical point is that if the stock falls to $40, you have the *right* to sell it (regardless of the market) at $50, preserving the original value of your stock. That is an admittedly good *right* to have, which is exactly why it has a price. The question is how much should that price be.

The answer is $5. Here is what happens if you pay $5 to purchase a right to sell your stock at $50. Say that in three months, the stock price

(1)   rises to $60. You sell the stock at $60 for a $10 profit. Subtracting the $5 you paid for the right, your net profit would be $5; or alternatively, say the price

(2)   falls to $40. You would have the right to sell the stock for $50 for a profit of $10. But you paid $5 for the right, so your net profit would be $5.

You see that the uncertainty of making *or* losing $10 is eliminated. Now, for a known payment of $5, which is the price of the *right*, the risk of loss is eliminated. Absence of uncertainty is the absence of risk. That is another way of saying that your position is *riskless*.

What I just described is the well-known option valuation problem, which had bedeviled academics until Fischer Black, Myron Scholes, and Robert Merton solved it in 1973. The "solution" meant answering the question we asked: How much should the right to buy or sell a stock at a given price at some future date be worth?

The Black–Scholes–Merton option-valuation formula has an imposing form and involves calculation of probability density functions. Its authors derived it using differential calculus. But the complexity comes only from the model of the stock price movement; otherwise, the concept of option valuation is no less or more than what we saw above.

With regard to the stock price, our assumption that price will become either $60 or $40 is simplistic to the point of being absurd. Stock prices change every day, and many times during the day. The more actively a stock is traded, the more frequently its price changes. To produce a realistic option price, Black, Scholes, and Merton had to use a realistic stock price model. They found it in the work of an early-twentieth-century French mathematician, Louis Bachelier. Bachelier's model is expressed as a differential equation.

What the model is saying is that in the short term, stock prices fluctuate up and down, but that their long-term trend is upward. That is a description that fit the behavior of the most of the stocks in the pre–HFT days.

Because Bachelier's model accurately captured the broad price behavior of stocks, the resulting option valuations made sense to traders and they began using them. The most important insight of option valuation is that an option can be replicated by a combination of cash and stock—"replicated" meaning that it can be synthetically created.

Portfolio managers took note of the new tool and the insight behind its valuation. These managers' bonus depends on their returns. More critically, like physicians who must first do no harm, portfolio managers first and foremost strive not to lose clients' capital. Such a loss would lead to redemption and to the decline in the size of the fund, with all the consequences that follow. An option-based method that limited their losses was thus very attractive to them. They began using it to hedge their portfolio in the late 1970s.

4. Program Trading and Market Crash

Program trading is computerized trading because it is *mathematical* trading: it follows an algorithm and thus lends itself perfectly to programming. The purpose of the strategy is to preserve the value of a portfolio. What *follows* from it—the unintended consequences—is the market instability, the potential for it to crash. That is because program trading synchronizes the action of all portfolio managers and thus, in a falling market, exacerbates the fall.

Take a fund manager who is entrusted with $100 to invest. The most damaging outcome for him, as we saw, is losing the principal. So, he has to make sure that under no circumstances will the value of his fund drop below $100. Generating return is a secondary concern.

In the previous example, we assumed a one-period horizon, at the end of which that stock was either $40 or $60. Now, we assume a two-period horizon. In each period the market will go up either by the factor $u = 1.1$ or decrease by the factor $d = 1/1.1$. Let us assume that the "market" measure by an index such as Dow Jones or S&P 500 is at 100. Starting from that level at time zero, the market would change as follows in the first period:

$$100 \times 1.1 = \$110 \text{ (point B); or}$$

$$100 \times 1/1.1 = \$90.91 \text{ (point C)}$$

And in the second period, starting from $110 (point B), either

$$110 \times 1.1 = \$121 \text{ (point D); or}$$

$$110 \times 1/1 = \$100 \text{ (point E)}$$

Starting from 90.91 (point C):

$$90.91 \times 1.1 = \$100 \text{ (point E); or}$$

$$90.91 \times 1/1.1 = \$82.63 \text{ (point F)}$$

To repeat, our object is not to let this portfolio fall below its starting value of $100.

The mechanics of option value will show that the portfolio manager would need $4.76 to achieve that goal. With that information, and starting with $104.76, the original $100 entrusted to him plus the cost of insurance, he proceeds as follows.

Period 0:

Buy 0.5238 shares of the market worth $100 \times \$0.5238 = \$52.38$.

Keep the remainder $(104.76 - 52.38 = \$52.38)$ in cash.

Period 1:

Market index rises to 110.

Use $52.38 cash to buy $52.38: 110 = 0.4762$ shares of the market.

With the previous 0.5238 shares, the manager now has $0.5238 + 0.4762 = 1$ share.

At the end of period 2:

If the market rises to 121 (D), the portfolio will be worth $1 \times 121 = \$121$.

If it falls to 100 (E), the value would be $1 \times 100 = \$100$.

In both cases, the objective is met.

Market index falls to $90.91.

Sell the 0.5238 share at $90.91 = \$47.62$.

With $52.38 cash, the total value of portfolio is $100.

Exit the market.

The objective of maintaining $100 value is achieved.

The most critical part of this process is point C. At that point, the market has fallen so much that it has reached the loss limit of the portfolio manager. It is true that from that point the market might rise to 100 (point E). But it might also drop to 82.63, and that is a chance that our manager cannot take. That would violate the starting condition of the problem, which is to preserve the value of the fund at $100. So he cashes his chips, so to speak, and leaves the market.

Our two-period strategy is for illustration. In reality, during market hours the trading, and with that the price changes, are continuous. In response, computer-based algorithms constantly adjust the portfolio to keep it riskless with reference to the latest prices. Hence the description of the strategy as *dynamic hedging*, as the hedge, defined by the ration of stocks to cash, constantly changes. Dynamic hedging, portfolio insurance and program trading are used interchangeably.

An important point here is the meaning of "riskless portfolio," which is vividly highlighted. A riskless portfolio is the one that is taken out of the market. Or, to put it differently, the risk of loss of principal is inherent to the market: to be capital is to be exposed to the risk of loss. The only way to eliminate the risk is *not to be* capital. And the way to do *that* is to leave the circuit of capital, which is done by converting it to cash—money—and leaving the market.

It is easy to see what would happen if all portfolio managers followed suit: the market would crash. That is what happened on October 19, 1987, when US stocks lost 25 percent of their value in a single trading day.

Market crashes are not a new phenomenon; historically they have been a fixture of the market since the rise of capitalism. But in the pre–program trading era, crashes, no matter how much they were "psychological" or the result of "herd mentality," had an economic underpinning. In that regard they were the harbingers of economic stagnation to come; for instance, the US market crash of 1929 preceded the Great Depression by a few years.

The 1987 crash seemed to be an exception. The market recovered shortly afterward, and there was no visible economic damage. Looking back a few years later, a hedge fund manager commented, "The stock market is supposed to be an indicator of things to come, a discounting mechanism that is telling you of what the world is to be. All that context was shattered. In 1987, the stock-market crash was telling you nothing."

What the crash revealed was the collapse of the existing market mechanism, although a trader could not see it or discern its meaning and significance. The system of buying and selling stock in the New York Stock Exchange was designed around "specialists," originally individuals and in later years large Wall Street firms that were in charge of "making a market" in a group of stocks that was assigned to them. IBM, for example, was given to a specialist who matched the "buy" and "sell" orders and earned a "spread" in each transaction. For example, he quoted the stock at "99 ⅞ x 100 ⅛," meaning that he was willing to buy IBM for $99.875 and sell it at $100.125. In each share, he thus made 25 cents. If on a particular day IBM traded, say, 100,000 shares, the specialist would make $25,000—generally risklessly, as he only matched the buyers and sellers.

You can see the similarity of the arrangement with our JP Morgan and currency example: an intermediary situating himself between buyers and sellers and collecting a fee for his "service." Of course, there was a much higher volume of trading in IBM stock than in currency deals, but the mechanics were the same.

Yet, the stock specialists were also different in one critical respect. Because their position was official, the privilege of their position for collecting generally riskless profit went hand in hand with the obligation of market making. In the hypothetical case that there were no buyers for IBM stock, the specialist in charge had to use his capital to buy it from the seller. Needless to say, he could lower the price to discourage unbridled selling, but technicalities aside, the obligation of his position was clear-cut and firmly in place.

The computer-driven selling of the 1987 crash pushed the prices beyond anything the specialist could tolerate. The mechanics of selling are not only synchronized, but also self-perpetuating: the further prices fall, the more stock must be sold, which further lowers the prices. So the specialists refused to honor the sell requests, and as the requests mounted, they walked out of their posts. Sell orders went unfilled, and as the market dropped, losses mounted.

Large institutions with access to the exchange floor were able to unload their positions. But small investors who had to rely on the telephone to convey the sell orders were hit hard. Their outcry three years later led to the creation of the Small Order Execution System, or SOES. Using SOES, retail investors could trade up to 1,000 shares of stock directly with market makers without having to call them.

There is no evidence that market makers understood the implications of the system. Despite some initial reservations, they generally supported it; they reasoned that computerized trading would increase the volume, and with that, their commissions. What happened in practice was something different altogether, setting the stage for the destruction of the market makers entirely.

SOES could not only place orders, but execute them as well. The screen showed the best bid and offered prices for the stock by four market makers, MM1 to MM4. The system was designed to rank the stock in the order of the best bid and offered prices. The 20 ¼ x 20 ½ bid and offer shown is the best price because it is the lowest a retail investor can buy (for 20 ½) or sell (at 20 ¼) a stock. The critical point is that these prices come from two *different* market makers. It is MM1 who is willing to buy the stock at the highest price (20 ¼) from the retail seller, while it is MM3 who is offering the best price (20 ½) for retail investors wanting to buy it.

Suppose now, as a result of some news, that the stock price increases and all market makers change their prices, except MM4 who keeps his or her bid/asked at the previous 19 ⅞ × 20 ⅞.

MM4 is now offering the stock at 20 ⅞. A SOES trader could then buy it from him for 20 ⅞ and immediately sell it to the highest bidder, MM1, who is paying 21 ¼ for the stock. The SOES trader realizes a profit of $375 on 1,000 shares. That was simultaneously buying low and selling high, the hallmark of speculative capital—only now, the table was turned on the market makers, and they were on the receiving end of the arbitrage.

As market makers began to realize the threat, they reacted to it in ways small and large, using all means available to them. The history of their fight, which lasted almost a decade, cannot be covered here, but it is instructive to mention some highlights. Despite the enormous power of established financiers, the force of speculative capital was greater still and eventually won the day.

Initially SOES traders were labeled "SOES bandits" by the financial press, whose sympathies were with the traditional traders:

> SOES has a provision that the SOES bandits – who are hardly the typical small investor – have been able to exploit very profitably. Basically, the system requires that brokers exercise constant vigilance in keeping current the prices. . . . A few-second delay by a broker in updating the price of a volatile stock is all a SOES trader needs to hammer the broker with repeated automatic orders to buy or sell. The hapless broker has to execute the orders regardless of whether they will be profitable. Nasdaq . . . argues that [SOES firms] distort prices. (Wall Street Journal 1995a, p. C1)

Note the language and that SOES "requires that brokers exercise constant vigilance in keeping current the prices." Unbeknownst to anyone, the stage was being set for the rise of automatic price updates, from which HFT would then follow.

The complaint about the SOES "bandits" went on for many years and took many forms, including the claims that SOES traders "ruin the market" through their extensive buying and selling activities:

> Extensive short term trading activities on the [SOES] system have adversely affected volatility and spreads, according to critics. If this activity causes significant losses to market makers, they will attempt to reduce and recoup these losses. To reduce the losses, market makers may spend more resources monitoring their participation in SOES, which would result in fewer deals per issue and a reduction in the depth of the market. To recoup losses, market makers may widen bid-ask spreads for all investors in stocks that are heavily traded in short-term trading tactics and possibly in other stocks as well. (Kothare and Laus 1995, pp. 42–53)

Of course, extensive trading had begun a decade ago with dynamic hedging. The genie was out of the bottle, and there was no going back.

Market makers also encouraged the regulators to stop SOES trading, complaining that regulators did not do enough: "The president of the STA [Security Traders Association], along with other traders, complained that the SEC has failed to address alleged problems in the Small Order Execution System. . . . Some market-makers claim that SOES traders abuse the system to 'pick off' big dealers who don't update their price quotations fast enough" (Wall Street Journal 1995c, p. B9). The critical point, though, was not about updating the prices. Market makers had quickly learned to be more "vigilant" and to update prices regularly. The "problem" was that speculative capital, now in the form of SOES traders, had begun the move toward reducing the historically established spreads between the bid and offered sides of the prices.

To elaborate this point, Stock X is quoted at 20 ¼ × 20 ½, indicating that the best bid/asked spread for the stock is ¼ or $.25. This is what the public saw. But these prices come from two *different* market makers: In our example, market maker MM1 provides the best bid at 20 ¼, while market maker MM3 provides the best asked, at 20 ½. The bid/asked spread for each individual market maker is considerably larger. In the case of market MM1, he or she is buying for 20 ¼, (as shown in row 1), but selling at 20 ¾ (row 2); thus, MM1's profit in every share is $.50. Market maker MM3 is even more egregious. MM3 is providing the best offer price at 20 ½, but his or her bid (the price MM3 is willing to pay to buy the stock) is 19 ⅞ (row 4); therefore MM3's profit in each share is $.75. If he or she traded 20,000 shares a day, about the average number for a standard stock in those days, MM3 would pocket $15,000 a day with very little effort. It was this windfall profit that SOES traders threatened to capture.

They did so by submitting a bid *between* the traders' prices. For example, they submitted a bid of 20 ⅜, which improved the best bid and offer of 20 ¼. In doing so, they began to cut into the market makers' profit by lowering the bid/asked spreads.

For a long time, market makers ignored those prices, which was a violation of the rules: customers who wanted to sell the stock were denied the opportunity to sell it at 20 ⅜ and had to settle for 20 ¼. Market makers who accepted better bids from outside were censured by their colleagues. The *Wall Street Journal* reported the story and, despite its pro-trader tone, was forced to admit that the practice was illegal:

> Major backing-away sanctions have been rare partly because so many of the backing-away complaints have come from . . . "SOES bandits," whom dealers accuse of bombarding the market . . . with orders at

dealers' expense. The 12 backing-away incidents in the Morgan
Stanley case all involved orders from SOES bandits, and the Lehman
matter is understood to derive from bandits' complaints, as well . . .
yet despite unsympathetic victims, backing away from quotation is
forbidden in the markets. (Wall Street Journal 1995b, p. A4)

Ultimately, futures pit traders, Nasdaq market makers, and New York Stock
Exchange specialists were merely "inefficiencies" that speculative capital
arbitraged away. The Nasdaq bid/asked controversy, for example, came to
a conclusion as a result of legal pressure; the market makers settled a lawsuit
by agreeing to pay almost $1 billion in fines: "A federal judge . . . granted
preliminary approval to 30 securities firms' $910 million settlement of a
class-action suit alleging that the firms fixed prices in the past on Nasdaq
Stock Market trades. . . . The investors' lawsuit alleged that more than three
dozen Nasdaq dealers conspired to widen spreads on trades involving 1,659
stocks" (Wall Street Journal 1997b, p. C13).

But speculative capital cannot stop arbitraging, or else it will negate
itself. Having broken the barrier of one-quarter spreads, it kept the pressure
to reduce the spreads even further. In doing so, it brought to an end the
centuries-old conventional profit margins in securities trading:

After more than centuries of using a system descended from Spanish
pieces of eight, American stock markets are now appear to be moving
toward having stocks priced . . . in dollars and cents. . . . If Wall Street
does move, it is widely expected that it would lead to better . . . prices
for investors. That gain would come at the expense of brokers, who
have resisted the move in the past. . . . A change in pricing could shrink
their profit margins. (NYT 1998, p. C1)

By the early 2000s, the spreads had fallen to a few pennies per trade and
were still heading lower. If the spread is a penny ($.01), buying and selling
10,000 shares of stock would generate only $100, too meager a sum to
sustain a market-making business. That is why and how market makers and
specialists were forced out of business. In their place came the new "SOES
traders." But because of the very low profit in each trade, the only way to be
profitable was to engage in more frequent trading, which, given the limited
numbers of hours the market was open, could only come through faster
trading. The stage was set for the rise of HFT.

5. The Rise of HFT

In HFT, the human element is taken out of the trading loop and replaced by
computers. More accurately, the human element is pushed out: it is humanly

impossible to monitor the price movement of thousands of stocks every one-thousandth of a second and place the order accordingly.

Like the Rothschild agent, the early phases of HFT relied on the brute force of speed. The early high-frequency traders intercepted the buy-and-sell order of institutional traders and submitted an order ahead of them. They profited when the original trade arrived and moved the stock slightly higher or lower, depending on whether it was a buy or a sell order. At this stage what mattered was "getting there first"—before others, before the opportunity was gone. The ensuing "arms race" for speed led to the impasse where all HFT firms reduced their execution time to the irreducible minimum imposed by nature. They even placed their computers next to the computers of the clearing houses to reduce the travel time, notwithstanding that their orders traveled at the speed of light. Statistics will allow us to gain some perspective on what is taking place in the markets.[11]

The Tabb Group, a consultancy, estimated in 2009 that high-frequency trading accounted for as much as 73 percent of the US daily equity volume, up from 30 percent in 2005 (Financial Times 2009, p. 23). With three-quarters of the daily volume being generated by HFT, this style has become the way equities in the United States are bought and sold. Meanwhile, a PhD thesis at Northwestern University's Kellogg School of Management concluded that twenty-six firms, controlling 75 percent of the HFT, were making about $3 billion annually on $30 trillion in trading volume (Financial Times 2010a, p. 21).

The most noteworthy aspect of these numbers is the trading volume. Divided by 260 trading days per year, we see that the daily trading volume is about 115 billion shares, or 5,000 shares every millisecond during the market hours. The profit margins have accordingly fallen to adjust to that volume; the profit margin of HFT firms is a fraction of a penny per share. That is reflected in the relatively small $3 billion profit for all HFT firms.

Perhaps not surprisingly, the complaints that rapid-fire trading is "ruining the market" are being heard again. Here is an official of a stock exchange, of all places, criticizing too much competition, which he says is due to fragmentation caused by HFT: "'Most of the world views our market structure as a joke,' said Larry Leibowitz, chief operating officer at NYSE Euronext. 'Our market is too fragmented. The challenge is, how much competition is too much competition,' he said" (Financial Times 2010d).

But the harm to the market structure, in the form of its increased instability, comes from an aspect of HFT that an exchange official would not realize. Two parallel developments must be recognized. On one hand, a large segment of finance capital employed through the traditional brokerage houses and financial institutions considers the interception of its orders, and the shaving off of even a fraction of a penny from its profits, a flagrant robbery. These institutions refused to be robbed and took actions to protect themselves. The only defense against faster predators, who feed on intercepting one's orders, is *not* to show the orders at all. Hence the rise of private exchanges, "dark pools" and internal settlement mechanisms, created as private venues for trading to keeps outsiders at bay.[12] These private trading clubs diminish the role of the "market" and impede "price discovery," that leitmotif of every finance professor who ever taught a course in a Western university.

But the most profound perversion of price discovery takes place when speculative capital works from within the markets and exchanges. In volume 1 of *Speculative Capital*, Saber points out that a system in equilibrium is a dead one, a static system incapable of generating any movement except through the intervention of an outside force. He goes on to say that by bringing "equilibrium" to markets through arbitrage, speculative capital neuters the markets in terms of the information content. This aspect of speculative capital's self-destructive tendency needs elaborating. We begin by noting the difference between physical and social destruction.

Physical destruction has finality. It brings the *physical aspect* of the story to an end: a beach is destroyed by the sea, and that is the end of the story. However, social systems are different. A social system is destroyed only when it is replaced.

Speculative capital destroys markets by replacing their traditional structure with one of its own making. The first step in the process is gaining access to the markets, which is made easy by the prospects of large trading volumes that speculative capital promises—and delivers. To attract high-frequency traders, exchanges are building data centers where traders can place their computer system—packed with algorithms—as close as possible to the exchange's trading system, shaving crucial microseconds off trading times (Financial Times 2010b, p. 1).

After the markets are "opened up," speculative capital settles in—even after the arbitrage opportunities are grazed out. There is no going back, as market makers and the specialist-based system are ruined. The market—now "efficient" precisely because it cannot be arbitraged—becomes a conduit for the movement and expansion of speculative capital. The point is that market prices set by speculative capital seem completely irrational to traditional traders and investors. Saber noted this point in volume 1 of *Speculative Capital* when he explained how "relative value" trading is arbitrage trading that either keeps the traditional traders out of the market altogether, or forces them to join arbitrage trading:

> "Lately, if you'd used almost any kind of absolute-valuation guidelines,
> you'd have kept out of this market altogether, and missed a lot of

the bull market," sighs Mr. Jandrain [who manages a stock fund for Banc One]. "The reality is that we're still at record [valuation] levels historically by nearly every measure, and you have to look for pockets of relative value."

"Relative value" trading – comparing one stock against similar stocks – is arbitrage trading. Banc One's Mr. Jandrain is being forced to disregard individual stock analysis with an eye to estimating its future growth, in favor of buying relatively undervalued or selling relatively overvalued stocks. He calls that "looking for pockets of relative value." But arbitrage by any name is arbitrage. In his quest for pockets of relative value in the equities market, Jandrain has assigned his fund to the ranks of speculative capital, thus guaranteeing that relative value trading, and, with it, the volatility of the stock market, will increase. (Saber 1999, p. 221)

In this way, the raison d'être of markets—the much-touted "price discovery"—is hollowed. The prices now convey little or no information about the companies and, by extension, the economy. While in 1999, at the time of the publication of *Speculative Capital*, few had noticed this phenomenon, the evidence is now difficult to ignore. Even the establishment newspapers are forced to acknowledge it:

What are the equity markets for these days? In the developed world, at any rate, they no longer seem trusted as a store of value or a source of income. Nor are they much use at providing capital to businesses, which should be their primary function.

The quality of information they provide is, meanwhile, deteriorating. Daily index movements are often a by-product of larger external forces. Individual stock prices tell us little, since they move in lock-step. And volume is meaningless, since may be half of it now consists of information-free "flash" trading. (Financial Times 2010c)

More still, HFT creates sudden and unexplained crashes. On May 6, 2010, the Dow Jones Industrial Average dropped more than 1,000 points in a few minutes. A joint SEC and CFTC report (2010) several months later blamed a broker in the Midwest buying a large number of future index contacts. Such "Mrs. O'Leary's cow" explanations satisfied no one.

The cause of the crash of the market in the age of HFT is HFT.

Consider this game. You are given $20 to take part in a game of three consecutive coin tosses. In each toss, you win $5 if you guess right and lose $5 if you do not. You must leave the game with at least $10.

If your first call is right, starting with $20, you will win $5 and end up with $25. In the second toss, if you win, you will have $30; else your money will be reduced to $20. After the third and last toss, depending on whether you start, you will end the game with $35, $25, or $15. In all cases, the condition of having at least $10 would be satisfied.

If your first call is wrong, you will end up with $15. If your second call is also wrong, you will be at only $10; that is the end of the line for you. Technically, though, the game is not over yet. One more toss is left, and if you guess right, you might end up with $15. But you cannot take that chance, because if you lose, you would violate the condition of leaving the game with at least $10. So there is no going forward, which is why it is no longer connected to the mesh "going forward."

You have no doubt recognized the mechanism of the portfolio insurance that we saw earlier, only that the number of tosses is not three but in the hundreds. Under that condition, the probability of arriving below $10 is infinitesimally small; imagine the probability of throwing two hundred consecutive "heads" in a game of coin toss.

That infinitesimally small probability also governs the probability of consecutive price decreases in algorithmic HFT trading. But that extremely small probability becomes realizable—it is magnified, if you will—in HFT where billions of trades take place every hour. HFT shrinks time by creating a condition of simulation in the market. We cannot conceive of one hundred consecutive "heads" in a game of coin toss. But we can simulate the game and, by repeating it tens and hundreds of billions of times, eventually arrive at one hundred consecutive "heads." Similarly, HFT constantly tests the crash conditions. Because there are so many players, the odds of a crash are infinitesimally small. But eventually, HFT arrives at it, as it inevitably must.

The unease about the markets reached the higher echelons of the government. On the anniversary of the May 2010 "Flash Crash," two US senators wrote,

> America's capital markets, once the envy of the world, have been transformed in the name of competition that was said to benefit investors. Instead, this has produced an almost lawless high-speed maze where prices can spiral out of control, spooking average investors and start-up entrepreneurs alike.
>
> The flash crash should have sounded an alarm. Unfortunately, the regulators are still asleep. (Kaufman and Levin 2011, p. A27)

Note the "lawless high-speed maze," a reference to the absence of officially designated market makers. The authors even take a swipe at the cherished "competition," which I said is the guise under which speculative capital self-destructs. Having perceived that point, they cannot develop it further, because they do not know speculative capital. So they turn to regulators— regulators who must have been asleep if all these terrible things happened.

But the regulators were not asleep; it is that there is nothing they could do. They, too, operate in a landscape shaped and defined by speculative capital. One year after the May 2010 Flash Crash,

> Securities and Exchange Commission chairwoman Mary Schapiro ... expressed dismay that active traders fled the stock market during the May 6 "flash crash." ... "The issue ... is whether the firms that effectively act as market makers during normal times should have any obligation to support the market in reasonable ways in tough times," Ms. Schapiro said in a speech earlier this month. (Wall Street Journal 2010)

But there is no issue, and it is not a matter of conduct.

Beginning with "conduct," the concept is meaningless—it does not apply. Conduct connotes freedom, and with it, choice. In the speculative capital–created, frenzied environment of the markets maintained by HFT, there cannot be any freedom, because there is no choice. It is, to use a popular expression, either speculative capital's way (i.e., HFT), or the highway. No one *not* in line with speculative capital's trading pattern will last a day in the markets. That is precisely the meaning of the market being "ruined."[13]

Saber emphasized this crucial point in his book:

> Because these attributes [being fast-paced, probing market for arbitrage opportunities to exploit] define speculative capital, the manager of speculative capital must employ it in activities that are consistent with these attributes.... Thus, in the absence of any real option, the manager of speculative capital turns into its agent, someone who nominally "runs" the speculative capital but must in fact follow its "agenda." Speculative capital becomes the grammatical subject of the sentence as if it were alive: speculative capital seeks arbitrage opportunities. Of course, it does so through its agent, the fund manager, but it is the speculative capital which determines the nature of its own employment and calls the strategic shots. (Saber 1999, p. 73)

As for the "issue" of whether traders should support the market at difficult times, the then-SEC chairwoman also missed the point. The entire point of the transformation of markets into its current shape, where the high-frequency traders dominate, is *not* to have anyone in charge. Speculative capital does not recognize any obligation, especially an obligation like supporting the markets, that is, *buying*, when prices are falling. Arbitrage is about "freedom" as speculative capital defines it: the ability to move at lightning speed from any market in the world to any other in search of profits, without having to explain and without being impeded. Regulators are right to have concerns, but their concerns will not carry the day. Functionally, practically, and, most important of all, ideologically, speculative capital has the final say in matters of markets, with results that are plain for everyone to see: a crash-prone market conveying no useful information, and thus serving no purpose, sustained by the feverish activity of the same HFT that perverted the prices in the first place. Such is the ironic state of affairs ultimately brought about by the self-destructive tendency of speculative capital.

Notes

1   "Since the financial crisis, regulators have focused on improving the transparency of opaque markets such as derivatives, which generate enormous profits for global banks. As a consequence, more markets are becoming computerized, opening the door to high-frequency or ultra-fast trading as technological knowhow is applied in new areas. The potential benefits to investors seem clear: trading will become cheaper and more transparent" (Financial Times 2013, p. 7).

2   "At a recent conference Alasdair Haynes, chief executive of Chi-X Europe, a trading platform, likened the market's obsession with speed to the dung-loving fungus. He was alluding to the rapid dealing of so-called 'high-frequency' traders in markets. The fungus propels its spores faster than anything in the natural world. But not in the technological world. Electronic trading is now faster" (Financial Times 2011b, p. 20).

3   In August 1971, President Nixon formally ended the convertibility of the dollar to gold, bringing the Bretton Woods system to an end. From 1971 until 1973, a sort of informal agreement between the central banks of the Western countries and Japan maintained a loose regime of fixed rates between their currencies. In 1973, that agreement, too, collapsed under economic/monetary pressure, and the currencies were thrown into the markets to find their equilibrium point.

4   This is an example employed to highlight a particular point. I naturally abstract from many factors such as transportation cost.

5   ¥3,600,000/320 = $11,125.

6    $10,000 × 320 = ¥3,200,000.

7   ¥3.2 billion/340 = $9.4 million.

8   This is an example in terms of details. Such transactions, in point of fact, did take place and gave rise to speculative capital.

9   Stocks were brought into the game late because banks in the United States were prohibited from trading stocks.

10   It is also called quantitative finance because of its mathematical structure.

11   The markets I have in mind here are specifically the US equities markets.

12   In internal settlement, the broker matches my order for buying one hundred Google shares with your order selling the same internally, and without transmitting them into the exchange.

13   The remaining 25 percent of trading volume that is not HFT-related is due to pension funds and other long-term investors.

References

Bernstein, P. (2005) *Capital Ideas: The Improbable Origins of Modern Wall Street*, Wiley.
Financial Times (2009) "SEC Eye Over High-Speed Trading," *Financial Times*, July 28.

————. (2010a) "High-Frequency Traders Battle to Make Big Returns," *Financial Times*, September 9.

————. (2010b) "Market Structures Face Test of Trust," *Financial Times*, October 18.

————. (2010c) "Behaviour of Equities Poses Questions," *Financial Times*, May 17.

————. (2010d) "SEC Passes 'Stub Quote' Rules," *Financial Times*, November 8.

————. (2011a) "ECB Warns on High-Speed Trading," *Financial Times*, February 24.

————. (2011b) "Super-Fast Traders Feel Heat from Competition," *Financial Times*, April 14.

————. (2013) "In Search of Fast Buck," *Financial Times*, February 19.

Kaufman, E. and C. Levin (2011) "Preventing the Next Flash Crash," *New York Times*, May 6.

Kothare, M. and P. A. Laus (1995) "Trading, Costs and the Trading Systems for Nasdaq Stocks," *Financial Analysts Journal*, Vol 51, No. 2.

New York Times (1997) "Fractions Edge Closer to Wall St. Extinction," *New York Times*, June 4.

Saber, N. (1999) *Speculative Capital*, Vol 1, *The Invisible Hand of Global Finance*, Pearson Education.

Samuelson, P. (1994) "Introduction," in R. Merton, *Continuous-Time Finance*, Blackwell.

Securities and Exchange Commission, Commodity Futures Trading Commission (2010) "Findings Regarding the Market Events of May 6, 2010," available at http://www.sec.gov/news/studies/2010/marketevents-report.pdf.

Wall Street Journal (1995a) "Nasdaq's 'SOES Bandits' Seek Recruits," *Wall Street Journal*, June 1.

————. (1995b) "NASD is Expected to Penalize Lehman For Failing to Honor Stock-Price Quotes," *Wall Street Journal*, September 6.

————. (1995c) "SEC Official Chides Nasdaq Traders for Complaining About Regulations," *Wall Street Journal*, May 20.

————. (1997a) "Trading Vast Volumes, Stock Firm Consults Only Its 'Black Box,'" *Wall Street Journal*, November 20.

————. (1997b) "'Securities Concerns' Settlement of Suit by Investors Wins Backing from Judge," *Wall Street Journal*, October 9.

————. (2010) "Keeping Traders in the Market Could Prove Challenging," *Wall Street Journal*, October 24.

PART IV

THE CRISIS AND THE EURO

CHAPTER 16

FROM THE CRISIS IN SURPLUS VALUE TO THE CRISIS IN THE EURO

Guglielmo Carchedi

In 2007–2008, the explosion of the speculative bubble was avoided by massive injections of "liquidity" (basically, the extension of credit) in the banking sector. However, banks used that liquidity for speculation, rather than lending it to the productive sectors. Starting from 2008, the European Central Bank lent the European banks money at a 1 percent interest rate. With that money, banks bought bonds issued by states with less-than-solid finances whose interest rates fluctuated between 2 percent and 5 percent. These banks gained enormously from the interest rate differentials. Yet their exposure to bad debts was such that more was needed, and the states had to contract further debts in order to save the banks. Consequently, the states' deficits and debts increased hugely. The states risked default and had to issue bonds at higher interest rates, thus falling into even greater debt. The pressure on banks was temporarily relieved, but a menacing crisis of sovereign debt emerged, and the states landed in a vicious circle. From 2007 to 2011, the total deficit of the countries in the Organisation for Economic Co-operation and Development (OECD) increased sevenfold, while their debt skyrocketed to a record US$43 trillion, almost equal to the world GDP. In the Eurozone, debts reached the level of US$7.7 trillion. It was within this context that the *euro crisis* emerged—the specific form taken in Europe by the global financial crisis. It is the risk of default of the sovereign debt of the weaker states, accompanied by the possible consequences for the structure of the Eurozone and for the survival of the euro. But why and how was the euro called into life, and what is its connection to the present crisis?

From the very beginning, the European project aimed at creating an economic bloc capable of counterbalancing the economic power of the United States (Carchedi 2001). One of the conditions was the creation of a single, strong currency that could become the rival of the US dollar. This was not merely a political question. Rather, it was basically a financial and economic one. Financially, a strong currency could have attracted international capital and could have created a European financial center able to challenge Wall Street. Economically, what was at stake was international seigniorage.

Since 1971 a substantial amount of dollars has been used (1) by other countries as international reserves; (2) as money circulating within the dollarized countries; and (3) as a means of payment on the international markets. However, these dollars have not been used to import goods and services from the United States. For more than forty years, the US trade balance has constantly been negative. Value (imported foreign commodities) is exchanged for a representation of value (dollars), but the latter is not transformed into actual value produced in the United States (US commodities). In this way, the United States appropriates value produced by other nations—recently in amounts totaling close to 6 percent of its GDP (fig. 16.1). This is *seigniorage*, the appropriation of international value by the nation whose currency is the international means of exchange and of international reserves; the currency of the economically dominant nation, the US. But inasmuch as the US lose their dominant position, the dollar's seigniorage is threatened.

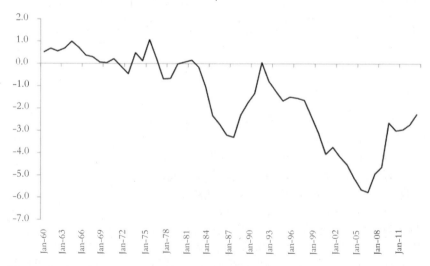

Figure 16.1. US current account (% of GDP), 1960–2013. Source: see appendix; author's calculations.

The euro has emerged as the only real challenger of the dollar's seigniorage. This challenge needed to rest on two interrelated pillars: the euro had to represent an economy on the same scale as that of the United States, and it also had to be a strong currency. It had to be strong even before it was born. To see this, we must deal with the precursor of the euro, the European currency unit (ECU). The ECU was introduced in 1978. It was not real money, like the dollar or the German mark (DM). Rather, it was basically money of account, virtual money. Officially, it was introduced for the settlement of accounts between the European central banks. But the dollar was already performing this function quite well. Thus, what the EU needed was not only its own money of account, but also a virtual currency that would be the precursor of a real currency—one that would already, in its potential state, have the features that would make it a challenger of the US dollar's seigniorage, once it would become a real currency.

At its inception, the ECU was created by accrediting to each central bank a quantity of ECUs equal to 20 percent of its gold reserves and 20 percent of its US dollar reserves. Once the ECU price of US$1 was found (we shall see shortly that it was set at ECU 1.3 for the US dollar), it became possible to compute the quantity of ECUs that each central bank swapped in exchange for its dollar and gold reserves. This was done by the European Monetary Cooperation Fund. These swaps were renewed four times a year, at the beginning of each quarter. Notice, incidentally, that the tying of the price of the ECU to that of the dollar and to that of the member states' dollar reserves was a recognition of the relative superiority of the US economy compared to the European ones. Let us consider the composition of the ECU.

In the ECU, all the currencies of the member states were represented in different quantities. These were the *bilateral central rates*. When it was introduced in 1978, the ECU had the composition shown in column A of table 16.1. Column B gives the exchange rate against the US dollar on December 1, 1978, the date the ECU was introduced. Column C is derived from dividing A by B and thus gives the equivalent in dollars of column A, that is, of the quantities of the national currencies going into ECU 1 expressed in dollars. The total of column C, that is, 1.3001831, is the value in dollars of ECU 1. Column D gives the value of ECU 1 in the different national currencies. It is obtained by multiplying the value of ECU 1 in dollars (1.3001831) by each rate in column B. Thus, ECU 1 was equal to DM 2.51689, FF 5.78516, and so on. Finally, column E is the expression in dollars of the weight of each currency in ECU 1. It is obtained by dividing each item in column C by the total (1.3001831).

A	B	C	D	E
0.828 DM	1.9358	0.427301	2.51689	32.90%
1.15 FF	4.4495	0.258456	5.78516	19.90%
0.0885 UKL	1.9364	0.1713514	0.671443	13.20%
109.0 ITL	853	0.1277842	1109.06	9.80%

0.286 HFL	2.1935	0.1359638	2.73494	10.50%
3.66 BFR	30.6675	0.1193445	39.8734	9.20%
0.140 LFR	30.6675	0.004565	39.8734	0.40%
0.217 DKR	5.3885	0.0402709	7.00604	3.10%
0.00759 IRL	1.9364	0.0146972	0.671443	1.00%

Table 16.1. Equivalents of national currencies of ECU 1and weightings. Source: author's calculations.

In spite of the introduction of the ECU, the member countries retained their national currencies with which they settled international accounts. They could devalue or revalue according to their need. Yet, the ECU set limits to this room for maneuver. Through their fixed value relative to the ECU (column D in table 16.1), national currencies had a fixed value relative to each other. These were called *cross central rates*. For example, DM 2.51689 were equal to FF 5.78516. Since the *market cross rates* diverged from the cross central rates due to the effect of the demand and supply for the different currencies, the member states undertook to keep their currencies' fluctuations within relatively narrow limits. These limits of fluctuations were called *bilateral limits*. To keep currencies within their bilateral limits, central banks and governments had to intervene. In the case of a weak currency, they resorted to restrictive monetary policies (a rise in interest rates or a credit crunch); to support operations using a diversity of currencies; to a tightening of fiscal and income policy; or, exceptionally, to the realignment of the central rate (devaluation). In the case of a strong currency, the opposite applied in each case.

Take the example of Germany. Given its higher productivity, it was more competitive on foreign markets, and German exports were not dependent on the devaluation of the DM. Italy's situation was the opposite. It had to resort to devaluation. But the high value of the ECU relative to the dollar and the relative fixity of the cross central rates greatly limited the less efficient country's possibility to devalue. Consequently, Italy, if it did not want to devalue by modifying its bilateral central rate, had either to accept a deterioration of its balance of trade, or to reduce the rate of inflation. Of course, Italy's predicament would have been eased if Germany had revalued the DM (so that the lira would have devalued relative to the DM, thus increasing its exports to Germany), but that was not in the interest of Germany. If the weight of defending the Italian bilateral central rate became intolerable, only one solution was left: to leave the ECU. This is what Italy did in 1992, only to be readmitted in 1996. Given that the weaker countries wanted to remain within the ECU area, Germany could thus set limits to the their capacity to devalue. This was the first aspect of the German leadership within the ECU.

The use of the ECU among the member states of the European System of Central Banks was the official circuit. However, when the private market started to use the ECU for commercial and financial dealings, the private circuit appeared. The ECU became a foreign currency that began to be used in the same way as other currencies—most particularly the US dollar. In this way, the ECU changed from a unit of account to a foreign currency. Even if its use for commercial settlements outside the European Economic Community remained limited, it is useful to see how this use posed limits to the weaker countries' freedom to devalue. For example, if the DM revalued relative to the dollar because of Germany's strong economic performance, the ECU also revalued. Exports in ECU would become more difficult, and less efficient countries (capitals) like Italy would meet more difficulties in exporting. These countries needed a weak ECU. If Italy devalued the lira, in order to weaken the euro, but Germany revalued the DM, then, given the greater weight of the DM than of the lira, the ECU would revalue. In the history of the ECU, the DM only revalued, the lira only devalued, and the ECU consistently revalued. This was the second aspect of the German leadership within the ECU. In short, the ECU was born a strong currency, and this was not by chance.

When in 1999, the ECU was transformed into the euro on the basis of ECU 1 = €1, the euro was born as a strong currency—a potential rival of the dollar as the currency of international exchange and reserves. It reflected, in a contradictory way, not only the economic interests of the new emerging bloc, but even more so those of Germany, whose strategic aim was the creation of an imperialist pole under its leadership as an alternative to that of the United States.

After its birth, the euro had to maintain its strong position. The conditions for this were that Germany keep its dominant economic strength, that the euro area be extended, and that the other Eurozone nations too remain or become internationally competitive. However, the euro was extended to countries that were far from enjoying the level of productivity—and thus of international competitiveness—needed to contribute to making the euro a strong currency. From the perspective of Germany, the reason was twofold. First, the weaker, less productive countries could not compete with Germany by resorting to competitive devaluation. The market for German goods would expand. Second, a wider Eurozone would have increased the international transactions settled in euros, thus increasing the demand for the currency and favoring its revaluation. This would have counterbalanced the dollarization of some Latin American countries. But while dollarization does not imply any US financial responsibility for the dollarized countries, the EU (and within it Germany) has become financially responsible within the Eurozone.

The present phase of economic depression has marked a pause in the struggle between the dollar and the euro. A weak dollar on the one hand weakens its role as the international currency, but on the other favors US exports. In the present crisis, the United States chooses a weak currency to spur exports, rather than a strong currency whose effect would be to defend the US dollar's role as an international currency—even more so because in the present conjuncture, due to Brexit, the solidity of the EU and thus of the euro has been placed at increasing risk. Moreover, the weakening or disappearance of the euro through a "disorderly" default of one or more Eurozone countries' financial systems could have devastating reverberations on the other side of the Atlantic. This is not to say that there is no longer rivalry between the two currencies. Rather, in the present conjuncture the struggle for seigniorage is less impelling than other, more immediate dangers, given also the increasing dangers to the survival of the EU and the euro.

At present, as another economic and financial crisis looms in the near future, the future of the EU depends also on the interests of the different factions of the Germany ruling elite. One faction, together with similar factions in the other financially strong countries, wants to reorient its long-term strategy, seeking the expansion of Germany toward China and Russia. There are several reasons for this move. First, both countries have immense reserves of raw materials. Second, the level of China's economic growth and the size of its market are way above those of the EU. China has huge potential both as a consumer market for German industrial products and as a field of investments.[1] Third, Germany's relative technological superiority is the ideal condition for the intertrade appropriation of Chinese surplus value. Fourth, if bilateral trade relations were to continue at the current pace, Beijing would become Germany's main trading partner by 2020 (Schibotto 2014). Fifth, for China, Germany is the European country with the best investment opportunities; China is the second-largest non-European investor in Germany after the United States. Finally, China's likely ultimate goal is to lessen US influence in Europe by forging its own close ties to the EU—and Germany is the strategic foothold in Europe. These are ideal conditions for German expansionism to scale down its interests in Europe and direct its attention to the East.

Arguably, the de-linking from the weak euro and the introduction of the Northern euro would be part of these new strategic interests. This is why "Germany," that is, this faction of its ruling class, pushes for (or at least does not oppose) the default of the weaker countries (including, but not limited to Greece) so that they leave the Eurozone. One way to do this is to impose, through international bodies, conditions upon countries undergoing dire financial difficulties that are genocidal, and in the end impossible to satisfy. The recent example of Greece is paradigmatic.

The best solution for this section of the Northern bourgeoisie would be for these countries to "eurorize" their economies—that is, to leave the Eurozone while retaining the euro (possibly the Northern euro)—similar to what occurred during the dollarization of some South American countries (Panama in 1904, Ecuador in 2000, El Salvador in 2001) that are not part of the US economic system.[2] The economic area within which the euro would be used would not shrink, while the strong countries would not be financially responsible for the weaker ones. But, so the reasoning goes, even if some of the weaker countries were to abandon the euro, the volume of transactions (with China, among other nations) would grow rather than shrink. The euro would become a strong "Northern" euro, capable of challenging the dollar also because the dollar is being weakened, as shown by its 2011 first downgrading. But while the dollar's weakening is relatively modest, the Euro might face an existential crisis.[3]

However, the default by the weak countries could unleash a chain reaction of bank failures that, given the interconnection of debts, could branch out into the stronger countries, including the United States. This could provoke the generalized financial crisis that it has been possible to postpone until now through huge extensions of credit. The strong countries would have to intervene, this time to salvage their own financial systems. It is probably because of these unknowns that the other faction of the German bourgeoisie prefers to keep the present euro even as a weaker currency. They hope that, given sufficient financial aid and anti-crisis (i.e., anti-labor) measures, the Eurozone will not fall apart and the euro will regain and reinforce its position vis-à-vis the dollar. Thus, the weak countries' default should be avoided. This is, in essence, the difference between the German hawks, on the one hand, and the hawks dressed up as doves, on the other.

These are capital's dilemmas. However, labor's concern should be different: the decision as to whether to retain the euro or not should be informed by a wider strategy, in which that decision is part of a program that challenges capitalist production relations and replaces them with socialist ones. This is the fundamental issue of political strategy, which cannot be dealt with here. What can be done here is to examine this issue as it is framed in contemporary economic debates—that is, from the perspective of the advantages and disadvantages of reverting to competitive devaluation, and its effects on a country's economic growth.

Those arguing for exiting the euro hold that the weak Eurozone countries' exports and economic growth have fallen because competitive devaluation is no longer an option. Exiting the euro and resorting to competitive devaluation would improve exports, production, wages, and profits. To evaluate this claim, let us assess whether, and in what measure, the introduction of the euro has affected the trade balance between Germany and Italy (Fig. 16.2).

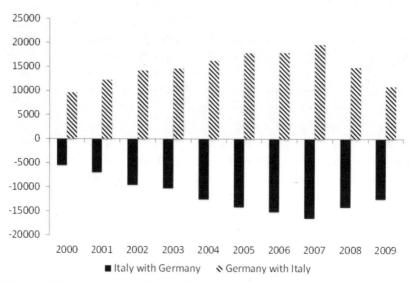

Figure 16.2. Germany–Italy trade balance (€ million), 2000–2009. Source: see appendix; author's calculations.

From 2000 to 2009, the Italian and the German trade balances have moved in opposite directions. However, the deterioration of the Italian trade balance with Germany cannot be ascribed only, or even mainly, to the impossibility to resort to competitive devaluation; this is shown by Germany's ability to penetrate non-EU foreign markets. In 2011 Germany had a surplus of €1 trillion, a record. Given that the Eurozone countries account for only 40 percent of its exports, Germany's ability to penetrate foreign markets is relatively independent of the lack of competitive devaluation of its Eurozone partners. Rather, Germany's trade surplus with the EU partners depends mainly upon its technological superiority.

"Labor productivity" has been defined in chapter 2 of this book as output divided by labor units. It applies, by definition, only to the productive sectors. Data on the productive sectors are available for the US economy but are lacking for other countries. Therefore, what follows has to rely on the available statistics, and thus on (1) GDP figures for the economy as a whole, and (2) labor productivity is defined as GDP divided by labor hours (L). Consider first the GDP in Italy and Germany (fig. 16.3); then the growth rates of GDP/L (fig. 16.4); and finally labor hours in Italy and Germany (fig. 16.5).

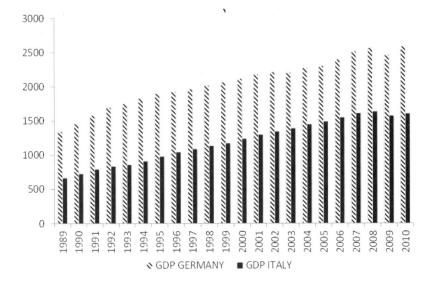

Figure 16.3. GDP in Italy and Germany (€ billion), 1989–2010. Source: see appendix.

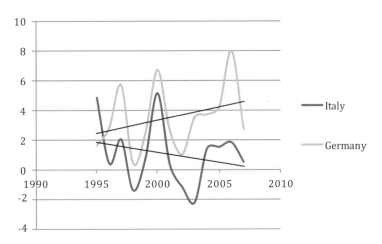

Figure 16.4. Growth rate of GDP/L in Italy and Germany, 1990–2010. Source: see appendix.

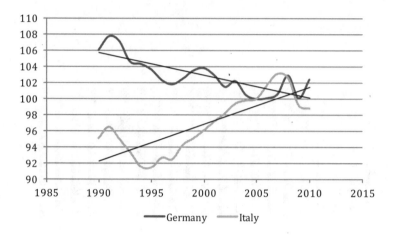

Figure 16.5. Labor hours in Italy and Germany (2005 = 100), 1985–2015. Source: see appendix.

In both countries, GDP grows (fig. 16.3). However, the increment in GDP can be due either to greater labor productivity or to a greater rate of surplus labor (mainstream economics does not distinguish between these two cases for obvious ideological reasons):

(1) In Germany, *GDP/L* grows (fig. 16.4) while labor hours decline (fig. 16.5). Therefore, the greater GDP (fig. 16.3) seems to have been due to greater productivity, something that does not rule out a greater rate of surplus value.[4]

(2) In Italy, *GDP/L* falls (fig. 16.4) while labor hours increase (fig. 16.5). Therefore, the greater GDP (fig. 16.3) seems to have been due to a greater rate of exploitation.

The same results hold also for the manufacturing sector. The value added per employee is €67,500 in Germany but €51,000 in Italy, while the hours worked in Italy are 1,778 per year, 360 more than in Germany (di Branco 2012, p. 3). So much for the "lazy southerners."

This is Italy's relative economic weakness: its growth rests on increasing exploitation, while that of Germany rests on higher labor productivity. Thus, it is mistaken to ascribe Italy's negative trade balance to the euro. The cause of Italy's negative performance is its backward technological base relative to Germany's, and the lack of competitive devaluation has been grafted onto this technological weakness. Why, then, have the weaker countries sought membership in the ECU first and then in the euro? Or, better said, why has their *capital* sought such membership?

Their capitalists knew, as they know nowadays, that they cannot compete with Germany on the technological level. They also knew that competitive devaluation causes inflation (see below), which in its turn leads to yet higher levels of competitive devaluation. They knew that the only way to compete internationally was to increase the national rate of surplus value of their labor force: this could be achieved, on the one hand, through longer working hours and higher intensity of labor, together with a compression of real wages; on the other, it could be attained through dismantling social security systems and increasing the legal possibility of arbitrarily dismissing laborers, called "labor flexibility." This predicament seems to be the consequence of the introduction of the euro. Therefore, anti-labor measures seem to originate in some distant, "European" bureaucracy, which deflects the attention from the weakness of capital. In reality, euro membership, rather then being the *cause*, is a *consequence* of the failure of the weaker countries' national capitals. Exiting the euro would not remedy this weakness. The question here is not whether the weaker countries should abandon the euro or retain it. Rather, my primary aim is to demystify the notion that the euro is the weaker countries' source of their predicament, and that exiting the euro would be a solution to that predicament.

Macroeconomics holds that greater export-led production spurs economic growth, but that this improvement can be limited or even annulled by a number of counteracting factors. For example, the depreciation of currency, on the one hand, reduces exports, but on the other, it increases imports. This could cause an inflationary movement. Or, other countries could resort to the same policy, thus canceling the devaluing country's original advantage. These could be called counteracting factors. But these factors do not dent the basic macroeconomic argument that devaluation spurs export-led production, and that this in turn stimulates consumption, investments, and thus economic growth.

This argument is erroneous. Greater production is not necessarily equal to economic growth in the exporting country, as the devaluing country loses value and its profitability falls. Profitability rises in the countries importing its cheaper commodities. Profitability falls not because less surplus value is generated, but because surplus value is lost by the country resorting to competitive devaluation. This thesis can be argued in three steps.

First, Marx's much maligned, and yet very robust, theory of production prices holds that when two commodities are exchanged at their production price (after the equalization of the profit rates), the manufacturer of the commodity produced with a lower organic composition loses value to the manufacturer of the commodity produced with a higher organic composition of capital. The focus here is on exchange within the same national economy and using the same currency. This theory can be applied mutatis mutandis to the international economy, and to different currencies as mediums of payment. Thus, there is a first source of appropriation of surplus value inherent in the formation of international production prices, much the same as in the case of national production prices. Let us abstract, as a first approximation, from different currencies. Given the formation of international production prices, if two commodities are exchanged at their production price, one produced in a country by a capital with a lower OCC and the other produced in another country by a capital with a higher OCC, that exchange implies a loss of value by the former to the latter capitalist (and thus in their national economies, as well).

Second, let us assume that the two countries have different currencies as means of payments. Suppose Italy exits the euro and reverts to the lira, while Germany keeps the euro. Suppose initially that ITL 1,000 = €1, that commodity *a* costs ITL 1,000 in Italy, and that commodity *b* costs €1 in Germany. The German capitalist exchanges €1 for ITL 1,000 and buys 1*a* (produced in Italy). The Italian capitalist receives €1 and with it buys 1*b* (produced in Germany). Under the assumption that these are international production prices, if the Italian producer makes 1*a* with a lower OCC than that used by the German producer to produce 1*b*, there is a loss of value from the Italian to the German producer. There is equilibrium in the two countries' balance of payment. But behind it, there is the Italian exporter's loss of value and its appropriation by the German importer. Therefore, there is a fall in Italy's value ARP and a rise in that of Germany. The equilibrium in the trade balance hides a worsening of the technologically weaker country's profitability.

Why, then, does the Italian capitalist in the example above resort to export? Suppose that the exporter has produced a given output, 2*a*, and that she cannot sell all of it on the domestic market. If 1*a* can neither be sold on the domestic market, nor exported because it is too expensive on the international market, then the exporter suffers a loss equal to the value of 1*a*. Therefore, the government can resort to competitive devaluation. While at the old exchange rate of ITL 1,000 = €1 the exporter could export only 1*a* (so that 1*a* was a loss because it remained unsold), at the new exchange rate of ITL 2,000 = €1 the entire output, 2*a*, can be exported.

Because the exporter receives ITL 2,000, she can sell the whole output, 2*a*. In terms of Italian lire, her rate of profit is the same as if she had sold 1*a* (previously unsold) on the domestic market. Thus her *money* rate of profit rises relative to when 1*a* was unsold. The same holds for the economy as a whole. However, the *value* rate of profit falls because 1*a*, and thus its value has been lost. The fall in the value rate of profit is hidden by the improvement in the money rate of profit. If 1*a* is a means of consumption, less is left for domestic consumption. If it is a means of production, the new cycle begins on a contracted scale. The initial euphoria due to the rising money profitability following competitive devaluation is bound to be followed by the deterioration of the economy caused by the same economic policy.

There is a Keynesian counterargument. Suppose that the initial output of 1*a* rises to 2*a* because of export-led demand. Differently from the assumption above, output increases by 1*a* because of foreign demand. Constant capital, variable capital (wages) and profits increase. The demand for assets and labor power rises, and this leads to higher consumption and investment. At this point the Keynesian multiplier is set in motion. A chain of further investments, production, and consumption—that is, economic growth—follows. This is the theory.

In reality, even if nominal wages and employment might increase due to this chain of investments, real wages (real not in the sense of deflated wages but in terms of the consumption goods available on the domestic market) fall. Thus, the employed labor force and nominal wages might grow, but real wages fall. This is the initial effect of competitive devaluation, which is unnoticed by the Keynesian multiplier. But consider the chain of (decreasing) investments following the first boost of export-led exports. What is further unnoticed by the Keynesian multiplier is that what jump-starts the economy is not only greater production, investment, and consumption, but also (and chiefly) a higher average profitability. And this depends on what has been called the "Marxist multiplier," namely, on whether at the end of the chain of induced investments the average OCC has risen (and the ARP fallen) or fallen (and the ARP risen). Given that each investor commissions the commodities she needs to the producers with lower prices, and given that these latter are those who use new techniques with higher organic composition, the most likely outcome is a fall in the average, or general, rate of profit. Empirical evidence supports this conclusion.[5]

In sum, due to competitive devaluation, the money rate of profit of the exporting capital improves together with the money-average rate of profit. Employment and investments in the exporting nation might also improve. But at the same time, in the exporting nation consumption and investment goods are lost, and with them the value contained therein. The value-average rate of profit worsens with the concomitant dangers of bankruptcies for the weaker capitals and a slowdown of economic growth. Such are the consequences of competitive devaluation.

The above shows how misdirected is the call in some quarters of the Left for exiting the euro and returning to the national currencies, in order to resort to competitive devaluation and restart economic growth (and employment)—possibly on the basis of the Keynesian multiplier. This is not to say that the weaker countries should keep the euro. Whether to stay in or to leave the euro is a decision that should be embedded in a wider strategy of radical change centred upon the transformation of the capitalist production relation.[6] In taking this decision, due notice should be taken of the real effect of competitive devaluation. Outside of this perspective, to exit or not to exit is meaningless question.

The real problem for the countries that rely on competitive devaluation is the inefficiency of their productive systems relative to stronger international competitors. This is capital's problem. Thus, labor (especially the trade unions) should not believe that this is also its problem, nor that the modernization of the productive apparatus would also be convenient to it because of the possibility of a pro-labor redistribution of a share of the (export-led) increased output. Increased productivity means increasing technological unemployment, and all the misery inherent in the tendency toward a falling ARP and crises. The laborers who have not lost their jobs might receive a greater share of the higher output. But by cooperating with capital in the modernization of capital's productive apparatus, they would become active members in international capitalist competition, and in the creation of technological unemployment.[7] Labor would participate in the downloading of the effects of technological innovations, not only upon itself, but also upon the weaker countries—with all the accompanying negative consequences for the laborers of those countries. Labor's problem is different. It should try to avoid bearing the cost of the crises by demanding better living and working conditions. But its perspective should be that labor's gains, far from being the way out of the slump, in fact weaken capital. This is one of the essential conditions for the formation of the consciousness necessary for a transition out of capitalism. Labor's struggle cannot but be anti-capitalist and internationalist.

Appendix: Statistical Sources

For general statistical sources, see Carchedi (2001).

Figure 16.1. Data 360 (2006) "U.S. Trade Balance as a Percentage of GDP," *Data 360*, available at http://data360.org/dsg.aspx?Data_Set_Group_Id=270.

Figure 16.2. Eurostat (2010) "External and intra-EU trade—statistical yearbook, Data 1958–2009, European Commission," *Eurostat*, available at http://epp .eurostat.ec.europa.eu/cache/ITY_OFFPUB/KS-GI-10-002/EN/KS-GI-10-002-EN.PDF.

Figures 16.3, 16.4, 16.5. http://stats.oecd.org/Index.aspx?DatasetCode=PDYGTH.

Notes

1   As the *Financial Times Deutschland* writes, "As long as the euro zone doesn't fall apart, and Europe's economy doesn't slump violently, the German companies have a chance at avoiding a crash. Demand from Europe has been weak for months, and German firms have managed to more or less handle it. This is partly

because they have globalized, with earnings in Asia making up for losses in Europe" (quoted in Allen 2012).

2   According to the dominant interpretation of Article 50 of the Lisbon Treaty, a euro-nation that would leave the euro would have to leave the EU. But nothing prevents a country from leaving the EU and retaining *unilaterally* the euro.

3   On August 1, 2011, Standard & Poor's cut the rating of US debt from AAA to AA+. From October 2010 to February 2012, Russia halved its US debt, and China is selling, too, even if it has still $1 trillion of US debt.

4   According to official German statistics, unemployment has fallen from 5.3 million in 2005 to 2.9 million in 2008 and 3.4 million in 2010. But these figures are cooked. In 2005, the Schröder government introduced a reform of the labor market. Before the reform, the unemployed received unemployment benefits equal to two-thirds of the last salary for up to three years. After the reform, the length of the unemployment benefit equal to two-thirds of the last salary has fallen to one year, after which time the benefit falls to half of the last salary and becomes conditional upon the capacity to work of the unemployed, defined as the capacity to work for three hours a day. In this way, the unemployed have been pushed onto the labor market at hunger wages, and about 2.9 million long-term unemployed have disappeared from the official statistics (see Lestrade 2010). According to another report, in 2008, 6.55 million employees worked for a wage below the low-wage threshold, an increase of 2.3 million since 1998 (Kalina and Weinkopf 2010). According to other figures, the workers holding Mini jobs increased by 47 percent between 1999 and 2009, while temporary workers increased by 131.4 percent (see OFS, n.d.). High productivity and high rates of exploitation: the ideal recipe for capital.

5   See Carchedi and Roberts, chapter 1 of this volume; and Carchedi, chapter 2 of this volume.

6   The supporters of the thesis that competitive devaluation spurs economic growth like to mention the case of Argentina. But Argentina's former finance minister Domingo Cavallo is clear: "Growth restarted and unemployment began to fall in 2003. But this was not due to the devaluation. The key factors were the depreciation of the dollar and good luck on the commodity prices. The price of soy—which is a price set in international markets—jumped from less than $120 a ton in 2001 to more than $500 a ton by the late 2000s. It is absolutely erroneous and misleading to attribute the rapid growth of Argentina during the last 8 years to the 'pesofication' and devaluation of 2002" (Cavallo 2011). See also Roberts, chapter 17 of this volume.

7   The same applies, with due modifications, to those authors who theorize an alliance between labor and small capital against big capital.

References

Allen, K. (2012) "Uncomfortable and Bitter Truth for German Economy," *Spiegel Online International*, July 27.

di Branco, M. (2012) "Italia maglia nera in Europa ma lavorialmo più degli altri," *Il Messaggero*, February 22.

Carchedi, G. (2001) *For Another Europe*, Verso.

Cavallo, D. (2011) "Looking at Greece in the Argentinean mirror," *VOX*, available at http://voxeu.org/index.php?q=node/6758.

Kalina, T. and C. Weinkopf (2010) "Niedriglohnbeschäftigung 2008," Universität Duisburg Essen, available at http://www.iaq.uni-due.de/iaq-report/2010/ report2010–06.pdf.

Lestrade, B. (2010) "Les réformes sociales Hartz IV à l'heure de la rigueur en Allemagne," *Ifri*, available at http://www.france-allemagne.fr/IMG/pdf/IFRI_ndc75lestrade .pdf.

Office fédéral de statistiques (n.d.) untitled table, OFS, available at http://cdn1.myeurop .info/sites/default/files/media/images/Capture_4.PNG.

Schibotto, E. (2014) "Germany and China Have an Emerging 'special relationship' which has the potential to go far beyond trade," *European Politics and Policy* (blog), London School of Economics, official website, available at http://bit.ly/WcogBs.

CHAPTER 17

THE EURO CRISIS IS A CRISIS OF CAPITALISM

Michael Roberts

1. Introduction

The euro crisis of 2009 to 2013 was a product of the slump in global capitalism, and the subsequent failure to recover is the same. Profitability in most capitalist economies is still well below the peak of 2007 (the US is the only exception), and for economies like Italy and Slovenia it is still heading downward. If you correlate profitability with growth after the end of the trough of the Great Recession from 2010 until 2015, the trend line is positively sloped (fig. 17.1). Estonia and Ireland have seen the biggest recovery in profitability (through austerity and through cutting wages and living standards, along with massive emigration of the unemployed). As a result, they have had the best GDP recoveries—such as they are. Where the recovery in profitability has been weak or nonexistent, real GDP has contracted the most.

The correlation between profitability and growth is much better than that between government spending and growth, the Keynesian indicator (fig. 17.2). Countries where government spending to GDP has increased since 2009 (through Keynesian-style stimuli), like Japan and Slovenia, have not grown at all, while there are many countries that applied austerity and reduced government spending to GDP after 2009 and have achieved some growth. There is no real correlation between growth and austerity (the trend line is almost flat), whatever Keynesian "multipliers" might indicate (Roberts 2012).

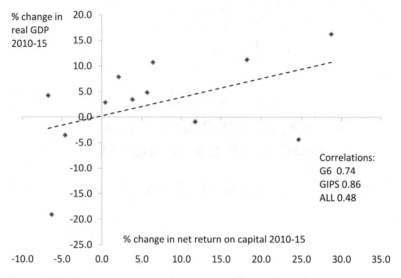

Figure 17.1. Eurozone economies: percent change in real GDP and percent change in net return on capital, 2010–15. Source: AMECO, author's calculations.

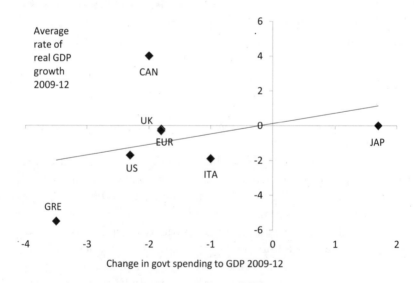

Figure 17.2. G7 and Eurozone average rate of real GDP growth and change in government spending (%), 2009–2012. Source: OECD and author's calculations.

The buildup of debt, not just for banks but also for the non-financial capitalist sector, has exerted downward pressure on the ability of Europe's capitalist economies to recover quickly, even after cutting jobs, closing down businesses and ending investment to reduce the cost of capital. The greater the growth in private sector debt before the crisis, the smaller the recovery has been. Balance sheet stress is heavier on the weaker Economic and Monetary Union (EMU) states, and on the financial centers of the United Kingdom and the United States.

The debt-servicing burden of the Eurozone periphery in 2015 accounted for almost 10 cents in every euro of revenues received by these governments. In the other thirteen Eurozone countries, the same burden averages only 3.5 percent, with the difference in the debt-service burden between the indebted periphery and the rest of the zone forecast to rise over the next five years. These high levels of debt service, even with lower interest rates, will erode highly indebted countries' ability to make investments and maintain social security nets. For example, Portugal's €7.3 billion interest bill exceeded its education spending and almost matched its health budget.

2. The Euro Project

There are special features involved in the euro crisis. Capitalism is a combined but uneven process of development. It is combined in the sense of extending the division of labor and economies of scale, and involving the law of value in all sectors, as in "globalization." But that expansion is uneven and unequal by its very mode, as the stronger seek to gain market share over the weaker.

The euro project aimed at integrating all European capitalist economies into one unit in order to compete with the United States and Asia in world capitalism with a single market and a rival currency. But one policy on inflation, one short-term interest rate, and one currency for all members is not enough to overcome the centrifugal forces of uneven capitalist development, especially when growth for all ceases and there is a slump. The professed aim from the beginning of the euro in 1999 was that the weaker economies would converge with the stronger in GDP per capita, and in terms of fiscal and external imbalances. But instead, the opposite has happened.[1]

The global slump dramatically increased the divergent forces within the Eurozone, threatening to break it apart. The fragmentation of capital flows between the strong and weak Eurozone states exploded. The capitalist sectors of the richer economies like Germany stopped lending directly to the weaker capitalist sectors in Greece, Slovenia, and elsewhere. As a result, in order to maintain a single currency for all, the European Central Bank (ECB; the official monetary authority) and the national central banks had to provide the loans instead. The Eurosystem's "TARGET2" settlement figures between the national central banks revealed this huge divergence within the Eurozone (fig. 17.3).

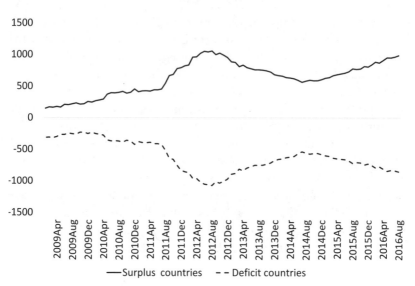

Figure 17.3. "TARGET2" net settlement balance in Eurozone (€ billion), April 2009–August 2016. Source: ECB.

Those who wish to preserve the euro project—like the European Commission, the majority of EU politicians and most capitalist corporations—recognize that the only way to do so is to extend the process toward more integration. That means having a "banking union" so that all the banks in the Eurozone are subject to control by the euro institutions like the ECB, and not by national government regulators.

Better still would be the establishment of a full "fiscal union," so that taxes and spending are controlled by Eurozone institutions and deficits in one EMU state are automatically met by transfers from surplus states. That is the nature of a federated state like Canada, the United States, or Australia. These transfers reach 28 percent of US GDP, as compared to the controlled and conditional transfers under EU budgets and bailouts of less than 10 percent of one state's GDP (fig. 17.4).

But the Eurozone does not have such a fiscal union, and there is little prospect of one. Instead, after much kicking and screaming, the Germans and the EU agreed to set up some fiscal transfer funds, first the European Financial Stability Facility (EFSF) and then the European Stability Mechanism (ESM). But these are not automatic fiscal union transfers; they are contingent on meeting fiscal targets in a Troika (EU, IMF, ECB) program, and national governments can still set their own budgets. And there has been growing opposition in Germany to shelling out cash for what they see as wayward countries who cannot get their public finances in order.

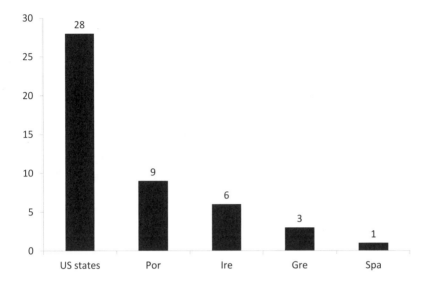

Figure 17.4. Internal automatic fiscal transfer as percent of GDP, 2015. Source: OECD.

3. The Policy of Austerity

The ECB, the EU Commission, and the governments of the Eurozone proclaimed that austerity was the only way Europe was to escape from the Great Recession. Austerity in public spending would force convergence too. But the real aim of austerity is to achieve a sharp fall in real wages and cuts in corporate taxes, thus raising the share of profit. The Estonian labor force was decimated as thousands left the tiny country to seek work elsewhere in Europe. Estonia also received over €3.4 billion in EU structural funds to finance infrastructure spending and employment. In this way, wage costs were lowered and profits raised.

That other poster child for "successful austerity," Ireland, achieved a partial export-led recovery by getting rid of its "excess" workforce in a similar way. By 2015, Irish emigration reached levels not seen since the dark days of the late 1980s.

Austerity could eventually deliver the required reductions in budget deficits and debt. But already there have been years of austerity, and very little progress has been achieved in meeting these targets or, more important, in reducing the imbalances within the Eurozone on labor costs or external trade to make the weaker more "competitive."

The adjusted wage share in national income, defined here as compensation per employee as percentage of GDP at factor cost per person employed, is the cost to the capitalist economy of employing the workforce (wages and benefits) as a percentage of the new value created each year. Every capitalist economy had managed to reduce labor's share of the new value created since 2009 (fig. 17.5). Labor has been paying for this crisis everywhere.

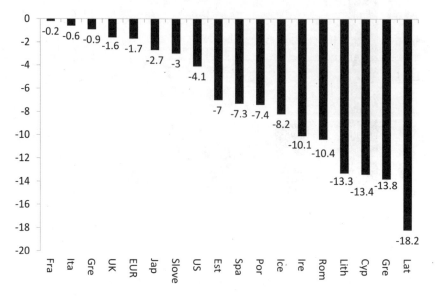

Figure 17.5. Reduction in labor's share of new value added (%), 2009–15. Source: AMECO, author's calculations.

Not surprisingly, it has been the workers of the Baltic states and the distressed Eurozone states of Greece, Ireland, Cyprus, Spain, and Portugal who have taken the biggest hit to wage share in GDP. In these countries, real wages have fallen, unemployment has rocketed, and hundreds of thousands have left their homelands to look for work somewhere else. That has enabled companies in those countries to sharply increase the rate of exploitation of their reduced workforce, although so far this has not been enough to restore profitability to levels before the Great Recession—nor has it been enough, therefore, to sustain sufficiently high new investment to get unemployment down to pre-crisis levels and these economies onto a sustained path of growth.

The major economies of Japan and the United States have also achieved a "moderate" reduction in wage share, which is helping to restore profitability. What is worrying for the capitalists of Italy or France is the failure to raise the rate of exploitation much at all. This failure is slowing the pace of return to profitability—no wonder Italy's economy continues to grind down and France is stagnant. And clearly Slovenian capitalism needs to do more to reduce wage share there if it is to recover profitability—at least as much as Portugal, Ireland, or Romania have.

In all these countries, governments are preparing an agenda of "labor market reform"—spending cuts and privatizations designed to hit labor's share in the national output—and there is more misery to come.

4. Emigration: The Safety Valve

One of the striking contributions to the fall in labor's share of new value has been from emigration. It has become an important contribution to reducing costs for the capitalist sector in the larger economies like Spain. Before the crisis, Spain was the largest recipient of immigrants to its workforce from Latin America, Portugal, and North Africa. Now that trend has been completely reversed.

Hundreds of thousands of migrants are heading back home every year, and the country's overall population has fallen for the first time since records began. Spain's population jumped from 40 million in 1999 to more than 47 million in 2010—one of the most pronounced demographic shifts experienced by a European country in modern times. The surge was almost entirely the result of migration from countries such as Ecuador, Bolivia, Romania, and Morocco. The number of foreigners living in Spain increased eightfold in just over a decade, while their share of the population soared from less than 2 percent in 1999 to more than 12 percent in 2009.

Now, increasingly, they are leaving Spain altogether. In 2008, one year after the start of the crisis, Spain still recorded 310,000 more migrant arrivals than departures. That number fell to just 13,000 the following year, before turning negative in 2010. In 2012 there were over 140,000 more departures than arrivals, and the pace of the exodus is picking up fast. According to the national statistics office, the foreign-born population stood at under 6 million in 2016, down from more than 6.5 million in 2009.

This net emigration acts a safety valve for Spanish capitalism—unemployment would be even higher without it. It helps the capitalist sector get down labor costs without provoking a social explosion. However, over the longer term this spells deep trouble for capitalist expansion in Spain. There remains a huge overhang of unfilled real estate from the property boom that triggered the crisis there. A falling population means that this form of unproductive capital will continue to weigh down Spain's recovery. And with a public sector debt-to-GDP ratio hitting 100 percent, there will be fewer workers to extract value to service that debt.

Unless the productivity of the smaller labor force can be raised, Spain's growth rate will be limited. While German capitalism has succeeded to some extent in coping with a falling population, Spanish capitalism will be less able. After all, most of the people emigrating are the skilled and more productive parts of the workforce. They are going to Germany, France, the

United States, and even Latin America. Maybe they will return, as many have done in the Baltic states or Ireland after past recessions ended. But given the length of this Long Depression, this time could be different.

The recession in the Eurozone, namely a contraction in real GDP, has made fiscal austerity programs self-defeating. As the denominator for fiscal deficit (GDP) has shrunk, the deficit ratios have risen, despite huge cuts in government spending and higher taxes. France, which promised to get below the 3 percent budget deficit-to-GDP target set by the Eurozone leaders, took until 2017 to achieve the target, much longer than forecast. Spain, which has been granted two separate delays in its timetable to hit the target, is still short of the target. Debt-to-GDP levels rocketed during the Great Recession but have failed to shrink since—on the contrary. The Eurozone sovereign debt ratio was 78 percent of GDP in 2009; in 2017 it was 87 percent. Spain's debt ratio was 52 percent in 2009 and 98 percent in 2017.

More importantly for labor, the euro crisis drove the area's average unemployment rate to 12.2 percent in 2014 from 7.3 percent in 2007, a more than 50 percent rise. In the last three years, the rate has gradually declined; but at 9 percent in 2017, it was still well above the pre-crisis level. Around one in six Spanish workers are unemployed, as are one in five Greeks.

5. The Keynesian Solution

The crisis in the Eurozone has been blamed on the rigidity of the single-currency area and on the strident "austerity" policies of the leaders of the Eurozone, Germany. But the euro crisis is only partly a result of the policies of austerity being pursued, not only by the EU institutions, but also by states outside the Eurozone, like the UK. Alternative Keynesian policies of fiscal stimulus and/or devaluation, where applied, have done little to end the slump and have still made households suffer income losses.

Austerity means a loss of jobs and services and thus income. Keynesian policies mean a loss of real income through higher prices, a falling currency, and eventually rising interest rates. Take Iceland, a tiny country outside the EU, let alone the Eurozone. The widely supported Keynesian policy of devaluation of the currency—a policy not available to the member states of the Eurozone—has still meant a 40 percent decline in average real incomes in dollar terms and nearly 20 percent in krona terms since 2007 (fig. 17.6).

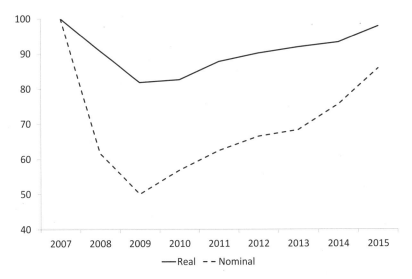

Figure 17.6. Iceland krona effective exchange rate (%, 2007 = 100), 2007–2015. Source: EU AMECO, author's calculations.

Restoring profitability is key for economic recovery under the capitalist mode of production. So which pro-capitalist policy has done best on this criterion? Let's compare Greece and Iceland. Iceland's rate of profit plummeted from 2005, and eventually in 2008–2009 the island's property boom burst; the banks collapsed along with it. Devaluation of the currency started in 2008, but profitability in 2012 remains well under the peak level of 2004, although there has been a slow recovery in profitability from 2008 onward. Greece's profitability stayed up until the global crisis took hold; then, it plummeted and only stopped falling in 2015. Profitability in "austerity" Greece and "devaluing" Iceland in 2015 was about the same, relative to 2005 levels (fig. 17.7). So you could say that both policies have been equally useless.

6. Greece Cannot Escape

At the end of January 2014, finance officials from the Troika (EU Commission, ECB, and the IMF) and the finance ministers of Germany and France held a secret meeting to discuss what to do about Greece. Greek government officials were not invited. They were trying to figure out how to tackle two issues threatening to unsettle the fragile economic recovery in Greece and the broader Eurozone: (1) how to press the Greek government to forge ahead with unpopular "structural reforms"; and (2) how to scramble together extra cash to cover a shortfall in the country's financing for the second half of the year, estimated at €5–6 billion. The meeting was inconclusive.

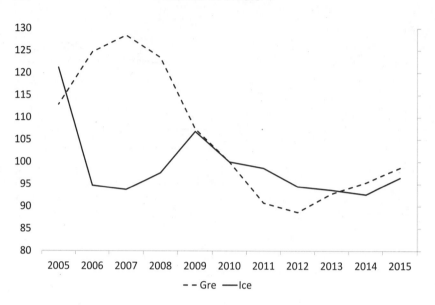

Figure 17.7. Net return on capital for Iceland and Greece
(%, 2005 = 100), 2005–2015. Source: AMECO.

Greece cannot escape the debt-deflation trap into which it has descended. Gross public and private debt relative to GDP has risen to record proportions and is still rising. Greek companies have the highest debt-to-equity ratio of modern economies at 235 percent, more than twice the Eurozone corporate average. These debt ratios are rising partly because the deficit on Greek government budgets has only just been closed, but mainly because nominal GDP growth remains very low.

The cruel irony is that Troika funds go to the Greek government through an "escrow" account (not controlled by the government), to be used to pay government creditors—who turn out to be other EU governments and banks! Less than 10 percent of the bailout funds have reached the Greek economy and the people.

Sure, the government managed to obtain a surplus (before interest payments on debt) in 2013. But, this budget "surplus" was only possible through extreme austerity cuts on government spending. Tax revenues still fell short of target. More important, as a recent Organisation for Economic Co-operation and Development (OECD; not part of the Troika) report argued, Greece has hardly recovered from its economic depression that began in 2010. Greek nominal GDP was $355 billion in 2008. In 2016 it was just $195 billion, a fall of 45 percent. This fall has driven up the Greek public debt ratio from 125 percent of GDP in 2009 to 182 percent in 2017.

The IMF forecast that by 2020 Greece's debt pile will still stand at the astronomical level of 177 percent of GDP, even if things go well. This is three times the level of debt set for Euro member states to meet by the end of next decade (2030). The OECD reckons that the Greek public sector must run a surplus of 4.5 percent of GDP from now in order to get its debt ratio down to the Troika target. The reality is that further austerity for another five years is both politically impossible and economically futile. Greece will never do it.

What is the alternative, then? Well, up to now Keynesian economists and many on the left have advocated that Greece needs to break with the euro and the German-led Troika bailout packages. Greece should restore the drachma and then devalue in order to boost exports and inflate away the real value of debt. In short, Greece should "do an Argentina" and default on its public debts. Two-thirds of the outstanding Greek government debt is held by the Eurozone bailout mechanisms and the IMF. The other third is mainly held by the Greek banks.

Two things spring from this alternative policy. First, was the Argentina option of 2002 a success? The experience of Argentina was partly exceptional, and the option eventually proved unsuccessful (Roberts 2012). Second, if the euro crisis is a crisis of capitalism, not just a problem of the euro as "too strong" a currency, then devaluation and debt default on its own would only be a temporary palliative for Greek capitalism—and no more pallatable for working people than euro-defined austerity, as it would mean hyperinflation and a collapse of businesses laden with euro debt. The current renewal of Argentina's crisis has confirmed that prognosis (Roberts 2014).

In a January 2015 election, the pro–Troika austerity, conservative government in Greece was replaced by an anti-austerity, anti-Troika, leftist government. This led to a new deal with the euro leaders to reduce the burden of Greek government-debt repayments to the ESM and euro governments, and to a small opening-up or "fiscal space" to partly reverse austerity measures. But even this will not revive Greek capitalism, which is not only on its knees, but is prostrate, with life-support mechanisms not working.

It's true that the crushing of the living standards and wage earnings of Greek households is making Greek industry more "competitive"—in 2017, the average hourly labor cost in Greece was €14.50, well below the Eurozone average of €$26.80, and way below the 2008 level of €16.80.

Greece is not tiny like Estonia, but it is still a relatively small capitalist economy, dependent on trade—mainly of processed minerals, pharmaceuticals, and food—as well as services like tourism. Austerity in Greece is supposed to be aimed at the public sector. But the reality is that it is private sector workers that have been hit the most. Public sector employment shrank from 693,000 in 2009 to 567,000 in 2015, an 18 percent drop. But private sector employment (a much larger share of the labor force) fell 800,000 between 2010 and 2014 as Greeks left the country and others lost their jobs. Getting labor costs down across the board was the real target of austerity.

7. Germany: The Success Story

The gap between the strong and the weak in the Eurozone has never been greater. Germany is the largest and most important capitalist economy in Europe, and it is the main creditor and funder of the Eurozone member states.

Germany's rate of profit fell consistently from the early 1960s to the early 1980s slump (down 30 percent)—much like the rest of the major capitalist economies in that period. Then there was a recovery (some 33 percent up—using Penn measures), with a brief fall during the recession of the early 1990s, followed by stagnation during the 1990s as West Germany digested the integration of East Germany into its capitalist economy (fig. 17.8). The real takeoff in German profitability began with the formation of the Eurozone in 1999, generating two-thirds of the rise from the early 1980s to 2007.

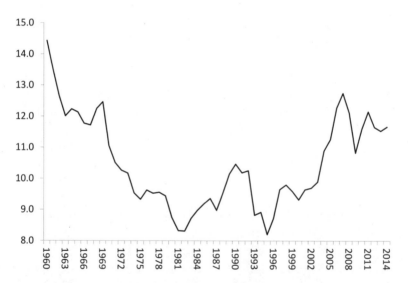

Figure 17.8. Germany: rate of profit on capital (%), 1960–2015. Source: Penn world tables, author's calculations.

German capitalism benefited hugely from expanding into the Eurozone with goods exports and capital investment until the Great Recession hit in 2008, while other euro partners lost ground (fig. 17.9). And once the east was integrated, Germany's manufacturing export base grew just as much as that of the new force in world manufacturing, China (fig. 17.10).

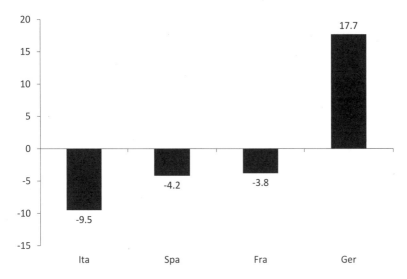

Figure 17.9. Change in rate of profit since EMU formation, 1999–2007 (%). Source: AMECO.

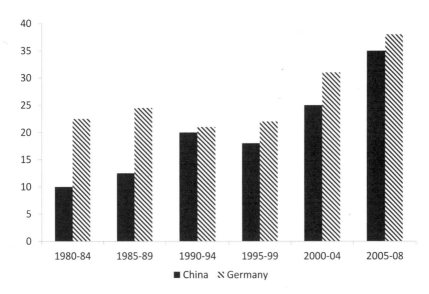

Figure 17.10. Exports to GDP (%), 1980–2008. Source: OECD.

The rise in the rate of profit from the early 1980s to 2007 can be broken down into a rise in the rate of surplus value of 38 percent, accompanied by only a small rise of 5 percent in the organic composition of capital. This is consistent with Marx's law of profitability, in that the rate of profit rises when the increase in the rate of surplus value outstrips the increase in the organic composition of capital. It seems that the ability to extract more surplus value out of the German working class while keeping the cost of constant capital from rising much was the story of German capitalism. In other words, constant capital did not rise due to innovations and investment in new technology; however, surplus value did—at first due to the expansion of the workforce from using imported labor from Turkey and elsewhere, and then later, from expansion directly into Europe.

The real jump in the rate of profit began with the start of the Eurozone. In this period, the organic composition of capital was flat, while the rate of surplus value rose 17 percent. German capital was able to exploit cheap labor within EMU but also in Eastern Europe to keep costs down. The export of plant and capital to Spain, Poland, Italy, Greece, Hungary, and so forth (without obstacle and in one currency) allowed German industry to dominate Europe, and even parts of the rest of the world.

Most importantly, the fear of the export of jobs to other parts of Europe enabled German capitalists to impose significant curbs on the ability of German laborers to raise their wages and conditions. The large rise in the German rate of profit was accompanied by a sharp increase in the rate of surplus value or exploitation, particularly from 2003 onward (fig. 17.11).

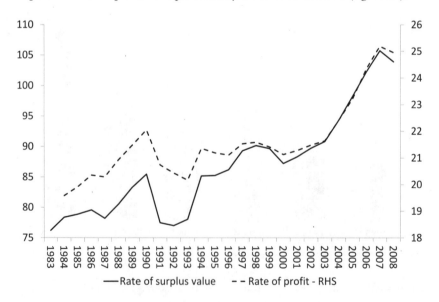

Figure 17.11. Germany: rate of profit and rate of surplus value (%), 1983–2008. Source: AMECO, author's calculations.

What happened from 2003 to enable German capitalism to exploit its workers so much more? In 2003–2005 the SPD-led government implemented a number of wide-ranging labor market "reforms," the so-called "Hartz reforms." The first three parts of the reform package, Hartz I–III, were mainly concerned with creating new types of employment opportunities (Hartz I), introducing additional wage subsidies (Hartz II), and restructuring the Federal Employment Agency (Hartz III). The final part, Hartz IV, was implemented in 2005 and resulted in a significant cut in the unemployment benefits for the long-term unemployed. Between 2005 and 2008, the unemployment rate fell from almost 11 percent to 7.5 percent; after barely increasing during the Great Recession, it then continued its downward trend, reaching below 5 percent at the end of 2016, although this is still higher than during in the Golden Age of expansion in the 1960s (fig. 17.12).

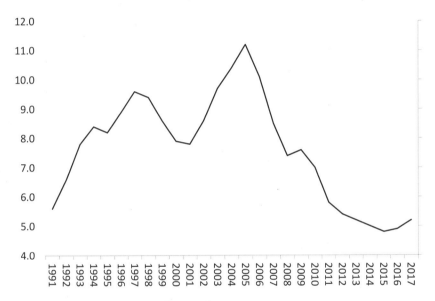

Figure 17.12. German rate of unemployment (%), 1991–2017. Source: AMECO.

The Hartz reforms were, then, a wonderful success—but not for labor. About one-quarter of the German workforce now receive a "low-income" wage, using a common definition of one that is less than two-thirds of the median—a higher proportion than all seventeen European countries, except Lithuania. A recent Institute for Employment Research (IAB) study found wage inequality in Germany has increased since the 1990s, particularly at the bottom end of the income spectrum. The number of temporary workers in Germany has almost tripled over the past ten years to about 822,000, according to the Federal Employment Agency. This is something we have seen across Europe—the dual labor system in Spain being the prime example.

So the reduced share of unemployed in the German workforce was achieved at the expense of the real incomes of those in work. The fear of low benefits if you became unemployed, along with the threat of moving businesses abroad into the rest of the Eurozone or Eastern Europe, combined to force German workers to accept very low wage increases, while German capitalists reaped big profit expansion. German real wages fell during the Eurozone era and in 2015 were still below the level of 1999, while German real GDP per capita rose nearly 30 percent.

8. Spain's Inquisition

In the Eurozone's fourth-largest economy, the rate of unemployment hit 27 percent in 2013 for the first time since records began. That's six million Spaniards without work in a population of forty-seven million. Youth (fifteen to twenty-four years) unemployment reached an astronomical 55 percent—only Greek youth are in a worse position for employment.

Even in 2017, the unemployment rate was still over 16 percent. And for the first time, permanent employment has started to fall as much as temporary employment in the deep economic recession that began in 2008, while long-term unemployment rose from 2 percent in 2008 to 14 percent in 2014 and was still around 8 percent in 2017.

The unemployment rate would be even higher, except that Spaniards are on their bikes and cars leaving the country to look for work elsewhere in Europe, or even Latin America. The rate of net emigration has reached 250,000 a year, draining the economy of some of the most educated and productive young Spaniards.

Spain's much-heralded economic boom saw 3.5 percent real growth per year during the 1990s. But it stopped being based on productive investment for industry and exports in the 2000s and turned into a housing and real estate credit bubble, just like Ireland's Celtic Tiger boom did. House prices to income peaked at 150 percent, nearly as high as Ireland. This has fallen back to 120 percent now, but Ireland has dropped to 85 percent. Household debt reached 90 percent of GDP. Non-financial corporate debt, including that of the developers, reached 200 percent of GDP, the highest in the OECD.

Housing construction doubled from 1995 to 2007, reaching 22 percent of GDP in 2007. Investment in real estate then fell from 12.5 percent of GDP in 2006 to 5.3 percent at end of 2012, well below the historic low of 7 percent in 1997. Oversupply of housing reached around 700,000 units in 2012 and was still 560,000 in 2015; and the backlog has not yet cleared. House prices fell 31 percent in nominal terms and 38 percent in real terms. During the property boom, credit grew at 20 percent a year, much faster than nominal GDP, which grew at about 7 percent a year. But lending collapsed beginning .

in 2008. The private sector has deleveraged its debt by 15 percent of GDP since the peak of 2008. But debt is still well above accepted international level of 160 percent. This is seriously holding back economic recovery. Capitalists won't invest if they have to meet heavy debt burdens. And Spanish corporations are most indebted among the major economies.

Much of the funding for the property boom came from abroad—mainly from other European banks, greedy to get a piece of the property cake. Spanish household savings and corporate profits were not nearly enough to fund the boom and all those consumer purchases that it enabled. Costs of production rocketed, and the real price of Spanish exports rose 20 percent from 2000 to 2009, increasingly pricing them out of world markets. So Spain's external deficit with the rest of Europe and the world mushroomed.

The current account deficit reached 10 percent of GDP in 2007, and net international liabilities (debt and equity) hit 92 percent of GDP, well above the recommended prudent level of 35 percent for a growing emerging economy. Gross external debt reached 167 percent of GDP in 2016, compared with 74 percent in 2000, nearly half of it in short-term loans. External debt interest to foreign banks sucks up 2.5 percent of GDP each year, and in 2017 the Bank of Spain had net liabilities to the Eurosystem at 40 percent of GDP. This is a huge burden.

And this is a burden that cannot be borne indefinitely, because of the hidden Achilles' heel of Spanish capitalism: the long-term decline in its profitability (fig. 17.13).

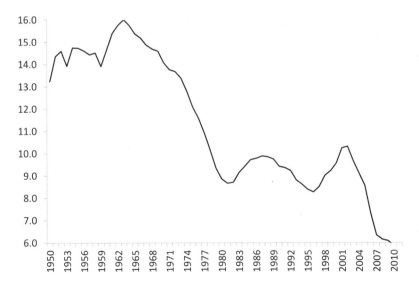

Figure 17.13. Spain: rate of profit (%), 1950–2010. Sources: extended Penn tables, AMECO; author's calculations.

Spanish capitalism was not a great success under the military rule of Franco. Profitability fell from the great heights of the Golden Age of postwar capitalism (as it did for all other capitalist economies from 1963 onward) in a classic manner, with the organic composition of capital rising nearly 30 percent, while the rate of surplus value fell by about the same. Eventually that led to the fall of Franco and, for a while, Spanish capitalism reversed the decline as foreign investment flooded in to set up new industries, relying on a sharp rise in the rate of exploitation brought about by plentiful surplus labor and a system of temporary employment contracts (while freezing permanent employment), the so-called dual labor policy.

The rate of exploitation rose over 50 percent leading up to 1996, helped by the foreign-led investment boom in the 1990s. This drove up the ratio of capital to labor (by 19 percent), as German and other capitalist companies relocated to Spain in search of cheaper labor and higher profits. That eventually put renewed pressure on the rate of profit. From 2000, profitability dropped sharply as wages squeezed profits in the boom of the 2000s.

Spanish capitalists switched to investing in property and riding on the cheap credit boom that disguised weakening profitability in the productive sector. The Spanish economic "miracle" came to a sorry end in the Great Recession, which in turn led to the property bubble burst, bringing about the banking crash. Indeed, it was in that order, unlike in the United States and the United Kingdom.

The aim of "austerity" and high unemployment is to restore Spanish profitability. It's a modern capitalist form of the Spanish Inquisition on the people. Corporate revenues dropped by €3 billion in 2012 (a 0.5 percent drop), but there was a €17 billion (5.0 percent) cut in wages to employees, so profits rose by €6 billion. Unit labor costs fell by 3.5 percent in 2012 as labor laws were introduced to make it easier to sack permanent staff and end the dual labor system—an ironic reversal of neoliberal policies. The aim, of course, is not to provide rights for temporary workers but to end them for permanent workers—leveling down.

Can lower wages and high unemployment eventually make Spanish exports more competitive and thus restore growth through exports? Spanish exports in real terms are up €26.3 billion from 2007 (+10 percent), but its imports are €64.4 billion lower (–20 percent). So lower wages and the cost of labor are helping trade, but this change in net trade has been paltry relative to the complete collapse of investment of €108 billion (–36 percent in real terms). The Spanish depression is a result of the collapse in capitalist investment.To reverse that requires a sharp rise in profitability. And until investment recovers, the depression will not end.

When unit labor costs are driven down sufficiently, enough weak companies are bankrupted, and exports are cheap enough, corporate profitability will rise from the ashes of the millions of unemployed, much lower living standards, decimated pensions, and destroyed public services, all of which have been burnt at the stake of capitalist accumulation. After years more of misery, the Spanish Inquisition will eventually have done its job.

9. Italy Deep in Stagnation

In some ways, Italy is in the direst position. Italian capital was in the doldrums even before the Great Recession, while profitability has been falling since 2000, and in 2008 the rate of profit fell below the level of 1963 (fig. 17.14).

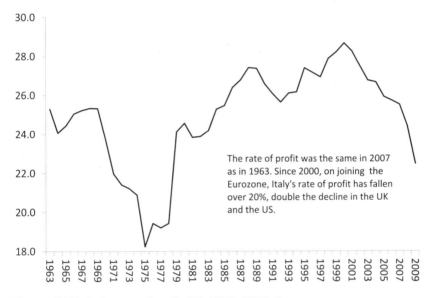

The rate of profit was the same in 2007 as in 1963. Since 2000, on joining the Eurozone, Italy's rate of profit has fallen over 20%, double the decline in the UK and the US.

Figure 17.14. Italy, rate of profit (%), 1963–2009. Sources: extended Penn tables, AMECO, author's calculations.

And since the trough of the Great Recession in mid-2009, Italy's rate of profit has fallen further; in 2017 it was 30 percent below the level of 2005, compared to 15 percent for the Eurozone as a whole. As night follows day, with profitability falling, net investment by Italy's capitalists dried up entirely. And since the end of the Great Recession, there has been no recovery in investment at all: real investment levels are now down 25 percent from their peak in early 2007.

The policies of austerity at first introduced by Berlusconi back in 2010, and then more vigorously by the bankers' man Mario Monti in 2012, failed even on their own terms. The public debt-to-GDP ratio continues to rise, and unit labor costs, which have been cut back sharply by austerity in other countries, continue to rise despite falling wages, because productivity is falling.

Italian capitalism remains paralyzed, and it is going to take drastic measures to raise profitability and productivity sufficiently to turn things around on a capitalist basis. Italy's only hope is that the rest of the Eurozone will recover and that this will spill over to Italy to improve its growth and employment.

10. The Tiny Members Suffer Most

The smaller member states of the Eurozone, like Ireland, Portugal, and Cyprus, have suffered badly. Tiny Slovenia, a nation of 2 million people wedged along the Alps, between Italy to the west and Austria to the north, is the only Balkan (ex-Yugoslav) country in the Eurozone. Slovenia has been relatively more prosperous than the other Balkan states and avoided the internecine wars that took place between Croatia, Serbia, Bosnia, and Kosovo after the collapse of the "communist" Yugoslav federation. It entered the EU and the Eurozone with great hopes of going forward. Then the global economic crisis erupted from 2007 onward. Slovenia seemed to avoid the worst for a while, but then it was hit with tremendous damage, and the economy was in a deep recession in 2011–2015.

The Slovenian economic crisis was very similar to that of Ireland. Slovenia's state-owned banks had been engaged in massive loans to Slovenian companies, mainly in construction and real estate, stimulating a huge commercial property boom that came crashing down when the global economic slump began. And just as in Ireland, it has been found that the politicians were in collusion with builders and developers to promote a crazy credit boom, taking a slice of the action for their troubles.

For a while this was covered up, but with unpaid loans reaching 20 percent of all lending, the banks were close to bust. A bailout of the banks amounting to at least €5 billion was necessary to avoid collapse. Of course, the EU and IMF came up with the usual "Irish solution": to hive off all the bad debts into a "bad bank" (which the taxpayer must "own"), while the cleansed banks are given funds to recapitalize, with the aim of selling them off to foreigners or others as soon as possible. The Slovenian government was left with a public sector debt that rose from 23 percent of GDP in 2008 to 83 percent in 2015 and that was still at 75 percent in 2017—a massive burden on taxpaying Slovenians.

And the level of debt built up in the credit boom has destroyed the ability of the banks to provide more credit for companies to fund investment. Fixed capital investment fell from 20 percent of GDP in 2009 to 18 percent in 2016, as the Slovenian capitalist sector went on strike or bust. That drop is second only to Ireland in the Eurozone. The depression was mega-sized for such a small country.

11. Will the Euro Survive?

There are two ways a capitalist economy can get out of slump. The first is by raising the rate of exploitation of the workforce enough to drive up profits and renew investment. The second is to liquidate weak and unprofitable capital (i.e., companies) or write off old machinery, equipment, and plant from company books (i.e., devalue the stock of capital). Capitalists attempt to do both in order to restore profits and profitability after a slump.

This is taking a long time in the current crisis, since the bottom of the Great Recession in mid-2009. Progress in devaluing and deleveraging the stock of capital and debt built up before is taking time and even being postponed by monetary policy. But progress in raising the rate of exploitation has been considerable.

Ultimately, whether the euro will survive is a political issue, depending on the majority view of the strategists of capital in the stronger economies and on the balance of class forces within the Eurozone. Will the people of Greece, Portugal, Spain, Italy, Cyprus, Slovenia, and Ireland endure more years of austerity, leading to the creation of a whole "lost generation" of unemployed young people, as has already happened in Greece and will happen in Spain, Italy, Portugal, and Slovenia?

Or will the electorate lose patience and remove pro-austerity, pro-Euro governments as in Greece (only to be disappointed)? The EU leaders and strategists of capital need economic growth to return soon, or further political explosions are likely. But, given the current level of profitability, this may not occur before the world economy drops into another slump. Then, all bets are off on the survival of the euro.

Notes

1   "During the years that followed the euro's introduction, financial integration proceeded rapidly and markets and governments hailed it as a sign of success. The widespread belief was that it would benefit both south and north – capital was finally able to flow to where it would best be used and foster real convergence. But in fact, a lasting convergence in productivity did not materialize across the European Union. Instead, a competitiveness divide emerged. As the financial crisis gripped the euro area in 2010, these and other problems came to the fore. . . . In fact, there has been little absolute real convergence in the euro area. Those euro area countries that had low per capita incomes in 1999 did not have the highest per capita growth rate" (Shafik 2013).

References

Organisation for Economic Co-operation and Development (OECD) (2013) "Economic Survey of Greece," *OECD iLibrary*.

Roberts, M. (2012) "Eurozone Debt, Monetary Union and Argentina," *The Next Recession*,   https://thenextrecession.wordpress.com/2012/05/10/eurozone-debtmonetary-union-and-argentina/.

————. (2014) "Argentina, Paul Krugman and the Great Recession," *The Next Recession*,   https://thenextrecession.wordpress.com/2014/02/03/argentina-paul-krugman-and-the-great-recession/.

Shafik, N. (2013) "Europe: Toward a More Perfect Union," *IMFdirect*, February 15, https://blogs.imf.org/2013/02/15/europe-toward-a-more-perfect-union/.

CONTRIBUTORS

Jonah Butovsky teaches quantitative methods and political sociology. He is affiliated with the Centre for Labour Studies at Brock University.

Guglielmo Carchedi, coeditor, was senior researcher in the Department of Economics at the Univesity of Amsterdam. His previous books include *Frontiers of Political Economy, Marx and Non-equilibrium Economics,* and *Behind the Crisis: Marx's Dialectics of Value and Knowledge.*

Maldonado Filho was an instructor at the Faculty of Economics and International Relations at the Federal University of Rio Grande do Sul, Brazil.

Abelardo Mariña Flores is a permanent professor in the School of Economics at the Autonomous Metropolitan University of Mexico City (UNAM).

Mylène Gaulard is a professor of economics at Centre de Recherche en Économie de Grenoble (CREG), Université Grenoble Alpes, France.

Sergio Cámara Izquierdo is a full-time professor of political economy at the Universidad Autónoma Metropolitana-Azcapotzalco, where he is the head of the Capitalist Society and Accumulation Area.

Vladimir Lautert is an analyst in geography and statistics at the Brazilian Institute of Geography and Statistics Foundation.

Esteban E. Maito is a graduate student in sociology at the Universidad de Buenos Aires, Argentina.

Thanasis Maniatis has been a professor of Marxist political economy in the Department of Economics of the University of Athens since 1996.

Adalmir Marquetti was an instructor at the Faculty of Economics and International Relations at the Federal University of Rio Grande do Sul, Brazil.

Juan Pablo Mateo Tome is a professor of applied economics at the University of Valladolid Segovia, Spain.

Steve Nash works in the financial services department of a major US state.

Tony Norfield worked in bank dealing rooms in the City of London for twenty years and was an executive director and the global head of foreign exchange strategy at a major European bank. He blogs at https://economicsofimperialism.blogspot.co.uk/.

Costas Passas works at the Labour Institute of the General Confederation of Greek Workers (INE–GSEE) and teaches in the Department of Economics, National and Kapodistrian University of Athens, and in the Greek Open University.

Michael Roberts worked in the City of London as a professional economist for over thirty years. As coeditor, his previous books include *The Great Recession: A Marxist View*; *The Long Depression*; and *Marx 200: A Review of Marx's Economics 200 Years after his Birth*. He blogs at https://thenextrecession.wordpress.com/.

Takuya Sato is a professor at the Faculty of Economics, Chuo University, Japan.

Murray E. G. Smith is professor of sociology at Brock University, Canada.

José A. Tapia is an associate professor of politics at Drexel University, Philadelphia, USA.

INDEX

ABOUT HAYMARKET BOOKS

Haymarket Books is a radical, independent, nonprofit book publisher based in Chicago.

Our mission is to publish books that contribute to struggles for social and economic justice. We strive to make our books a vibrant and organic part of social movements and the education and development of a critical, engaged, international left.

We take inspiration and courage from our namesakes, the Haymarket martyrs, who gave their lives fighting for a better world. Their 1886 struggle for the eight-hour day—which gave us May Day, the international workers' holiday—reminds workers around the world that ordinary people can organize and struggle for their own liberation. These struggles continue today across the globe—struggles against oppression, exploitation, poverty, and war.

Since our founding in 2001, Haymarket Books has published more than five hundred titles. Radically independent, we seek to drive a wedge into the risk-averse world of corporate book publishing. Our authors include Noam Chomsky, Arundhati Roy, Rebecca Solnit, Angela Y. Davis, Howard Zinn, Amy Goodman, Wallace Shawn, Mike Davis, Winona LaDuke, Ilan Pappé, Richard Wolff, Dave Zirin, Keeanga-Yamahtta Taylor, Nick Turse, Dahr Jamail, David Barsamian, Elizabeth Laird, Amira Hass, Mark Steel, Avi Lewis, Naomi Klein, and Neil Davidson. We are also the trade publishers of the acclaimed Historical Materialism Book Series and of Dispatch Books.